A History of the

The Berliner Ensemble was founded by Bertolt Brecht and his wife Helene Weigel in 1949. The company soon gained international prominence, and its productions and philosophy influenced the work of theatre-makers around the world. David Barnett's book is the first study of the company in any language. Based on extensive archival research, it uncovers Brecht's working methods and those of the company's most important directors after his death. The book considers the boon and burden of Brecht's legacy and provides new insights into battles waged behind the scenes for the preservation of the Brechtian tradition. The Berliner Ensemble was also the German Democratic Republic's most prestigious cultural export, attracting attention from the highest circles of government, and from the Stasi, before it privatized itself after German reunification in 1990. Barnett pieces together a complex history that sheds light on both the company's groundbreaking productions and their turbulent times.

DAVID BARNETT is Reader in Drama, Theatre and Performance at the University of Sussex. He is the author of *Brecht in Practice: Theatre, Theory and Performance* (2014), *Rainer Werner Fassbinder and the German Theatre* (Cambridge, 2005) and *Literature versus Theatre: Textual Problems and Theatrical Realization in the Later Plays of Heiner Müller* (1998). He has also edited the ninth volume of Brecht's collected plays in English, the *Berliner Ensemble Adaptations* (2014). He writes extensively on political and postdramatic theatre in Europe and has published articles in *Modern Drama* and *Contemporary Theatre Review* on Brechtian and post-Brechtian theatre.

Cambridge Studies in Modern Theatre

Series editors

Maria Delgado, *Queen Mary University of London*
Simon Williams, *University of California, Santa Barbara*

The new Cambridge Studies in Modern Theatre series explores, through the discussion of theatre, what it has meant to be modern over the last two centuries. Encompassing a global range of theatrical exchange, cultural productivity and historiography, it encourages contributions that probe both the aesthetic and sociopolitical dimensions of performance. Studies will cover not only plays, but operas, musicals, dance, circus and public ceremonies and rites and incorporate new inflections in Theatre Studies that recognise the importance of space, architecture and time. Building on the first wave of books published under David Bradby's editorship, the series will generate a dialogue as to what constitutes a global theatrical culture within modernity and how local cultures help constitute that global context. It also seeks to explore how theatre operates as an active agent in the political and social world, by bringing communities together and formulating agendas, both in the cultural and social field.

Founding editor

David Bradby

Advisory board

Maggie Gale, *University of Manchester*
Carl Lavery, *University of Glasgow*
Erin Mee, *New York University*
Mark Ravenhill
David Savran, *City University of New York*
Joanne Tompkins, *University of Queensland*
Patricia Ybarra, *Brown University*
Ted Ziter, *New York University*

Books published

Brian Crow and Chris Banfield, *An Introduction to Post-Colonial Theatre*
Maria DiCenzo, *The Politics of Alternative Theatre in Britain, 1968–1990: The Case of 7:84 (Scotland)*
Jo Riley, *Chinese Theatre and the Actor in Performance*
Jonathan Kalb, *The Theatre of Heiner Müller*
Claude Schumacher, ed. *Staging the Holocaust: The Shoah in Drama and Performance*

A History of the Berliner Ensemble

David Barnett

CAMBRIDGE
UNIVERSITY PRESS

CAMBRIDGE
UNIVERSITY PRESS

University Printing House, Cambridge CB2 8BS, United Kingdom

One Liberty Plaza, 20th Floor, New York, NY 10006, USA

477 Williamstown Road, Port Melbourne, VIC 3207, Australia

314-321, 3rd Floor, Plot 3, Splendor Forum, Jasola District Centre, New Delhi-110025, India

79 Anson Road, #06-04/06, Singapore 079906

Cambridge University Press is part of the University of Cambridge.

It furthers the University's mission by disseminating knowledge in the pursuit of education, learning and research at the highest international levels of excellence.

www.cambridge.org
Information on this title: www.cambridge.org/9781107663763

© David Barnett 2015

First published 2015
First paperback edition 2017

A catalogue record for this publication is available from the British Library

Library of Congress Cataloging in Publication data
Barnett, David, 1968–
A history of the Berliner Ensemble / David Barnett.
   pages   cm. – (Cambridge studies in modern theatre)
Includes bibliographical references and index.
ISBN 978-1-107-05979-5 (hardback)
1. Berliner Ensemble.   2. Brecht, Bertolt, 1898–1956 – Criticism and interpretation.   I. Title.
PN2656.B4B275   2015
792.0943 – dc23   2014034059

ISBN 978-1-107-05979-5 Hardback
ISBN 978-1-107-66376-3 Paperback

For Georgina, my wife,
and for Geoff Westgate,
because a mention in the Acknowledgements
simply isn't enough

Contents

Figures

Acknowledgements

The sheer time necessary to research a study like this does not arise from the occasional term of leave. I am therefore indebted to the British Academy for the award of a Research Development Award (BARDA) that permitted me twenty months to trawl the archives of Berlin between January 2010 and August 2011. I am also grateful to the Arts and Humanities Research Council for the Fellowship (AH/I003916/1) that allowed me to write up my findings from October 2011 to August 2012. Thanks are also due to the Alexander von Humboldt Foundation, which generously contributed to my research expenses while in Germany. The School of English at the University of Sussex has also graciously made funds available to pay the publisher's image surcharge.

My archival work has been aided and abetted by many professionals:

Academy of the Arts:	Elgin Helmstaedt, Maren Horn, Frau Kopp, Konstanze Mach-Meyerhofer, Iliane Thiemann, Susan Todd and Sabine Zolchow
Berlin City Archive:	Sabine Preuß
Berliner Ensemble Archive:	Petra Hübner
Bertolt Brecht Archive:	Dorothee Aders, Asja Braune, Gesine Bey, Uta Kohl, Anett Schubotz, Helgrid Streidt, Synke Vollring and Erdmut Wizisla
Brecht Research Centre:	Jürgen Hillesheim
Deutsches Theater Archive:	Karl Sand
Federal Archive:	Sylvia Gräfe, Isgard Löffler, Johanna Marschall-Reiser, Solveig Nestler, Jana Pautsch and Uta Räuber
Stasi Archive:	Anja Facius

In addition, I am most grateful to John Rouse for sharing with me his wonderful collection of unpublished interviews with members and former members of the Berliner Ensemble. I also extend my gratitude to all those who agreed to let me interview them: Uta Birnbaum, Wolf Bunge, Friedrich Dieckmann, Werner Hecht, Werner Heinitz, Hans-Jochen Irmer, Claus Küchenmeister, Jörg Mihan, Peter Raue, Hans-Georg Simmgen, Rolf Stiska, Stephan Suschke, Vera Tenschert, Holger Teschke, Hilmar Thate, B. K. Tragelehn, Carl Weber and Manfred Wekwerth. I also thank all those who have permitted me to quote from unpublished sources, and they include the Bertolt Brecht Estate and the Suhrkamp Verlag, who have permitted me to use unpublished material from Brecht. While I have endeavoured to contact as many sources as possible, some have eluded my efforts. They are welcome to contact me post publication.

I have had great support in this project from Geoff Westgate who read the whole manuscript, José Macián, who read the first seven chapters, and a battery of expert readers who offered me their views and suggestions on a number of individual chapters: Laura Bradley, Steve Giles, Tom Kuhn, Moray McGowan, Meg Mumford, Steven Parker and Denise Varney.

Series editors Maria Delgado and Simon Williams have been a great help and source of encouragement, as have Cambridge University Press' commissioning editor, Vicky Cooper, and her team of production assistants. In addition I would like to thank Andrew Hadfield for drawing my attention to the now sadly defunct BARDA scheme; Nick Royle for emboldening me to apply; Belinda Freda and Amelia Wakeford in the Sussex Research Office for their excellent advice on making grant applications; and to Hermann Wündrich at the Berliner Ensemble for his many fascinating insights into the German theatre system.

 BRITISH ACADEMY
for the humanities and social sciences

 Arts & Humanities
Research Council

Unterstützt von / Supported by

Alexander von Humboldt
Stiftung / Foundation

Abbreviations

AdK	Akademie der Künste (Academy of Arts)
BArch	Bundesarchiv (Federal Archive)
BBA	Bertolt Brecht Archive
BE	Berliner Ensemble
BEA	Berliner Ensemble Archive
BFA	Bertolt Brecht, *Große kommentierte Berliner und Frankfurter Ausgabe*, ed. by Werner Hecht, Jan Knopf, Werner Mittenzwei and Klaus-Detlef Müller (Berlin and Frankfurt/Main: Aufbau and Suhrkamp, 1988–2000) (= Complete Works in German. References give volume and page numbers)
BoP	Bertolt Brecht, *Brecht on Performance*, ed. by Tom Kuhn, Steve Giles and Marc Silberman (London: Bloomsbury, 2014)
BoT	Bertolt Brecht, *Brecht on Theatre*, ed. by Marc Silberman, Steve Giles and Tom Kuhn, 3rd edn (London: Bloomsbury, 2014)
Briefwechsel	Helene Weigel, *'Wir sind zu berühmt, um überall zu hinzugehen'. Briefwechsel 1935–1971*, ed. by Stefan Mahlke (Berlin: Theater der Zeit, 2000)
BStU	Bundesbehörde für Stasi-Unterlagen (Federal Authority for Stasi Documents)
DAK	Deutsche Akademie der Künste (German Academy of Arts, the first incarnation of the AdK)
DT	Deutsches Theater (Berlin)
ESA	Ekkehard Schall Archive
FDA	Friedrich Dieckmann Archive
FRG	Federal Republic of Germany
GDR	German Democratic Republic
GI	Geheimer Informator (secret informer for the Stasi)
GmbH	Gesellschaft mit beschränkter Haftung (limited liability company)

GMS	Gesellschaftlicher Mitarbeiter für Sicherheit (social collaborator on security for the Stasi)
HMA	Heiner Müller Archive
HWA	Helene Weigel Archive
IM	Inoffizieller Mitarbeiter (unofficial collaborator with the Stasi)
Journals	Bertolt Brecht, *Journals 1934–1955*, ed. by John Willett (London: Methuen, 1993)
JTA	Joachim Tenschert Archive
KO	Komische Oper (Comic Opera, Berlin)
KVP	Kasernierte Volkspolizei (Garrisoned People's Police)
LAB	Landesarchiv Berlin (Berlin City Archive)
Letters	Bertolt Brecht, *Letters 1913–1956*, ed. by John Willett (London: Methuen, 1990)
MWA	Manfred Wekwerth Archive
NVA	Nationale Volksarmee (National People's Army)
RBA	Ruth Berghaus Archive
SAPMO	Stiftung Archiv der Parteien und Massenorganisationen der Deutschen Democratischen Republik (Charitable trust for the archive of the parties and mass organizations of the German Democratic Republic – hosted by the Bundesarchiv)
SED	Sozialistische Einheitspartei Deutschlands (Socialist Unity Party of Germany)
StaKuKo	Staatliche Kunstkommission (the GDR's State Art Commission)
TiW	Theater in der Wende (Theatre in the *Wende*)
Werke	Heiner Müller, *Werke*, ed. by Frank Hörnigk (Frankfurt/Main: Suhrkamp, 1998–2008). References give volume and page numbers

Introduction

The Berliner Ensemble: a theatre company like no other

If one were to gather together the most significant theatre companies of the twentieth century, the Berliner Ensemble (BE), founded by Bertolt Brecht and his wife, Helene Weigel, in 1949, would surely find itself near the top of the list. 'Significant' here may denote not only companies that expanded the theatre's performance vocabulary, but also influenced the work of theatre-makers around the world through their productions, organization and/or philosophy. As will be shown, the BE amply satisfied all these criteria. Its inaugural season initiated a steady stream of innovative work that was later acknowledged internationally after tours to Paris and London in the mid 1950s. Brecht's death in 1956 caused widespread anxiety that the experiment would end, but the tenacity of Weigel and the willingness of the assistants Brecht had nurtured meant that the BE continued making theatre and developing the method he had established in his seven years as artistic director. As the only company in the world dedicated to Brecht's theories and practices, the BE became a distinctive and much fêted institution, attracting the interest of Peter Brook, the Living Theatre and Dario Fo (see pp. 192–3 and 324–5), amongst others, and of audiences worldwide for its regular foreign tours.

It is this distinctiveness that makes the BE such an attractive cultural phenomenon. Brecht returned to Germany in 1948 having spent fifteen years – the period of the Third Reich and its immediate aftermath – in exile in both Europe and the United States, largely cut off from practical work in the theatre. In this time, he had been theorizing the principles of a new theatre, and he finally got the opportunity to put his ideas into practice in 1949. Brecht's influence was pervasive and defined the aesthetic and political profile of the new company, during the last years of his life and for decades after his death in 1956. His ability to deliver a fresh, vibrant approach to making theatre set the BE apart from any other stage in Germany and, indeed, far further afield. This was quickly recognized by audiences and critics alike. Yet Brecht's practice was based on a method, not an array of devices, and so every production probed new formal and thematic problems, extending Brecht's theatrical means in the context of the particular play in question. The direction was never formulaic and thus the productions could always surprise and often provoke.

But Brecht looked further than just his own practice as a director. From the outset, he cultivated enthusiastic and able young collaborators, who were initially employed to assist him. Brecht's aim was to develop an active creative team that would learn from him before acting independently on their own projects. Before long, Brecht entrusted productions, under his supervision, to remarkably young colleagues as a means of promoting new ways of looking at his method. The strategy was successful: after he died, Brecht's assistants donned their mentor's mantle and led the BE out of the uncertainty brought about by the great loss. Thus, the BE was not simply a vehicle for Brecht to test out his ideas, it was a dynamic institution where the exchange of views and engagement in experiment helped to secure a liveliness in production, based on a new set of dramaturgical principles. Over time, however, Brecht's posthumous presence became an inhibiting factor. The BE itself had raised expectations about what spectators would encounter in a theatre dedicated to a single practitioner's ideas, and the pressure continually to produce radical and engaging work in the shadow of the master took its toll. A major crisis concerning the direction and sustainability of the company began in 1966 that had dire effects on both the productions and the personnel, but it is nonetheless remarkable that it took a whole decade after Brecht's death for creative fatigue finally to set in.

The productions did not, of course, exist in a vacuum: the BE was making theatre in the German Democratic Republic (GDR) for the first forty years of its existence. The socialist state, founded scarcely a month after the BE in October 1949, followed the Soviet model and developed systems of political control that pervaded every level of society. The BE was certainly committed to the cause of socialism, and the authorities backed and encouraged the company for the most part, but the BE's probing examination of dramatic material meant that it would rarely offer work that could be considered 'propaganda'. Consequently, the BE's relationship to the Sozialistische Einheitspartei Deutschlands (Socialist Unity Party of Germany – SED) was one that had to be negotiated and renegotiated as the party's agenda changed. In its first years, for example, the BE enjoyed the support of the SED before it found itself a target for ideologically driven attacks on the very ways that it made theatre. The relationship with the SED was also differentiated, due to the many agencies charged with supervising the company over the years. The BE's history is thus also closely linked to the ways in which the party treated it. Yet this was not a one-way, reactive process; ever since the triumphs on tour in Paris and London of the mid 1950s, the BE could use its international reputation to strengthen its position in matters of cultural policy. The SED always necessarily had the upper hand, yet it had in the BE a company that could stand its ground when it needed to, due to its international profile, its fame and its connections.

The BE offers itself as an intriguing and contradictory object of inquiry. It struggled to impose its dialectical approach to theatre-making, but made an indelible mark on theatre history. It preached the invigorating principles of Brecht's method, but could not liberate itself from the millstone of Brecht's reputation. Its aesthetics were informed by Marxist thought, but came into conflict with a socialist government.

Looking beyond the proscenium arch

Given the standing of Brecht and the BE, it is extraordinary that the scholarly literature contains so little on this company. Christoph Funke provides a general overview of the BE's time at the Theater am Schiffbauerdamm in a book on the theatre building and the theatre-makers it hosted, rather than on the BE itself.[1] Petra Stuber features the BE in her insightful account of theatre in the GDR, but it is only one company amongst others.[2] John Fuegi's is the only book solely devoted to Brecht's practices as a director, but he actively de-politicizes them,[3] something against which I argue in the first four chapters of this study. Elsewhere directors and actors have written memoirs of their time with Brecht and/or the BE, and scholars have studied particular aspects of specific productions or directorial approaches. So, despite a number of useful and less useful forays, that will be cited in subsequent chapters, there has been no systematic investigation or examination of a much-celebrated theatre company whose work, practices and organization influenced theatre-makers around the world.

The aim of this study is to offer the kind of systematic investigation envisaged by Ric Knowles in which the performed event is not seen in

---

[1] See Christoph Funke, 'Das Berliner Ensemble am Schiffbauerdamm 1954–1992', in Funke and Wolfgang Jansen, *Theater am Schiffbauerdamm. Die Geschichte einer Berliner Bühne* (Berlin: Christoph Links, 1992), pp. 165–207.

[2] See Petra Stuber, *Spielräume und Grenzen: Studienzum DDR-Theater* (Berlin: Christoph Links, 1998).

[3] See John Fuegi, *Bertolt Brecht: Chaos according to Plan* (Cambridge: Cambridge University Press, 1987), particularly pp. 110–86.

isolation, but as the intersection of many different and potentially con-flicting interests.[4] I have chosen to start with the BE's theatre work, the method and the productions that made it famous, as a way of illuminating the many contexts and frames of reference that informed the company. In order to understand why its productions were so significant, one has both to look behind the scenes and to leave the theatre building. The BE's internal structures were subject to Brecht's revolutionary ideas, and these were reflected in the ensemble playing on stage. The repertoire, which was constructed for a socialist society, naturally originated in the BE, but had to be approved by state institutions, and so an ideological dimension was present on both sides of that equation. The BE's interna-tional profile also affected what it was and was not allowed to perform, and the SED also sought to influence the people who occupied strate-gic positions, both overtly through its officials and covertly through the recruitment of well-placed Stasi informers (although this practice only really started once Brecht was dead, and intensified in the wake of the Prague Spring of 1968). After the fall of the Berlin Wall in 1989, the BE had to deal with a new set of social, political and economical contexts as it struggled to come to terms with the reunified, capitalist Germany.

Consequently, a contextualized study needs to deal with a variety of factors that manifested themselves on stage, in the rehearsal room, the BE's various departments, the byzantine structures of the SED, and the wider world. In short, the BE was a focal point for a number of forces, and it is only by engaging with these multifarious impulses that a rounded account may be given. The reader will thus find references to the BE's own rehearsal and production documentation, internal minutes and letters, theatre reviews, and a mass of communication to, from and within the SED, including its covert agency, the Stasi and, later, with the Berlin Senate, as well as interviews with some of the BE's most important associates.

The scope of the study

This study is, broadly, a chronological one. The BE's history, however, includes a caesura that is worth identifying here. From 1949 until her death in 1971, Weigel was the BE's *Intendantin* (the feminine form of *Intendant*, 'general manager'). The years up to that point represent the 'Brecht phase': Brecht introduced and developed a method for making theatre that close collaborators continued and extended after his death.

---

[4] Ric Knowles, *Reading the Material Theatre* (Cambridge: Cambridge University Press, 2004).

While the method was to accompany production work after 1971, other ideas challenged 'orthodox' Brechtianism in the early 1970s, occasionally in the 1980s, and again in the 1990s. The years after Weigel's death thus represent the company's 'post-Brecht' phase. The study concludes in 1999, fifty years after the BE's founding. While I will dwell on that year as an end-point in the Conclusion, I merely note here that the new *Intendant*, Claus Peymann, sought to liberate himself and the company from Brecht's direct influence and thus his first productions in 2000 mark the end of the 'post-Brecht' phase.

The study is not only interested in how the BE, as an institution, developed over time. It is also concerned with the practical theatre work of Bertolt Brecht, an under-researched field for a practitioner so significant and well known. The first seven chapters of the book ask how Brecht reconciled his theoretical ideas and his practice over the course of many productions, and how these techniques and methods developed after his death. The second seven focus on the dissatisfaction with some of Brecht's approaches and the varying attempts to address them while retaining Brecht's dialectical worldview and his faith in the changeability of people and society.

The BE's history itself is a fascinating one, not only for the kinds of theatre that generated international attention, but also for the ways in which the BE's distinctiveness arose within the GDR. The history of the BE is also a history of the SED's cultural policies, its ability to implement them, and the sanctions it was and was not able to deploy with respect to its most prestigious cultural entity. The BE, of course, experienced the GDR's major crises, both in national and cultural-political terms. It sought to engage with the workers uprising of 17 June 1953 and lauded the building of the Berlin Wall in 1961. It was also the victim of a witch-hunt in the early 1950s that obsessively sought out 'formalism' in the arts and was censured by the SED's XI Plenum of late 1965. The BE was a unique theatre in the history of the GDR, but it was also subjected to policies that affected the theatre system as a whole. As such, analysis of the BE can also comment on more general aspects of the authorities' cultural ambitions.

Readers will notice that the study is a necessarily compressed history, due to the amount of material available and the need to fashion it into a narrative that covers half a century replete with incident within and without the BE. There is also insufficient space to consider all the productions in the fifty seasons under discussion, but such exhaustive chronicling would not have been desirable, either. Instead, I have focused on both the productions that were received with much fanfare, as well as those that offer different perspectives on the BE's output. Readers may find that their favourite productions either do not appear or only serve as points of reference. I can only counter that I have attempted to offer a representative mix of theatrical work. As the reader may well expect, a study that aims to construct a new narrative of the company provides a selection that recognizes not only the BE's acknowledged achievements, but also lingers on some of the lesser-known projects that deserve greater attention.

There are also areas that have been deliberately neglected in order for the focus to remain on the distinctiveness of the BE's productions and the conditions under which this distinctiveness developed. For the most part, I have not considered the history of the BE's many tours, for example, and only concentrate on those to Paris and London in the mid 1950s that established the company internationally.[5] In addition, I note the problems the BE encountered when it could not travel abroad in the wake of the erection of the Berlin Wall. I also treat the productions themselves in terms of their rehearsal, original performances and reception, yet the BE continually returned to the productions, which could run for years at a time. The 'Abendberichte' ('evening reports'), often compiled by the company's assistants, bear witness to changes over the years, but the reader will have to be satisfied with the knowledge that this process took place rather than be initiated into the various stages of post-premiere development. Such a description would only be possible in individual accounts of particular productions. In addition, I have chosen to examine preparation, rehearsal, and performance rather than offer in-depth analyses of the plays themselves. Similarly, I have subordinated the music that accompanied the productions and innovations in scenography that ran alongside the development of the BE to the dynamics of acting and directing.[6] Again, these elements could provide material for complete studies in themselves.

The book opens with a chapter that considers the ways in which Brecht approached his new theatre company as an opportunity to implement ideas and ways of working that had occupied him during his exile from

[5] For a broader consideration, see David Barnett, 'The Politics of an International Reputation: The Berliner Ensemble as a GDR Theatre on Tour', in Christopher Balme and Berenika Szymanski-Düll (eds.), *Theatre, Globalization and the Cold War* (Basingstoke: Palgrave, forthcoming).

[6] For further discussions of both aspects, see, for example, Friedrich Dieckmann, 'Komponenten am Berliner Ensemble', in Dieckmann, *Die Freiheit – ein Augenblick: Texte aus vier Jahrzehnten*, ed. by Therese Hörnigk and Sebastian Kleinschmidt (Berlin: Theater der Zeit, 2002), pp. 85–95; Joachim Lucchesi and Ronald K. Schull, *Musik bei Brecht* (Frankfurt/Main: Suhrkamp, 1988); Friedrich Dieckmann, *Karl von Appens Bühnenbilder am Berliner Ensemble: Szenenbilder, Figurinen, Entwürfe und Szenen photos zu achtzehn Aufführungen* (Berlin: Henschel, 1973).

Germany. Chapter 2 examines the founding of the company, its first season as a case study of the varieties of performance work on offer, and the existential problems the BE faced before it was a year old. Chapters 3 and 4 consider Brecht's work with the BE and the political battles in which it found itself embroiled. Because the BE was Brecht's theatre and the early years establish the tone, parameters, and principles for the work in the decades to come, the study begins with a detailed examination of the period in which Brecht was artistic director. This provides the foundation for understanding the BE as the 'Brecht theatre' it became after his death. Brecht's spirit haunted the BE until the end of the 1990s: without an appreciation of how Brecht directed or envisaged the structures of the company, it may be difficult to fathom subsequent developments that both consciously and unconsciously took up or reacted against Brecht's influence. All subsequent chapters explore the way the BE operated under a most divergent group of leaders.

As is the case with any historical investigation, it would be impossible to tell the company's complete story. I have had to be selective, due to sheer volume of information available in the various archives, interviews and literature, but believe that any omissions do not fundamentally undermine the cumulative picture of the company that emerges over the chapters. The indefinite article in the study's title acknowledges this position from the outset. I hope that the reader will enjoy the breadth and the depth of the chapters without ruing the inevitable gaps, and that the history's richness will suggest a sense of the BE's remarkable achievements and the value they may have to theatre-makers and audiences today.

1   The Berliner Ensemble as an opportunity to establish a new type of theatre

Ambitions after exile

Bertolt Brecht left Germany and went into exile on 28 February 1933. He had been preparing for such an eventuality earlier that month, although the event that brought about his immediate departure was the blaze that gutted the seat of government, the Reichstag, the day before.[1] That the Nazis could undertake such an action to secure power was enough to tell Brecht, as a prominent critic of the party, that he was no longer safe in his homeland. He returned to Germany, via France and Switzerland, for the first time in late August 1948.

His fifteen years of exile offered him precious little contact with the theatre. His attempts to intervene in the New York production of *Die Mutter* (*The Mother*) in 1935 ended in chaos, and he was banned from attending rehearsals. In 1936, he participated more productively in rehearsals of his play *Die Rundköpfe und die Spitzköpfe* (*Round Heads and Pointed Heads*) at the Theater Riddersalen in Copenhagen; he played a similar role in Parisian productions of *Die Dreigroschenoper* (*The Threepenny Opera*) and *Die Gewehre der Frau Carrar* (*Señora Carrar's Rifles*) in 1937. While in exile in the United States, he worked closely with the actor Charles Laughton on *Leben des Galilei* (*Life of Galileo*), and the production premiered in Beverly Hills under the direction of Joseph Losey in 1947. Brecht, who had directed several productions in the Weimar Republic, had not directed a single play during his exile.

Instead of working in the theatre, Brecht had been writing for and about it. Many of the plays on which Brecht's reputation as a dramatist rests were written in this period. His theoretical reflections on and aspirations for the theatre were also fashioned, thought through and developed away from a rehearsal room or an audience. He was certainly keen to have his unstaged plays produced in professional theatres, but, as their production histories show, it was neither his priority to launch them on

---

[1] See Werner Hecht, *Brecht Chronik 1898–1956* (Frankfurt/Main: Suhrkamp, 1997), pp. 346 and 349.

an unsuspecting public in quick succession after returning from exile nor to take directing credits exclusively for himself. Instead, he was far more concerned with implementing a series of reforms to the theatre as it existed at the time in order to change the nature of theatre-making itself. The years of exile had allowed Brecht to speculate on what a new theatre might look like and how it might function. Having tentatively moved back to Berlin in October 1948, Brecht formulated the idea of a establishing a permanent theatre company in December, although it would take a further five months and much negotiation with the East German authorities before the company was officially recognized and supported.

The advantages of such an entity were obvious. Brecht's plans for a new theatre could not be realized after productions in different theatres as a freelance director. A theatre company of his own could offer all the basic structures necessary for sustained practice and research: it would have regular access to rehearsal and performance facilities; a stable leadership to guide and nurture a creative team; an ensemble of actors to engage with novel modes of understanding their characters and fresh approaches to rehearsal; and a dedicated infrastructure to support the productions themselves. As it would turn out, this ideal state only came about once the Berliner Ensemble (BE) was finally given its own theatre buildings, over four years after its founding in September 1949. However, the establishment of a permanent company did offer Brecht an amount of stability, and with this he was able to bring about some remarkable changes to the processes of making theatre in a relatively short period.

Brecht's ideas for a new theatre, theorized in and, to an extent, prior to his exile can be understood in terms of the ways directors and actors rehearsed, their aims for performance, how a theatre is organized, and how labour might be divided in such an institution. This chapter explores the ways in which Brecht sought to reconcile his theoretical ambitions with the concrete reality of a theatre company.

The director and the ensemble

Brecht's understanding of an ensemble was the product of the way he thought about the director's relationship with the actors. One of Brecht's concerns was the common belief that good directors came to the first rehearsal with a completely thought-through vision of the production, which would then be transmitted to the actors. This was a standard method of the time, one exemplified by one of the most innovative and well-respected German directors of the twentieth century, Max Reinhardt. He 'worked out all the details of a new production in his head long before rehearsals began' and noted them down in what he called his 'Regiebuch' ('directing book').[2] Brecht, on the other hand, argued that the director 'should insist that at any one time several solutions be considered'.[3] He proposed, in a radical departure from accepted practice, that the director and the cast work inductively on the dramatic material. The inductive process is predicated upon the movement from observation towards the tentative establishment of patterns and principles. As Antony Tatlow notes: 'in Brecht's open, inductive process, reality, like the work of art, is not given; it must be interpreted, engaged with, constructed, produced'.[4] The inductive method is one that is particularly well suited to the work of art, an object that strives to make connections from the often unexpected behaviour of different people in different situations. The inductive method of direction was thus one focused on discovery. In order to achieve this, Brecht sought to instil a naïve attitude both in himself and in the actors at the beginning of the rehearsal process: 'the correct starting point is the zero point'.[5] By approaching the contradictory impulses of a play without a definitive interpretation, the director *and* the actors could work together to discover how to perform the dramatic material.

The idea of 'togetherness' is closely tied to the concept of ensemble, yet Brecht's ideas on this diverged from those of his fellow directors around 1930:

Some theatres have tried to foster an 'ensemble spirit'. What this usually boils down to is that all the actors are expected to sacrifice their own egoism 'for the good of the play'. It is actually much better to mobilize this egoism in each and every actor.[6]

Brecht recognized that rather than restricting the actors with misplaced deference to other cast members, he would do better to activate them all. Indeed, when working at the BE, he told an actor that a productive contradiction existed between the collective desire to stage a play and the individual actor's desire to represent his or her position: 'everything lives off this contradiction'.[7] Again, the director is not concerned with controlling the actors, but rather empowering them to make discoveries that can be used productively in performance.

---

[2] J. L. Styan, *Max Reinhardt* (Cambridge: Cambridge University Press, 1982), p. 120.

[3] Brecht, 'Haltung des Probenleiters (bei induktivem Vorgehen)', BFA, 22: 597; *BoT*, p. 212.

[4] Antony Tatlow, 'Bertolt Brecht Today: Problems in Aesthetics and Politics', in Tatlow and Tak-Wei Wong (eds.), *Brecht and East Asian Theatre* (Hong Kong: Hong Kong University Press, 1982), pp. 3–17 (13).

[5] Brecht, 'Über das Ansetzen des Nullpunktes', BFA, 22: 244; *BoT*, p. 161.

[6] Brecht, 'Über die Probenarbeit', BFA, 21: 388; *BoT*, p. 50.

[7] Brecht, 'Die Regie Bertolt Brechts', BFA, 23: 164; *BoP*, p. 228.

Brecht also linked ensembles to a new way of making work, one inflected by his ideas on modernity. While I will not go into these in detail, they are, put somewhat crudely, concerned with a shift brought about by changes in European society. The sovereign individual of the bourgeois nineteenth century gave way to the interconnected individual of the more socialist twentieth, and Brecht believed that this shift had transformed the creative process: 'the act of creation has become a collective creative process, a continuum of a dialectical sort in which the original invention, taken on its own, has lost its importance'.[8] Brecht's war on the originality of the individual visionary was based in the collective process he cultivated: an ensemble pooled its members' many and varied experiences as a means of generating realistic material, ratified by the group, rather than fanciful singular speculation.

Brecht's decisions for staging plays at the BE were, however, often determined by the availability of preferred actors for lead roles. His plans for his own *Life of Galileo* were regularly postponed until 1955 because he was unable to secure a strong lead for the title role. Brecht was also keen to attract major actors to his ensemble. John Fuegi has tried to arraign Brecht for his 'reliance on stars',[9] as a way of undermining the centrality of ensemble in the BE's practice. Käthe Rülicke, one of Brecht's assistants, also registered surprise when she reported Brecht's fondness for stars, but then wrote 'ensemble doesn't mean everyone has the same ability, only that every role has the correct actor and that they are all in balance with each other'.[10] Brecht could recognize different degrees of talent and set about making sure that they could work productively together. Indeed, some of his casting decisions deliberately put his most talented performers in minor roles in order to allow less experienced actors to observe how they worked with smaller parts. Ernst Busch, one of Brecht's favourite actors and the one he finally persuaded to take on Galileo, made a minor appearance in the last scene of Johannes R. Becher's *Winterschlacht* (*Battle in Winter*) that premiered in January 1955, for example.

Brecht's affection for Busch, and indeed for many other actors, stemmed from the way that they could bring their biography to a role and contrast it with that of their characters. Brecht roundly criticized what he perceived to be Stanislavsky's insistence on an actor erasing his or her personality to inhabit a character fully.[11] He was fascinated by difference, the

---

[8]   Brecht, 'Antigonemodell 1948', BFA, 25: 76; *BoP*, p. 167.
[9]   Fuegi, *Chaos according to Plan*, p. 135.
[10] Käthe Rülicke, 'Brecht: 25-4-51', undated, BBA 1340/54. All translations from German are mine unless otherwise acknowledged.
[11] See Brecht, 'Über die Bezeichnung "restlose Verwandlung"', BFA, 22: 178–9.

cleavage between elements on stage, as a way of interrupting sustained relationships, be they between the actor and the role, or between the spectator and the actor. The end in both cases was to stimulate the spectator out of a position of passive consumption by offering productively inconsistent material from the stage. Thus Brecht praised Busch because he brought his proletarian biography on stage, along with his role.[12] He found this so fascinating that he entreated Busch to play the patrician general Coriolanus in his adaptation of the play, but Busch turned him down.[13] The revelation of the actor's personality was not only reserved for those with an expansive collection of life experiences. Regine Lutz was a doctor's daughter from a comfortable suburb in Zurich. Brecht auditioned her while he was at the Zurich Schauspielhaus in 1948 and asked her to deliver a poem. Having completed the task, she was asked to read the poem as if she had never read a poem before.[14] Brecht was interested in the friction between the young bourgeois woman and the effort it would take to suppress her background. He clearly saw something in the incongruity that he liked, and she was later invited to join him as a founding member of the BE. To Brecht, the mark of real actors was that they desired and were able to portray people very different from themselves.[15] Here he valued the objective of putting distance between actor and role.

Once the BE had been established, Brecht's theoretical ideas took concrete shape by engaging the ensemble as a whole, regardless of the different experiences of its membership. Brecht instituted a practice that quickly took hold as a standard rehearsal method there. Manfred Wekwerth, who joined the BE as an assistant director in 1951, noted concisely how the process worked: 'the actors are to make "offers". The director develops [the offers] through correction. To repeat: the *Fabel* [the interpreted events of the play] decides everything. The final understanding of a character only comes about through this interplay'.[16] This, then, is the inductive method at its most fundamental: actors offer performances based on the given dramatic situation. The director provisionally 'corrects' the offers in a bid to approach satisfactory acted solutions, but these solutions are always open to further alteration.

[12] See Brecht, journal entry for 7 February 1954, BFA, 27: 349; *Journals*, pp. 457–8.

[13] See Manfred Wekwerth, *Schriften: Arbeit mit Brecht*, second, revised and expanded edition (Berlin: Henschel, 1975), p. 201.

[14] Lutz, in Joachim Lang and Jürgen Hillesheim, *'Denken heißt verändern . . .': Erinnerungen an Brecht* (Augsburg: Maro, 1997), p. 79.

[15] See Brecht, '[Was einen Schauspieler ausmacht]', BFA, 23: 186; *BoT*, p. 271.

[16] Wekwerth, *Schriften*, p. 111.

Lutz recounts that Brecht effectively banned discussions at rehearsals and instead sought the actors' 'offers' as a physical articulation of the position they would otherwise have argued.[17] The result of such a demand redefined the role of the actor. Actor Käthe Reichel said that actors had to 'learn to think "dramaturgically"' under Brecht.[18] That is, they were no longer the passive vessels into which the director's ideas were to be poured. Instead, they were active co-producers of meaning, and this perpetual call to action was designed to engage both mind and body in the exploration not only of their own roles, but of the roles of the rest of the ensemble. Brecht's understanding of an ensemble not only dynamized the actors by actively soliciting their contribution, but transformed the way that they conceived of their own function.

'Actor training' at the BE

The differences between the BE's work and that of rival theatres, like Berlin's Deutsches Theater or Volksbühne, may give the impression that Brecht founded a 'training school' of sorts for his new company. The training he gave, however, was not formal: it entailed neither classes nor specific schedules of exercises, but was, for want of a better word, inductive. Consequently, the phrase 'actor training' may be considered inaccurate. As John Rouse writes: 'Brecht was far less concerned with acting method than he was with the interpretive basis of the actor's work'.[19] This significant observation challenges the view that there is a 'Brechtian acting style' by suggesting that what one sees on stage is the result of an interpretive process rather than the deployment of specific acting stratagems. Brecht was involved in a process of acclimatizing the actors to an integrated process of interpreting the contradictions of their roles and relationships with other characters rather than constructing an acting methodology per se.

Sensitizing the actor to a less character-focused approach to performance was a central element in Brecht's implementation of new theatre practice. The basic Marxist position that the individual is the ensemble of social relations meant that character never came from the individual in isolation, but from the individual's contact with other individuals

---

[17] See Regine Lutz, *Schauspieler – der schönste Beruf: Einblicke in die Theaterarbeit* (Munich: Langen Müller, 1993), p. 234.

[18] Käthe Reichel, in Christa Neubert-Herwig, '"Wir waren damals wirklich Mitarbeiter"', in Neubert-Herwig, *Benno Besson: Theater spielen in acht Ländern*, pp. 33–6 (33).

[19] John Rouse, 'Brecht and the Contradictory Actor', *Theatre Journal*, 36:1 (1984), pp. 25–42 (26).

and social institutions.[20] That said, these interactions had to conform
to Brecht's notion of realism, and so he advocated the role of observation as a key skill in the actor. He appreciated that the process was
not a simple one: observation was actually about noting differences, not
similarities, such as those between '*relaxed* and *loose, quick* and *hurried,
imaginative* and *digressive*'.[21] This approach was designed to make the
actor more aware of nuance, but the process did not stop there. While
Brecht acknowledged that identification was one form of observation,
he preferred an actor's observation to centre on other people.[22] Such a
method conferred an extra layer of distance of which Brecht approved –
one can be more critical of others than of oneself. In order to bring this
about, Brecht suggested that actors rehearse each other's roles, that men
rehearse women's roles and vice versa.[23] Observation here is focused on
difference, on how a man's execution of an action may diverge from a
woman's.

As far as can be ascertained, Brecht did not encourage rehearsing
role reversals of gender with the BE, but he did entertain other ideas
designed to bring out differences between actors and their characters.
The aim here, as before, was to expose types of behaviour critically for
the spectator by contrasting the actor with the character and not allowing
them to merge seamlessly. Lutz tells the story of how Brecht invited her
to choose a role from *Die Tage der Kommune* (*The Days of the Commune*).
As a young actor, she understandably chose two young characters, one a
larger and one a smaller role. She reports how Brecht was disappointed
that she had not chosen Mme Cabet, the fifty-year-old lead.[24] The BE
never staged the play in Brecht's lifetime, but she notes how successful
this strategy was in practice when Carola Braunbock, another young
actor, played the old peasant woman in *Der kaukasische Kreidekreis* (*The
Caucasian Chalk Circle*).

A contrastive method employed more frequently at the company was
that of alternating two different actors in the same role. The initial plan
for casting Puntila in the BE's first production was to alternate the actors
Willy A. Kleinau and Leonard Steckel until, as I will show in the next
chapter, Brecht realized he could not work with Kleinau. Over the years,

[20] See Brecht, 'Rollenstudium', BFA, 22: 601.
[21] Brecht, '*Messingkauf* – Fragment B 75', BFA, 22: 746; *BoP*, p. 68.
[22] See Brecht, 'Kleines Organon', BFA, 23: 86; *BoT*, p. 246; and Brecht, in Anon., 'Über
die Arbeit am Berliner Ensemble', in Werner Hecht (ed.), *Brecht im Gespräch: Diskussionen und Dialoge* (Berlin: Henschel, 1979), pp. 154–74 (159), respectively.
[23] See Brecht, 'Kleines Organon', BFA, 23: 88; *BoT*, p. 247; and Brecht, '*Messingkauf* –
Fragment B 66', BFA, 22: 740–1; *BoP*, p. 66, respectively.
[24] See Lutz, *Schauspieler*, p. 233, and p. 235 for the subsequent reference.

actors were paired more successfully and the flyers for the 1954 production of *Don Juan* show that the two lead roles alternated on different nights.[25] This was a structural feature of many BE productions and one aimed at the actor rather than the spectator (who may have been blissfully ignorant of the dual casting). Actors could observe their peers' approach to a particular character and consequently note the differences between the two performances.

The process of sublimating theories formulated in exile into practice was an ongoing process at the BE. Actor Angelika Hurwicz noted that the first impression she got of Brecht's work appeared to be

entirely one of a normal director, different from conventional direction only perhaps in his greater patience. It was only after some time that Brecht's characteristics as a director converged from many single qualities to a complete whole.[26]

This almost imperceptible shift of accent in direction initially passed Lutz by, too, as she recorded in a letter home to her parents, written a couple of days after rehearsals started for *Puntila*. She describes rehearsal methods that would endure at the BE: of starting with setting out the actors on stage and trying several reconfigurations, of actors being encouraged to make suggestions[27] (something she found both surprising and welcome). She concludes, however, with a remarkable line: 'and everything, really and truly, for the sake of *art*'.[28] As the next chapter shows, *Puntila* was anything but an example of *l'art pour l'art*, but Lutz as an actor was clearly unaware of the politicized nature of Brecht's direction.

A similar motif can be found in a letter written while she was rehearsing *Der Hofmeister* (*The Tutor*), a play set in the late eighteenth century, but which was not merely a 'costume drama'. She describes how she took off her shoes 'with all due Prussian care'.[29] Lutz is invoking historicization, a Brechtian practice in which actions and opinions are contextualized historically as a way of demonstrating how behaviour and values are different in different historical periods. Except, of course, Lutz never calls her action 'historicization'. Her letters and Hurwicz's observation show how many of the actors were involved in the enactment of theory

---

[25] See the two flyers in Christa Neubert-Herwig (ed.), *Benno Besson: Jahre mit Brecht*, pp. 114 and 116.

[26] Angelika Hurwicz, 'Brechts Arbeit mit dem Schauspieler', in Hubert Witt (ed.), *Erinnerungen an Brecht* (Leipzig: Reclam, 1964), pp. 172–5 (172).

[27] They were not yet called 'offers' at this early stage of the BE's history.

[28] Lutz to her parents, 19 September 1949, BBA Lutz file 'Briefe Berlin Aug. 1949–Nov. 1950'.

[29] Lutz to her parents, 16 March 1950, ibid.

without being able to name it. Instead, they were introduced to a set of practices and were then invited to locate themselves within them.

By 1954, Brecht commented about rehearsal:

> There is a strict ban on achieving a desired effect. Actors can't resist it for too long. They start to get embarrassed when offers they make that have nothing to do with reality are taken as impudence.[30]

While Brecht's insistence on realism is clear, it is his process of enforcing it that is of more importance here. He develops a practice that simultaneously seeks input that is tentative and naïve while discouraging ideas that are forced or pursue a line of action that runs contrary to the material itself. Brecht thus 'trained' his actors by suggestion, rather than explication, in a mode predicated on contextualized experimentation. The process certainly achieved transformative results. Ekkehard Schall, one of the BE's most famous leading actors, arrived, according to Rülicke, as 'a young, screwed up, pathos-ridden actor . . . How he was taken apart'.[31] I shall go into more detail about Brecht's practices as a director on pp. 31–7 below.

The picture of Brecht the educator that emerges from his approaches to the ensemble counters that of Brecht the dictator that has been invoked elsewhere. James K. Lyon, for example, writes: 'Brecht began to style himself as a teacher to a whole generation of young actors and directors. But despite his rejection of the old-style, tyrannical German schoolmaster . . . he came to resemble that very model'.[32] As a justification for this view, Lyon notes how Brecht did not suffer dissent (a claim Lyon does not support with argument or examples), set his assistants homework tasks, and threatened them when he considered them to fall below his standards. I can only assume that Lyon is referring to a letter of 1952 in which Brecht reproaches the assistants for laziness and not taking advantage of the BE's opportunities.[33] While this letter is stern, it ends by asking for suggestions as to what *Brecht* can do to improve the situation,

---

[30] Brecht, in Anon., 'Über die Arbeit am Berliner Ensemble', in Werner Hecht (ed.), *Brecht im Gespräch*, pp. 154–74 (159).

[31] Rülicke, in Erdmut Wizisla, 'Gespräch mit Käthe Rülicke-Weiler über Helene Weigel und Bertolt Brecht am 8.11.1984 in ihrer Berliner Wohnung [with Matthias Braun]', undated, 38 pages (36), HWA FH 70. I have and will be talking of 'Rülicke' in the text when referring to her experiences at the BE before she married Fritz Weiler.

[32] James K. Lyon, 'Brecht in Postwar Germany: Dissident Conformist, Cultural Icon, Literary Dictator', in James K. Lyon and Hans-Peter Breuer (eds.), *Brecht Unbound: Presented at the International Bertolt Brecht Symposium held at the University of Delaware February 1992* (Newark: University of Delaware Press, 1995), pp. 76–88 (84).

[33] See Brecht, 'Über die Arbeit der Dramaturgen, Regisseure, Assistenten und Schüler des Berliner Ensemble', BFA, 23: 220–1.

however. Lyon's claims apply to the treatment of the assistants rather than to the actors, and they ignore testimony from those who worked closely with Brecht, who describe him as a facilitator of learning rather than a dictator of dogma. Directing assistant Egon Monk, for example, notes how Brecht dynamized his own work and promoted 'initiative' in the actors.[34]

Brecht's close collaborator and sometime mistress Ruth Berlau lists the words she most frequently heard Brecht use in rehearsal: 'show, try out, contradiction, dry, speak, *Fabel*, why?, why?, and again: why?'.[35] This short list may contain imperatives to cool down delivery ('dry', 'speak'), but it is more concerned with activity, activation and interrogation. The inclusion of 'contradiction' and '*Fabel*' show that Brecht not only set down parameters linked to his dialectical worldview, but also sought input in terms of practice to answer the recurring question 'why?'. This is not tyranny, but an insistence on dialogue. Benno Besson and Claus Küchenmeister, both assistants in the 1950s, praise Brecht for his ability to make those with whom he worked productive.[36] Käthe Reichel notes that Brecht was never afraid of showing his ignorance in rehearsal,[37] something borne out by the BE's rehearsal documentation.[38]

In the light of the evidence, it can be seen that Brecht's method of rehearsing at the BE was hardly authoritarian, although it was certainly challenging and demanding. Brecht was convinced that talent could not be taught as such, merely given tasks to complete.[39] When it came to his actors, he set the task of realizing the text in all its contradictoriness. He encouraged their active contribution, and contributed himself. It was very much learning by doing, with Brecht undoubtedly in the central position, but a position which was not only able to admit its own weaknesses, but also structure ways of working whose outcomes would garner the BE an international reputation.

---

[34] See Monk, in Carola Stern, *Männer lieben anders: Helene Weigel und Bertolt Brecht* (Reinbek: Rowohlt, 2000), p. 13; and Monk, in Lang and Hillesheim, '*Denken heißt verändern...*', p. 103.

[35] Berlau, in Hans Bunge, *Brechts Lai-Tu: Erinnerungen und Notate von Ruth Berlau* (Darmstadt: Luchterhand, 1985), p. 288.

[36] See Besson, in Thomas Irmer and Matthias Schmidt, *Die Bühnenrepublik. Theater in der DDR*, ed. by Wolfgang Bergmann (Berlin: Alexander, 2003), p. 39; and Claus Küchenmeister, in Ditte Buchmann, Wera and Claus Küchenmeister, '*Eine Begabung muß man entmutigen...*' (Berlin: Henschel, 1986), p. 39.

[37] See Reichel, in Lang and Hillesheim, '*Denken heißt verändern...*', p. 142.

[38] See, for example, the problems encountered towards the end of *Katzgraben* on 3 and 7 March 1953 in Käthe Rülicke's documentation, n.p., BEA File 13.

[39] See Brecht, 'Aufbau einer Rolle. Laughtons Galilei', BFA, 25: 10; *BoP*, p. 153.

Appointing young collaborators and the definition of talent

Brecht's desire to articulate, interrogate and develop his practice was not only a question of his own self-understanding. Brecht was an artist who thrived on the energy of collaboration, and so practice was always something into which he entered with a group of like-minded, but critical, associates. Like-mindedness here suggests an interest in the social possibilities of theatre, not the character-based fare offered at most other theatres. The drive to make the creative staff productive rather than reactive extended beyond the actors.

Brecht wanted to open up a dialogue about fundamental questions facing a theatre under socialism, but this could only be carried out in an atmosphere where exchange of ideas was possible. Returning from exile and with very little known about his work at the time, Brecht may well have been brimming with ideas, but a reception of his plays and his theories was yet to take place. The praise lavished on his own Berlin production of *Mother Courage* in early 1949 had brought him a great deal of attention and had stimulated curiosity, especially amongst young people interested in a new kind of theatre. Monk reports that he attended the dress rehearsal of the production because all acting students in Berlin had been invited.[40] Brecht capitalized on this enthusiasm and sought to train a battery of assistants as a means of introducing, developing and propagating his practice.

The appointment of the assistants was a process that had no formal procedure. I have found no evidence to support Mary Luckhurst's claim that 'Brecht systematised a large and complex training operation, carefully selecting mostly young individuals of distinction and promise'.[41] On the other hand, Werner Mittenzwei's contention that employment 'often came about quite spontaneously'[42] paints slightly too casual a picture, although, on the surface, that is how things certainly seemed. There are examples of how the potential assistant's lack of formal interview did not betoken a slipshod approach to appointment. Wera Skupin, one of the BE's first *Meisterschüler* (a term to which I will return in Chapter 3), reports how she had been recommended to Brecht by the author Michael Tschesno-Hell. She was disappointed by her meeting with Brecht in which he asked her more about her life and opinions than

[40] See Egon Monk, *Regie Egon Monk. Von 'Puntila' zu den Bertinis: Erinnerungen* (Berlin: Transit, 2007), p. 24.
[41] Mary Luckhurst, *Dramaturgy: A Revolution in Theatre* (Cambridge: Cambridge University Press, 2006), p. 129.
[42] Werner Mittenzwei, *Das Leben des Bertolt Brecht oder der Umgang mit den Welträtseln*, vol. 2 (Berlin: Aufbau, 1997), p. 386.

her prose and poetry. It was only later that she learned that Tschesno-Hell had already provided Brecht with such material,[43] and so Brecht had already been able to establish a mark of her talent. Thus, the process was not quite as open-ended as one might have thought, although the 'interview' was fleeting and anything but orthodox. Brecht's fascination with a person's biography, his belief in their ability and their interest in his work were decisive factors. Other examples of this confluence can be seen in the appointment of Skupin's future husband, Claus Küchenmeister, and Manfred Wekwerth.[44] It is also possible that a lack of professional theatrical experience, coupled with commitment and enthusiasm, meant that Brecht would not have to 'undo' practices inimical to his own.

As time went on, the appointment process became slightly more skills-orientated. Carl Weber, who joined as an assistant in 1952, tells of how he had to describe scenes he had seen at the BE, and Uta Birnbaum had to prepare a comparison between Farquhar's *Recruiting Officer* and Brecht's adaptation *Pauken und Trompeten (Trumpets and Drums)*.[45] In both cases, the tasks would have been unusual exercises in a more conventional theatre, yet typical of those set to directing and dramaturgical assistants at the BE. If one considers Weber's task, one may have expected an analysis rather than a description, but Brecht appears to have been far more concerned with Weber's powers of observation. Analysis, which was unquestionably important at the BE, was perhaps deemed a skill that could not be developed without a good eye.

The unconventional appointment process was partly concerned with identifying talent, but talent as defined from Brecht's perspective. Käthe Rülicke reports Brecht's formula: 'hard work + interest = talent'.[46] Brecht's position, referred to earlier, that talent could not be taught, but only set tasks, suggests that he was keen to harness diligence and enthusiasm, and channel them into his own theatrical enterprise through exercises concerning the particular features of a given theatrical project.

'Training' the assistants at the BE

Brecht's initial plan for his new company was to engage experienced directors who would work either together with or independently of him, while he also developed young talent as assistants. Benno Besson recalls

[43] See Buchmann *et al.*, *'Eine Begabung'*, pp. 25–9.
[44] Claus Küchenmeister, unpublished interviews with the author, 4 November 2010; and see Manfred Wekwerth, in Hans-Dieter Schütt, *Manfred Wekwerth* (Frankfurt/Oder: Frankfurt Oder Editionen, 1995), p. 67.
[45] Carl Weber and Uta Birnbaum, unpublished interviews with the author, 28 May 2010 and 28 August 2010, respectively.
[46] Brecht, in Käthe Rülicke, '[Diary]', undated, n.p., BBA 1264/10.

how he initially rejected the job title of 'assistant director' as it usually denoted little more than the dogsbody who fetched the director's coffee.[47] Brecht, however, had far greater ambitions for his assistants: they were implicitly charged with working through his method and making use of it both with the BE and any other company they might encounter in their professional careers. For the most part, Brecht decided on whether they would train as directors or dramaturges,[48] but the dividing line between directing and dramaturgy at the company was also deliberately blurred. Assistant dramaturges, for example, were to attend rehearsals and their contribution, according to Rülicke, was 'obligatory. Everyone did everything'.[49]

A short yet important document that was circulated to the company's six assistants at the end of the BE's first month tells much about Brecht's understanding of his trainees' tasks and his aspirations for them. Entitled 'Pflichtbesuch' ('compulsory attendance'), the paper opens by stating that the assistants had to attend a certain Herr Bergmann's lectures in addition to a fortnightly series of in-house talks and discussions that was to begin on 27 September 1949.[50] The first considered one of Brecht's essays and its relationship to *Mister Puntila and his Man Matti*, the BE's first production, and so the link between theory and practice was established early. In addition, the document dispelled the idea that the assistants' training conformed to a fixed scheme: 'the individual's own desire to explore particular areas of interest is a part of achieving good results for the group'. The document proposed that its readers might want to organize the lecture series themselves or recommend further reading, amongst other things. In addition, suggestions were 'requisite . . . in order to enrich the individual's theoretical "toolkit" and make it serviceable'. This is another reference to the reciprocal relationship between theory and practice, embedded into the assistants' work ethic from the outset. This early set of directives and proposals was to set the tone for 'training', that is, training was not so much a question of passively absorbing material, but actively acquiring it.

This impulse can be found in four further areas of activity set for the assistants. The first was writing up '*Notate*'. The normal German word for

---

[47] See Besson, in Irmer and Schmidt, *Die Bühnenrepublik*, p. 39.
[48] Hans Bunge, unpublished interview with John Rouse, 18 May 1988, p. I-1.
[49] Käthe Rülicke-Weiler, 'Anfänge des Berliner Ensembles', in Rainer Mennicken, *Peter Palitzsch* (Frankfurt/Main: Fischer, 1993), pp. 57–61 (58).
[50] [Brecht?], 'Pflichtbesuch', 25 September 1949, n.p., BEA File 2. All subsequent references are to this document. Note that information in square brackets indicates that no information was supplied at source, but was added by me, based on contextual evidence. The inclusion of a question mark where necessary indicates that the information I have provided is merely likely.

notes taken in a rehearsal is '*Notizen*'. Brecht coined this term as a way of describing a special kind of note. Indeed, Monk reports that he had never heard the word before, and Küchenmeister in turn had it explained to him by Monk.[51] *Notate*, when properly taken, were not slavish records of rehearsals, but selective analyses and reflections. Both Peter Palitzsch and Hans Bunge recount that the submission of *Notate* to Brecht was initially a process in which Brecht offered comments of his own and counter-suggestions.[52] Palitzsch felt that he was benefitting from Brecht's input and that he learned a great deal through the exchange, something at odds with Lyon's reduction of such activity to the status of 'homework'. Once the assistants had understood the form and function of the *Notate*, they no longer submitted them to Brecht's scrutiny. For Monk, they provided the basis and the critique for the following day's work.[53]

The second set of activating tasks was work on compiling *Modellbücher* ('model books'). These were pictorial documentations of productions in which photographs and the text appeared alongside each other, sometimes with a commentary as to why a certain directorial decision had been taken. The books, in their most elaborate forms, were available to buy, and the *Modellbücher* of the productions of *Antigone* in Chur and *Mother Courage* in Berlin are reprinted in volume 25 of Brecht's collected works in German. Examples compiled for in-house use, which are today held in the Brecht and BE archives, tend either to include only photographs or photographs and text from the play in question. This is not the place to debate either the *Modellbücher*'s form or function, but to note the pedagogical value Brecht ascribed to them. In the book *Theaterarbeit*, Brecht wrote a short essay called 'Photographability as Criterion'. In it, he posits the idea that photographs of productions only make sense if the 'basic action' ('*Grundvorgang*') is readable; otherwise one records either too much irrelevant material, as in naturalism, or emptiness, as in stylized productions.[54] While these views are certainly open to debate, the important point is that photography in the theatre became a means of guaranteeing the clear meaning of the performances on stage. Rehearsals were extensively photographed, as the BE photographic archive at the Brecht Archive amply testifies,

---

[51] See Monk, *Regie Egon Monk*, p. 59; and Claus Küchenmeister, unpublished interview with the author, 4 November 2010.
[52] Peter Palitzsch, unpublished interview with John Rouse, 7 June 1988, p. II-2–3; and Hans Bunge, unpublished interview with Rouse, 18 May 1988, p. III-9.
[53] See Monk, *Regie Egon Monk*, p. 87.
[54] See [Brecht], 'Fotografierbarkeit als Kriterium', in BE/Helene Weigel (eds.), *Theaterarbeit: 6 Aufführungen des Berliner Ensembles* (Dresden: Dresdner Verlag, 1952), p. 343; *BoP*, p. 237.

and the choice of photographs to be included in any one *Modellbuch* was enormous.

Berlau recounts how Palitzsch pored over a large selection for hours, evaluating their relative merits. On the back of this, she recommended him to Brecht, who employed him as a dramaturge with special responsibilities for design.[55] Brecht regarded not only a keen sense of observation, but also vast reserves of commitment essential qualities in an assistant. Angela Kuberski notes that there was 'no norm' for the manufacture of *Modellbücher*,[56] which suggests that finding a suitable form was also a task for the assistants. It should be added, however, that while some of the staff registered the usefulness of making the books,[57] I have found no reference to this being an overly pleasurable activity. Uta Birnbaum calls it 'tough work',[58] and both Brecht and Weigel complained about delays in *Modellbuch* production at various times.

The third form of 'training' for assistants was interrogative discussion. Rehearsal was usually prefaced by a meeting, but this was, perhaps surprisingly, not a stringent preparation of how to approach the particular scenes in the schedule. Rather, Brecht and his assistants tended to discuss politics and current events. These 'enlivening stimuli'[59] triggered all manner of associations and chance connections that could then be considered in the light of the impending rehearsal. Palitzsch expands on this: 'it was never only about the scene to be rehearsed, but that was our point of departure and we always came back to it'.[60] The discursive form helped to free up ideas and try to connect life and art in a concrete fashion. Assistants also took part in more focused discussions. One such is available in print and features Brecht and twelve others, including actors, assistants and more established BE personnel preparing Molière's *Don Juan*.[61] Brecht's role is not, however, to dominate the discussion, but rather to provoke it. As Peter W. Ferran notes: 'what is most instructive about this discussion, with its constant posing of contradictions to apparent conclusions, is that it does not seem urged to settle these matters'.[62]

---

[55] Ruth Berlau, in Bunge (ed.), *Brechts Lai-Tu*, p. 232.

[56] Angela Kuberski, 'Brechts Modellbücher und die Folgen', *notate*, 6 (1984), pp. 4–5 (5).

[57] See Palitzsch, in Stephan Suschke, 'Ich hielt mich nie für ein Genie', *Theater der Zeit*, 2 (2002), pp. 30–2 (31).

[58] Uta Birnbaum, unpublished interview with the author, 28 August 2010.

[59] Manfred Wekwerth, unpublished interview with the author, 14 June 2011.

[60] Palitzsch, in Peter Iden, *Peter Palitzsch: Theater muß die Welt verändern* (Berlin: Henschel, 2005), p. 55.

[61] See Anon., 'Über die Komik in *Don Juan*', in Hecht (ed.), *Brecht im Gespräch*, pp. 126–33.

[62] Peter W. Ferran, 'Molière's *Don Juan* adapted for Brecht's Berliner Ensemble', *Contemporary Theatre Review*, 6:2 (1997), pp. 13–40 (22).

Brecht fired off a series of questions that continually queried his collaborators' assumptions as a model of how one retains a dialectical liveliness in the production process. The aim was to open up the material in the hope that his directing staff would replicate the method in the rehearsal room.

The final task that an assistant had to carry out was to write 'Abendberichte' ('evening reports'). These formed a part of the BE's quality control mechanism, a way of ensuring that productions retained their freshness over their often lengthy runs. While I will discuss questions of monitoring quality on pp. 157–60, Chapter 5, I will merely note here that the assistants' role in writing such a report was to use their observational skills to identify divergences from the usual performance and suggest modifications that could add to or bring out more from the production. The reports were primarily descriptive, although assistants were encouraged to evaluate what they had seen as well.

'Training' for the assistants was formally similar to that for the actors. Brecht did not set down a regime as such, but asked the assistants to observe what he was doing and to draw conclusions in an ongoing process of interrogation. While the actors received a concrete reaction to the 'offers' they made, in that they were either accepted or rejected, the assistants embarked on a longer learning process that promoted independent thought, analysis and evaluation. Brecht was not teaching his approach to directing as such, but rather articulating its principles practically and eliciting constructive and productive responses. These responses in turn would provide the assistants with points of reference for their own practice.

Not just a job, or the BE as a way of life

Brecht did not believe that theatre was an activity for which one 'clocked on' and 'clocked off'. While the actors were used to rehearsing during the day and performing when required in the evening, the assistants were called upon to work all hours, just, to make this clear, as Brecht and Weigel did. According to Hans Bunge, who started as an assistant dramaturge, Brecht demanded '100% commitment and enthusiasm',[63] something he also expected of himself. Küchenmeister summarizes the position concisely: 'the theatre was the priority, not you'.[64] The focus on the work over the individual had much to do with Brecht's ambitions for the BE as a whole. While there was certainly no sense that the audience

---

[63] Hans Bunge, unpublished interview with John Rouse, 18 May 1988, p. II-5.
[64] Claus Küchenmeister, unpublished interview with the author, 4 November 2010.

would leave a performance of *Mother Courage* and collectively abolish war, Brecht wanted art to play a role that pervaded his audience's lives by refashioning their consciousness. His theatre was designed to make the spectator a curious, questioning, and active member of society, having developed those attributes over time watching his productions. He sought to reduce the gap between art and life, something Peter Bürger identifies as a distinguishing feature of the historical avant-garde.[65] It is clear, however, that Brecht's theatre was not aesthetically extreme like that of the expressionists or the surrealists, so here one may identify a different method of folding art into life. Brecht forged this link first and foremost in the BE itself: only when his collaborators viewed their work as essential, rather than merely as a means of earning a wage, might their art itself attain the centrality in the spectators' lives for which Brecht strove.

Such complete dedication affected what it meant to be in the employ of the BE. Mittenzwei extrapolates that the need to relax outside of work 'was, for [Brecht], merely another expression of a lack of interest, of laziness'.[66] Thus, one may interpret Lyon's claim, quoted on p. 16, that Brecht aped the authoritarian teachers he claimed to despise by treating his assistants like school pupils, with a little more sensitivity to context. For Brecht, the new company had the potential to reintegrate art into his audience's lives, and this process was to start with art's integration into the lives of his co-workers. When he found that they sometimes treated their jobs like jobs and not central parts of their lives, he registered his disappointment.[67] I am not seeking either to condone or condemn this possibly monomaniacal behaviour, rather to show the ramifications of Brecht's commitment to his project.

Brecht's view was not necessarily one shared by everyone else, and the BE's logbook shows that seven actors and three assistant directors left the company after its first year.[68] Wolfgang Bömelburg, a member of the technical staff since 1951, complained to his union about the hours he had to work, but found that complaining did not change anything.[69] He, however, seems to have been taken with the BE's infectious work ethic after all and continued to work at the BE until the 1990s. For those who chose to remain, the opportunity to be involved in the collective work outweighed its demanding nature.

---

[65] See Peter Bürger, *Theory of the Avant-Garde*, trans. by Michael Shaw (Minneapolis: University of Minnesota Press, 1984). Originally published in German in 1974.

[66] Mittenzwei, *Das Leben des Bertolt Brecht*, vol. 2, p. 399.

[67] See, for example, Brecht to the directors and dramaturges of the BE, c. 1954, BFA, 30: 667.

[68] See the entry for 31 August 1950, n.p., BEA File 'Logbücher 50–52'.

[69] Wolfgang Bömelburg, unpublished interview with John Rouse, 24 May 1988, p. II-17.

The 'social' structure of the BE also helped to perpetuate the demands for commitment. While families had run theatres before, they had never been so well supported by subsidy. Brecht and Weigel were able to 'domesticate' the work with the BE due to their position at the company's head. The charismatic yet boisterous father and the nurturing yet firm mother served to transform working relationships into senses of obligation, underpinned by support and encouragement. This family structure puts paid to suggestions that the BE was in some way a utopian band of equals. However, a family can also open up channels of dialogue, and so this was not a top-down structure for paternalist *diktat*, as was the case in most other German theatres at the time in which strict hierarchies were, had been and would be the order of the day for some time. The metaphor of an organizational structure as 'familial' naturally has its limits and should not be taken too literally; the relationships at the BE *resembled* those of a family. While Weigel called herself the mother of the ensemble (but only once Brecht was dead), Brecht preferred to see himself as a teacher, although not, as we have already seen, in a conventional sense.

What marks the BE as different from any other company at that time was that it did not simply view itself as an institution that staged plays. Manfred Pauli, who undertook work experience at the BE under Brecht, calls it 'a craftsman's workshop ["Handwerksbetrieb"] or a research laboratory'.[70] Fredric Jameson considers the BE a 'master class' to which the audience 'is invited only on selected occasions'.[71] This emphasis on process over product, and the value of reflection and refinement mark the BE as a perpetual training ground rather than a simple manufacturer of productions. Its commitment to what Schiller called an 'aesthetic education' meant that it was doing far more in terms of developing practice and attitudes than establishing and consolidating a singular way of working. Its peculiar interpersonal structures may be traced back to this premise. The idea of the BE as family or as school are both useful in understanding its unique way of producing bonds (meant in both the positive and negative senses) between those involved in the company's work. However, one must not lose sight of the material situation at the BE either. Egon Monk counsels us to remember what was actually happening at the time: 'I was [Brecht's] assistant; he was definitely my boss'.[72]

---

[70] Manfred Pauli, *Unterwegs zu Brecht: Rekonstruktion einer Annäherung* (Schkeuditz: Schkeuditzer Buchverlag, 2012), p. 35.

[71] Fredric Jameson, *Brecht and Method* (London: Verso, 1998), p. 63.

[72] Monk, in Lang and Hillesheim, *'Denken heißt veränden . . .* ', p. 103.

The different kinds of institutional structures did bring about important changes in the way that the BE made theatre. What emerged, after a short time, was a process of *Mitbestimmung* ('collective decision-making'), something that would only emerge in the Federal Republic of Germany in the late 1960s and effectively disappear by the early 1970s.[73] *Mitbestimmung*, as practised later in the West, can be understood in connection with the student movement of 1968, the rebellion against parental authority and institutional hierarchy. Its appeal to leaderless collectives sowed the seeds of its own decline. *Mitbestimmung* at the BE had an altogether different context and was not blighted by revolutionary romanticism. No one at the BE would deny that Brecht was the central figure. His ideas and practice informed and inspired the work from the outset. He had more experience and understanding than his assistants on account of their age and lack of contact with working theatres. His centrality was a given, but this did not prevent the creation of processes to which his collaborators could actively contribute. The following example, however, demonstrates the nature and limits of the arrangement. Over time, the assistants were invited to participate in the casting process. A table would be compiled that listed every assistant's suggestion for every role. Yet this did not lead to a 'democratic' outcome, where the most popular choices got the parts. The director always made the final decision, but the process of collecting the opinions of others helped to inform it.

Contribution from everyone was essential, and Brecht was not reticent about promoting his assistants and giving them productions to direct early in their careers. This was a way of making them independent, that is, of being able to take what they had learned and to develop it further. Brecht admired the fact that Meyerhold and Vakhtangov, who had learned to direct under Stanislavsky, had taken his principles in new and exciting directions.[74] All the same, Brecht was the ultimate arbiter in meetings, but as set designer Hainer Hill puts it, Brecht listened to all opinions during dramaturgical conferences and then reached a decision based on how useful the proposals were for the issue at hand.[75] Hierarchies were therefore weakened rather than eliminated, but the fact that discussion took place and was treated seriously meant that Brecht's views could also be challenged and modified.

[73] See David Barnett, *Rainer Werner Fassbinder and the German Theatre* (Cambridge: Cambridge University Press, 2005), pp. 175–8, for a short account of the rise and fall of the practice.

[74] See Brecht, '[Stanislawski – Wachtangow – Meyerhold]', BFA, 22: 285.

[75] Hainer Hill, unpublished interview with John Rouse, 23 June 1988, p. III-8.

Brecht's vocabulary for the stage: an introduction

Before considering Brecht's directing practice, it is important to understand a series of terms that helped Brecht approach the business of staging
plays and that feature regularly in the documentation of the BE's production work.[76] All the terms are informed by Brecht's Marxist worldview,
one based on understanding the world and people in terms of perpetual
processes of change. These processes are what Brecht called 'dialectical';
and it is to this term, which Brecht took from Hegel and Marx, that I will
now turn because it offers the philosophical basis for all the key concepts
that follow.

The dialectic accounts for changes in human existence over time. In
abstract terms, an entity, the thesis, exists concretely in space and time.
Over time another entity, the antithesis, comes into being and the relationship between the two is one of contradiction. Change comes about
when the contradiction becomes too great and something new takes
its place: the synthesis of thesis and antithesis. In its turn, the synthesis becomes a new thesis, is met by a new antithesis, and the two are
then resolved into a new synthesis in a process that never ends. The
dialectical worldview sees individuals and society in a process of sustained dialogue which, through contradiction, brings about change in
perpetuity. This philosophy is political because it proposes that both
human behaviour and society are unfixed, a relationship which affects
the exercise of power. Thus, put rather simply, if human beings change
society, they will also change themselves, as the conditions under which
people function will help to produce different behaviours. Contradiction is at the heart of the dialectic, and so Brecht was keen to investigate
this relation in connection with characters' own inconsistencies, relationships between characters, and relationships between characters and social
situations.

A dialectical understanding of people and events implies that surface
reality that is reproduced in naturalist performance cannot be trusted
because everything on stage is the result of social processes, the interaction between individual and society. Brecht thus wanted to get behind
appearances and tease out what might have brought them about. Carl
Weber offers a useful definition: '"Fable" was, of course, Brecht's preferred term designating a play's plot as it is retold on stage from a specific point of view . . . a fable was always to reveal the contradictions of a

---

[76] For a more detailed explanation of the terms, together with practical examples, see
David Barnett, *Brecht in Practice: Theatre, Theory and Performance* (London: Bloomsbury,
2014).

plot'.[77] The *Fabel* (which I will keep in German so as to avoid the misleading associations of the English 'fable') is thus an interpreted extrapolation taken from the plot of any given play. It rereads the events (and not the characters) and uses them as a guide for the director and the actors. In effect, it becomes the production's meta-narrative to which all else defers. Brecht was clear on this point when he wrote, reflecting on the work of the BE: 'we work out situations, and the *Fabel* has the final say. We construct the *Fabel*, not the characters that are then thrown into the *Fabel*'.[78] Brecht maintained that a work of art had to defend itself 'against the most unartistic of questions' in order to assert itself as worthy of the title.[79] That is, questions of a sociological or historical nature were asked of the work when establishing the *Fabel*, as to whether people would really behave in such ways in such situations, and only then could production work proceed. In the same note, Brecht also recognized that the 'magnitude [of a work of art] emerges in its variability, or rather in its service to varied interests that are antithetical to one another'. The *Fabel* was therefore open to a number of readings; there was no single interpretation.

Brecht developed what would become known as the 'erzählendes Arrangement'[80] ('narrative arrangement'), that is, the grouping of actors on stage into meaningful units to communicate the dialectical tensions in play at any particular point in the *Fabel*. Brecht sketched his aspiration for this idea in the 1930s in a way that covers several important features, before later settling on the term '*Arrangement*':

Epic theatre uses the simplest possible groupings, ones that clearly reveal the meaning of the incidents portrayed. It abandons 'random', 'life-like', 'casual' grouping: its stage does not reflect the 'natural' disorder of things. Its goal is the opposite of natural disorder: natural order. The ordering principles are of a social and historical nature.[81]

Brecht proposes that a successful *Arrangement* is one that is readable, whose elements stand in clear relationships to each other. Chance details obscure meaning, as does a slavish deference to an imitation of the way events take place outside the theatre. However, he does not then suggest that the director should engage in elaborate stylization – he contrasts natural disorder with natural order. Eric Bentley observed in this context

---

[77] Carl Weber, 'The Actor and Brecht, or: The Truth Is Concrete', *Brecht Yearbook*, 13 (1984), pp. 63–74 (71).

[78] Brecht, 'Über unsere Inszenierungen', BFA, 23: 192; *BoT*, p. 274. I have substituted '*Fabel*' for the translators' 'plot'.

[79] Brecht, '[Die Fabel]', BFA, 23: 193; *BoT*, p. 275.

[80] See Manfred Wekwerth, *Theater in Veränderung* (Berlin: Aufbau, 1960), pp. 93–116.

[81] Brecht, 'Anmerkungen zur *Mutter* [1938]', BFA, 24: 155; *BoT*, p. 87.

that Brecht's 'pet hate was actors in a straight line or symmetrically disposed across the stage'.[82] On the contrary, Brecht's understanding of realism dictated that the representations on stage were recognizable – that is, natural – yet arranged in such a way that the meaning behind the surface was *also* visible. His note that historical and social factors influence the *Arrangement* connects it inextricably to the *Fabel*. Maarten van Dijk counsels, however, not to view the *Arrangement* as something fixed or static, but as an active representation of competing interests: 'Brecht thought the essential principle of blocking was montage. Not composition but decomposition..., a selection of... elements placed together so as to comment on each other'.[83] Van Dijk points to the life-like liveliness Brecht strove for and dispels the misapprehension that the *Arrangement* reduced the plenitude of the action to something static or mechanical. As Rouse points out, the progression of the *Arrangements* traces the dialectical relationships between characters.[84]

While the *Fabel* probed the surface of a play's action, a different term opened up the contradictions of a character: *Gestus*. Meg Mumford offers the following definition: '*Gestus* entails the aesthetic gestural presenta-tion of the socio-economic and ideological construction of human iden-tity and interaction', adding that is it 'the externalization of the socially significant'.[85] That is, the actor's body is involved in a dynamic relation-ship with its social contexts as a way of establishing a visible connection between the two. The body is no longer in some way neutral, but actively shows its insinuation in its environments. The actor emphasizes certain physical postures and gestures as a way of pointing to connections that lie beyond the scope of naturalistic representation. *Gestus*, however, is quite a slippery term whose meaning Brecht never firmly established. As Mumford observes: 'in Brecht's writings, the *Gestus* concept appears to embrace a wide variety of activities'.[86] Mindful of these slippages, I will refer to *Gestus* in the context of the actor's overall posture only. That is, the *Gestus* of, say, a postman, might reveal something about his class

---

[82] Eric Bentley, *The Brecht Memoir* (Evanston, IL: Northwestern University Press, 1989), p. 54.

[83] Maarten van Dijk, 'Blocking Brecht', in Pia Kleber and Colin Visser (eds.), *Re-interpreting Brecht: His Influence on Contemporary Drama and Film* (Cambridge: Cambridge University Press, 1990), pp. 117–34 (123).

[84] See John Rouse, *Brecht and the West German Theatre: The Practice and Politics of Interpre-tation* (Ann Arbor: UMI, 1989), p. 36.

[85] Meg Mumford, 'Gestic Masks and Brecht's Theater: A Testimony to the Contradictions and Parameters of a Realist Aesthetic', *Brecht Yearbook*, 26 (2001), pp. 143–71 (144 and 145 respectively).

[86] Meg Mumford, *Showing the Gestus: A Study of Acting in Brecht's Theatre* (Unpublished PhD Thesis, University of Bristol, 1997), p. 23.

and the nature of his work, just as the *Gestus* of a head teacher might
tell an audience something different about her social provenance and
status.

Gestus will generally remain fixed during a production because characters cannot change their class, although a drastic turn of events, such
as unemployment or a win on the lottery, may radically change a character enough to change their *Gestus*. A character's *Gestus*, however, also
comprises a repertoire of *Haltungen*. The concept of *Haltung* was central
to Brecht's understanding of what actors did on stage and is translated
into English both as 'attitude' and 'bearing'. The German word combines what is usually a mental state in English (attitude) with physical
expression (bearing), and I shall retain the German *Haltung* so as not
to emphasize either aspect unduly. The most important tenet of *Haltung*
is that it is never passive; it denotes a relationship *towards* someone or
something; as the 'someone' or 'something' changes, so will the *Haltung*.
In the Marxist tradition, people are an assemblage of the *Haltungen* they
display, and because the *Haltungen* might be contradictory, they may surprise members of the audience into asking how a character they thought
they knew behaved in unexpected ways. After all, a character embodies
the contradictions of any given society. Actors were thus charged with
developing an overall *Gestus* that situated their character in a play's given
social environment and a series of *Haltungen* that revealed the contradictions of that position.

Brecht interpreted the world through the perspective of materialist
dialectics.[87] Monika Buschey, drawing on an interview with Lutz, notes
that Brecht was interested in playing causes and not effects on stage.[88]
I will thus propose that Brecht's was an 'undogmatic' or 'heterodox'
Marxism. That is, while Marxism informed the structuring of dialectical performance as articulated in the *Fabel*, *Arrangements*, *Gestus* and
Haltungen, Brecht tended to leave his clearly articulated questions open;
it was the spectator's job to synthesize or resolve them. As Wekwerth
observes, Brecht 'didn't like anything pre-chewed, it took away his pleasure in eating'.[89] In other words, theatre cannot do all the thinking for
the spectator; it can offer material, but that material cannot be processed
to such a degree that it is simply consumed by the spectator without
reflection or effort.

---

[87] See Brecht, 'Kleines Organon', BFA, 23: 82; *BoT*, p. 242.
[88] See Monika Buschey, *Wege zu Brecht: Wie Katharina Thalbach, Benno Besson, Sabine
      Thalbach, Regine Lutz, Manfred Wekwerth, Käthe Rülicke, Egon Monk und Barbara Brecht-
      Schall zum Berliner Ensemble fanden* (Berlin: Dittrich, 2007), p. 44.
[89] Wekwerth, *Schriften*, p. 69.

Brecht's rehearsal and directing practices

Brecht's theoretical positions affected the way he conducted rehearsals as director. I have already noted how he promoted the practice of actors making 'offers' as a way of engaging the ensemble in the more inclusive and active staging of plays (see pp. 12–13), but this was just one, albeit central, part of his approach to directing.

Brecht's redefinition of the relationship between the director and the actor re-echoed through the rehearsal process as a whole. Conventional practices were jettisoned in the name of rehearsing a production inductively. Brecht was keen for the actors to make discoveries in rehearsal, rather than to arrive with preconceived ideas about their characters or the situations. The read-through, the occasion at which actors would usually bring their pre-meditated characterizations to the rest of the cast, took on a different function. Angelika Hurwicz recalls the initial read-through of *Mother Courage*, where the actors were instructed simply to read the play: 'that was it. No debates about the diction or the "specific demands of the play"'.[90] The read-through was purely an exercise in orientation; no one was asked to interpret, but only to listen to themselves and the other actors. The emphasis on discovery fed into the early rehearsal process too: actors under Brecht were not asked to learn their lines too quickly. Scripts were often present in the rehearsal room and the prompter played an important role in the early stages.[91] Brecht feared that learning lines before sufficient rehearsal had taken place would cement interpretation before it had been properly established over time.

After the read-through, the actors participated in the 'Stellproben' ('rehearsals of positioning') at which the director put together early *Arrangements*. While the actors could certainly contribute to this type of rehearsal, they were far more involved in the 'Detailproben' ('rehearsals of details'). Here the director worked inductively with the cast on bringing out the 'details' of the characters' relationships to each other under the conditions set out by the *Fabel*.[92] The idea of a 'detail' is connected to Brecht's understanding of semiotic synecdoche in the theatre: 'the *distinguishing features* stand as realistic parts to the realistic whole'.[93] The German word for detail, 'Merkmal', contains a particle from the verb

[90] Angelika Hurwicz, in Renate Seydel, . . . *gelebt für alle Zeiten: Schauspieler über sich und andere* (Berlin: Henschel, 1975), p. 334.

[91] See Wolf Kaiser, unpublished interview with John Rouse, 11 May 1988, p. I-1; and Willi Schwabe, unpublished interview with Rouse, 1 July 1988, p. I-1-2.

[92] See BE/Helene Weigel (eds.), *Theaterarbeit*, pp. 256–8 (*BoP*, pp. 230–2), for a schematic, fifteen-point list of elements that comprised the realization process at the BE.

[93] Brecht, '[Die Auswahl der einzelnen Elemente]', BFA, 22: 253.

'merken', 'to notice' – and so the details were not in some way minor or accidental, but significant and designed to catch the spectator's eye. Indeed, no lesser a spectator than Lee Strasberg, the great exponent of the American Method acting, observed approvingly of the production of *The Caucasian Chalk Circle* when it toured London in 1956: 'there is no attempt at completeness in the physical staging, which consists entirely of selected details'.[94] Brecht picked out only the most important aspects of a relationship, something rooted in his emphasis on clearly showing *Gestus* and *Haltung*. Helene Weigel, however, notes that one can have too much of a good thing and that she almost destroyed her own Mother Courage by building too many details into the performance.[95] An excess of meaning had the same effect as a dearth – the character and its relationships became unreadable.

The discovery of dialectical contradictions was another way of accentuating discrepancies in a character's behaviour, rather than passing them over. One such way of identifying moments of contrast was when the actor observed that the character did 'not' do one thing, 'but' did another. For example, in *The Caucasian Chalk Circle* the servant Grusha does 'not' walk away from the royal child who has been abandoned, 'but' takes him into her care. 'Doing good' is revealed to be the result of a struggle, rather than a natural response. Actors can show that they are not doing one thing, but another and thus open up the contradictions involved in making decisions. Brecht recommended the 'not/but' technique as a way of building a character.[96] Lutz reports that her understanding of character at the BE was defined by two concepts: '"Drehpunkt" und "Bruch"' ('"turning point" and "break"'); she adds that the difference between the two was merely a question of degree, not quality.[97]

Fuegi, who is prepared to countenance that dialectics were involved in the actors' work at the BE, gives a remarkably flattened account of them. He asserts that if a character were painted in a particularly positive light in one rehearsal, then Brecht would search for more negative elements in the next.[98] This description lends the process a mechanistic dimension, concerned only with crude notions of balancing a character's polarized attributes. Käthe Rülicke offers a far more complex insight when describing the way in which a positive character might be portrayed: 'it's not a question of whether the positive hero may be shown as

[94] Lee Strasberg, *At the Actors Studio: Tape-Recorded Sessions*, ed. by Robert H. Hethman (New York: Viking, 1965), p. 384.
[95] See Weigel, in Hecht (ed.), *Helene Weigel: Eine grosse Frau des 20. Jahrhunderts* (Frankfurt/Main: Suhrkamp, 2000), p. 31.
[96] See Brecht, 'Kleines Organon', BFA, 23: 87; *BoT*, pp. 246–7.
[97] Lutz, *Schauspieler*, p. 120.   [98] See Fuegi, *Chaos according to Plan*, p. 158.

a "secret" drinker or someone who treats his wife badly, on the contrary, it's a question of showing *the positive as a process*, as a development'.[99] The difference between the two descriptions is telling. For Fuegi, dialectics is little more than a question of an artificially created roundness, of locating good and bad in everyone. For Rülicke, good and bad do not simply exist in conditions of mutual suppression, but are produced by forces with which the hero has to interact. This version is intimately connected to Lutz's experience of 'turning points' and 'breaks' – change comes about through situations that transform their participants. That is how dialectical rehearsal was understood at the BE.

Brecht favoured the procedure of having actors make 'offers' to each other as a way of activating them and developing their sensitivity to the material in the context of the *Fabel*. Brecht, of course, still had to offer help and guidance of his own in rehearsal, and here, again, one finds a director unwilling to spoon-feed his cast with definitive instructions but to make use of suggestive direction. This he undertook in two modes.

The first is the obvious one: he gave verbal assistance. Claus Küchenmeister remembers a scene, later cut, in *The Caucasian Chalk Circle* in which the actor playing a smuggler was having difficulties: 'Brecht then explained to the actor very seriously: smugglers are essentially traders. And that was the sum of his direction'.[100] Brecht did not tell the actor what to do or how to speak the lines, but gave him a social reference point that could stimulate a set of responses.

The second type of help offered came in the form of 'vormachen', 'acting out' the character to the actor. Melanie Hinz notes a passage in Regine Lutz's book on acting in which Brecht acts out a movement, and Lutz praises Brecht's skills: 'Brecht steals the show with his performance... The director's performance is met with humility... He sets the yardstick of a "successful portrayal"'.[101] If we ignore the fact that Lutz herself states how directors who were also actors could inhibit actors with their virtuosity when acting out parts and that Brecht never inhibited her,[102] Hinz still fundamentally misunderstands both Lutz's delight and Brecht's intention. Many of Brecht's assistants and actors have commented on his performance abilities. Reichel, mixing her metaphors, says that Brecht offered images 'on which [the actors] could move as if on

---

[99] Käthe Rülicke-Weiler, *Die Dramaturgie Brechts: Theater als Mittel der Veränderung* (Berlin: Henschel, 1966), p. 178.

[100] Claus Küchenmeister, in Buchmann *et al.*, *'Eine Begabung'*, p. 62.

[101] Melanie Hinz, 'Vorspiel und Nachahmung auf Probe', in Hinz and Jens Roselt (eds.), *Chaos und Konzept: Proben und Probieren im Theater* (Berlin: Alexander, 2011), pp. 72–96 (79).

[102] See Lutz, *Schauspieler*, pp. 88 and 234, respectively.

a railway track'.[103] She registers the ease with which the ideas could be taken up, but elsewhere she mentions a quality that was similar to his verbal instructions: 'he always ran up onto the stage. But he didn't want us to copy him. He wanted to provide a spark'.[104] So, one is led to ask how he managed to combine ease of use with suggestive (rather than concrete) actions. Hurwicz talks of a 'dryness', or perhaps better, 'understatedness' in his performance while Monk says his actions were 'almost always exaggerated'.[105] Carl Weber adds that Brecht often spoke the lines in gibberish.[106] At the heart of Brecht's performance was, as Lutz adds, an implied *Haltung*, 'but you could distil [it] and develop it further'.[107] Thus, actors who had learned to play with *Gestus* and *Haltung* could read Brecht's either over- or understated demonstrations and redirect the example into something specific. Brecht was not, then, as Hinz argues, involved in inhibiting the actor with his virtuosity. Instead, he enlivened the actor with his own gestic renditions which were performed in such a way that direct imitation was impossible.

Brecht set his gestic directions to individual actors in the context of their social relationships. The dialectical standpoint that the smallest social unit is not one, but two people informed this approach. Interaction causes change, and the BE's productions embodied this dictum. In the *Messingkauf* Brecht asserted that actors had to be interested not only in themselves, but in their partners on stage because characters develop through their relationships to each other.[108] He asks the actors to demonstrate their debt to the other characters by tracing the dialectical tensions in the dialogue, rather than concealing them under a veneer of unchanging 'character'. Thus Ekkehard Schall praised Weigel for her generosity to her partners, despite playing leading roles herself.[109]

Enhancing the rehearsal process

The great problem with the movement from *Fabel* to *Arrangement* to the development of suitable *Gestus* and *Haltung*, which carefully unfold throughout a performance, is that it could become a de-humanized and de-humanizing process in which actors merely went through a series of

[103] Reichel, in Lang and Hillesheim, '*Denken heißt verändern . . .* ', p. 141.
[104] Reichel, reported in Buschey, *Wege zu Brecht*, p. 66.
[105] Hurwicz, in Seydel, *. . . gelebt für alle Zeiten*, p. 334; and Monk, *Regie Egon Monk*, p. 57.
[106] Carl Weber, unpublished interview with the author, 28 May 2010.
[107] Lutz, in Holger Teschke, '"Bei Brecht gab's immer was zu lernen": Regine Lutz im Gespräch mit Holger Teschke', *Dreigroschenheft*, 1 (2009), pp. 5–7 (7).
[108] See Brecht, '*Messingkauf* – Fragment B 77', BFA, 22: 747; *BoP*, p. 66.
[109] See Schall, in Anon., 'Ekkehard Schall am 28.9.1981 in seiner Berliner Wohnung im Gespräch mit Matthias Braun', undated, 31 pages (3), HWA FH 32.

rigid motions. Brecht was not unaware of this danger and wanted performances to flow.[110] With an emphasis on episodic action and very close
attention to detail, the productions themselves ran the risk of atomiza-
tion. Actors and the creative team could become so fixated on getting
particular gestures and actions correct that they would lose sight of the
overall shape of a production. An anonymous *Notat* of 1951 recorded
this predicament when the BE revived *Puntila* with a new lead actor:

Our tempo is the same throughout, it's mechanical. That comes from the way
we rehearse. We separate out the individual scenes to give them more detail. We
now need to introduce differentiation. At other moments calmness again. The
tempo must vary.[111]

What is interesting about this observation is that it does not criticize the
actors per se or ask them to do anything different directly. Instead, the
problem is structural – the details are fine and should be retained, but it is
their overall presentation that requires further attention. Brecht's solution
was the institution of a 'Durchsprechprobe' (a 'speak-through') which
was used after the more conventional 'Durchlaufprobe' ('run-through')
had detected the problems in the first place.

   The aim of such a measure was to reintroduce lightness to the performance, and to get away from the studied concentration required to
articulate contradiction and social specificity. In a *Durchsprechprobe*, the
actors were usually asked to run the scenes, retaining both the *Arrangements* and their established gestures, but without investing them with too
much energy, while acting and delivering their lines at speed.[112] The
result of a successful *Durchsprechprobe* is set out in this anonymous observation from the first production of *Puntila*:

The actors were tired. That's why they performed what they'd learned (very)
mechanically. As the actors were not interested in coming across earnestly, all the
unnecessary emoting disappeared as well . . . This was the funniest performance
by far.[113]

The comment appears paradoxical: by performing learned actions
mechanically, the actors freed themselves from mechanical performance.
The key factor at this stage in the process was that the actors were not
asked to focus as such, but to loosen up, at speed. Consequently, the

---

[110] See, for example, Brecht, 'Abnehmen des Tons', BFA, 23: 174; *BoP*, p. 233.
[111] Anon., '48. Probe 24.10.51 I', n.p., BEA File 2.
[112] See Angelika Hurwicz, in Hurwicz and Gerda Goedhart, *Brecht inszeniert: 'Der kaukasische Kreidekreis'* (Velber: Friedrich, 1964), n.p.
[113] Anon., 'Sonnabend 5-11–49, 2. Hauptprobe BB EE CN . . .', 3 pages (3), BEA File
2.

enactment of learned movements gained a new, lively quality. In addition, the reduction of unrequited emotion pared the performances down so that the social relationships became clearer. Former assistant Carl Weber notes that such runs also gave the actors 'a keen sense of the show's rhythmic pattern'.[114] The relaxed yet pacey 'speak-through' suspended the actors' usual mode of performing and allowed them to see themselves and each other with fresh eyes. They could then import the lightness back into their performances while also having gained a better understanding of the production's structure as a whole.

Once a BE production had reached the requisite standard, Brecht reactivated a practice he had instituted as a director in the Weimar Republic. Laura Bradley reports that his 1932 production of *The Mother* did not open with the premiere or a press night, but was presented in four closed performances first.[115] While there are no records of the function of these previews from that time, a substantial hint is given later in *Theaterarbeit*. Here it states that the BE sought an audience of working people from factories and students in its closed previews. The company then engaged them in discussion after the performance with a view to using responses and reactions in further rehearsals.[116] The connection with the theatre's audience, especially with working and young people, was a further example of Brecht's commitment to reduce the gap between art and everyday life. He had hoped that his theatre was not extraneous to his audience's lives, but integrated or even integral. This aspiration was made clear in one of his earliest pieces of advice to Regine Lutz. She had scarcely arrived in Berlin before Brecht told her which newspapers to read 'to become acquainted with my audience'.[117] Brecht's advice and his hopes may well have been blue-eyed or illusory, but they provide undeniable testimony to his need for connection and reciprocal exchange between the institution and the audience.

Yet, even once the previews and the premiere had passed, Brecht did not consider the process over. He said as much in his notebook: 'it isn't a question of turning the production into a product – on the contrary, it's about provoking changes that can influence the development of the mode of performance and make it perceptible'.[118] His commitment to

---

[114] Carl Weber, 'Brecht as Director', *The Drama Review*, 12:1 (1967), pp. 101–7 (104).

[115] See Laura Bradley, *Brecht and Political Theatre. 'The Mother' on Stage* (Oxford: Oxford University Press, 2006), p. 30.

[116] See Anon., 'Phasen einer Regie', in BE/Helene Weigel (eds.), *Theaterarbeit*, pp. 256–8 (258); *BoP*, p. 231.

[117] Lutz to her parents, 25 August 1949, BBA Lutz file 'Briefe Berlin Aug. 1949–Nov. 1950'.

[118] Brecht, *Notizbuch 48–49*, BBA 811/32.

dialectics meant that the very concept of a 'production' itself required redefinition because it was never considered finished. The traditional end-point of rehearsals was merely a staging post for Brecht. He returned to productions like *Mother Courage* and *Puntila* with new actors and new ideas to see how the dialectical tensions within the productions could be re-evaluated and re-performed.

The BE as a Brechtian theatre company

It may sound tautological to call Brecht's theatre company 'Brechtian', but that is only the case once the meaning of 'Brechtian' has been clearly established. It is not unusual to find the adjective attributed to a performance, yet its meaning is often misguided or simply incorrect. Consider the following examples:

In a Brechtian coup de théâtre, the director Richard Jones and designer Miriam Buether turn the lights on the audience, casting us as the town's burghers at a rancorous public meeting.[119]

Though he probably would not like the term, [Stewart] Lee is the most Brechtian of comedians, exposing the mechanics of his art at every turn.[120]

In both examples, the 'Brechtian' is a quality concerned with banishing illusion, yet this could apply to many modes of performance that are non-naturalistic and that often pre-date Brecht. Michael Patterson critically notes a more commercial use of 'Brechtian' and asks: 'can one claim that Brecht's legacy is anything more than a matter of employing a more or less fashionable label to enhance theatre work ranging from performance art to agitprop?'[121] Whether Brecht is indeed 'fashionable' any more is raised by newspaper reviewer Michael Billington, writing fifteen years after Patterson's essay. Billington contended in 2009 that, in some circles, '"Brechtian" these days has come to mean "slow, ponderous, didactic"'.[122] There is clearly no agreement in this small sample of usages, yet a common feature of all the deployments of the adjective is that they do not mention politics. This is surprising, to say the least,

---

[119] Tim Auld, '*Public Enemy* at the Young Vic', *The Telegraph*, 18 May 2013.

[120] Stephanie Merritt, 'Stewart Lee: Much A-Stew About Nothing – review', *The Observer*, 10 November 2013.

[121] Michael Patterson, 'Brecht's Legacy', in Peter Thomson and Glendyr Sacks (eds.), *The Cambridge Companion to Brecht*, 1st edn (Cambridge: Cambridge University Press, 1994), pp. 273–87 (276).

[122] Michael Billington, 'When Did "Brechtian" Become Such a Dirty Word?', *The Guardian*, 20 October 2009.

given how politics and society pervade Brecht's thinking about theatre and the way it represents the world.

Yet one should also be wary of attaching the word 'Brechtian' directly to what one sees on stage. It is at this point that it is worth differentiating between method and style. Käthe Rülicke, Manfred Wekwerth and Werner Hecht have all made the argument that Brecht's was a method and not a style.[123] This distinction suggests that all the features observed in performance were products of a way of working, epiphenomena, not a collection of required and necessary performance devices. Monk summarizes the position concisely: 'there was always a basis, but it was developed anew for every production'.[124] This 'basis' was the dialectical investigation of the text and its contexts, and the investigation was a critical one. Brecht had counselled against a 'mistaken reverence for the playwright' in the 1930s.[125] This was a view he maintained at the BE although it was not only manifested in a series of adaptations of other people's plays and a willingness to rewrite his own. The exhortation to the actor to be critical of certain positions was a concrete means to step back from conventional readings and sally forth towards new, more 'realistic', that is, dialectical ones.

Consequently, the meaning of 'Brechtian' (and, by extension, 'Brechtianism') I will be employing in the rest of the book is defined by the dialectical method of approaching theatrical representation, rather than any particular instances of its realization. This decouples the 'Brechtian' from formal features associated with the productions themselves and returns the adjective to its philosophical starting point, rather than to a mistaken connection with a style. A Brechtian theatre is thus one concerned with placing dialectics at the heart of its analysis, its rehearsals and its productions. The 'Brechtian' becomes a yardstick that helps to chart the developments of the BE over the decades and to establish when the BE indeed ceased to be a Brechtian theatre company any longer.

---

[123] See Käthe Rülicke-Weiler, *Die Dramaturgie Brechts*, p. 221; Manfred Wekwerth, 'Berliner Ensemble 1968. Oder: was blieb von Brecht?', *Theater heute*, 1 (1968), pp. 16–19; and Werner Hecht, *Aufsätze über Brecht* (Berlin: Henschel, 1970), p. 81.

[124] Monk, unpublished interview with John Rouse, 10 June 1988, p. II-8.

[125] Brecht, '[Der Nullpunkt]', BFA, 22: 245; *BoT*, p. 162.

2 The founding and the first season of the Berliner Ensemble

Prelude to a return to Germany

Brecht had already expressed an interest in returning to the business of theatre directing while still an exile in the USA. In a letter of late 1946 to his old friend, the set designer Caspar Neher, he named the Theater am Schiffbauerdamm in Berlin as a possible venue for future activity.[1] This was where Brecht had scored his only major hit to date with the world premiere of *Die Dreigroschenoper* (*The Threepenny Opera*), directed by Erich Engel in 1928. The letter also included an important prerequisite: Brecht suggested that he and Neher prepare for their return in Italy or Switzerland with theoretical work and the occasional production. And this was precisely what happened. The day after his appearance before the House Un-American Activities Committee on 30 October 1947, Brecht left the United States for Europe. He sojourned in Zurich for about a year, where he would set down the 'Kleines Organon für das Theater' ('Short Organon for the Theatre'), his longest theoretical work to be published in his lifetime. He directed his adaptation of *Antigone* in Chur on 14 February 1948 and his own *Herr Puntila und sein Knecht Matti* (*Mr Puntila and His Man Matti*) in Zurich later that year on 5 June. The preparatory period ended with the huge success of *Mutter Courage und ihre Kinder* (*Mother Courage and her Children*) at the Deutsches Theater in the Eastern sector of Berlin on 11 January 1949, directed by Brecht and Erich Engel.

This account might seem to suggest that Brecht was following some kind of 'master plan' that would culminate in the founding of the BE, yet it is difficult to believe that that was the case. Brecht was certainly adept at turning opportunities to his advantage, and so the route to the BE was probably more down to fortuitous circumstances coupled with his ability to make the most of them.

---

[1] See Brecht to Caspar Neher, end of October/1 November 1946, BFA, 29: 401–2; *Letters*, p. 417.

The short period before the protracted founding of the BE was nonetheless the ideal preparation for Brecht for a number of reasons. The work on the 'Organon' allowed him to marshal his ideas on theatre that had accrued during his exile and to offer the theatre world an elaborate 'calling card'. He was then able to deploy and assess his skills as a director on three occasions. The first two were fairly understated affairs – the production in Chur ran for a humble four performances before going on to a single afternoon matinee in Zurich. It was not, however, success as such that Brecht craved, but an opportunity to test his theory, his practice and indeed his leading actor, Helene Weigel. According to Ruth Berlau, Zurich's Kurt Hirschfeld would not cast Weigel in *Puntila* as Brecht had wished, possibly because he feared a poor performance after so many years away from the stage.[2] Brecht, on the other hand, used *Antigone* as a way of preparing Weigel for the role of Mother Courage (as well as re-activating his relationship with designer Neher).[3] Carola Stern notes that the process and realization of the *Antigone* project indeed gave Weigel her confidence back,[4] and she was thus in a stronger position to tackle the demanding role of Courage a few months later.

Brecht's approach to directing in Chur was also marked by an interest that went beyond the stage, despite the shortness of the run. Hans Curjel wrote that Brecht was concerned 'with the theatre as institution, with the consumer and with the environment in which it exists'.[5] That is, Brecht was keen to investigate the theatre's role in the life of Chur, to understand theatre's social functions. This impulse would return, amplified, once the Berliner Ensemble was established.

The production of *Puntila* not only served Brecht as a way of reacquainting himself with the practice of direction, but also allowed him to take what he had learned from *Antigone* and expand on it; *Puntila*'s larger cast, more intricate plotting, and lengthier script set greater and more complex tasks. While Hirschfeld was credited as director, Brecht was in fact the creative force behind the production, as attested to by Erwin Leiser, who sat in on rehearsals.[6] Brecht was not wholly satisfied with his work in Zurich, and this can be seen in his choice to re-stage the play as the BE's first production.

Mother Courage at the Deutsches Theater was Brecht's final preparation before he and Weigel founded the BE, and it showed just how much he

---

[2] See Ruth Berlau, in Bunge (ed.), *Brechts Lai-Tu*, p. 211.
[3] See Brecht, journal entry for 16 December 1947, BFA, 27: 255; *Journals*, p. 377.
[4] See Stern, *Männer lieben anders*, p. 146.
[5] Hans Curjel, in Clemens Witt (ed.), *Gespräch auf der Probe* (Zurich: Sanssouci, 1961), p. 10.
[6] See Erwin Leiser, in ibid., p. 42. Brecht was denied the directing credit because he did not possess a Swiss work permit – see Werner Hecht, *Brecht Chronik*, p. 823.

had learned from his two previous directorial outings. The production was phenomenally successful: it attracted packed audiences and a great many enthusiastic reviews.[7] The strength of the response that can be ascribed to both the technical brilliance of the production work and, as Sabine Kebir suggests, the remarkable resonance of the subject matter: she sees the play as a dark mirror for the spectators, reflecting themselves as people who, like Courage, went along with a war without critical insights or awakenings.[8] Contrary to what some commentators believe,[9] *Courage* was not the BE's first production, as the company was yet to be formed. I shall not discuss either the rehearsals or the aesthetics of this important production for this reason.[10] Even critic Hans Daiber's contention that 'the Berliner Ensemble existed in fact already from the time of the Berlin production of *Courage*' does not reflect the practical difficulties that had to be negotiated in order to constitute the BE in the first place.[11]

The immense popularity of the production, however, was perhaps the most compelling factor in the formation of the BE in that it demonstrated how a committed writer-director could attract a large audience while maintaining high production values and dealing with serious issues. Petra Stuber notes how Brecht became 'a representative figure in Berlin' and started to feature regularly in ongoing discussions.[12] This suggests that key decision-makers at that time considered his theatre to be a part of their own cultural programme. However, the transformation from an intention to form a company to its realization was to prove difficult and hard-fought.

'Theaterprojekt B.'

The first record of a concrete plan to form a theatre company came in a letter Brecht sent to composer Kurt Weill on 6 December 1948.[13] An entry in Brecht's journal of 12 December 1948 enlarged on the project.

[7] The production also unleashed a more negative critical debate around Brecht's theatre as a whole, driven by Fritz Erpenbeck. However, this ideological attack could not take anything away from the overwhelmingly positive reaction to the production.
[8] See Sabine Kebir, *Helene Weigel. Abstieg in den Ruhm. Eine Biographie* (Berlin: Aufbau, 2000), p. 223.
[9] See, for example, Sarah Bryant-Bertail, *Space and Time in Epic Theater: The Brechtian Legacy* (Rochester, NY: Camden House, 2000), pp. 68 and 85.
[10] It has already been the focus of many illuminating analyses over the years, however. The most extensive, to my knowledge, is: Peter Thomson, *Brecht: 'Mother Courage and her Children'* (Cambridge: Cambridge University Press, 1997), pp. 59–80.
[11] Hans Daiber, *Deutsches Theater seit 1945. Bundesrepublik Deutschland, Deutsche Demokratische Republik, Österreich, Schweiz* (Stuttgart: Reclam, 1976), p. 123.
[12] Petra Stuber, *Spielräume und Grenzen*, p. 60.
[13] See Brecht to Kurt Weill, 6 December 1948, BFA, 29: 480; *Letters*, p. 451.

He wrote that he was working with the *Intendant* (general manager) of the Deutsches Theater Berlin, Wolfgang Langhoff, on a '*Studiotheatre* to be attached to the *Deutsches Theater*'.[14] For an aesthetically conservative director like Langhoff, this signified quite a radical experiment. Brecht also intended to attract well-known German émigré actors, build his own ensemble, and set up a theatre for children in order to develop an epic mode of performance. These initial plans were to be fleshed out more fully in a document entitled 'Theaterprojekt B.', which is undated, but which was almost certainly written around this time due to the similarities in terminology and ideas. It is unclear whether the 'B' stands for 'Berlin' or 'Brecht', but I suspect, from the number of collaborators Brecht sought, that the former is more likely.

The document opens with an ambitious claim: the theatre project will help make Berlin the cultural centre of Germany.[15] More particularly, Brecht appealed to his potential Soviet backers by suggesting that the new company would be interested in staging Russian, Polish and Czech plays, although he specifically mentioned works by Gorky, Lorca, O'Casey and himself. Another idea designed to appeal to the authorities was Brecht's plan to attract leading actors and designers to his new project. Of the ten names mentioned, Brecht actually managed to secure eight – the actors Peter Lorre and Oskar Homolka did not make the journey east. Brecht did note that they might need to be paid in foreign currency, while sweetening the financial pill by proposing a modest-sized permanent ensemble of 20–5 actors. He was nonetheless aware that there was no theatre building for him and his new company, and so he suggested attachment to a large theatre 'to allow for an interchange of actors'.

These proposals were designed to offer an attractive prospect to both Berlin and the Soviets, yet his further ideas, in their candour, perhaps betray his own optimistic naïvety (meant in the more negative, un-Brechtian sense). Brecht noted that the new company's approach would be focused on 'a realistic, new mode of performance' and its development. Here he is clearly referring to his own new practices, ones that were yet to be seen in Germany. He then proposed that by its second year of existence, the new company could produce '*Modell* productions with which it could tour Germany'. The *Modell* was a means of offering an imitable production, in which Brecht's new methods could be passed on to other theatre practitioners as a basis for their own work. In addition,

---

[14] Brecht, journal entry for 12 December 1948, BFA, 27: 290; *Journals*, p. 409.
[15] See Brecht, 'Theaterprojekt B.', undated, n.p., LAB C Rep 120 1504. All subsequent references and quotations relate to this unpaginated document. The document is reproduced in full (in German) in Werner Hecht, *Brecht und die DDR. Die Mühen der Ebenen* (Berlin: Aufbau, 2013), pp. 20–1.

Brecht was already thinking about the company's potential function as a theatrical beacon before it had even been founded, in his desire to have its work 'recorded, disseminated and made available to provincial theatres'. Here Brecht is perhaps showing his own ambition a little too openly: he was proposing the wholesale export of his new methods, without having gauged how popular they were with the authorities. In addition he noted how ensemble members 'are to receive philosophical schooling', which was to be voluntary in the first year and mandatory in the second. The philosophy in question was unambiguous – lectures given by Marxists were considered 'necessary', again a nod to the confluence of his thought and that of the Soviets.

Of course, Brecht had every reason to want to propagate his new practices which he saw as socialist and progressive, but he betrays no wariness of the hostility his work might provoke in the coming years. While Brecht, of course, did not possess a crystal ball, he did have the experience of the 'expressionism debate' of the late 1930s, in which he found an opponent in György Lukács,[16] the Hungarian literary theorist whose definition of realism Brecht found restrictive and outdated, and whose divorce of form from content he deemed execrable.[17] Brecht's explicit presentation of his plans not only to develop, but also to propagate his work was an ambitious statement of intent and something of a gamble at the same time.

Founding the Berliner Ensemble

Creating a new ensemble from scratch was never going to be easy, especially in a Germany devastated by war and uncertain of its financial future. There were no empty theatres for the new company to use, either. The sole building that was scheduled to be rebuilt, the Volksbühne am Rosa-Luxemburg-Platz, overran optimistic restoration plans by several years and was only reopened in 1954. On top of this, political relations in the Soviet zone were also in a state of flux with various authorities flexing their political muscles before a stricter hierarchical order emerged after the formal establishment of the German Democratic Republic (GDR) on 7 October 1949.

The 'Theaterprojekt B.' document was discussed with the mayor of what was to become East Berlin, Friedrich Ebert, on 6 January 1949,

---

[16] See Eugene Lunn, *Marxism and Modernism: An Historical Study of Lukács, Brecht, Benjamin and Adorno* (Berkeley and Los Angeles: University of California Press, 1982), pp. 75–127.

[17] See Brecht, 'Über Georg Lukács', BFA, 22: 483.

that is, before the premiere of *Courage*. According to Brecht, Ebert neither welcomed him nor bade him farewell, and referred to his proposal
only once, and at that dismissively.[18] Wolfgang Langhoff was also present,
as was Fritz Wisten, the *Intendant* of the Theater am Schiffbauerdamm.
Wisten was a Jewish survivor of a Nazi forced labour programme who
had had an amount of success at the theatre, particularly with a production of Lessing's *Nathan der Weise* (*Nathan the Wise*) in September
1945. Despite these credentials, Brecht viewed him as a representative
of the bourgeois theatre[19] which he was trying to supplant with his own
methods. The meeting was also attended by three representatives of the
dominant Socialist Unity Party (SED), including Anton Ackermann, a
senior member of the SED's executive Zentralkomitee (Central Committee), and Kurt Bork, one of Brecht's associates from the Weimar Republic
who was responsible for theatre in various capacities within the SED from
1946. The Deutsches Theater included a smaller venue, the Kammerspiele (chamber theatre) and this, together with the Deutsches Theater
itself and the Theater am Schiffbauerdamm, were all mooted as venues
by the SED functionaries for Brecht's 'Gastspiele'. This is the standard
German term for a theatre tour, yet it was clearly inappropriate for what
Brecht envisaged, as it pre-supposed that his company would have a base
from which to tour. His earlier idea of his company being 'attached'
to another theatre reflected his needs far more accurately. The meeting
left the central question of where Brecht's new, but as yet unconstituted
theatre company could work unanswered.

East Berlin was administered by the Magistrat von Gross-Berlin
(Municipal Authority for Greater Berlin). The Central Committee and
its ministries would later become the seat of power in the GDR, but at this
time, such questions were open, and the Municipal Authority exploited
the situation to exert its own influence. Bork, who worked in the authority's cultural office, communicated the main points of the meeting to a
city councillor, Max Kreuziger, a week later.[20] Brecht rejected the offer
of working in the *Kammerspiele* as he reportedly considered it 'completely
unsuitable', something which, according to Bork, effectively torpedoed
the project before it had even got started. However, he was keen to stress
the importance of keeping Brecht in Berlin, not only for the calibre of his
work, but also for 'its extraordinary propaganda value'. Kreuziger added
a comment to the letter noting that Brecht's ability to attract a number

---

[18] See Brecht, journal entry for 6 January 1949, BFA, 27: 296; *Journals*, p. 415–16.
[19] See Christoph Funke and Wolfgang Jansen, *Theater am Schiffbauerdamm*, pp. 145–6.
[20] All subsequent information taken from Kurt Bork to Max Kreuziger, 13 January 1949,
       LAB C Rep 120 1529.

of prominent actors to Berlin was important to offset those leaving for the West, although setting up a new ensemble would not be cheap. From the outset, then, functionaries explicitly linked Brecht's significance to his usefulness for them.

There was a flurry of activity in the following weeks, fuelled in part by the interest generated by the premiere of *Courage*. Brecht found a vocal supporter in the charismatic young philosopher Wolfgang Harich. At the tender age of twenty-five, Harich had written an impassioned plea for Brecht's plans to work at the Schiffbauerdamm to Ackermann. Citing Bork's name in Brecht's favour, Harich listed Brecht's supporters, who argued for his ability to enliven the theatre in Berlin.[21] The financial aspect was mentioned, as was an ethical one. Alexander Dymschitz, a Soviet culture officer who ostensibly supported Brecht's work, had told Harich three days earlier that he was not prepared to force Wisten, as a victim of Nazi persecution, out of the Schiffbauerdamm, a theatre that Wisten had built up 'literally out of nothing'. Dymschitz would later claim that it was Brecht who made this high-minded argument,[22] but this is a retrospective fantasy. Brecht had his eye on the Schiffbauerdamm. Harich reported that Brecht would tolerate, rather than serve under Wisten as *Intendant* if Brecht's new company were attached to the Theater am Schiffbauerdamm. That meant that Wisten would not be allowed to interfere in the slightest with the new company's artistic direction. Brecht was thus either not interested in respecting Wisten and his experiences during the Nazi period or felt that they were not the point in question. In either case, he wanted to ignore the *Intendant* while nonetheless making use of his facilities.

Harich also reported that Dymschitz would have to drop the project if Brecht was not prepared to cooperate with others. However, Dymschitz stated that this was his personal view as the Soviet Military Administration in Germany (SMAD), of which he was a part, did not want to get involved in what it perceived to be a German matter. He nonetheless said he supported 'a little plot' to help Brecht. Harich, in typically forthright terms, said Wisten's rights were far outweighed by those of Berlin's theatre audiences. In his autobiography, Harich wrote that Ackermann rejected the letter out of hand for ideological reasons concerning

---

[21] Wolfgang Harich to Anton Ackermann, 17 January 1949, BArch NY 4109/89; also published as 'Brief an Anton Ackermann' in *Sinn und Form*, 50:6 (1998), pp. 894–903. The subsequent quotation attributed to Dymschitz is also taken from this letter.

[22] See Alexander Dymschitz, 'Ein gewöhnliches Genie', *Theater der Zeit*, 14/1966, p. 14. The article was written to commemorate the tenth anniversary of Brecht's death, and its author appears to look back on events through rose-tinted glasses.

SED cultural politics,[23] which I will address in the next chapter. Harich's 'conspirators' met with Bork on 17 January 1949 and persuaded him to support Brecht's cause by lobbying for access to, but not total control of, the Theater am Schiffbauerdamm.[24] Harich, together with the essayist Paul Rilla, decided to promote Brecht and his work through a series of newspaper articles.[25] Harich's two-pronged strategy had the desired effect of reviving Brecht's project, which had looked dead in the water after the meeting with Ebert earlier that month. Bork had heard from a high-ranking party official that the SED's Central Secretariat had approved the realization of 'Theaterprojekt B.' at the Theater am Schiffbauerdamm while Wisten remained *Intendant* and until he could be moved to another theatre.[26]

There may have been positive mutterings before this meeting because Brecht was writing to actors, designer Caspar Neher, and director Berthold Viertel, inviting them to join him at the Theater am Schiffbauerdamm for the next season well before formal approval was granted.[27] The problem was that the space issue had still not been resolved, and there seemed to be no practicable way of reconciling both Brecht's and Wisten's needs.[28] In a memorandum of early February 1949, Bork acknowledged that both Wisten and Brecht refused to work with each other and that, once again, the project had stalled. He asked the Deutsches Theater to cancel all contracts made in Brecht's name.[29]

By 14 February, things were back on track. A meeting had agreed 'a special arrangement' for 'Theaterprojekt B.' and the finer points were settled at a further meeting attended by Ackermann, Brecht, Weigel and Walter Kohls, the administrative director of the Deutsches Theater. The group agreed to the creation of a new ensemble under the leadership of Helene Weigel, which would indeed be attached to the Deutsches Theater, but with a budget of its own. Rehearsals were to begin on 1 September and the initial repertoire consisted of *Die Niederlage* (*The Defeat*, a play that would later become Brecht's *Die Tage der Kommune – The Days of the Commune*), Gorky's *Vassa Zheleznova* and Brecht's *Puntila*. The subsidy for the new company was estimated at one million German

[23] Wolfgang Harich, *Ahnenpass: Versuch einer Autobiographie*, ed. by Thomas Grimm (Berlin: Schwarzkopf & Schwarzkopf, 1999), p. 183.
[24] See Bork to Kreuziger, 19 January 1949, LAB C Rep 120 1529.
[25] Harich, *Ahnenpass*, p. 185.
[26] See Bork to Kreuziger, 7 February 1949, LAB C Rep 120 1529.
[27] See, for example, Brecht to Caspar Neher, 25 January 1949, BFA, 29: 492; *Letters*, pp. 454–5 (which dates the letter as 28 January).
[28] See Bork to Kreuziger, 22 February 1949, LAB C Rep 120 1529.
[29] Bork, 'Betrifft: a) Volksbühne Berlin b) Projekt "B" (Brecht)', February 1949, 5 pages (2 and 4), LAB C Rep 120 1529.

marks, and SMAD said that the Municipal Authority should supervise, that is, finance the new ensemble itself.[30] Although the plans were yet to be ratified, and these would cause further consternation, Bork started to work on the new ensemble's behalf and sought office space for the new company at the end of February.[31]

April began with a letter from Stefan Heymann, a member of the Central Committee's Cultural Department, to Bork announcing that the Politburo had approved the formation of a new ensemble. It was to come into effect on 1 September 1949 with a budget of 1,125,500 marks plus an additional 340,000 marks for start-up expenses.[32] Bork was asked to support this decision, and so he submitted a proposal to the Municipal Authority in April to establish the new ensemble. It was returned to him unapproved because Mayor Ebert and Councillor Kreuziger were not prepared to foot the bill.[33] It is important to note that at the time of the administrative toing and froing, the state that would be known as the GDR had not actually been founded. This was also the time of the Berlin Blockade in which the Soviets prevented Western powers from using road and rail to access West Berlin. In short, the SED had not properly secured its monopoly on power and was already involved in one of the first major battles of the Cold War. The Municipal Authority itself was an SED institution, yet it had sufficient power to rebuff a decision made by the highest German political body in the Soviet zone, something that would be unthinkable in subsequent years. It forced the Central Committee to work on a new funding solution.

Ernst Held, another cultural functionary, had noted on 28 April that the Municipal Authority's decision was a serious obstacle to the realization of the plan, especially as Weigel, acting upon the Central Committee's decision, had already signed contracts with actors and technicians.[34] Walter Ulbricht, who would head the Central Committee from 1950, thus urgently appealed to Heinrich Rau, the chairman of the Deutsche Wirtschaftskommission (German Economic Commission), to reach a decision on funding, which was now to include an annual sum of $10,000 to pay for guest actors from the West. This detail is not to be overlooked: foreign currency was expensive and a commitment to securing

---

[30] See Bork to Kreuziger, 18 February 1949, LAB C Rep 120 1504; and [Stefan] Hey[mann], 'Aktennotiz', [on or shortly after 16 February 1949], n.p., HWA File 161.

[31] Bork to Hans Hessling, 28 February 1949, LAB C Rep 120 1504.

[32] See Stefan Heymann to Bork, 1 April 1949, HWA 161.

[33] See [Bork], 'Magistratsvorlage [unnumbered]', [April, 1949], 2 pages; and Bork to Ernst Held, 19 April 1949, both documents: LAB C Rep 120 1504.

[34] Ernst Held, 'Aktenvermerk', 28 April 1949, HWA 161.

such amounts signalled the importance of the project to the authorities. Ulbricht added that 'the political aspect of the matter' had been cleared with the Soviets.[35]

In the middle of May, Bork was finally able to issue a certificate confirming the legal existence of the BE which was now under the control of the Verwaltung für Volksbildung (Department of People's Education), whose remit included cultural policy.[36] The department was equivalent to a ministry at the time and thus represented an SED governing organ. Its status thus ruled out any further interventions from the Municipal Authority. Stuber has demonstrated that this administrative switch from the obvious first choice of a funder and overseer for the BE, the Municipal Authority, to the more centralized body was the result of necessity, rather than preference. She notes its importance because the switch was brought about by the most senior members of the SED: future GDR president Wilhelm Pieck, SED joint chairman Otto Grotewohl, and Ulbricht.[37] It was, as Friedrich Dieckmann observes, a combination of SED weakness at the time and tacit Soviet support that led to the founding of the BE.[38] Consequently, Mary Luckhurst is mistaken in her assertion that the BE started its life with 'an educational remit',[39] because its funding and supervision by the Department of People's Education was an existential prerequisite, not a political choice. The attachment to the department associates the company with a narrow public role that was actually at odds with the way it would make theatre and the way that the SED would later respond to its productions. While Brecht was certainly interested in the pedagogic aspects of his theatre, they were rarely concerned with transmitting information or doctrine.

Assembling and naming the new company

In late January 1949, buoyed by the success of *Courage* and the way it had reinvigorated 'Theaterprojekt B.', Brecht continued his campaign to attract high-profile actors and directors from the West. For the most part, he was successful; the only major figure he was unable to persuade at this early stage was the German director with whom he had collaborated in the Weimar Republic, Erwin Piscator. From late February, Brecht was out of Berlin courting actors in Zurich for his new company and only

[35] Walter Ulbricht to Heinrich Rau, 29 April 1949, HWA 161.
[36] See Bork, 'Bescheinigung', 18 May 1949, LAB C Rep 120 1504.
[37] Stuber, *Spielräume und Grenzen*, pp. 63–4.
[38] See Friedrich Dieckmann, *Wer war Brecht? Erkundungen und Erörterungen* (Berlin: Aufbau, 2003), pp. 155–70 (169).
[39] Luckhurst, *Dramaturgy*, p. 128.

returned to Berlin at the end of May, and so left Helene Weigel to manage the ructions at home. Brecht gained agreement from potential ensemble members with whom he had already worked in Zurich, while he also exploited the Swiss calm to concentrate on his writing. His approach was certainly tailored to each potential recruit. Director Berthold Viertel was assured of a wealth of privileges for artists in December 1948 and offered the title of 'head director' in January 1949.[40] Brecht sought to enthuse actor Leonard Steckel, who had played Puntila under Brecht in Zurich, with the prospect of building on the progressive staging traditions established during his exile in Switzerland.[41] Yet he was more direct with Benno Besson, who would become one of Brecht's first directing assistants. Besson's former wife, Iva Formigoni, recalls that Brecht and Weigel had painted the devastated Berlin in the bleakest of terms so that the Bessons would have no illusions about working there.[42] Brecht was clearly being quite tactical here, stressing the positives to older friends and those who may only be working as guests, while preparing those whose skills he hoped to develop over time for the stark realities of the situation in Berlin.

Weigel was also working hard in Berlin to prepare the way for the new company. Once she had been given a tentative green light in early February, she began actively recruiting personnel and establishing administrative structures.[43] Even before office space had been secured, she was working from the partially bombed-out Hotel Adlon in which she had been billeted. She had also employed a head of administration, Elfriede Bork, known informally as 'Blacky' because of her jet-black hair. Her husband, Kurt Bork, had suggested his wife for the position.[44] Kurt, who was so closely involved in the establishment of the BE, would accompany the development of the company until the late 1960s, when he lost his portfolio for theatre, having risen to the lofty position of Deputy Minister of Culture. It is difficult to know whether the offer of his wife's administrative services was a deliberate move on Kurt's part to maintain an inside connection with the BE from the very outset. Margaret Sejte-Eilers believes that the friendly proximity of Brecht, Weigel and

[40] See Brecht to Berthold Viertel, 14 December 1948 and 25 January 1949, BFA, 29: 483 and 493, respectively; *Letters*, pp. 452 (which dates the letter 7 December) and 455.

[41] See Brecht to Leonard Steckel, 24 January 1949, BFA, 29: 490; *Letters*, p. 454.

[42] See Iva Formigoni, in Christa Neubert-Herwig, '"Er wollte schon 1942 Theater machen"', in Neubert-Herwig, *Benno Besson: Theater spielen in acht Ländern. Texte – Dokumente – Gespräche* (Berlin: Alexander, 1998), pp. 30–2, here p. 31.

[43] See Helene Weigel to the German Department of People's Education, 28 July 1949, BBA uncatalogued file 'Aktuelles'.

[44] See Helene Weigel, in Werner Hecht, *Helene Weigel*, p. 33.

the Borks 'worked to the mutual advantage of these four individuals'.[45] At certain times later in their relationship, however, it was far more a case of particular members of the quartet gaining an advantage by either exploiting the social connection or ignoring it altogether. Nonetheless, this is not to deny that there was a mostly cordial relationship between Weigel as the BE's *Intendantin* and Bork as a high-ranking cultural functionary.

It is not clear precisely when Helene Weigel became *Intendantin*. In Heymann's letter to Bork of 1 April 1949, the Politburo's decision includes the phrase 'under the leadership of Helene Weigel'.[46] She attended a meeting of *Intendanten* on 11 April 1949 before her company had even been constituted, and so she probably undertook her early administrative work with the implicit understanding of her role.[47] The party used the name 'Helene-Weigel-Ensemble' as a shorthand in lieu of an agreed designation in late April 1949,[48] a formulation at odds with the more generic terms 'Projekt B.' and 'Brecht-Theater' which were circulating that February.[49] The change of reference point indicates that the SED had been told that Weigel was to head the new company and this does not seem to have raised any hackles within the party, even though she was not a member of the SED herself. The decision was Brecht's. Weigel told Werner Hecht that he had admired her formidable organizational skills while they were in exile.[50] Werner Mittenzwei makes a keen observation on Brecht's choice:

He needed someone who had him in mind in all planning decisions and when resolving purely practical problems without having to discuss everything in advance. There had to be someone at the top who understood him completely, but did not have the ambition to seek to determine policy themselves.[51]

A page later, Mittenzwei notes that the price Weigel paid for this new position was a smaller number of major acting roles. Sarah Bryant-Bertail suggests that this division of labour led to Weigel undertaking a host of

---

[45] Margaret Setje-Eilers, '"Wochenend und Sonnenschein": In the Blind Spots of Censorship at the GDR's Cultural Authorities and the Berliner Ensemble', *Theater Journal*, 61: 3 (2009), pp. 363–86 (375).

[46] Stefan Heymann to Bork, 1 April 1949, HWA 161.

[47] See Anon., 'Vereinbarungen in der Besprechung mit den Theater-Intendanten am 11.4.1949', 11 April 1949, 2 pages, BArch NY 4036/680.

[48] See Ernst Held, 'Aktenvermerk', 28 April 1949, and [Walter] U[lbricht] to Heinrich Rau, 29 April 1949, both in HWA 161.

[49] See, for example, Bork to Kreuziger, 18 February 1949, LAB C Rep 120 1504; and Stefan Heymann, 'Aktennotiz', [soon after 16 February 1949], n.p., HWA 161.

[50] See Helene Weigel, in Werner Hecht, *Helene Weigel*, p. 32.

[51] Werner Mittenzwei, *Das Leben des Bertolt Brecht*, vol. 2, p. 362.

unglamorous tasks while 'Brecht was free to do only the artistic work, as well as taking most of the credit for the success of the theatre'.[52] This binary view is somewhat at odds with the evidence. While the BE's administrative files certainly show what a full-time job Weigel's was, there is little to indicate, before the BE's crisis of the late 1960s, that she did not enjoy it. One finds professional pride and indeed a great pleasure in playing the role of a great company's public face. Käthe Rülicke, who joined the BE in 1950 as an assistant, reports that Brecht could not stand it when Weigel behaved like that, even though it was often necessary.[53] On the other hand, it is difficult to support the view that Brecht took anything but immense *private* satisfaction in the success of the BE. There would be several occasions when he deliberately encouraged his assistants to direct instead of himself or left out directing credits for himself despite his own considerable input.

While Weigel was busy setting up the company, the search was on for a name. Ruth Berlau asserted in 1959 that she had coined the name 'Berliner Ensemble': '[the suggestion] came about quite simply. Because people were always saying that we needed to have an ensemble in place if we wanted to make good theatre, the name pretty much suggested itself'.[54] Berlau is not a terribly reliable witness, due to her alcoholism and fragile mental state, and it is difficult to ascertain that she did suggest the name; however, her sentiments certainly ring true. The idea of an ensemble lay at the heart of Brecht's theatre project. In a letter of March 1949 to the actor Maria Wimmer, Brecht talks of founding 'a new Berlin ensemble', which is then abbreviated to 'N.B.E.' in a letter courting the theatre director Jacob [sic] Geis written slightly later, as if it had already become the acknowledged title.[55] The 'Berliner Ensemble', liberated of the adjective that would have become anachronistic over time, only featured officially for the first time in the contract that founded the company.

The contract itself was signed on 24 September 1949, that is, a little over three weeks after the founding date of 1 September.[56] The lag between a list of objections Weigel returned to the Department of People's Education in July and the final agreement in late September may indicate

---

[52] Bryant-Bertail, *Space and Time*, p. 65.
[53] See Rülicke, in Anon., 'Interview Matthias Braun mit Käthe Rülicke-Weiler, 1978 und 1984, über Helene Weigel/Bertolt Brecht', undated, 40 pages, here p. 23.
[54] Ruth Berlau, in Bunge (ed.), *Brechts Lai-Tu*, p. 218.
[55] See Brecht to Maria Wimmer, March 1949, and Brecht to Jacob Geis, March/April 1949, BFA, 29: 508 and 511 respectively.
[56] See Paul Wandel and Helene Weigel, '[Contract founding the Berliner Ensemble]', 24 September 1949, 3 pages (3), BBA uncatalogued file 'Aktuelles'.

the amount of negotiation required to push through her amendments.[57] Many of these were of a practical nature, and they aimed to ensure benefits for the BE, such as getting the Deutsches Theater to pay for the BE's costume, props and set manufacture, but one alteration concerned cultural politics and deserves special attention. In the draft contract, the BE was required to stage 'exemplary productions of particularly significant contemporary plays'.[58] Stuber deciphers this code and translates it as actually meaning 'plays by Brecht'.[59] Here the word 'exemplary' is the clue as it refers to Brecht's idea of productions as imitable models. The plan to limit the BE by reducing its repertoire's scope was easily circumvented, and the final contract listed the BE's main task as 'the nurture and advancement of progressive theatre culture'. This broader formulation, written very much in the language of the SED, allowed the BE to diversify its repertoire and engage with older works, something that would have been the traditional province of the Deutsches Theater. This clause would later create problems, with regard to the loaded question of the German 'Erbe' ('cultural heritage') in general and the production of Goethe's *Urfaust* in particular.

At the time of signing the contract, Weigel could be satisfied that all her suggestions for amendments had been accepted. Such a situation again shows the relative weakness of the SED, which granted all the concessions, something that would have been most unlikely once it set about entrenching its power in the early 1950s.

The Berliner Ensemble opens with new offices and a new repertoire

After all the negotiations, the false dawns, and the great effort required to found the Berliner Ensemble, 1 September 1949 finally arrived with very little fanfare. Egon Monk, who was employed at the age of twenty-two as an actor, recalls that the day was 'so unceremonious' that one would not have known that there was anything important happening at all.[60] Brecht was in Munich, setting up a production of *Courage* there, and Weigel was busy preparing the tour of the Berlin *Courage* to Brunswick and Cologne, which would take place at the end of the month. There

---

[57] See Helene Weigel to the German Department of People's Education, 28 July 1949, BBA uncatalogued file 'Aktuelles'.
[58] Anon., 'Vertrag', undated, 2 pages (1), BBA uncatalogued file 'Aktuelles'.
[59] See Petra Stuber, 'Helene Weigel und ihre Rolle als Intendantin zwischen 1949 und 1954', *Brecht Yearbook*, 25 (2000), pp. 253–75 (258).
[60] Egon Monk, *Regie Egon Monk*, p. 41.

were no speeches to mark the momentous day, only a cast list for the first
production, *Puntila*, hung on a wall of the BE's new, temporary offices.

There was no room in the Deutsches Theater for a second, separate
administrative unit, and so the BE was allocated space in the side wing of
the building that housed the club reserved for Berlin's artists, the Möwe,
on 18 Luisenstraße. According to official documents it included ten office
rooms, three guest rooms, one lounge, and a rehearsal stage.[61] Half the
small stage area was taken up by rostra and a billowing grey curtain
hung from the back wall.[62] Rehearsal conditions were rudimentary and
cramped, and were to become a bone of contention before the year was
out, but at that time, they were all that the state could provide. It should
be noted that the BE's better-known 'Probenhaus' ('rehearsal building'),
a refurbished drill hall on 29 Reinhardtstraße, was only completed in
1951.

Puntila was mooted as a potential production back during negotiations
with the SED, together with Brecht's version of Nordahl Grieg's play,
The Defeat, which would later be completely reworked as *The Days of the
Commune*, and Gorky's *Vassa Zheleznova*. Brecht had initially planned to
open his first season with *Commune*, followed by *Vassa*, and *Puntila*.[63]
The choice of the latter two plays was obvious to Brecht as they were
both productions that had recently been staged in Zurich. As already
noted, Brecht directed *Puntila* in 1948, and so it would have been both
fresh in his mind and ripe for critical reassessment. Its final position
in the initial plan was due to the limited availability of Brecht's Puntila
in Zurich, Leonard Steckel. And while Brecht had nothing to do with
the Swiss production of *Vassa*, he planned to bring in another director,
his friend Berthold Viertel. He also invited one of the great German
actors, Therese Giehse, to reprise her role as the play's eponymous anti-
hero. Both Viertel and Giehse had been in exile during the Nazi period
and featured in Brecht's list of guest artists from the 'Theaterprojekt B.'
document.

One can only speculate as to why *Commune* was Brecht's first choice
for the opening production, but the reasons do not seem too obscure.
First, it was a new play and could thus combine new drama with a new
company. Second, it was an overtly partisan play that signalled its own
politics clearly: it follows the rise and fall of the Paris Commune of 1871.
Its shifting canvas between the plight of the poor people of Paris and their

---

[61] See Anon., untitled, [March 1950], 4 pages (1), BArch DR 2/8237.
[62] See Alfred Doll, 'Helene Weigel und das "Berliner Ensemble"', *Vorwärts*, 28 November
1949.
[63] See Brecht to Weigel, 25–26 February 1949, BFA, 29: 501–2; *Letters*, pp. 459–60.

political ambitions as delegates to the Commune displayed a commitment to the material causes of the uprising. The ultimate defeat served as a warning against a revolutionary romanticism that presumed the act of establishing the Commune was enough to sustain it against forces that sought to preserve their privileges and the system that perpetuated them. Yet already by April 1949, Brecht was having second thoughts. He decided to change the order of productions, favouring *Puntila* as the company's new opener while retaining *Commune* nonetheless. He considered his initial running order too controversial.[64] That said, he valued *Commune* for its pedagogical value, calling it 'a training play for the ensemble' that would offer many small yet rounded parts and in which actors from the Deutsches Theater could perform 'but in the style of the New Berliner Ensemble'.[65] That Brecht's interest in the play extended beyond the themes and forms to its use-value for a nascent ensemble already tells us something important about his understanding of how the early repertoire was to work.

Commune itself, however, would never be staged by the BE in Brecht's lifetime, although it remained a plan for the next couple of years. Its 'controversial' nature was acknowledged by no less a body than the Central Committee in 1951. It decreed that Brecht's proposal to stage the play 'requires a fundamental review'.[66] While I will return in the next chapter to the climate that gave rise to such an instruction, I will note here that the instruction itself did not initiate a review at all. Just as in most official documents, be they the GDR's or other governments', code words and euphemism help to hide actual meanings. Here 'review' (and a 'fundamental' one at that) meant that the plan was to be condemned to the wastepaper bin. Joachim Werner Preuß reads the SED's decision as one based in its own political dogma. He notes how Brecht pays homage to an heroic collective that acts 'without prompting or leadership'.[67] 'Leadership' was a crucial issue in the depiction of revolutionary movements while the SED was cementing its power in the early 1950s. At stake was the proposition that socialism could be established without informed and firm leadership, something that would have made the SED superfluous or redundant. The tacit banning of *Commune* meant that Berlin audiences would not be offered the option of considering that position at all. It is possible that the play could also have been considered defeatist, not

---

[64] See Brecht to Weigel, 21 April 1949, BFA, 29: 513–14; *Letters*, pp. 468–9.
[65] Brecht to Weigel, April–May 1949, BFA, 29: 519; *Letters*, pp. 469–70.
[66] Trautzsch, 'Protokoll Nr. 91 der Sitzung des Sekretariats des ZK am 2. August 1951', undated, 19 pages (9), SAPMO BArch DY 30/J IV 2/3/220.
[67] Joachim Werner Preuß, *Theater im ost-/westpolitischen Umfeld; Nahtstelle Berlin 1945–61* (Munich: iudicum, 2004), p. 777.

the optimistic fare promoted by the party. (It will be clear on pp. 181–3, Chapter 6, however, just how useful the play proved for the BE but a decade later when it was used to justify the construction of the Berlin Wall.)

Brecht, Engel, Neher and *Puntila*

The celebrated production of *Courage* that had given 'Theaterprojekt B.' such a fillip had been co-directed by Brecht and Erich Engel. Brecht, whose predilection for collaboration extended over much of his creative life, invited Engel back to co-direct *Puntila*. One might conclude that the two had a similar approach or outlook to direction, but this was not really the case. While they shared similar political positions, Engel was a far more restricting director. Weigel asserted that she could not have rehearsed *Courage* solely under Engel as he made it difficult for the actors to make suggestions – his approach was more akin to that of a conventional director who had a pre-existing vision of what he wanted to achieve.[68] Werner Hecht notes that Engel did not direct inductively like Brecht and preferred to coach the actors by making them repeat his understanding of a character's delivery, rather than encouraging them to reach their own solutions.[69] It is thus worth asking why Brecht considered working with Engel again, let alone on the BE's first production. The answer may be found in the complementarity between the two directors. Monk observes that Engel was far more concerned with what he heard and consequently focused on the dialogue while Brecht worked on the visual elements of 'gestures and *Haltungen*'.[70] In other words, Brecht was involved in a dialectical relationship with his co-director in which the physical details he developed might be offset in some way by the vocal delivery suggested by Engel. The tension between the two directing foci was intended to generate productivity through difference. However, it would be wrong to view this relationship as an equal partnership, at least in terms of the finished production: Brecht was undoubtedly the senior partner.

Another collaborator with whom Brecht had also previously worked was the designer Caspar Neher. I have refrained from qualifying 'designer' here with the word 'set' because the sketches that were to inform some of the BE's first productions were not primarily concerned with the stage's architecture. Brecht noted his own indebtedness to

---

[68] See Weigel, in Hecht (ed.), *Helene Weigel*, pp. 28–9.
[69] See Hecht, in ibid., p. 76.   [70] Monk, *Regie Egon Monk*, p. 50.

Figs. 2.1 and 2.2. Realizing the plan: the similarity between Neher's sketch and the scene as performed is unmistakable. Sketch of *Mr Puntila and His Man Matti* and the performance in November 1949.

Neher's sketches as the basis for the production of *Antigone* in Chur.[71] Susanne de Ponte describes precisely the function that some of these sketches played with respect to Neher's work on *Puntila*, scenes 3, 7 and

[71] Brecht, '*Antigonemodell 1948*', BFA, 25: 76 (footnote); *BoP*, p. 167.

8: 'with these [sketches], Neher represents the course of a single scene with such attention to detail that a kind of storyboard, a chain of sensual, gestic images of the action is at hand'.[72] It was Neher's ability to find the central gestic moments of an action sequence that appealed to Brecht. Neher, like Brecht, started with the situation, rather than the characters and thus emphasized the ways in which certain behaviours were produced by their circumstances.

If we look at Neher's sketch that shows Matti defending four of the female characters before an imaginary judge in the form of a pitchfork (see Fig. 2.1), we can see a set of relationships, something that Brecht then used as a concrete basis for his staging (see Fig. 2.2). The complex of *Haltungen* provided Brecht with a readable set of through-lines for any given scene. Their liveliness, as the example shows, was not limited to a single relationship but, here, encompasses communication within the group of women, between Matti and the women, and Matti and the 'judge'. Monk reports, in connection with the rehearsals of *The Tutor*, that Brecht would rather wait for Neher's sketches than proceed without them.[73] Hans Curjel believed Brecht saw Neher as 'his second self'.[74] This was because their aims for and realization of theatre were so close. Neher helped to convert Brecht's texts into images; Brecht went on to turn the images into performance.

Brecht had assembled a team that offered three complementary yet discrete centres of creativity. Before I consider the fruits of their labour, I will turn to the play itself and some of the ideas that informed the production. *Puntila* is a drama about social division and how power is wielded in a class-based society. The play's central conceit concerns the Finnish landowner Puntila who is a savage capitalist when sober, but a friend of the worker when drunk. This inconsistency lends the play a comic edge, despite some of the more vicious decisions taken by the sober Puntila. The scenes follow his exploits, and focus on the relationship with his working-class chauffeur, Matti, who eventually leaves Puntila's service at the end of the play. Puntila's daughter Eva is also an important character. She is initially engaged to the Attaché, a chinless but well-born idiot, but falls for Matti, who in turn finds that her class prevents her from becoming a suitable wife to a working man like him. The play is a *Volksstück*, an untranslatable term which approximates to a 'play of or for the people', due to its broad range of social types.

---

[72] Susanne de Ponte, *Caspar Neher – Bertolt Brecht. Eine Bühne für das epische Theater*, ed. by the Deutsches Theatermuseum, Munich (Berlin: Henschel, 2006), pp. 87–8.

[73] See Egon Monk, 'Caspar Neher und Bertolt Brecht auf der Probe', *Frankfurter Rundschau*, 27 August 1966.

[74] See Hans Curjel, in Witt (ed.), *Gespräch auf der Probe*, p. 11.

As already noted, one of the reasons why Brecht chose this play was his recent experience of staging it himself. He was not, however, completely satisfied with the result. He believed that Puntila ran the risk of being perceived as a mainly sympathetic character 'with some nasty traits when sober'.[75] That is, Brecht wanted to dispel an undialectical reading of the character as somehow naturally good. Erwin Geschonneck, the actor who played Matti in the BE production, recalls that Brecht was also unhappy with the actor who played Matti in Zurich for being 'too servile and superficial'.[76] Brecht was convinced that Puntila should not overshadow Matti and that in fact Matti possessed the 'intellectual superiority' in the relationship.[77] Brecht therefore set about clarifying the dialectical tensions the second time around in order to produce a more combative class-conscious comedy.

It is worth lingering on the implications of class consciousness for Brecht's theatre. As a Marxist, Brecht committed himself to two positions which, in his day, were complementary, but which today undermine each other. These were a dialectical worldview and the proletariat's place in it. The dialectic is a mechanism that continually redefines reality by synthesizing contradictions in perpetuity. It is a radical way of envisaging history because established orders can give way to new formations, and therein lay the Marxists' revolutionary optimism. In this narrative, the proletariat's historical role was to drive change and bring about a fairer society in which oppression and exploitation were rejected. The dialectic was thus loaded in the favour of working people, and Marxist art was required to be 'parteilich' ('partisan' in a more positive, 'partial' in a more negative translation). A problem arises, however, when eliding the dialectic with this (or indeed any other) historical narrative: teleology. Rather than using the dialectic experimentally to uncover possible syntheses, Brecht was convinced that history, through the Soviet example and now through the GDR, was confirming Marxism's aims, and he was happy to put the dialectic at the service of the proletariat. At the time, there was little to contradict the conflation of form (the dialectic) and content (the victory of the proletariat) – socialism was on the march. But with hindsight, one sees just how misused the dialectic could become when its terms were marshalled by an historical narrative, rather than serving the contradictions of a play's material itself without prejudice. This

---

[75] Brecht, 'Steckels zwei Puntilas', BFA, 24: 310.
[76] Erwin Geschonneck, *Meine unruhigen Jahre*, ed. by Günter Agde (Berlin: Dietz, 1984), p. 151.
[77] Brecht, 'Notizen über die Züricher Erstaufführung', BFA, 24: 302.

self-imposed limitation will also present itself in Brecht's productions of *The Mother* and *Katzgraben* in Chapters 3 and 4, respectively.

Aspects of Brechtian directing practice as exemplified by *Puntila*, or: making theatre politically

Despite having two directors and an active formative contributor in Neher, *Puntila* was marked by Brecht's imprint in its political aims, its aesthetics, and its mode of rehearsing. The first formal rehearsal of 19 September 1949 did not go well as problems quickly emerged with the first actor to rehearse Puntila. Willy A. Kleinau had previously played the character in Hamburg, and was proposed for the role by Ruth Berlau, who had seen the production. The problem with Kleinau was that he was unable to move away from the earlier production and would not respond to Brecht's direction, believing that he should merely repeat that which had found favour with the audience in Hamburg.[78] Kleinau's portrayal of Puntila as a likeable drunk was precisely what the new production was trying to avoid.[79] Leonard Steckel, who was Brecht's Puntila in Zurich and was due to alternate the role with Kleinau, came to Berlin in early October, after Kleinau had been dropped from the production. His openness and willingness to modify his Zurich Puntila energized the work on the production. Steckel's arrival prompted alterations to the existing *Arrangements*,[80] and this tells us something important about the reciprocal relationships within Brecht's working method. Performance usually proceeded from the *Arrangements*, but they were not unalterable and did not exist in isolation. Steckel's input profoundly redefined the central character's possibilities, and so the team re-set the *Arrangements* to take advantage of this fact.

The rehearsal documentation reveals many of the central features of Brecht's work as a director, and so I shall examine these as a complex designed to realize a dialectical production. One of the main questions that arose concerned the status of what it meant to be a human being in a class-based society. The way the audience perceived Puntila's 'humanity' had been a weakness of the Zurich production, and Brecht was keen to reveal this humanity as a social, rather than as a natural product. He was therefore very much involved in the *Verfremdung* of the character, that is, making the familiar strange, surprising the audience with unexpected

[78] See Berlau, in Bunge (ed.), *Brechts Lai-Tu*, p. 224–5.
[79] See Anon., *'Puntila* – Stellprobe – 1. Bild 19.9.49 (B. E. N.)', undated, n.p., BEA File 2.
[80] See Koval, 'Sonnabend 8. Oktober 1949', undated, n.p., ibid.

contradictory qualities or behaviour. In a preparatory note on the play, one finds that Puntila should appear 'strange' because he becomes a human being when drunk. Yet in the same document, the writer also states that Eva makes 'the strange discovery' that Matti is also a man.[81]

Matti, too, was implicated in exposing the interplay of class and the establishment of 'the human'. A concrete example of the way in which Brecht tried to bring this about is to be found in a direction to the actors that has a suggestive gestic quality. Matti sees Puntila drunk for the first time in the first scene. It would have been tempting for the worker to have embraced the humanity of his employer, but that was not what was suggested. Instead one reads: 'meeting of two patrols, reconnaissance in no-man's land'.[82] The image evokes mutual suspicion and uncertainty, neither side is sure of what it is encountering. However, Brecht's was not a theatre of static states, but of dynamic changes, and so the scene developed out of an atmosphere of wariness into one that was lighter. Matti is described as 'later amused because Puntila is actually amusing and funny'.[83] A tentative friendship had been established, but this was neither easy nor inevitable.

Brecht based his realism on a materialist view of the world, and so he insisted that everything on stage had material causes. The final scene, before the epilogue in which Matti quits Puntila's service, involves Matti constructing an image of Finland's mount Hatelma at Puntila's behest. The mountain is made of Puntila's furniture and there are many valuable objects for Matti to use. Geschonneck thought that alcohol played its part in the wanton destruction, but he was advised that 'a certain *vengefulness*' was not to be overlooked.[84] It is not that Geschonneck was imagining a cause – alcohol may well have been a contributory factor – rather, Brecht wanted to locate the action in a social context and to build in a 'not/but' to emphasize Matti's class-based motivation. Earlier in the scene, Puntila, sober and vicious, had sacked Surkkala, a left-wing worker he had employed when drunk, leaving him and his four children without an income. Surkkala had not appeared in the Zurich version, but had been included in Berlin to emphasize class antagonism.

On other occasions, Brecht paid close attention to the productive tension that could arise from decoupling meaning from delivery. The scene 'Tales from Finland', for example, was an important one to Brecht.[85] It

---

[81] Anon., untitled, undated, 2 pages (1 and 2, respectively), ibid.

[82] Anon., '*Puntila* – Stellprobe – 1. Bild 19.9.49 (B. E. N.)', undated, n.p., ibid.

[83] Anon., 'Zu *Puntila* Regie', undated, n.p., ibid.

[84] Anon., 'Bühnenprobe Deutsches Theater Sonnabend 24. September 1949...', un-dated, 4 pages (1), ibid.

[85] See Brecht to Konrad Schrader, 14 March 1953, BFA, 30: 120.

features stories narrated by four female characters that reflect on issues of injustice in the social sphere. After the production, assistant Peter Palitzsch wrote that the directors did not make these characters comic and they were not treated critically, like the other characters.[86] One might then expect a jarring piece of propaganda, but he continues: 'the scene should emerge tenderly and strangely: the women are right'. The directors achieved this in the following way: 'the accusation is not in the tone, which remains easy-going, but in the construction of the [respective] tale'.[87] In other words, while the women may well have been right in their criticism, the audience was not required to empathize with them to reach this conclusion, but to discover the correctness from the lines themselves.

Brecht's emphasis on showing was also present in this first production. Puntila's dialectic, the contradiction between alcohol-induced humanity and clear-headed capitalism, was recognized early in rehearsal: '"this tyrant" would like nothing more than to get out of his own skin; *we* have to *show* this skin'.[88] Puntila's acquisitiveness, love of power and the status quo are not, then, pleasant or easy, even if they have brought him great wealth and influence. Rather, they are a burden that isolates him, and makes his drunken behaviour necessary. Again, a socially predicated 'not/but' lies at the heart of the character. The audience had to be made aware that this was the case in order to understand the character in all its complexity. This meant moving beyond 'pure' character towards a greater integration of the social environment into his distinctive traits.

One of Brecht's favourite targets of 'showing' were rituals. He wanted to stage such procedures as strange because they were social constructions that could reveal particular values of a given society. Rehearsal of the second scene, in which Puntila drives home and Matti unloads a suitcase full of bottles, did not ignore the special moment: 'setting down the precious suitcase is a special ceremony'.[89] By turning a possibly routine action into something notable, Brecht highlighted the relationships between master and servant, and between human beings and objects in the eyes of a wealthy landowner.

Brecht often strove to express a clarity of meaning on stage, and this started with the composition of the scene. As already noted, the directors constructed *Arrangements* in such a way that they were readable. Consequently, one finds in the documentation: 'as a point of principle: we try

---

[86] See Peter Palitzsch, 'Finnische Erzählungen', in BE/Helene Weigel, *Theaterarbeit*, pp. 29–31 (29). The following quotation is on the same page.

[87] Anon., '*Puntila* VII. Bild, Stellprobe 17.9....', undated, 2 pages (2), BEA File 2.

[88] Anon., '*Puntila* – Stellprobe – 1. Bild 19.9.49 (B. E. N.)', undated, n.p., ibid.

[89] Anon., '*Puntila*. II. Bild, Stellprobe 20.9. BB CN P/K', undated, 2 pages (1), ibid.

to keep the groupings in place until the necessity for a change presents itself.[90] Because the *Arrangements* were so crucial as visual indices of the *Fabel*, any alteration had to be born of a change in circumstance. Actors were encouraged not merely to move for movement's sake, but to move for a reason. As Eric Bentley observes, to Brecht movement *is* action.[91] The imperative for clarity was also extended to the individual actors. One of Geschonneck's suggestions was turned down 'because the desired effect would have been blurred by too many secondary meanings'.[92] The opposing sides of the dialectic had to be clearly articulated, and a muddling of the terms would obscure its contradictions for both the actors and the audience. The kind of input Brecht welcomed can be seen in a suggestion by Engel that the team adopted. He wondered whether a fence could be placed on stage as 'a sign of the limits of possession',[93] that is, despite his onstage dominance, Puntila's power was not unbounded, and there were others like him abroad. This is an example of a realistic detail.

Taken together, the features discussed above offer an overview of some of the key issues involved in staging under Brecht's leadership. The common threads running between them betoken a sharp focus on the social dimension, the primacy of showing, and the productive splitting of different sign systems. What should be clear is that everything performed on stage was designed primarily with the audience in mind – the *mise en scène* and the actors all served the purpose of clear communication. Yet it should not be ignored that this was the clear communication of complex relationships, not simplified propaganda.

The prevalence of the social dimension in this, and indeed every subsequent production that Brecht directed or oversaw, helps elucidate the concept of 'making theatre politically'. This formulation, which I have deliberately differentiated from 'making political theatre', shifts the emphasis from content to form. Often, Brecht is considered a purveyor of political theatre, that is, theatre with overtly political themes. While this may be generally true, the idea of making theatre politically is concerned with revealing power relations in more prosaic or less consciously political areas. Brecht sought to politicize the action on stage, whether it had a political subject matter or not. So, the way that a working man talks to the daughter of a landed property owner deployed the gestic components to contextualize the exchange and its developments socially, regardless

[90] Anon., '*Puntila* VIII. Bild, Stellprobe. 23.9. BB und Assistenten. P/K', undated, n.p., ibid.

[91] See Bentley, *The Brecht Memoir*, p. 55.

[92] Anon., '*Puntila*, Donnerstag, 22. September 1949. BB EE + Assistenten', undated, 4 pages (3), BEA File 2.

[93] Engel, in Anon., 'Mittwoch 21. Sept: Skandal auf Puntila IV. Bild', undated, n.p., ibid.

Fig. 2.3. A Brechtian stage: combination of realistic props, an otherwise empty set, gestic acting and projection. *Mr Puntila and His Man Matti*, November 1949.

of whether he was talking about politics or love. Nothing is 'innocent' any more, but inculcated in a series of social codes that permit or proscribe the behaviours on stage. The emphasis on showing, on displaying these relations, was a key feature of Brecht's intention for his theatre: behaviours would be highlighted on stage so that spectators might recognize the more covert manifestations of the political in the everyday world.

The production itself offered episodic scenes to the audience, each combining realistic set and furniture accoutrements, set on an otherwise bare stage, against a large, framed, projected drawing by Neher that was different for each setting. The drawings were more metaphorical than illustrative, as in the second scene, set inside Puntila's estate. Here three identical wall-mounted hunting trophies, narrow, bleached skulls in triangular formation, looked down on proceedings (see Fig. 2.3). The stage thus offset recognizable surroundings with a form of visual commentary, much as the actors' talents were intended to illuminate the action, standing at a distance from their roles. Actors representing the privileged

characters occasionally wore prosthetics and gave more grotesque performances, denoted a 'loading' of the dialectic in favour of the workers.
Otherwise, however, the production made use of the stylization implicit
to Brecht's theatre: carefully staged *Arrangements* and the deliberateness
of *Gestus* and *Haltung* served to give everyday situations and actions the
qualities of something special, to draw in the spectators' curiosity and to
invite their questions.

Puntila premiered on 12 November 1949 on the main stage of the
Deutsches Theater, after less than two months' rehearsal. It was a
great success, and its social inflection did not go unnoticed. A typical
response may be found in a comment from Susanne Hess-Wyneken who
wrote:

> there is no confusion in the politics; Brecht clearly and strictly divides the classes,
> both social and human. With wonderful breadth, Brecht constructs not a drama,
> but a depiction of conditions in which a sharply observed realism is treated
> critically and heightened grotesquery gives rise to all manner of humour.[94]

The primacy of social conditions over human drama noted here is tribute
to Brecht's attempts to emphasize the process and not the end-point of
the scenes, social mechanisms, rather than their localized vicissitudes. A
very different approach, however, was taken by Berthold Viertel, who
directed the BE's second production.

Vassa Zheleznova and Brecht's aesthetic pluralism

Maxim Gorky's *Vassa Zheleznova* was originally written in pre-
revolutionary Russia and tells of a family's downfall. The plot follows
the matriarch of a family, the eponymous anti-hero, and her attempts to
keep her shipping business afloat while the rest of her largely degenerate
family threaten to sink it with their wayward behaviour. Vassa herself
is anything but sympathetic, and her final demise hardly elicits pity; at
one point she convinces her paedophile husband to kill himself so as to
avoid the scandal that would ruin the business. Gorky revised the play
in 1936 and included, amongst other things, a new character, Vassa's
daughter-in-law, a revolutionary called Rachel. She presented a positive
counter-figure and one who could look forward to the revolution with
well-founded hope.

Like most of Gorky's work, the play was, broadly speaking, naturalistic,
and Brecht invited a fairly conventional, but not unexceptional director
to stage the work. Both the choice of play and director have rightly led
commentators to note how the BE started with a broad, undogmatic

---

[94] Susanne Hess-Wyneken, 'Bert Brechts *Herr Puntila und sein Knecht*', *Berlin's* [*sic*] *Modenblatt*, 1 (1950), p. 22.

conception of how it was going to make theatre. Paul Rilla, for example, wrote in 1949, 'that Brecht's artistic method is not a doctrine to which the development of the theatre is sacrificed'.[95] It should be noted, however, that the play's content was critical of the Russian bourgeoisie. The BE's initial aesthetic eclecticism was not to be applied to any given subject matter. Matthias Braun notes that Stanislavsky was an important figure for Viertel and that Viertel had no great liking of Brecht's directorial ideas.[96] In a letter to Brecht accepting the commission, he said that he had no intention of using the methods of epic theatre, but added that historical distancing would be his means to create the desired political effect.[97] That is, by portraying the details of the relationships accurately in the past, he would be able to point to the play's importance in the present by contrasting the two periods.

According to a report on the rehearsals, Viertel's approach to direction made use of psychological identification and wanted to create its Russian specificity through 'atmosphere and setting',[98] that is, not through concrete situations or behaviour. Actors were off book quickly, just as in a more conventional rehearsal process, and Viertel wanted them to start with an image of their character which would be developed as the weeks progressed.[99] In short, Viertel was happy to proceed with character-based theatre, something Brecht resisted fiercely. This had a negative effect on the consolidation of the ensemble, and one reviewer wrote that the production was carried by the 'individual achievement' of Therese Giehse as Vassa.[100] Regine Lutz, who played Vassa's infantile daughter Ludmilla, charted a development in her relationship to Viertel over the rehearsal period in letters to her parents. At first she noted the challenge of playing 'such a psychological role'.[101] She then praised Viertel for giving her great freedom to explore the role by herself before realizing that this was quite 'risky, as I really have too little practical experience'.[102] Lutz's excessive gestures and characterization were duly criticized in the press.[103] Viertel's 'hands-off' style of direction allowed her to spiral out of control.

---

[95] Paul Rilla, *Essays: Kritische Beiträge zur Literatur* (Berlin: Henschel, 1955), p. 413.
[96] See Matthias Braun, 'Berthold Viertels erste Berliner Nachkriegsinszenierung: *Wassa Schelesnowa* am Berliner Ensemble: Ein dokumentarischer Bericht', *Kleine Schriften der Gesellschaft für Theatergeschichte*, 36 (1991), pp. 31–51 (32–3).
[97] See Berthold Viertel to Brecht, 11 August 1949, BBA 211/71.
[98] Anon., 'Probenbericht', undated, 6 pages (1), BEA File 3.   [99] See ibid., p. 2.
[100] Gerhard Kaiser, 'Eine verlöschende Welt', *BZ am Abend*, 22 December 1949.
[101] Lutz to her parents, 20 November 1949, BBA Lutz file 'Briefe Berlin Aug. 1949–Nov. 1950'.
[102] See Lutz to her parents, 29 November 1949; and Lutz to her parents, 9 December 1949, respectively, BBA Lutz file 'Briefe Berlin Aug. 1949–Nov. 1950'.
[103] See, for example, Friedrich Luft, 'Gorki: Stadien eines Verfalls', *Die neue Zeitung*, 23 December 1949.

Fig. 2.4. A conventional set for a conventional production: director Berthold Viertel pursues his own aesthetic agenda. *Vassa Zheleznova*, December 1949.

Viertel was offering fairly standard fare: a costume drama played within a naturalistic box set with a great actor stealing the show (see Fig. 2.4). The premiere on 23 December 1949 in the Deutsches Theater's chamber theatre was, however, very well received with many critics pointing to the implications beyond the specificity of the play itself. This position is perhaps best summed up by one reviewer who wrote that the production was not about a private family tragedy: 'here it's more about the life or death of a rotten, disintegrating world'.[104] What this and several similar reviews show is that the choice of play was more important than its aesthetic realization. Staging a play about a degenerate bourgeois family in decline in the newly founded GDR meant that its reception was overdetermined from the start. That is, it was so clear as to how one was to respond to such subject matter that the production was doomed to success before the first night.

Carl Weber calls the choice of play 'a gesture towards the Russian military administration',[105] which is certainly likely. Brecht told Viertel that the Russians very much enjoyed the production.[106] The combination of

---

[104] Horst Lommer, 'Zwei Welten', *Tägliche Rundschau*, 23 December 1949.
[105] Carl Weber, 'Brecht and the Berliner Ensemble – the Making of a Model', in Peter Thomson and Glendyr Sacks (eds.), *The Cambridge Companion to Brecht*, second edition (Cambridge: Cambridge University Press, 1994), pp. 175–92 (178).
[106] See Brecht to Viertel, 17 January 1950, BFA, 30: 10; *Letters*, p. 487.

an ideologically sound drama, coupled with a bravura performance from Giehse as a leading émigré actor, was going to do the BE no harm at all. In addition, Fritz Erpenbeck, in the SED's newspaper *Neues Deutschland*, was full of praise for the turn away from epic theatre and very much hoped that more BE productions would follow Viertel's dramatic, psychological style.[107] Erpenbeck was one of the SED's most vociferous critics of Brecht and his theories, and so Viertel's approach to directing may well have had a strategic advantage, too. With Viertel as a regular guest director, the BE could have presented itself as an aesthetically broad church, fighting the good fight in a variety of manners. Viertel did not, however, return to the BE, despite pleas from Brecht and Weigel, and, as Braun concludes 'the result was that a distinctive psychological style was hardly developed'.[108] Brecht had tried to enlist both Engel and Erich von Stroheim to direct the next production,[109] but ended up having to take the helm himself. The development of a more Brechtian theatre continued by default.

The process of adapting *The Tutor*

The third and final production of the BE's first season completed a journey backwards through time from contemporary Finland via pre-revolutionary Russia to Enlightenment Prussia. J. M. R. Lenz wrote *Der Hofmeister* (*The Tutor*) in 1774, and although it is now recognized as a shining example of *Sturm und Drang* ('storm-and-stress') drama, it was something of a curiosity that had rarely been staged before 1950. Lenz drew on his own experiences as a private tutor to write a drama about how such figures were exploited by their wealthy patrons with a view to reforming the situation. In addition, the play contains one of the most remarkable actions in the German repertoire when Läuffer, the eponymous tutor, castrates himself offstage in a bid to control his desires. Despite this episode, Lenz called the play a comedy, and one of the endings suggests that Läuffer will find childless happiness with the beautiful Lise. Brecht was already drawn to the play in 1940 when he

---

107 See Fritz Erpenbeck, 'Mit unerbittlicher Konsequenz', *Neues Deutschland*, 24 December 1949.
108 Braun, 'Viertels erste Berliner Nachkriegsinszenierung', p. 47.
109 See Erdmut Wizisla, 'Gespräch mit Willi Schwabe über Helene Weigel und Bertolt Brecht am 27.11.1978 im Berliner Ensemble [with Matthias Braun]', 1981, 38 pages (28), HWA FH 26; and Lutz to her parents, 10 January 1950, BBA Lutz file 'Briefe Berlin Aug. 1949–Nov. 1950'.

praised its realism, although he considered it a tragedy at the time.[110] This was because Läuffer allows himself to suffer humiliation and degradation in his work at the hands of the ruling class. To Brecht, the castration was metaphorical, too: an intellectual made himself impotent and thus ended any possible resistance to the existing class system.

Tragedy was a problematic genre for Brecht because it ascribed fatalistic categories to situations that humans themselves had created.[111] Brecht offered a social explanation: 'the *tragic* domain is curtailed when society bumps up against the limits of its potency'.[112] That is, the tragic is both a social and an historical category that actually points to the constraints and inadequacies of a given society, rather than to the shortcomings of the human beings in question. In other words, by playing situations, rather than characters, Brecht's stagecraft was in an ideal position to criticize what was taken for tragic drama and recontextualize it. This was not, however, Brecht's first solution to the problem of tragedy in this case; instead, he decided to adapt the text.

This study, as I set out in the Introduction, is not primarily concerned with ways in which writers or adapters constructed their plays, but rather with the ways the Berliner Ensemble staged them.[113] In this case, however, it is worth dwelling on the adaptation process because the treatment of *The Tutor* would itself become a model of how the company approached many original plays for the following two decades. Adaptation, as opposed to cutting and re-jigging, offered the company an active method of direct intervention. The aim was to refashion dramatic material into a form that allowed Brechtian stagecraft to work more efficiently and effectively.

A brief description of the adaptation process reveals its complexities and demonstrates Brecht's restless development of the written material. Brecht worked on initial drafts of the adaptation in autumn 1949 and arrived at a complete version in late December.[114] He did not consider it finished and handed it on to Benno Besson and Egon Monk for further work in January 1950. The tasks he set them are illuminating. While the first was merely to reduce the playing time by 30 minutes, the following three tell far more about the problems Brecht was confronting:

---

[110] See Brecht, 'Notizen über realistische Schreibweise', BFA, 22: 632. He wrote a more satirical poem of the same year, 'Über das bürgerliche Trauerspiel *Der Hofmeister*', BFA, 11: 270–1, in which the play was still considered tragic.

[111] See Brecht, '*Messingkauf* – Fragment B 13', BFA, 22: 711; *BoP*, p. 35.

[112] Brecht, '*Messingkauf* – Fragment A 22', BFA, 22: 829; *BoP*, p. 120.

[113] For a more detailed consideration of the adaptation itself, see Arrigo Subiotto, *Brecht's Adaptations for the Berliner Ensemble* (London: MHRA, 1975), pp. 15–43.

[114] See Brecht, journal entry for 22 December 1949, BFA, 27: 309; *Journals*, p. 425.

1. reduce playing time by 30 minutes;
2. clearly establish the central *Fabel* (the account of the real events) so that it is easily understandable, while retaining the elegance of the sequence of the scenes;
3. arrange the subplots around the central *Fabel* so that they illuminate and explicate the latter smoothly without interrupting it;
4. eliminate the untypical, accidental or purely pathological features in the motivation of the action and the characters.[115]

The emphasis on clarity is key to the exercise, but this should not be mistaken for simplification. Just as the actors at the BE were encouraged to pick out only the most salient points of dialectical contradictions, so were the adaptors. This meant that a hierarchy of meaning had to be established around the play's central themes and actions so that the subplots functioned to support and add new perspectives. The mention of 'elegance' attests to Brecht's need to retain the beauty of the work of art. Finally, the fourth point again focuses on clarity by getting rid of what seems extraneous detail, but the inclusion of 'purely pathological features' points to an ideological agenda as well. The pathological was, to Brecht, an area that could not be treated in his theatre because it suggested a purely personal deficiency and thus had no social component. Decades later, Deleuze and Guattari posited a relationship between mental illness and capitalism, for example, in their *Anti-Oedipus* and *One Thousand Plateaus*, which together form the *Capitalism and Schizophrenia* project. Yet in Brecht's day, Freudian psychiatry was dismissed as bourgeois in the East,[116] and Brecht did not hesitate to banish anything deemed to be singularly psychological from his stage.

Laurence Kitching traces the evolution of the adaptation and finds two complete drafts that preceded rehearsals, followed by a further three that emerged during the rehearsal period, and a final published text, which slightly amended the last rehearsal draft.[117] John Rouse notes: 'the changes from text to text, as the production team absorbed what they were learning in rehearsals, were hardly minor'.[118] He remarks that the epilogue, a commentary spoken by the actor playing Läuffer, written

---

[115] This is probably an original document, but its status is not clearly signalled in Christa Neubert-Herwig (ed.), *Benno Besson: Jahre mit Brecht* (Willisau: Theaterkultur, 1990), p. 65.

[116] See, for example, Heike Bernhardt, 'German Democratic Republic: Absorbing the Sins of the Fathers', in Jacob D. Lindy and Robert Jay Lifton (eds.), *Beyond Invisible Walls. The Psychological Legacy of Soviet Trauma* (New York: Taylor & Francis, 2001), pp. 59–89.

[117] See Laurence P. A. Kitching, *'Der Hofmeister': A Critical Analysis of Bertolt Brecht's Adaptation of Jacob Michael Reinhold Lenz's Drama* (Munich: Wilhelm Fink, 1976).

[118] See John Rouse, *Brecht and the West German Theatre*, p. 76.

in rhyming couplets, was added very late; up until then, the team was using the more generalized epilogue from *The Good Person of Szechwan*.

The process clearly exhibits a dialectical interaction between text and performance: contradictions between text and rehearsal were reconciled in the form of a new draft that was then subjected to the rehearsal process before, again, a new textual synthesis emerged. A playwright's text, often the defining category in rehearsal, defers to the political aims of the production and is modified to realize them. A reflection on the process notes:

> These changes were mostly not the result of theoretical concerns, but the product of the continual perfection of the *Arrangement*, the increasing elegance of the way we staged the *Fabel*, the errors observed in the social dimension, the desire to confer lightness upon the production etc.[119]

It is worth remembering that this was also a collective process. While Brecht was undoubtedly in charge,[120] his collaborators[121] were integral, as were the members of the ensemble who played the twenty-strong cast. The published version 'is only two thirds the length of the original and well over half of this is new'.[122]

Staging German history

Brecht as a dialectician was convinced that the experience of history had a profound effect on human beliefs, values and behaviour. Therefore, any action that took place in the past needed to show that performative category crucial to Brecht: difference. He proposed that the events on stage be placed in their historical context and called the process 'Historisierung' ('historicization').[123] On the one hand, historical discrepancies fuelled Brecht's Marxist optimism; if the spectators could become aware of these contrasts, they could understand that their own society was subject to historical change, too. On the other, the world of the past presented on stage had to connect with a contemporary audience in some way, lest it be dismissed as outdated and irrelevant. As John J. White points out: 'processes of *Verfremdung* and *Historisierung* need to be

---

[119] Anon., '*Hofmeister*: Textänderungen während der Proben', undated, 14 pages (1), BEA File 4.

[120] See Besson, in Neubert-Herwig (ed.), *Jahre mit Brecht*, p. 68; and Monk, unpublished interview with John Rouse, 10 June 1988, pp. II-3–4.

[121] The list of collaborators in the BFA includes Ruth Berlau and Caspar Neher: BFA, 8: 320.

[122] Subiotto, *Brecht's Adaptations*, p. 18.

[123] Brecht, 'Kleine Beschreibung einer neuen Technik der Schauspielkunst, die einen Verfremdungseffekt hervorbringt', BFA, 22: 646; *BoT*, p. 187.

shown to be ways of treating the present, rather than just the past'.[124] That is, it is not so much a question of recreating an accurate image of the past as demonstrating that that past also has a bearing on the experience of the contemporary audience. Brecht realized that the only way to signal historicization was to apply *Verfremdung* frequently in order to make what could have been perceived as familiar strange.[125] His elision of historicization and *Verfremdung* has implications beyond staging the past. The production of *Puntila*, for example, was just as historical as any other of Brecht's productions, only in this case Brecht was historicizing the present.

Historicizing the past brought forth different problems from historicizing the present, in that the past, to quote the opening line of L. P. Hartley's *The Go-Between*, is 'a foreign country: they do things differently there'. The solution could not be cosmetic; Brecht criticized modern-dress productions as superficial 'costume play[s]'.[126] He insisted on staging credible differences, which were in part suggested by historical research conducted by the assistants, although he also relied on issues of class antagonism. For *The Tutor*, Brecht could easily make use of particular historical qualities associated with Prussia. Performing pointed social divisions, enforced by an overweening submission to authority, would suggest a Germany that was familiar, yet comically exaggerated enough to produce the desired distance. After all, one of the central themes of the play is that Läuffer has internalized social pressures to such an extent that, despite his intelligence and learning, he and no one else carries out the castration. Brecht's intention was to dramatize 'die deutsche *Misère*' ('the German *misère*'), that is, a specifically German political impoverishment that was reflected in its people's failure to lead and complete a revolution successfully, as seen in the Peasants War of 1524–6 and the failed March Revolution of 1848. Brecht was certainly aware that there had not been a popular uprising in the last days of World War Two,[127] and socialism was imposed upon eastern Germany from 'above' by the occupying Soviets. The production of *The Tutor* was to chronicle how human beings abased themselves in deference to oppressive social structures. However, in the spirit of Brecht's rejection of tragedy as a timeless genre, he would reinstate Lenz's play as a comedy to confront

---

124 John J. White, *Bertolt Brecht's Dramatic Theory* (Rochester, NY: Camden House, 2004), p. 96.
125 See Brecht, 'Verfremdungseffekte in der chinesischen Schauspielkunst', BFA, 22: 207; *BoT*, p. 156.
126 Brecht, 'Über experimentelles Theater', BFA, 22: 541; *BoT*, p. 134.
127 See Brecht, 'Vorwort zu *Turandot*', BFA, 24: 409.

the audience with a past that was sadly ridiculous, rather than bleakly unchangeable.

Regine Lutz wrote to her parents of the remarkable concentration she applied in rehearsal to attain the required precision in her acting.[128] The production was elaborate in its attention to detail as a way of giving eighteenth-century Prussia a particularity and a peculiarity that the audience could compare to its own experience of the present. One such generalizing detail, which has attracted an amount of critical attention, is a series of bows Läuffer performs towards his potential employers at the beginning of the play. Rouse gives a full account of this complicated gesture which allowed the actor both to present the self-humiliation and offer a commentary on it.[129] Sarah Bryant-Bertail concludes that Läuffer 'is forced to perform ceremonies that make a spectacle of his own debasement'.[130] Historical settings gave Brecht the opportunity to emphasize ceremonial acts because they were more unfamiliar to the contemporary spectator; in performing such rituals the actors could display their deference to and, at times, their contempt for social institutions.

The production opened on 15 April 1950 on the main stage of the Deutsches Theater, and garnered nothing but plaudits for a new style of theatre that clearly distinguished itself from the other Berlin stages. One reviewer summed up the effects of the historicization concisely:

Bertolt Brecht has subjected *The Tutor* to an adaptation that transposes the play out of the sensual and vital atmosphere of the storm-and-stress theatre onto the sparse, barely illusionist *Modell*-stage that bears his own imprint. In doing this, the play's intellectual substance has not been touched, on the contrary, it has rather been emphasized more strongly – and definitely with greater clarity .[131]

Brecht had carefully drained the storm-and-stress movement of its wild emotion and energy by offering the play to the audience as an object of curiosity. Yet this transformation did not turn the production into something cold and distant, but actually enlivened its reception. Brecht's tactic of contrasting text and delivery served to heighten the production's impact, not to deaden it. Some reviewers found the caricature of some of the characters, which Brecht engaged to open them up to criticism, either too exaggerated or too self-conscious, but still had to admit that the production was fresh and exciting.[132] Another facet the reviews frequently

---

128 See Lutz to her parents, 7 March 1950, BBA Lutz file 'Briefe Berlin Aug. 1949–Nov. 1950'.
129 See Rouse, *Brecht and the West German Theatre*, pp. 37–9.
130 Bryant-Berail, *Space and Time*, p. 95.
131 Walter Thomas, 'Enthüllung der "teutschen Misere"', *BZ am Abend*, 15 April 1950.
132 See, for example, ic [*sic*], 'Aufgefrischter Sturm und Drang', *Neue Zeit*, 16 April 1950.

mentioned was how well the predominantly young ensemble worked as a unit.[133] The troupe, which was scarcely half a year old, was showing how focus and commitment could trump inexperience given the right leadership and rehearsal regime. Brecht referred to himself, Neher, Monk and Besson as the show's 'Regiekollegium' ('council of directors'),[134] and wanted to credit Monk and Besson as directors on the programme, but they refused due to the defining role he had played. However, because he could not countenance appearing alone after such profitable collective work, he co-opted Neher, and so both were credited as directors.[135]

Langhoff drops a bombshell

It would be difficult to consider the BE's first season anything but a triumph. Brecht as artistic director and Weigel as *Intendantin* had overseen three diverse, high-quality and well-received productions, brought guest stars from the West to the GDR, and introduced a group of young actors and assistants to a new way of making theatre. And all this was achieved without a theatre of their own. It is perhaps understandable, then, to see why commentators have often assumed that the BE had a productive, friendly relationship with the Deutsches Theater (DT).[136] This view, however, could not have been further from the truth. One of the bases for this opinion is the perceived generosity of Wolfgang Langhoff as the DT's *Intendant* towards the 'homeless' Brecht, which Mittenzwei calls both humane and comradely.[137] Stuber, however, has comprehensively demonstrated that this was not the case. Langhoff did not in fact attend the key meeting at which the DT was considered the best temporary home for Brecht's new company, and it was the SED and not Langhoff that proposed the option in any case.[138] Indeed, she concludes that Langhoff played the 'master of the house' with respect to Weigel,[139] despite their ostensibly similar status in their theatres' respective hierarchies.

The BE had scarcely been working at the DT for four months before it experienced its first major crisis. The company's very existence was under threat due to a power play initiated by none other than Langhoff. He had tried to take advantage of the contract Weigel signed with the

[133] See Friedrich Luft, 'Ein ABC der deutschen Misere', *Neue Zeitung*, 16 April 1950.
[134] Brecht, 'Anmerkungen', BFA, 24: 357.
[135] See Monk, in Lang and Hillesheim, *'Denken heißt verändern...'*, p. 103.
[136] See, for example, Manfred Berger, Manfred Nössig, Fritz Rödel, *et al.*, *Theater in der Zeitenwende. Zur Geschichte des Dramas und Schauspieltheaters in der Deutschen Demokratischen Republik 1945–1968*, vol. 1 (Berlin: Henschel, 1972), p. 180.
[137] See Mittenzwei, *Das Leben des Bertolt Brecht*, vol. 2, p. 32.
[138] See Stuber, *Spielräume und Grenzen*, pp. 58–9 and 61.
[139] Stuber, 'Helene Weigel und ihre Rolle', p. 262.

SED to found the BE; its ninth clause stipulated that the contract was to last for a year in the first instance, and could be extended at the latest by 15 January 1950.[140] With this date in mind, Langhoff moved quickly. The Municipal Authority, as the agency responsible for the DT, sent a letter to Weigel in early January with an enclosed report, dated 30 December 1949, from Kurt Bork to Councillor Max Kreuziger.[141] The report described the logistical difficulties Langhoff had encountered and demanded the BE's expulsion from the DT by the end of the season. Trouble was brewing earlier, however: a government document of mid December already mooted a plan to move the BE.[142]

The Municipal Authority's first proposal, rather than seeking any form of arbitration between the two companies, suggested that the BE move to East Berlin's Komische Oper (KO), roughly a kilometre south of the DT. The plan took for granted that the BE would no longer be working at the DT and set out detailed conditions of a future relationship between the BE and the KO.[143] It identified work that would need to be carried out at the KO, which included a new acoustic treatment to suit the demands of an acting company and the construction of a dedicated rehearsal space. It is not clear how the BE responded to this offer. A document entitled 'Fragen für Felsenstein' ('questions for Felsenstein', the KO's *Intendant*) sets out thirteen specific points and queries, suggesting that, with their backs to the wall, Weigel and Brecht had to treat the proposal seriously.[144] The BE also asked its backer, no longer the Department, but since 1950 the Ministry of People's Education, to invite other theatres in the county of Brandenburg for discussions about sharing facilities, a strategy the Ministry welcomed.[145]

Brecht was nonetheless incredulous. He drafted a letter (which appears not to have been sent) that outlined his disbelief and shock. He contended that the BE and DT had worked together 'without any friction' and that the BE had brought the DT two critical *and* financial successes that had been registered beyond Germany's frontiers.[146] While unable to fathom Langhoff's motives, Brecht continued that having his company

[140]   See Paul Wandel and Helene Weigel, '[Contract founding the Berliner Ensemble]', 24 September 1949, 3 pages (3), BBA uncatalogued file 'Aktuelles'.

[141]   Schwarz to Helene Weigel, 2 January 1950, ibid.

[142]   See Max Burghardt, 'Betrifft: Berliner Ensemble', 17 December 1949, n.p., BArch DR 2/8237.

[143]   See Bork to Max Kreuziger, 30 December 1949, BBA uncatalogued file 'Aktuelles'.

[144]   See Anon., 'Fragen für Felsenstein', undated, 2 pages, ibid.

[145]   See Max Burghardt and Schulze to Bork, 21 January 1950, BArch DR 2/8237.

[146]   Brecht, '[Zusammenarbeit mit dem Deutschen Theater]', BFA Registerband: 741. All subsequent quotations refer to this source. The document is undated, but was probably written in January 1950 in response to the letter from the Municipal Authority.

play at different theatres was 'ignoble' and offered no way for the BE to develop an audience. He also declined the opportunity to work under Fritz Wisten at the Theater am Schiffbauerdamm with the rather haughty remark that the theatre 'doesn't measure up to our artistic standards'. Yet while Brecht set out his position and Weigel sought a solution, it is almost certain that Langhoff's plan remained largely hidden from the rest of the BE. Monk notes palpable tension only *after* the first season, something echoed by Lutz in a letter written in July 1950.[147]

The Ministry reassured Weigel that it wanted the BE to continue its work beyond the 1949/50 season. Yet it noted that the accommodation question was still open and that it would endeavour to make cooperation with the DT work, should no alternative venue be found.[148] By March, Langhoff had written to the Minister himself, Paul Wandel, outlining his reasons for severing ties with the BE, a relationship he tellingly called 'a solution of necessity' in the first place.[149] He listed the rehearsal time and roles his actors had had to forego, the overstretched technical resources, and the psychological strain of having two leaderships in one theatre. He offered to tender his resignation if his plan was not accepted. Wandel, who supported Brecht and his work, told Langhoff that a failure to solve the problem could lead to the dissolution of the BE, something he could not allow. He wrote that it would be bad for Berlin and the GDR, and that it would have major political ramifications. He also asked Langhoff to reconsider his resignation.[150] Langhoff stayed in the post, yet this had its own significance in the GDR's cultural politics, as will become evident in the discussion of *Urfaust* in the next chapter.

Correspondence during March and April betrays the urgent search for a solution involving different levels of the administration. Kurt Bork, now responsible for theatre matters at the Ministry, continued to lobby for the BE. In a letter to the SED's Central Secretariat, he recognized the BE's unique status and argued that it was the only theatre in the GDR that set itself the task 'of turning its co-workers into conscious co-workers for a new society'.[151] A month later he cited the production of *The Tutor* as indisputable proof of the need to ensure the survival of the company.[152] The BE could also call on an old friend, the critic Herbert

---

[147] See Monk, in Stuber, *Spielräume und Grenzen*, p. 65; and Lutz to her parents, 4 July 1950, BBA Lutz file 'Briefe Berlin Aug. 1949–Nov. 1950'.
[148] See Ministerium für Volksbildung to Weigel, 3 February 1950, BBA uncatalogued file 'Aktuelles'.
[149] Wolfgang Langhoff to Paul Wandel, 15 March 1950, BArch DR 2/8237.
[150] See Paul Wandel to Wolfgang Langhoff, 28 March 1950, BArch DR 2/8237.
[151] Bork to Stefan Heymann, 27 March 1950, BArch DR 2/8237.
[152] See Bork to Herbert Volkmann, 18 April 1950, BArch DR 2/8237.

Ihering, who was, at that time, the head dramaturge at the Deutsches Theater. In a personal letter to his *Intendant*, he pointed out that the BE was of value to the GDR, but also to Langhoff in that he would be credited with enabling the work of such a company.[153] Weigel drew on her personal connections with the highest-ranking officials in a bid to defend the BE. Consequently, Wilhelm Pieck, the president of the GDR, brought her proposals to the Politburo, the state's most senior executive body. He reported with regret that the only solution was to stay either with Langhoff or Wisten because there were no other theatres available, and the GDR could not undertake further major building work due to its limited financial resources.[154] She also turned to Minister Wandel stating that the constant uncertainty was making work impossible and putting off potential guest artists. Brecht was now refusing to work, having put so much effort into building up the BE in the first place. She ended by placing the ball firmly in Wandel's court: 'I ask you to tell me what to do'.[155] Agreement was reached by June 1950 after the Ministry conferred with Alexander Abusch, a member of the Politburo. It stated that the BE would have access to the DT's chamber theatre for three days a week and that a rehearsal stage would be built near the DT. However, this was only to be a temporary arrangement; the authorities had to consider what would happen to the BE in the 1951/52 season.[156] As it turned out, the BE would remain at the DT for a few more years as the relationship normalized, although this was not without frequent internal bickering over resources.

A rehearsal stage for the BE was one of Weigel's key demands for remaining at the DT, and its presence runs through the correspondence about the crisis. Despite the Secretariat's approval of the measure,[157] the Ministry of Planning had refused to release the sum of 80,000 marks required to renovate the former drill hall at 29 Reinhardtstraße. Herbert Volkmann of the Ministry of People's Education made some interesting arguments, designed to wrest the funds from Minister Heinrich Rau. First, the use of an existing building which would be converted into a rehearsal space already delivered a large saving. Second, the space was only temporary, and it would be used to further the GDR's official Stanislavskian acting doctrine when the Theatre Institute in Weimar moved to Berlin. He also noted that he hoped that the Volksbühne would

---

153   See Herbert Ihering to Langhoff, 6 May 1950, AdK Wolfgang Langhoff Archive 171.
154   See Wilhelm Pieck to Weigel, 27 March 1959, *Briefwechsel*, p. 54.
155   Weigel to Wandel, 22 May 1950, BArch DR 2/8237.
156   See Herbert Volkmann, 'Aktenvermerk', 9 June 1950, n.p., BArch DR 2/8237.
157   See Baumann, 'Protokoll Nr. 113 der Sitzung des Sekretariats am 9, Juni 1950', undated, 10 pages (5), SAPMO BArch DY 30/J IV 2/3/113.

be rebuilt by 1951 to allow Wisten to move there and for the BE to take over the Theater am Schiffbauerdamm. Third, he reminded Rau that Walter Ulbricht had expressly supported this solution.[158] The letter had the desired effect and construction work was swift. A newspaper article mentions the new 'Probenhaus' ('rehearsal building') in January 1951.[159] One of its first guests was an amateur group from Köthen that staged Brecht's *Señora Carrar's Rifles* on 21 February.[160] The play was directed by Manfred Wekwerth, whom Brecht invited to join the BE as an assistant after seeing (and criticizing) the production and who would become its *Intendant* in 1977.

The BE had survived its first season, but had to use its nascent reputation together with its influential connections to guarantee its future. That the Politburo and indeed the Minister of People's Education himself were involved in the rescue signals the degree to which the highest echelons of GDR polity monitored and intervened in cultural activities. At this time, they strove to find an agreeable outcome to the BE's accommodation problems. This high-level support was not to last, and the BE found itself embroiled in a series of cultural battles in the following years, in which it was no longer to be defended, but harassed.

[158] See Herbert Volkmann to Heinrich Rau, 24 August 1950, BArch DE 1/59945.
[159] See Alfred Doll, 'Ihre Kunst gilt dem Volke', *Nachtexpreß*, 29 January 1951.
[160] See Weigel to Egon Rentzsch, 17 February 1951, SAPMO BArch DY 30/IV 2/9.06/188.

3   The Berliner Ensemble's years at the Deutsches Theater: 1949–1953

Helene Weigel as *Intendantin* in the BE's early years

The role of *Intendantin* entailed looking after the internal running of the Berliner Ensemble itself while dealing with the Deutsches Theater, the SED, and the public. This division of duties did not, however, radically affect the manner in which Weigel either administered the BE or represented it to other bodies. Irene Ebel, Weigel's personal assistant since 1964, acknowledges a form of communication that also manifested itself earlier in her boss' tenure: 'she hardly ever wrote personal letters. The theatre always played a role'.[1] Petra Stuber notes, with respect to Weigel's correspondence, that in her style 'the private and the official were bound together inextricably'.[2] Many of her dealings betrayed this mixture of registers, something that was disarming in that her correspondents did not quite know with whom they were talking, the private person or the *Intendantin*. Heinrich Goertz, one of Fritz Wisten's staff, alleged that Weigel had joined the SED 'to achieve her demands'.[3] However, Weigel was never a member of the SED, and so the successes of her dealings are probably better attributed to her skilful rhetorical strategies and the force of her personality, rather than to any sense of political obligation from the authorities.

As already noted, Brecht nominated Weigel as *Intendantin* with the intention that she would act autonomously while keeping to his agenda. This she achieved in a variety of ways. She was happy to innovate, like Brecht, in the way actors were treated, for example. She instituted regular mandatory voice, singing, and movement classes for the ensemble, something vocal tutor Helga Generlich considered unique in a theatre of the

---

[1] Ebel, in Matthias Braun, 'Notat zu einem Gespräch mit Irene Ebel über HW am 21.2.1983', undated, n.p., HWA FH 55.
[2] Petra Stuber, 'Helene Weigel und ihre Rolle', p. 265.
[3] Heinrich Goertz, 'Wie Brecht sich das "Schiff" unter den Nagel riß', *Die Welt*, 9 December 1972.

time, as opposed to an acting school.[4] On an institutional level, Weigel demonstrated her toughness when negotiating with Berthold Viertel on the production of *Vassa*. He had made it a condition of his employment that his new wife Elisabeth play Anna, a role already assigned to Angelika Hurwicz.[5] Brecht was keen to engage Viertel as a director and to develop a more lasting connection between the director and the BE, but this did not stop Weigel from resisting Viertel's attempt at blackmail. Weigel prevailed and proved that she was no pushover as *Intendantin*. This firmness extended to more material concerns as well. In a letter to Stefan Heymann of the Central Committee, she ironically described herself as a 'thrifty housewife' who was trying to get the most out of her public subsidy.[6] In a document probably written in spring 1950, the BE noted that it had actually underspent its projected budget by 6,247 marks[7] (or roughly €3,100 in 2014)[8] per month. Weigel's fiscal responsibility, which was almost certainly born of budgetary privations in exile, extended to pay negotiations, too. She did not indulge her actors' salary claims and planned to report to the Ministry of Culture in 1954 that actors who wanted to move from the DT to the BE could not expect a pay rise.[9]

That is not to say that Weigel was unconcerned about her staff. For example, the SED had offered the BE a small allocation of holiday homes for the summer of 1956. The criteria for acceptance were that the nominated staff had either won major prizes in the GDR or were high earners. Weigel complained about the very notion of privilege in the GDR and bemoaned the fact that the offer was not made to younger colleagues who could not afford holiday homes on their wages.[10] The same egalitarian impulse extended to the technical staff. One of her stage workers recalls how accommodation on tour in Rügen was divided between officers' quarters intended for the actors, and barracks for the technical

---

[4] See Helga Generlich, 'Stimmbildung und Sprecherziehung', in BE/Weigel (eds.), *Theaterarbeit*, pp. 390–3 (390).

[5] See Sabine Kebir, *Abstieg in den Ruhm*, p. 236.

[6] Weigel to Stefan Heymann, 1 August 1950, SAPMO BArch DY 30/IV 2/9.06/188.

[7] Anon., '[interim internal report on the Berliner Ensemble]', [c. March/April 1950], 4 pages (1), BArch DR 2/8237.

[8] Historical comparisons provided here and elsewhere are taken from http://fxtop.com/de/historische-wechselkurse.php?MA=1. Officially, marks in the East were exchanged on a 1:1 basis with those of the West, although black market trading understandably drove down the value of the GDR's currency.

[9] See [Weigel], 'Für die Besprechung am Freitag, 22.10.[1954] Ministerium für Kultur', undated, n.p., BBA uncatalogued file 'Aktuelles'.

[10] See Weigel to Günther, 3 February 1956, BBA uncatalogued file 'Schriftwechsel Ministerium für Kultur 1954–58'.

personnel. Weigel was outraged at the demarcation and insisted on equal treatment for all her staff.[11]

Weigel also took an active interest in the BE's collective health. This was particularly evident in cases of alcohol and tablet dependency, which were not infrequent at the BE and other Berlin theatres. Here it was evident that Weigel wanted to make sure that her talented ensemble remained able to work and perform at the high levels demanded by the company's burgeoning reputation. Weigel had championed the anti-alcohol drug Antabus and put it to use together with her own powers of persuasion. However, she could not offer transfusions of willpower, and Regine Lutz noted how one actor who had been Weigel's 'poster boy for Antabus' relapsed after the summer break in 1955.[12]

As discussed earlier, Weigel's adoption of the role of 'mother' of the ensemble was something of a double-edged sword. Her care and concern personalized relationships in ways that could be beneficial to those in favour, but detrimental to those who were not. It is difficult to assert that Weigel deliberately developed this role with definite ends in mind. However, Christine Herold writes that over time the deployment of such motherliness helped her to get the most out of the BE.[13] The ability to exert power that went beyond the professional, especially within an institution such as a theatre company, meant that she was able to ask for more than was contractually stipulated. Actor Willi Schwabe perhaps bests sums up the two sides of the relationship: 'we loved her like a mother and we feared her like a mother'.[14]

Weigel served to support Brecht and develop the structures in the BE in order to nurture his new ideas for making theatre. The same, however, could not quite be said of Brecht. While he praised Weigel as an actor, a note-giver during final rehearsals and an *Intendantin*, he actively undermined her intellectual abilities and her opportunities to contribute to the conceptual questions of his productions. Hans Bunge noted that Brecht encouraged the assistants to look down on Weigel, and Werner Hecht felt the persistent presence of this attitude in the 1960s.[15] Peter Voigt, who was an assistant under Brecht, recounts an incident when he made a set of suggestions in rehearsal that Brecht

[11] See Wolfgang Bömelburg, *Hobellied für Bertolt Brecht. Ein Theatertischler erzählt* (Berlin: Eulenspiegel, 1997), p. 37.
[12] Lutz to her parents, 14 August 1955, BBA Lutz file 'Briefe ab Jan 1955 bis Dez 1956'.
[13] See Christine Herold, *Mutter des Ensembles. Helene Weigel – ein Leben mit Bertolt Brecht* (Cadolzburg: Ars Vivendi, 2001), p. 169.
[14] Willi Schwabe, in Seydel, . . . *gelebt für alle Zeiten*, p. 384.
[15] See Hans Bunge, unpublished interview with John Rouse, 18 May 1988, p. III-8; and Werner Hecht, unpublished interview with the author, 13 May 2010.

enthusiastically embraced. Yet they were not his suggestions, but Weigel's. She had summoned him to her office to communicate them; she knew that Brecht would not have listened if they had come straight from her mouth.[16] One can only presume that she had chosen Voigt as the youngest assistant at the time because he had been least exposed to the atmosphere Brecht had nurtured. It is worth adding that Weigel had no pretensions about being a great thinker and relied on her senior staff to comment on theoretical issues after Brecht's death, but her total exclusion from such matters was a regrettable piece of short-sighted prejudice on Brecht's part while he was alive.

Managing the relationship with the Deutsches Theater

After the upheavals of the BE's first season, Weigel had her work with the DT cut out. The solution to the tensions between the DT and the BE was hardly a solution at all. In effect both companies continued to work under the same conditions that led to the falling out, with the one exception that the BE now had the 'Probenhaus' (rehearsal building) to ease pressure on rehearsal space. Both companies still needed access to the DT's stages and this caused an amount of friction for the duration of the BE's residence at the DT.[17]

Weigel was not intimidated by Langhoff, despite his show of strength during the BE's first season. Instead, she was determined to make the best of a bad lot. Agreement had scarcely been reached with Langhoff in 1950 before she asked the DT to let the BE's lighting specialist advise on the renovation of the DT's chamber theatre.[18] The following year, she actively lobbied for the DT to build an orchestra pit and to refurbish its projection room, amongst other things.[19] On the one hand, she insisted on maintaining the high technical quality of BE productions, which demanded state-of-the-art equipment. On the other, she conducted herself not like a guest at the DT, but as a partner with full rights to determine its use of resources. Langhoff, however, did not recognize these rights completely and let Weigel know the limits of her power on various occasions.

---

[16] See Peter Voigt, 'Der Zögling. Ein Filmtext', Sinn und Form, 2 (2004), pp. 221–39 (223).
[17] See, for example, Weigel to Langhoff, 25 August and 23 October 1952, BBA uncatalogued file 'Aktuelles'.
[18] See [Weigel] to Walter Kohls, 1 August 1950, ibid.
[19] See Weigel to the Deutsches Theater, 26 April 1951 and [Weigel] to Walter Kohls, 13 June 1951, both ibid.

Perhaps the low point of the relationship came in 1952. The BE decided to revive *The Tutor*, a production which had run for 72 performances over the course of a year, even though the actor playing the eponymous hero, Hans Gaugler, had returned to Switzerland. Weigel wanted to return the production to the repertoire and asked a senior member of the DT technical staff what needed to be done to the set to make it ready for use.[20] She was staggered to learn that it had been completely recycled and complained to the DT's head of administration, Walter Kohls.[21] Kohls justified the 'recycling' of the set by stressing the scarcity of resources and the absence of Weigel's lead actor. He added that revivals tended not to be commercially viable, and so he would not endorse a new build.[22] This argument was hardly valid; the BE had revived *Mother Courage* in 1951, a show that continued to draw large crowds, and *The Tutor* had already been very popular. Weigel's parting remark was that the DT had acted without any discussion or consultation,[23] something that underlined the problem at the heart of the episode. Keen not to see a repeat of such an action, Weigel asked Kohls not to destroy the set of another production, *Das Glockenspiel des Kreml* (*The Kremlin Chimes*), when it reached the end of its run in 1953.[24] This production was not revived, and the direction to store and maintain the set may well have had a punitive intent.

The BE as an institution was not averse to using its own underhanded tactics on occasion. The company had developed a special kind of playbill which it considered an important complement to the productions. The programmes were deliberately designed to be small enough to be carried in a pocket or a bag, and spectators were to be offered them when they bought their ticket, in advance of the performance.[25] Like so much at the BE, it reflected a fundamental rethink of the way the elements of theatre could work together. Shortly after the dispute about the *Tutor* set, Kohls established that the budget centre for BE programmes, which was contractually paid for by the DT, was overdrawn by more than 100 per cent. Kohls reminded the BE that such costs were supposed to have been cleared in advance and informed the company that he had instructed the printers no longer to accept any further orders from the BE.[26] However, barely a year later, he discovered that the BE had secretly

---

[20] See [Weigel] to Karl Ruppert, 4 June 1952, ibid.
[21] See [Weigel] to Walter Kohls, 6 June 1952, ibid.
[22] See Kohls to Weigel, 9 June 1952, ibid.
[23] See [Weigel] to Kohls, 17 June 1952, ibid.
[24] See Weigel to Kohls, 24 June 1953, ibid.
[25] See 'Das Programmheft', in BE/Weigel (eds.), *Theaterarbeit*, p. 225.
[26] See Kohls to Herr Moll, 22 July 1952, BBA uncatalogued file 'Aktuelles'.

started using a different firm of printers.[27] Weigel's thrifty management of her own company's finances did not necessarily extend to those of the DT.

This lack of concern may well have been the product of the ongoing friction over resources. There was, however, another aspect to the uncomfortable relationship between the two companies. Egon Monk considered the DT (and indeed the Schiller-Theater in West Berlin) 'quite simply old-fashioned, leaden, creaking in comparison to us', an attitude that spurred BE members on to do more than their contracts required.[28] The sentiment is echoed in many other voices, from assistants and actors: they all felt a special quality when working with Brecht, and this was publicly affirmed by their success. There is no doubt that the BE had an aura of cockiness about it, founded upon an understandable sense of self-worth. Yet this swagger did not make the ensemble many friends. Benno Besson describes the BE as having 'eine Igelstellung'.[29] This is a term taken from the military and describes a 'hedgehog position', that is, soldiers in a circle with their rifles pointing outward. This is not the image of a theatre company on the march, but one on the defensive. Its achievements were starting to attract unwanted attention from the GDR's cultural authorities.

The SED's attack on 'formalism'

The SED had already taken a great interest in the BE. Its highest-ranking politicians were instrumental in securing the funding necessary for its foundation, and they were also closely involved in the quest to find a solution to the crisis sparked by Langhoff in the BE's first season. This interest reflected the SED's self-understanding of its role in GDR culture, rather than a sense of allegiance to Brecht and the BE. To the SED, to ensure that the new socialist society progressed in line with its doctrines, nothing could be allowed to develop without supervision. At the time, the BE was staging high-quality, left-orientated productions. Yet as the SED aligned its policies more with those of the Soviet Union, the relationship with the BE changed radically, as imported dogma set the tone for cultural policy. In Moscow, Andrei Zhdanov had enforced the tenets of socialist realism with more stick than carrot. The two issues that most profoundly

---

[27] See Kohls to Walter Gelmar, 2 June 1953, ibid.

[28] Monk, *Regie Egon Monk*, p. 140.

[29] Besson, in Irmer and Schmidt, *Die Bühnenrepublik*, p. 40. The term was already associated with the BE in 1952: a reviewer noted that Brecht had assumed an 'Igelstellung' with respect to the press (G. W., 'Berliner Ensemble spielt *Urfaust*', *Neue Zeit* 26 April 1952).

affected artistic production in the young GDR were formalism and the treatment of the *Erbe* ('cultural heritage', discussed below). To call a work of art 'formalist' was to accuse it of emphasizing form over content, or in more contemporary parlance, style over substance. Formalism was a means to attack modern art that Zhdanovite socialists considered to be bourgeois and 'decadent'. Decadence betokened a loss of faith in a bright socialist future, and modernism, as an artistic response to uncertainty and relativism in the human and physical sciences, could be read as a reflection on a world in turmoil.

Brecht had already been subject to such charges. As noted in Chapter 2, he had been party to the debate on expressionism in the late 1930s, which also included a treatment of formalism (see p. 43). However, this debate was far from over, and it resurfaced for Brecht after the premiere of *Courage* in Berlin. Fritz Erpenbeck, a critic well regarded by the authorities and thus potentially a dangerous voice, had in 1949 accused the play of exhibiting the toxic quality 'volksfremde Dekadenz' ('a decadence alien to the people').[30] That Wolfgang Harich could take him to task shortly afterwards[31] indicates that free public discussion was still possible at that time in the Soviet zone. The problem, to the official ideologues, was that *Courage* did not offer anything positive because its protagonist never learns from her experiences. To Brecht, this was a clear index of the play's realism: 'misfortune on its own is a bad teacher. Its pupils learn hunger and thirst, but rarely hunger for the truth or a thirst for knowledge'.[32] To Brecht, the audience should view her with scepticism and question the roots of her blindness.

At this point, it is worth noting that Brecht did not oppose the rejection of formalism. He supported the position in 1939 and offered an unpublished definition in 1951 that did not diverge from that of the SED.[33] He did observe, however, how the campaign itself had been deformed by the triumph of dogma over artistic practice: 'the discussion about formalism is not helped by the fact that the wrong people are supporting the right side, and the wrong arguments are being presented for the right position'.[34] He identified how a valid discussion was being

[30] Fritz Erpenbeck, 'Einige Bemerkungen zu Brechts *Mutter Courage*', *Die Weltbühne*, 4:3 (1949), pp. 101–3, here p. 103.
[31] See Wolfgang Harich, 'Trotz fortschrittlichen Wollens...', *Die Weltbühne*, 4:6 (1949), pp. 215–19.
[32] Brecht, 'Die Courage lernt nichts', BFA, 24: 273.
[33] See Brecht, 'Über reimlose Lyrik mit unregelmäßigen Rhythmen' BFA, 2: 363; *BoT*, p. 174; and '[Formalismus und Formung]', BFA, 23: 147.
[34] Brecht, 'Notizen über die Formalismusdiskussion', BFA, 23: 141; *Brecht on Art and Politics*, p. 311.

instrumentalized, although he did not ponder the reasons why. In a book published in the GDR in 1978, Werner Mittenzwei offers a critique of the formalism debate that remains within the aesthetic realm: new socialist works were measured by traditional norms.[35] Petra Stuber looks behind the surface and concludes that the debate 'was nothing other than an instrument for stabilizing the GDR or rather cementing the SED's central authority'.[36] Her explanation signals that championing or denouncing certain works of art was actually a smokescreen for power politics. Yet this historically dependent fickleness with respect to what was acceptable did not remain in the realm of the theoretical: policy was directly to affect Brecht and the BE.

Brecht presented a problem for the SED because his work with the BE was founded upon a dialectical definition of reality. His refusal to toe the party line and his preference instead for inductive discoveries in rehearsal meant that the productions could not be regulated by imposing conceptual constraints, such as the exhortation for plays to feature positive heroes and happy (socialist) endings. The campaign against Brecht and his theatre was conducted both publicly and behind the scenes. Hostile criticism appeared in newspapers, with the SED's Johanna Rudolph writing in *Neues Deutschland*, while Erpenbeck's attacks mainly appeared in the GDR's only theatre magazine, *Theater der Zeit*. Rudolph's review of Brecht's *The Mother* in 1951 at the BE denied that the use of projections was formalist, but still equated the elements of epic theatre she identified with abstraction, a synonym for formalism.[37] The GDR officially adopted a campaign against formalism after the Central Committee's fifth conference from 15 to 17 March 1951, at which Weigel also spoke, without mentioning formalism explicitly.[38] The illusion of free speech was exposed by the conference's outcome: the argument was stacked so clearly in the SED's favour that there was never any question that the campaign would not become official policy. The less apparent means used to combat Brecht were formulated behind closed doors, however, and these mostly took place under the auspices of a new government agency.

---

[35] See Werner Mittenzwei, *Der Realismus-Streit um Brecht. Grundriß der Brecht-Rezeption in der DDR 1945–1975* (Berlin and Weimar: Aufbau, 1978), p. 54.

[36] Stuber, *Spielräume und Grenzen*, p. 128.

[37] See Johanna Rudolph, 'Wertvolle Bereicherung des Berliner Theaterlebens', *Neues Deutschland*, 14 January 1951.

[38] See Hans Lauter, *Der Kampf gegen den Formalismus in Kunst und Literatur, für eine fortschrittliche deutsche Kultur* (Berlin: Dietz, 1951), pp. 64–8. This book is the authorized protocol of the conference. It is almost certain that Brecht wrote Weigel's contribution.

Theaterarbeit, or how the SED tried to stifle the BE

The Ministry of People's Education had a remarkably broad remit and the SED decided to divide up its responsibilities into more manageable areas in the summer of 1951. In May of that year, the Politburo approved the formation of the 'Staatliche Kommission für Kunstangelegenheiten' ('State Commission for Artistic Matters'), alternatively known as the 'Staatliche Kunstkommission' or StaKuKo, as a body to formulate, implement and police cultural policy.[39] It was a coincidence that, at the very same Politburo meeting, the SED authorized the cultural hardliner Wilhelm Girnus 'to undertake continuous political work with Bert Brecht and to give him help', that is, decoded, to spy on and influence him. Yet it was no coincidence that the two items came about around the same time. Both register a movement towards control, something essential to the SED's struggle for dominance in its early years. The BE, as a theatre formerly under the purview of the Ministry, was now to be supervised by the StaKuKo. Harich notes that the StaKuKo's leadership was not well inclined to Brecht: the chairman, Helmut Holtzhauer, despised what he considered Brecht's modernist theatre, and another senior figure, Ernst Hoffmann, had the task of suppressing non-orthodox art.[40] Trumpeted in *Theater der Zeit* as a defender of the GDR's culture against formalism and cosmopolitanism (that is, art not rooted in national traditions),[41] it was the commission's more clandestine manoeuvres that were designed to frustrate the BE's work. It complemented the Central Committee's agenda to present a united front.

An illuminating example of this cooperation can be found in the treatment of the BE's book *Theaterarbeit*. The title means 'work in the theatre', which may not strike the reader as terribly exceptional today. However, Peter Palitzsch maintains that at the time 'the common view was: theatre's just something you do'.[42] Brecht wanted to use the experience he had gained with the BE as a means of propagating his approaches and practice, and raising the company's profile. The book was to document the BE's early work and offer a range of views on the concrete measures employed to bring about a new theatre. The well-illustrated book contains a series of short essays, descriptions and analyses, rather than a grand narrative. What Fuegi calls 'rather haphazard'[43] was a

---

[39] Anon., 'Protokoll Nr. 46 der Sitzung des Politbüros der Zentralkomitees am 2. Mai 1951', undated, 2 pages (2), SAPMO BArch DY 30/J IV 2/2/146. The following quotation is taken from the same page.

[40] See Harich, *Ahnenpaß*, pp. 210–11.

[41] See the special supplement that accompanied *Theater der Zeit* 15 (1951).

[42] Palitzsch, in Iden, *Peter Palitzsch*, p. 60.   [43] Fuegi, *Chaos according to Plan*, p. xiii.

deliberate attempt to represent the many elements that came together in the rehearsal process. The emphasis on practice was in part a strategy to deflect attention from Brecht's theories, which had already proved controversial in the GDR. Indeed, the very positive review of *Theaterarbeit* in *Theater der Zeit* praised the absence of theoretical essays (as well as the openness approaching the company's theatrical methods).[44] This was not the only tactical move on the part of the BE. Detlev Schöttker notes the absence of the word '*Verfremdung*' in favour of others terms that were less contentious.[45] The book also appeared under the editorship of 'Berliner Ensemble/Helene Weigel', yet Schöttker argues that this had nothing to do with the collectivity that ran through the company. Rather, it was concerned with keeping Brecht's name away from the editorship.[46] Instead, Brecht appeared amongst a five-person 'Redaktion' ('editorial committee'), but did not publicly associate himself with final editorial decisions. There is, however, no question that Weigel alone would have been at sea coordinating and supervising the 435-page volume.

The work was originally to be called *Theaterchronik des Berliner Ensembles* (*Theatre Chronicle of the Berliner Ensemble*).[47] By June 1951, Brecht had settled on the single name *Theaterarbeit*, but this did not find favour with the authorities, a month before the official formation of the StaKuKo; the title was deemed to be far too broad and inclusive. The name by which the volume is known today (*Theaterarbeit: Sechs Aufführungen des Berliner Ensembles – Six Productions by the Berliner Ensemble*) was the direct result of State intervention, implemented by none other than Brecht and Weigel's 'friend', Kurt Bork.[48] He wrote of how Brecht's method must not be considered the single recognized method of making theatre in the GDR and that the book should not be propagated as Brecht had intended. He made three proposals: the name change, that the DT and the KO produce rival editions (which never appeared) to reduce the book's impact, and that the publisher carry all the costs without a subsidy. However, just to underline the cynicism at work here, it is worth mentioning that Bork welcomed the interest the BE's book would find in West Germany.

[44] See Ilse Galfert, '*Theaterarbeit – Sechs Aufführungen des Berliner Ensembles*', *Theater der Zeit*, 11 (1952), pp. 14–17 (16).
[45] See Detlev Schöttker, 'Brechts *Theaterarbeit*: Ein Grundlagenwerk und seine Ausgrenzungen', *Weimarer Beiträge*, 53:3 (2007), pp. 438–51 (442).
[46] Ibid., p. 441.
[47] Berliner Ensemble and Dresdner Verlag, 'Vorvertrag', signed on 2 April 1951, 2 pages, BBA 2093/5–6.
[48] See Bork to Egon Rentzsch, 7 July 1951, HWA 161.

The Central Committee's Cultural Department came to a similar conclusion about *Theaterarbeit* the following year. It agreed to let the volume
appear, but to prevent it from receiving any funding.[49] The reason for
this decision was linked clearly to a familiar charge: the same agenda
item in the minutes opens with the instruction to compile 'a report on
the work of the formalist Brecht circle'. A more menacing tone was introduced when the meeting suggested that the book be subjected to 'special
analysis', concluding that 'criticism of the handbook is to be prepared'.
It seemed as if another campaign were in the offing. The 'criticism' was
not published, but then, it seems that little on the book was. Weigel
wrote to her friend, the critic and dramaturge Herbert Ihering, registering the now customary lack of reviews and encouraging him to lead
the charge.[50] Brecht, clearly unaware of the government agencies' plans,
wrote to Holtzhauer at the StaKuKo to ask what more could be done to
promote the book, noting that it was in no way only written for special-
ists, but designed to make the theatre experience all the more enjoyable
for the new audience, too.[51]

Previously, Brecht had contacted friend and academic Hans Mayer
inviting him to write an essay about *Theaterarbeit*.[52] A year later, Mayer
had proposed to publish the essay in two parts for the magazine *Aufbau*.
In addition, editor Bodo Uhse had asked him for 'a comprehensive statement' on Stanislavsky, something that led him to withdraw the essay and
his association with the magazine.[53] As it happened, reviews did eventually appear, and extracts from five positive ones may be found in the
Brecht Archive.[54] *Theaterarbeit* went on to become the most important
document published on the practical work of Brecht and the BE. Plans
to bring out an English translation in 1957, on the back of the BE's
successful tour to London, were never realized.[55]

Party dogma and the rejection of *The Mother*

To all appearances, the BE's production of Brecht's *The Mother* should
have represented the kind of work the SED would welcome. The play is
the story of a Russian mother, initially unsympathetic to the revolutionary

---

[49] See Anon., 'Beschluß-Protokoll des Abteilungsbesprechung vom Freitag, dem 2.
Februar 1952', undated, 2 pages (2), SAPMO BArch DY 30/IV 2/9.06/11. The following quotations also come from the same page.
[50] See Weigel to Herbert Ihering, 25 April 1952, AdK Herbert-Ihering-Archiv, 2776.
[51] See Brecht to Helmut Holtzhauer, 7 July 1952, BFA, 30: 130.
[52] See Brecht to Hans Mayer, 25 May 1952, BFA, 30: 125–6.
[53] Hans Mayer to Brecht, 9 February 1953, BBA, 731/75.
[54] See BBA 683/11–12. All the extracts are unhelpfully undated.
[55] See Peter Palitzsch to Verlag der Kunst, 29 March 1957, BBA uncatalogued file 'HW
A-L 1960'.

cause, who gains insights and develops class consciousness, and in doing so becomes a revolutionary herself. Laura Bradley entitles the chapter on the production in her book on *The Mother* 'courting the audience'.[56] By this, she means that both in terms of the show's aims and its aesthetics, Brecht, who was the sole director, was actually going against his usual method. He had told Wekwerth that he wanted to use the production to overturn years of anti-communist propaganda.[57] By presenting the story without the devices he usually employed to create critical distance, Brecht was departing from his own performance principles. The production was certainly dialectical, but this was a loaded dialectic that favoured the mother and did not seek to interrogate her position or her politics. In effect, the audience was encouraged to sympathize with her and to accompany her on the journey to awareness and activity in the name of the Russian Revolution. However, as Bradley notes, the reasons for the less abrasive treatment of the subject matter had its roots in a production of the same play, directed by Brecht's collaborator, Ruth Berlau, in Leipzig in January 1950.[58] Her more politically radical *Mother* had alienated representatives of the SED, and Brecht thus made changes that he (mistakenly) believed would remedy the reception of the production in Berlin.

The unusually sparse *Notate* for the production underline this position. There are criticisms, such as 'Mother too intellectual' and '"untenable" – we need real emotion here'.[59] Indeed, even the actor/audience relationship underwent a change: 'everything direct to the mother. No longer in relation to the spectator. Changed historical situation'.[60] The re-erection of the fourth wall was connected to the new historical situation, that of the GDR under the SED. Here, the production signalled that it actively turned epic theatre into something more conventionally dramatic in order to address the situation of the workers in a socialist and not a capitalist state. Indeed, Wera Küchenmeister remembers the lengths to which Brecht went in order to attract more working people to this production.[61]

The premiere on 13 January 1951 was mainly well received. The staging of *The Mother*'s dialectical journey and the use of epic narration

---

[56] For a full description and analysis, see Laura Bradley, *Brecht and Political Theatre*, pp. 67–83.

[57] See Manfred Wekwerth, *Erinnern ist Leben. Eine dramatische Autobiographie* (Faber & Faber: Leipzig, 2000), p. 90.

[58] See Bradley, *Brecht and Political Theatre*, pp. 63–4.

[59] Wera Küchenmeister, entries for 6 and 9 November 1951, in Küchenmeister, 'Persönliche Aufzeichnungen, Notate, Arbeit mit Brecht', BBA E 47/77–102, here 81 and 84, respectively.

[60] Küchenmeister, entry for 24 November 1951, ibid., BBA E 47/98.

[61] See Küchenmeister, in Ditte Buchmann *et al.*, *'Eine Begabung'*, p. 96.

Fig. 3.1. A stylized set foregrounds its own artifice: Brecht's understanding of realism is at odds with that of the Party. *The Mother*, January
1951.

meant that the production was not to be mistaken for a piece of naturalism (see Fig. 3.1), but the way that Brecht treated the characters
and events was qualitatively different from his more sceptical practices
discussed in the two preceding chapters. Walther Pollatschek praised the
triumph of the production over Brecht's theories and wrote how Weigel
in the lead role of the mother 'didn't stand next to her character, but
inhabited it completely'.[62] Another reviewer noted the tension between
epic dramaturgy and a more empathetic set of depictions when observing
that Brecht both applied 'his theory of epic theatre and distanced himself
from it as the same time'.[63]

If Brecht had regretted the lack of distance between the audience
and Mother Courage, he revelled in this relationship with respect to
the mother. It would seem that Brecht was making political theatre,
rather than making theatre politically, with the spectator led through the
play's dialectic of political awakening. Monk found that the play had been
'directed "past" the real lives of the GDR populace'.[64] It is difficult to see
The Mother as anything but a deliberate staging strategy on Brecht's part,

[62] Walther Pollatschek, 'Die Bühne als Anleitung zum Handeln', *Tägliche Rundschau*,
    14 January 1951.
[63] Anon., 'Das kommunistische ABC', *Telegraf*, 14 January 1951.
[64] Monk, *Regie Egon Monk*, p. 143.

born of tacit SED pressure while acknowledging his political sympathies, too. It thus possibly signalled a new type of epic theatre for the BE, one that did not reject dialectics, but introduced greater proximity between the stage and the audience in a bid to win over audience members critical of the new socialist order.

One may have thought that the production would have found favour with the SED and demonstrated a harmony with their politics. On one area of policy, this was not the case. Sabine Kebir reports that a scene in which the mother tears up a Bible was cut after the premiere because it was at odds with the SED's 'Bündnispolitik' ('policy of forging alliances') with its Christian constituents.[65] This interference was based on the play's content, and while it is hardly defensible, one can understand how the party sought to cultivate potential opponents to its ethos by denying them alienating moments in a production well inclined towards communism. However, the SED had not finished with *The Mother*, despite the production's affirmative aesthetics.

Egon Rentzsch of the Central Committee wrote to Walter Kohls, the administrative manager of the DT, in early 1951 to ask him to keep tickets available at short notice 'whenever the Politburo is about to reach decisions on theatre matters'.[66] He mentioned *The Mother* twice in the letter, which was written the day before the conference at which the campaign against formalism was officially sanctioned. There, Politburo member Fred Oelssner attacked the production by name and criticized its interpretation of realism. He went on to ask whether the form in fact corresponded to what was conventionally understood as theatre, preferring to view it as a mongrel, mixing drama and narrative.[67] The SED did not tolerate an epic theatre, even in the service of socialism. It is no surprise to read that the Central Committee resolved to keep the number of performances to 'the bare minimum'.[68] However, despite the decision, its implementation was more difficult. *The Mother* ran for 113 performances until May 1955 and was revived in 1957. By 1958 the production had been officially rehabilitated after the dogmatic attacks of the early 1950s: Kurt Bork booked a closed performance for the fifth SED party conference.[69]

---

[65] Sabine Kebir, *Abstieg in den Ruhn*, p. 248.

[66] Egon Rentzsch to Walter Kohls, 14 February 1951, SAPMO BArch DY 30/IV 2/9.06/188.

[67] See Fred Oelssner, in Hans Lauter, *Der Kampf gegen den Formalismus*, p. 51.

[68] Trautzsch, 'Protokoll Nr. 91 der Sitzung des Sekretariats des ZK am 2. August 1951', undated, 19 pages (9), SAPMO BArch DY 30/J IV 2/3/220.

[69] See Bork to Weigel, 25 March 1958, BBA uncatalogued file 'HW Briefw. 1–6/1958'.

While it is tempting to see the SED's criticism as part of an orchestrated campaign against the BE, the protocol recommending the reduction of *Mother* performances also censured Berlin's Komische Oper and the Nationaltheater in Weimar, where no less than Shakespeare and Schiller were deemed too problematic. The treatment of the BE was a part of a larger plan to rein in what was viewed as non-conformity to cultural dogma. That said, the GDR authorities had particular problems with the BE, too. While *The Mother* inadvertently incurred the SED's wrath, the production of a German classic revealed how a more predictable source of contention could touch sensitive cultural nerves.

Urfaust and the 'mistreatment' of the German cultural heritage

Earlier I mentioned that the campaign against formalism was allied with an attack on cosmopolitanism (see p. 86). The SED considered the neglect or indeed the outright denial of national traditions in art 'volks-fremd' ('alien to the people' – the term Fritz Erpenbeck used as a weapon against *Courage* in 1949), because art is 'only' inspired by the people. The antidote to cosmopolitanism was the celebration and nurture of the *Erbe*, the cultural heritage. The official pronouncement on precisely what this entailed was narrow and conservative, more bourgeois than socialist. Brecht, not surprisingly, had a more radical view of what it meant to engage with works of the past. In a journal entry of 1942, he arraigned the physicist Hans Reichenbach for objectifying the culture of the past. He wrote: 'culture must lose the character of a commodity in order to become culture again'.[70] Brecht had earlier proposed that the treatment of the *Erbe* necessitated struggle.[71] He realized that different cultures appropriated the cultural past to different ends, and thus socialists could not just take over values attributed to works by bourgeois society, but needed to establish their own. The process of appropriation was not in some way neutral, but partisan. However, Brecht's view on this active process diverged considerably from that of the SED, too.

Up until 1950, the authorities' relationship to Brecht with respect to their position on the *Erbe* had been ambiguous. On the one hand, Brecht had been criticized in 1949, following the publication of the 'Short Organon', for having the audacity to apply his theories to the

---

[70] Brecht, journal entry for 22 August 1942, BFA, 27: 122; *Journals*, p. 255.
[71] See Brecht, '[Ein eigentümlicher Hang zum Idyllischen]', BFA, 22: 494.

performance of Shakespeare and not limiting them to his own plays.[72] On the other, the production of *The Tutor* had been lauded: Brecht's method *could* be applied successfully and productively to a classic text. While Stuber believes that the retention of Lenz's classical form protected the production from brickbats,[73] Brecht was still directing a radically adapted text that departed from the original by virtue of its many innovations and alterations. I would suggest that it was far more the case that Lenz's play was not well known and consequently possessed virtually no cultural capital. The high quality of the BE's production further spoke in the show's favour. But when the BE turned its attention to Goethe, the most hallowed poet in the German repertoire, and to his Faust, the German equivalent of Hamlet, only the most naïve of observers could have imagined a problem-free reception from the SED.

Brecht's emphasis on a process of appropriation, defined by usefulness and, as will become clear, predicated on dialectical realism, opposed the SED's proscription of what were non-negotiable criteria. Faust was the perfect embodiment of what was more generally known, in socialist parlance, as the 'Vollstreckungstheorie' ('completion theory').[74] This teleological idea connected progressive elements in the *Erbe* to their realization or 'completion' in a socialist state. Faust's 'striving' to better himself and his society reflected on the nation, which was striving for a society without exploitation and the fulfilment of Goethe's humanist vision. Consequently, Faust's positive credentials were untouchable. Any deviation in interpretation on the page or the stage would lead to trouble.

At first glance, the choice of *Urfaust* may seem an odd one for a materialist like Brecht. It tells the tale of a frustrated scholar who makes a deal with the devil to gain more knowledge. Devils and magic clearly have no place in a materialist world, but Brecht was more concerned with the social aspects of the play and how they affected an understanding of human aspiration and its consequences. Brecht reportedly found that '*Urfaust* is more realistic [than *Faust*], the story of a magician'.[75] This apparently contradictory summation proposes that we accept the magical elements of the play while treating them as if they were real to expose relationships and attitudes.

[72] See Martin Hellberg, 'Armer Kean! Die anorganischen Thesen Bertolt Brechts', *Theater der Zeit*, 10 (1949), pp. 10 and 14 (14).
[73] See Stuber, *Spielräume und Grenzen*, p. 147.
[74] See Ingeborg Cleve, 'Subverted Heritage and Subversive Memory: *Weimarer Klassik* in the GDR and the Bauerbach Case', in Christian Emden and David Midgely (eds.), *German History, Literature and the Nation* (Berne et al.: Peter Lang, 2004), pp. 355–80 (367).
[75] Brecht, in [Manfred Wekwerth?], 'Brecht über *Faust* und *Urfaust*', 16 February [1952], n.p., BEA File 9.

Urfaust was not the standard version of Goethe's *Faust* material. It had been first discovered in the late nineteenth century and amounts to a collection of early scenes written between 1772–5, that is, during the 'storm-and-stress' period. Goethe returned to the drafts later in his life and the more famous first part of the tragedy was written between 1797 and 1805. While the two versions share common features, *Urfaust* is a fragment that captures a rougher, less 'classical' treatment of the characters and the action. The unfinished nature of the text appealed to Brecht, too. No stranger to fragments himself,[76] Brecht was reported to have said: 'everything must be fragmentary and sketch-like'.[77] The choice of the unfinished and incomplete version meant that the audience would have to fill in the gaps and adjust to unfamiliar articulations of scenes and speeches that were otherwise a standard part of their literary education. The difference between *Urfaust* and *Faust I* was thus a productive one to Brecht. In addition, he was also convinced that *Faust I* was not actually a play to be performed, but one to be read, and asserted 'there's not even an actor who's famous for playing Faust' – as opposed to the many actors celebrated for their Mephistopheles, the devil figure.[78] That is, Brecht wanted to refocus the production onto Faust and his world, and not let Mephisto steal the show as usual.

Brecht had charged Egon Monk to direct the play and hoped that it, like *The Tutor* before it, would help prepare the young ensemble for the challenge of staging Shakespeare.[79] To Brecht, Shakespeare was the great realist, and there was no way to negotiate his complexity other than to rehearse other classical plays as an exercise in learning through doing. With such a great responsibility on his shoulders, Monk found himself working together with Brecht, who is mentioned extensively in the rehearsal notes.[80]

The BE staged two versions of *Urfaust*, one in Potsdam in 1952, the other in Berlin in 1953. Bernd Mahl describes the discrepancy in approach thus: the Potsdam production emphasized Faust as charlatan and seducer, whereas the one in Berlin had learned from the more icon-oclastic interpretation and developed something more dialectical: 'the

---

[76] Volume 10 of the BFA, which takes up two physical books, is exclusively dedicated to Brecht's unfinished projects.

[77] Brecht, in Anon., 'Brecht über *Faust* (*Urfaust*), Jan. 1952', undated, 4 pages (4), BEA File 9. The reference in the next line has the same source.

[78] Brecht, in [Wekwerth?], 'Brecht über *Faust* und *Urfaust*', 16 February [1952], n.p., BEA File 9.

[79] See Monk, *Regie Egon Monk*, p. 168.

[80] This relationship is confirmed by Hans Mayer, the eminent *Germanist*, who attended some of the rehearsals in Berlin, in Mayer, *Erinnerung an Brecht* (Frankfurt/Main: Suhrkamp, 1996), p. 106.

tragic contradiction and conflict was seen in the fact that Faust had to engage the services of the devil to realize his humanist ideals'.[81] The focus on Faust in both readings is clear, but I will return to the reasons for the shift in emphasis below. In my analysis of rehearsal, however, I will not be discussing the differences in the interpretations, but rather the commonalities in approach to the material in order to understand the basis of Monk and Brecht's 'realistic' treatment of the play.

The magical elements presented a problem for materialists, but a brief survey of three fantastical elements gives a rounded picture of how Monk and Brecht dealt with them. In the very first scene, Faust turns to magic as a way of overcoming his earthbound restrictions. He first summons the earth spirit, who is too powerful for him and who pays him no attention in any case. He then turns to the devil. To the production team, this was the difference between white and black magic, something that could be communicated in two different *Haltungen*: 'solemn and noble' versus 'feverish and criminal'.[82] One may choose to criticize the distinction made, but the signifying strategy is clear: communion with a magical force of nature trumps the movement towards darker elements and their power to corrupt. The BE was thus dramatizing a choice rather than pondering the existence or otherwise of magic.

Once Faust has attained magical powers, he exercises them for the first time in the scene 'Auerbach's Cellar', which involves a group of drunken students. Käthe Rülicke described the action thus:

1. Attempt at magic
2. It is successful
3. Repulsed by this
4. Leaves[83]

The breakdown of the action tells a clear story. Faust is uncertain about his abilities, but once he has demonstrated his command of them, he shows that they do not please him, and he emphasizes this by exiting. The action is clear and it is also social: his need for magic, as seen earlier in the play, is an expression of his dissatisfaction with his earthly existence. The drunken students in the cellar are indicative of the conditions against which Faust is rebelling. The team also developed details of their own. Manfred Wekwerth noted that their Mephisto was not an important devil: 'our devil is a lower devil. Doesn't have his own enchanted horses, has to rent them. We're treating all the sorcery realistically'.[84] Once again, one

---

[81] Bernd Mahl, *Brecht und Monks 'Urfaust'-Inszenierung mit dem Berliner Ensemble 1952/53* (Stuttgart and Zurich: Belser, 1986), p. 20.

[82] Anon., *'Urfaust'*, undated, n.p., BEA File 9.

[83] Käthe Rülicke, 'Zu *Urfaust* – Notate von Rülicke', undated, pp. 1–3 (2), ibid.

[84] Wekwerth, *Schriften*, p. 109.

observes how potentially supernatural phenomena were brought down to earth – hell hath a pecking order and an economy, too.

The concretization of the fantastical complemented the realistic portrayal of social relations between Faust, as bourgeois academic, and Gretchen, a woman of the lower orders, whom he seduces, impregnates and abandons. One of the most famous scenes between the two contains an exchange where Gretchen asks Faust about his views on religion. Rülicke describes how they rehearsed two possibilities for Gretchen: 'clever: with folk wisdom = she is critical and unmasks [Faust's] idealist flight of fancy as a prevarication. Or she can just be dim = she doesn't understand him'.[85] It is no surprise that the team settled on a 'strengthening of her scepticism'. In either eventuality, however, one notes the focus on the interaction, not on Faust's ambivalent speech itself.

By the final scene in the dungeon, where Gretchen has been incarcerated for infanticide, the production sought another shift in emphasis. Gretchen chooses to remain in the cell awaiting her death sentence despite Faust's attempt to rescue her with the help of Mephisto's magical powers. The conventional temptation was to portray Gretchen as raving and desperate, having killed her child. This more traditionally 'theatrical' interpretation did not satisfy the BE. The final lines were instead to show how Gretchen rejected Faust 'not because they are estranged, but because she understands him'.[86] This 'enlightened' ending read Gretchen's experiences as a learning process – that death in the dungeon was preferable to a life with Faust. Such a conclusion was one more indication of how the traditional and SED-sanctioned interpretation of Faust as untouchable progressive humanist had been discarded in the name of Brechtian realism. The production's reception in Potsdam and Berlin reflected the view that the BE had committed a substantial act of heresy.

Rejection (almost) across the board: *Urfaust* as cultural pariah

The Potsdam production had its premiere on 23 April 1951 and ran for thirteen performances. The first reviews were generally positive. One critic enjoyed 'the sensible reduction of mysterious metaphysical romanticism to a minimum', while another called the production 'more relevant than ever'.[87] The reviewer went on to praise the lack of mawkishness and

[85] Käthe Rülicke, '*Urfaust*', 27 January 1953, 2 pages (1, as is the following quotation), BEA File 9.
[86] Wekwerth, *Schriften*, p. 110.
[87] Hade, 'Gastspiel des "Berliner Ensembles"', *Märkische Union*, 26 April 1952; and sigy, 'Der *Urfaust* in Landesbühne Potsdam', *Märkische Volksstimme*, 29 April 1952.

exuberance, and observed 'all sympathy resides with this girl, the typical victim of the bigoted and self-satisfied German middle class'. The BE had made clear its social contextualization of the tragedy. But this reading, founded in the BE's materialism, was to offend those bound to the SED's cultural strictures. The Potsdam theatre's own party organization wrote an open letter to the editor of the *Märkische Volksstimme* and spelt out the problem in no uncertain terms: 'we are of the opinion that the true humanist ideas of our classic authors must be realized when critically and creatively appropriating our cultural heritage in order to prompt an effect that will positively activate the audience'.[88] The authors of the letter overlooked the contradiction between a critical treatment of the text and the inescapable outcome of the process, but this was not important to them. An official group had criticized the BE's treatment of the *Erbe* and the production was thenceforth tarred with that brush.

The BE leadership was either unaware or undeterred by the letter. Weigel wrote to the StaKuKo in June to suggest they transfer the production to the Theater am Schiffbauerdamm to avoid burdening the DT. She proposed that the BE use that theatre's main stage while it rehearsed in the BE's *Probenhaus*. A note in pen, written a week after receipt and passed on to hardliners Hans Rodenberg, Fritz Erpenbeck and Wilhelm Girnus read 'suggest rejection of performance in Berlin due to the reviews'.[89] Erpenbeck, however, wrote to Weigel telling her that the BE could not perform the production at the Theater am Schiffbauerdamm for logistical reasons.[90] Around the same time, the StaKuKo also considered targeting Brecht with a conference on the *Erbe*, but, in a letter, Kurt Bork wisely dissuaded his boss from pursuing the plan because he felt the agency was not actually qualified for such a discussion.[91]

The StaKuKo had put the BE's plan for a Berlin *Urfaust* on hold, but the BE persisted and later shifted the performance venue to the DT. In the meantime, the BE worked on its new interpretation, which avoided the more negative portrayal of Faust in Potsdam. By now it must have become evident that major changes were required. However, Langhoff wrote to Weigel shortly before the Berlin premiere on 13 March 1953 to tell her that he would not allow the production to appear in the evening schedule and that he would only countenance matinees or closed

---

[88] SED-Parteiorganisation, 'An die Kulturredaktion der *Märkischen Volksstimme*', *Märkische Volksstimme*, 29 April 1952, in Mahl, *Brecht und Monks 'Urfaust'-Inszenierung*, p. 189.

[89] Weigel to StaKuKo, 17 June 1952, instruction in pen by Willi Lewin appended 23 June 1952, BArch DR 1/6084.

[90] See Fritz Erpenbeck to Weigel, 30 June 1952, BArch DR 1/6084.

[91] See Bork to Helmut Holtzhauer, 15 July 1952, BArch DR 1/6042.

performances. The reason he gave was that it would conflict with the DT's own production of *Faust I*.[92]

It is difficult to ascertain whether the SED colluded with Langhoff in restricting performances because there appears to be no documentary evidence to suggest this. However, at this juncture, Langhoff was something of a compromised figure. While in Swiss exile, he had known Noel Field, whom the SED later accused of being an American spy. The 'Noel Field affair' was actually a front to purge the SED of exiles who had stayed in the West during the Nazi era, rather than in the East; the latter were considered more reliable for having chosen the Soviet Union. Langhoff found himself relieved of all party duties and positions in the summer of 1950, but was allowed to remain *Intendant* of the DT. His initial strident defence against the charges was superseded by a letter of self-criticism that bordered on self-humiliation.[93] It is difficult to view this sea-change as anything other than the result of official pressure. While history was to show that the Field affair had no basis in fact, Langhoff would have still been deemed suspect at the time of the *Urfaust* production. Stuber argues that Langhoff was retained at the DT to stand up to Brecht.[94] If this were the case – and it probably was – he certainly proved his worth.

The rehearsals at the DT had already generated disquiet. In a letter that has now been lost, the DT's technical staff complained to Brecht on the day of the dress rehearsal about some of the more humorous scenes, which violated the implicit decorum that was felt due to Goethe.[95] Brecht wrote an open letter in reply defending the use of humour as long as it was put to critical use.[96] Monk does not believe that the technicians sent the letter, because Brecht got on well with them, and suspects the DT's own party group of using them as a front.[97] Interestingly, the dress rehearsal was also attended by members of the StaKuKo who reportedly made no objections to what they had seen.[98] It is unclear whether they merely kept their reservations to themselves because they knew that the performances were to be restricted to a very limited audience. This is likely, especially in the light of the damning reviews that were to follow.

[92] See Langhoff to Weigel, 10 March 1953, BBA uncatalogued file 'Aktuelles'.
[93] See letters from Langhoff to the SED on 31 August and 8 September 1950, AdK Wolfgang-Langhoff-Archiv, 189.
[94] See Stuber, *Spielräume und Grenzen*, p. 100.
[95] See [Isot Kilian], 'Betr.: Verlauf der Verhandlungen über die Aufführung des *Urfaust*', 6 May 1953, 2 pages (1), BEA uncatalogued file 'Aktuelles'.
[96] See Brecht, 'Humor und Würde', BFA, 24: 430.
[97] See Monk, *Regie Egon Monk*, p. 169–70.
[98] See [Kilian], 'Betr.: Verlauf der Verhandlungen', p. 2.

The production's programme in Berlin contained articles that set out the BE's motives and methods. Brecht defended the choice of *Urfaust* even though it was a fragment because that genre included 'master-pieces', such as Büchner's *Woyzeck*.[99] In the same essay, he noted how the unfinished form militated against 'Einschüchterung durch die Klas-sizität' ('an intimidation by the classics') and on the contrary encouraged fresh new discoveries. In another essay, he more openly engaged with the production's bad press in Potsdam and noted that the Berlin production dialectically examined the positive sides of Faust and his radical ideas and feelings.[100] The invitation to a new interpretation and the emphasis on the positive fell mainly on deaf ears, or rather, on very few ears at all. Langhoff's strategy to limit the audience had been successful and the production was given a mere six times in Berlin.

The only two extant reviews of the Berlin production are closely aligned to the party standpoint. A transcription of a review on the radio men-tioned formalism in the realization of the *Erbe* and concluded that the play had lost any trace of Goethe's humanism.[101] Johanna Rudolph, in the SED's paper *Neues Deutschland*, made similar comments and found that the production displayed 'an anti-national foundation, alien to the people'.[102] She was also careful to observe that while Monk was a young director, he was nonetheless working under the experienced eye of his master. All of a sudden, Brecht became a modern Socrates, corrupting the youth of Berlin. Perhaps the most shocking response to the Berlin production came from the young audience Brecht wanted to attract to the BE. A transcription of a post-show discussion with students reveals attitudes that seem to be the product of cultural prejudice, rather than intellectual curiosity. It is unfortunately impossible to determine whether the students had been specially selected by the party or whether they were a representative group, although the latter is more likely from the lack of uniformity in the questions. Yet while the responses were not all negative and were indeed critical, the conservatism betrayed an educational appa-ratus that instilled a set of official values. The students certainly had a view of what performing a storm-and-stress play should entail and were disappointed by the Brechtian lack of feeling and emotion.[103]

---

[99] Brecht, 'Ist die Aufführung des Fragments gerechtfertigt?', BFA, 24: 432.
[100] See Brecht, 'Ein dialektisches Moment in der Darstellung', BFA, 24: 433.
[101] See Anon., 'Wir blenden auf', undated, radio station unknown, BBA File 9.
[102] Johanna Rudolph, 'Weitere Bemerkungen zum *Faust*-Problem', *Neues Deutschland*, 27 May 1953.
[103] See Anon., 'Diskussion über den *Urfaust* mit Studenten am 19.3.53 im Probenhaus', undated, 6 pages (1), BEA File 9.

The *Urfaust* affair signalled that the SED would not tolerate open infractions of its cultural policy. The network of institutions, from the theatres to the press and the academy, put an end to any chance of a productive engagement with the performances. Brecht had been targeted in a similar campaign in 1951 when his opera *Das Verhör des Lukullus* (*The Trial of Lucullus*) had been officially prevented from performance at Berlin's Staatsoper.[104] However, the process surrounding *Urfaust* was a different one: no ban was issued. Instead, the SED wielded what we now call 'soft power' by making performance so difficult that the show simply could not go on. The BE did not produce another classic text from the German tradition until 1970. This is not to suggest that the authorities could implement policy by persuasion and pressure all the time – there are examples of bans both before and after *Urfaust* in the GDR. Rather, the process around *Urfaust* represented one available option that allowed the SED to avoid the potential controversy and negative publicity surrounding a ban while still achieving its desired objective.

Assistants and the development of directorial independence

That Egon Monk was allowed to direct a project as contentious as *Urfaust* is remarkable. Monk was twenty-four when the production premiered in Potsdam, but by then he had already directed one full-length show with the BE in 1951. That, in turn, had followed his production of *Puntila* in Rostock in 1950. Monk's trajectory tells us much about Brecht's ambitions for his young collaborators and the ways in which he realized them.

That Monk 'directed' *Puntila* in Rostock requires qualification. He had been an important assistant in the BE production and had closely observed the rehearsal process. Brecht sent Monk to Rostock as his 'representative' to observe and advise on the production because Brecht could not find the time to direct in Rostock himself.[105] Monk started to intervene by directing 'behind the back' of the original director when it became clear that the latter understood precious little about Brecht's theatre.[106] His wealth of first-hand experience and his possession of the *Modellbuch* meant that he was charged with realizing an existing production with a new cast in a different theatre. This is not to deny Monk's

---

[104] For a complete documentary account of the affair, see Joachim Lucchesi (ed.), *Das Verhör in der Oper. Die Debatte um die Aufführung 'Das Verhör des Lukullus' von Bertolt Brecht und Paul Dessau* (Berlin: Basisdruck, 1993).

[105] Egon Monk, unpublished interview with John Rouse, 10 June 1988, p. I-6.

[106] See Esther Slevogt, 'Ritterschlag mit dem Damokelsschwert: Egon Monk und Bertolt Brecht, 1949–1953', *Brecht Yearbook*, 37 (2012), pp. 163–77 (170).

input into the production; Brecht was profoundly aware that using a *Modellbuch* did not entail a simple process of transplantation. He wrote that the productive employment of a *Modellbuch* was 'a particular kind of art'.[107] However, the difference between devising *Arrangements* and *Haltungen*, and adapting them betokened a creative gradation, and so Monk's first work as a director was actually an extended, unsupervised training opportunity. And he was not the only assistant to be sent off to other theatres at that time: Heinz Kuckhahn directed *Mother Courage* in Dessau and *Puntila* in Dresden,[108] and French-speaking Benno Besson was dispatched to Paris to work on various projects.[109] Monk, however, was the first to be entrusted with a production of his own at the BE.

The distance between directing from a *Modellbuch* and directing from scratch was great. Monk's directorial debut was a complex project that boiled down and joined together two plays by Gerhart Hauptmann: *Der Biberpelz und Roter Hahn* (*The Beaver Coat and Conflagration*). One was a comedy, the other a tragicomedy; the difference in genre did not help the production. While it would not be fair to call the production a flop, it certainly failed to measure up to the quality of the BE's previous productions. Reviewers noted that the two halves did not fit well together and that Hauptmann's careful satires were treated somewhat ham-fistedly by the BE.[110] The company's own records report a modest reception to the premiere on 24 March 1951: the seven curtain calls may sound impressive, but compared to those of *Puntila* (32 on its premiere) and *The Tutor* (55 on its premiere),[111] the applause was relatively sparse. The production itself was doomed to a curtailed run when the Hauptmann estate intervened and withdrew the performance rights. The BE had overstepped the limits of the contract which permitted 'dramaturgical arrangement' rather than a full-blown adaptation.[112]

Monk was not the first choice for the role of director. Brecht had originally wanted Berthold Viertel to return.[113] Viertel was not impressed by the adaptation and concluded that he was not the right man for the job.[114] Brecht may well have turned to Monk as a last resort, but the

---

[107] Brecht, 'Couragemodell 1949', BFA, 25: 172; *BoP*, p. 184.
[108] See Bork to Stefan Heymann, 27 March 1950, BArch DR 2/8237.
[109] See entry for October 1950, BEA File 'Logbücher 50–52', n.p.
[110] See Rudolf Harnisch, 'Gerupfter *Biberpelz* und *Roter Hahn*', *Tägliche Rundschau*, 29 March 1951; and R.K., '*Biberpelz* und *Roter Hahn* von Gerhart Hauptmann', *Nacht-Expreß*, 24 March 1951.
[111] Figures taken from Anon., *Vorstellungsbuch 1950 1951*, n.p., BBA uncatalogued item.
[112] Dr Hirschfeld to Weigel, 25 April 1951, BBA 725/25.
[113] See Brecht to Viertel, end of August and November 1950, BBA 1280/5–7 and 22, respectively.
[114] See Viertel to Brecht, 10 December 1950, BBA 2773/1–2.

production's relative failure was not a mark of Monk's own failure. He had been set a difficult task and had learned a great deal, enough for Brecht to invite him to direct *Urfaust* the following year. After the fall-out from the performances in Potsdam, Brecht charged Monk with a production of his politically and aesthetically safer play, *Señora Carrar's Rifles* that opened on 16 November 1952. (That Weigel reprised the role of the eponymous lead that she had given at the play's premiere in 1937 further served to protect the production from criticism.) Monk's extended period of 'training' reflects Brecht's longer-term faith in what he had identified as talent.

Monk reports that Brecht told him and Besson: 'stand on your own two feet and take over from me!'[115] The project to nurture young talent had two main aims: Brecht wanted to pass on and develop his approach to making theatre, and he also wanted to direct less often himself. The two aims are linked, of course, and in order to achieve both, Brecht had to give his assistants assistance, mainly in the form of input when attending their rehearsals. Initially, Brecht was a major presence in such rehearsals, yet as time went on, he strategically withdrew. In a notice to the BE of late 1955, he wrote with reference to the young directors: 'people shouldn't downplay my part in their productions, but they shouldn't overestimate it either'.[116] His position is well illustrated by one of his most successful assistants, who went on to become a distinguished inter-national director himself. Benno Besson recounts how Brecht refused to take a directing credit for the help he gave him: '"I only helped you do what you wanted to do. I would've done it differently"'.[117] Brecht's 'help' did thus not dictate aesthetic decisions as such, but instilled a set of principles. Besson's work with the BE had dialectical clarity, but could not be mistaken for Brecht's own productions. Brecht was happy to sup-port a certain type of practice without insisting on the ways in which it was realized. To have used his young directors as surrogates for his own direction would have robbed them of crucial experiences and pre-vented them from experimenting. The work of his most accomplished assistants as directors in their own right (Egon Monk, Benno Besson, Peter Palitzsch and Manfred Wekwerth) bears witness to the success of Brecht's strategy; he did not produce epigones, but passed on certain ways of understanding theatre that his assistants reinterpreted and made productive.

---

[115] Monk, in Lang and Hillesheim, *'Denken heißt verändern. . . '*, p. 103.
[116] Brecht, 'Aushang [3]', BFA, 23: 359.
[117] Besson, in Irmer and Schmidt, *Die Bühnenrepublik*, p. 44.

The move towards independence started, as noted above, with the strategic dispatch of 'emissaries', but a chance invitation for Besson led to the development of a different tactic. He was out of favour at the BE in 1950 having lost the *Notate* to the *Tutor* rehearsals. He had received a request from the theatre at Rostock to direct a play of his choice and chose Molière's *Don Juan* as a text ripe for adaptation. Brecht got involved, however, when Besson began to translate the play into German with Brecht's collaborator from the Weimar Republic, Elisabeth Hauptmann.[118] The production was such a success that Brecht asked Besson to stage it with the BE and, as it happened, it opened the BE's first season at its new theatre building in 1954. What this episode established was a practice that would become something of a tradition at the BE: young assistants, having gained a grounding in the BE's approaches to making theatre, were sent out to provincial theatres in order to work through plays and their production with a view to staging them later in Berlin. Perhaps the most significant example of this practice took place in 1958 when Palitzsch directed the world premiere of Brecht's *Der aufhaltsame Aufstieg des Arturo Ui* (*The Resistible Rise of Arturo Ui*) in Stuttgart. Wekwerth wrote a very critical appraisal of the production,[119] for whose indelicate style he apologized a year later.[120] The point was that remedying the perceived faults of the original production formed the basis for a new production, one that would write theatre history and prove that there was still life in the BE after Brecht's death in 1956 (see pp. 160–4, Chapter 5).

The idea of 'trying out' a production elsewhere before realizing it at the BE might give the impression that the BE suffered from delusions of grandeur; rather than taking a risk itself, it passed on the possibility of a flop to 'less important' theatres while sharing 'its' human resources so that they might benefit. There is certainly an element of that in the practice, but one should not overlook the developmental aspect either. Smaller theatres offered younger directors a chance to work outside the glare of the BE and to workshop a complete production before considering the changes that would need to be made back at the BE. Over time, these theatres made the requests for BE directors themselves, testifying to the value they derived from the arrangement, too. The process was not always successful, though: to Besson, his production of *The Good Person*

[118] See Besson, in Anon., 'Gespräch mit Benno Besson am 17.11.1987 im Kleinen Saal der Akademie der Künste der DDR', *Material zum Theater*, 16 (1988), pp. 66–80 (67).
[119] See Wekwerth, *Schriften*, pp. 144–7.
[120] See Wekwerth to the BE and Party Leadership, 30 November 1959, AdK JTA, uncatalogued box 'BE interne Korr./Dramat. 1959–1970'.

of Szechwan worked far better in Rostock (1956) than it did in Berlin (1957).[121]

The *Meisterschüler* myth

The understanding of the BE as a school certainly has a basis in fact. Brecht considered himself a teacher of sorts, and this intention was set out in the 'Theaterprojekt B.' document, discussed on p. 43 in Chapter 2. That his teaching was not conventional, that he had no 'curriculum' as such, meant that the very nature of the lesson could not be communicated in phrases, but rather through experience. There is an amount of debate surrounding the term 'Schüler' ('pupil' or 'student') at the BE. Both Egon Monk and Hans Bunge deny the use of the term at all,[122] while Wekwerth often refers to the retention of himself, Besson and Palitzsch at the BE after Brecht's death as the 'Schülervariante' ('student option').[123] The untranslatable term 'Meisterschüler' adds to the sense that the BE was more formally a school, yet this term, too, is deceptive. '*Meisterschüler*' is taken from the apprenticeship process where the gifted apprentice studied under a master with a view to becoming a journeyman or later a master him or herself.

The Deutsche Akademie der Künste (German Academy of the Arts – DAK) was established in the GDR in 1950, and Brecht was a founding member. As such, he was instrumental in bringing the *Meisterschüler* scheme to life. He proposed that full members, the *Meister*, should be entitled to take on *Schüler* who would be supported by stipends before the DAK was established.[124] Mary Luckhurst asserts that the *Meisterschüler* represented the top level of a three-tier hierarchy of training for dramaturges, suggesting that the *Meisterschüler* formed an 'élite', taken from arts academies.[125] Brecht's letter to the education minister, Paul Wandel, proposed that the *Meisterschüler* only required the equivalent of secondary school leaving certificates.[126] It was in fact Kurt Bork at the StaKuKo who suggested that *Meisterschüler* possess university degrees together with

---

[121] See Besson, in Anon., '"Einige Stücke inszeniert man eben mehrmals"', in Neubert-Herwig (ed.), *Benno Besson: Theater spielen in acht Ländern*, pp. 107–25 (108, 119 and 122).

[122] See Monk, in Lang and Hillesheim, '*Denken heißt verändern . . .* ', p. 103; and Bunge, unpublished interview with John Rouse, 18 May 1988, p. I-1.

[123] For example, Wekwerth in Lang and Hillesheim, '*Denken heißt verändern . . .* ', p. 187.

[124] See Brecht to Arnold Zweig, June/July 1949, BFA, 29: 537; *Letters*, p. 478.

[125] Mary Luckhurst, 'Revolutionising Theatre: Brecht's Reinvention of the Dramaturg', in Peter Thomson and Glendyr Sacks (eds.), *The Cambridge Companion to Brecht*, second edition(Cambridge, Cambridge University Press, 1994), pp. 193–208 (201).

[126] See Brecht to Paul Wandel, 24 May 1951, BFA, 30: 72; *Letters*, p. 502.

evidence of a particular talent or aptitude.[127] It would appear that Bork did not prevail; Brecht proposed the untrained B. K. Tragelehn for a vacant place as a *Meisterschüler* in directing and merely appended his date of birth and postal address.[128] Brecht's recommendation sufficed.

In the same letter to Wandel, Brecht proposed that the *Meisterschüler* participate in the usual theatre activities undertaken by the other directing and dramaturgical assistants,[129] and reports from the *Meisterschüler* and assistants bear this out.[130] The descriptions of the work with the BE that both *Meisterschüler* Wera Küchenmeister in dramaturgy and her husband Claus in directing gave at a DAK meeting sound remarkably similar to the experiences of the other assistants. Wera said that Brecht wanted 'his students to "pinch" important things from him', and Claus reported that Brecht considered it essential for his students to play a defined role in production work in order to learn from it.[131] The cultural authorities opposed this open form of education in favour of defined classes and learning outcomes.[132] The Performing Arts Section of the Academy insisted on a special class for Brecht, and it seems that the authorities could not stop it.

To Claus Küchenmeister, the only difference between the *Meisterschüler* and the assistants was that the former were subordinated to Brecht while the latter, as least officially, came under Weigel's jurisdiction as *Intendantin*.[133] The lack of differentiation in the BE sadly did not extend beyond the company. The status of *Meisterschüler* may actually have attracted the authorities looking for ways to put Brecht under pressure. Two *Meisterschüler* were arrested and gaoled on trumped-up charges during the GDR's properly Stalinist phase in the early 1950s. Horst Bienek was sentenced in April 1952 to 25 years for, as Jochen Staadt put it, 'criticism of Stalinist cultural politics', although he was released three years later.[134] Klaus Pohl was implicated in a spurious spying charge and sentenced to four years in 1953. He was released just

[127] See Bork to Rudolf Engel, 20 July 1951, BArch DR 1/6082.
[128] See Brecht to Rudolf Engel, 5 July 1955, BFA, 30: 360.
[129] See Brecht to Paul Wandel, 24 May 1951, BFA, 30: 73; *Letters*, p. 503.
[130] See *Meisterschüler* Claus Küchenmeister, in Buchmann *et al.*, '*Eine Begabung*', p. 32; or assistant Egon Monk, unpublished interview with Rouse, p. I-5.
[131] Wera and Claus Küchenmeister, in Anon., 'Zusammenkunft der Meisterschüler der Sektion Darstellende Kunst und der Sektion Dichtkunst am 22. März 1954...', undated, 4 pages (1 and 3, respectively), AdK AdK-O 132.
[132] See Anon., 'Protokoll über die Sektionssitzung am 19. Juni 1951...', 21 June 1951, 3 pages (2), AdK AdK-O 54.
[133] Claus Küchenmeister, unpublished interview with the author, 4 November 2010.
[134] Jochen Staadt, '"Arbeit mit Brecht" – "daß wir uns auf den Standpunkt der Gesellschaft stellen." Brecht, Weigel und die Staatliche Kommission für Kunstangelegenheiten', in

over a year later.[135] Stephen Parker believes that Pohl's arrest in particular was a deliberate 'intimidation of Brecht'.[136]

If there were a hierarchy, as Luckhurst suggests, then the *Meisterschüler* element did not reflect an elite status. While Monk, Wekwerth, Palitzsch and Besson have all erroneously been called '*Meisterschüler*' over the years,[137] these 'trainees', the most successful of Brecht's assistants, were not a part of the *Meisterschüler* programme at all. *Meisterschüler* B. K. Tragelehn did go on to have a career as a director that spanned the German-speaking countries, but Claus Küchenmeister went into film, his first love, rather than theatre, despite his experiences with the BE. Pohl and Bienek fled the GDR after their appalling treatment. Others, such as Wera Küchenmeister (dramaturgy), Heinz Kahlau (poetry) and Dieter Berge (acting) had successful careers in the GDR, but did not achieve great renown. The perceived privilege of being a *Meisterschüler* with the BE did not reflect a privileged relationship within the BE. Talent was the main criterion, and those who shone and made the most of their opportunities went on to secure national and international reputations.

Guests from the West, guests from the East

Brecht used his ability to attract high-profile guests to the BE as a way of making his project more appealing to the Soviet and German authorities in 1949. Having secured Berthold Viertel, Therese Giehse and Hans Gaugler in the BE's first season, he found that the flow of prominent theatre people from the West soon dried up. The problem of playing at the BE was highlighted in an incident surrounding a proposed prologue to the BE's production of Heinrich von Kleist's *Der zerbrochene Krug* (*The Broken Jug*). Two BE dramaturges, Käthe Rülicke and Claus Hubalek, compiled the short piece, based on documentary material from

Staadt (ed.), *'Die Eroberung der Kultur beginnt!' Die Staatliche Kunstkommission für Kunstangelegenheiten der DDR (1951–1953) und die Kulturpolitik der SED* (Frankfurt/Main et al.: Peter Lang, 2011), pp. 351–78 (360).

[135] See Anon., '[protocol of the case against Peter Lefold and Klaus Pohl]', undated, file pp. 242–56 (256), BStU MfS AU 87/54, vol. 3; and Anon., telex communication, 21 December 1954, file p. 52, BStU MfS AU 87/54, vol. 7.

[136] Stephen Parker, 'A Life's Work Curtailed? The Ailing Brecht's Struggle with the SED Leadership over GDR Cultural Policy', in Laura Bradley and Karen Leeder (eds.), *Brecht and the GDR: Politics, Culture, Posterity* (Rochester NY: Camden House, 2011), pp. 65–82 (76).

[137] See, for example, Gerhard Schoenberner, 'Frühe Theaterarbeit', *Marburger Hefte zur Medienwissenschaft*, 21 (1995), pp. 6–18 (6), for Monk; Birgit Haas, *Theater der Wende – Wendetheater* (Würzburg: Königshaus & Neumann, 2004), p. 131, for Wekwerth and Palitzsch; and Werner Wüthrich, *Bertolt Brecht und die Schweiz* (Zurich: Chronos, 2003), p. 163, for Besson.

the West German news magazine, *Der Spiegel. Bonn im Spiegel (Bonn in 'Der Spiegel'/in the Mirror)* dramatized allegedly corrupt practices that led to the small town of Bonn being chosen as the FRG's capital rather than Frankfurt.[138] The plan was to preface Kleist with a contemporary example of how the law was made to bend to the advantage of those in power. Rehearsals started in April 1951, months before those for *The Broken Jug*, but were interrupted by a tour in May.[139] Fritz Erpenbeck had got wind of the plan and, without mentioning the prologue by name, suggested that it would be sacrilege to bolt a new piece 'onto this splendid work from our national *Erbe*'.[140] Later in the year, the Central Committee was similarly sceptical and suggested that Brecht be no longer permitted to stage 'further performances of mixed plays'.[141] By 'mixed', they meant the combination of two plays, such as *The Beaver Coat and Conflagration* and the proposed union of *Der Spiegel* and Kleist. In both cases, the criticism was based on the possible damage that 'additions' could do to the *Erbe*. It seems that the potential for *Bonn im Spiegel* to sully relations with the FRG was not an overt factor.

By the end of 1951, with *Broken Jug* rehearsals in progress, the *Bonn* project was postponed and Monk was charged with writing a new adaptation in early 1952.[142] There are no records to suggest that Monk did revise the text, and it was never performed. Wekwerth reports that the prologue was cancelled at Giehse's request; Mittenzwei believes that it was because she feared for her acting career in the West.[143] Kebir writes that a Western actor who planned to perform in the film version of *Mother Courage* was actively threatened by a senator from West Berlin and decided against working in the GDR.[144] It is unclear whether Giehse was 'spoken to' or whether she was merely responding to the chilly climate of the Cold War. In either case, this episode illustrates that the application of cultural pressure was not only the preserve of the GDR; the FRG could also wield 'soft power' to further its own ends by manipulating symbols in the real conflict between the two German states.

---

[138] Various drafts and plans written by Käthe Rülicke and Claus Hubalek are to be found in BBA 613/1–28.

[139] See Rülicke, '[Diary]', BBA 1264/8.

[140] Fritz Erpenbeck, 'Anknüpfen – aber wie? Unser klassisches Erbe in Theorie und Praxis', *Theater der Zeit*, 9 (1951), pp. 4–8 (7).

[141] Trautzsch, 'Protokoll Nr. 91 der Sitzung des Sekretariats des ZK am 2. August 1951', undated, 19 pages (9), SAPMO BArch DY 30/J IV 2/3/220.

[142] See entries for December 1951 and January 1952, in BEA File 'Logbücher 1950–52'.

[143] See Manfred Wekwerth, *Erinnern ist Leben*, p. 106; and Mittenzwei, *Das Leben des Bertolt Brecht*, vol. 2, p. 389.

[144] See Kebir, *Abstieg in den Ruhm*, p. 240.

Giehse herself was invited to direct the production of *The Broken Jug*, a peculiar decision for an actor who had never directed before. She had played one of the leads, Marthe Rull, under Viertel's direction in Salzburg in August 1951. Weigel, a close friend, invited Giehse to direct in September, and it is clear from the letter that the directing role was to take precedence over the acting because Weigel suggested Giehse alternate her leading role with Angelika Hurwicz.[145] Indeed, Weigel reported that Giehse did not want to act at all.[146] Carl Weber views the move as purely tactical: to deflect attention from Brecht and *his* relationship to the *Erbe*.[147] By using a big, international name, the BE could shield itself from accusations about the treatment of *The Broken Jug* by ascribing them to someone who was not even a citizen of the GDR.

The problem was that Giehse was not a director, and her approach to historical material was naturalistic, not dialectical. Regine Lutz offers an insider's view of events; she played another main character, Eve. At first, she admired Giehse's resolution,[148] that is, she directed like a traditional director, telling the actors what to do. A couple of weeks later, she noted the problems of working with a director who neglected work on the kinds of details to which she had become accustomed.[149] Brecht started to attend rehearsals in December when Giehse began to rehearse her role as Marthe. He redirected much of what had already been fixed, and Lutz acknowledged that despite her initial annoyance at his interventions, she found them sensible, clear and effective.[150] Once Brecht had seen a complete run, he condemned it as having the quality of an acting school's production and set about making further major changes. The *Notat* for one of Brecht's earliest rehearsals is full of interventions that emphasize social difference and the dialectical nature of the characters. One finds, for example, 'emphasizing the class issue: Walter puts Adam straight in such a way that he can't be heard by the peasants'.[151] Brecht's concern for detail in class relations meant that hierarchies became clearer than in Giehse's more psychological approach to the play as a character drama: Walter, the visiting legal official has power over the local judge Adam, but this power cannot be used to undermine Adam before those of a lower class whom he has to judge.

---

[145] See Weigel to Therese Giehse, 29 September 1951, *Briefwechsel*, p. 38.
[146] See Weigel to Brecht, 16 October 1951, BBA 1340/109.
[147] See Carl Weber, 'Brecht and the Berliner Ensemble', p. 182.
[148] See Lutz to her parents, 4 November 1951, BBA Lutz files 'Briefe ab Feb. 1951 bis Nov. 1954'.
[149] See Lutz to her parents, 22 November 1951, ibid.
[150] Lutz to her parents, 26 December 1951, ibid.
[151] Anon., 'Probe *Zerbrochener Krug* 3.1.52', undated, 6 pages (3), BEA File 7.

Contrary to the impression Werner Hecht gives,[152] Giehse was most offended that Brecht had taken over 'her' direction,[153] yet she retained the directing credit. Even today, Giehse's most recent biographer insists that she directed 'with particular care' to show that directing was not merely a male preserve.[154] It is likely that if she had actually directed, Armin Kuckhoff, the future rector of the Theatre Academy in Leipzig, may not have condemned the production so definitively.[155] That said, the production ran for 107 performances after its premiere on 23 January 1951 and was revived later in 1953 with a new leading lady (Hurwicz), because Giehse did not return to work with the BE. In contradistinction to Kuckhoff's ideological critique, the reviewers of the time saw the production as a welcome revision of the *Erbe* and praised the new light cast on one of the few great German comedies.[156]

The BE's history has shown that Viertel was the only guest director who brought a style wholly alien to Brecht's to a production. This might suggest that from *Vassa* onwards, the BE inevitably steered a course towards Brecht, but his collected letters include invitations to at least three directors who were not associated with his approach to making theatre.[157] It is, of course, possible, that these invitations had a tactical intention – by diluting a sense of aesthetic 'purity', Brecht could work in greater peace on his own productions. Yet Brecht also wrote the invitation to Hans Schweikart when he was already quite ill in 1956, and this instance may represent a way of reducing his own workload at the BE. In any case, none of the directors ended up working with the BE, and this might have something to do with its geopolitical situation. On the one hand, director Ludwig Berger said in 1951 that 'the highest authorities in the West put paid to my wonderful plans'.[158] Wilful obstruction thus prevented exchange between West and East. On the other, personal objections also played a role. Weigel invited actor Erich Ponto to appear as a guest with the BE in 1954. He had played Peachum in the world premiere of *The*

---

[152] See Werner Hecht, *Brecht Chronik*, p. 993, in which he states, without a reference, that Giehse invited Brecht to direct the final rehearsals.

[153] See Lutz to her parents, 6 January 1952, BBA Lutz files 'Briefe ab Feb. 1951 bis Nov. 1954'.

[154] Renate Schmidt, *Therese Giehse: Na, dann wollen wir die Herrschaften mal was bieten! Biographie* (Munich: Langen Müller [sic], 2008), p. 213.

[155] See Armin G. Kuckhoff, 'Unsere Stanislawski-Diskussion', *Theater der Zeit*, 8 (1953), pp. 19–23 (20).

[156] See, for example, J. Weinert, 'Wiederentdeckung eines deutschen Klassikers', *National-Zeitung*, 29 January 1952.

[157] See Brecht to Leopold Lindtberg, 25 April 1950; Brecht to Günter Rennert, 27 March 1954; and Brecht to Hans Schweikart, 8 June 1956, BFA, 30: 23, 235, and 462, respectively.

[158] Ludwig Berger, in Preuß, *Theater im ost-/westpolitischen Umfeld*, p. 755.

Threepenny Opera, but declined to leave Munich in 1954 because he did not agree with the political nature of Brecht's theatre.[159] All the same, the BE did manage to attract at least one A-list guest early on: the French mime Marcel Marceau gave a workshop in December 1951 and helped choreograph a production for children the next month.[160] Marceau, of course, was not subject to specifically intra-German tensions.

In the same season that Giehse 'directed' *The Broken Jug*, the BE invited actor and singer Ernst Busch to direct *The Kremlin Chimes* by the Soviet author Nikolai Pogodin. The play itself is thin and unsatisfying: set after the Russian Revolution, Lenin seeks to electrify the new state to bring it into the twentieth century. The play climaxes when he delivers a speech, and the Kremlin chimes play 'The Internationale'. It is easy to dismiss this choice of play as 'Konzessionstheater' ('theatre as a concession'),[161] but the choice of both play and director was not without its dangers. Weigel noted changes that the BE had to make after criticism from the Soviet ambassador, and the StaKuKo offered tips on authenticity in the production shortly before the premiere (see Fig. 3.2).[162] This apparently affirmative play still had the potential to attract criticism, rather than automatically garner plaudits. And Busch, like Giehse, was an untried director and thus a potential risk. The BE was trading on his good name as a politically committed actor and singer, although he, too, would provoke the SED's wrath with his record label 'Lied der Zeit' in the months after the premiere. The BE assigned Wekwerth to assist and almost certainly to rein Busch in. Weigel warned Busch 'be careful what you do. Directing this play is not only a matter for you'.[163] Brecht himself intervened in the direction, again without credit, to ensure that the production worked on stage, and the *Notate* suggest similar alterations to those made to *The Broken Jug*.[164] The point here is that a great deal of energy was invested in this production to 'get it right' – the mere performance of a propaganda play was not enough to ensure a tactical advantage for the BE and ran the risk of alienating the StaKuKo further. Indeed, Bork would not release funds to provide the BE with specially adapted scenery that could be used to tour the production.[165] This indicates that the authorities did not view the show

---

[159] See Erich Ponto to Weigel, 6 February 1954, *Briefwechsel*, p. 63.
[160] See logbook entries for these months, BEA File 'Logbücher 1950–52'.
[161] Jochen Staadt, '"Arbeit mit Brecht"', p. 364.
[162] See Weigel, in Werner Hecht, *Helene Weigel*, pp. 40–1; and Willi Lewin to Weigel, 24 March 1952, HWA SM 23/7.
[163] Weigel to Ernst Busch, 10 March 1952, HWA SM 23/1.
[164] See various documents concerning the production, in AdK Ernst-Busch-Archiv, uncatalogued files.
[165] See Bork to BE, 30 June 1952, BEA File 8.

Fig. 3.2. Placating the implacable: an apparently propagandist production, with its realistic depiction of the central historical characters, still encounters criticism. *The Kremlin Chimes*, March 1952.

as a political or fiscal priority. The attempt at mollifying the SED was not a success, something that was perhaps connected to the persistence of Brecht's dialectical directions evident in the production.

The contentious influence of Stanislavsky on the Berliner Ensemble

The Soviets had championed Stanislavsky's acting theories, which were focused on achieving what Brecht would have called 'naturalism', as the only methodology of realizing realism in the theatre. Brecht's realism was more concerned with representing the dialectical social mechanisms that produced the appearances Stanislavsky sought to reproduce. The tension between Brecht and Stanislavsky has become a much discussed topos in Brecht scholarship, and I do not intend to revisit old debates about whether or not the two figures can be reconciled. Instead I am more concerned with the concrete impact of Stanislavsky on Brecht at the BE, something that cannot be understood solely in terms of either cultural politics or theatre practice, but by viewing the two in conjunction with each other.

Renate Ullrich shows that an article written in 1946 by Alexander Dymschitz, the Soviet cultural officer who had also supported Brecht, conferred upon Stanislavsky's acting methods 'very quickly something official and at the same time something missionary-like'.[166] The trouble was that such canonization led to nothing but artistic failure because the question of process, of appropriation, had been ignored.[167] While Brecht was reflecting upon and challenging his own practice, the acolytes of Stanislavsky believed in a simplistic implementation of hallowed principles.[168] Despite this imposition from the Soviet Union, the undeniable success of the BE as a bastion of a different approach to theatre continued to provoke hostility. Here it is worth remembering that cultural policy dovetailed political expediency with aesthetic simplicity. At this early stage of the GDR's history, the implementation of any directive was closely related to the SED's exercise of power. Any deviation from the norm was, by definition, an implicit critique of the wisdom and authority of the party. Yet at the same time, a drive to an aesthetic that remained on the naturalistic surface meant that the authorities could canalize art as propaganda and thus reduce the possibility of theatre generating 'dangerous' secondary meanings. This may account for the Soviets' championing of such an unpolitical theorist and practitioner as Stanislavsky.

The BE was such a thorn in the SED's side that the StaKuKo convened a conference on Stanislavsky in 1953 as a way of publicly bringing the issue to a head. However, it would be a mistake to assume that this was a conference at which the various parties actually conferred. Helene Weigel's contribution, written by Brecht, was defensive and stressed the points of contact between Brecht and Stanislavsky.[169] The BE was well aware that it could not oppose the Stanislavsky agenda in public. In addition, knowledge of Stanislavsky was not a prerequisite for the conference in any case. On the contrary, Stuber argues that ignorance was a positive boon in the eyes of the StaKuKo because it could transmit its own version through its selected speakers.[170] She also notes that this was far more a conference on Brecht than Stanislavsky as he became the direct or indirect point of reference for almost all the papers.[171] The BE was clearly under pressure, yet Brecht was still able to register his resistance

[166] Renate Ullrich, '"Und zudem bringt Ihr noch den genialen Stanislawski in Verruf." Zur Kanonisierung einer Schauspielmethode', in Birgit Dahlke, Martina Langermann and Thomas Taterka (eds.), *LiteraturGesellschaft* [sic] *DDR: Kanonkämpfe und ihre Geschichte(n)* (Stuttgart and Weimar: Metzler, 2000), pp. 104–45 (114).
[167] See ibid., p. 105.   [168] See Hans Daiber, *Deutsches Theater seit 1945*, p. 127.
[169] See extracts from her speech in Weigel, 'Gemeinsam studieren', *Theater der Zeit*, 5 (1953), pp. 7–8.
[170] See Stuber, *Spielräume und Grenzen*, p. 164.   [171] See ibid., p. 168.

as a member of the DAK. In a sitting of early 1953, when the StaKuKo was preparing the conference, Brecht rejected the monolithic orthodoxy of Stanislavsky as a dogma and pleaded for support for all effective, alternative approaches,[172] implicitly including his own in the open formulation. All the same, the official view dominated, something that has led Matthew Philpotts to stress the tactical nature of Brecht's interest in Stanislavsky.[173] Yet while this was almost certainly a contributory factor, it was by no means the only one.

Brecht's relationship with Stanislavsky underwent a series of changes. Open hostility in the 1930s and 1940s gave way to a far more pragmatic approach. Meg Mumford argues that, while acknowledging the pressure exerted by the SED, Brecht actually found much that was useful to him in Stanislavsky's work.[174] This is reflected, for example, in his positive response to Stanislavsky's later theory of physical actions[175] in which character is developed through external gestures, something Brecht would have associated with his own concept of *Gestus*. It becomes increasingly clear that Brecht started to view Stanislavsky through his own prism and suggested that his Russian colleague was in fact a (partially) dialectical director who used *Verfremdung* without actually knowing it.[176] At the same time, Brecht still could not locate the social moment in Stanislavsky's work,[177] and this, ultimately, represents the line between the two that could never be crossed. Hans Martin Ritter sums this up neatly; the Stanislavskian actor's basic justification for being on stage is intentionally to embody the proposition 'ich will' ('I want to').[178] While this desire was certainly present on the stage of the BE, it was always contextualized by the dialectic of individual and society, the 'I' was never sovereign, but part of a greater system of interconnections.

Consequently, Brecht's use of Stanislavsky was critical and circumspect. Wera Küchenmeister reports that Brecht asked her with genuine interest about her experiences with Stanislavsky's teachings as a

---

[172] See Brecht, in Anon., 'Arbeit in der DAK', undated, 12 pages (6), AdK AdK-O OM 3.

[173] See Matthew Philpotts, '"Aus so prosaischen Dingen wie Kartoffeln, Straßen, Traktoren werden poetische Dinge!": Brecht, *Sinn und Form*, and Strittmatter's *Katzgraben*', *German Life and Letters*, 56:1 (2003), pp. 56–71 (62).

[174] See Meg Mumford, 'Brecht Studies Stanislavsky: Just a Tactical Move?', *New Theatre Quarterly*, 11: 43 (1995), pp. 241–58 (243).

[175] See Brecht, '[Stanislawskis Theorie der physischen Handlungen]', BFA, 23: 228.

[176] See Brecht, 'Klassische Ratschläge Stanislawskis' and 'Zu Stanislawski', BFA, 23: 224 and 225, respectively.

[177] See Brecht, 'Stanislawski-Studien [6]', BFA, 23: 230.

[178] Hans Martin Ritter, 'Bertolt Brecht – Unterm Strasberg begraben. Abwichlung oder Entwicklung der Brechtschen Theatertheorie in der Schauspielerausbildung?', *Brecht Yearbook*, 17 (1992), pp. 63–74 (68).

student in Weimar,[179] where the Russian director was the only theorist taught there. Even Fritz Erpenbeck, the critic who never ceased to
criticize Brecht in the pages of *Theater der Zeit*, was invited to discuss
Stanislavsky with the BE's actors.[180] But just like almost everything else
Brecht encountered, Stanislavsky provided useful *material* that could be
appropriated for his theatre, and this is why one should not necessarily
over-emphasize his importance at the BE, something even Brecht himself
sought to do in the '*Katzgraben*-Notate', discussed below.

Stanislavsky 'in practice': a productive appropriation at the BE

Mumford notes how Stanislavsky influenced the portrayal of the crowd
scenes in the production of *Der Prozeß der Jeanne D'Arc zu Rouen 1431*
(*The Trial of Joan of Arc at Rouen, 1431*), a BE adaptation of a radio play by
Anna Seghers, in late 1952.[181] Unfortunately, there is very little material
in any of the archives that documents the rehearsal process, and so it is difficult to understand precisely which methods were deployed and in which
ways. One note, however, does describe the desire 'to make a socially differentiated group of people out of the "mass" that one often encounters as
a dim-wittedly murmuring chorus in the theatre'.[182] Stanislavsky sought
to bring realism to all aspects of a performance, and so the 'humaniza-
tion' of the crowd represents an application of his theories to a specific
dramaturgical problem. The extent to which Stanislavsky was put at the
disposal of Brecht's approach to making theatre in the crowd scenes is
evident in two responses to them. The production's credited director,
Benno Besson, emphasized how each of the seven representative individuals who made up the crowd developed and transformed their *Haltung*
towards Joan as the play progressed.[183] So, while he subjected the crowd
members to approaches taken from Stanislavsky, his aim was nonetheless
one focused on the clear demonstration of dynamic dialectical contradictions and syntheses over time. Indeed, Besson noted that directing
this play as a whole introduced him to dialectics in the most concrete
of terms.[184] Johannes Goldhahn considers the treatment of the crowd

---

[179] See Wera Küchenmeister, in Lang and Hillesheim, '*Denken heißt verändern . . .* ',
p. 69.
[180] See Rülicke, in Anon., 'Interview Matthias Braun mit Käthe Rülicke-Weiler, 1978 und
1984, über Helene Weigel/Bertolt Brecht', undated, 40 pages (27), HWA FH 80.
[181] See Mumford, 'Brecht Studies Stanislavsky', p. 245.
[182] Anon., 'Über die Volksszenen', undated, BBA 681/6.
[183] See Besson, in Neubert-Herwig, *Benno Besson: Jahre mit Brecht*, p. 148.
[184] See Besson, in André Müller, *Der Regisseur Benno Besson* (Berlin: Henschel, 1967),
p. 22.

naïve (in Brecht's positive sense) as a way of seeing a hitherto faceless mass anew.[185] The changes in *Haltungen* of a collection of individuals over time allowed spectators to follow a complex of interests; the focus shifted from person to person due to the impact of events on the different social types.

The production that is usually cited as the one that used Stanislavsky most thoroughly is Erwin Strittmatter's *Katzgraben* (the name of a rural village), directed by Brecht himself. The choice of play itself marked something new for the BE: it was a contemporary play written by a GDR citizen about problems solved by socialism on German soil. The play is set in the Soviet zone before the founding of the GDR and revolves around the democratic decision to support or oppose the building of a road to connect Katzgraben with the local town. Three representatives of the surviving social order offer differing perspectives on the action: a smallholder, a farmer with a medium-sized farm, and a wealthy farmer. Over the course of the play, the power of the wealthy farmer diminishes and the village benefits from the investment and guidance of the Party. However, as even the StaKuKo noted, there is no real conflict in the play.[186] The four acts simply run through a series of events in which consciousness changes over time with the establishment of the Party's own resources, and the whole of the final act is nothing but a celebration of the Party's successful work.

This was Strittmatter's first play, and he was later known as a great novelist, not a dramatist. Brecht himself registered doubt from Monk and Palitzsch as to whether the BE could make productive theatre out of such weak dramatic material and was sceptical of Strittmatter's decision to rewrite the play in verse.[187] It would appear that his response to the textual challenge was to see whether Stanislavsky's ideas could be used to create such interesting human characters on stage that they overshadowed the obvious shortcomings of the script.

Some critics, however, have rather overstated the role of Stanislavsky in the staging process. This is largely due to the importance ascribed to the so-called '*Katzgraben*-Notate'. Werner Hecht considers them a record of all aspects of the process 'in their entirety'.[188] The problem with this view

---

[185] See Johannes Goldhahn, 'Nachdenken über Naivität', Brecht-Zentrum der DDR (ed.), *Brecht 85: Zur Ästhetik Brechts. Fortsetzung eines Gesprächs über Brecht und Marxismus. Dokumentation* (Berlin: Henschel, 1986), pp. 212–23 (217).

[186] See Helmut Holtzhauer to Brecht, 5 February 1953, BArch DR 1/6029.

[187] See Brecht to Rülicke, 13 December 1952; and Brecht, journal entry for 22 July 1952, BFA, 30: 154 and 27: 333, respectively; *Journals*, pp. 444–5.

[188] Werner Hecht, '"Der Pudding bewährt sich beim Essen". Brechts "Prüfung" Stanislawskis 1953', in Ingrid Hentschel, Klaus Hoffmann and Florian Vaßen (eds.), *Brecht*

is twofold. First, the '*Katzgraben*-Notate', extensive as they are,[189] were originally compiled for publication (although the production's lukewarm reception postponed the plan indefinitely). They thus deliberately foreground the engagement with Stanislavsky for obvious reasons connected with the cultural climate of the time. Second, the actual *Notate*, written for the creative team and the cast during the rehearsal process, do not appear in the '*Katzgraben*-Notate' at all. This part of the documentation has rarely been discussed in connection with the production, yet it reveals much because it was never intended for publication.

It is evident that Brecht engaged more fundamentally with Stanislavsky here than at any other time in his directing career. The apparatus to the '*Katzgraben*-Notate' includes full character biographies for three of the main characters, written by Strittmatter himself.[190] This exercise was designed to give the characters depth, but the descriptions really only tell the actors what they already could have guessed – there are no major surprises in their backgrounds or their relationships, and so the exercise was somewhat tautological. Elsewhere, Regine Lutz writes that she took part in a workshop many years after the production with the founder of American Method acting, Lee Strasberg, yet that she only knew about Stanislavsky 'from hearsay'.[191] The impression given by the '*Katzgraben*-Notate' is that Stanislavsky was on everybody's lips, but it seems that, just like Brecht's use of his own theories, he was not mentioned by name and became merely another way of working. This was not a telegraphed engagement with a new practitioner, but an addition to the BE's working methods.

In Käthe Rülicke's detailed documentation of *Katzgraben* in the form of *Notate*, one finds almost all the features of a more conventional Brechtian rehearsal process. Scene titles, such as 'Tobacco More Important Than Seed Potatoes' and 'Mrs Mittelländer Studies the People' helped the actors negotiate the *Fabel*, especially in the initial rehearsals that constructed the *Arrangements*.[192] Indeed, the centrality of the *Arrangement* persisted over any sense that Stanislavskian individuals now populated the stage. At one point of crisis, where rehearsal simply could not proceed, the team decided to work on a new *Arrangement* as the starting point to a solution.[193] Dialectics and the emphasis on the social still dominated

---

& *Stanislawski und die Folgen. Anregungen für die Theaterarbeit* (Berlin: Henschel, 1997), pp. 57–71 (63).

[189] They can be found in BFA, 25: 401–90. Extracts in English are in *BoP*, pp. 249–75.

[190] See BFA, 25: 554–8.   [191] Lutz, *Schauspieler – der schönste Beruf*, p. 44.

[192] Käthe Rülicke, '[documentation of *Katzgraben* rehearsals]', undated, n.p., entry for scene I/i/1, 26 February 1953, BEA File 13.

[193] See ibid., entry for scene III/ii/8, 7 March 1953.

and one *Notat* clearly states that the Mittelländers' problems do not arise from their characters, but from their situation in 1947. One also finds evidence of the 'loaded dialectic' in the same rehearsal, as Rülicke wrote 'of course we are showing these [problems] in a partisan fashion, but we can't blithely dismiss the difficulties or make light of them'.[194] The dialectical reconciliation of realism and artifice was also a key feature; Rülicke observed how the actors were to enjoy the rhythms of the verse without sacrificing the character's naturalness to the verse form.[195] (By way of comparison, the *Notat* in the '*Katzgraben*-Notate' for the very same rehearsal makes no mention of the *practice* of speaking verse. Instead it emphasizes the political importance of having people from lower down the social ladder speaking like characters from Shakespeare, Goethe and Schiller, and the poetological effects of having to condense language in verse.)[196]

Gestus and *Haltung* also recurred as pointers for the actors and one finds the customary attention to social detail. For example, the Großmann family, the large farm-owners, are Christians, and Großmann cut a cross into their bread before he sliced the loaf. Brecht reportedly said 'customs are always good', in that the ritual tells the spectator more about the characters' place in society. In the same rehearsal, Brecht worked carefully on the line 'the Farmers Aid is delivering seed potatoes' so that Großmann showed how he both disapproved of the socialist assistance programme, but was happy to accept its wares.[197] It would have been easy for the actor to have delivered the line positively, but Brecht insisted on the dialectical approach – the capitalist may spurn the socialists, but will nonetheless take whatever he wants from them.

In short, Rülicke's documentation signals no great move away from one methodology towards another, although, as with *The Mother* before it, it shows Brecht's search for a realistic dialectical theatre aimed at a socialist and not a capitalist society. If I had only read Rülicke's *Notate* and not the '*Katzgraben*-Notate', I would not have been aware that Stanislavsky's theories were present at all. Of course, the evidence provided above shows that Brecht was engaging with Stanislavsky's ideas as they were understood in the GDR at the time, and this reveals something about what Rülicke chose to include in her own documentation, too. However, the emphasis on Brechtian approaches suggest that Stanislavsky was actually

---

[194] Ibid., entry for scene I/i/1, 31 March 1953.
[195] See ibid., entry for the same scene, 8 April 1953.
[196] See Brecht, '*Katzgraben*-Notate', BFA, 25: 426; *BoP*, p. 258.
[197] See Brecht, in Rülicke, '[documentation of *Katzgraben* rehearsals]', undated, n.p., entry for scene I/iv/1, 5 March 1953, BEA File 13.

someone Brecht found helpful, but who did not wholly satisfy Brecht's own demands of a politicized theatre.

Carl Weber also compiled *Notate* for the production, and these tend to echo those of Rülicke's as to the style of and approach to rehearsals. He notes one important philosophical idea that talks to the relationship between Stanislavsky and Brecht: 'in each scene, we must show a human issue in a general sense that doesn't seem at all political at first. It will become evident that the human is connected to the political'.[198] This comment puts Stanislavsky in context. The human qualities Brecht sought to bring onto the stage in all their liveliness and complexity were always manifestations of greater political relations. Brecht was still 'making theatre politically'. An actor could not enter a scene without appreciating his or her social position, and while that might not emerge straight away, it would reveal itself as the performance went on. Weber's mention of 'a general sense' already militates against seeing characters as hermetically sealed individuals. We view their individual experience of situations, which are common to particular societies at particular points of their history, and therein lies the value of the performance: the audience can abstract beyond the specific scene and characters, and understand the social mechanisms that affect them, too.

Brecht, socialist realism and the GDR after 17 June 1953

Katzgraben was not well received in the press after its premiere on 23 May 1953 and was only given thirty-seven times in its initial two-year run. Yet Brecht was convinced that he was making a major contribution to contemporary socialist theatre. His support for the project was, given the scepticism of Monk and Palitzsch, the driving force for the production, and his decision to reflect on the process in the '*Katzgraben*-Notate' indicates the centrality he ascribed to the work. Without doubt, the play itself was not terribly good, and reviewers pointed to the problem identified by the StaKuKo: it lacked a powerful central conflict.[199] However, Brecht believed that his approach to staging the play compensated for its shortcomings, and this is also evident in the rehearsal material cited above. What the production of *Katzgraben* (and indeed others discussed earlier) articulated was a commitment to a new way of working in the theatre that would seem to ally Brecht with the SED's fundamental artistic principle

---

[198] Carl Weber, '[*Notate* on *Katzgraben*]', undated, n.p., entry for 19 March 1953, BBA 550/62.

[199] See, for example, Karl Reinhold Döderin, 'Die Moritat vom bösen Kulaken', *Neue Zeit*, 3 June 1953.

of socialist realism. In the following argument, I will not suggest that Brecht or the BE were consciously striving to realize the SED's vision, but that elements of the BE's practice overlapped with the party line to such an extent that the BE actually satisfied a series of criteria without actually satisfying the SED.

There were three official criteria that helped define socialist realism: the work of art had to have the qualities of 'Parteilichkeit' ('partisan-ship'), 'Volksverbundenheit' ('a closeness to the people') and display 'Typisches' ('typicality').[200] I have already noted how Brecht's dialectic was partisan and how his practice of previewing shows to working people and students attempted to integrate their views into the final stages of rehearsal. However, 'the people' is such a broad term that it is all too easy to homogenize it. The production of *The Tutor*, for example, was a great success in Berlin, where Brecht's theatre was already developing an audience. But when the production toured Weimar in July 1950, an article noted that while working people appreciated the production at a festival for factory workers, they had no connection with it and found it difficult to understand.[201] *Volksverbundenheit* was a slippery criterion that artists could never fully satisfy, following the adage that one can never please all the people all the time, regardless of what the SED thought.

Typicality was also a central part of Brecht's theatre. His concept of *Gestus* was concerned with connecting the individual with the social, and the 'realistic detail' suggested a similar process of abstracting the general from the particular. Brecht elaborated on typicality in a note of 1951: 'historically significant (typical) people and events may not be the most frequent on average or the most obvious, but those that are decisive in society's developmental processes'.[202] Brecht's understanding links typi-cality to the other two criteria for socialist realism by redefining typicality in terms of significance rather than high statistical incidence. Significant people or events tie them to the socialist narrative, although, to Brecht, this was not one-sided flag-waving. Later in the same piece, he acknowl-edged that significance did not merely apply to those aspects that serve socialism, but to those that seek to hinder it as well, otherwise typicality would not reflect reality. Typicality was thus, in his eyes, the discovery of social and political issues in the everyday, so that they may be emphasized in performance and used to sensitize the audience's consciousness.

---

[200] The terms still had currency in 1978 and appear with lengthy definitions in Manfred Berger *et al.*, *Kulturpolitisches Wörterbuch*, second, expanded edition (Berlin: Dietz, 1978), pp. 545–7, 746–8, and pp. 683–8, respectively.
[201] See Karl Sippel, 'Kritik der Werktätigen am *Hofmeister*', *Das Volk*, 12 July 1950.
[202] Brecht, 'Das Typische', BFA, 23: 141.

In short, Brecht was a socialist realist in that he satisfied the three criteria listed above. The question, then, arises as to why he was pilloried so
often and so vociferously. The answer is sadly simple: Brecht's reading of
socialist realism differed from that of the SED. Brecht certainly agreed
with its principles and defined the category in terms of its active contribution to the realization of socialism through art.[203] But he was always
concerned with process and activity, while the SED anchored socialist realism's tenets in specific approved and consequently static forms.
Hence, Brecht protested in 1954 against the dogma of realizing socialist
realism's aims solely through Stanislavsky's methods[204] and criticized the
authorities' version of socialist realism in 1953 'as a style they're trying
to impose on artists of the most diverse kinds'.[205] For Brecht, socialist
realism was not government propaganda, but the activating exposure of
social contradictions, framed by the progressive cause of socialism.

SED dogma in the cultural sphere was to suffer a body blow as the
result of popular discontent in the economic and political spheres. Less
than a month after the premiere of *Katzgraben*, the events of 17 June
1953 shook the young state to its core. The protests, initially driven by
workers who were told to work harder for less pay, led to a strike and
calls for the removal of the government, bolstered by propaganda from
Western radio. The events were as close as the GDR came to a revolution
and they traumatized the SED in ways that would re-echo throughout
its rule. The need to secure its power led to both a cultural thaw, but, in
the wake of the uprising in Hungary in 1956, a return to the hard line.
Greater acts of entrenchment, such as the expansion of the Stasi and the
building of the Berlin Wall, can also be traced back to 1953. And while I
do not want to dwell on this complex historical moment and its causes,
Brecht's relationship to it is important.

Brecht famously sent a letter to Walter Ulbricht that was censored
for publication in *Neues Deutschland*: his display of loyalty to the SED
appeared in print; his more critical suggestion about governmental dialogue with the masses did not.[206] A meeting was held at the BE and
Brecht, uncharacteristically, made a speech in which he reportedly told
the assembly that they had to support the GDR, warts and all, as there
was no superior alternative to socialism.[207] In addition, the BE offered
practical assistance to the SED by proposing to supervise programmes
on the country's radio station to counter the propaganda emanating from

---

[203] See Brecht, 'Sozialistischer Realismus auf dem Theater', BFA, 23: 286.
[204] See Anon., 'Arbeit in der DAK', undated, 12 pages (9), AdK AdK-O OM 3.
[205] Brecht, '[Gegen den Zwang zum sozialistischen Realismus]', BFA, 23: 265.
[206] See Brecht to Walter Ulbricht, 17 June 1953, BFA, 30: 178; *Letters*, p. 515–16.
[207] See Claus Küchenmeister, in Buchmann *et al.*, '*Eine Begabung*', p. 69.

the West.[208] GDR radio wanted nothing to do with the BE's plan and continued to play only music on 17 and 18 June. However, despite these open shows of support, Brecht blocked a knee-jerk declaration of confidence in the SED on the afternoon of 17 June at the DAK and insisted that mistakes in cultural policy be openly discussed.[209] This strident position betrays both Brecht's understanding of the watershed the GDR had reached and his intention to capitalize on it. Meredith A. Heiser-Duron lists Brecht's achievements after this date, which included helping to shut down the StaKuKo and replace it with the Ministry of Culture.[210] The SED had to make concessions in its cultural policies, something that did not give artists carte blanche by any means, but that derailed the public campaign against formalism and the dogmatic pursuit of the *Erbe*, and freed up a more public debate in the media. Perhaps Brecht's relationship to the SED and the GDR post crisis is best summed up in an observation Rülicke made in her diary: 'after 17 June 53, Brecht thought long and hard about how Marxism's principles could be publicized most effectively'.[211] Brecht sought to highlight the philosophical system and the mechanisms that would bring about a more just society. By going back to dialectical basics, Brecht hoped to regain the people's faith in Marxism, and not necessarily in the SED.

A thaw of sorts would follow, although it would not last long. However, even by the time of the uprising, a disaffected Monk had already left the BE without any discussion with Brecht and headed to the West. Bienek and Pohl had been arrested, and, as I will discuss in the next chapter, the very future of the BE had been cast in doubt by SED power politics.

[208] See Anon., 'Für Besprechung mit Rundfunk', 17 June 1953, BBA 732/31–2.
[209] See Anon., 'Improvisierte erweitete Präsidiumssitzung am Mittwoch, den 17. Juni 1953', undated, BBA 1493/12–13.
[210] See Meredith A. Heiser-Duron, 'Brecht's Political and Cultural Dilemma in the Summer of 1953', *Communications for the International Brecht Society*, 30: 1 and 2 (2001), pp. 47–57 (55).
[211] Käthe Rülicke, '[Diary]', BBA 1264/21.

Brecht's last seasons at the Theater am
Schiffbauerdamm: 1954–1956

Back from the brink: the Berliner Ensemble's move to
the Theater am Schiffbauerdamm

The Berliner Ensemble's position before 17 June 1953 was precarious.
It had incurred the SED's wrath for making theatre in a variety of ways
that did not correspond to the official line. Journalist Christoph Funke's
contention is that 'without its uncompromising insistence on its distinctiveness, the Berliner Ensemble would not have survived'.[1] It was, on
the contrary, that very distinctiveness that was getting the BE into trouble, as most clearly evidenced by the problems surrounding *Urfaust*. The
company survived due to the SED's uncompromising insistence on its
own rightness, which ultimately provoked the uprising in June and the
concessions the SED was forced to make in its wake. The BE survived
because of this change in the political situation, which worked to its
advantage.

As already noted, the Theater am Schiffbauerdamm, the theatre in
which the BE still performs to this day, had been Brecht's chosen venue
for his new company well before it was founded. The residency at the DT
was a temporary solution to a problem that could only be solved by giving
the BE a theatre of its own. From the outset, the SED had intended to
rebuild the Theater am Rosa-Luxemburg-Platz so that Fritz Wisten could
transfer there and the BE could take over at the Schiffbauerdamm. The
building work was well behind schedule, and a realistic plan for a move
only emerged in 1953. Up until then, the BE had always been the first
choice to occupy the soon-to-be vacated Theater am Schiffbauerdamm.

Things took a surprising turn in March 1953 when the Bezirksleitung
der SED in Groß-Berlin (District Leadership of the SED in Greater
Berlin) decided to move Wisten to the new Volksbühne am Rosa-
Luxemburg-Platz and install the theatre ensemble of the Kasernierte
Volkspolizei (Garrisoned People's Police – KVP, a forerunner to the

---

[1] Christoph Funke, in Funke and Jansen, *Theater am Schiffbauerdamm*, p. 170.

GDR's National People's Army) in the Theater am Schiffbauerdamm.[2] The Politburo ratified the decision taken on 9 April 1953 twelve days later.[3] The District Leadership worked in tandem with the Municipal Authority to administer Berlin, yet while the latter mainly concerned itself with practical matters, the former was a political and ideological agency, founded when the SED established 'Bezirke' ('Districts') in 1952. That the plan came from this quarter is peculiar, in that one would have expected higher governmental organs (either the StaKuKo or the Central Committee) to have initiated such a major change in policy. However, it is quite possible that the idea was passed down from one of these bodies to give the impression that the decision came from the grassroots of Berlin itself.

There is no record of what the SED intended for the BE. Was it to remain at the DT until things reached some kind of breaking point? Was it to be shut down? The successful repression of *Urfaust* in 1953 might have led the SED to think it was gaining the upper hand. Peter Palitzsch certainly felt that sustained official criticism threatened the BE fundamentally.[4] Käthe Rülicke registered similar fears in her diary.[5] Manfred Wekwerth asserted publicly that he had seen letters signed by Walter Ulbricht dissolving the BE.[6] (However, in an interview I conducted with him, he later denied all knowledge of the letters.)[7] Uncertainty and anxiety about the BE's future were affecting morale.

However, the Central Committee's section on literature and art had suggested in mid July 1953 that the BE, not the KVP, move into the Theater am Schiffbauerdamm.[8] While its reasons are not given in the document, Wilhelm Girnus, whom the Central Committee had instructed to spy on Brecht in 1951, made a report directly to Ulbricht later in July that may shed a little more light. Having informed on Brecht's

---

[2] See Martin Helas to Egon Rentzsch, 23 March 1953, SAPMO BArch DY 30/IV 2/9.06/188.

[3] See Trautzsch, 'Protokoll Nr. 22/53 der Sitzung des Politbüros des Zentral-Komitees am 21. April 1953', undated, 13 pages (12), SAPMO BArch DY 30/J IV 2/2/318. However, there is no evidence to suggest that confidential minutes of this sort were passed on to *Intendantin* Weigel as Jan Knopf asserts (see Jan Knopf, *Bertolt Brecht. Lebenskunst in finsteren Zeiten* (Munich: Hanser, 2012), p. 503). No letters or documents register the shock or rage that Weigel or Brecht would have expressed at such news.

[4] See Palitzsch, in Iden, *Peter Palitzsch*, p. 61.

[5] See Werner Hecht, 'Das Vergnügen an einer ernsten Sache: Ein Leben im Dienste Brechts – Erinnerungen von und an Käthe Rülicke', *Der Tagesspiegel*, 3 November 1992.

[6] See Wekwerth, in Lang and Hillesheim, *'Denken heißt verändern...'*, p. 173; and in Hans-Dieter Schütt, *Manfred Wekwerth*, p. 84.

[7] Taken from Wekwerth, unpublished interview with the author, 14 June 2011. It is difficult to know why Wekwerth denied all knowledge, although he was particularly sensitive to any of my questions concerning the SED.

[8] See HB to Martin Helas, 15 July 1953, SAPMO BArch DY 30/IV 2/9.06/188.

profound criticism of SED cultural policy, Girnus argued that 'in view of the international ramifications' it would be 'untenable' to deny Brecht his own theatre in the long run.[9] Girnus was primarily contemplating an international scandal if the decision to bar Brecht from the Schiffbauerdamm were made public. He tried to soften the blow by suggesting that the SED had to expose Brecht by giving him a proper theatre, so that he could not use poor facilities or lack of resources as an excuse for his 'primitivism and Puritanism'. Girnus considered his argument to have 'an educative function' that would be effected by 'our criticism' in the media. So, while Girnus did not bring about the change in plan itself, his letter at least helps to explicate it. An almost unheard of *volte face* took place in the Central Committee: it reversed its previous decision that August and put the Schiffbauerdamm at the BE's disposal.[10] As Preuß notes: 'a KVP theatre remained a fiction that was never mentioned again'.[11]

Brecht appears to have been unaware of the District Leadership's original plan; there is nothing in his letters or journal that even mentions what would have been a remarkable affront. Perhaps smelling blood just ahead of the uprising on 15 June 1953, he wrote to Otto Grotewohl, the joint chairman of the SED, and lobbied for the Theater am Schiffbauerdamm, deploying an international argument, as Girnus would subsequently.[12] He suggested that the SED could publicly refute foreign press speculation about a rift between himself and the Party if the latter supported the move. Weigel also wrote to Kurt Bork at what was still the StaKuKo in the hope that the BE would be moved and indicated that the company would need more actors and technicians, although, as it would turn out, her proposal was quite modest.[13] That Brecht and Weigel's efforts coincided with the State's own back-pedalling reflects the profound effects of 17 June on both sides of the argument.

Weigel and Wisten as *Intendanten* were officially informed of the Politburo's (revised) decision at a meeting at the beginning of September. The as yet unconstituted Ministry of Culture would now supervise the BE, while the Volksbühne would remain under the control of the Municipal Authority. That is, the BE retained its prestigious 'Staatstheater' ('theatre of the state') status while the Volksbühne kept the more parochial title of 'Stadttheater' ('theatre of the city'). Weigel told the meeting that

[9] Wilhelm Girnus to Walter Ulbricht, 27 July 1953, SAPMO BArch DY 30/IV 2/2.026/40. The following quotations are taken from this letter.
[10] See Trautzsch, 'Protokoll Nr. 4/53 der Sitzung des Sektretariats des Zentral-Komitees am 19 August 1953', undated, 6 pages (4), SAPMO BArch DY 30/J IV 2/3/50.
[11] Preuß, *Theater im ost-/westpolitischen Umfeld*, p. 494.
[12] See Brecht to Otto Grotewohl, 15 June 1953, BFA, 30: 177–8; *Letters*, p. 515.
[13] See Weigel to Bork, 30 July 1953, BArch DR 1/6089.

she intended to call the company the 'Berliner Ensemble am Schiffbauerdamm' to establish its identity at its new location.[14]

The battle for the *Probenhaus*

If the BE and the DT thought that their problems of co-existence were
now behind them, they were mistaken. The DT wanted to reclaim
the rehearsal building specially erected for the BE during its sojourn
at the DT, the *Probenhaus* on 29 Reinhardtstraße. Initially, it seemed as
if the DT would be granted its wish; Bork told Wolfgang Langhoff while
making arrangements for the BE's move that he thought the BE would
no longer need the facility.[15] This, presumably, was because the BE was
to be furnished with its own new rehearsal stage at the Schiffbauerdamm.
Problems arose before the BE could start work there, however: the new
rehearsal stage was unusable, due to poor design and construction, and
so Weigel proposed that the BE and DT share the *Probenhaus* on the
condition that the BE had priority.[16] The problems with the BE's new
facilities were not fabricated, and Weigel listed the many deficiencies in
a letter to Alexander Abusch, a Deputy Minister of Culture.[17]

By September 1954, the Ministry insisted that the *Probenhaus* now
belonged to the DT and allocated Weigel funds to improve her own
rehearsal space.[18] Langhoff rubbed salt into this open wound by inverting
Weigel's earlier offer: he wrote that the BE could use the *Probenhaus* whenever the DT was not using it, although his letter indicates that the *Probenhaus* was not yet under the DT's control.[19] Weigel had not been informed
of the imminent transfer of the facility from the BE to the DT and
complained to both Langhoff and the Minister of Culture, Johannes R.
Becher. She argued that the *Probenhaus* was so closely associated with
the BE 'that it's already an historical scandal to make this demand'.[20]
The hyperbole aside, Weigel was busy stylizing the BE's reputation into
one that was not to be overshadowed by Langhoff's claims. In a further
letter to Minister Becher, Weigel framed the dispute in an international
context, claiming that to the outside world the *Probenhaus* was a unique
gift from the GDR and that it must remain bound to Brecht and his

[14] See Ludwig, 'Protokoll einer Besprechung am 1.9.1953 unter Leitung von Herrn
Holtzhauer', 1 September 1953, 2 pages (2), ibid.
[15] See Bork to Langhoff, 26 October 1953, BBA uncatalogued file 'Aktuelles'.
[16] See Weigel to Langhoff, 8 February 1954, *Briefwechsel*, p. 64.
[17] See Weigel to Alexander Abusch, 30 April 1954, ibid., p. 65.
[18] See Fritz Apelt to Weigel, 10 September 1954, ibid., p. 66.
[19] See Langhoff to Weigel, 27 September 1954, ibid., pp. 67–8.
[20] Weigel to Langhoff, 28 September 1954, ibid., p. 68.

company. Whether anyone outside East Berlin knew anything about the *Probenhaus* is itself questionable. The letter concluded with the haughty tone previously identified in the BE's attitude towards the DT: 'should Langhoff not share Brecht's opinion of Brecht, he could perhaps be put straight'.[21] The tone, however, was Brecht's and not Weigel's. The original draft was written by Brecht,[22] and it shows just how involved he was in the more serious issues surrounding the BE.

The authorities were certainly a model of indecision. Back in March, Bork noted that the DT *should* get the *Probenhaus*, but that Brecht would protest vigorously, and so the BE should actually keep it with the DT permitted access at agreed times.[23] Bork later enquired about whether the BE's defective rehearsal facilities at the Schiffbauerdamm could be upgraded, but was told on expert advice that this would not be possible.[24] Minister Becher's private secretary Fritz Apelt officially told Weigel that the *Probenhaus* would go to the DT in August,[25] but it would seem that Weigel prevailed in the end: a BE memorandum states that the BE was to retain the *Probenhaus* and would only offer it to the DT when the BE could spare it.[26]

A solution to the DT's own rehearsal space problems was found a year later: a new stage was built at a cost of 200,000 marks. However, Bork noted that other options could not be realized due to Weigel's intransigence in ceding the BE's rehearsal space.[27] For example, before the new build had been agreed, Langhoff was obliged to ask Weigel for access to the *Probenhaus* for rehearsals. These had become necessary due to re-casting of roles in existing productions. Weigel sardonically replied that the BE would need the space for its own rehearsals of this kind after the DT had poached two of its lead actors.[28] The boot was now firmly on the other foot, and Weigel was not going to hide the fact.

This tussle and the BE's eventual victory shows how Brecht's name and the BE's short yet illustrious history could be deployed to overturn official decisions in the wake of 17 June 1953. The BE possessed cards that could trump those of the DT, and with a theatre of its own, it was

---

[21] Weigel to Johannes R. Becher, October 1954, ibid., p. 70.
[22] See Brecht, [Untitled draft letter], undated, without catalogue number, Brecht-forschungsstätte Augsburg. The line I have quoted is an addition to the typescript in Brecht's hand.
[23] See Bork to Alexander Abusch, 19 March 1954, BArch DR 1/18169.
[24] See Bork to Knoll, 17 July 1954; and Knoll to Bork, 27 July 1954, ibid.
[25] See Fritz Apelt to Weigel, 10 August 1954, *Briefwechsel*, p. 66.
[26] See Elfriede Bork, '[Memorandum]', 25 October 1954, n.p., BBA uncatalogued file 'Aktuelles'.
[27] See Bork to Alexander Abusch, 27 September 1955, BArch DR 1/18169.
[28] See Weigel to Langhoff, 1 August 1955, BBA uncatalogued file 'Aktuelles'.

able to consolidate its reputation and display its artistic as well as its political power.

The Berliner Ensemble's new start at the Theater am Schiffbauerdamm

The Theater am Schiffbauerdamm is a neo-Baroque theatre, festooned with stucco mouldings. The pompous architecture very much appealed to Brecht: not only was the stucco a mark of conscious theatricality, but the idea that working people could watch his theatre from bombastic boxes reflected the transformed social relations in the new socialist society.[29] The theatre's proscenium arch also emphasized the act of showing, as the action would always inhabit an overt frame. One feature that did not please Brecht was the imperial eagle above what was once the Kaiser's box. Unable to remove it because the theatre was a listed building, he instructed a technician simply to paint a diagonal red cross over the emblem to strike it out.[30] The cross remains to this day as a symbol of Brecht's republicanism and represents a better solution to the problem in hindsight. Weigel was keen to update the new theatre's technical capabilities in order to realize the BE's productions as Brecht intended. Sound engineer Helmut Schlafke reports that the BE built a small recording studio in one of the auditorium's boxes in 1954, which was then extended in 1955 to accommodate the aural demands of *Winterschlacht* (*Battle in Winter*).[31] He also notes that Brecht got the bright, white lighting he craved,[32] although it was only after Brecht died that the theatre was able successfully to test 1000W luminaires that brought the GDR, at least in one theatre, up to the level to which the FRG had already become accustomed.[33]

The BE opened at the Schiffbauerdamm with a production of Molière's *Don Juan* in Brecht's adaptation on 19 March 1954. The show featured Erwin Geschonneck, the proletarian actor who played Matti in the BE's first ever production, in the title role. He found the part challenging, due to the divergence between his own biography and the social position of Don Juan as aristocrat.[34] Brecht's casting suggestion, emphasizing his

---

[29] See Brecht to Lion Feuchwanger, October/November 1954, BFA, 30: 276; and Brecht, in Anon., 'Über die Arbeit am Berliner Ensemble', in Hecht (ed.), *Brecht im Gespräch*, pp. 154–74, here p. 174.

[30] See Bömelburg, *Hobellied*, p. 45.

[31] Helmut Schlafke, unpublished interview with John Rouse, 24 May 1988, p. II-1.

[32] Ibid., p. II-14.

[33] See [Weigel] to Kurt Bork, 29 November 1957, BBA uncatalogued file 'HW Allg. Schriftwechsel 1957'.

[34] See Geschonneck, *Meine unruhigen Jahre*, p. 156.

predilection for difference, paid off, and the contrasts were praised in the press.[35] The production was hardly radical, but its humour and precision proved a solid and popular choice for the opening show in the BE's new home.

Don Juan was followed by one of the BE's best-known productions, *Der kaukasische Kreidekreis* (*The Caucasian Chalk Circle*). Brecht, assisted by Wekwerth, started rehearsals on 17 November 1953, and the play premiered on 7 October 1954. Although the dates give the impression that rehearsals lasted for almost a year, this is not actually the case. Rather, there were four phases: (i) 17 November–15 December 1953; (ii) 11 January–11 March; (iii) 29 April–22 June; and (iv) 22 August–6 October 1954,[36] so, roughly six months in total, which is, of course, not a short period at all. The third phase should actually have been the final one, but the State Workshops could not provide the BE with sets and costumes in time, and so while previews took place, there was no premiere.[37]

Brecht's production of *The Caucasian Chalk Circle* marks an important refinement of his dialectical theatre. In 1954, Brecht noted that the most interesting read of that year had been Mao's *On Contradiction*.[38] Friedemann Weidauer has asserted that Brecht's public approval of the essay is not enough to confirm a shift to Maoism, and that merely stating that the essay 'reaffirmed Brecht's trust in the dialectic' tells us nothing terribly new.[39] Yet it was not the case that Mao merely reinforced Brecht's theoretical model of reality: the text both changed the way Brecht viewed the dialectic in theory and fundamentally influenced the way he translated it into practice. Mao declared that all dialectics were not equal. Brecht adopted Mao's term 'Hauptwiderspruch' ('main contradiction') and urged theatre-makers to consider how it was to be resolved in revisions to the 'Short Organon' in 1954.[40] The introduction of a hierarchy into the dialectical method represents a restriction of its unsystematic mechanism by interpreting it in terms of a master narrative and a series of supplementary ones. Meg Mumford has drawn attention to this limitation when she identifies 'something closed about the performed structure of opposition, as if the promise of offering up multiple options had been

[35] See, for example, Lothar Kusche, '*Don Juan* am Schiffbauerdamm', *Die Weltbühne*, no date supplied, pp. 502–4 (503).

[36] Dates taken from Hans Bunge, 'Tagebuch einer Inszenierung', BBA 944/1–105, 945/1–101, and AdK Bunge-Archiv File 1145.

[37] See Bunge, 'Tagebuch', BBA 945/85.

[38] See Brecht, '[Antwort auf eine Umfrage nach dem besten Buch 1954]', BFA, 23: 339.

[39] See Friedemann Weidauer, 'Brecht's (Brush with) Maoism', *Brecht Yearbook*, 36 (2011), pp. 189–99 (192 and 197, respectively).

[40] Brecht, '[Weitere Nachträge zum "Kleinen Organon"]', BFA, 23: 293; *BoT*, p. 260.

Fig. 4.1. Loaded dialectics: a gestic, visual contradiction in the play's most recognizable scene. *The Caucasian Chalk Circle*, October 1954.

replaced by a presentation of "the" alternative, the "socially efficacious" way of behaving, the "better" social solution'.[41] It may well be the case that Brecht saw the 'main contradiction' of labour and capital as eminently well suited to theatre work in the GDR, but this was certainly not the only contradiction one could ascribe as 'main' (gender and ethnicity are two obvious rival contenders, should one choose to order the complexities of the dialectic hierarchically). Brecht's binary dialectics received theoretical support from a contemporary communist classic in the form of Mao's short book, and Brecht sought to ascribe economics-driven readings to the contradictions of *The Caucasian Chalk Circle* (and, indeed, subsequent productions). If, for example, one considers the photograph of the 'chalk circle test' itself (see Fig. 4.1), it is clear that the

---

[41] Meg Mumford, 'Brecht on Acting for the 21st Century: Interrogating and Re-Inscribing the Fixed', *Communications from the International Brecht Society*, 29: 1 and 2 (2000), pp. 44–9 (45).

acquisitive governor's wife pulls the child as if he were a commodity, emphasizing the financial nexus in the scene. The dialectical promise of the theoretical writings became ever more compromised as Brecht coloured its opposing terms with ever more pre-determined meaning.

The Caucasian Chalk Circle at the BE has been described and analysed by two scholars, John Fuegi and Meg Mumford,[42] and I will therefore comment on certain aspects of its reception, together with that of *Don Juan*, to show the altered conditions under which the BE was working in the wake of 1953. *Don Juan* was an adaptation of a classic text, yet it did not attract the kinds of criticism associated with *The Broken Jug* or *Urfaust*. Instead, one finds reviews emphasizing the freshness of the interpretation and its social contextualization.[43] A little like the production of *Vassa Zheleznova*, critics viewed the production as a document of a class in decline, but this time, the BE chose to portray this comically. Hermann Martin found the interpretation agreeable and stated that the play had been directed 'in a partisan fashion'.[44] The BE's rehabilitation was made all the more complete when the production featured as the company's first ever front-page cover on the GDR's theatre magazine *Theater der Zeit*, followed by a positive review in the next issue.[45]

Despite the possible impression that the GDR had suffered a sudden irreversible outbreak of cultural liberalism, there is evidence to suggest that there was life in some old arguments yet when regarding the reception of *The Caucasian Chalk Circle*. The editors of the BFA attribute to the overwhelming thrust of the GDR responses to the production 'the character of a reckoning' with epic theatre, its forms and its means.[46] The SED's newspaper, *Neues Deutschland*, did not even print a review of the production. Yet Fritz Erpenbeck, who had left the StaKuKo because he felt too bound by the official line,[47] was happy to reprise his customary critiques of Brecht's mixture of epic and dramatic elements in his review in *Theater der Zeit*, and warned the director that he was approaching an

---

[42] See Fuegi, *Chaos*, pp. 132–67, for an account that seeks to expunge any trace of theory (even though Bunge's record *does* include reference to *Verfremdung* – see Bunge, 'Tagebuch', BBA 945/93 – and other theoretical terms); and Meg Mumford, *Bertolt Brecht* (Abingdon and New York: Routledge, 2009), pp. 91–129, for a more balanced description and analysis.

[43] See, for example, Jürgen Rühle, '*Don Juan* – ausgegraben und aufgeputzt', *Sonntag*, 11 April 1954.

[44] Hermann Martin, 'In die Hölle mit Don Juan', *BZ am Abend*, 29 March, 1954.

[45] See cover of *Theater der Zeit*, 4 (1954); and H.-D. Sander, '*Don Juan*', *Theater der Zeit*, 5 (1954), pp. 44–6. The same issue celebrated the 200th performance of *Mother Courage*.

[46] The editors, 'Wirkung', BFA, 8: 469.

[47] See Susanne Misterek, *Polnische Dramatik in Bühnen- und Buchverlagen der Bundesrepublik Deutschland und der DDR* (Wiesbaden: Harrassowitz, 2002), p. 46.

artistic 'dead end'.[48] Hans Bunge recalls how he felt incensed by the review and wrote a rebuttal, although this was not at Brecht's behest.[49] Brecht had been reluctant to conduct his battles in the GDR's press and preferred to let his theatre speak for him instead.[50] The SED also found the production problematic, but for thematic, rather than formal reasons. According to Heiner Müller, Alexander Abusch was stunned by the play's utilitarian epilogue, which he linked with the arguments white South African racists made about themselves as being better suited to governing than black Africans.[51]

Elsewhere, the BE's adoption of an image by Picasso was fanning old flames, too. Picasso had been associated with the BE since its inception; Brecht had insisted that its productions at the DT have Picasso's dove of peace draped on the curtain, not only for its obvious meaning, but also, according to Wolfgang Bömelburg, to differentiate BE productions from those of the DT.[52] The new Picasso image, which was used in BE publicity materials, depicted four differently coloured faces looking outwards with another dove of peace in the middle. A message in a number of languages wished peace to all nations. However, the abstract nature of the image provoked a series of letters both attacking the BE for and defending it against the charge of formalism. It is perhaps a sign of the BE's newfound self-confidence that it printed nine of these in the programme to *The Caucasian Chalk Circle*.[53] The formalism campaign had effectively ended with the dissolution of the StaKuKo in 1953, and its replacement with the Ministry of Culture in 1954. However, it seems that its ideas reverberated beyond its lifespan in the popular, political imagination.

The BE's relationship with amateur theatre

Alongside the productions of *Don Juan* and *Chalk Circle* on the BE's main stage, other work was being offered as studio performances. The deliberate shift to a less formal environment reflected the different status

---

[48] Fritz Erpenbeck, 'Episches Theater oder Dramatik?', *Theater der Zeit*, 12 (1954), pp. 16–21 (17).

[49] See Hans Bunge, in Anon., '[Conversation between Hans Bunge and Matthias Braun]', undated, 31 pages (23), HWA FH 21.

[50] See Ernst Kahler, in Charlotte Braun, 'Gespräch mit Ernst Kahler über Helene Weigel und Bertolt Brecht am 2.7.1980 in Berlin [with Matthias Braun]', undated, 24 pages (6), HWA FH 56.

[51] See Heiner Müller, *Krieg ohne Schlacht*, *Werke*: 9: 98.

[52] See Bömelburg, *Hobellied*, p. 20.

[53] Seven of the letters, together with the image itself, can be found in Friedrich Dieckmann and Karl-Heinz Drescher (eds.), *Die Plakate des Berliner Ensembles 1949–1989* (Hamburg: Europäische Verlagsanstalt, 1992), pp. 229–30 and p. 191, respectively.

of the work. The BE engaged with the potential problems of amateur theatre in three short productions, although it had actually started this work
while still at the DT. When Brecht wrote about amateur theatre, he was
talking about workers theatre, of untrained men and women improving
themselves through art. He believed that the professional theatre should
help these groups by sharing its experiences and enriching the amateurs'
production process. He was also of the opinion that both traditions could
learn from each other.[54] However, there is little evidence of a reciprocal arrangement in the BE's approach; instead, one only finds the BE
offering versions of its own dialectical theatre in simplified forms for the
benefit of the amateurs.

The first palpable contribution the BE made to amateur performance
was the publication of a book written by Wekwerth that sets out, step
by step, how an amateur group might approach staging Hauptmann's
Der Biberpelz (The Beaver Coat).[55] The Zentralhaus für Laienkunst
(the Centre for Amateur Art) in Leipzig had commissioned Wekwerth,
although he had never actually worked on the production of the play with
amateurs.[56] This initial position perhaps best demonstrates just how little
dialogue there was between the BE as a professional company and the
amateur theatre. In the same vein, Käthe Rülicke also outlined the BE's
plans for a connection with amateur theatre in the year Wekwerth's book
was published (1953): the BE was searching for suitable plays that could
be performed by professionals in such a way that amateur groups could
re-stage them themselves without great difficulty. She added that the BE
hoped to publish a special series of *Modellbücher* to give the groups access
to the BE's materials.[57]

At the time, the BE was developing three pieces: the medieval adaptation *Hans Pfriem oder Kühnheit zahlt sich aus (Hans Pfriem, or Bold-
ness Pays Off)*, the nineteenth-century Berlin farce *Schuster Pinne in der
Patsche (Cobbler Pinne in a Pickle)* and the twentieth-century political
piece *Hirse für die Achte (Millet for the Eighth Army)*. The three were
staged by young directors (Rülicke, Angelika Hurwicz and Wekwerth,
respectively). There is little material on *Schuster Pinne*, but *Pfriem* and
Hirse were published as *Modellbücher*.[58] Both books are beautiful objects

---

[54] See Brecht, '[Das Laientheater der Werktätigen]', BFA, 23: 190.
[55] See Wekwerth, *Wir arbeiten an Gerhart Hauptmanns Komödie 'Der Biberpelz'*, ed. by the
      Zentralhaus für Laienkunst (Halle: Mitteldeutscher Verlag, 1953).
[56] Wekwerth, unpublished interview with the author, 14 June 2011.
[57] See Rülicke, 'Die Laienspielbrigade im Berliner Ensemble', *Volkskunst*, 2: 12 (1953),
      pp. 24–5.
[58] See Martino Hayneccio, *Hans Pfriem der Kühnheit zahlt sich aus*, with *Notate* by Käthe
      Rülicke (Leipzig: Friedrich Hoffmann, 1955); and Loo Ding *et al.*, *Hirse für die Achte*,
      with additional material by Manfred Wekwerth (Leipzig: Friedrich Hoffmann, 1956).

and do not betray in the slightest that the GDR suffered from a paper shortage. The format of the *Pfriem* book is extraordinary: when this book is open, the right-hand page is in fact a double page folded in on itself. When folded, the page as it stands is blank, awaiting the amateur group's notes; unfolded, one finds photos and a commentary on directorial decisions. The text itself is on the corresponding left-hand page. Such a book presented itself as deliberately unfinished, awaiting, as it was, input on the blank pages from the troupe staging the play. The *Millet* book is not quite as elaborate, although it includes all those elements in more standard form. It does, however, contain a pull-out supplement that features colour illustrations of the main characters in costume and the set. The GDR's Amt für Literatur (Office for Literature) supported their publication with a subsidy,[59] something refused to the BE's *Theaterarbeit* earlier in the 1950s. Such official approval reflects both the impact of 17 June 1953 on earlier dogmatic positions and the SED's more pragmatic enthusiasm to encourage amateur art through the best of examples.

A conference celebrating two years of the Centre for Amateur Art strongly supported the BE's endeavours. In an article that did appear in *Neues Deutschland*, in April 1954, the author reported that many amateur groups at the conference had requested that the BE send them its documentations as quickly as possible and praised the 'exemplary example' set by the BE, after such a long wait in the GDR.[60] The connection with the amateur stage extended until the late 1950s when Weigel appointed a dramaturge, Herbert Fischer, with the remit of supporting amateur groups in the GDR, West Berlin and the FRG.[61] Fischer appears to have remained at the BE until at least 1960 when he directed Brecht's *Die Ausnahme und die Regel* (*The Exception and the Rule*) with two BE actors in the lead roles and amateurs playing everything else.[62] By this time, the relationship had become at least a little more reciprocal.

However, the interest in amateur theatre in the mid 1950s and its diminution in importance in the early 1960s reflects an important shift in the BE. Initially, the BE was keen to act as a cultural dynamo, using

---

[59] See Rülicke, 'Aktennotiz', 14 January 1956, BBA 771/22.

[60] See Siegfried Gläss, 'Eine hilfreiche Hand für unsere Dramatischen Zirkel', *Neues Deutschland*, 27 April 1954.

[61] See Anon., 'Beschlußprotokoll der Besprechung mit den Regieassistenten am 22. September 1958', undated, 3 pages (2), BEA File 'Protokolle Dramaturgie Sitzungen 1957–1964'.

[62] See Uta Pintzka, 'Aus der Arbeit unserer Brigaden', 2–3 ([1960]), 50 pages (43), HWA 113.

its profile not only to expand its own sphere of influence, but to make a concrete contribution to theatre culture in other areas, too. Brecht sought to spread the impact of his new theatre as widely as possible, although, as is evident, he was more willing to disseminate his own practice, rather than to learn from the practice of others. After his death and without his impetus, the BE's ambitions became more limited and conventional in terms of what theatre as an institution could do.

The international dimension: the BE's early tours and the breakthrough in Paris and London

As the 'Theaterprojekt B.' document bears out, Brecht had always understood touring to be an important part of his new company's activities. The ability to perform beyond Berlin was a way of both spreading what he considered exemplary practice and raising the company's profile. The BE started touring the FRG before the company was a month old, and of the eleven German cities it visited in 1950, six were in the West. At the time, the SED had been pursuing a policy that aspired to reunify Germany, and it would seem that the BE allowed itself to play its own small role in this larger context. However, the BE was not immune to the negative aspects of SED policy either. It successfully presented *The Tutor* in Leipzig in March 1951, yet the original plan had been to perform *The Mother*. The Ministry of People's Education had insisted on the change 'a few days before departure',[63] presumably due to the SED's hostility to the production, noted in the previous chapter. The BE did tour *The Mother* in three GDR cities later that year, so one can appreciate that policy was at best fluid in such domestic matters.

It is the BE's international touring programme that established its reputation without and bolstered it within the GDR. Before 1949 was over, the Department, as it still was, of People's Education toyed with the idea of the BE touring Budapest.[64] This did not take place. The BE's first trip beyond German soil was to neighbouring Austria where it performed *The Tutor* in September 1950 at the left-wing Neue Scala theatre in Vienna, a home to many returned émigrés. In a way, then, this was not a 'proper' foreign tour as such – the audience understood the language, and the staff and actors were very much a part of a politically committed German theatre tradition. The first attempt to tour beyond the German-speaking countries came to nothing as a result of political antagonism. A tour to Venice in 1951 was apparently wrecked by interference from

---

[63] See logbook entry for March 1951, BEA File 'Logbücher 50–52'.
[64] See Anon., untitled, 15 November 1949, 44 pages (41), BArch DR 2/8237.

Italy's conservative prime minister, De Gasperi, despite the intervention of the Biennale's director.[65] (Venice would become something of a 'bogey' destination over the years: it similarly refused to host the BE in the wake of the erection of the Wall despite protests from fans outside the theatre.)[66] After this false start, the BE became the first German theatre company to tour Poland, and it took *Mother Courage*, *The Mother*, and *The Broken Jug* in December 1952. Rülicke reports that Brecht considered it important to tour socialist countries in order to find out whether work written under capitalism had any 'meaning' for them.[67]

It is a mark of the chaos in the GDR in 1953 that this was the only year the BE did not tour in its entire history. Yet, it more than made up for the deficit in June 1954 when all the hard work of the previous seasons catapulted it into the international limelight. The BE took both *Courage* and *Jug* to Paris, but it was the former that predominantly garnered the praise. The tour was clearly important to the BE, and the company was keen to show off productions that were of the highest possible standard. That meant manufacturing a revolving stage that could be taken abroad,[68] in order to replicate the Berlin *Courage* as accurately as possible. The Parisian audience was already familiar with the play from a production directed by Jean Vilar, the founder of the Festival d'Avignon and the Théâtre National Populaire. However, one reviewer wrote that while he did not want to denigrate Vilar's achievement, the BE's was far superior.[69] Another commented on the BE as performing theatre of which one had previously only dreamt, and a young Roland Barthes noted the distinction between the constriction of the characters on stage and the freedom of thought in the audience.[70] The only major paper to find fault with the production was the conservative *Le Figaro*,[71] although this seemed thoroughly out of step with the popular reception at the Théâtre Sarah Bernhardt. Indeed, so popular was the BE that it returned the following June with *The Caucasian Chalk Circle*, to even

[65] See Anon., '*Mutter Courage* nicht in Venedig', *Informationen Deutsches Friedenskomitee*, 29 (1951), pp. 43–4.

[66] See Weigel to Bork, 5 December 1964, BBA uncatalogued file 'HW BE-MfK 1961–67'.

[67] Rülicke, in Erdmut Wizisla, 'Gespräch mit Käthe Rülicke-Weiler über Helene Weigel und Bertolt Brecht am 8.11.1984 in ihrer Berliner Wohnung [with Matthias Braun]', undated, 38 pages (16).

[68] See Bömelburg, *Hobellied*, pp. 48–9.

[69] See Guy Leclerc, 'Paris a Fait un Accueil Triumphal aux Acteurs Berlinois de *Mère Courage*', *L'Humanité*, 1 July 1954.

[70] See Anon., 'Un Festival D'Erreurs', *L'Express*, 24 July 1954; and Roland Barthes, 'Théâtre Capital', *Observateur*, 8 July 1954, respectively.

[71] See Jean-Jacques Gautier, 'Au Festival de Paris *Mère Courage* de Bertolt Brecht', *Le Figaro*, 1 July 1954.

greater adulation: this time the same reviewer at *Le Figaro* wished that the BE would stay longer.[72]

Brecht had been sharply criticized in the West for supporting the SED in the part-published letter to Ulbricht of 17 June 1953. In a letter written to his old friend Lion Feuchtwanger after the second Paris tour, he noted that 'since Paris there's no real danger in staging a play of mine in Western Europe'.[73] He considered himself vindicated; his belief in letting the theatre do the talking instead of fulminating himself in public had paid off. In the same letter, he noted that Peggy Ashcroft, John Gielgud and George Devine of the English Stage Company had spoken to him during their tour of Berlin and were very keen to bring the BE to England. The plan was quickly realized and the BE were guests at London's Palace Theatre for a three-week residency from 27 August to 15 September 1956. The BE's repertoire reflects its confidence insofar as, in addition to its two Paris hits, *Courage* and *Chalk Circle*, it included its adaptation of George Farquhar's *The Recruiting Officer*, *Pauken und Trompeten* (*Trumpets and Drums*). The British critics mixed appreciation for the new possibilities of theatre with a scepticism towards what they understood to be Brecht's theoretical ambitions.[74] The experiment with *Trumpets* was not entirely successful due to the language barrier – the BE performed in German without surtitles or translators; its comedy was more difficult to apprehend for speakers of English. The tour did gain the company one notable admirer, Kenneth Tynan, for whom Brecht was to become a point of reference in his subsequent theatre criticism.[75] Tynan later brought the BBC arts programme *Monitor* to the BE to film a twenty-minute item in 1960.[76] Important figures in GDR television promised to support the plan as it would reflect well on the GDR abroad.[77] This factor was, of course, of prime importance to the authorities and can be seen in their relationship to the BE after its international success.

Laura Bradley writes that the BE's ability to tour the West meant that it was able to go to places that the GDR's diplomats could not;[78] the

[72] See Jean-Jacques Gautier, 'L'Allemagne de l'est présente: *Le Cercle de Craie Caucasien*', *Le Figaro*, 22 June 1955.
[73] Brecht to Lion Feuchtwanger, 28 September 1955, BFA, 30: 378; *Letters*, p. 549.
[74] See, for example, John Barber, 'The Extraordinary Leading Lady who Startled London Last Night', *Daily Express*, 28 August 1956.
[75] See Kenneth Tynan, 'Braw and Brecht', *Observer*, 2 September 1956.
[76] See Kenneth Tynan to Weigel, 18 October 1960, BBA uncatalogued file 'HW M-Z 1960'.
[77] See Heinz Adameck and Werner Fehlig to Weigel, 21 November 1960, ibid.
[78] See Laura Bradley, *Cooperation and Conflict. GDR Theatre Censorship 1961–1989* (Oxford: Oxford University Press, 2010), p. 3.

state would not properly be recognized until the détente of the early 1970s. James Smith views the BE as 'a particularly valuable bargaining chip for the GDR' in such dealings.[79] While both authors are writing about the BE in the 1960s, official documents show that this was also the case earlier. Brecht's international reputation was a factor in the BE securing the Theater am Schiffbauerdamm. After the about-turn on that question, the SED's support came in more concrete forms. The GDR was not a wealthy country at this time, and the acquisition of hard foreign currency cost it dearly. Nonetheless, the authorities realized the potential importance of the BE abroad and made a plentiful supply of French Francs available to support the first Paris tour.[80] Such assistance over the years was rewarded both in public adulation and private communication. In 1956, the impresario Peter Daubeny, who had brought the BE to London, wrote to Minister Becher to report the tour's success. He also noted that members of the British government had seen the BE's performances.[81] The GDR did not, of course, have bottomless pockets and this prevented what would have been the first ever trip of a GDR theatre to the USA in 1959.[82] In this case, the cost in terms of foreign currency outweighed the prestige of such a cultural coup.

The BE itself also benefitted from international interest. Peter Huchel reports that Brecht considered the BE and Huchel's journal *Sinn und Form* 'the best visiting cards the GDR has'.[83] The effect of the Paris tour was, almost instantly, to raise the BE's standing in the eyes of the State. This coincided with the post-1953 cultural thaw, and so it is difficult to ascertain whether the lack of criticism from the SED can be attributable solely to the BE's international success. However, there is no doubt that it certainly helped. The BE was becoming stronger as an institution in its own right, something that would play to its advantage in its dealings over the years. It could thus refuse a one-month residency in Paris in 1959 because it would have adversely affected production work in Berlin.[84] However, it also recognized its role as a standard-bearer for the GDR. The Central Committee was made aware that the BE had postponed a performance in the FRG on 10 September 1960 to mark the death

[79] James Smith, 'Brecht, the Berliner Ensemble, and the British Government', *New Theatre Quarterly*, 22: 4 (2006), pp. 307–23 (311).
[80] See Alexander Abusch, in Anon., 'Notat zu Gespräch mit Alexander Abusch am 31.1.79', undated, n.p., HWA FH 15.
[81] See Peter Daubeny to Johannes R. Becher, 17 September 1956, BArch Dr 1/8227.
[82] See Irene Gysi to Weigel, 4 August 1959, BArch DR 1/7851.
[83] Peter Huchel, in Stephen Parker and Matthew Philpotts, *Sinn und Form. The Anatomy of a Literary Journal* (Berlin and New York: de Gruyter, 2009), p. 30.
[84] See Bork to the Dept. of Cultural Relations, 9 October 1959, BArch DR 1/18249.

of the GDR's president Wilhelm Pieck.[85] Pieck had publicly supported
the BE in its early years by regularly attending productions,[86] and so
the public demonstration of respect had a political and also a personal
meaning.

The BE and the GDR were involved in a symbiotic relationship regarding touring and the reflected glory it brought. The GDR could show how
progressive culture could blossom under socialism, and the BE could
improve its own standing both at home and abroad. It is thus worth noting that while touring might be considered an appendage in the history of
most theatre companies, it actually played a major role in that of the BE.
It strengthened the BE's position domestically with the SED and raised
its profile internationally, creating interest, audiences and imitators. After
Paris and London, the BE was indisputably the GDR's most prestigious
cultural export and it would remain thus until the GDR was dissolved in
1990.

A failed attempt to avoid directing: Becher's *Winterschlacht*

Brecht's health in the GDR had never been terribly robust, and he particularly suffered from heart complaints in the last years of his life.[87] In
the wake of the lengthy rehearsals for *Chalk Circle*, Brecht reportedly told
Besson in confidence that he did not intend to direct any more sizeable
plays, preferring his young assistants to direct instead.[88] He had, however, already lined up a guest to direct the next production, Johannes
R. Becher's *Winterschlacht (Battle in Winter)*. The play is set around the
Battle of Moscow (1941–2) and follows Johannes Hörder, a middle-class
soldier whose experiences of Nazi aggression finally drive him to disobey
a barbaric order to bury pro-Soviet partisans alive and to shoot himself
dead instead. Brecht had seen the play performed in Leipzig in 1954
and was not taken by the production. He wrote to the playwright, who
was now also Minister of Culture, to tell him that the BE could stage
the play better and informed him that he would have his young team
work on the text.[89] Brecht had invited Czech communist Emil Burian

---

[85]   See Siegfried Wagner to Alfred Kurella, 12 September 1960, SAPMP BArch DY 30/IV
       2/2.026/67.
[86]   See Erwin Geschonneck, in Lang and Hillesheim, *'Denken heißt verändern...* ', p. 49.
[87]   See Stephen Parker, 'What was the Cause of Brecht's Death? Towards a Medical His-
       tory', *Brecht Yearbook*, 35 (2010), pp. 291–307.
[88]   See Lutz to her parents, 3 October 1954, BBA Lutz file 'Briefe ab Feb. 1951 bis Nov.
       1954'.
[89]   See Brecht to Johannes R. Becher, 2 February 1954, BFA, 30: 229; *Letters*, p. 527.

to re-stage the play he had successfully directed in Prague in November
1952. Brecht was most enthusiastic about his guest and believed that his
young actors would learn a lot from his colleague.[90] Hopes were also
high at the Ministry of Culture, where a letter shows how Burian and his
set designer were to travel to Berlin without an assistant director. The
Ministry believed that guest directors worked more successfully with a
German assistant.[91] As it would turn out, the decision would bring the
production to the brink of disaster.

Burian, the politically reliable guest, was a rather conventional director.
In one rehearsal, he asked that the actors delve deeply into their characters
to understand them and permitted them to move wherever they felt was
correct rather than sticking to the *Arrangements* he had sketched. He
reportedly mused: 'this scene it is not about a political, but a human
conflict'.[92] It is clear that Burian was not treating an important historical
play in an historicized manner, but rather like a timeless human tragedy.
Rülicke recalls that the production was 'the most difficult' that the BE had
attempted to date because it was confronting an audience of Germans
with their own shortcomings for not rising up against the Nazis.[93] Thus
the BE required a specifically German production, rather than one that
generalized the horrors of war as a timeless human tragedy.

Burian announced, only after arriving in Berlin, that he also had commitments back in Prague, and so the BE's assistants were charged with
maintaining the scenes while he was away. Brecht, of course, could not
keep himself away from his assistants' rehearsals, but was staggered by
what he saw. Lutz provides a first-hand account. The actors were off
book, but were moving around the stage without any sense of purpose:
'it was so funny – everyone was laughing. Except Brecht. He was livid'.[94]
She reports that the whole cast was against his 'interference', but he
proceeded calmly and reasonably from scene to scene and transformed
the production with great lightness in a very short time. She concludes
that she learned more in those few days than she had in her six years
at the BE. Brecht explained his alterations to Burian at a rehearsal he
attended on 1 December, and one may detect both anger and pride in
his admonishment:

---

[90] See Brecht to Emil Burian, 20 September 1954, BFA, 30: 270; *Letters*. p. 532.
[91] See Frau Jäger to the BE Secretariat, 13 September 1954, BBA 738/133.
[92] Anon., 'Notate *Winterschlacht*', undated, pencil note 'Burian', 15 pages (7, 9b and 14
      (quotation)), BEA File 18.
[93] Rülicke, 'Historisierende Lesarten von J.R. Bechers *Winterschlacht*', *notate*, 1 (1988),
      pp. 18–19 (p. 18).
[94] Lutz to her parents, 28 November 1954', BBA Lutz file 'Briefe ab Feb. 1951 bis Nov.
      1954'.

What I didn't understand was changed. The audience can't understand what the actors don't understand . . . That wasn't the fault of the actors. In that I brook no contradiction. I know my actors, I built this theatre from nothing.[95]

An 'agreement' was reached on the very same day: Burian would leave the production, and the BE would continue to work using certain of Burian's ideas 'in a comradely spirit'.[96] The document was a compromise, designed to spare Burian's blushes, because Brecht, co-directing with Wekwerth, had to engage fundamentally with the work already done in order to historicize the tragedy.[97]

The production (premiere 12 January 1955) moved away from the grotesquery of *Puntila* and the exaggeration of *Chalk Circle*, both of which criticized the ruling classes by presenting their representatives in prosthetics or masks. Here Brecht committed to an understanding of realism that emphasized different modes of behaviour, rather than overt theatrical nods to the audience. This direction was very much in keeping with the themes of the play and the painfulness of the action in the memories of the audience.

The central problem was the portrayal of the Nazis. The actors initially wanted to 'show' their relationship to the *Wehrmacht* by ironizing their lines, but a chance moment in rehearsal with co-director Manfred Wekwerth led to a different kind of portrayal: the soldiers needed to be heard over the noise of a real motorcycle on stage and thus had to roar our their lines. This produced 'the committed tone' required to present the soldiers' enthusiasm for their tasks.[98] However, this was not a naturalist treatment of the text. Hörder, played by Ekkehard Schall in his first lead role with the BE (see Fig. 4.2), was directed to approach his part dialectically, as 'a sympathetic young man who nonetheless spoke and acted in the manner of a Nazi'.[99] Thus Schall presented the central figure not anchored in some way to 'characteristics', but caught between certain more positive qualities and the pressures of a barbarous army. The army itself offered Brecht an institution for analysis, and thus its workings could be unpacked to show the kinds of behaviour it produced: 'this colossal chain of command with its particular customs, military ranks and traditions has to be right not only because the majority of our audience are familiar with it, but all the more so because our hero

[95] Brecht, in Heinz Kahlau, 'Notate *Winterschlacht*', undated, 35 pages (6), BEA File 18.
[96] Brecht, '[Über die Zusammenarbeit mit Burian]', BFA, 24: 450.
[97] For a fuller discussion of this process, see David Barnett, 'Undogmatic Marxism. Brecht as Director at the Berliner Ensemble', in Bradley and Leeder (eds.), *Brecht and the GDR*, pp. 25–43 (35–9).
[98] Heinz Kahlau, '*Winterschlacht* Notate', undated, n.p., BEA File18.
[99] Anon., 'Zur *Winterschlacht*', undated, BBA 940/13.

Fig. 4.2. The first of many: Ekkehard Schall (left) plays Johannes Hörder in his first lead role at the BE. *Battle in Winter*, January 1955.

is stuck in its mechanisms'.[100] As a result, the army did not emerge as an evil monolith, but as a stratified microcosm of a class-based society. In one scene, for example, the officers were directed to get drunk in a stiff, disciplined manner, as opposed to the regular soldiers, who reeled around the stage. Elsewhere, in the domestic scenes set away from the front in Germany, Brecht cast the working-class Carola Braunbock as Hörder's bourgeois mother. She complained to Brecht that she had been miscast as a fine lady, to which Brecht replied: 'you of all people can do that better than properly well-to-do people'.[101]

The production proceeded from dialectical analysis, but selected its theatrical means in order to show off contradictions in what the directors considered the most appropriate forms. While Braunbock was allowed to 'show the join' between herself and her character, the actors playing the Nazis had to emphasize the complex contradictions of their class, and it was the interaction between officers and men that exposed the fault lines running through the *Wehrmacht*. The production thus demonstrates how Brecht was not bound by particular performance modes, but proceeded from concrete social tensions to offer the audience different experiences of the materialist dialectic.

Battle in Winter was, as one might expect, mainly warmly received in the East while criticized in the West as a waste of a good production on a poor play. This position has been framed as 'politically expedient', as a thank you to the State in which playwright Becher was a minister.[102] What these charges fail to understand is the process behind the production. The documentation amply demonstrates the lengths to which Brecht and Wekwerth went to create a lively piece of theatre, aware of its obligations to its German audience, rather than to its author, whose work was extensively adapted, after all. Lyon's claim that Brecht 'overlooked artistic standards'[103] is baseless. Had he wished merely to flatter Becher, he would have let the Czech director continue his work and bathe in the reflected glory of Burian's humanist production.

The two critical voices in the East German reviews were to be found in *Neues Deutschland*, which considered the BE's divergences from Becher's original flawed,[104] and in *Theater der Zeit*. The latter commissioned a review by a dramaturge from Leipzig who, although he did not work

---

[100] Brecht, 'Schwierigkeiten, denen Burians Konzeption in Berlin begegnet', BFA, 24: 449.

[101] Brecht, in Anon., 'Notate *Winterschlacht*', undated, 14 pages (3), BEA File 18.

[102] Preuß, *Theater im ost-/westpolitschen Umfeld*, p. 598; and see Daiber, *Deutsches Theater seit 1945*, p. 132.

[103] Lyon, 'Brecht in Postwar Germany', p. 77.

[104] See Horst Knietzsch, 'Eine deutsche Tragödie', *Neues Deutschland*, 18 January 1955.

on the Leipzig production of *Battle*, nonetheless compared the two and found the BE's lacking.[105] It is to the magazine's credit that it published a counterblast from Palitzsch and Wekwerth, criticizing the reviewer for not revealing his professional provenance and noting that he had been contracted by the eternal Brecht critic, Fritz Erpenbeck.[106] Feuds within the GDR had not entirely disappeared, then, but the BE's right to reply here, as with Bunge's response to Erpenbeck's polemic on *Chalk Circle* earlier, showed that there was space in the media for a debate that would not have been possible in the early 1950s.

Time runs out: the final productions under Brecht's leadership

The BE staged two major productions before Brecht's death, Farquhar's *Trumpets and Drums* on 19 September 1955 and Synge's *The Playboy of the Western World* (staged at the BE as *Der Held der westlichen Welt*), both of which appeared in specially adapted versions.

Trumpets was revised specially for Regine Lutz, and she played Victoria Balance, the britches role in the restoration comedy. Lutz describes the difficulty of performing the three personae that Brecht told her to keep separate: '1. girl from a good family 2. plays the soldier 3. often falls out – addressing the audience – of the britches role'.[107] Mumford reads the socially complex role-play as a way of using the actor's body as critical weapon: 'the multiple subjects contributed not only to the display of gender as social costume, but also to the linking of imperialist politics with male colonializing behaviour'.[108] The gestic acting was able to provide a shifting point of reference in the manufacture of masculinity and military aggression, particularly when focused through the female body.

Farquhar's action was transplanted from the early eighteenth century to the Revolutionary America of 1776; the new version thus placed British imperialism in a context that was more concrete to the German spectator. Putting the socialist audience on the side of the nascent USA was an interesting decision on Brecht's part, in that its historicizing aims would appear to have set it up for another quarrel with the SED. Carl Weber sees the praise of the US constitution encoded in the play as a direct critique

---

[105] See Günter Kaltofen, '*Die Winterschlacht*', *Theater der Zeit*, 2 (1955), pp. 53–5.
[106] See Palitzsch and Wekwerth, 'Leipziger Allerlei', *Theater der Zeit*, 3 (1955), pp. 19–23.
[107] Lutz to her parents, 13 February 1955, BBA Lutz file 'Briefe ab Jan. 1955 bis Dez. 1956'.
[108] Meg Mumford, '"Dragging" Brecht's *Gestus* Onwards: A Feminist Challenge', in Steve Giles and Rodney Livingstone (eds.), *Bertolt Brecht Centenary Essays* (Amsterdam: Rodopi, 1998), pp. 240–57 (249).

of the GDR.[109] However, the SED was far more concerned that the play
was in some way pacifist. The FRG was remilitarizing and founded the
Bundeswehr a month after the premiere, and the GDR followed suit in
1956 with the formation of the *Nationale Volksarmee* (National People's
Army – NVA). Carl Wege notes that the premiere was actually put back
by four months so that it could be performed 'in a version purged of any
possible misinterpretation'.[110] That said, Rülicke still had to convince a
Pole who wanted to translate the play of its un-pacifist stance in 1956,[111]
and so perhaps the text was not quite as unambiguous as was hoped.

The production of *Playboy* (premiere 11 May 1956) was a deliberate
attempt to get away from a folkloric reading, as was traditionally the case
in the performance of the play, and to apply the laws of the dialectic to
the action. Christie Mahon comes upon a rural village in Ireland and
announces that he has killed his father. The remarkable nature of such a
deed and the skill with which Christie tells his tale turn him into a hero
with the locals. When his father actually arrives, he threatens to kill the
father for real, something that then repulses them. In a series of *Notate*,
Wekwerth, who directed together with Palitzsch, showed his theoretical
adroitness. The most important point they chose to emphasize was that
it was the environment that created the hero; the mechanism of Christie's
rise and fall had to be shown.[112] Wekwerth described the dynamics of the
dialectic in abstract terms in the titles to his notes, as in the formulation
'*negation of the negation*', that is, the resolution of dialectical contradiction
into a new synthesis. However, he also concretized such philosophical terminology. For example, he observed that as long as Christie is celebrated
as a hero, his father rejects him. But when the villagers reject Christie
as a parricide, his father regains his son: he rejects the rejection. History
brings about vigorous change.

Despite all the theoretical meditation on dialectical movement, the
performance itself was not abstract or woolly. The *Notat* of a meeting
Brecht attended reveals that the specially commissioned songs were not
to have the jarring effect of those in *The Threepenny Opera*, but should
be a logical part of the action itself.[113] The songs were contributing to
the realistic conditions the BE wanted to portray. The overall aim was,
as usual, to play the situation, rather than the characters, and the need

[109] Carl Weber, unpublished interview with the author, 28 May 2010.
[110] Carl Wege, 'Spielplan(politik) und Inszenierungskalkül des Berliner Ensembles zwischen 1952 und 1956', in Thomas Jung (ed.), *Zweifel – Fragen – Vorschläge: Bertolt Brecht
anläßlich des Hundersten* (Frankfurt/Main: Peter Lang, 1999), pp. 93–8 (97).
[111] See Rülicke to Barbara Witek-Swinarska, 1 March 1956, BBA 713/119.
[112] See Wekwerth, *Schriften*, p. 131. The following example is taken from p. 132.
[113] See Anon., 'Die Musiknummern', undated, n.p., BEA File 22.

to get Ireland 'right' was a prerequisite for displaying the mechanisms at work in the construction of heroes amongst the rural poor.

The production was mainly well received, but the programme that accompanied the show drew an amount of criticism.[114] Its attempt at topicality, by equating Christie with Hitler as a 'hero' who had been made by the people, were crass and detracted from the quality of the production itself, which never otherwise broke frame through direct commentary on other instances of 'heroism'. Ultimately, it was the production itself that led to a five-year run of 105 performances. Perhaps the greatest praise came from the Dublin Festival Company, which visited East Berlin in 1960. Actor Donal Donelly acknowledged that while the BE production diverged greatly from the Irish tradition, there was still something 'typically Irish' about it.[115]

After these two successes, Brecht began rehearsing *Leben des Galilei* (*Life of Galileo*), a production I will discuss in the next chapter. Rehearsals commenced on 14 December 1955. Brecht was ill from 19 to 23 February 1956, and Benno Besson took over while he was away. Besson, however, could not work with the strong-willed Ernst Busch, who played Galileo, and suggested that Erich Engel take over. Brecht reportedly replied 'Engel can hone away, but he doesn't understand me'.[116] On 27 March, because he did not like the way Busch was working, Brecht stopped the rehearsal early; it was to be his last. Engel took over from the ailing Brecht on 29 March. Everyone expected that Brecht would convalesce and recover, to take up rehearsals again, but this was not the case. He died on 14 August 1956 and left a void that nobody in the BE was certain could be filled.

---

[114] See, for example, Sabine Lietzmann, 'Der Mann, was seinen Papa killte', *Frankfurter Allgemeine Zeitung*, 17 May 1956.

[115] Donelly, in Anon., 'Irisches Lob für Berliner Ensemble', *Der Morgen*, 2 October 1960.

[116] Besson, in Neubert-Herwig (ed.), *Benno Besson: Theater spielen in acht Ländern*, p. 35.

5   Developing the Brechtian legacy: 1956–1961

The SED's problematic apotheosis of the dead Brecht

Brecht was buried on 17 August 1956 and, in accordance with his wishes, no words were spoken at the grave. However, there was no shortage of speeches the following day at the memorial service. Two prominent orators set the agenda for what would become an official attempt to neutralize Brecht's critical legacy and canalize Brecht for the GDR. That Walter Ulbricht spoke was at once understandable, given that he was *de facto* the State's most senior politician and that the BE had become *the* jewel in the GDR's cultural crown, and an affront, due to his hostility towards the BE in the preceding years. Indeed, Rülicke recalled in 1958 that Minister Paul Wandel had deliberately kept Brecht and Ulbricht apart for fear of the irreparable damage such a meeting might cause.[1] Ulbricht's speech honoured 'the most important dramatist of the day', and he noted 'the duty to provide him with a space to realize his creative plans in the Berliner Ensemble'.[2] That Ulbricht had approved the plan to station the KVP in the Theater am Schiffbauerdamm instead of the BE was conveniently forgotten, of course. Brecht the theorist was also quietly omitted in favour of the great playwright and the campaigner for world peace. The BE, an institution now effectively impossible to silence due to its international profile, was implicitly charged with continuing its work without the millstone of Brecht's theories.

The more surprising choice of funeral eulogist was György Lukács, the Hungarian theorist and literary critic, whom Brecht, as late as 1955, had criticized for his deleterious effect on modern literature.[3] Lukács' speech 'celebrated a Brecht who had succeeded in spite of his own

---

[1] See Rülicke, in Anon., ' Gespräch über Bertolt Brecht mit Käthe Rülicke am 13. Dezember 1958', undated, 48 pages (34), SAPMO BArch DY 30/IV 2/2.024/49.

[2] Ulbricht, in Anon., 'Ansprache des Ersten Stellvertreters des Vorsitzenden des Ministerrats, Walter Ulbricht, auf der Staatsfeier zum Gedächtnis von Bertolt Brecht am 18. August 1956', undated, 3 pages (1 and 2, respectively), BArch NY 4182/1387.

[3] See Brecht to Wolfgang Harich, 5 January 1955, BFA, 30: 295–6, *Letters*, p. 534.

intentions, in spite of his own theory of epic theatre'.[4] Both speakers clearly hoped that Brecht's official canonization would retain the plays without the potentially subversive baggage of the theory with its power dialectically to question and challenge historical and political issues. The SED's responses to Brecht's ideas, rather than his plays, in the following years bears ample witness to this desire. Three years after Brecht's death, Weigel complained to Hans Grümmer at the Central Committee's Cultural Department about Comrade Drohma at the District Leadership in Berlin. He had proposed 'an ideological examination' to establish 'whether Brecht's methods were applicable to other theatres and other plays [than Brecht's]'.[5] Weigel threatened to stand down as *Intendantin* if the party was about to launch a new 'campaign against Brecht'. Grümmer assured Weigel that that was not the case and that the Party's relationship to Brecht remained exactly the same as in Ulbricht's oration. Which was something of an ambiguous guarantee.

An official declaration in 1960 at a conference on acting contended that Brecht had been fully rehabilitated thanks to the BE's exemplary productions of his work.[6] However, later that year, all mention of Brecht had been excised from a revised draft of another official conference's programme, a position that an unnamed official found 'shameful'.[7] Kurt Bork, who had risen to the rank of Deputy Minister in 1962, was also someone who did not acknowledge the 'rehabilitation' in its entirety. He objected to the mention of the term 'the theatre of the scientific age' in a message from Weigel for World Theatre Day in 1966, which she had submitted to the Ministry, as required, in advance.[8] He conceded, however, that there was no chance that she would remove the phrase because Brecht had coined it and that she was nonetheless a useful international advocate for the GDR. A year later, Bork advised against the Acting Academy in Halle introducing a course on the value of Brecht's theory and practice for contemporary theatre: 'I consider it necessary to oppose

---

[4] Stefan Mahlke, 'Klassisch = Episch: Brecht als Agent seiner Produktion', in Birgit Dahlke, Martina Langermann and Thomas Taterka (eds.), *LiteraturGesellschaft* [*sic*] *DDR: Kanonkämpfe und ihre Geschichte(n)* (Stuttgart and Weimar: Metzler, 2000), pp. 146–72 (152).

[5] Hans Grümmer, 'Aktennotiz', 23 May 1959, 2 pages (1), SAPMO BArch DY 30/IV 2/2/026/67. The following quotation and reference are taken from pp. 1 and 2, respectively.

[6] See Hans Pischner, in Anon., 'Rede des Stellvertreters des Ministers, Professor Pischner, für Schauspielkonferenz, Januar 1960 in Berlin', undated, 70 pages (8), BArch DR 1/7851.

[7] Anon., 'Aus den Thesen zur Schauspielkonferenz – Januar 1960', [c. September 1960], 2 pages (2), SAPMO BArch DY 30/IV 2/2.026/67.

[8] See Bork to [Minister of Culture] Klaus Gysi, 11 January 1966, BArch DR 1/8845.

such tendencies shrewdly and to correct them'.[9] The 'shrewd' nature of the opposition meant that the process should take place as covertly as possible, so as not to ruffle Weigel's or anyone else's feathers from afar.

These examples reveal that what Brecht's theories and ideas about theatre represented continued to discomfort the authorities for well over a decade after his death and echo Ulbricht's and Lukács' tacit attempts to reduce their effects in 1956. It was primarily the BE's efforts to continue, develop and disseminate Brecht's work that kept the connection between theory and practice alive. Yet the BE's future success was far from inevitable in the wake of Brecht's death, and the theatre had to negotiate a series of thorny questions as to how it was to survive its great loss.

The quest for new artistic directorship

Brecht's death did not leave the BE without a leader: Helene Weigel was still *Intendantin*, and it fell to her to find someone to replace the seemingly irreplaceable creative heart of the company. According to Wekwerth, Erich Engel's plan was to bring in a high-profile international director, but Weigel decided on the 'Schülervariante' ('the student option'), that is, for Wekwerth, Palitzsch and Besson, Brecht's *Schüler*, to steer the BE's artistic direction.[10] Elsewhere, Wekwerth names the potential applicants as Wolfgang Langhoff, Gustav Gründgens and Rudolf Noelte, candidates whom Weigel vetoed despite SED approval.[11] Wekwerth's is, however, a somewhat simplified and misleading account of events, contradicted by a series of developments which only came to an end with the building of the Berlin Wall.

I have found no evidence of great directors descending upon the BE. Instead Weigel wrote to Bork shortly before the BE departed for its tour to London asking whether Engel's film commitments in the GDR would prevent him from assuming the role of artistic director at the BE.[12] An agreement to free Engel from half his filming obligations was confirmed in a letter just over a month later.[13] Weigel thus did not opt for the *Schülervariante*, as Wekwerth asserts, but supported one of Brecht's established collaborators as a way of publicly continuing Brecht's traditions at the BE.

---

[9]   Bork to Willi Schrader, 7 February 1967, ibid.
[10] Wekwerth, in Lang and Hillesheim, *'Denken heißt verändern...'*, p. 187.
[11] See Wekwerth, *Erinnern ist Leben*, p. 146–7.
[12] See Weigel to Bork, 22 August 1956, BArch DR 1/6067.
[13] See Bork to Alexander Abusch, 2 October 1956, ibid.

According to Besson, Ernst Busch came up to him at Brecht's funeral wake and said 'those still alive are laughing'.[14] By this he meant that those who survived Brecht were now eyeing the vacant throne. The *Schüler* were not simply going to accept Weigel's decision to back Engel. Carl Weber and Wekwerth both report that Besson believed himself to be Brecht's natural successor.[15] This was presumably because he was the most experienced of Brecht's former assistants and had directed more productions by himself than any other assistant at the BE. However, for a short period, a more united front formed against Engel, and this can be seen during the BE's tour of the Soviet Union in the early summer of 1957. Engel had been rehearsing *The Good Person of Szechwan* with Käthe Reichel, who played the lead roles of Shen Te and Shui Ta, without director Besson's knowledge. She wrote: 'trouble is certainly unavoidable and, as Manfred [Wekwerth] thinks, now also desirable, since it's turned out that Engel's got a contract as artistic director and head director for next year'.[16] However, at the same time, tension was developing between Wekwerth and Besson, too.

Uta Birnbaum, who arrived as an assistant at the BE in 1955, and Hans-Georg Simmgen, whom Wekwerth engaged as an actor and assistant in 1957, both attest to the existence of Besson and Wekwerth factions in 1957.[17] The first major clash revolved around Besson's production of *Szechwan*, which premiered on 5 October 1957. As previously stated, Besson was not terribly satisfied with the Berlin production (see pp. 103–4), but Wekwerth was most critical of what he saw as an un-Brechtian production: in Berlin, *Szechwan* lacked the naïvety of Rostock and set about to demonstrate that the good person, Shen Te, and the evil person, Shui Ta, could not be reconciled,[18] rather than presenting them as complementary oppositions of the same dialectic. Palitzsch also offered Besson a series of orthodox Brechtian critiques days before the premiere, suggesting, for example, that the actors were playing characters rather than situations.[19] The interventions indicate that deviation from Brecht's principles would receive short shrift from the two former *Schüler*. Weigel also signalled her intentions towards the Besson camp. According to Kebir, Reichel was fired from the BE on the day of the *Szechwan* premiere.[20]

---

[14] Besson, in Irmer and Schmidt, *Die Bühnenrepublik*, p. 40.
[15] Carl Weber and Wekwerth, unpublished interviews with the author, 28 May 2010 and 14 June 2011, respectively.
[16] Käthe Reichel to Benno Besson, 26 May 1957, AdK Besson-Archiv File 140.
[17] Uta Birnbaum and Hans-Georg Simmgen, unpublished interviews with the author, 28 August 2010 and 21 July 2010, respectively.
[18] See Wekwerth, *Erinnern ist Leben*, p. 157.
[19] See Palitzsch to Besson, 2 October 1957, BEA File 25.
[20] See Kebir, *Abstieg in den Ruhm*, p. 300.

This was Weigel's way of punishing both Besson and Reichel, whose open secret was that she was one of a coterie of young women with whom Brecht had had an affair during his years at the BE. I shall return to this subject presently.

By 1958, Besson wrote an ultimatum to Weigel, demanding certain conditions that had to be satisfied for him to continue working at the BE. The ultimatum concerned his directing a production of Brecht's *Mann ist Mann* (*Man Equals Man*), which he had recently staged in Rostock. He insisted that the production take precedence over any other major work and that he co-direct with either Wekwerth or Palitzsch, 'so as to realize the desired collective collaboration'.[21] Weigel's reply was certainly conciliatory, and she hoped that they could reach an agreement.[22] His mention of the collective signals the new direction that the BE was taking. Beforehand, Brecht was the undisputed leader who commissioned his assistants to direct or co-direct whenever he was not directing himself. The BE now lacked such a centre; Engel, while formally head director was himself not in the best of health and could not provide a replacement for Brecht. The solution to Engel's lack of presence was to construct a collective leadership, although this experiment could hardly be called successful.

The minutes of a meeting held in late 1958, ostensibly to discuss how the standards of the BE's work were to be maintained, actually reads like a list of orthodox Brechtian doctrines: the retention of the centrality of the *Fabel*; measures to be taken to banish naturalism in rehearsal; and the safeguarding of realism as Brecht understood it.[23] The emphasis on the collective was also clear. Besson was sceptical about this concept at the BE and saw it merely as the name Weigel gave to 'the united front of the day' that she deployed to quell dissent.[24] In the same document, he criticized Wekwerth for his speed in making himself the most prominent former assistant and for 'the mechanical spread of Brecht's traditions'. Earlier, Besson had imagined himself, Wekwerth and Palitzsch as a triumvirate with a right of veto with respect to Weigel's decisions.[25] This position was no longer tenable once Wekwerth started to jostle for the position of first amongst equals, and Besson's time at the BE came to an end in 1959.

---

[21] Besson to Weigel, 21 August 1958, BBA uncatalogued file 'HW im Haus 1958'.
[22] See Weigel to Besson, 1 September 1958, ibid.
[23] See Isot Kilian, 'Bericht über die Besprechung vom 30.11.58 bei Frau Weigel', undated, n.p., ibid.
[24] [Besson], untitled, undated, n.p., AdK Besson-Archiv File 51.
[25] See [Besson], 'Gespräch am 12ten April [1958?] mit BPO', undated, n.p., ibid.

Besson had proposed staging Molière's *Georges Dandin* in 1958, a play about a rich peasant who dreams of upward social mobility through marriage to a young noblewoman. Besson's idea was to overturn a romantic view of the character and to include a series of intermezzos in the form of dumb-shows, dances and songs to present the varieties of upper-class life to which Dandin aspires.[26] In embryo, he was sketching a form he would pioneer to great acclaim in the early 1970s at the Volksbühne, the 'Spektakel' ('extravaganza'), in which several types of performance overlap and intersect to create something greater than the sum of its parts. The plan was rejected outright, and this triggered Besson's departure.[27] By this time, Weigel was no longer interested in a collective, but a firm artistic base. Many years later, during a more enduring crisis, she told Wekwerth that she had chosen him as her most important collaborator and that the decision had proved to be the right one.[28] Her active engagement to support Wekwerth shows that she was looking to re-establish a central figure to stabilize the company. In hindsight, Wekwerth regretted Besson's ejection and said: 'I unjustly applied my own yardstick [that is, the insistence on the collective] because I got bored when working by myself'.[29]

The third member of the erstwhile collective, Peter Palitzsch, also found the years after Brecht's death difficult. He was less vociferous than either Wekwerth or Besson, but was still an important figure in the BE's artistic leadership as a creative force in his own right. According to Wekwerth, Palitzsch was deeply unhappy that no real collective had been formed after Brecht's death.[30] He consequently took an extended break from the BE and directed ten productions in the FRG from November 1957 to April 1961.[31] Palitzsch did co-direct the most important production of the post-Brecht, pre-Wall years, *Arturo Ui*, in 1959, but this did not prevent him from staying in the West (see pp. 171–3, Chapter 6), where he was directing Brecht's *The Trial of Joan of Arc* in Ulm when the Wall was built.

The departures of both Besson and Palitzsch show that the *Schülervariante*, the response to Engel's inability and/or unwillingness to step into Brecht's shoes, fell apart relatively quickly. The criticism of

---

[26] See Besson, in Neubert-Herwig, *Benno Besson: Jahre mit Brecht*, p.140.
[27] See Isot Kilian, 'Bericht über die Besprechung bei Frau Weigel am Freitag, dem 9. Januar 1959', undated, 2 pages, marked 'vertraulich' ('confidential'), BEA File 'Protokolle Dramaturgie Sitzungen 1957–1964'.
[28] See Weigel to Wekwerth, 23 May 1968, *Briefwechsel*, p. 208.
[29] Wekwerth, *Erinnern ist Leben*, p. 158.
[30] See Wekwerth to the BE and Party Leadership, 30 November 1959, AdK JTA 'BE interne Korr./Dramat. 1959–1970'.
[31] See Iden, *Peter Palitzsch*, pp. 199–202.

Besson started in 1957 and Palitzsch's dissatisfaction can be dated to the same year. By 1961, Wekwerth was the only full-time director left at the BE (Engel directed two major productions, in 1960 and 1962, but by then he was more a guest and cannot be considered a functioning part of the BE's leadership).

Over the years since Brecht's death, Helene Weigel, the BE's other *Intendanten* and staff, reviewers and critics have frequently supported or opposed decisions and actions based on the premise that they were or were not what Brecht 'would have done'. This is perhaps an inappropriate criterion to apply in the field of production work, where one simply cannot predict how Brecht would have adapted his practice to changing social and historical contexts. But on the question of the BE's organization, it is clear that Weigel did not realize Brecht's hope for a plurality of directorial styles, capable of co-existence under the same roof. She had not sought to reconcile or even to tolerate contradiction amongst the *Schüler*, but to favour one over the others.

Weigel was also settling old scores, although one should be circumspect as to her motives and the extent of her 'campaign', if it can be called that at all. Brecht had been liberal with his affections at the BE (as he had indeed been earlier in his life), conducting affairs with actor Käthe Reichel, dramaturge Käthe Rülicke, and actor-turned-assistant Isot Kilian, sometimes concurrently. Brecht's old flame Ruth Berlau was also in Berlin, as was Elisabeth Hauptmann, although he had not been amorously involved with her since the Weimar Republic.[32] Reichel's dismissal seems to have come as a response to both her association with Besson and her relationship with Brecht. Rülicke had actually withdrawn herself from the BE after Brecht died, maintaining only a loose relationship to the company, but she inquired about whether she could return permanently in 1964. Weigel wrote that her instinctive response was to decline because she had left the BE without discussion.[33] Here it appears that Weigel felt betrayed by Rülicke during a particularly difficult time for the company, rather than venting a long-standing resentment about the affair. Indeed, Kilian, Brecht's final lover, was kept on at the BE and provided invaluable help to Weigel in the overall administration of the productions. Any trace of enmity seems to have remained private, if it existed at all, and their relationship was cordial, until Kilian left on principle following the BE's worst crisis in the late 1960s.

---

[32] This information is not quite certain, but Hauptmann-expert Paula Hanssen told me that this was likely to have been the case, in an email of 16 March 2012.
[33] See Weigel to 'dear friends', 19 June 1964, AdK JTA 'BE interne Korr./Dramat. 1959–1970'.

Weigel did not even terminate Berlau's contract with the BE upon Brecht's death, even though she had issued an official warning about Berlau's drunkenness in 1955 and criticized her for haranguing John Heartfield and Gerda Goedhart in 1956.[34] Weigel even drew up a free-lance contract for Berlau in September 1957, which was very accommodating and included a range of tasks, including photographing productions, working with young actors, and co-directing a studio production.[35] All the same, Berlau left without telling Weigel in the same month. Elisabeth Hauptmann, who had only become a full-time member of the BE in 1954,[36] was a trusted colleague to Weigel, who sought her advice on a range of matters, and who had a positive influence on the assistants.[37]

The upheaval surrounding Brecht's death led to a range of personnel changes over time, yet the BE faced a more immediate problem back in 1956: how to continue Brecht's work on *Life of Galileo*.

A switch of directors: Engel completes Brecht's *Galileo*

Brecht had planned to stage *Galileo* for some years. Weigel mentioned the technical demands of producing the play to the DT in 1950, and Brecht told Caspar Neher that he intended to premiere the play in December of that year.[38] He had hoped that his Puntila of 1949, Leonard Steckel, would reprise the title role he had played in Zurich in 1943, yet an inability to secure a suitable Galileo had led to the plan's continued deferral.[39] By 1955, Brecht convinced the slender Ernst Busch to play the corpulent scientist, and *Galileo* took precedence over another major project: Brecht's *Coriolan*.[40] However, by this time, Brecht was ailing and had intended to avoid directing lengthy plays after the exertion of *The Caucasian Chalk Circle* in 1954. His solution, in lieu of finding another director, was to use the *Modellbuch* of his Los Angeles production with

---

[34] See Weigel to Ruth Berlau, 3 June 1955 and 14 December 1956, BBA uncatalogued files 'HW Brief W 1954/5' and 'HW Allg. + Aush. Haus 1956/57', respectively.

[35] See Weigel to Ruth Berlau, 11 September 1957, BBA uncatalogued file 'HW + and. Allg. SV Haus 1957–6 '58'.

[36] See Paula Hanssen, *Elizabeth Hauptmann: Brecht's Silent Collaborator* (Bern et al.: Peter Lang, 1995), p. 128.

[37] See Wekwerth, *Schriften*, p. 27. He includes himself, Palitzsch and Besson.

[38] See Weigel to Walter Kohls, 1 August 1950, BBA uncatalogued file 'Aktuelles'; and Brecht to Caspar Neher, July 1950, BFA, 23: 29; *Letters*, p. 493.

[39] See, for example, Brecht to Fritz Kortner, 5 May 1951; and Brecht to Alexander Bardini, 28 January 1953, BFA, 30: 69 and 163, respectively; *Letters*, p. 501–2 for the letter to Kortner.

[40] See [Weigel] to Wolfgang Langhoff, 31 October 1955, BBA uncatalogued file 'Aktuelles'.

Charles Laughton in 1947 as the solid foundation on which to build the production.[41]

Meisterschüler B. K. Tragelehn followed the rehearsal process and observed the customary detail with which Brecht worked, such as the dialectical treatment of the character of the Little Monk who turns his back on the Church in favour of Galileo: 'this really is a genuine crisis of conscience: you are an honest Christian. A son of poor parents, the Church paid for your studies. And now, all of a sudden, this benefactor's been called into question'.[42] This role, like many of the others, was a difficult one, and Tragelehn reflected on the subject of great actors: 'nothing is obvious to them – everything is open to question. Thus *Verfremdung* is also present in their approach to building a character, not only in the result for the audience'.[43] However, Tragelehn later noted that Brecht's direction demanded empathy from the actor playing Cardinal Bellarmin, although he qualified this with the phrase 'at this stage of rehearsal'.[44] It is thus clear that while Brecht was happy to proceed from a set of *Arrangements* that had already proved their worth, he had to work very carefully with the actors to make sure that they could inhabit those *Arrangements* with characters that were fresh and the product of intense investigation of their social contradictions.

Yet this process proved difficult to carry out in the case of Busch. Brecht rated the actor for bringing his proletarian biography to the roles he played. He was not, however, a 'natural' Brechtian actor. Ekkehard Schall noted how Busch did not defer to his acting partners and how actors needed to find the appropriate means to keep him in check.[45] He would also come to rehearsal having read up extensively on the historical Galileo[46] and argue the toss with Brecht about scientific principles. Fuegi contends that there was no difference between Busch and 'a Stanislavsky-trained actor',[47] but this assertion suggests one has to be either one type of actor or the other. Busch certainly prepared in a way Brecht found unproductive because he arrived with fixed ideas about his character in isolation, rather than in relation to the others. Yet Rülicke registered Busch's distance to the role as well, when he continued to refer to Galileo in the third person, rather than the first.[48] Rülicke makes

---

[41] See B. K. Tragelehn, 'Notate', undated, n.p., BEA File 23, who notes that Brecht initially stuck rigidly to the documented *Arrangements*.
[42] Ibid., entry for 15 December 1955.   [43] Ibid., entry for 16 December 1955.
[44] Ibid., undated entry for 'Montag'.
[45] See Ekkehard Schall, in Lang and Hillesheim, *'Denken heißt verändern . . .'*, p. 151.
[46] See Rülicke, 'Probenbeginn: 14.12.1955', BBA 2071/28.
[47] John Fuegi, *Choas according to Plan*, p. 152.
[48] See Rülicke, '21.12.55', BBA 2071/49–50.

an interesting observation concerning Busch's curious combination of Brecht and Stanislavsky: 'he is always trying to work out how Galileo might have felt. What's remarkable is that he didn't try to reproduce his own feelings, but tried to work out and show the feelings Galileo might have had'.[49] On the one hand, Busch concentrated on his own character and its feelings, rather than on the more Brechtian preference for a character's actions. On the other, he engaged with his character as other and sought to display the feelings rather than simply to embody them. Brecht was aware of this contradiction and seemed to view Busch as an actor for whose very soul he was struggling. Rülicke wrote about Brecht's final rehearsal, which he stopped early, in terms of Brecht's frustration with Busch's lack of concentration, which he ascribed to Busch's more conventional experiences at the DT.[50]

On the production as a whole, Brecht did not want the play simply to represent anti-clericalism or anti-Catholicism. On the contrary, he aimed to give Galileo wholly credible opponents in order to understand the historical tensions of the time. *Galileo* was to be a study of power and what happens when someone challenges it. Brecht reportedly acknowledged the contradictions central to the play's *Fabel* when considering the figure of the Pope, who was himself a natural scientist: 'this is a thoroughly progressive Pope. Circumstances force him to defend a wholly reactionary decision',[51] that is, to threaten Galileo with torture to make him recant his scientific truths. Brecht had originally cast the DT's *Intendant* Wolfgang Langhoff as the Pope and records show that he did rehearse the role while Brecht was still alive. This direct experience may have changed his attitude towards Brecht and his theatre because he developed a greater openness towards it and its methods after Brecht died. Brecht also deliberately cast a young, vibrant actor in the role of the Grand Inquisitor in order to avoid 'that [old] age serves in some way as an excuse or a reproach in addition to the things they [the senior members of the Catholic Church] do'.[52] But Galileo was not to present a purely positive voice of reason himself.

According to Käthe Rülicke, Brecht summed up the *Fabel* of the play in the English rhyme 'Humpty Dumpty'.[53] That is, once Galileo had recanted, there was no way for him to repair the damage, he could not be 'put back together again'. Consequently, the production as a whole was

---

[49] Rülicke, '28.12.55', BBA 2071/141.
[50] See Rülicke, '1. Szene 27.3.56', BBA 673/55.
[51] Brecht, in B. K. Tragelehn, 'Notate', BEA File 23, entry for 7 January 1956.
[52] Brecht, in ibid., same entry.
[53] Rülicke, '*Leben des Galilei*. Bemerkungen zum Schlußszene', *Sinn und Form*, Zweites Sonderheft Bertolt Brecht (1957), pp. 269–321 (319).

concerned with building Galileo up in order to tear him down, although, as always, the character was not simply one thing or another, but dialectically both at the same time. As Brecht reportedly put it: 'by the end, he is a champion of science and a social villain'.[54] He removed his own play's more optimistic final scene in a bid to heighten the ambivalence.

Rehearsals were cut short after Brecht was forced to withdraw due to bad health. Weigel wrote to Bork a week after Brecht's death to ask permission for Erich Engel to continue the work on *Galileo*,[55] and rehearsals restarted on 2 October 1956. For Rülicke, the change of directorial style was something of a shock to the system. She noted that she found it virtually impossible to write *Notate* for Engel: 'where Brecht directed actions (in a clear way), Engel directed states'.[56] She added that this was not to take anything away from his sterling work, but that some of the more dialectical moments were getting lost. On the other hand, Besson praised Engel's firmness and unwillingness to indulge the actors, especially Busch.[57] Engel's more conventional direction, which, in contrast to Brecht's, did not encourage the overly active participation of the actors, was a means of cutting down on Busch's suggestions and holding him to Brecht's movements and gestures.

The premiere on 15 January 1956 was much lauded. The sets were designed after sketches made by Caspar Neher, and the engraved copper walls would become an intertextual reference point in later BE productions. Critic Friedrich Luft admired the way that Engel was able to rein in some of Brecht's own exaggerated devices in a more moderate, but no less illuminating performance.[58] Luft and Sabine Lietzmann both noted how well Engel had successfully completed the open task.[59] Another reviewer was pleased to see the full engagement of the ensemble and the centrality of the social aspect, here in the portrayal of the Church as not bad in itself, but as a product of the times.[60] The review in *Neues Deutschland*, which appeared a whole fortnight after the premiere, both praised Engel's direction while sniping about certain details. It also sought to criticize some of the Western reviewers who found analogies between the

---

[54] Brecht, in ibid., p. 282.
[55] See Weigel to Bork, 21 August 1956, BArch DR 1/8227.
[56] Rülicke, 'Kleine Notate zur Probe von Engel', undated, BBA 2071/16. The following reference is taken from BBA 2071/15.
[57] See [Benno Besson], untitled, undated, n.p., AdK Besson-Archiv File 51.
[58] See Friedrich Luft, 'Brechts *Galileo Galilei* von beklemmender Aktualität', *Die Welt*, 17 January 1956.
[59] See ibid.; and Sabine Lietzmann, 'Wenn die Wahrheit zum Angriff geht . . .', *Frankfurter Allgemeine Zeitung*, 18 January 1956.
[60] See Karl Reinhold Döderlin, 'Am Anfang der wissenschaftlichen Epoche', *Neue Zeit*, 22 January 1956.

representation of the Church and the GDR's Politburo.[61] Despite the lack of whole-hearted approval in that paper, the production generated large audiences and ran for almost five years. The BE had not yet proven that it had survived Brecht's death, but it had been able to show that it had recovered from the shock.

The twin pressures of low productivity: making and maintaining productions that would last

The BE had never been a terribly productive theatre company in terms of the number of new productions it realized. In its first years this was partly due to a scarcity of rehearsal and stage space; it could not develop a full repertoire because it shared facilities with the DT. In the seasons the BE spent at the Schiffbauerdamm until Brecht died, productivity remained, however, at under three major shows per year, a figure that contrasted negatively with other theatres in Berlin at the time.[62] And in the years between Brecht's death in August 1956 and the erection of the Berlin Wall in 1961, the company managed to bring a mere seven major productions to the stage. The average would not rise significantly until Ruth Berghaus became *Intendantin* in 1971.

Weigel explained the reason for the relative dearth of new productions to Kurt Bork in 1958: 'our productions are difficult, most painstaking, and to all intents and purposes each one is a world premiere, and we must retain the right to work like this'.[63] Her comment is rooted in the 'special' nature of work at the BE. The company did not simply 'put on plays', but spent much time processing and developing texts before exposing them in rehearsal to the Brechtian process of 'discovering' what contradictions they might contain. Vsevolod Vishnevsky's *Optimistische Tragödie* (*Optimistic Tragedy*), which premiered on 1 April 1958, was submitted to extensive adaptation in order to craft its *Fabel*. Only once this element was in place could practical work proceed. Weigel's use of 'world premiere' stresses how the directors and actors tried to assume nothing in advance and work through problems from scratch, naïvely, just as Brecht had done since 1949. The concluding clauses of her justification are also telling: to her, the generous conditions that permitted such low productivity were not a privilege, but a right. This assumption was based on the BE's national and international reputation: with slowness and care came

---

[61] See Henryk Keisch, 'Bertolt Brechts *Leben des Galilei*', *Neues Deutschland*, 29 January 1956. Lietzmann compared the Curia in the production to the Politburo.

[62] The DT, for example, averaged ten productions per year on its two stages in the 1950s. Data supplied by its archivist, Karl Sand.

[63] Weigel to Bork, 23 May 1958, *Briefwechsel*, p. 101.

quality and respect. The statistics certainly tend to support this view –
some of the major productions ran and ran:

> *Chalk Circle*: premiere 7 October 1954. 175 performances to 22
> December 1958
>
> *Galileo*: premiere 15 January 1957. 242 performances to 2
> December 1961
>
> *Arturo Ui*: premiere 23 March 1959. 532 performances to 13
> January 1974
>
> *Threepenny Opera*: premiere 23 April 1960. 497 performances to
> 10 July 1971

The fact that Brecht wrote the plays helped to attract interest from home
and abroad. In the wake of his death and the great success of the BE's
tours, the time spent getting his plays 'right' was rewarded by long runs.
These in turn reduced the pressure to stage more productions. However,
long runs themselves were not easy to manage, and the BE instituted a
range of measures to maintain the productions' quality in the long term.
Brecht, and to a great extent Wekwerth and Palitzsch, rehearsed inductively. Actors made discoveries together with the director(s), and this
helped to cement the productions' many details because the actors were
aware of why they were performing specific moves, gestures and deliveries. On the other hand, Erich Engel, who directed, amongst other things,
the long-running *Threepenny Opera*, rehearsed mainly by giving the actors
direct instructions that they then had to carry out and store. His productions were far more difficult to 'maintain' because the actors lacked
a concrete connection between the performances and their rationale.

As already noted, the assistants were often charged with writing
'Abendberichte' ('evening reports'), also known as 'Abendregie'. Rülicke
said that the reports ensured that the essentials of a scene were present
in performance although this was not a mechanical process in itself.[64]
Indeed, Claus Küchenmeister noted that the reports also included obser-
vations that could lead to productive changes once the reports had been
read.[65] However, Ekkehard Schall, complaining about what he saw as
the drop in quality of *Arturo Ui*, recognized the problems to which such
systems could become prone: 'the evening reports for productions in
repertory have become superfluous without actually being so, they've
turned into a paper exercise'.[66] Schall lamented the way that the quality

[64] See Rülicke, in Erdmut Wizisla, 'Gespräch mit Käthe Rülicke-Weiler über Helene
Weigel und Bertolt Brecht am 8.11.1984 in ihrer Berliner Wohnung [with Matthias
Braun]', undated, 38 pages (24), HWA FH 70.
[65] See Claus Küchenmeister, in Buchmann et al., '*Eine Begabung*', pp. 38–9.
[66] Ekkehard Schall to Weigel, 25 April 1965, *Briefwechsel*, p. 144.

control mechanism started to become a drudgery, rather than a creative contribution to the maintenance of the work. This was certainly something of an enduring problem at the BE. Weigel noticed 'signs of decline' in *Galileo* in 1958.[67] An attempt to supplement the *Abendberichte* was the creation of an in-house group, the 'Brigade zur Erhaltung der Qualität der Aufführungen' ('Brigade for the Maintenance of the Productions' Quality') in late 1959.[68] Actor Hilmar Thate was the co-chair of this group, together with Ekkehard Schall. Thate hoped that the group would introduce a sense of co-responsibility to the process of maintaining productions in the long term. The chairs also wanted to integrate more actors into the quality control process, rather than merely leaving the task to the assistants, directors and dramaturges who wrote the *Abendberichte*.[69] Convening the group proved difficult in the theatre, due to the actors' rehearsal commitments, and it seems that it did not have a major effect on what was a repetitive process of performing the same show for years on end.

The long-running productions proved to be both a blessing and a curse. While the Ministry of Culture criticized the BE for its low productivity, it still registered a pleasing increase in audience numbers and a corresponding decrease in subsidy per spectator (from 1,777 marks in 1957 to 1,511 marks in 1960). Between 1957 and 1960, takings rose by 37 per cent while costs increased only by 18 per cent. The BE filled 93.8 per cent of its seating capacity in 1959 and a remarkable 98 per cent in 1960. And while it missed its target for the number of performances that year (297 instead of 310), it considerably surpassed the Ministry's target for income (taking 1,001,300 marks, a surplus of 228,200 over the target of 773,100).[70] This was a pattern that would repeat itself throughout the 1960s. The BE was in rude financial health on account of its popular productions. Consequently, the Ministry could accept low productivity because the productions themselves proved so attractive. The other side of this coin was that the BE tended to keep its successful shows in repertory for a great deal of time, and this had adverse effects on the ensemble and the quality of the productions over time. New roles were hard to come by, and the idea of developing the actors became increasingly difficult. The BE thus found itself caught up in something of a creative vicious circle: it could not risk trimming time reserved for preparation or

---

[67] Weigel to Lothar Bellag, 3 April 1958, ibid., p. 100.
[68] Hilmar Thate, 'Versuch neuer Arbeitsweisen', *Theater der Zeit*, 3 (1960), pp. 47–50 (48).
[69] Hilmar Thate, unpublished interview with the author, 19 July 2011.
[70] Statistics taken from Anon., 'Protokoll über die durchgeführte Revision der Haushalts- und Finanzwirtschaft. Zeitraum 1.1.58–31.12.1960', 5 April 1961, 25 pages (mostly 2–5), BArch DR 1/18164.

rehearsal by producing more shows for fear that its productions would lose their longevity and appeal. But there were only so many long-running Brechtian 'blockbusters' that the theatre could turn to, and so the policy had a limited shelf-life in any case. This became more than apparent in the mid 1960s, and the working pattern established in the mid 1950s would almost prove to be the undoing of the company when it tried to stage Brecht's *Die heilige Johanna der Schlachthöfe* (*Saint Joan of the Stockyards*) in 1968. However, a decade before that, the BE was busy trying to consolidate its reputation, and one production in particular would resonate around the world.

Proof delivered: Wekwerth and Palitzsch direct *Arturo Ui*

The BE had chalked up some successes in the wake of Brecht's death; both *Galileo* and *Szechwan* had been well reviewed and attended. Between the two shows came a collective production of Brecht's montage of scenes, *Furcht und Elend des Dritten Reichs* (*Fear and Misery of the Third Reich*), with five young directors staging ten of the scenes. These, too, had been well received, and the production as a whole had a special function: it formed the prelude to *Der aufhaltsame Aufstieg des Arturo Ui (The Resistible Rise of Arturo Ui)*. *Ui* is a play that satirizes and examines the rise of Hitler through the Chicago gangster, Arturo Ui. The play is a darkly comic allegory derived from episodes in German history, such as the Reichstag fire in 1933, and Brecht believed, as Wekwerth noted, that the BE had to perform his grim depiction of conditions under the Nazis, *Furcht und Elend*, before unleashing the clownesque *Ui*.[71] Brecht realized that the production could be misinterpreted or accused of trivializing an historical catastrophe, and his reservations were productively integrated into the preparation and rehearsal processes at the BE.

Wekwerth directed the production together with Palitzsch, who had stepped down as head dramaturge in order to concentrate on directing. Joachim Tenschert, who later formed a creative partnership with Wekwerth, came to the BE in the late summer of 1958 to take up Palitzsch's old position.[72] Wekwerth told me that the joint direction was a concrete attempt to 'bind' Palitzsch to the BE.[73] This was a logical conclusion in

---

[71] See Wekwerth, *Schriften*, p. 142.
[72] See Joachim Tenschert, in Manfred Dosdall, 'Gespräch mit Joachim Tenschert über Helene Weigel am 5.7.1983 in Berlin [with Matthias Braun]', undated, 30 pages (2 and 29), HWA FH 61.
[73] Wekwerth, unpublished interview with the author, 14 June 2011.

the face of Palitzsch's burgeoning commitments in the West. The partnership, according to Hilmar Thate, who played Ui's sidekick Giri, was well balanced, with each director keeping the other in check while nonetheless making productive contributions to the production.[74] The two directors decided to adapt Brecht's text, rather than to retain the original. The Nuremberg trials, for example, had exposed the close collusion between the Nazis and big business, and so more emphasis was placed on that relationship. Rülicke suggested that they cut the appearance of Roma's ghost, as the sequence, which reflected Ui's guilty conscience, added little to the play.[75] This was not a major BE adaptation, more a dramaturgical tying up of loose ends, something Brecht was unable to carry out because he had not rehearsed the play himself.

Rehearsals began in early November 1958 with the usual Brechtian construction of the *Arrangements*. Wekwerth, in the preparatory stage that began in September, had criticized sketches for the *Arrangements* for caricaturing the Nazi period. Instead, he preferred the drafts 'that imbue gangster *Haltungen* with Nazi attributes'.[76] This observation was crucial to the production as a whole because it struck at the heart of the problems of staging an allegory. Step by step, the play charts Ui's rise by transforming real events into allegorized analogies, such as when Ui, having conquered Chicago, annexes Cicero, just as Hitler, having conquered Germany, annexed Austria. If one considers the role of the spectators, such a play can become profoundly unproductive because they believe they have done their work merely by identifying the connections between the play and history. In this case, the reception of the play becomes little more than a tautological exercise in confirming one's historical knowledge, rather than opening up the mechanisms that led to Hitler's rise. Clearly Brecht did not intend such a viewing process because he called Ui's rise 'resistible', that is, he wanted the audience to see past the allegorical connections and consider the ways in which dictators can be stopped. Wekwerth's observation about the *Arrangements* represents a move away from allegory. Instead he sought to offer the audience a complex interpenetration of Nazism and the gangster genre. The key term in his note is '*Haltung*', which emphasizes modes of behaviour and not personal traits. Indeed, critic Dieter Kranz makes an important distinction in his comments on the production: Ekkehard Schall as Ui 'did not play the great criminal, but the perpetrator of great

[74] Hilmar Thate, unpublished interview with the author, 19 July 2011.
[75] See Rülicke, 'Notizen von Frau Rülicke zur Bearbeitung des *Arturo Ui*', November 1958, 6 pages (1), BEA File 27.
[76] [Wekwerth] to Palitzsch, 22 October 1958, ibid.

crimes'.[77] Ui was defined by his actions and not as some kind of essentially evil Nazi character.

Rehearsals themselves continued along Brechtian principles. The directors were keen to deploy dialectical contradiction to open up the events on stage. In the court scene, for example, the defence lawyer was directed to act highly professionally so that his ultimate failure could be seen not as owing to incompetence, 'but due to the brutality of the opposing party'.[78] The dynamic use of contrast pervaded the production. At the funeral of Dullfeet, murdered by Ui's men, the gangsters themselves needed to show their distress as 'great and genuine' in order to demonstrate 'the "value" of bourgeois feeling'.[79] Thus, by removing any trace of artifice in the performance, the directors were actually pointing to the artifice of grieving for someone the mourners had murdered in this case.

Brecht, in a note to the play, counselled that it should be played 'in the *grand style* . . . preferably with obvious harkbacks to the Elizabethan theatre'.[80] This was another way of distancing productions from a reduction to simple allegory, and the BE team was keen to realize Brecht's instruction. Joachim Tenschert's report on a run-through points to the qualities the directors associated with the 'grand style'. He called the opening scene 'not big, not objective, not Shakespearean enough'. Elsewhere he noted: 'over long passages, the performance is small, accidental, naturalistic'[81] (which are effectively synonyms for each other here). The two responses suggest that the frame for the production had to have a broad, exemplary quality; there was no room for private gestures or expressions. A year into the run, Wekwerth asked the cast to banish all irony from their performances and to play 'the actions seriously, earnestly, and with moral gravity as if you were performing one of Shakespeare's Histories'.[82] The instruction underlines the tension between the theatricality of the production's frame (the 'Grand Style') and the realistic details contained within it. Only by insisting on the characters' sincerity could the production point to the ironies that would be received by the audience, not knowingly delivered on stage. Such a grand style was also written into the performance of one of the best-loved scenes of the play, where an actor teaches Ui how to declaim speeches in public. The idea

---

[77] Dieter Kranz, *Berliner Theater: 100 Aufführungen aus drei Jahrzehnten* (Berlin: Henschel, 1990), p. 35.

[78] Anon., '[*Notat* for 9 December 1958]', undated, n.p., BEA File 27.

[79] Hans-Georg Simmgen, 'Besprechung über die Musik', 23 December 1958, n.p., ibid.

[80] Brecht, '[Hinweis für die Aufführung]', BFA, 7: 8; Brecht, 'Notes', *Collected Plays*, ed. by John Willett and Ralph Mannheim, vol. 6. (London: Methuen, 1994), p. 353.

[81] Joachim Tenschert, 'Durchlaufprobe am 2.3.1959', undated, 11 pages (2 for both quotations), BEA File 27.

[82] Wekwerth to the cast, 25 March 1960, ibid.

here was to present Ui before his lesson as someone who speaks naïvely and realistically. The actor, however, teaches him to speak like '"a ham at a courtly theatre", so that something grotesque comes about that Ui allows himself to be persuaded that the unnatural tone is the right one because it is more demagogically seductive'.[83] The directors were concerned with showing the process and the decision-making involved in Ui's vocal (and, indeed, gestural) transformation. From that scene on, the audience would be able to contextualize Ui's un-ironically delivered speeches as conscious, reasoned products, predicated upon political efficacy.

As is often the case, there was a nervousness surrounding the opening night on 23 March 1959. In a letter to the actors on the production's 450th performance, Wekwerth recalled that they had doubted a production that they considered too 'directly political'.[84] His observation suggests that they did not necessarily appreciate the delicate contrast between their 'serious' acting style and the ironies it generated. All the actors appeared in clown-like make-up. The scenes themselves were all carefully constructed to offer a series of tableaux (see Fig. 5.1), a readable succession of significant moments in the action. Wekwerth and Palitzsch managed to combine an almost forensic treatment of the action, as represented in the stage images, with an intense liveliness in their actors. These were *tableaux vivants* in the most literal sense of the phrase. As such they took up Brecht's imperative to show relationships and situations clearly while injecting them with all the complexities and contradictions of the characters. Schall proved to be a master of physical acting, articulating Ui's *Gestus* through a series of repeated and modified *Haltungen* that continually offered the audience new ways of understanding his place in the production.

The reviews reveal how the BE struck the delicate balance between the absurd machinations of the gangsters and the darker reality that lurked behind them. The production combined 'idiocy . . . and great dangerousness', it was 'transparent and ghostly', 'horrifying and amusing'.[85] The contradictions could not have been clearer. The production also displayed an interesting dialectic in the performance of its cast as a whole. The central role of Ui made Ekkehard Schall's reputation overnight:

---

[83] Joachim Tenschert, 'Notate von den Durchlaufproben am 16. + 17.3.1959 *Ui*', undated, 8 pages (6), ibid.
[84] Wekwerth to the cast, 28 November 1969, ibid.
[85] Christoph Funke, 'Das Gangsterstück im großen Stil', *Der Morgen*, 25 March 1959 (first quotation); and Friedrich Luft, '*Der aufhaltsame Aufstieg des Arturo Ui*', *Die Welt*, 26 March 1959 (second and third quotations).

Fig. 5.1. The dramaturgy of the *Arrangement*: tableau is used extensively in the production as a means of framing the *Fabel*'s social contradictions. *The Resistible Rise of Arturo Ui*, March 1959.

his physical acting, exaggeration and modulated deliveries won plaudits aplenty, yet the large supporting cast was in no way overshadowed by the bravura performance. The leads complemented the supporting actors in an ensemble production that paid such close attention to detail that all the actors had a chance to shine.

More importantly, perhaps: the production established the BE as a theatre that had survived Brecht's death and that had been able to stage one of his great plays to the standard to which the audience had become accustomed over the years. Wekwerth and Palitzsch had proven themselves worthy heirs to an interpretation of the Brechtian legacy (that is, one Besson may not have shared), and Weigel criticized the lack of recognition for the directors in the *Neues Deutschland* review to Minister of Culture, Alexander Abusch.[86] It was clear that the team had achieved something great. International 'confirmation' followed when the BE returned to Paris, the scene of its first great international triumph, in June 1960, and won the first prize in the official competition for its production of *Ui*.

---

[86] See Weigel to Alexander Abusch, 5 May 1959, *Briefwechsel*, p. 107.

Enduring tensions between the SED and the BE

The lukewarm review in the party's newspaper of what would become a much-toured and much-lauded production reflected the relationship between the BE and the SED at the time. It was not that the SED was openly hostile to the company, more that its ways of working never properly aligned themselves with the SED's demand for control. There was a remarkable exchange between the BE and the Ministry of Culture in 1958, for example. The BE had wanted to produce Brecht's first major hit, *The Threepenny Opera*, back in 1956, in response to public demand, but Brecht believed that this was not possible because they simply did not have a new take on the play.[87] Weigel wanted to have it staged in 1958 to mark the sixtieth anniversary of Brecht's birth,[88] yet she faced opposition from Abusch himself. The Minister considered the plan 'untenable' and justified his curious opinion thus: the play was the product of a different phase of Brecht's writings, and so the BE would be muddying the clear political programme it had developed over the years. He also noted that this would be latched upon by the 'the Western press',[89] so the international dimension, as was often the case, influenced the decision. In the very same month, however, the Ministry granted the theatre in the small town of Rudolstadt permission to perform the play. This detail underlines the pragmatic nature of Abusch's position: it was not the play itself, but its function in context that mattered. Although Weigel had asked Bork to put in a good word on the subject with Abusch,[90] the Ministry remained implacable. A plan to stage *Ui*, *The Threepenny Opera* and *Man Equals Man* in the 1958/59 season met resistance at a meeting in late September 1958. While the Ministry had no problem with *Ui*, it considered that the other two proposals did not possess 'the slightest connection to the problems of the day'.[91] To an extent, the Ministry was right. In a note to the production, once it was finally approved, Erich Engel wrote that his attempt to incorporate material from Brecht's *Dreigroschenroman* (*Threepenny Novel*) failed because it diverged too greatly from the play, and so he returned to his 1928 production,[92] rather than establish a new approach.

[87] See Brecht to Emil Burian, 25 May 1956, BFA, 30: 454.
[88] See Wolfgang Pintzka, *Von Sibirien in die Synagoge. Erinnerungen aus zwei Welten* (Teetz: Hentrich & Hentrich, 2002), p. 116.
[89] Alexander Abusch to Weigel, 18 March 1958, *Briefwechsel*, p. 98.
[90] See Weigel to Bork, 23 May 1958, ibid., p. 102.
[91] Rainer John, 'Aktennotiz über ein Gespräch mit dem Berliner Ensemble am 19.9.58', 22 September 1958, n.p., BArch DR 1/18081.
[92] See Erich Engel, 'Über die Neuinszenierung', in Werner Hecht (ed.), *Brechts 'Dreigroschenoper'* (Frankfurt/Main: Suhrkamp, 1985), pp. 168–71 (168–9). The following quotation is taken from p. 168.

While he stressed that he wanted to criticize the 'the pervasion of capital in all human relationships', it is easy to understand why the authorities would question the concept's relevance in a socialist state. However, that the Ministry even sought to prevent a production of one of Brecht's great plays reflects its narrow, instrumentalized view of culture's functions.

I have found no Ministry documents that acknowledge the approval of *The Threepenny Opera* for performance, and so I can only speculate on the reasons why the production was allowed to go ahead after all (premiere 23 April 1960). It would be difficult to dismiss the effects of *Ui*'s success, a production that had re-established the BE's reputation and that had also been very well received in the Western media. Abusch's sensitivity to international repercussions may well have influenced the decision, together with the popular demand for the show. *Neues Deutschland* seemed, however, to re-echo the Ministry's original critique when it called the play 'not yet the work of one involved in the class struggle' while acknowledging that the production did not romanticize its lead, Mack the Knife.[93] The precision and detail of the show drew praise, but some critics in the West were becoming suspicious of this quality. Sabine Lietzmann wrote that 'everything was superbly, expertly, and accurately presented. But it lacked teeth and fire'.[94] Friedrich Luft called this 'the curse of perfection'.[95] The BE had always been concerned with exactness in its productions because it valued clarity, particularly when articulating dialectical contradictions. The new critiques suggest that the degree of perfection was making everything so readable that the audience's work was already being done for it on stage. Such criticism did not, however, adversely affect the show's reception; it ran and ran, proving itself to be a big hit with audiences.

Yet even when the SED was not on the offensive, it had the power to threaten the BE, despite the success of its productions. I noted at the start of this chapter that the Ministry of Culture sponsored a conference on acting in January 1960. The BE's preparation for this betrays great anxiety, similar to that experienced before the Stanislavsky conference of 1953. In the minutes of a meeting at the BE in 1959, one finds the instructions 'we must urgently collect what Brecht wrote on Stanislavsky' and that any discussion at the conference 'has to be robustly steered towards Stanislavsky *and* Brecht'.[96] It is worth noting an important difference

---

[93] Henryk Keisch, '"Lebensgefühl" gestern und heute', *Neues Deutschland*, 5 May 1960.
[94] Sabine Lietzmann, 'Der kunstvoll ausgestopfter Haifisch', *Frankfurter Allgemeine Zeitung*, 30 April 1960.
[95] Friedrich Luft, 'Alte Theaterliebe rostet leider doch', *Die Welt*, 28 April 1960.
[96] Anon., 'Protokoll der Besprechung bei Frau Weigel am 15.11.1959', undated, 3 pages (2 for both quotations), BEA File 'Protokolle Dramaturgie Sitzungen 1957–1964'.

between the conditions under which the two conferences were held. In the latter case, the BE at least felt that it had the power to influence the debate; in 1953 there had been no space for debate at all. As it happened, the BE's fears were unfounded, and the conference passed without controversy. In an internal memorandum written after the conference, an anonymous BE author noted that the conference chair had said: 'every theatre has to find its own way, there isn't a formula'.[97] Regardless of that rather generous interpretation of how theatre worked in the GDR, the BE's reaction betrays both the trauma of the campaigns of the early 1950s and the fact that the SED had successfully regrouped in the wake of 17 June 1953. Its authority and power were fully re-established. It could still make a theatre like the BE quake, even without due cause.

The curious case of the Berliner Ensemble and Friedrich Dürrenmatt

Brecht reportedly wondered in 1956 whether Friedrich Dürrenmatt's play *Der Besuch der alten Dame* (known in English as *The Visit*) would be suitable for the BE.[98] It had premiered in Zurich in January of that year with Therese Giehse in the lead role. Its subject matter certainly would have appealed. A billionaire, Claire Zachanassian, returns to the destitute small town that rejected her as a poor unmarried mother. She offers the town a large sum of money on one condition: that somebody rights the wrong that was done to her many years before. She asks that one of the denizens murders the father of her child, Alfred Ill, who denied paternity in court and won with the help of bribed witnesses. The corrosive effect of capital is evident both in Zachanassian's revenge and in the crime that provoked it.

Negotiations with Giehse were ongoing in 1958,[99] and she agreed to play the lead the following year, noting that Dürrenmatt had agreed to the plan.[100] The Ministry was happy to have Giehse as a guest at the BE, but not in a play by Dürrenmatt.[101] No reason was given for this decision, but, at that time, the GDR was keen to develop its own new writing rather than to import contemporary plays from the West. Weigel,

---

[97] Hans Pischner, in Anon., 'Notizen über Theaterkonferenz', 8 February 1960, 2 pages (1), ibid.

[98] See Erwin Leiser, 'Der freundliche Frager', in Witt (ed.), *Gespräch auf der Probe*, pp. 42–8 (47).

[99] See Anon., '[Notice-board notice]', 20 May 1958, BBA uncatalogued file 'HW Briefw. 1–6/1958'.

[100] See Weigel to Alexander Abusch, 7 December 1959, *Briefwechsel*, pp. 108–9.

[101] See Elfriede Bork, 'Anruf Ministerium für Kultur Abt. Theater Kurt Bork', 5 January 1960, BBA uncatalogued file 'HW M-Z 1960'.

however, suspected that the play itself, rather than the author, presented a stumbling block and wrote to both Bork and Abusch and asked them to reconsider.[102] She enclosed a short document supporting the choice of play with her letter to Abusch. Its arguments were somewhat curious at times. While it opened with the reasonable observation that all the relationships in the play were 'for sale', it continued that the play was 'to our knowledge the only realistic play about the Economic Miracle'.[103] The Economic Miracle was the historical phenomenon in which the devastated FRG transformed itself into an economic powerhouse in the space of a decade. Dürrenmatt, however, was Swiss and was writing about financial relations in the West in general. In addition, the document related Dürrenmatt to Gogol (and his play, *The Government Inspector*), manufacturing a relationship with the progressive *Erbe*. The play was also to offer a counterpoint to another play the BE was planning to stage, *Frau Flinz*. The arguments seem to have been successful; Joachim Tenschert noted that the BE was in contact with Dürrenmatt to secure the performing rights in May 1960.[104]

It is not clear when rehearsals started on the production, but early 1961 seems likely, as in late January, the premiere was pencilled in for 10 April 1961.[105] By this time, Giehse was no longer associated with the project, and the lead role was to be played by Agnes Kraus. The BE was so committed to rehearsing *The Visit* and *Frau Flinz* that it even decided against touring England that spring.[106] It also proposed to adapt the text, and drafted two letters to Dürrenmatt asking in the first that he permit their changes and in the second that they merely discuss them.[107] The growing caution with respect to a playwright with an international reputation suggests that the BE might have hesitated in its plan to adapt Dürrenmatt. The company may have feared that it would incur his anger at the implicit criticism of his much-performed play as it stood and that he might consequently withdraw the rights. It is unclear whether either

---

[102] See Weigel to Bork, 6 January 1960; and Weigel to Abusch, 14 January 1960, ibid.

[103] See [Wekwerth and Palitzsch?], '[On *The Visit*]', 13 January 1960, 2 pages (1), BEA File *'Besuch der alten Dame'*.

[104] See Joachim Tenschert, 'Die wichtigsten Punkte aus dem Bericht der Dramaturgie auf der Sitzung des Künstlerischen Beirats am 9. Mai 1960', undated, 3 pages (2), BEA File 'Protokolle Dramaturgie Sitzungen 1957–1964'.

[105] See Isot Kilian, 'Bericht über Dramaturgie-Besprechung am Dienstag 24.1.1961', undated, n.p., ibid.

[106] See Alfred Kurella, 'Aktennotiz', [c. 3 February 1961], n.p., SAPMO BArch DY 30/IV 2/2.026/67.

[107] See Palitzsch, Wekwerth and Hans-Georg Simmgen to Friedrich Dürrenmatt, 4 February 1961; and Palitzsch to Dürrenmatt, 13 February 1961, both in BEA File *'Besuch der alten Dame'*.

of the letters were sent. In any case, the BE did not produce the play. There is no record in either the Dürrenmatt archive or the archive of his publisher that attests to his cancelling the performance rights. The production, for which meetings had been held regarding the music, set and costume, imploded. Director Hans-Georg Simmgen told me that this was his first solo project, having been an assistant at the BE since 1957, and he simply was not up to the task.[108] He had little idea of how to rehearse such a difficult play and could not answer the actors' questions about his directions. Wekwerth told me that there was also a problem with Agnes Kraus.[109] He had hoped to use the proletarian actor to contrast her roots with the sudden acquisition of billions, but she was not able to carry it off.

This is a remarkable episode. The BE had struggled to gain approval from the Ministry and considered the politest ways of persuading a world-famous playwright to agree to an adaptation of his world-famous play. The company had also postponed a tour of England. Yet despite all the effort and investment, the BE entrusted the complex production to an assistant who soon realized that he was out of his depth. The BE found itself with a hole in its plan for the season and had to write off all the monies expended. However, it would seem that this was not a terribly big problem, as the plan was never resuscitated; Wekwerth ran it past the Central Committee in 1963, but nothing came of the suggestion.[110]

Instead of staging Dürrenmatt, the BE pursued only its second piece of new writing from the GDR, Helmut Baierl's comedy, *Frau Flinz*, which he wrote with help from Wekwerth. This was, like *Katzgraben* before it, another piece of propaganda that effectively told the story of *Mother Courage* in reverse. Frau Flinz 'loses' her five sons not to war, but to the demands of GDR socialism before they return to her, happy and fulfilled. Helene Weigel helped to ensure its success by taking the title role, although its premiere had to be put back after she collapsed through exhaustion.[111] This sugary fantasy was praised by the Ministry ahead of its eventual premiere on 8 May 1961.[112] GDR playwrights Peter Hacks and Volker Braun were not able to convince Baierl and Wekwerth to have

---

[108] Hans-Georg Simmgen, unpublished interview with the author, 21 July 2010.
[109] Wekwerth, unpublished interview with the author, 14 June 2011.
[110] See Wekwerth to Hans Grümmer, 27 September 1963, BEA File 'Dramaturgische Durchschläge für Frau Weigel ab 15. Jan. 1963–1970'.
[111] See Bork to Hans Bentzien, 25 April 1961, BArch DR 1/8630.
[112] See W., 'Punkte von der Kollegiumssitzung des Ministeriums für Kultur am 4.4.1961', undated, n.p., BBA uncatalogued file 'HW BE-MfK 1961–67'.

one of Flinz's sons flee to the West,[113] like so many other GDR citizens who took advantage of the open border. Little did they know that some three months after the premiere such action would no longer be possible: on Sunday, 13 August 1961, the SED sealed the frontier with the West with the Berlin Wall.

[113] See Kebir, *Abstieg in den Ruhm*, p. 305.

6   Making theatre politically after the Berlin Wall: 1961–1965

The Berlin Wall and its impact on personnel at the Berliner Ensemble

With hindsight, it might seem that the GDR authorities had telegraphed the building of the Berlin Wall to the cultural sector. In the field of the performing arts, the Ministry of Culture surveyed theatres, opera houses and other institutions for the number of staff who were living in West Berlin in May 1961, three months before construction started on 13 August.[1] According to the responses, the Berliner Ensemble submitted its twenty-seven names sometime in June. Today it is clear that the Ministry was pre-emptively assessing the impact that the closure of the border would have on the GDR's ability to keep its venues open. Yet it is difficult to ascertain who knew the ends to which the information was to be used. Kurt Bork was aware that something significant was afoot because the document to which I have referred notes concern about how the Staatsoper and the Komische Oper were to play on, considering the large numbers of West-dwelling staff at those institutions. However, such surveys were not unusual in themselves. For example, the Ministry had asked the BE for details of its West Berlin members ahead of its tour to Halle in 1959.[2] The theatres and opera houses probably thought that this was just another bureaucratic hoop through which they were required to jump. What the survey did not identify was the potential for additional East German staff either to defect or to remain in the West because they were already working there as guests. This was the case for Peter Palitzsch and Carl Weber, who were directing Brecht plays in Ulm and Lübeck, respectively. It would seem from the evidence that the authorities and the BE were not that concerned about Weber's decision; instead they focused on the loss Palitzsch represented practically as a director and symbolically as a Brecht *Schüler*.

[1] See Bork, 'Betr.: Theater, Orchester, Zirkus, Museen . . .', [July 1961], 4 pages, BArch DR 1/18001. An attached list of replies is dated 6 July 1961 and marked 'confidential'.
[2] See Ille Rustler to the Ministry of Culture, 17 June 1959, BArch DR 1/18018.

Initially, Manfred Wekwerth proceeded as if the Wall had had no impact on Palitzsch and his work at the BE. In a letter written barely two weeks after the border was closed, Wekwerth told Palitzsch that they needed to sort out the *Fabel* for the next major BE project, Brecht's *Coriolan*. He also noted that the BE would not be publicly protesting against the rumoured Brecht boycott in the FRG: 'after all, why should we be surprised that, in a revolutionary situation, counterrevolutionaries behave in a counterrevolutionary manner?'[3] Wekwerth's blasé tone may surprise us today, but for many committed socialists, the Wall was not in itself a bad thing. Hilmar Thate, who would leave the GDR to work in the West in the wake of the Biermann affair of 1976 (see pp. 295–6, Chapter 9), believed that the Wall would actually allow greater freedom and democracy in the GDR because the state could now proceed with its own business without the pressure exerted by an open border.[4] Such illusions were sometimes slow to fade. The banning, straight after its premiere on 30 September 1961, of Heiner Müller's *Die Umsiedlerin* (*The Resettler*), for its critical stance on elements of GDR society, did little to puncture optimism: the BE's 'Parteileitung' ('local party leadership') sent a letter denouncing the play and its production to the Ministry.[5]

By early September, the BE still hoped to convince Palitzsch to return. A memorandum of a meeting with Minister Hans Bentzien records that the GDR press should be instructed to refrain from making any mention of Palitzsch, lest it prevent him from reconsidering his position.[6] A plan was hatched to have Wekwerth meet his directing partner in Austria or Scandinavia, that is, not on German soil.[7] Wekwerth had initially turned his back on Palitzsch 'definitively', but he then sought to convince him to return 'with his very best efforts'.[8] (This information is to be found in Wekwerth's Stasi file, and I will return to the Stasi's connection with the BE in the following chapter. Here it is worth noting that Stasi intervention may have changed Wekwerth's attitude towards his colleague in the interests of the BE and the GDR. Yet by November, Wekwerth was referring to Palitzsch's decision as treachery.)[9]

[3] Wekwerth to Palitzsch, 26 August 1961, BBA uncatalogued file 'Korr 54–66'.
[4] See Hilmar Thate, with Kerstin Retemeyer, *Neulich, als ich noch Kind war: Autobiografie – Versuch eines Zeitgenossen* (Bergisch Gladbach: Gustav Lübbe, 2006), p. 160.
[5] See Helmut Baierl to Eva Zapff, 5 October 1961, marked 'confidential', BBA uncatalogued file 'Korr 54–66'.
[6] See Anon., 'Zu einem Gespräch mit Min. Bentzien am 4.9.61', undated, n.p., BBA uncatalogued file 'HW BE-MfK 1961–67'.
[7] See Weigel to Bork, 12 September 1961, ibid.
[8] Anon., 'Auskunftsbericht', 27 December 1962, file p. 61, BStU MfS AIM 2927/69, vol. 1.
[9] See Wekwerth to Helmut Baierl, 12 November 1961, AdK MWA 'Korr. BE'.

Palitzsch was in no mood to compromise and rejected an offer to meet in Oslo by arguing that the Wall was not a measure designed to combat the West, but the GDR's own workers.[10] The BE's response to his final decision was a vitriolic open letter, published in *Neues Deutschland*, that reproached him for leaving the country in which the '[Arturo] Uis' had been politically and economically disempowered and concluded in trenchant style: 'we have suffered losses. We have made up for them'.[11] The BE had not, however, made up for the loss. Despite the GDR press blackout and the BE's continued efforts, the West German *Tagesspiegel* reported that Palitzsch was not going to return to the GDR. The BE tried to get Kurt Palm, the head of the costume department at the GDR's State Workshops, to replace Palitzsch,[12] but he did not want to return to the GDR either. And while the authorities insisted that actors living in West Berlin either move to the GDR or have their contracts cancelled, a 'special arrangement set up by the Ministry'[13] allowed Erich Engel to remain in the West while directing at the BE. Exceptions were made where necessary, it seems.

Head of Administration at the BE, Hans Giersch, painted a picture of the effects of the Wall on the BE's personnel in November. While he acknowledged that he had not yet discussed contracts with all West Berliners, he could establish that the company had lost nineteen staff, including four instances of 'Republikflucht' ('flight from the Republic'), which included Palitzsch[14] and Weber, and two actors. Eight West Berliners decided to stay at the BE. The company was planning to employ four new actors in the 1962/63 season, including Gisela May, who went on to enjoy an international reputation as a chanteuse singing Brecht's songs, and Renate Richter, who would marry Wekwerth and become one the BE's leading actors later that decade and again when her husband was appointed *Intendant* in 1977.[15] Despite the relatively modest damage done in terms of lost ensemble members, the repertoire was nonetheless in trouble: the company needed to rehearse new actors to replace those who stayed in the West, and deal with bouts of illness. However, the BE

---

[10] See Palitzsch to Wekwerth and Joachim Tenschert, 24 September [1961], AdK JTA 'Korr. mit Inst.'.

[11] Künstlerischer Beirat [the BE's Artistic Advisory Council], 'Offener Brief an Peter Palitzsch', *Neues Deutschland*, 4 October 1961.

[12] Anon. to Kurt Palm, 4 September 1961, BBA uncatalogued file 'Korr 54–66'.

[13] Hans Giersch to Ministry of Culture, 7 February 1962, BArch DR 1/18001.

[14] Technically, Palitzsch (like Weber) had not left the GDR illegally; he had stayed away when the opportunity presented itself while directing in the West.

[15] All personnel information in Hans Giersch, untitled, 17 November 1961, 3 pages, BArch DR 1/18001.

took pains to avoid the Western media attributing the disruption to the Wall, something that could be 'interpreted maliciously'.[16]

The events of 13 August 1961 did have a negative effect on the BE's ability to realize its plans. The triumvirate of young directors who looked like they would lead the company after 1956 was no more, and Manfred Wekwerth was without a directing partner. The East German audience had to wait over a year for the BE's next major production; the audience in the West had to wait considerably longer.

The Wall and the problem of touring

One of the BE's great attractions to the SED was that the company was regularly invited to tour politically important countries, including those in which the GDR was not diplomatically recognized. The many countries making invitations wanted to see innovative and high-quality theatre, something that made the BE the GDR's most prestigious cultural export. The construction of the Wall had a direct effect on the BE's ability to tour the West, and the problems lasted for years, rather than months. With the exception of a one-night performance of the first *Brecht-Abend* (see below) in Helsinki in 1962, the BE did not travel beyond the Warsaw Pact countries again until 1965, when it returned to London to be welcomed back like the prodigal son. The effects of the Wall were felt almost immediately. In what looks like a text for a press release, the BE noted that its performances at the Venice Biennale scheduled for September 1961 had been cancelled. The Italian authorities had withdrawn entry visas at the last minute 'to our great astonishment'.[17] Weigel received personal apologies from the Biennale's head, who asked whether a postponement, rather than a cancellation would be possible.[18] The BE did not return to Venice until 1966.

The BE, and indeed any GDR theatre, had to negotiate two hurdles in order to tour non-communist Europe: the West Berlin 'Travel Board', the gateway to the West administered by the three remaining allies, and the host country's own immigration departments. The BE failed to clear both of these for a planned tour of Denmark in 1963. Danish coalition politics played its part here: the Minister of Justice reportedly turned down the visa application in September although the Prime Minister was

[16] [Weigel?] to Ministry of Culture, 9 October 1961, BBA uncatalogued file 'HW BE-MfK 1961–67'.
[17] Anon., untitled, [September 1961], n.p., BBA uncatalogued file 'D 1/61–9/62'.
[18] See Adolfo Zajotti to Weigel, 11 September 1961, ibid.

said to have supported the tour.[19] In any case, the Travel Board refused visas at the West German end.[20]

The story of the BE's prolonged absence from the UK in the early 1960s shows how pressure came both from within and without the British government. James Smith, whose assiduous work on the subject looks back to how the UK authorities sought to frustrate the tour of 1956 as well, writes that the Foreign Secretary blocked the issue of travel visas to the BE for a trip to the Edinburgh Festival without the Prime Minister's knowledge. The news of the refusal began to leak around the time of the Profumo affair in 1963, and the government found itself overwhelmed by 'a wave of negative publicity'.[21] Prime Minister Harold Macmillan felt that decisions that should have been taken by the UK were instead being 'bullied' out of them by the FRG.[22] Against the backdrop of this pressure, the National Theatre invited the BE to London in January 1964. Kenneth Tynan, who was the literary manager at the National Theatre, reported that Laurence Olivier was delighted at the prospect of a tour in August.[23] By this time, the issue of visas for GDR artists had become so contentious that it was debated in the House of Commons on 3 and 25 February 1964,[24] and the government decided to relax travel regulations in March.[25] However, this plan to tour the West was also scuppered by the Travel Board.[26]

An interesting footnote to the proposed 1964 tour of London concerns the role of the SED in the business of another Warsaw Pact country's cultural affairs. Tynan had warned Weigel that a Polish troupe would be bringing a production of *Arturo Ui* to London in May. This plan was in fact already known to the Ministry of Culture; Kurt Bork feared that a Polish *Ui* would make the need for a home-grown GDR production superfluous and thus undermine the GDR's struggle against travel restrictions.[27] Weigel was also aware of the tour and wrote to the Viennese-born director of the Polish *Ui*, Erwin Axer, someone whom she

[19] See Anon., untitled, *Stuttgarter Zeitung*, 17 September 1963; and Anon., 'Krag [the Danish PM] will Brecht-Ensemble sehen', *Frankfurter Allgemeine Zeitung*, 23 September 1963.
[20] See Anon., 'Berliner Ensemble nach Kopenhagen', *Volksstimme Österreich*, 3 October 1963.
[21] James Smith, 'Brecht, the Berliner Ensemble, and the British Government', p. 316.
[22] Harold Macmillan, in James Smith, ibid., p. 319.
[23] See Kenneth Tynan to Weigel, 22 January 1964, BArch DC 20/7718.
[24] See the official record of proceedings in parliament, *Hansard*, vol. 688, no. 44, pp. 812–13 and vol. 690, no. 61, pp. 392–402, respectively.
[25] See James Smith, p. 320.
[26] See [Weigel] to Alexander Abusch, 17 April 1964, BArch DC 20/7718.
[27] See Baum, 'Aktennotiz', 8 January 1964, n.p., BArch DC 20/7716.

and Brecht had met on a trip to Poland in 1952.[28] She noted both that he had not sought permission to take the production to London and, more importantly, that it was tactical for London to develop a hunger for Brecht which only the BE could satisfy. This blatant statement of self-interest was concluded with a plea for Axer's solidarity with the GDR.[29] The director replied that he *had* applied for the rights and that he considered he was very much acting in Brecht's interests.[30] In addition, GDR Deputy Minister for Foreign Affairs, Herbert Krolikowski, reported that the Polish Foreign Minister was also in favour of the tour.[31] Yet despite the Polish support, Bork told Weigel later that year that it was the Ministry of Culture's intervention that prevented the tour.[32] Axer's response was never to direct Brecht again.

The incident shows that the BE could align its position with that of the GDR authorities when it served its interest, how resolute the GDR authorities were in fighting the travel ban, and how far they were prepared to go in negotiations to secure the primacy of the BE as a GDR theatre company. It is hard to overlook the irony that the same party that imposed widespread travel restrictions on almost all its populace expended so much time and energy to ensure the travel privileges of a single theatre company. Ultimately, the SED got its way, and the BE was much fêted when the boycott was finally lifted and it returned to London in 1965.

The *Brecht-Abende* and other shorter productions

In response to its own low productivity and the attendant problems this created, the BE hit upon a format that could enliven the fatigued ensemble and the samey repertoire. It began to work on pieces with shorter rehearsal periods and less orthodox Brechtian material that did not demand the deference accorded to the 'great' plays.

The *Brecht-Abende* (Brecht Evenings) actually emerged from a practical necessity. A performance of *Galileo* had to be cancelled at very short notice, and the BE was not able to inform theatre-goers in good time. Ernst Busch together with other actors sang or recited their favourite songs and poems by Brecht, and, according to Wekwerth: 'the success was astounding'.[33] The impromptu event led to the compilation

[28] See Werner Hecht, *Brecht Chronik*, p. 1004.
[29] See Weigel to Erwin Axer, 16 January 1964, BArch DC 20/7716.
[30] See Erwin Axer to Weigel, 5 February 1964, ibid.
[31] See Herbert Krolikowski, 'Aktennotiz', 21 January 1964, ibid.
[32] See Bork to Weigel, 21 October 1964, BArch DR 1/8688.
[33] Wekwerth, *Schriften*, p. 175.

of the first *Brecht-Abend*, simply subtitled 'Lieder und Gedichte 1914–1956' ('Song and Poems 1914–1956'). It had its first performance on 26 April 1962. The evening included roughly forty items, with the programme nonetheless indicating a degree of flexibility in the note 'subject to change'. The choice of material was certainly partisan, although it was not exclusively composed of rousingly militant pieces. Indeed, a selection from the *Buckower Elegien* (*Buckow Elegies*), the poems written in the wake of 17 June 1953, was included, although the performers did not recite the ones famously critical of the SED, like 'Der Radwechsel' or 'Die Lösung' ('Changing the Wheel' or 'The Solution'). The GDR press, which seems to have been the main body covering the show, was uniformly enthusiastic. One reviewer observed the relaxed atmosphere that accompanied the evening and regretted that the performance had to take place on stage, preferring closer communion with the actors.[34] Another reported the twenty-minute applause that followed the *Abend*.[35] The review in *Neues Deutschland* was also very favourable and noted that the programme indicated that this was just 'Brecht-Abend Nr. 1'.[36]

The GDR audience certainly had to wait for the next instalment, which built on the success of the format and the positive responses to it by expanding both the scope and ambition of the second *Evening*. There was no formal plan for how the BE was going to follow up its initial success; the company merely believed it was an idea worth developing. Young directors Manfred Karge and Matthias Langhoff, one of Wolfgang Langhoff's sons, set the second *Evening* in motion when they asked Weigel whether they could work with actors who were not involved in Erich Engel's production of Brecht's major play *Schweyk im Zweiten Weltkrieg* (*Schweyk in the Second World War*). The new *Evening*, entitled 'Über die großen Städte' ('On the Great Cities'), came in two halves. The first echoed the previous *Brecht Evening* in that it consisted of recitations and songs, here related to the *Evening*'s theme. The second half presented a novelty, the reconstitution of Brecht's *Das kleine Mahagonny* (*The Little Mahagonny*), that is, the *Songspiel* version of Brecht and Kurt Weill's opera *Aufstieg und Fall der Stadt Mahagonny* (*Rise and Fall of the City of Mahagonny*). This is a stripped-down version which only includes songs and linking texts written by Brecht, rather than dialogue. Weill scholar David Drew had already unearthed the six songs and four intermezzos that form its musical heart. The problem with the plan was that there was no extant script for the linking texts, something Karge and Langhoff

---

[34] See Lothar Heinke, 'Ohne Puder und Perücke', *Der Morgen*, 28 April 1962.
[35] See Anon., 'Begeisterung mit Brecht', *BZ am Abend*, 27 April 1962.
[36] Elvira Mollenschott, 'Große Kunst der kleinen Form', *Neues Deutschland*, 27 May 1962.

discovered upon visiting the Brecht Archive. They thus decided to write their own in a 'Brechtian' style, based on the reminiscences of Weigel and Elizabeth Hauptmann, who saw the original production in 1927. The directors cheekily went back to Weigel claiming that they had discovered the texts themselves. Weigel reportedly said they looked familiar.[37]

The evening premiered on what would have been Brecht's 65th birthday, 10 February 1962, a day that opened with the ceremonial renaming of the area in front of the BE as 'Bertolt-Brecht-Platz'.[38] This evening, like the first, was warmly received, and reviewers were again impressed by the relaxed manner in which it was conducted.[39] The only dissenting voice was Rainer Kerndl at *Neues Deutschland*.[40] Karge and Langhoff paraphrased his critique at a party meeting in the BE on 15 February as 'formalist ideas and their realization'.[41] The indignation did not end in the BE. Former Minister Alexander Abusch publicly criticized Kerndl in *Neues Deutschland* and asserted that the show 'turns content and form into an inextricable dialectical unity'.[42] Such a high-ranking intervention suggests the hand of Weigel, who had good connections with the upper echelons of the SED. On the other hand, the counter-comment may have come directly from the SED, as it, after all, was basking in the reflected glory of the celebration around Brecht's anniversary, too.

Both *Evenings* were popular and were performed over fifty times in runs of roughly four years. The third *Evening* was the most ambitious yet, and also, as will become evident, the BE's most personal. Werner Hecht, who was editing a new collection of Brecht's theoretical writings, suggested performing the *Messingkauf*. As John J. White puts it:

the nature of this grandiose project and Brecht's failure to complete it go hand in hand... *Der Messingkauf* attempts to expound, illustrate and *perform* theory by means of an ingenious presentational strategy largely dictated by the theatrical medium that is at the same time the work's subject matter.[43]

---

[37] See Manfred Karge, in Manfred Dosdall, 'Gespräch mit Manfred Karge über seine Zusammenarbeit mit Helene Weigel am 9.1.1988 im Burgtheater Wien [with Matthias Braun]', 17 pages (5–6), HWA FH 85; and Anna and Matthias Langhoff, '"Der Gummimensch kommt in Sicht"', *Theater der Zeit*, 3 (1998), pp. 36–9 (37).

[38] See Anon., 'Berlin ehrt Bertolt Brecht', *Berliner Zeitung*, 11 February 1963.

[39] See, for example, -ler [*sic*], 'Die Welt feiert unsern Brecht', *National-Zeitung*, 12 February 1962.

[40] See Rainer Kerndl, 'Brecht-Abend des Berliner Ensembles', *Neues Deutschland*, 12 February 1962.

[41] Manfred Karge and Matthias Langhoff, 'Über eine Kritik im *Neuen Deutschland*', undated, n.p., BEA File 33.

[42] Alexander Abusch, 'Brecht im Geiste Brechts', *Neues Deutschland*, 17 February 1962.

[43] John J. White, *Bertolt Brecht's Dramatic Theory*, pp. 240–1.

Hecht had his work cut out: Brecht took up and went back to the *Messingkauf* project at various times from 1939 to 1955, and the many fragments fill over 170 pages in the standard edition.[44] The project did not merely stop with the production of a workable and playable script, however. The BE included three 'demonstrations' of practice, taken from its own repertoire, and five exercises for actors, three that appear in the *Messingkauf* itself and two devised by the BE.[45] This was a complex and ambitious project, which was also, in part, a response to audience demand as recorded in earlier post-show discussions.[46]

The decision was taken to stage the project in September 1963 in the belief that it would have a very short run.[47] The BE was of the opinion that this would be a show for a more specialist audience, and Weigel wanted Wekwerth and his team of young directors to present it on the *Probebühne* ('rehearsal stage'), which had a capacity of 100. Wekwerth, however, rehearsed on the main stage behind Weigel's back and provoked her ire when she found out. She was only placated by the positive reviews.[48] It turned out that she would have much of which to be proud. The show ran for 100 performances between its premiere on 12 October 1963 and its last night on 17 June 1970. Over this time, the script was continually reviewed and revised, and the project represented the BE's attempt to communicate its own 'secrets' by performing theory to enthusiastic audiences.

The engagement with the fragment and its development over time betokened the special relationship between the BE and Brecht's performance philosophies. Kenneth Tynan had asked whether an English-language *Messingkauf* would be performable. Elisabeth Hauptmann argued against the plan, writing that the show could not be easily transferred because it was the result of the BE's own experiences.[49] This sentiment was echoed shortly after the *Messingkauf* left the repertoire. The great director of Brecht's plays in the West, Harry Buckwitz, asked whether he could use the BE's version in Zurich and received a similar

---

[44] See Brecht, *Der Messingkauf*, BFA, 22: 695–869.
[45] For a full description and analysis of the *Evening*, see David Barnett, 'Brechtian Theory as Practice: The Berliner Ensemble stages *Der Messingkauf* in 1963', *Theatre, Dance and Performance Training*, 2:1 (2011), pp. 4–17.
[46] See Elvira Mollenschott, 'Vergnügliches Theatergespräch', *Neues Deutschland*, 28 September 1963.
[47] See Anon., 'Dramaturgie-Sitzung am 19.8.1963', undated, 4 pages (1), BEA File 'Dramaturgie '65–69/65–66 Protokolle/Briefe 63–64'.
[48] See Werner Hecht, *Helene Weigel*, pp. 84–5.
[49] See Elisabeth Hauptmann, 'Zu Tynans Brief', 10 February 1964, n.p., BEA File 34.

reply to Tynan from Joachim Tenschert.[50] The BE was convinced that the *Evening* was a product of its own unique response to experiences garnered from years of hard work.

The BE's audience had to wait over four years for the next *Brecht Evening*. Karge and Langhoff directed another fragment, *Der Brotladen* (*The Bread Shop*), a world premiere that opened on 13 April 1967 and enjoyed similar success and a similar run to that of the *Messingkauf*. The fifth and final *Evening* was conversely a very damp squib and reflects the malaise at the company in the late 1960s. Designed to celebrate the 20th anniversary of the GDR, *Das Manifest* (*The Manifesto*) featured Brecht's versification of Marx's *Communist Manifesto* together with a selection of poems, prose, songs and scenes. It premiered on 1 October 1969 and ran for the next four days playing evening and afternoon slots. Critics were mainly underwhelmed; one wrote that the show lacked 'dynamism, passion, originality'.[51] It was perhaps this lacklustre treatment of a tired format that led to its demise.

However, before moving on from this more compact and flexible form, I will linger briefly on a variation developed in the mid 1960s, which was intended to be the first of a series, but which was not to be continued. The first 'Nachtschicht' ('Night Shift') was named after a popular song of the early post-war years, 'Also wissen Se nee' ('Don'tcha know') by Bully Buhlan, and this period provided the backdrop for a loose collection of songs and sketches. The emphasis was on entertainment, and a compère linked the different items. There was a definite lightness to the evening, and the compère stressed that the audience was in for a Brecht-free evening. He humorously offered spectators their money back if they detected a *Verfremdung* or a free ticket for anyone who uncovered a *Gestus*.[52] The evening was the brainchild of Peter Sodann, who would become a successful *Intendant* himself in the GDR of the 1980s. At the time, however, Weigel had taken him under her wing; he had been arrested and imprisoned for nine months for his part in a satirical cabaret group in 1961. He began rehearsals, but Wekwerth took them over, as Sodann reports: 'they feared the worst; at the end of the day, the BE wasn't a bourgeois pleasure palace'.[53] Indeed, the positive reviews from East and West still noted a didactic tone amongst the jollity: 'forgetting [the privations of the post-war period] with a smile, so as not to forget — that was the evening's dialectic. We were in the BE after all'.[54]

[50] See Joachim Tenschert to Harry Buckwitz, 2 September 1970, ibid.
[51] Christoph Funke, 'Der Dichter und seine Zeit', *Der Morgen*, 3 October 1969.
[52] See first version of the compère's text in BEA File 37.
[53] Peter Sodann, *Keinehalben Sachen. Erinnerungen* (Berlin: Ullstein, 2009), p. 145.
[54] Christoph Funke, 'Also wissense, ja!', *Der Morgen*, 12 February 1965.

Coming out with guns blazing: *Die Tage der Kommune* as a defence of the Wall

The first *Brecht Evening* was not only a useful gambit to help expand and enhance the BE's repertoire, it also represented the first new piece of work after the erection of the Wall. Its commitment to Brecht and his politics was a rousing, but not uncritical statement of solidarity with the state in which he had chosen to settle. In this sense, the *Evening* echoed Brecht's full letter to Ulbricht on 17 June 1953. Yet the BE could not survive on new evenings of songs and poems alone, however well performed and well received they were. The company's first major post-Wall production was to present a resolute front and necessitated a change of production plan. Wekwerth's letter to Palitzsch of late August 1961, quoted above, noted that the BE was busy preparing Brecht's unfinished *Coriolan*. By November planning had begun on *Die Tage der Kommune* (*The Days of the Commune*), the play about which the SED had had grave doubts in 1951. Wekwerth and Besson had co-directed the play in Karl-Marx-Stadt in 1956, although it had not been terribly successful. By 1958 at the latest, the SED considered the play fully rehabilitated and suggested it, together with *Saint Joan of the Stockyards*, as a replacement for *The Threepenny Opera* and *Man Equals Man* in the BE's proposed production plan.[55] The decision to switch from *Coriolan* to *Commune* did not receive any objections in 1961.

Wekwerth's experience of Karl-Marx-Stadt led him to the conclusion that the BE would have to adapt Brecht's text because he believed that he and Besson had not worked on a bad production, but on a bad play.[56] One of the major additions to the Berlin production was the inclusion of documentary material taken from the protocols of the Paris Commune itself. Here the *Fabel* was not to change; the additional text was there to bolster it. Manfred Karge reported Wekwerth's basis for the production: 'we can't think we know better. We shouldn't talk of the characters' mistakes, nor overly emphasize them; our criticism must be objective: these are mistakes made in a non-revolutionary situation'.[57] The production's *Fabel* becomes clear if one analyses the quotation's final point first: all the action takes place 'in a non-revolutionary situation', a time at which history was not 'ripe' for revolution, in Marxist parlance. In other words, the material situation of the Communards drove them to insurrection,

[55] See Hans-Rainer John, 'Aktennotiz über ein Gespräch mit dem Berliner Ensemble am 19.9.58', 22 September 1958, n.p., BArch DR 1/18018.
[56] See Wekwerth, in Kranz, *Berliner Theater*, p. 72.
[57] Wekwerth, in Manfred Karge, 'Gespräch mit Wekwerth (9.11.61)', undated, n.p., BEA File 31.

but the absence of an organized communist party meant that they were doomed to failure: history was not ready for a popular revolution in 1871. Consequently, their actions, unbeknownst to them, could never succeed, yet, as the quotation shows, it was their valiant efforts, rather than their political naïvety that was to be the focus of the production.

Wekwerth, who thrived in directing partnerships, teamed up with head dramaturge Joachim Tenschert, and they proceeded to work on the performance implications of the *Fabel*. These were evident to critic Dieter Kranz: the directors 'had managed to pull off a remarkable feat by combining a demonstrative didactic acting style with the methods of Stanislavsky'.[58] Such a combination may remind the reader of Brecht's 1951 production of *The Mother* in its careful manipulation of audience sympathies. The production of *Commune* strategically deployed empathy to attach the spectators to the flawed revolutionaries in order to guide them away from undue criticism and towards admiration for the Communards. As Laura Bradley notes: 'Wekwerth sought to win his spectators' sympathy for the Communards in Brecht's play, on the assumption that if the spectators wanted the Commune to continue, they would accept the means necessary to achieve that end'.[59] The critical aspect retained by the production invited the audience to understand the reasons why the uprising failed.

Rehearsal was due to start on 1 January 1962 for a premiere in mid March.[60] After a not inconsiderable 212 rehearsals, the production finally went up on 7 October 1962. The BE was not concerned with delivering its response to the Wall that quickly; instead, as had become the 'tradition' over the years, it strove to craft a production that would endure and reward the exertion of the creative team and the actors. *Commune* ran for almost nine years. The production certainly had a Brechtian edge in that it emphasized action, deeds and contradictory situations over local colour. What almost every review noted was the production's relationship to very recent history. GDR critics viewed the show as a defence of the 'the protective measures of 13 August 1961' and understood that the Communards failed due to 'indecision and naïvety' – they used force too late (unlike, by extension, the GDR).[61] Another East German reviewer noted the optimistic thrust: the Paris Commune as 'the first battle on the

[58] Dieter Kranz, *Berliner Theater*, p. 70.

[59] Laura Bradley, 'A Different Political Forum: East German Theatre and the Construction of the Berlin Wall', *Journal of European Studies*, 36: 2 (2006), pp. 139–56 (150–1).

[60] See Anon., '*Tage der Kommune*: Brigadensitzung am 5. Dezember 1961', undated, 8 pages (2), BEA File 31.

[61] Karl Mennerich, '*Die Tage der Kommune*', *Freiheit*, 9 October 1962; and Helmut Ullrich, 'Auf den Barrikaden von Paris', *Neue Zeit*, 9 October 1962, respectively.

way to victory'.[62] The ultimate seal of approval was delivered by no less a politician than Walter Ulbricht who enthused about the production to Weigel.[63]

A Western reviewer, on the other hand, pointed to the way in which the aesthetics helped to carry the production's pro-Wall stance: 'you are transported by the perfection, by the sober brilliance of the production; you are concerned about the amount of agitation that this brilliance supports'.[64] Again one observes the ways in which well-rehearsed artistic perfection was used not to open up a dialectic but, on the contrary, to narrow it and make it serve political ends. However, it was not only the East that had a propagandist agenda. Many Western papers were quick to point out that Wolfgang Langhoff had started playing the role of Langevin in *Commune* almost a year after the premiere. The SED had stripped Langhoff of the DT *Intendanz* earlier in 1963 after it banned Peter Hacks' play *Die Sorgen und die Macht* (*Worries and Power*). The title of one article indicates the general thrust of the inter-German sniping: '*Intendant* Langhoff Now Simple Actor'.[65]

Shakespeare at the Berliner Ensemble: *Coriolan* as an unqualified success?

After the premieres of *Commune* and *Schweyk in the Second World War* in the autumn of 1962, the BE's audience had to wait almost two years for the next major production, *Coriolan*. Indeed, the wait for this particular play was a considerable one; Brecht began adapting Shakespeare's *Coriolanus* in 1951, but a combination of official disapprobation in the same year[66] and a dearth of suitable actors to play the title role led him indefinitely to postpone the project.[67] By the 1960s both problems had been resolved. The Ministry actually praised the plan to stage *Coriolan*[68]

---

[62] Walther Pollatschek, '*Tage der Kommune*', *Berliner Zeitung*, 10 October 1962.

[63] See Kebir, *Abstieg in den Ruhm*, p. 331.

[64] Dieter Hildebrandt, 'Ist die Mauer eine Barrikade?', *Frankfurter Allgemeine Zeitung*, 24 October 1962.

[65] Anon., 'Intendant Langhoff jetzt einfacher Schauspieler', *Hamburger Abendblatt*, 9 September 1963.

[66] See Trautzsch, 'Protokoll Nr. 91 der Sitzung des Sekretariats des ZK am 2. August 1951', undated, 19 pages (9), SAPMO BArch DY 30/J IV 2/3/220.

[67] See Rülicke, in Anon., 'Interview Matthias Braun mit Käthe Rülicke-Weiler, 1978 und 1984, über Helene Weigel/Bertolt Brecht', undated, 40 pages (9), HWA FH 80.

[68] Publisher Siegfried Unseld suggested that editor Elizabeth Hauptmann differentiate Brecht's play from Shakespeare's by dropping the 'us' in a letter of 1959 (see the Editors: BFA, 9: 344). I will maintain this practice for clarity.

as an engagement with the *Erbe*[69] and the BE had a viable Coriolan in the star of *Ui*, Ekkehard Schall. What the company lacked was a viable text.

Wekwerth was not satisfied with Brecht's unfinished adaptation and felt that the BE could improve on what he considered to be some of Brecht's false emphases. I do not wish to examine the adaptation process here and will instead point out some of the problems that the adaptation wanted to address. Wekwerth, who had seen the unsuccessful world premiere of Brecht's adaptation in Frankfurt am Main in 1962, noted a 'tendency to idealize the people that should counterbalance Shakespeare's idealization of the nobility'.[70] The BE did not want to show the people as 'Revoluzzer' (an untranslatable German term, usually used disparagingly towards revolutionaries who do not have the wherewithal to conduct a revolution), nor as Brecht's own 'revolutionaries', but a group that had 'a revolutionary *Haltung*'.[71] The representatives of the common people were thus to show that they could develop productive political behaviour, but that this was neither given nor inevitable.

Coriolan himself presented a great problem, primarily due to the perceived status of protagonists in general in the works of Shakespeare. Matthias Langhoff identified an unchangeability in the character that 'demands a mode of acting unknown to our theatre'.[72] The point of view persisted into rehearsals where an anonymous *Notat*-taker wrote that Coriolan 'is of a fixity that pervades his diction and his gestures, he's become a montage of this fixity, constructed from naïve and contradictory behaviour'.[73] Thus the BE's solution was to present the unchangeable figure in all possible contradictory richness, although this is a peculiar point to have reached in the first place for a company with the BE's intellectual heritage. Nancy C. Michael writes: 'neither Shakespeare's Coriolanus nor Brecht's Coriolan has a place in society, Coriolanus because he will not condescend, Coriolan because he will not adapt'.[74] This position, not an uncommon one in Western Brecht criticism, imputes to Coriolan

---

[69] See W., 'Punkte von der Kollegiumssitzung des Ministeriums für Kultur am 4.4.1961', undated, n.p., BBA uncatalogued file 'HW BE-MfK 1961–67'.

[70] Wekwerth, 'Zu einem Punkt der *Coriolan*- Bearbeitung Brechts', in Anon., 'Schauspielermaterial', [October 1963], 84 pages (70), BEA File 36.

[71] Anon., '[*Notat* for 3 April 1963]', in ibid., p. 80.

[72] Matthias Langhoff, 'Über die Darstellungsweise des *Coriolan*', 22 November 1963, in Anon., 'Zweites, ergänzendes Material zur *Tragödie des Coriolan* im Berliner Ensemble', undated, n.p., BEA File 36.

[73] Anon., 'coriolan [sic]', 16 March 1964, n.p., ibid.

[74] Nancy C. Michael, 'The Affinities of Adaptation: The Artistic Relationship between Brecht's *Coriolan* and Shakespeare's *Coriolanus*', *Brecht Yearbook*, 13 (1984), pp. 145–54 (152).

an intransigence that borders on existentialism, in which human subjects have complete freedom of choice over all their decisions. In this reading, Coriolan has the power to choose whether he changes or not, something that contradicts the very nature of the dialectical process. The dialectic does not work exclusively on the conscious mind, and adaptability in human beings is a prerequisite for dialectical movement: its advance cannot simply be held up because a particular character chooses not to be subject to a mechanism that is historically irresistible. It is not, then, that Coriolan is unable to adapt; he, by definition, adapts to every change of circumstance that runs through the play. His problem is that he continually makes the wrong choices in a society that indulges his individualism. In this understanding of the dialectic, individualism is the tragic component of the play, in that the hero only views it positively, while society takes a far more pragmatic approach to it. That the BE chose to follow an undialectical reading of Coriolan's character is surprising, and its decision merely to offer a contradictory kaleidoscope is ahistorical at best.

One attempt to contextualize the Roman Coriolan was to re-emphasize the rivalry with Aufidius, the leader of the Volscians. Wekwerth believed that this helped to undermine Coriolan as a singular hero by framing his need for victories socially.[75] The victories were not in some way abstract, but concrete means of achieving greatness in Rome over a named opponent. After all, the character gains the honorary title 'Coriolan' from his defeat of Aufidius at the Battle of Corioli, and this offered the production another opportunity to engage in materialist analysis.

Brecht had not rewritten the battle scenes, preferring to consider them on stage, in rehearsals that were never to take place. Wekwerth and Tenschert observed that some productions did not stage the battle scenes in the belief that one should simply take Coriolan's martial mastery in good faith. They continued that the BE did not share this view and wanted the spectator to reach that opinion having seen him 'at work'.[76] The Brechtian emphasis on exposing the ceremonial as social code allowed a dialectical view of the battle to emerge: 'we show the savagery [of the battle] as ceremony, the chaos as order, that is only to be created by experts in warfare'.[77] Action as social process helped to undermine a

---

[75] See Wekwerth, *Schriften*, p. 203.

[76] See Wekwerth and Tenschert, in Anon., 'Interview zwischen einem Redakteur des Bayrischen Runkfunks München und Wekwerth/Tenschert am 16. September [1964] im Berliner Ensemble', undated, 3 pages, BEA File 36.

[77] Anon., 'September 1963', in Anon., 'Schauspielermaterial', [October 1963], 84 pages (82), ibid.

mythologizing reading of Coriolan in favour of one firmly rooted in his expertise.

Wekwerth and Tenschert entrusted the battle scenes to an assistant director, Ruth Berghaus. Berghaus scholarship has long considered this to be her first work at the BE, but she was in fact responsible for the crowd scenes in *Commune* beforehand.[78] She had trained as a dancer and had been an intern at the BE between 1951 and 1953.[79] She thus combined a sense of physicality with Brecht's performance principles. This is evident in a direction she gave to the actors of these scenes, who were mostly acting students gaining experience at the BE: 'we're supposed to be showing how barbaric the fight was and how the different warriors behave differently, not how savage or barbarous our actors can be'.[80] The emphasis on showing action and not characters was a priority, as was a Brechtian impulse to historicize, as Berghaus noted: 'a battle is not taking place, on the contrary we are showing how a particular battle took place'.[81] The difference between the immediacy of the former and the careful artistry of the latter denotes the care Berghaus took to stage action sequences that were not to be mistaken for a real battle, but to demonstrate its workings.

Composer Paul Dessau, Berghaus's husband and erstwhile Brecht collaborator, wrote the music for the battle scenes, which was percussive and raucous. At this time, the BE, which was always interested in making use of the latest technology in its productions, tested a stereo system to heighten the impact of Dessau's non-illustrative soundtrack.[82] It should not be forgotten that in October 1963 the Beatles had recorded their first ever stereo record, 'I want to hold your hand', at the cutting-edge Abbey Road studios.[83] The BE was only ten months behind the capitalist West. However, the price of the stereo unit from Switzerland was prohibitive and the BE's engineers suggested they build their own.

The production finally premiered on 25 September 1964. Its centrepiece was a tower, mounted on the BE's revolving stage: one side was

---

[78]   See Tenschert and Wekwerth to Hans Giersch, 7 November 1963, BEA File 'Dramaturgie Durchschläge für Frau Weigel ab 15. Jan. 1963–1970'.

[79]   See Corinne Holtz, *Ruth Berghaus. EinPorträt* (Hamburg: Europäische Verlagsanstalt, 2005), p. 143–4.

[80]   Ruth Berghaus, 'Notat für Schauspieler', 3 March 1964, BEA File 36.

[81]   Ruth Berghaus, 'Notat-*Coriolan*: 1.3.[1964] Schlachtproben', undated, n.p., AdK RBA 921/2.

[82]   See Anon., '[Report on stereo testing at the BE on 8 August 1964]', undated, n.p., BEA File 36.

[83]   See Ian MacDonald, *Revolution in the Head. The Beatles' Records and the Sixties*, third, revised edition (London: Vintage, 2008), p. 102.

Fig. 6.1. Exposing the general's expertise: the choreography of the battle scenes sets out Coriolan's mastery of the art of war. *Coriolan*, September 1964.

a white stone portal, the other dark wooden gate. Much of the action played out against this central set item. The sparseness of the otherwise white cyclorama allowed the actors to set out the carefully staged *Arrangements*, with the battle scenes in particular unfolding as a series of tightly choreographed yet energetic set pieces (see Fig. 6.1). The physicality of the action complemented the gestic performances to lend the production a controlled muscularity that, again, allowed Schall to shine. His Coriolan articulated the pride of the character, as spectators would have expected, but the strength of the interpretation contextualized the quality squarely in the Rome of the play. The general was anchored in his society as a figure who had overplayed his hand, unable to appreciate that the majority of the people only valued him for one particular talent. The precision of the work applied to the interaction between individual and society, a hallmark of the BE, allowed audiences to view the play with fresh eyes: no longer were characters the focus as individuals, but their complex place in the antagonistic city states that populated the ancient world. The show was not only of historical interest; the clarity of the relationships also created a window onto the present, as the theme of self-assumed indispensability resonated with spectators. In a world of burgeoning individuality, what was considered a strength in the West was subjected to critique on the BE's stage.

It is also worth noting that this production was 'transplanted' to the National Theatre in London in the early 1970s, where the same directing team staged the play with an English cast. One reviewer noted: 'Wekwerth's and Tenschert's creation fits neither the text it's been given [Shakespeare's original, not Brecht's adaptation] nor the company which has been strait-jacketed into it'.[84] This not uncommon response from the British press underlines just how well the direction suited the ensemble at the BE. Its traditions of gestic acting helped to dovetail a socially based interpretation with a set of performative abilities, crafted to realize it.

For the most part, the production was very well received in Berlin. Elvira Mollenschott wrote in her review for *Neues Deutschland* that 'rarely . . . were expectations so high':[85] the BE's first Shakespeare had been a long time coming, but had not disappointed. FRG critic Urs Jenny noted a total absence of 'a purely mechanical application of the Brechtian method', indeed he registered his surprise at how critically Brecht's own adaptation had been treated.[86] The main point of critique was the casting of a guest from the Volksbühne, Manja Behrens, as Coriolan's mother, Volumnia. Helene Weigel took over the role for the London tour because, despite her dislike for the character, she appreciated that the BE could not afford to make mistakes, especially when offering its own Shakespeare to the English.[87] This was Weigel's last major new role and one for which she was much celebrated.

The immediate adulation aside, there were two more critical voices who, independently of each other, touched on similar points. In the East, Friedrich Dieckmann accused the set design, which literally revolved around the revolving tower, of running the risk of representing nothing due to its multipurpose ubiquity.[88] In effect, he was referring back to the older criticism, levelled at Engel's *Threepenny Opera*, that (in *Coriolan* visual) perfection could blind spectators to an absence.[89] He went on to

---

[84] Ronald Bryden, 'Off the Peg Coriolanus', *The Guardian*, 9 May 1971.
[85] Elvira Mollenschott, 'Zweier großer Dramatiker würdig', *Neues Deutschland*, 27 September 1964.
[86] Urs Jenny, 'Der ersetzbare Held', *Süddeutsche Zeitung*, 28 September 1964.
[87] See Tenschert, in Manfred Dosdall, 'Gespräch mit Joachim Tenschert über Helene Weigel am 11.7.1983 in Berlin [with Matthias Braun]', undated, 34 pages (11), HWA FH 63.
[88] See Friedrich Dieckmann, '*Die Tragödie des Coriolan*: Shakespeare im Brecht-Theater', *Sinn und Form*, 17: 3 and 4 (1965), pp. 463–89 (488).
[89] This point is also made and argued in Darko Suvin, 'Brechtian or Pseudo-Brechtian: Mythical Estrangement in the Berlin Ensemble Adaptation of *Coriolanus*', *Asaph*, 3 (1986), pp. 135–58 (148).

criticize what he perceived to be a considerable shift in the BE's ethos: it had changed from being a radical workshop in the 1950s to 'a representative institution whose fame has become something legendary across the whole of Europe'.[90] Klaus Völker in the West raised the 'accusation of artistic dogmatism and of mechanical perfectionism in the practical work'.[91] He also criticized the company's lack of productivity as a disadvantage for the actors and noted that in Brecht's lifetime the productions were much debated, whereas now artistic brilliance meant that everybody seemed to like them. Völker is the first person to coin a term that would haunt the BE later that decade, that the company could become a 'Brecht Museum'.

What the two critics describe is difficult to reconcile with the glowing reviews of the production. However, they had seen many BE productions and were in a good position to raise these reservations. My account of the realization process shows that much time and effort was spent on both the adaptation and rehearsals,[92] and there is little trace of a mechanical process at all. However, the two critics both point to issues that certainly revisited the BE, and so perhaps they were able to detect failings, present at the time, that would only increase and multiply in the future. They may have taken the shine off the production, but it proved to be another great hit, given 276 times over fourteen and a half years, and toured extensively abroad. Indeed, this was perhaps the BE's final production that drew renown from around the world until Heiner Müller's *Arturo Ui* in the mid 1990s.

Exclusivity and orthodoxy: the Berliner Ensemble's 'divine right' to Brecht

Dieckmann's criticism pointed to something of a lethal process for lively theatre-making: fame had turned the BE from a radical institution into a 'representative' one. One can certainly discern such a shift in certain sentiments in the BE's correspondence of late 1963. Weigel had written to Wolfgang Heinz, who succeeded Langhoff as *Intendant* at the DT, telling him that he would be welcome to play *Puntila* at the BE, but not at the DT: 'and that on principle'.[93] It is worth considering why the BE

---

[90] Dieckmann, *'Die Tragödie'*, p. 481.
[91] Klaus Völker, 'Wohin geht das Berliner Ensemble?', *Theater heute*, 11 (1964), pp. 34–5 (35). All following references are taken from this page.
[92] The first batch of material for the actors to read (see n. 70) notes that new work started on the adaptation in January 1963, for example.
[93] Weigel to Wolfgang Heinz, 15 November 1963, *Briefwechsel*, p. 133.

felt itself uniquely charged with the task of exclusively staging Brecht's plays.

Hans-Rainer John, the head dramaturge at the DT, had written to the BE asking whether the DT could perform the plays by Brecht that the BE did not intend to stage. The BE's head dramaturge, Joachim Tenschert, wrote an extensive reply explaining why the BE would not be granting other East Berlin theatres the rights to stage Brecht. His opening position was that the BE was interested in Brecht's complete dramatic output, which was curious in the first place, because the BE had neither planned nor shown any interest in the work that preceded *The Threepenny Opera* (1928) at that time. Tenschert then made the argument that their policy was not predicated on eliminating competition:

> to us, it's not a question of having productions based on a different approach to Brecht's plays running alongside the BE's in Berlin, but of embedding our approach, primarily with our audience.[94]

He supported this position by telling John that the BE was carefully exploring Brecht's method, which was not 'simple to adopt', but required time and training both in the ensemble itself and in the spectators who were learning how to view Brecht's plays.

Tenschert's positions betray some interesting contradictions. While no one would begrudge the BE its desire to develop its understanding of 'Brecht's method', he, like Weigel did to Heinz, treated the BE's approach as if it were the only legitimate exegesis. Consequently, his denial of a fear of competition becomes debatable: if the BE were successfully working through Brecht's method as an unambiguous system, then other Berlin theatres would present either pale imitations or productions which could not be considered 'Brechtian'. If, on the other hand, the BE were only pursuing *one* possible avenue, however effective it had proven, then its implicit claims to authority (and concomitant prestige) would be undermined by success from other Berlin theatres. This exclusivity was based on a belief that the BE was the true heir to Brecht's theory and practice, something that the DT was to call into question (see pp. 199–201, Chapter 7).

The BE's pious veneration of the Brechtian method was satirized by the GDR writer Peter Hacks in a story written in 1961–2 and 1966, 'Ekbal, oder: Eine Theaterreise nach Babylon' ('Ekbal, or: A Theatre Trip to Babylon'). Hacks' comic allegory, where Babylon stands for Berlin, contains an episode that recounts the death of the Eurasian saint,

---

[94] Tenschert to Hans-Rainer John, 12 November 1963, BBA uncatalogued file 'Korr 54–66'.

Bebe[95] (Brecht), whose last will and testament decreed the preservation of four qualities in his theatre: 'greatness, revolutionary power, vitality, and care'.[96] The will was distributed to his heirs, but the parchment got lost over time. High Priest Wewe (Wekwerth) retained the exhortation to 'care' and had the other three qualities declared heretical. Hacks' allegory saw Brechtianism as a religion at the BE, the company that dictated its precepts by 'divine right'. The tendency towards orthodoxy found its confirmation in Tenschert and Wekwerth's reply to John, who had proposed that *Theater der Zeit* publish their correspondence. They told him in no uncertain terms that they wrote articles and essays when they needed to, and did not publish letters: 'in any case, the arguments we've presented are nothing new; you can read up on them in Brecht's published writings'.[97] Again, a tone of arrogance in communications from the BE is notable, which here masked its own debatable positions.

Interest from home and abroad: confirmation of the Berliner Ensemble's reputation

East Berlin may well have had a special status when it came to staging Brecht, but other theatres in the GDR regularly received BE directors as guests who disseminated Brecht's practice without the sustained preparation upon which Tenschert insisted. The Ministry of Culture had been happy to endorse Brecht's tradition of sending BE directors out to the provinces, and indeed beyond. In 1957, it requested that a BE director stage *Mother Courage* in Bulgaria.[98] A similar invitation for Wekwerth to direct the same play in Moscow arrived the following year.[99] Wolfgang Pintzka was dispatched to Görlitz, where the BE was promoting a more regularized relationship with the theatre there in 1960, and three years later, while he was still at that theatre, the Ministry promoted him to *Intendant* at the theatre in Gera.[100] The authorities had found that the BE and its programme of developing young directors could be most useful in a small country with a lot of theatres. Regardless of old ideological disputes, the BE offered qualified, competent directors who could be relied upon to deliver.

---

[95] Pronounced in German like the letters BB.
[96] See Peter Hacks, *Die Erzählungen* (Hamburg: Lutz Schulenburg, 1995), pp. 47–86 (64).
[97] Wekwerth and Tenschert to Hans-Rainer John, 21 November 1963, BBA uncatalogued file 'Korr 54–66'.
[98] See Bork to Weigel, 30 November 1957, BBA uncatalogued file 'HW Allg. Schriftwechsel 1957'.
[99] See Bork to Weigel, 12 May 1958, BBA uncatalogued file 'HW Briefw. 1–6/1958'.
[100] See Pintzka, *Von Sibirien*, pp. 129–31 and 133.

GDR theatres did not only demand well-trained staff from the BE. The *Modellbücher* were also much sought after. This was a very different situation from that which had confronted Brecht on the publication of the *Antigonemodell* in 1949: he sold fewer than 500 copies.[101] This dispiriting statistic probably cooled Brecht's ardour and led to the fact that the *Courage* and *Galileo Modellbücher* were only published after his death. The BE's unpublished in-house *Modellbücher* were certainly in demand in the late 1950s, on the back of both the BE's international success and the surge of interest following Brecht's death. Statistics compiled by the BE show that in the years from 1964 to 1967, the company sent the *Modellbücher* of twenty-three different productions to 165 theatres. Sixty-three remained within the GDR, twenty-nine went over the border to the FRG, and seventy-three were sent further afield to Europe and beyond, to Cuba, Argentina, the USA, Turkey, Ceylon (as was), Israel, and Egypt.[102] The BE also received 729 visitors to its archive from 1964 to 1969, just under half of whom came from the FRG and the rest of the world. The company found it difficult, however, to deal with so many people, and this was noted as early as 1961 when the need to create an 'Overseas Section' was mooted to relieve pressure on the BE's dramaturgy department.[103] The Ministry of Culture was so keen to cultivate foreign interest in the BE that it proposed the idea of a 'Brecht Scholarship' to support theatre people from abroad to work at the BE for 1–2 years. Two to three places were to be offered each year, although the Ministry actually wanted to sponsor more. The BE was cautious about overstretching its own resources and suggested the lower figure.[104]

High-profile and innovative theatre-makers also wanted to direct at or bring shows to the BE. The archive shows that Jean Vilar offered to stage Brecht's *Turandot* in 1963, Peter Brook registered his interest in directing something from the English canon through Kenneth Tynan in 1966, and Luigi Nono proposed staging his *Floresta* in 1967.[105] Weigel wanted

[101] See Klaus-Detlef Müller, 'Brechts Theatermodelle: Historische Begründung und Konzept', in Jean-Marie Valentin and Theo Buck (eds.), *Bertolt Brecht. Actes du Colloque Franco-Allemandtenu en Sorbonne...* (Bern: Peter Lang, 1990), pp. 315–32 (318).
[102] Anon., 'Berliner Ensemble – Modellbücher-Ausleihe', undated, n.p., BEA File 'Modellbücher: Archiv-Statistik'. The following untitled document is also kept in this file.
[103] [Weigel?], 'Notizen zu einem Gespräch mit Minister Hans Bentzien am 23. Mai 1961', undated, 2 pages (1), BBA uncatalogued file 'HW BE-MfK 1961–67'.
[104] See Werner Hecht, 'Besprechung im Ministerium für Kultur über Studienmöglichkeiten am Berliner Ensemble', 4 October 1965, 3 pages, AdK JTA 'BE interne Korr./Dramat. 1959–1970'.
[105] See Anon., 'Dramaturgie-Besprechung am 10.6.1963', undated, 3 pages (2), BEA File 'Dramaturgie '65–69/65–66 Protokolle/Briefe 63–64'; Kenneth Tynan to Wekwerth, 23 May 1966, BEA File 'Dramaturgie Wekwerth Allgemeines – Schriftwechsel 1964–68/69'; and [Wekwerth] to Paul Dessau, 2 June 1967, ibid., respectively.

to invite the Living Theatre in 1964, on the back of their winning a prize at the Théâtre des Nations in 1961 for their production of Brecht's *Im Dickicht der Städte* (*In the Jungle of the Cities*).[106] The Ministry later reported that it had nothing against the experimental company playing at the BE,[107] although Bork also handwrote a simple 'nein!' next to the proposal for a production by Brook.[108] As it turned out, none of these guests actually worked with or at the theatre, and one can only speculate that either the expense of buying hard foreign currency to pay the guests, official politico-aesthetic objections and/or problems with schedules led to the failure of realizing these ambitions.

The explosion of domestic and international interest in one of the world's most exciting theatre companies was based on its concrete achievements, as demonstrated by its productions in the GDR and on tour. However, this work had to be sustained in order for its reputation to remain tangible rather than to slip into theatre lore. One solution to this was to produce more regularly and to diversify beyond the limits of Brecht's dramas while retaining the Brechtian method.

Documentary drama, Heinar Kipphardt, and the GDR: *Oppenheimer* and the XI Plenum

The reaction to the elephantine gestation period of *Coriolan* was a new production that spent a relatively short period in rehearsal, a mere three months. Yet Heinar Kipphardt's *In der Sache J. Robert Oppenheimer* (*In the Matter of J. Robert Oppenheimer*) was a play that presented the SED with two different, yet unintentionally related problems. The play was one of the major harbingers of a resurgent wave of documentary drama in Germany that sought to approach the complexities of modern life by capturing its contours in factual sources. In this case, Kipphardt drew on the official record of a hearing to determine whether Oppenheimer, the physicist who had managed the US atomic bomb programme from 1942 to 1945, should retain his security clearance in 1954. The problem for the SED was the documentary mode itself: Kipphardt's attempt to render the situation *without* bias lacked by definition a partisan stance on atomic weapons, the US state and its security apparatus.

Wekwerth consulted the Ministry of Culture for permission both to stage the play and to stage it ahead of the Volksbühne, which had also

[106] See Weigel to Bork, 19 October 1964, BArch DR 1/18249.
[107] See Heinz Schröder, 'Aktennotiz', 15 December 1964, 2 pages (2), ibid.
[108] Bork, 'Helene Weigel', 1 December 1965, n.p., BArch DR 1/8849. No reason is given for the rejection.

signalled an interest. He first connected the play to Brecht's *Galileo* by noting the common theme of the social responsibilities of scientists. He then argued that the experience of the *Messingkauf* meant that the BE now possessed the techniques to stage conversations, the main mode of communication in the play, as engaging interactions. His final point was that the BE had registered its interest first.[109] The Ministry wrote in a memorandum that the play could indeed be produced in the GDR if it was thoroughly historicized.[110] That is, the play was written in the West for Western audiences and was more about Oppenheimer's morals than the political context that brought about the hearing and the decision it reached. In short, the Ministry, internally at that time, was in favour of a thoroughly Brechtian approach to the material. An anonymous report in the Central Committee's archive unequivocally favoured the BE as the theatre best prepared to stage the play 'with the necessary distance and criticism'.[111] Even Walter Ulbricht backed the BE over the Volksbühne on this production, which says something about how certain aspects of the Brechtian tradition had bedded down in the circles of power by the mid 1960s.[112]

Kipphardt himself brought an amount of ideological baggage to the discussion as well. He had previously been the head dramaturge at the DT, but illegally left the GDR in 1959 after SED interference in the DT's repertoire and adverse criticism of one of his plays. Kipphardt was, in the SED's language, a 'Republikflüchtling' (an 'escapee from the Republic'), and Kurt Hager, the most powerful figure in cultural politics from the early 1960s until 1989, banned his entrance to the GDR in 1964.[113] Kipphardt's status as *persona non grata* did not, however, automatically disqualify the play from performance, and sometime afterwards, Hager's decision must have been rescinded, as BE documentation shows that Kipphardt attended rehearsals on at least five occasions.[114]

The nature of the production process seemingly suggested that the BE and the SED were singing from the same songbook: the need to historicize and politicize the neutrality of documentary drama was key. Ruth Berghaus, who was one of the two directing assistants assigned to the process, noted: 'the mode of delivering the speeches is to be derived

---

[109] See Wekwerth to Heinz Schröder, 17 November 1964, BArch DR 1/18249.
[110] See Willi Schrader, 'Ergänzung zur Notiz vom 3.12.1964 über Kipphardts *Oppenheimer*', undated, 2 pages (1), ibid.
[111] Anon., untitled, [early December 1964], 2 pages (2), SAPMO BArch DY 30/IV A2/9.06/113.
[112] See Gero Hammer to Heinz Schröder, 14 December 1964, ibid.
[113] See Kurt Hager to Weigel, 28 May 1964, SAPMO BArch DY 30/IV A2/2.024/32.
[114] See BEA File 38 for rehearsals at the end of March and the beginning of April 1965.

from the *Haltungen*, not from the speeches. The words that are spoken are the product of thought processes'.[115] Directors Wekwerth and Tenschert were thus interested in creating tensions between word and *Haltung*. They wanted to open up Kipphardt's documentary dramaturgy in order to reveal the political attitudes that underlay it. Wekwerth also wrote that the production as a whole was an experiment in which the BE had chosen a special form, that of the drawing room drama, in order to generate a lightness in the acting.[116] The intention here was to contrast the apparent ease of speech encoded in the hearing's protocol with the hard facts at the heart of nuclear research and its practical consequences.

The production's historicizing approach only converged with the SED's up to a point, however. The team acknowledged that productions in the West had been criticized for how sympathetically Oppenheimer and, conversely, how negatively the FBI could be portrayed. In the interests of dialectical realism, the BE wanted to redress this balance by showing that the USA had 'a certain right to the atom bomb' and that that made the decision to deny Oppenheimer clearance all the more difficult.[117] Such a reading, that sought to give the hearing realistic depth, simply did not condemn the USA clearly enough for the SED, and this would lead to problems after the East German premiere on 12 April 1965.

The BE nonetheless retained its critique of Oppenheimer, and reused the etched copper walls of the 1957 production of *Galileo* (see Fig. 6.2) to suggest a connection between the two scientists, an idea reportedly supplied by the celebrated Italian director of Brecht, Giorgio Strehler.[118] Wekwerth wanted to portray Oppenheimer's scientific greatness *and* his historical limitations. The production was well received. In the East, a reviewer noted how the documentary aesthetic had not been punctured by the BE's approach, 'but brought out in its sober poignancy'.[119] Another praised how the BE avoided the temptation to make the production more sensuous or emotional, and enjoyed the ways in which the verbal relationships and the *Haltungen* did that work amply.[120] Western critics were also positive. The title of one review, 'Without an Anti-American Edge', reflected the BE's insistence on the production's

---

[115] Ruth Berghaus, '[Notat]', 25 January 1965, BEA File 38. This, and certain other *Notate* were also published in *Theater der Zeit*, 10 (1965), pp. 21–3. This *Notat* appears on p. 23.
[116] See Wekwerth to Wolfgang Langhoff, 17 April 1965.
[117] Anon., 'Besprechung vom 11. Januar 1965', undated, 5 pages (4), BEA File 38.
[118] See Wekwerth, in Anon., 'Dramaturgie-Sitzung über *Oppenheimer* am 13.1.1965', undated, 7 pages (5), ibid.
[119] Helmut Ullrich, 'Schlüsselfigur der Epoche', *Neue Zeit*, 15 April 1965.
[120] See Christoph Funke, 'Die Wissenschaft – ein Krüppel?', *Der Morgen*, 18 April 1965.

Fig. 6.2. Intertextual set design: copper walls from the 1957 production of *Galileo* implicitly criticize the nuclear physicists. *In the Matter of J. Robert Oppenheimer*, April 1965.

realism.[121] Others noted how producing a play by a *Republikflüchtling* in the GDR went hand in hand with the permission to stage recent productions of potentially controversial work like Peter Weiss's *Marat/Sade* and Rolf Hochhuth's *Der Stellvertreter* (known as both *The Deputy* and *The Representative* in English).[122] The West welcomed a cultural thaw. This, however, did not last long.

Between 16 and 18 December 1965, the Central Committee of the SED held its eleventh Plenum, a meeting that was originally supposed to consider economic issues, but instead turned its attention to cultural politics. It has gone down in GDR cultural history as a significant turning point, a very public re-establishment of the SED's power in this field.[123] Shortly before the Plenum, a lesser-known meeting took place, and it was there that Kurt Hager roundly criticized the BE's production of *Oppenheimer*. He asserted that it lacked 'any real class perspective' and

[121] Dietmar E. Zimmer, 'Ohne antiamerikanische Spitze', *Die Zeit*, 16 April 1965.
[122] See, for example, Dieter Hildebrandt, 'Oppenheimer, ein Nachfahrer des Galilei', *Frankfurter Allgemeine Zeitung*, 21 April 1965.
[123] See, for example, Werner Mittenzwei, *Die Intellektuellen. Literatur und Politik in Ostdeutschland 1945–2000* (Berlin: Aufbau, 2003), p. 218.

was a play 'that blurred any demarcation of fronts' by viewing the USA and the USSR as equals, both seeking nuclear weapons.[124] Kurt Bartel dovetailed the critique with his contention that the play was written by a traitor, something that the BE's Helmut Baierl disputed.[125] Walter Ulbricht countered that Kipphardt's status was irrelevant; the problems were down to the BE's unwillingness to cut the play 'correctly'.

While the main attacks in the Plenum itself affected the GDR's film industry, theatre was not entirely untouched. The two main targets were Peter Hacks' *Moritz Tassow* and Heiner Müller's *Der Bau* (*The Building Site*). Ernst Schumacher notes that the mostly unreported third play was Volker Braun's *Kipper Paul Bauch* (*Trucker Paul Bauch*).[126] This drama had been developed and rehearsed at the BE, but found its rehearsals halted in the wake of the Plenum on 12 January 1966. Attempts to revive the process later in 1966 and 1969 came to nothing.[127] Two days after the Plenum ended, the Ministry of Culture set about formulating policy. It requested information on *Bauch* and asked which measures could be taken to remove 'ideologically false positions' in *Oppenheimer*.[128] The BE, however, was given the right to reply and responded not to the Ministry, but to the Central Committee's Cultural Department. The BE's local party leadership concluded that the production did not generate 'negative effects' and should thus be neither changed nor cancelled.[129] The arguments seem to have worked, and the production continued to be performed until mid 1969.

The Central Committee had played an important part in both the banning of Müller's *The Resettler* and the removal of Wolfgang Langhoff from the DT's leadership in the wake of 13 August 1961. Yet the unambiguous direction of the Plenum for cultural policy as a whole marked an apparent return to the 'bad old days' of the early 1950s, when central intervention was deemed necessary to ensure conformity. Minister Hans Bentzien lost his post in January 1966 and was replaced by Klaus Gysi in a bid to curb the liberal agenda that had briefly crept into GDR culture. However,

---

[124] See Kurt Hager, in Anon., 'Humanismus und Realismus in der Literatur der Deutschen Demokratischen Republik', undated, 129 pages (72), SAPMO BArch NY 4204/17.
[125] See Kurt Bartel and Helmut Baierl, in ibid., pp. 74 and 115, respectively. Ulbricht's comment is taken from p. 115.
[126] See Ernst Schumacher, 'DDR-Dramatik und 11. Plenum', in Günter Agde (ed.), *Kahlschlag. Das 11. Plenum des ZK der SED 1965. Studien und Dokumente* (Berlin: Aufbau, 1991), pp. 93–104, here p. 100.
[127] See Anon., 'Besprechung: *Die Kipper* am 3. November 1969', undated, 16 pages, BEA File '*Die Kipper: Konzept. Material*'.
[128] Hans Starke to Heinz Schröder, 20 December 1965, BArch DR 1/8844.
[129] Anon., 'Aktennotiz über Ansprache mit dem Genossen Helmut Baierl am 5.4.1966', 7 April 1966, n.p., SAPMO BArch DY 30/IV A2/2.024/32.

despite the Plenum, the BE was nonetheless given the opportunity to account for itself, the Central Committee at least tolerated its arguments and did not cancel *Oppenheimer*. The more prominent presence of the Central Committee in late 1965 heralded its greater involvement in 'difficult' matters and decisions in the future, as Wolfgang Langhoff and the DT had already experienced to their cost earlier in the decade. It would thus present an additional layer of supervision to that of the Ministry when the BE entered its most serious and sustained crisis in the second half of the 1960s.

7   Years of crisis: 1966–1971

Competition for the Berliner Ensemble at last: *Purple Dust* and a challenge from Benno Besson

To all appearances, the BE was a most unusual theatre company. It was dominated by the work and implemented the practice of a single artist, and it produced considerably fewer major productions than any of its rivals in East Berlin (see n. 62, Chapter 5). However, the unconventional focus and remarkably low productivity had proven to be a domestic and an international success, and had promoted a sense that the arrangement was in some way sustainable. One factor that helped foster this illusion was the marked lack of competition from the Deutsches Theater, the Volksbühne, and the smaller Maxim-Gorki-Theater (which was founded in 1952 to present a Stanislavskian counter-model and 'corrective' to the BE).[1] By the 1960s, however, things started to change, and the instrument of this change was none other than Benno Besson.

Having been forced out of the BE, Besson directed in the GDR as well as in the FRG, Switzerland, and Italy. In the GDR, Besson tended to work at the DT, and he scored a hit with critics and audiences alike in 1962 with Aristophanes' *Peace* in Peter Hacks' adaptation. Three more productions there allowed him to experiment with his practice; he then staged one of the GDR's freshest and best-received productions of the 1960s, *The Dragon* by the Russian Yevgeny Schwartz, which premiered on 21 March 1965. This fairytale for adults created huge interest in a form of Brechtian performance that had an ebullience and lightness to it without neglecting dialectics or precision. The DT had finally gained an imaginative and able director who (indirectly) threw down the gauntlet to the BE. Besson challenged its orthodoxy and its exclusivity in all things Brechtian. The BE's next production would betray the extent of the challenge in that, for the first time in its history, the BE was reacting to the work of another theatre, rather than setting the agenda itself.

[1] See Preuß, *Theater im ost-/westpolitischen Umfeld*, p. 499.

The plan to stage Sean O'Casey's *Purple Dust* (*Purpurstaub* in German) predated its premiere on 14 February 1966 by some years. Brecht mentioned the playwright by name in the 'Theaterprojekt B.' document, and Weigel wrote to the playwright personally in 1960 asking for his permission to have three of his plays, including *Purple Dust*, translated anew into German.[2] A more concrete plan to stage the comedy emerged in 1961 when the BE invited the Komische Oper's Joachim Herz to direct, although he later declined.[3] The BE returned to the play in 1963, but Wekwerth was unclear about how they might interpret its *Fabel*.[4] The play is about two English stockbrokers who buy a castle in Ireland and attempt to furnish it in 'olde-worlde' Tudor style. They try to impose their distorted vision on ancient customs and are contrasted with the Irish workmen employed to carry out the renovation. All is lost in the final act when a storm destroys the castle and all that is left of their colonial dreams is a pile of purple dust.

It is difficult to understand the difficulty Wekwerth had with the *Fabel* as the play is a fairly straightforward satire on wealth and its effects on the moneyed classes, and on their view of older cultures. The solution to his intellectual quandary was to have Hans-Georg Simmgen, the assistant responsible for the cancellation of *The Visit* in 1961, direct the play in Gera as a test to see whether it could be brought back to Berlin. This Simmgen did in 1964, where he worked together with the young set designer, Andreas Reinhardt. This was Reinhardt's first design and it contributed greatly to the success of the production: the castle's gradual deterioration and ultimate collapse were exquisitely engineered,[5] and both Simmgen and Reinhardt were invited to re-stage the production at the BE.

Rehearsals did not follow the BE's usual principles. Uta Birnbaum had noted that 'the beauty of the dialogues, the great exchanges tempt a staging of the dialogue'.[6] That is, the action was no longer the focus. Ruth Berghaus also recorded a lack of dynamism in rehearsal that was making the *Arrangements* uninteresting.[7] A year later, Wekwerth sent a letter to all working on the production to tell them that Simmgen had requested

---

[2] See Weigel to Sean O'Casey, 30 January 1960, BBA uncatalogued file 'HW A-L 1960'.

[3] See Joachim Tenschert to Joachim Herz, 17 March 1961, BBA uncatalogued file 'D 1/61–9/62'.

[4] See Anon., 'Dramaturgie-Sitzung am 30.8.1963', undated, 3 pages (2), BEA File 'Dramaturgie '65–69/65–66 Protokolle/Briefe 63–64'.

[5] See Friedrich Dieckmann, *Theaterbilder: Studien und Berichte* (Berlin: Henschel, 1979), p. 45.

[6] Uta Birnbaum, 'Bemerkungen zu Proben *Purpurstaub* aus der Woche 2.–7.11.65', 14 November 1964, 2 pages (1), BEA File 39.

[7] See Ruth Berghaus, 'Notat *Purple Dust* [sic] vom 26.11.64', undated, n.p., ibid.

help from him. The letter was defensive with Wekwerth denying he was '"coming and going to turn everything on its head"'.[8] A section, co-signed by Simmgen, attested that he was the one who asked Wekwerth for assistance. It reads, however, somewhat like a forced confession, which, according to Simmgen, it virtually was. Wekwerth had been rehearsing alone with some of the actors, including his wife, Renate Richter, and Simmgen felt that it was no longer his production.[9]

After the premiere on 14 February 1966, Weigel and Alexander Abusch both criticized Wekwerth for staging shallow humour. Wekwerth replied to Weigel: 'I, however, find that jokes that arise from well-observed details aren't gags'.[10] The critics were divided on this matter, although there was no doubt that the BE was engaging in a comic form that did not resemble anything it had hitherto produced. One commented: 'slapstick is used as a means of satirical revelation. Exaggeration makes the action clear'.[11] Another bemoaned that 'this time, the art of acting has been replaced by the art of performing gags'.[12] In addition, references and comparisons to the Deutsches Theater found their way into the reviews for the first time.[13]

Yet while competition with the DT inflected this production, a more minor detail from the rehearsals quietly heralded another aspect of the BE's decline. In one scene, Wekwerth had originally intended to have a grass-roller hurtle apparently unstoppably towards the audience before veering off at the last moment. Weigel protested vigorously against this 'shock effect'.[14] She was as one with Brecht on this point, who objected to the limited value of shock in the theatre and associated it with what he perceived as the inefficacy of surrealism and the tired tricks of the bourgeois theatre.[15] Weigel's insistence on following Brecht so closely reflected her own conservatism in the matter of interpreting Brecht's aesthetics, and this would have a disastrous effect on her relationship with Wekwerth over time.

---

[8] Wekwerth to the cast of *Purple Dust*, 26 October 1965, ibid. The following section is also in this letter.

[9] Hans-Georg Simmgen, unpublished interview with the author, 21 July 2010.

[10] Wekwerth to Weigel, 18 February 1966, BEA File 39.

[11] Helmut Ullrich, 'Nachts, wenn die Sintflut kommt', *Neue Zeit*, 17 February 1966.

[12] André Müller, 'Gelächter – auf Kosten der Komödie', *Deutsche Volkszeitung*, 1 April 1966.

[13] See, for example, Ernst Wendt, 'Konkurrenz der Tiere', *Stuttgarter Zeitung*, 4 March 1966.

[14] See Wekwerth, *Erinnern ist Leben*, pp. 222–3.

[15] See Brecht, '*Messingkauf* – Fragment B 163', BFA, 22: 825; *BoP*, p. 110; and 'Kleines Privatissimum für meinen Freund Max Gorelik', BFA, 23: 38; *BoT*, p. 147.

Friction with the assistants: the shape of things to come

In the entry for 1968 on the biographical page of his website, Manfred
Wekwerth asserts that Helene Weigel forced three assistants, Uta Birnbaum, Hans-Georg Simmgen and Guy de Chambure, out of the BE
without his knowledge.[16] As will become evident, by 1968, things had
reached a head between Wekwerth and Weigel, and this had led to fac-
tional divisions at the very heart of the BE. Wekwerth considered all three
to be his *Schüler*, but his contention regarding Weigel's actions deserves
closer scrutiny.

Uta Birnbaum had assisted on various BE projects, but was given her
chance to direct alone in 1966. She had previously directed Brecht's
Man Equals Man with acting students at the Berliner Arbeiter-Theater
in 1964, and Tenschert thought that she could re-stage the play at the
BE.[17] Birnbaum told me that the BE needed a new production and
looked to her because Wekwerth, Manfred Karge and Matthias Langhoff
were all tied up with different projects.[18] Rehearsals did not progress
smoothly, however; Birnbaum felt that her work was being undermined.
In a letter to Weigel in late August 1966, she wrote that people outside the
production should not interfere with her work as she needed to find her
feet by herself.[19] Later that year she repeated the accusation and added
that she feared the BE merely wanted a rehashed version of Brecht's own
1931 production.[20] Again, one notes a conservatism in Weigel, a desire
to hold on to Brecht's *Modell*, rather than to allow experiments with
different forms. Birnbaum was right to suspect Weigel of harbouring an
aesthetic animosity towards her; Weigel later asked Werner Hecht for his
help to arm her with a solid arsenal of Brecht sources in her 'battle' with
Birnbaum.[21]

By the premiere, on Brecht's birthday, 10 February 1967, Weigel had
registered her criticism of the production's conclusion, but Birnbaum
insisted that either it stayed or the production would be cancelled.[22]
Wekwerth was, on the other hand, pleased with the production and
ironically congratulated himself 'for having worked successfully on my

[16] See Wekwerth, 'Manfred Wekwerth', www.manfredwekwerth.de/biographisches.html (accessed 28 March 2012).
[17] See Tenschert to Uta Birnbaum, 25 November 1964, BEA File 41.
[18] Uta Birnbaum, unpublished interview with the author, 28 August 2010.
[19] See Uta Birnbaum to Weigel, 30 August 1966, *Briefwechsel*, p. 180.
[20] See Uta Birnbaum to Weigel and Tenschert, 24 October 1966, ibid., p. 182.
[21] See Weigel to Werner Hecht, 28 December 1966, BBA uncatalogued file 'HW Haus 1966'.
[22] Uta Birnbaum, unpublished interview with the author, 28 August 2010.

own obsolescence'.[23] In the press, Wekwerth's pride at developing a new generation of directors was greeted with a degree of scepticism, as one reviewer noted:

Yet [the second generation of BE directors] create nothing new, they are students who have grown into an established tradition and now already play on the keyboard of pre-formed expressive technique with virtuosity.[24]

Dieckmann and Völker's critiques regarding museum-like tendencies at the BE, made a couple of years earlier with respect to *Coriolan*, were starting to become more widely accepted.

The premiere, however, did not mark the end of the tension with Weigel. A letter from Kurt Bork to Minister of Culture Klaus Gysi contained information of a party thrown by Wekwerth's wife, Renate Richter, at which Birnbaum allegedly released a barrage of insults directed towards Weigel, who was not present. It included the sentiment that things would be a lot better at the BE if Weigel were dead. As a result of hearing about the tirade, Weigel fired Birnbaum with immediate effect.[25] No one is credited with supplying the information about the party. The insults attributed to Birnbaum were never substantiated, however, and because they had to be relegated to hearsay, the sacking could not be justified. A meeting between Bork, Birnbaum and Isot Kilian discussed future plans. Birnbaum apologized for her behaviour, but acknowledged that it was 'doubtless the expression of an unpleasant situation'.[26] Birnbaum stated that she wanted to continue working at the BE and that she would respect Weigel's authority. It appeared that a truce had been called, but Birnbaum was discussing the termination of her contract not a month later.[27] She still entertained the idea of directing Büchner's *Dantons Tod* (*Danton's Death*) in 1969, but as a guest. A meeting held in August 1968 seemed to be approaching agreement on the production, but by this time, Birnbaum was already in discussion with the DT about moving there, although she was prepared to let the BE use her preparatory notes.[28]

Elsewhere, Hans-Georg Simmgen found himself marginalized in the final months of rehearsals for *Purple Dust*. His next project was similarly frustrating. The BE had initiated an exploration of Brecht's fragments, including *Der Brotladen* (*The Bread Shop*) and *Das wirkliche Leben des*

---

[23] Wekwerth to Uta Birnbaum, 25 February 1967, BEA File 41.
[24] Urs Jenny, 'Pyrrussieg eines Theaterelefanten', *Süddeutsche Zeitung*, 13 February 1967.
[25] See Bork to Klaus Gysi, 19 April 1967, BArch DR 1/8849.
[26] Birnbaum, reported in Bork to Weigel, 21 April 1967, ibid.
[27] See [Weigel?], '[Memorandum]', 16 May 1968, n.p., BBA uncatalogued file 'HW Haus 1968'.
[28] See Anon., untitled, 30 August 1968, 2 pages, ibid.

Jakob Gehherda (*The Real Life of Jacob Gehherda*) in early 1967. *Brotladen* became the fourth *Brecht Evening*, but *Gehherda*, on whose team Simmgen served, came to nothing after a whole forty-nine rehearsals. On the one hand, its dream sequences proved difficult to stage,[29] on the other, pressure on rehearsal space from other productions meant sacrificing this one in their favour.[30] Simmgen told me that he personally had no ideas for the play and ended up thoroughly confused by it.[31]

Guy de Chambure was a minor French aristocrat who had seen the BE in the 1950s when the company toured Paris.[32] He was never given a production of his own to direct at the BE although he was involved in a project, which was later abandoned, to stage Heiner Müller's *Philoktet* (*Philoctetes*) in the mid 1960s.[33] He also ran into trouble with the Ministry of Culture in 1966 when he planned to direct Peter Hacks' *Moritz Tassow* in the FRG.[34] The play had been cancelled at the DT in the wake of the XI Plenum and was thus effectively banned in the GDR. Weigel told the Ministry in 1966 that she would have fired de Chambure two years earlier,[35] but it seems that his time had finally come in 1968.[36]

It is true that Wekwerth understood all three assistants, Birnbaum, Simmgen and de Chambure, had come under attack from Weigel for their association with him.[37] However, there is little to show that Birnbaum and Simmgen were forced out of the company or that their relationship with Wekwerth had played a defining role. Birnbaum simply could not get on with Weigel, which led to an impossible working relationship. Simmgen did not receive enough work at the BE and left the company voluntarily to work at the Maxim-Gorki-Theater.[38] De Chambure is the only assistant whom Weigel actively encouraged to leave, yet even in this case, she refrained from calling for his resignation until at least four years after her original intention. In short, this was not a campaign as such, but a set of circumstances that led to a radical depletion of Wekwerth's younger allies in 1968. The reasons for the souring of the relationship

---

[29] See Klaus Erforth, Hans-Georg Simmgen, and Pieter Hein, 'Über den Gang der Überlegungen und Versuche zum *Gehherda*-Fragment', 10 June 1967, 4 pages (2), BEA File 42.

[30] See Weigel, '[Memorandum]', 25 May 1967, 2 pages (2), BEA File 'Dramaturgie '65–69/65–66 Protokolle/Briefe 63–64'.

[31] Hans-Georg Simmgen, unpublished interview with the author, 21 July 2010.

[32] See Ditte von Arnim, *Brechts letzte Liebe. Das Leben der Isot Kilian* (Berlin: Transit, 2006), p. 170.

[33] See BEA File 184 for a variety of documents on the project.

[34] See Bork to Weigel, 15 April 1966, BBA uncatalogued file 'HW BE-MfK 1961–67'.

[35] [Weigel] to Herbert Micklich, 9 September 1966, ibid.

[36] See Weigel to Guy de Chambure, 20 August 1968, *Briefwechsel*, p. 210.

[37] See Wekwerth to Weigel, [1967? 1968?], n.p., possibly a draft, AdK JTA 'BE interne Korr./Dramat. 1959–1970'.

[38] Hans-Georg Simmgen, unpublished interview with the author, 21 July 2010.

between Weigel and Wekwerth were complex. They involved Wekwerth's desire to break out of Weigel's narrow definition of Brechtian theatre, but they were also connected to another issue, which was more personal to Weigel.

The Berliner Ensemble as a 'family theatre': the troubled production of *Johanna*

Back in the late 1950s, Benno Besson had criticized the state of the BE after Brecht's death in an unpublished note and considered the company a 'private company, subsidized by the State'.[39] He felt that Weigel's power as Brecht's widow had conferred a status on the BE that was simply out of step with the political principles of the GDR. I have not found any further criticism of the BE in this vein around the same time, but as the tide began to turn against the BE in the mid 1960s, an increasing scepticism developed towards Weigel and the way she appeared to favour members of her family over the ensemble in casting decisions.

Ekkehard Schall, the BE's leading man, was Brecht and Weigel's son-in-law: he had married their daughter Barbara in 1961. Barbara had been given the female lead in *Playboy of the Western World* in 1956, but had not taken such a major role since then. In 1966, the BE started rehearsing *Mother Courage* with Barbara as the prostitute Yvette and Weigel's step-daughter Hanne Hiob set to play dumb Kattrin. Wekwerth complained to Weigel about the decisions and suggested what he considered better actors (including his wife) to replace them.[40] The situation had not been resolved a week later, and he turned to Kurt Bork at the Ministry of Culture, pointing out that Weigel had cast the roles without consultation with the creative team. He wrote that there was 'a line with respect to Helli [Weigel] and her family that, for the sake of Brecht's theatre, you can't cross'.[41] The dispute was resolved by substituting a revival of *The Mother* for *Mother Courage*.[42] Wekwerth was able to prevail in this case, but the BE's next major Brecht production raised the stakes and led to a situation where no one would triumph.

Die heilige Johanna der Schlachthöfe (Saint Joan of the Stockyards) was one of the few major plays by Brecht that the BE had not staged by the late 1960s (if one excludes the complete gamut of his pre-Marxist work). It had had its world premiere at the Schauspielhaus, Hamburg, in 1959 with Hanne Hiob as the eponymous heroine. Plans were hatched

---

[39] [Besson], untitled, undated, n.p., AdK Besson-Archiv File 51.
[40] See [Wekwerth] to Weigel, 24 October 1966, BArch DR 1/8847.
[41] Wekwerth to Bork, 3 November 1966, ibid.
[42] See Wekwerth to Bork, 16 December 1966, ibid.

to bring Hiob to the BE shortly afterwards to reprise the role, but in a very different production.[43] In 1960, Hiob wrote to Weigel to tell her that she feared overexerting herself if she were to take on the role while playing another elsewhere.[44] Her concerns about her health would prove to be well-founded, not in 1960, but later that decade when the BE finally rehearsed the production.

By 1965, Weigel had the anniversary of Brecht's seventieth birthday in 1968 on her mind. She wanted the BE to stage a production that would celebrate both his and the company's achievements at a special event, the *Brecht-Dialog*, which was to be held over the week of the anniversary. Weigel wrote to Bork at the Ministry to ask his permission to cast Hiob as Joan (and as Kattrin in *Courage*) in May 1966.[45] Wekwerth, for whom Hiob would become an immense problem over time, appears to have supported the decision at first, using her casting in *Joan* as an enticement when he invited an Austrian actor working in West Germany to play the male lead, Mauler.[46] In addition, Weigel cast herself, daughter Barbara, and son-in-law Ekkehard Schall in the production. However, Wekwerth's initial problem was neither Hiob nor the rest of the family, but the play itself.

Joan, in its standard published form, is a play set in the Chicago of the late 1920s and is Brecht's attempt to analyse the mechanisms of capitalism through the prism of the meat markets and the monopoly held by Mauler. Joan, a lieutenant in a Salvation Army–type organization, does her best to counter him morally, but realizes too late that morality leads only to reforming a mendacious system; what is needed is revolution to get rid of it entirely. Wekwerth was concerned about how to direct a play like this when the FRG was economically stable and had been so for many years. He sought advice from no other than Peter Palitzsch and asked whether strict historicization was the answer.[47] Previously, he had invited Egon Monk to direct, noting Hiob's interest positively, and suggesting that Palitzsch might play a role as well.[48] None of the directors came to his aid, and so Wekwerth teamed up with Tenschert

---

[43] See Werner Hecht, *Helene Weigel*, pp. 110–11.

[44] See Hanne Hiob to Weigel, 14 August 1960, *Briefwechsel*, p. 114.

[45] See [Weigel] to Bork, 24 May 1966, BBA uncatalogued file 'HW BE-MfK 1961–67'.

[46] See Wekwerth to Hanns Ernst Jäger, 2 August 1966, BEA File 'Dramaturgie Wekwerth Allgemeines – Schriftwechsel 1964–68/69'.

[47] See Wekwerth to Palitzsch, 1 June 1966, ibid.

[48] See Wekwerth to Monk, 8 December 1965, file pp. 76–7, BStU MfS AIM 2927/69, vol. 1. Wekwerth (see pp. 213–15) was a Stasi informer, but this intercepted letter, included in his own Stasi file, was accompanied by a report critical of Wekwerth's independent 'pan-German cultural work' (Stange, 'Manfred Wekwerth, Berliner-Ensemble', 15 December 1965, file p. 74, ibid.). I will consider the Stasi's role in the BE below, but

one more time and set about finding a way into the text he feared had become overtaken by history. Weigel nonetheless insisted that it had to be performed as part of the BE's project of staging all major plays by Brecht.

Wekwerth consulted the archive and found a version of the play that located the action at the turn of the century. This allowed him to emphasize the events of the play as parable rather than use them to illustrate an economic crisis he deemed out of date. The production was to shift the emphasis from economics to the ways in which ideology conditioned and manipulated situations and people.[49] Such a move was reflected in certain production decisions: the stock exchange, for example, was to attain the status of a cathedral of capitalism: 'Joan is surprised by the peculiarities of a world which is not, as expected, a bloody, but a sacred one'.[50] The emphasis on ritual and ceremony represented an attempt to focus on the ways capitalism extended beyond the purely practical into other realms that helped it perpetuate itself.

Yet while Wekwerth struggled with a re-reading of the text, problems were emerging with Hiob. Tenschert criticized her for acting purely for herself and not together with the rest of the ensemble.[51] Rehearsals themselves were lacklustre in the autumn of 1967, and Hiob was absent through illness for the eighteen rehearsals conducted in February 1968. There would be no *Joan* at the *Brecht-Dialog*. Wekwerth took advantage of this to suggest a change of lead to Weigel.[52] In a letter to actor Felicitas Ritsch, he rejected her suggestion that Christine Gloger should take the role and instead put forward his wife, Renate Richter, as a possible double-casting for the role.[53] By March, Wekwerth, too, was ill, suffering from heart problems, and shortly after passed the directing baton to Tenschert.[54] Bernhard Reich, one of Brecht and Weigel's friends from the Weimar Republic, reflected on the rehearsals he had seen and offered a distanced view of events. He deemed Hiob wrong for the role in its

---

this shows that it was not beyond the Stasi's remit to spy on its own informers, however reliable it considered them to be.

[49] See Wekwerth, 'Nach der Durchsicht des *Johanna*-Materials', 19 October 1966, 3 pages (1), BEA File 46.

[50] Dorothea Langhoff and Piet Drescher, 'Probennotat vom 11.10.1967 – Vor der Viehbörse', undated, n.p., ibid.

[51] See Tenschert, in Matthias Braun, 'Gespräch mit Joachim Tenschert über Helene Weigel am 14.11.1983 in Berlin [with Matthias Braun]', undated, 50 pages (14), HWA FH 64.

[52] See Wekwerth to Weigel, 6 February 1968, BEA File 'Dramaturgie Wekwerth Allgemeines – Schriftwechsel 1964–68/69'.

[53] See Wekwerth to Feliticitas Ritsch, 26 February 1968, ibid.

[54] See Wekwerth to the BE leadership, 17 April 1968, AdK MWA 'Korrespondenz mit Institutionen'.

new version, but criticized Wekwerth, whom he respected, for ponderous direction. He believed that Wekwerth aped Brecht's insistence on trying out the same scene in a variety of approaches, yet without having concrete reasons for doing so.[55] Hiob was well enough to return in May and June, and after a grand total of 153 rehearsals, the production premiered on 21 June 1968. Having been employed on full pay as a guest actor since 1967, Hiob performed the role all of five times, in part because she was ill again after the premiere, in part because Norbert Christian, who played another main role, was ill in the autumn of 1968.

The production received a mixed reception, and Hiob was more criticized than praised. Worries surfaced about the emphasis on aesthetic perfection over Brechtian analysis and that the *Arrangements* were becoming peripheral because the tension between Joan and Mauler was not working.[56] Despite the poor press, the BE decided that so much time and money had been invested in the production that it needed to be revived in 1969. Originally, Weigel had pursued the familial option of retaining Hiob, but was told that all the company's major committees were against the plan.[57] Christine Gloger, the actor Wekwerth had previously rejected, played Joan, and reviewers warmly welcomed her performance. On the production as a whole, one critic considered it 'more a premiere than a revival', and another wrote of the 'growth of a production'.[58] The BE had managed to salvage the show, which went on to play for a further forty-five performances until 1972.

Despite the eventual success of the production, the rehearsal process itself had brought together a series of problems, and in the light of this, Wekwerth undertook one risk-laden act: he tendered his resignation to Weigel while on sick leave in May 1968.[59] A second letter followed less than a month later to dispel any suggestion that his decision to allow the *Joan* rehearsals to continue while he was ill be construed as even tacit support for Hiob.[60] Wekwerth's resignation was concerned with far more than Weigel's questionable casting decisions, but before considering the full-blown crisis at the BE, for which symptoms abound in the *Joan* production, I will consider some further instances of disquiet.

[55] See Bernhard Reich to Weigel, 22 March 1968, *Briefwechsel*, pp. 201 and 203.
[56] See Michael Stone, 'Perfektion als Selbstzweck', *Christ und Welt*, 12 July 1968; and Christoph Funke, 'Kühle Legende ohne Sinnlichkeit', *Der Morgen*, 21 June 1968.
[57] See Gisela May to Weigel, 11 April 1969, HWA File 173.
[58] Günther Bellmann, 'Gewichte besser verteilt', *BZ am Abend*, 11 December 1969; and Christoph Funke, 'Mißbrauch der Naivität', *Der Morgen*, 16 January 1970, respectively.
[59] See Wekwerth to Weigel, 16 May 1968, *Briefwechsel*, pp. 204–8.
[60] See Wekwerth to Weigel, 6 June 1968, ibid., pp. 209–10.

Making a crisis out of a drama: the SED bans
Johann Faustus

1968 also marked the seventieth anniversary of Hanns Eisler's birth. Celebrations took place across the GDR for a composer who had, amongst other things, collaborated extensively with Brecht, and they were coordinated in Berlin by the Academy of Arts (DAK). Originally, the BE had planned an event that was to include songs, chamber music and '*Faust*-Ausschnitte' ('extracts from *Faust*').[61] This referred to Eisler's *Johann Faustus*, an opera whose libretto he published in 1952 and which had drawn similar ire from the SED as the BE's *Urfaust* (see pp. 96–100, Chapter 3). This was due to the opera's negative portrayal of its Faust figure, something considered a 'crime' against the *Erbe* at the time. By August 1968, when one might have thought such dogmatism were a thing of the past, the BE decided on a scenic reading of the whole *Faustus*, something questioned a month later by the DAK.[62] The Ministry of Culture believed that the decision had been taken by Weigel alone, as Wekwerth, Tenschert and the party leadership at the BE were all unaware of it.[63] The BE was on tour in the USSR as the Ministry urgently set about cancelling the event, and officials attempted to contact the company via the GDR's embassy in Moscow.[64] Bork wrote to Weigel the day after the BE returned and referred to a speech that Minister Klaus Gysi had made on 28 August in Weimar, the home of German Classicism where Goethe lived and worked for much of his later life. In the speech, Gysi expressly criticized Eisler's *Faustus*, and so Bork contended that the planned reading would present an affront to the Minister.[65] On the same day that Weigel proposed a discussion of the matter, Bork issued a 'Weisung' ('directive'), the authorities' euphemistic term for a ban. In a handwritten letter, he asked Weigel to withdraw her plans 'sensibly'.[66] Here 'sensibly' meant with as little fuss as possible.

This was not to be the case. Weigel was not satisfied by the flimsy explanation given concerning the Minister and noted in a letter to Gysi that hers was a theatre 'that had proved its political credentials over many

[61] See Anon., 'Protokoll der Aussprache über die Vorhaben anläßlich des 70. Geburtstages Hanns Eislers (6.7.1968) am 2.6.1967 in der Deutschen Akademie der Künste zu Berlin', undated, n.p., BEA File 104.
[62] See [Weigel] to Karl Hössiger, 12 August 1968; and Hössiger to Weigel, 18 September 1968, ibid.
[63] See Karl-Heinz Hafranke to Bork, 17 September 1968, BArch DR 1/8849.
[64] See Willi Schrader, 'Notiz', 9 September 1968, ibid.
[65] See Bork to Weigel, 20 September 1968, BEA File 104.
[66] Bork to Weigel, 24 September 1968, ibid.

years'.[67] Indeed, it would be difficult to see how the proposed reading was anything other than Weigel's celebration of a dead communist composer. Meetings subsequently took place inside the BE, whose members, too, were unable to fathom the reason for the ban. Manfred Karge and Matthias Langhoff, the directors of the reading, together with the thirteen actors involved (including big names like Ekkehard Schall and Hilmar Thate) took the unusual step of writing directly to the Minister to protest against the ban and the lack of clarification, on the day on which the reading was originally scheduled to take place.[68] This move exposed another rift within the BE: in a letter to Weigel critical of her protest letter, the BE's Parteileitung (Party Leadership), with Ruth Berghaus as its secretary, placed itself firmly on the side of the SED.[69] The factionalism was symptomatic of the divisions within the BE, which now pitted a group of some significant actors against the Party Leadership. This body had already tipped off the Central Committee about the letter sent to the Minister. Arno Hochmuth at the Central Committee felt that the *Faustus* plan was another example of 'subjectivist and anarchistic tendencies and acts' that were taking place under Weigel's nose.[70] He suggested to the Ministry that they make Wekwerth artistic director as a way of combating what he considered the malign potential for Karge and Langhoff to take over the BE. This was five months after Wekwerth's first letter of resignation and so, as is now clear, the letter was more tactical than literal.

There was more at stake to the authorities than the mere reading of a play that might contradict a recent speech made by the Minister. An official noted that the performance had to be seen 'in the light of the situation in Czechoslovakia'.[71] Soviet tanks had rolled into the country on 21 August 1968 to counter the reformist measures of the communist government under Alexander Dubček, otherwise known as the Prague Spring. This momentous political event split opinion in the ensemble. Minister Gysi had visited the BE before it departed for its tour of the USSR in August to obtain 'eine Stellungnahme' ('a statement') from the leading artists of the company.[72] Here, again, the seemingly neutral language was nothing of the sort: missing from the word 'statement' were

[67] [Weigel] to Klaus Gysi, 25 September 1968, ibid.
[68] See Karge, Langhoff *et al.* to Klaus Gysi, 6 October 1968, SAPMO BArch DY 30/IV A 2/2.024/74.
[69] See Ruth Berghaus to Weigel, 10 October 1968, BEA File 104.
[70] Arno Hochmuth to Klaus Gysi, 10 October 1968, SAPMO BArch DY 30/IV A 2/2.024/74.
[71] Jochen Genzel, 'Information', 27 September 1968, ibid.
[72] Gerhard Brähmer, 'Information über die Situation im kulturellen Bereich', 23 August 1969, LAB C Rep 902 2567.

the words 'of support'. The SED's District Leadership in Berlin was so concerned about the potential for dissent, or at least neutrality, that it kept almost daily written updates on the mood in Berlin's theatres to see who was siding with whom.[73] The Central Committee noted that Weigel had not made a 'statement' herself; she gave the reason 'that she didn't know enough about the events'.[74] Wekwerth, on the other hand, not only supported the Soviet invasion, but wrote to the Board of the Verband der Theaterschaffenden (Theatre-Makers' Association) encouraging them officially to endorse the measures.[75] The matter was a tendentious one, and support or opposition to it could have repercussions, as seen in the discussion of *Sieben gegen Theben* (*Seven against Thebes*), below.

Weigel's initial response to the *Faustus* problem, as reported by the GDR's cultural attaché in Moscow, was to tell officials not to overestimate the effect of a single reading in a theatre.[76] This, of course, is precisely what the Ministry and the Central Committee did. Rather than allowing the event to pass unnoticed or with little fanfare, the authorities provoked antagonism from and within the BE. Weigel was scandalized that the SED could doubt the BE's political position, but the party was actually betraying just how sensitive it was to the merest vibrations in the seismic waves generated by the Prague Spring.

The Stasi and its relationship to the BE

As Laura Bradley observes, the SED in part linked the Prague Spring to the activities of Czech artists and intellectuals and so, in the wake of the invasion, Stasi surveillance of individuals and institutions involved in the cultural field expanded rapidly.[77] This was the case when Manfred Karge and Matthias Langhoff directed *Seven against Thebes*, but the Stasi was present in the BE some years before 1968.

In the early 1950s, the Ministerium für Staatssicherheit (Ministry of State Security), better known today as the Stasi, was not overly involved in matters of culture and only dedicated significant numbers of staff to this area in the wake of the uprising in Hungary in 1956.[78] The earliest record connected to the BE concerned a report on the actor

---

[73] See ibid. for the reports.
[74] Anon., 'Betr. Künstler, die sich gegen die Maßnahmen der Verbündeten der CSSR geäußert haben oder die einer Stellunnahme ausgewichen sind', 27 September 1968, 7 pages [incomplete] (2), SAPMO BArch DY 30/IV A 2/9.06/28.
[75] See Wekwerth to Walter Vogt, 26 August 1968, BArch DR 1/8847.
[76] See Dr Tautz to Klaus Gysi, 18 September 1968, BArch DR 1/8849.
[77] See Laura Bradley, *Cooperation and Conflict*, pp. 76 and 118.
[78] See Joachim Walther, *Sicherungsbereich Literatur. Schriftsteller und Staatssicherheit in der Deutschen Demokratischen Republik*, revised edition (Berlin: Ullstein, 1999), pp. 169–74.

Curt Bois, sent personally by Walter Ulbricht to Wilhelm Zaisser, the head of the Stasi, in 1950.[79] Bois intended to work with the BE the following year, playing Puntila. In 1951, Kurt Bork issued a pass to allow the bearer, a member of the Ministry of State Security, to attend a performance of Brecht's *Lukullus*.[80] This instance of Stasi intervention was not covert, however: an official who had to sign for the pass was dispatched to monitor the stage. As discussed earlier, the 'agent' sent to spy on Brecht was Wilhelm Girnus, who was, to my knowledge, not a member of the Stasi, but someone who reported directly to Ulbricht and the Politburo. In the early years of the GDR, then, surveillance of Brecht and the BE was somewhat ad hoc. Around the same time, Weigel and Brecht also considered the Stasi to be an institution fighting the good fight. Just before 17 June 1953, the couple actively sought the Stasi's assistance in a letter after a case of suspected sabotage.[81] A person unknown had deliberately disconnected a microphone that relayed the sound of the glockenspiel in the pro-Soviet *The Kremlin Chimes*. This flustered the actor playing Lenin and thus ruined the performance's grand finale.[82]

The Stasi gained information on the BE in two ways. It deployed its own officers, as when it officially vetted, together with the theatre's leadership, the names of actors and technicians due to be sent outside the GDR on tour. Far more frequently, however, it recruited informers, who were generically known as IMs ('Inoffizielle Mitarbeiter', 'unofficial collaborators'), though a range of designations was used over the years for variations on and gradations of the same function. The first such report I have found on the BE is somewhat genteel. Written in late 1953, the author bemoans a waste of resources when the BE rejected expensive sets and costumes for *Don Juan*, while nonetheless acknowledging that realistic productions needed the correct accoutrements.[83] Over the years IMs were recruited, such as actor Erich Franz (1957), assistant Isot Kilian (1958), and head of administration Hans Giersch (1966),[84] as well as various members of the acting and technical staff. It is

---

[79] See Walter Ulbricht to Wilhelm Zaisser, 23 October 1950, SAPMO BArch NY 4182/931. The file on Bois itself is missing.
[80] See Bork to the Deutsche Staatsoper, 12 February 1951, in Lucchesi (ed.), *Das Verhör in der Oper*, p. 66.
[81] See Weigel to Wolfgang Langhoff, 12 June 1953, *Briefwechsel*, p. 60.
[82] See [Wekwerth? – signature unclear], '[Report of *The Kremlin's Chimes* on 11 June 1953]', 12 June 1952, n.p., BEA File 'Abendberichte'. I have found no further record of whether the case was solved or even investigated.
[83] See [signature unclear], 'Betr.: Brecht-Ensemble', 6 October 1953, file p. 429, BStU MfS AKK 8661/76, vol. 2.
[84] See BStU MfS AIM 6564/61, vols. 1 and 2 for Franz; MfS AIM 4635/81 for Kilian; and MfS AIM 2872/69, vols. A and P for Giersch.

remarkably difficult to reach conclusions that generalize the motives, behaviour or self-understanding of individual IMs. While some were fanatics who believed they were informing to secure socialism, others informed for material benefit and advancement. Even the nature of the information varies hugely. In what seems to be a one-off report in 1966, soon-to-be former head of personnel at the BE, Lilo Rudolf, made all manner of claims about her personal life and that of others, and about Weigel's relationships with her staff. The handling officer, however, noted that the views and opinions, which followed the break-up of an affair and preceded Rudolf's redeployment, were 'greatly tinged with personal issues' and should thus be viewed with scepticism.[85] Others provided more objective material: both Franz and Kilian proffered information on BE actor Otto Fuhrmann, who was targeted by the Stasi because of his sexuality.[86] The Stasi files, on which this section and others, later in the study, are based, thus call for careful reading, interpretation and triangulation with other sources to establish their veracity and usefulness.

One of the most interesting examples of how difficult it is to evaluate an IM is presented by Manfred Wekwerth, who is the earliest recruited informer I have found at the BE. Technically, he started out as a provider of a 'konspirative Wohnung', a place where secret meetings could take place.[87] By 1961, he was formally made a 'Geheimer Informator' ('secret informer' – GI), a position he had already informally held 'for a long time'.[88] By 1969, he became a 'Gesellschaftlicher Mitarbeiter für Sicherheit' ('social collaborator on security' – GMS).[89] This was a designation introduced in 1968 to accommodate particularly well-known GDR citizens into the IM system. Thus, while GMSs had a high profile, they could still be used to pass on secret information, but were not engaged in active espionage as such. Despite public protestations to the contrary,[90] Wekwerth's handwritten 'Verpflichtung' ('obligation' to remain silent about his secret work), signed probably more by design than by accident on Brecht's birthday, is to be found in one of the three extant files that

---

[85] Armin Neumann, 'Bericht', 11 May 1966, file pp. 409–12 (412), BStU MfS AKK 8661/76, vol. 2.

[86] See, for example, Karl Brosche, 'Bericht vom Treff', 21 January 1958, file p. 60, BStU MfS AIM 6564/61, vol. 1; and Brosche, 'Anwerbungsbericht', 30 December 1958, file pp. 102–3 (102), BStU MfS AIM 4635/81.

[87] See Jürgen Kallies, 'Bericht zur Anwerbung einer KW', 1 December 1956, file p. 25, BStU MfS AIM 2927/69, vol. 1.

[88] Müller and Arnim Neumann, 'Vorschlag zur Umregistrierung der KW "Manfred" zum GI', 20 November 1961, file p. 53, ibid.

[89] See Hartmann, 'Ablagevermerk', 24 January 1969, file p. 94, ibid.

[90] See Wekwerth, in Schütt, *Manfred Wekwerth*, p. 252, or the direct refutation 'Anstatt einer Antwort', *Neues Deutschland*, 9 June 1993.

mostly record his reports to Stasi handlers.[91] Wekwerth was keen both to join the ranks and show his own initiative. He criticized an attempt to contact him at the BE because the agent was too 'noticeable' and insisted that he write his own *Verpflichtung* rather than have it dictated to him.[92] In 1962 he reported that he wanted to improve the work of the BE together with the Stasi, and that he would only carry out tasks for the Stasi if he clearly understood the reasons for them.[93] He was not, then, someone who merely took orders, but actively engaged in the business of providing information.

Wekwerth, like most of the other IMs at the BE, could contribute tittle-tattle to the Stasi, such as that Weigel had fired three minor female actors on the spot for running a brothel for their male colleagues in 1962.[94] Yet, more often, he used his Stasi connections to discuss other matters, such as the behaviour of *Intendanten* in Berlin's theatres or his criticisms of both the Stasi and the SED's District Leadership.[95] Wekwerth was thus not merely informing, but trying to play a role in what he considered the improvement of both the State and the theatres. Yet while Wekwerth did not actually spill as many beans as possible or denounce enemies at every opportunity, his willingness to engage with the Stasi is still problematic. After all, the very act of seeing the Stasi as a legitimate conversation partner led in part to its entrenchment and normalization in GDR society as a whole.

One of the most interesting reports in Wekwerth's files concerns his own wariness of the Stasi. He found it difficult to trust his former handler Jürgen Kallies after an attempt to recruit the actor Wolf Kaiser through Wekwerth backfired spectacularly in October 1959. Once Kaiser had tentatively agreed to help the Stasi,[96] he reportedly confessed all before Weigel 'from which arose considerable difficulties for the GI, too'.[97] Thus, Weigel was aware that Wekwerth was both connected to the Stasi and that he had been recruiting at least one member of the ensemble. That said, there is no evidence to indicate that she treated him differently

---

[91] See Wekwerth, '[*Verpflichtung*]', 10 February 1956, file p. 126, BStU MfS AGM 11468/89. At first he was only a 'Kontaktperson' before he was fully integrated as an informer later that year.

[92] Jürgen Kallies, 'Bericht zur Anwerbung einer KW', 1 December 1956, file p. 25, BStU MfS AIM 2927/69, vol. 1.

[93] See Anon., 'Auskunftsbericht', 20 April 1962, file pp. 54–6 (55), ibid.

[94] See Armin Neumann, 'Treffbericht', 5 April 1962, file pp. 10–12 (11), BStU MfS AIM 2927/69, vol. 1 part 2. While handler Neumann wrote the report, the information was supplied by Wekwerth.

[95] See Armin Neumann, 'Treffbericht', 10 February 1964, file pp. 27–33 (29 and 31), ibid.

[96] See Jürgen Kallies, 'Treffbericht', 21 July 1959, file pp. 30–1, BStU AP 7296/74.

[97] Armin Neumann, 'Aktenvermerk', 18 November 1967, file pp. 51–2 (51), BStU AIM 2927/69, vol. 1, part 2.

afterwards; he was still entrusted with major projects. There is also nothing in his files to suggest that he used the Stasi as a weapon against Weigel in the late 1960s. Both these positions reveal something important about the role of the Stasi at the BE: neither Wekwerth nor Weigel overstressed its significance. Its existence was taken as read, and the two appear to have dealt with it thus.

As should be evident from the brief account of Stasi activity at the BE under Weigel's *Intendanz*, there is very little evidence of officers initiating active operations beyond recruitment. The Stasi was 'in no way a state within a state',[98] that is, it did not act independently of the higher powers, and, at the BE at least, was merely one of at least five agencies that monitored the company, the others being, roughly in order of influence, the Cultural Department of the Central Committee, the Ministry of Culture, the District Leadership in Berlin, and the Municipal Authority for Greater Berlin. As a result, the Stasi procured and provided information that might not have been gleaned from elsewhere, but rarely intervened in the running of this theatre. It is possible that the BE was so prestigious that the official agencies felt they had at least sufficient contact and influence in the first place. Conversely, the BE knew it had to answer to so many masters that it had little room to be actively subversive. So unavoidable was the relationship between the SED and the BE that I have discovered only one Stasi operation in the BE's history that aimed to affect the company's work, and I will consider that in the discussion of Volker Braun's *Großer Frieden* (*The Great Peace*) on pp. 307–14, Chapter 10. Even at the height of the crisis surrounding Ruth Berghaus's *Intendanz* in the mid 1970s, the Stasi 'merely' gathered information. My future references to the Stasi will consequently use the views of the secret service and its informers to shed further light on the work and the workings of the BE.

Two further 'difficult' productions

Karge and Langhoff's next project after *Faustus* was Aeschylus' *Seven against Thebes*, a production that Wekwerth had originally proposed.[99] This was the BE's first foray into the drama of antiquity and was almost certainly inspired by the success of Besson's Greek productions at the DT, of which his most recent, Sophocles' *Oedipus Rex* (adapted by Heiner Müller), had been a great success in January 1967. Karge and

---

[98] Roger Engelmann *et al.*, *Das MfS-Lexikon. Begriffe, Personen und Strukturen der Staatssicherheit der DDR* (Berlin: Christoph Links, 2011), p. 262.
[99] See Weigel to Hans Giersch and Tenschert, 15 March 1968, *Briefwechsel*, p. 199.

Langhoff were originally interested in the play's focus on a battle between brothers.[100] Preparation for the production started before the *Faustus* affair erupted, but was then influenced by the events in Prague. Helmut Baierl, a new recruit to the Stasi's network of informers, made a detailed report about the *Faustus* affair in October 1968 and pointed forward to Karge and Langhoff's next project. He supplied a copy of the text and asked his handler to consider the final section in particular. The directors were pushing their own agenda 'to perform negative, topical aspects under the cover of a classical text'.[101] Karge and Langhoff had written a new ending for the chorus which 'castigates itself for having shirked its civic responsibility by failing to speak out earlier, when it might have made a difference'.[102] The influence of the Prague Spring is clear: the passage criticizes popular passivity in the face of external pressure. Bradley, in the article from which I have just quoted, gives a thorough account of the censorship of this self-critical position. She describes how forces loyal to the SED at the BE managed to bring about textual changes in the face of Weigel's opposition, and how Weigel nonetheless helped to save the production, which was a remarkable achievement in itself. I will thus consider the ways in which the ructions affected the BE as a company.

In many ways, the fault lines exposed by the *Faustus* affair were merely reproduced in the bid to rein in the two directors and have them change the text into something less allegorically reflective of the Prague Spring. At its most basic, the internal conflict revolved around two groups: Weigel, who protected Karge and Langhoff, and Wekwerth, who joined forces with the BE's Party Leadership (which, at the time, was headed by Ruth Berghaus). However, as already noted on several occasions, internal disputes always found their way into the various agencies that governed and monitored cultural production in the GDR.

The problems with *Thebes* centred mainly on the chorus's final speech and the ways in which its sentiments could manifest themselves in the production as a whole. Wekwerth demanded a written 'Konzeption' ('conceptual plan') which he viewed as a means of controlling the general direction of the show. Bork at the Ministry of Culture had written to Weigel in December 1968 to tell her that the *Konzeption* she submitted merely confirmed existing doubts and that a new one would be required. At the same time, he warned her about resistance from Wekwerth and the BE's Party Leadership.[103] While the Ministry was not fully backing

[100] See Laura Bradley, '"Prager Luft" at the Berliner Ensemble? The Censorship of *Sieben gegen Theben*, 1968–9', *German Life and Letters*, 58:1 (2005), pp. 41–54 (44).
[101] Arnold Klemer, 'Operative Information Nr. 1130/68', 17 October 1968, file pp. 22–4 (23), BStU MfS Bln. Abt. XX A 477-4.
[102] Bradley, '"Prager Luft"', p. 45.
[103] See Bork to Weigel, 3 December 1968, SAPMO BArch DY 30/IV A 2/2.024/74.

Weigel, because it simply could not support Karge and Langhoff's critical stance, Bork nonetheless communicated a desire to help Weigel (the reasons for this will become apparent below). At present, however, it is important to note that the Ministry, represented by Bork, did not seek to threaten or coerce Weigel, but to encourage her to 'do the right thing'. The Central Committee monitored events, too, very much keeping itself abreast of developments. It did not want a repeat of the *Faustus* affair, fearing that two outright bans would only exacerbate the divisions that were already present in its showpiece theatre. However, while the Central Committee tended to favour Wekwerth over Weigel (and the Ministry took the opposite position), it did not support him completely. It agreed that a new *Konzeption* had to be submitted, but it was worried about Wekwerth's own ambitions with respect to the leadership of the BE.[104] In both cases, the agencies were calling for the same thing, but with different emphases; that is, they put policy over personality, although the latter also played a role.

The question of how the BE positioned itself with respect to the various official agencies had become more complicated, too. Hitherto, the two main bodies that supervised the BE were the Ministry of Culture and, on more serious matters, the Central Committee. In early 1967, the Ministry, which looked after the most important Berlin theatres as 'Staatstheater' ('theatres of the State'), proposed to transfer them to the Municipal Authority in order to effect a restructuring of the Ministry itself. It noted that one problem was a concern on the part of the *Intendanten* that they would lose prestige by becoming 'Stadttheater' ('theatres of the city').[105] The shift, which also extended to the devolution of powers from the Ministry to city councils in the rest of the GDR, was to take place in the spring of 1969.[106] The idea was that local agencies would have a closer relationship with their theatres and thus be better equipped to supervise and advise them. In the case of the BE, this meant attracting more interest from the District Leadership as well as the Municipal Authority. In effect, however, the Ministry and the Central Committee continued their involvement, and so the various factions at the BE sought support from all four official bodies, even before the official devolution of responsibility.

The difference between the Municipal Authority and the District Leadership was primarily one of quality. The former mainly managed the day-to-day running of Berlin. The latter was a more political and ideological

[104] Both positions can be found in: Arno Hochmuth to Erika Hinckel, 16 January 1969, SAPMO BArch DY 30/IV A 2/9.06/113.

[105] See Willi Schrader, 'Vorschläge zur Verbesserung der Leitungstätigkeit und der Arbeitsweise der Abteilung [Theater]', 31 January 1967, 7 pages, BArch DR 1/17549.

[106] See Anon., untitled, [late 1968/early 1969], n.p., BArch DR 1/18065.

body, charged with ensuring that policy and its execution corresponded to the SED's wishes at a local level. Ruth Berghaus and the BE's Party Leadership were closely connected to the District Leadership, which was a powerful body itself, due to its location in the GDR's capital city. In two successive reports of early December 1968, it is clear that the BE's Party Leadership was keeping the District Leadership abreast of developments.[107] Wekwerth was also active in keeping the District Leadership well informed when he reported the Party Leadership's success in forcing Karge and Langhoff to submit a new *Konzeption*,[108] although he was also well connected to the Central Committee. Weigel had a good relationship with Bork (and, to an extent, with Minister Gysi) in the Ministry and also worked closely with Horst Oswald at the Municipal Authority. The steady disclosure of sometimes confidential information led to annoyance and antagonism between the various agencies themselves. In a leak of a private meeting between the BE's Party Leadership and Bork, the former reported to the District Leadership that Bork had told them that Gysi had criticized the BE's Party Leadership for acting 'anarchistically'. In addition, Gysi reportedly called Weigel 'the most famous woman in the world'.[109] Hyperbole aside, the Minister was pointing out a major barrier to the SED enforcing its will: Helene Weigel was Brecht's widow and the internationally recognized face of the BE. Whatever the party wanted to achieve, it would not achieve it without at least some willingness on her part. It feared that she could use her reputation and connections as a way of causing them embarrassment and/or more concrete trouble.

Wekwerth and the BE's Party Leadership eventually got their way after a series of meetings and the application of pressure: Karge and Langhoff were forced to submit a new *Konzeption* and change the play's closing lines. The official agencies found that despite their differing strategies, the 'right' decision had been reached, and the Central Committee charged the District Leadership with monitoring the run-up to the premiere of *Thebes*.[110] Later, the Stasi, which had been following developments with interest,[111] made two reports on the production which finally opened on 28 May 1969. The first found it derivative of Besson's *Oedipus* and its stylized approach (see Fig. 7.1) and mannered deliveries generally

---

[107] See Roland Bauer to Paul Verner, 3 December 1968; and Gerhard Brähmer to Paul Verner, 5 December 1968, SAPMO BArch DY 30/ IV A 2/2.024/74. All the named figures are members of the District Leadership.

[108] See Wekwerth to Paul Verner, 26 December 1968, ibid.

[109] Gysi, in Gerhard Brähmer to Paul Verner, 16 December 1968, LAB C Rep 902 2860.

[110] See Arno Hochmuth to Roland Bauer, 19 May 1969, ibid.

[111] At one point, a handler requested that more IMs be deployed: see Arnold Klemer, 'Operative Information Nr. 1288/68', 19 December 1968, file pp. 27–9 (29), BStU MfS Bln. Abt. XX A 576–9.

Fig. 7.1. Scandal averted: a potentially controversial production loses its bite with stylized performances that also lost the audience. *Seven against Thebes*, May 1969.

confusing for the audience; the second was more critical, identifying 'decadence' and concluded '*that in the capital of the GDR, in Brecht's renowned theatre, un-Brechtian theatre is being produced*'.[112] Newspaper reviewers overwhelmingly agreed with the first Stasi report.

The most ironic part of this turbulent period in the BE's history is that the BE, in theory, had a practical counter-example to deploy against *Thebes*, the socialist realist play *Johanna von Döbeln*. It was written, like *Frau Flinz* before it, by Helmut Baierl together with Wekwerth. Originally commissioned in 1962 on the back of the success of *Flinz*,[113] it had been through many drafts and was finally ready for performance in 1969. As noted in Chapter 5, *Flinz* was a parody of *Mother Courage*; *Döbeln*, in turn, was a parody of *St Joan*, with a naïve Joan of Arc figure confronting the problems of a GDR factory in the small town of Döbeln. The play would seem to have been just the kind of positive contemporary drama the Ministry was so keen to promote, but this was not the case.

Unlike the censure of *Thebes*, there were no parties within the BE fighting for or against the production, and so the authorities presented a united front of criticism. The Ministry linked the play to works criticized at the XI Plenum in 1965; the District Leadership drew the BE's attention to the 'questionable positions' both in the play and the production; and the Central Committee's representative agreed with Minister Gysi that the play presented a distorted picture of the GDR.[114] The unanimity of opinion on *Döbeln*, however, was qualitatively different from the criticism of *Thebes* as potentially dissident. The authors, who, after all, were loyal GDR citizens and Stasi informers to boot, were deemed to have been gravely mistaken about the play, rather than actively oppositional. Remarkably, the only dissenting voice was the one that was probably never heard: that of the Stasi's own 'theatre critic', who was probably not an IM as no code name accompanied the reports. The review concluded that the production was 'a step forward despite all its failings'.[115] The Ministry of Culture did not recommend a ban to the Central

[112] See Lüdersdorf, 'Einschätzung der Inszenierung des Theaterstückes *7 gegen Theben*, Regie Langhoff/Karge', 29 May 1969, file pp. 31–2; and Arnold Klemer, 'Operative Information Nr. 356/69', 30 May 1969, file pp. 33–5 (34), BStU Bln. Abt. XX A 477–4.
[113] See Heinz Schröder to Weigel, 24 September 1964, BBA uncatalogued file 'HW BE-MfK 1961–67'.
[114] See Karl-Heinz Hafranke, 'Erste kurze Einschätzung... von Helmut Baierls *Johanna von Döbeln*', 14 October 1968, 6 pages, BArch DR 1/8849; Anon., 'Betreff: Teilnahme an der Generalprobe zu *Johanna von Döbeln* im Berliner Ensemble am 25.3.69', 27 March 1969, 2 pages (1), LAB C Rep 902 2860; and Herbert Werner to Arno Hochmuth, 16 April 1969, SAPMO BArch DY 30/IV A 2/9.06/113.
[115] Lüdersdorf, 'Einschätzung der Komödie *Johanna von Döbeln*. Autoren: Baierl/Wekwerth', 24 April 1969, file pp. 79–82 (82), BStU MfS AP 3788/73.

Committee, however, but a strategic reduction of performances with a view to eliciting yet another revision of the text.[116]

The two productions, which premiered within two months of each other, show how the SED dealt with material that offended its sensibilities in two different ways. That two projects could create such problems (three if one includes the banned *Faustus*) points to a crisis of leadership at the company. Weigel had allowed work at the BE to attract substantial disapprobation from without while presiding over increasingly dissatisfied and disconcerted factions within. While there were more than two factions involved in the crises, they nonetheless came to a head in the clash between Wekwerth and Weigel.

Weigel's weakness and Wekwerth's gamble

The crisis at the BE had various causes and symptoms, as the previous sections make clear. At its heart, however, was any theatre's basic function: to produce lively theatre. Such liveliness might be measured by the quality of work and the frequency of its production. The BE, up until the mid 1960s, excelled in the former while neglecting the latter. This imbalance may have been queried by the authorities, but was mitigated by the very large audiences the company was able to attract. Yet as the quality of the BE's productions started to fall, something thrown into relief most markedly by Besson's brand of Brechtianism at the DT, low productivity ground inexorably to near stasis. The BE found itself at a junction which led to either orthodoxy or innovation. Weigel steered a more conservative course, preferring tried and tested methods. Wekwerth wanted to move away from an exclusive focus on Brecht's work while still pursuing an extended exploration of Brecht's methods.

Weigel's conservatism can in part be traced back to a section of Brecht's will,[117] which she liked to paraphrase on occasion: 'keep the Ensemble for as long as you consider it to be the Berliner Ensemble'.[118] This exhortation rested on crucially undefined premises, but seems to have stayed with Weigel as a mantra during the crisis. Its eschatological thrust certainly caused anxiety. Wekwerth was already discomfited by the possibility of Weigel dissolving the BE in 1967. He wrote to the BE's head of administration noting that no contracts had been signed that ran beyond 1968. He sought assurances that all was well with the company.[119] By 1968,

---

[116] See Herbert Werner to Arno Hochmuth, 16 April 1969, SAPMO BArch DY 30/IV A 2/9.06/113.
[117] See [Otto Müllereisert], '[report of Brecht's oral will]', 15 August 1956, BBA 1646/48.
[118] Weigel to Eduard Fischer, [1964], *Briefwechsel*, p. 133.
[119] See Wekwerth to Giersch, 28 February 1967, BEA File 'Dramaturgie Wekwerth Allgemeines – Schriftwechsel 1964–68/69'.

there was already talk at the District Leadership that Weigel was ready to close the BE because it had fulfilled 'Brecht's purpose'.[120] By late 1969, top officials from the Municipal Authority, District Leadership and the Minister of Culture presented mutually exclusive views on the subject at a meeting chaired by Kurt Hager from the Central Committee. On the one hand, Horst Oswald of the Municipal Authority reported that Weigel planned to lead the BE for years to come. On the other, Paul Verner of the District Leadership believed that Weigel was intending 'to wind up the BE as a theatre in the near future'.[121] In a letter of 1970, however, Weigel privately dismissed the 'doomsday' option. She described the rumoured opinion that she would leave the BE and the GDR for her native Austria as 'the height of idiocy'.[122] It is difficult to know whether any truth can be ascribed to Weigel's reported threats either to close the BE or to leave the GDR. Things may well have been said in the heat of the moment, but there is no concrete evidence to support the view that Weigel planned to act on them. If anything, one finds ample material to show how Weigel struggled to retain control of the BE and, under pressure, to reform leadership structures.

Yet in such a volatile and unstable environment, Wekwerth saw the opportunity to exert his own influence. As already noted, Wekwerth tendered his resignation twice in the space of a month in the summer of 1968. The first letter detailed his dissatisfaction with the state of the BE and included lengthy criticism of the way the company was being led. The second letter was more concerned with the problems surrounding *Joan* as a symptom of a far broader malaise. Weigel rejected the first resignation,[123] but seems to have ignored the second. It is hard to read Wekwerth's letters as serious attempts to leave the BE; they are far more indications that change was needed, couched in the most serious of terms. Later in 1969, Wekwerth noted that he had discussed his resignation with both the Central Committee and the District Leadership, using it as a lever to bring about new leadership practices at the BE.[124]

The question of leadership at the BE was a central issue to Wekwerth for both professional and personal reasons. Professionally, reform would have helped steer the BE away from the crisis; personally, it would have

---

[120] Weigel, reported in Gerhard Brähmer to Paul Verner, 23 May 1968, LAB C Rep 902 2860.
[121] Paul Verner, in Anon., 'Ergänzendes Protokoll zur Beratung über die Berliner Theatersituation am 23 October 1969 bei Genosse Kurt Hager', undated, 5 pages (1), SAPMO BArch DY 30/IV A 2/2.024/30.
[122] Weigel to Fredrik Martner, 7 February 1970, *Briefwechsel*, p. 231.
[123] See Weigel to Wekwerth, 23 May 1968, ibid., p. 208.
[124] See Wekwerth to Hans Rodenberg, 15 May 1969, SAPMO BArch NY 4204/59.

enhanced his own position. Whether he sought to snatch the crown from Weigel is an open question. This may have been an ambition, but the more realistic prospect was for him to assume Brecht's old role: Wekwerth would have been responsible for all artistic decisions while Weigel looked after the practical side of the company. Weigel was certainly in a weakened position having interfered with *Man Equals Man* and insisted on casting Hiob in *Joan*. Indeed, in a letter of May 1968, she reported that Bork had asked: 'why have you isolated yourself so?'.[125]

The question of leadership in general was also an issue the SED was addressing. An official paper had outlined directions for cultural politics in the theatre after the XI Plenum. Along with signalling the desire to move control from the Ministry to local agencies, its author noted that leadership in the theatre needed to be 'wissenschaftlich'.[126] This word can be rendered in English not only as 'scientific' or 'scholarly', but also as 'objective'; each translation suggests an attempt to reduce the subjectivity of leadership in the theatres. Of course, the SED merely proposed substituting one set of subjectivities, those of a predominantly ageing *Intendanz*, with those of its own. Wekwerth, however, was keen to ally himself with the SED's position. In a letter to Weigel, he stressed: 'to me it's not a question of particular people or particular positions, but about objective leadership'.[127]

Wekwerth's analysis of the situation at the BE,[128] which he submitted to the SED, but not to Weigel at first, was hardly an analysis at all, if one understands 'analysis' to mean an examination of complex phenomena broken down and accounted for with well-founded arguments. Instead the extensive document was a serious conceptual proposal for the future of the company, which rarely included direct personal criticism of Weigel and was often innovative and engaging. He criticized performing Brecht's plays for their own sake and proposed extending Brecht's method to non-Brechtian and contemporary plays. The document ended with a plan for 'production groups with greater autonomy' that would supplement a stronger leadership structure, formed of experts in their creative and administrative fields. By the time Weigel finally got sight of the document, she was dismissive. She called it 'the self-righteous, arrogant missive'

125 Weigel to Elfriede Bork, 24 May 1968, *Briefwechsel*, p. 209.
126 Anon., 'Betr.: Bericht an den Staatsrat über kulturelle Entwicklung in der Deuschen Demokratischen Republik', 5 August 1966, 14 pages (11), BArch DR 1/18020.
127 Wekwerth to Weigel, 11 December 1968, BArch DY 43/1011.
128 See Wekwerth, 'Versuch einer Analyse der bisherigen Arbeit des Berliner Ensembles und einer Konzeption für die nächsten Jahre', 6 June 1968, n.p., SAPMO BArch DY 30/IV A 2/2.024/74. All subsequent references and quotations are taken from this document.

and found the proposal for a new leadership structure better suited to a 'scholarly institute' than a theatre.[129] Weigel did not address the issues concerning Wekwerth's aesthetic plans for the future.

Crises of leadership were not restricted to the BE, and documents show the SED's broader plans for replacing *Intendanten* elsewhere in Berlin, too.[130] Yet while a generational issue affected the leadership of the GDR's flagship theatres, the specific question at the BE presented a unique set of problems, due to its special status as the GDR's most recognizable cultural export. However, the party was caught in something of a double bind. On the one hand, it could not simply remove Weigel for fear of scandal and international disapproval. On the other, it could not engineer a shared leadership as envisaged by Wekwerth because of its own position on the matter: the SED had a central policy concerning leadership that pervaded all areas, from the Politburo downwards. The Central Committee thus noted that Wekwerth's proposal for the BE did not recognize 'the principle of the single leader who has to have complete authority in the running of a socialist theatre'.[131] This point of doctrine bolstered Weigel and had the full support of Kurt Bork.[132] Indeed, a meeting had been organized for early 1969 at which BE members believed that they were to have their say on the state of the company. Bork, however, opened the discussion with the Ministry's position that the *Intendantin* was to retain sole power and thus closed down the discussion before it had started.[133] Such an endorsement, even though the SED had been busy speculating about possible replacements for Weigel,[134] shored up her position, and in May 1969, she finally accepted Wekwerth's year-old resignation. Interestingly, she informed Minister Gysi a day before she contacted Wekwerth himself.[135] Her publicly stated reasons concerned what she considered Wekwerth's 'turning away from Brecht', which underlined her own aesthetic conservatism, and his 'attempts . . . to expand his field of control'.[136] The break with Wekwerth unfortunately coincided with

[129] Weigel to Tenschert, Pilka Häntzsche, and Hans Giersch, [1969], *Briefwechsel*, pp. 223 and 224.
[130] See, for example, Bork to Klaus Gysi, 7 December 1968, BArch DR 1/8764.
[131] Arno Hochmuth to Erika Hinckel, 16 January 1969, SAPMO BArch DY 30/IV A 2/9.06/113.
[132] See Bork to Willi Schrader, 15 January 1969, BArch DR 1/8847.
[133] Uta Birnbaum and Werner Heinitz, unpublished interviews with the author, 28 August 2010 and 13 July 2010, respectively.
[134] See, for example, Anon., 'Entwurf einer Vorlage an das Sekretariat des ZK der SED: "Konzeption für die weitere Entwicklung der Berliner Theater"', 3 September 1968, 8 pages (5–6), BArch DR 1/18065.
[135] See Weigel to Klaus Gysi, 7 May 1969; and Weigel to Wekwerth, 8 May 1969, HWA File 20.
[136] Weigel to 'dear friends, dear colleagues', 29 April 1969, AdK JTA 'BE interne Korr./Dramat. 1859–1970'. The date on the letter predates those to Gysi and

the discovery that he had contracted tuberculosis. His enforced leave led to an ugly set of exchanges predicated on Weigel's initial unwillingness to issue Wekwerth sick pay from the BE fund.[137]

On receiving Weigel's letter accepting his resignation, Wekwerth tried to back-pedal, stating that his move did not imply that he would leave the BE completely, but would keep the door open for work as a guest director, a position he had indeed articulated earlier.[138] But Weigel was in an uncompromising mood, and her decision was final, even though it was opposed by the SED's most senior cultural functionaries.[139] In fact, her continued leadership of the BE still caused senior party members an amount of consternation. This was due to the uncertainty about her plans for the BE and the recognition that the party could not actually remove her from the post. Head of the District Leadership, Paul Verner, suggested forcing her out, but Alexander Abusch registered grave doubts about associating her impending seventieth birthday with public quarrels. Hager warned against an 'international scandal', and Gysi reminded the cabal that Weigel still held all the rights to Brecht.[140] In short, the fig leaf of socialist leadership principles had been removed: the Party acknowledged that it was Weigel's power, drawn from her unique status as Brecht's widow, rights holder and *Intendantin* of the BE that protected her. Even so, the battle with Wekwerth had left her weakened and short of friends, and she would have to accede to reforms in the light of the internal fallout from the events of the past year.

Attempts to repair the damage: the departures and the arrivals

The BE haemorrhaged key staff in the late 1960s. I have already discussed the circumstances under which three of Wekwerth's assistants had left the company, and others were to follow. A sample of names and reasons taken from an internal BE document show the breadth of the problem. Actor Günter Naumann said that he could only work with *both* Weigel and Wekwerth; Renate Richter, Wekwerth's wife, criticized

---

Wekwerth. Either the date is wrong, the letter remained a draft, or Weigel sought to pre-empt internal criticism.

[137] See [Weigel] to Herbert Fechner, 2 September 1969, ibid. In the end, payment was made on the condition that Wekwerth did not extend or renew his contract with the BE.

[138] See Wekwerth to Tenschert, 2 May 1969, ibid.; and Wekwerth, 'Eine ergänzende Erklärung', 4 October 1968, n.p., LAB C Rep 902 2860.

[139] See, for example, Kurt Hager to Weigel, 29 May 1969, SAPMO BArch DY 30/IV A 2/2.024/74; and Klaus Gysi to Weigel, 19 May 1969, HWA File 20.

[140] See Anon., 'Ergänzendes Protokoll zur Beratung über die Berliner Theatersituation am 23 October 1969 bei Genosse Kurt Hager', undated, 5 pages, *passim*, SAPMO BArch DY 30/IV A 2/2.024/30.

an 'unprincipled atmosphere'; Gisela May (who actually remained at the BE) bemoaned the lack of artistic opportunities; and dramaturge Werner Heinitz noted that he had found a new position elsewhere.[141] Tenschert gives the impression that the departures of the late 1960s were a sign of solidarity with Wekwerth,[142] but the reasons given in this small sample indicate that this was not the case across the board. Rather, the BE was so directionless and demoralized that many left because they simply could not see the benefit of staying on.

The note concerning Heinitz hides an amount of intrigue behind its simple formulation. He was subject to disciplinary proceedings connected to Wekwerth's manoeuvrings while still at the BE. Wekwerth had convened meetings to develop the repertoire behind Weigel's back. Heinitz had signed a document in which Wekwerth reported negotiations with film director Frank Beyer to direct a production at the BE. In addition, dramaturge Helmut Rabe, who was also a part of Wekwerth's faction, admitted that he had been secretly in discussion with playwright Volker Braun. Weigel said: 'I will not tolerate two leaders in this house'.[143] Heinitz was confident at the hearing because he had researched his employment rights and found himself not to be in breach of contract.[144] Weigel had also consulted legal experts at the Ministry and was forced to issue a caution rather than the severe reprimand she had initially intended to serve.[145] Heinitz, although reprieved, could read the writing on the wall and chose to seek alternative employment.

Others, such as well-respected actors (Hilmar Thate, Bruno Carstens and Norbert Christian), directors (Alexander Stillmark, Klaus Erforth and Alexander Lang), dramaturges (Helmut Rabe and Isot Kilian) and a set designer (Pieter Hein) also left the BE in this period. Manfred Karge and Matthias Langhoff jumped ship as well. They had initially planned to work with Besson at the DT in 1968, but *Intendant* Wolfgang Heinz had reportedly broken off negotiations, lest he sour relations with the BE.[146] Later that year, the District Leadership reported that Karge and

---

[141] All four are reported in Anon., 'Verschiedene Gründe der Kündigungen', [late 1969], n.p., BBA uncatalogued file 'HW Haus 69'. The paragraph on Richter has been crossed out in pen.

[142] See Tenschert, in Braun, 'Gespräch mit Joachim Tenschert', p. 23, HWA FH 64.

[143] Weigel, in Anon., 'Notizen über eine Unterredung mit Dr. Werner Heinitz am 9.4.69', undated, 10 pages (2), BBA uncatalogued file 'HW Haus 69'.

[144] Werner Heinitz, unpublished interview with the author, 13 July 2010.

[145] See Weigel to 'dear friends', 6 May 1969, BBA uncatalogued file 'HW Haus 69'.

[146] See Arnold Klemer, 'Operative Information Nr. 723/68', 21 August 1968, file pp. 175–6 (176), BStU MfS AP 11958/81. This may or may not be true: Heinz was no friend of Besson and may have been frustrating attempts to strengthen his own faction at the theatre.

Langhoff had broken off negotiations because they thought Wekwerth was leaving the BE.[147] The SED certainly viewed the pair with suspicion and, in the light of the *Faustus* affair, wanted to entrench Wekwerth as artistic director to counter their presumed influence.[148] By March 1969, Helmut Baierl had informed the Stasi that the pair had reached agreement with Besson to join him at the Volksbühne in the coming season.[149] It is likely that Karge and Langhoff were unaware of their perceived power, and even if they were, they were unwilling to use it, preferring the fertile artistic ground of the Volksbühne to the well-worn furrows of the BE.

The spate of departures left the BE a shadow of its former self. Even though Weigel was fully protected by her international reputation, she still had to rebuild the BE if it were to be able to function properly again. She chose to form a 'Direktorium' ('directorate') to increase productivity and rebuild confidence at the BE with new directors, dramaturges and a deputy for the *Intendantin*.[150] She wanted to include Wolfgang Pintzka, who had served at the BE earlier in the 1960s, and Peter Kupke, a director who was the *Intendant* in Potsdam and who directed a very well-received *Caucasian Chalk Circle* there in 1966. The dramaturgy department was also re-populated: Hans-Jochen Irmer and Karl Mickel both joined in 1970. A more unexpected proposition was that of Friedrich Dieckmann. Dieckmann, as noted on pp. 188–9, Chapter 6, had written a highly critical article about *Coriolan* and the BE. In the wake of this, the production's designer, Karl von Appen, whose work Dieckmann had criticized, actually sought contact with him because he shared Dieckmann's concerns about the use of his design.[151] Appen recommended Dieckmann to the BE, and supported him in the face of Weigel's post-*Coriolan* scepticism.[152] That said, the dramaturge-in-waiting was only appointed in 1972. An even more fascinating prospect was not to be realized in Weigel's lifetime: she wanted to bring Heiner Müller to the BE.[153] Brecht's most adept successor could have had quite an effect on Weigel by extending the possibilities of the 'Brechtian', but this was not to be. Müller would join the BE as dramaturge under

147 See Gerhard Brähmer to Paul Verner, 16 December 1968, LAB C Rep 902 2860.
148 See Arno Hochmuth to Klaus Gysi, 10 October 1968, SAPMO BArch DY 30/IV A 2/2.024/74.
149 See Arnold Klemer, 'Operative Information Nr. 179/69', 11 March 1969, file pp. 173–4 (174), BStU MfS AP 11958/81.
150 See Weigel, '[Memorandum]', [September 1969], *Briefwechsel*, p. 217.
151 Friedrich Dieckmann, unpublished interview with the author, 17 November 2010.
152 See [Weigel] to Tenschert, 27 November 1969, BBA uncatalogued file 'HW Haus 69'.
153 See [Weigel] to Hans Giersch, 19 August 1970, BBA uncatalogued file 'HW Haus 1970'.

Ruth Berghaus, who was appointed Weigel's deputy to start the 1970/71 season.[154]

While Weigel was rebuilding the BE, she managed to alienate and lose one of her closest allies. The first new major production after *Thebes* was Büchner's *Woyzeck*. Weigel had unilaterally employed the film director Helmut Nitzschke to stage the play. Tenschert noted that he did not find Weigel's way of choosing the play or the director acceptable as there was no consultation with him, other directors or dramaturges.[155] At an early meeting, he criticized Nitzschke's version of Büchner's fragment, saying that he should read the latest research on the topic.[156] On the same day, he asked head of administration Hans Giersch to relieve him of his role as Head Dramaturge.[157] By 1970, Tenschert was not being invited to dramaturgical meetings, including one in which a paper he had submitted was to be discussed.[158] On the same day, he wrote directly to Weigel, complaining that Karl Mickel had been appointed dramaturge against his express wishes, and again asked to be relieved of his role as head dramaturge.[159] Werner Hecht assumed this role, although he deliberately chose the title 'the Leader of the Dramaturgy Department'.[160] Later that year, Weigel informed the Municipal Authority that she would not be taking Tenschert on tour to the FRG despite admittedly good work rehearsing *Commune* because he had been critical of the BE in public on their recent tour of Poland.[161] Tenschert left the BE shortly afterwards.

The question that arises from this sudden exclusion of Tenschert is what might have provoked it. In the battle between Weigel and Wekwerth, Tenschert, who had co-directed with Wekwerth since 1961, had surprisingly sided with Weigel. He offered Karge and Langhoff advice on how to get *Thebes* produced and had supported Weigel at the hearing with Heinitz.[162] Yet apparently without warning, Weigel had turned on him. The one indication available for why this happened comes from Tenschert himself. In an interview, he said that he had had a private conversation with Weigel and asked her to take Wekwerth back, however

[154] For a discussion of her rise, see pp. 231–4, Chapter 8.
[155] See Tenschert to Weigel, 10 November 1969, BEA File 50.
[156] See Anon., 'Dramaturgie-Sitzung am 20 November 1969', undated, 3 pages (1), ibid.
[157] Tenschert to Hans Giersch, 20 November 1969, BBA uncatalogued file 'HW Haus 1970 [sic]'.
[158] Tenschert, 'Aktennotiz', 2 March 1970, BEA File 50.
[159] See Tenschert to Weigel, 2 March 1970, BBA uncatalogued file 'HW Haus 1970'.
[160] Werner Hecht, unpublished interview with the author, 8 June 2011.
[161] See [Weigel] to Horst Oswald, 11 November 1970, BBA uncatalogued file 'HW Allg. Briefw. 1970'.
[162] See [Tenschert] to Manfred Karge and Matthias Langhoff, 7 December 1968, BEA File 48; and Anon., 'Notizen über eine Unterredung mit Dr. Werner Heinitz am 9.4.69', undated, 10 pages (2), BBA uncatalogued file 'HW Haus 69'.

difficult that might have been. She replied: 'the man has offended me too deeply'.[163] He reflected that everything went downhill after that. Weigel, it seems, felt that she could not work with someone who even considered a rapprochement with Wekwerth.

With Tenschert out of the way, Weigel tried to fashion new structures at the BE. A handwritten sketch outlines a series of groups (directing, dramaturgy, prognosis [i.e., planning], set, and music) under a five-person 'Rat der Intendanz' ('Council for the *Intendanz*').[164] Weigel, however, did not see that plan realized. After a successful tour of France, where she performed the title role in *The Mother*, she returned seriously unwell. She had been diagnosed with bronchial cancer at the beginning of 1971[165] and died on 6 May 1971. Her death marked the end of a bitter period in the BE's history in which her imposing personality was unable to rescue the company from a downward spiral; indeed, it was a contributory factor.

It is perhaps easy to downplay Weigel's contribution to the BE in the light of her final years as *Intendantin*, which were hardly glorious. Yet it should not be forgotten how her determination secured the company's future after Brecht's death in 1956 and how her decisions led to the realization of productions that would assure the BE's reputation as a purveyor of innovative, high-quality theatre. She sensibly withdrew from directorial decisions up until the mid 1960s and allowed her directing team the space to define the BE's aesthetic and political direction. Without her stewardship, the company could well have lost its commitment to Brecht and his methods, and declined into just another Berlin theatre.

In the wings, however, stood Weigel's deputy, Ruth Berghaus. She had staged two Brecht productions in 1971: *Im Dickicht der Städte* (*In the Jungle of the Cities*) and *Die Gewehre der Frau Carrar* (*Señora Carrar's Rifles*). The first was the GDR's initial attempt to stage this most unruly play; the second was a conscious defiance of the BE's own *Modell* production of 1952. The stage was set for upheaval as the BE approached its first season without Weigel.

---

[163] Weigel, reported in Matthias Braun, 'Gespräch mit Joachim Tenschert', p. 24, HWA FH 64.

[164] See Weigel, '[Sketch of New Management Structures]', HWA File 164, also reprinted in Hecht, *Helene Weigel*, pp. 118–19.

[165] See Herold, *Mutter des Ensembles*, p. 228.

8   A new beginning: 1971–1974

Continuities/discontinuities

By 1971, the BE, whether it liked it or not, had become the GDR's showpiece theatre company. It made theatre politically and had become so globally renowned that the SED fed it with money in return for international recognition and adulation. The crisis at home, however, generated great anxiety as to whether the golden goose would stop laying its eggs, and the SED had to find the 'right' new leader who could bring the BE back from the brink. The death of Helene Weigel led to the appointment of only the second *Intendant* in the Berliner Ensemble's almost twenty-two-year history. Weigel rarely defined artistic policy, and when she did, especially in a last years of her leadership, it proved divisive and led to crisis. However, her constant presence promoted the establishment of a tradition because she provided the environment in which certain ways of thinking about making theatre could flourish, while others were eschewed or ignored. The establishment of the BE as a 'Brecht theatre' after Brecht's death in 1956 owes much to Weigel's efforts to further her husband's work, and the period of her *Intendanz* not only associated Brecht's plays with the BE but, more importantly, Brecht's method with the Theater am Schiffbauerdamm.

Weigel's successor was thus entrusted with furthering the Brechtian legacy. Such an ambition was also of concern to the SED. Since the mid 1950s, the BE had become one of the world's most important theatre companies, due to the reception of its work internationally, and the party was keen to capitalize on the kudos this position brought to the GDR and to bathe in the reflected glory. The BE was thus *politically* obliged to further Brecht's work, too. Neither the BE nor the SED could determine how the company was to be led in any specific way because the new leadership itself would have to negotiate its artistic principles over time. However, it was clear that Brechtianism as it had been practiced in the late 1960s was in need of reappraisal. The techniques and approaches were looking tired, and the company was increasingly accused of having become a lifeless museum, rather than a vibrant site of theatrical discovery. But the change that was to take place was not only concerned with reviving the BE's flagging fortunes, but with a critique of the Brechtian method as it had been practiced previously.

Brecht's directorial approaches themselves were, of course, a product of their time. They shared the optimism of the early GDR, that a better society had been founded in which exploitation was to be banished, and human endeavour could advance without capitalist alienation. Brecht's method included elements of this optimism, particularly in the way he interpreted social contradiction on stage. That Brecht 'loaded' his dialectic in favour of implicitly socialist solutions reflected his hopes for a better future, but diminished the possibilities of a theatre for active spectators. His directing practice was thus productively informed *and* wilfully limited by his worldview. Quite how his attitudes may have changed in the light of the Hungarian Uprising of 1956 that inspired his friends Wolfgang Harich and Walter Janka to demand greater liberalization in the GDR (which in turn led to their incarceration) is unclear. Would he have stuck to his interpretive positions or directed them to criticize the SED's stewardship? The problem with the BE's relationship to Brecht under Weigel is that such questions were never asked and the method was never subjected to fundamental analysis.

As time went on, the GDR's totalitarian system had not proved itself to be the vanguard of a liberated workers' republic, but signalled the old problems of authoritarianism and paternalism. Artistic practice could not suddenly challenge the SED explicitly, of course, but it could interrogate the problems of socialism dialectically as it had the problems of capitalism. Such a theatre would call Brecht's political opinions into question while retaining at least some of his political forms.

The appointment of Ruth Berghaus

The crisis of the late 1960s had left Weigel much weakened and she was obliged to make structural changes to the BE's management in order to stabilize the company after the departure of key directors, actors and other staff. The BE was not alone in implementing new approaches to leadership, and recently appointed dramaturge Hans-Jochen Irmer noted in 1970 that rival Berlin theatres, the Deutsches Theater and the Volksbühne, were improving the communication flow between the leadership and the ensemble, and democratizing decision-making, respectively.[1] The GDR was certainly still following the Leninist mantra

---

[1] See Hans-Jochen Irmer, 'Perspektivpläne der Berliner Theater', 24 November 1970, 5 pages, BEA File 'Spielplan Überlegungen Bergh'.

of 'democratic centralism',[2] because it kept the individual leadership of the *Intendant* at the centre of a theatre's power structure. However, the State acknowledged, perhaps in line with social changes in the 1960s, such as the development of youth culture and a more engaged professional class, that paternalistic leadership required more than blind faith in the figurehead. The experience at the BE had certainly exposed the problems of allowing one person too much singular power, especially when that person was not a Party member herself.

Part of the BE's new system involved creating the post of deputy to the *Intendantin*. Ruth Berghaus, who had served as the BE's Party Secretary since 1967 and worked as a director at the BE, was appointed Weigel's deputy at the beginning of the 1970/71 season. As procedure dictated, the Ministry of Culture approved Berghaus's appointment, although this was hardly a surprise, given her political pedigree. She could be depended upon at least to keep an eye on Weigel, who, as far back as 1953, had not been deemed politically reliable,[3] a view that persisted well into the 1960s.[4] However, Weigel had her own choice of successor, and this was Wolfgang Pintzka. He was a director who trained at the BE and went on to lead the theatre in Gera. By 1970, he had been brought back into the management of the BE at Weigel's behest, and she wanted him to take over the leadership of production work, not Berghaus, whom she considered unsuitable for the task at the time.[5] Indeed, one of Weigel's two final documented letters, written five days before she died, named only Pintzka in connection with the BE's leadership.[6]

The Ministry of Culture had other ideas. According to a report written for the Stasi, a mere two days after Weigel's death, Berghaus had already been made interim *Intendantin*.[7] The informant was the BE's head of administration, Hans Giersch, and he testified to what he considered to be the correctness of the decision: Berghaus was looking after the State's interests by sealing the rooms in which Weigel worked and which contained her personal possessions. However, the question was still open

[2] See Michael Waller, *Democratic Centralism: An Historical Commentary* (Manchester: Manchester University Press, 1981), for a history and survey of the term and its diffuse usages in socialist states.
[3] See Kurt Bork, 'Betr.: Helene Weigel', 25 September 1953, n.p., LAB C Rep 124–02 16677.
[4] See [signature unclear], '[Untitled report on Weigel]', 20 January 1969, file pp. 399–400, BStU MfS AKK 8661/76, vol. 2.
[5] See Helene Weigel to Horst Oswald, 29 July 1970, *Briefwechsel*, p. 237.
[6] See Weigel to Elfriede Bork, 1 May 1971, ibid., p. 244.
[7] See Arnold Klemer, 'Aktuelle Hinweise auf die Situation im Berliner Ensemble nach dem Tode der Prof. Helene Weigel', 8 May 1971, file pp. 12–15 (12–13), BStU MfS AKK 8661/76, vol. 1.

as to who would ultimately be named Weigel's successor. Giersch noted that there was much speculation on this question and Weigel's daughter, Barbara Brecht-Schall, was reported to have said that she would not grant the company the rights to a single Brecht performance should Manfred Wekwerth return as *Intendant*.[8] Brecht-Schall's threat was to be the first of many.

Nothing is known about the appointment process itself; there are no official documents that minute discussions or even list candidates. There was, however, some vigorous lobbying from one quarter. Wolfgang Harich, the young philosopher who had demanded that Walter Ulbricht, the First Secretary of the Central Committee, resign in 1956 and who was imprisoned for his views in 1957, had been loosely associated with the BE after his release in 1964, between 1965 and 1971.[9] He had moved in with BE actor and singer Gisela May in 1966 and wrote a series of long and initially confidential letters advocating her suitability for the newly vacant position. These were addressed to senior SED figures, such as Kurt Hager, the final authority on cultural matters, and Hans Rodenberg, a member of the Staatsrat (the Council of State), for example.[10] It is difficult to know how these letters were received by their addressees: May almost certainly did not appear on anyone's list of candidates, and rambling letters that were partisan to the point of mania would hardly have made her any more attractive. Harich also sent a bizarre chart to Rodenberg comparing May, Berghaus, Wekwerth, the director Benno Besson, and the BE's lead actor Ekkehard Schall for the post of *Intendant*. Stuck together with tape, the sheets list a series of seventy-three criteria ranging from the sensible ('Member of the SED? . . . Well known to experts in the field?') to the downright absurd ('Free of decadent tendencies? . . . Another woman, like Helli?').[11] A cursory browse of the anonymous list reveals an obsessive, extended survey of minutiae, which was undoubtedly penned by Harich because it employed the same terms as his letters and clearly favoured May. Corinna Holtz, however, attributes the document to the Politburo, the GDR's highest executive committee.[12] This was more ranting than reasoning, and there can be

[8] See ibid., file, p. 15.   [9] See Wolfgang Harich, *Ahnenpaß*, p. 65.
[10] See Wolfgang Harich to Kurt Hager, 8 May 1971, SAPMO BArch DY 30/IV A 2/2.024/74; and Harich to Rodenberg, 9 June 1971, SAPMO BArch NY 4204/79.
[11] [Wolfgang Harich], 'Wer ist am besten geeignet, Nachfolger Helene Weigels als Intendant des Berliner Ensembles zu werden?', n.p., SAPMO BArch NY 4204/79. The term 'decadence' harks back to the SED's formalism campaign of the early 1950s and shows how Harich retained dogmatic terms to attack experimental art in the GDR.
[12] See Corinna Holtz, *Ruth Berghaus*, p. 160.

no suggestion that the document entered the decision-making process at all, except perhaps as comic relief.

Whatever did happen behind the scenes, Ruth Berghaus was confirmed by the Berlin City Council on 1 July and by the Berlin's Municipal Authority on 7 July as *Intendantin* of the Berliner Ensemble.[13] The justification for her appointment was suitably bland, mentioning pro forma how her political and artistic experiences and abilities provided the prerequisites for leading the BE.[14] Harich dispatched a blistering attack on Berghaus shortly after the formal announcement, again using the language of the 1950s' formalism campaign in places.[15] Giersch's report to the Stasi following the appointment told of the positive response from the ensemble, that Pintzka supported her fully, but that Berghaus had got wind of Harich's letters, which had also been sent to dramaturge Werner Hecht and actor Ekkehard Schall. May considered collecting signatures in support of Berghaus to demonstrate her loyalty, yet this did not happen as the action could have exposed divisions in the ensemble.[16] So, although the appointment was not necessarily controversial, the ensemble itself was still recovering from the crisis of the previous five years, and Berghaus could not begin her spell with a unified company behind her.

A new *Intendantin* for a new GDR: Berghaus redefines the relationship to Brecht

It is nothing but a coincidence that in the same year, 1971, Helene Weigel died, Ruth Berghaus became *Intendantin*, and Erich Honecker won his power struggle with Walter Ulbricht to become, with the support of the Soviets, First Secretary of the SED's Central Committee. Honecker's GDR, as will become apparent, was just as concerned with control and authority as Ulbricht's, yet, in its early years, Honecker seemed to suggest that he was a more liberal leader. On cultural matters, he set out his credentials in a now infamous speech of December 1971 in which he declared: 'if one proceeds from the solid position of socialism, there can be, in my opinion, no taboos in the field of art and literature'.[17] Honecker

---

[13] See Anon., 'Stenografisches Protokoll der 18. (ordentlichen) Tagung der Stadtverord-netenversammlung von Gross-Berlin am 1 Juli 1971', undated, 178 pages (177), LAB C Rep 100–01 117; and Rücker, 'Beschlußprotokoll für die 15. (ordentliche) Magis-tratssitzung am Mittwoch, dem 7. Juli 1971 . . .', 8 July 1971, 7 pages (7), LAB C Rep 100–05 1466.

[14] See Anon., 'Begründung', undated, n.p., ibid.

[15] See Harich to Hager, 10 July 1971, SAPMO BArch DY 30/IV A 2/2.024/74.

[16] See Wilhelm Girod, 'Operative Information Nr. 831/71', 19 July 1971, file pp. 24–6, BStU MfS Bln. Abt. XX A 480–11.

[17] Erich Honecker, 'Schlußwort auf der 4. Tagung des ZK der SED', *Neues Deutschland*, 18 December 1971.

would also open up the GDR to the West in the early 1970s by responding positively to initiatives from West Germany's Chancellor Willy Brandt. Yet as Joachim Walther notes in his study of the Stasi's relationship to GDR writers, the new openness merely meant that the security services adopted more subtle means of exerting influence, which should not be confused with a more humane approach to their work.[18] The BE was still under surveillance, and this was to burgeon under Honecker's reign.

However, the appointment of Berghaus over the more conventional Wolfgang Pintzka indicated either a desire to engage with an artist who was more experimental or a blindness to this quality in the name of a political reliability that had been ascertained covertly in 1970 and 1971.[19] Whichever of these was the case, Berghaus took over the BE with two recent productions of plays by Brecht under her belt that signalled her approaches to dealing with both the company's totemic founder and the business of staging drama in general in the GDR of the early 1970s. Although her production of *Señora Carrar's Rifles* premiered four and a half months after *In the Jungle of the Cities*, I shall consider *Carrar* first due to its engagement with the tradition of staging Brecht at the BE.

Carrar had its premiere on 15 June 1971, barely a month after Weigel's death, and had been part of the production schedule while Weigel was still alive. Weigel herself had starred as the eponymous heroine in the BE's production of 1952, having played the same role at the play's world premiere in Paris in 1937, and she reprised the role in Copenhagen a year later. The 1952 production had been what Brecht termed a *Modell*, a production which was exemplary of how one could stage the play. Indeed, in 1952 an authorized documentation in three sections was published of the productions in Paris, Copenhagen, and an amateur appropriation of the *Modell* in the GDR.[20] The play itself is not the most subtle of Brecht's works and follows Carrar's political awakening. Reluctant to enter the Spanish Civil War because her husband died from bullet wounds sustained in war, Carrar joins the struggle after one of her sons is killed while fishing by General Franco's men. However, the play's *Modell* character was radically called into question well before it was staged anew at the BE. Directors Hartwig Albiro and Piet Drescher considered the text

[18] See Joachim Walther, *Sicherungsbereich Literatur*, pp. 97, 101, and 141.
[19] See Philipp, 'Ermittlungsbericht', 24 August 1970, file pp. 7–8; and H. W., 'Berghaus-Dessau, Ruth – Stellv. Intendantin u. Regisseur', 6 January 1971, file, p. 20, both documents BStU MfS Bln. Abt. XX A 480–11.
[20] See Bertolt Brecht and Ruth Berlau, *Die Gewehre der Frau Carrar* (Dresden: Verlag der Kunst, 1952).

in 1969, in response to popular demand from GDR schools on whose literature syllabus *Carrar* had featured for some years. This was because the SED had successfully assimilated *Carrar* into the framework of socialist realism, unlike the rest of Brecht's dramatic *oeuvre*. The directors believed that the production of 1952 could only serve 'as orientation . . . it can't be elevated to the level of artistic yardstick for a contemporary . . . treatment of the play'.[21] They identified a problem with the aesthetics of the past, something Berghaus pursued two years later in a production that consciously jettisoned the BE *Modell* in favour of a production that was intended to speak to or provoke the audience of the day.

The 1952 production was well known for its attempt to recreate the milieu of a Spanish fishing village; Weigel even learned how to sew nets and displayed the skill every evening. Berghaus resisted this attention to detail with a radical change of perspective: for her, the connection between the stage and the audience was the concrete establishment of the Carrar family's class and the actions that emerged from this status. As a result, the set was stripped back in order to emphasize proletarian poverty. As assistant Peter Konwitschny put it: 'the "noblesse" of the *Modell* has no function today';[22] consequently the naturalistic details were to be replaced by the harsh realities of a family living in straitened circumstances. The Carrars used the few props in a variety of ways to underline their social position – mustard pots doubled as glasses, for example. This new grittiness derived from Berghaus's materialist aesthetic that connected attitudes and opinions to the body: 'we have to show that people only believe something when they suffer directly, not through words'.[23] She was thus keen to show the interaction of material deprivation and the evolution of class consciousness. In line with this, she cut one of the play's classic lines where Carrar identifies the reason for her son's murder: his shabby cap betrayed that he was proletarian to his murderers. Berghaus believed that this detail overegged the pudding because her production had already emphasized the social dimension.[24] The cut was also a signal that she was departing from the *Modell* and was prepared to take risks with respect to certain more conservative notions of the BE's traditions to make her production work.

[21] Hartwig Albiro and Piet Drescher, 'Einige Überlegungen zu *Gewehre der Frau Carrar*', 28 May 1969, n.p., BEA File 54.

[22] Peter Konwitschny, 'Notat zum Bühnenbild und [zu den] Kostümen 21.4.71 . . .', 27 April 1971, n.p., AdK RBA 945.

[23] Berghaus, in Peter Konwitschny, 'Notat Carrar (13.3.71)', undated, 3 pages (2), BEA File 54.

[24] See Berghaus, in Jörg Mihan, 'Foyergespräch nach der Generalprobe von *Die Gewehre der Frau Carrar* am 12.6.71', undated, 5 pages (2), ibid.

The emphasis on creating a realistic version also led to a fundamental rethink of the function of word and deed. Berghaus considered this to be a play about waiting, something she identified in Brecht's prologue to the play, set in a camp for Spanish refugees in France.[25] Here, inmates wonder why the Czechoslovakians did not fight back when the Germans invaded, and one of their number recounts the story of Carrar and how she almost waited too late to act. When questioned about the dominance of silence in the production, Berghaus replied 'decisions are made after gaps, to bring that to consciousness', and she added: 'silence has different functions: reflection, provocation, not wanting to answer'.[26] The emphasis on silence was thus a provocation for the spectators, too, in that it had no single, readable meaning. They were encouraged to engage with a play, familiar to many from school, afresh.

The reception of the stripped-down production was certainly mixed. Brecht expert Ernst Schumacher welcomed a *Carrar* which 'boldly negates' the *Modell*. He detected a careful play of dialectical tension in the new approach to Señora Carrar: 'the more she refuses to see, the more insights her partners have to bring to bear'.[27] This example of a 'not/but' tapped directly back into Brecht's theoretical arsenal as a way of showing the contradictions of the action. A reviewer from the FRG also welcomed the fact that Berghaus had distanced the production 'from the fussiness of that "impulse of showing" that in recent years . . . had become ossified into a pedantic insistence on pointing the finger'.[28] Elsewhere, in both East and West, the means through which Berghaus achieved her ends were also being questioned. One reviewer criticized 'the impression of an all too monotonous dryness' in the delivery.[29] The critic at the SED's own newspaper, *Neues Deutschland*, accused the production of formalism and noted that Brechtian means 'occasionally became opaque and gave rise to more questions than answers'.[30] That is, the devices did not lead the spectator to answers, but often left the play's questions open. Another critic noted that the fact that directors were not allowed to stage Beckett or Ionesco in the GDR should not encourage them to experiment with such approaches 'on the most unsuitable of objects'.[31] The transfer of

---

[25] See Berghaus, in Konwitschny, 'Notat Carrar (13.3.71)', here p. 3.

[26] Berghaus, in Mihan, 'Foyergespräch', pp. 1 and 2, respectively.

[27] Ernst Schumacher, '*Die Gewehre der Frau Carrar*', *Berliner Zeitung*, 24 June 1971.

[28] Rolf Michaelis, 'Ein Stück zum Parteitag', *Frankfurter Allgemeine Zeitung*, 19 June 1971.

[29] Michael Bilstein, 'An die Gewehre', *RheinischeMerkur*, 9 July 1971.

[30] Rainer Kerndl, 'Theater in Berlin', *Neues Deutschland*, 9 July 1971.

[31] Anon., 'Beurteilung die [*sic*] Aufführung *Die Gewehre der Frau Carrar* (Brecht)', 2 September 1971, 2 pages (2), AdK RBA 947-1.

authority from the stage to the auditorium was clearly unwelcome in more doctrinaire quarters.

Jörg Mihan, on behalf of the BE, conducted an investigation into the reactions of its predominantly young audience and found that the pupils responded most positively to the more naturalistic and dynamic sections of the production.[32] Earlier, Mihan had reached the conclusion that the pupils encountered two key problems: first, that they found it difficult to piece together the individual elements of the performance into a meaningful whole, and second, that what they saw did not correspond to the interpretation offered in schools.[33] Berghaus had constructed her production as a montage, rather than as an aesthetically coherent whole in a bid to offer a variety of new perspectives on the material. Brecht favoured montage himself, yet Berghaus pushed his ideas further to give the production's elements a level of autonomy that surpassed her inspiration's own achievements. Berghaus thus maintained a link with Brecht, but sought to radicalize his ideas for a new period. To understand her reasons, I will now turn to the BE production of *In the Jungle of the Cities* that casts more light on her approach in general to staging plays per se, rather than just Brecht in particular.

Although Brecht wrote *Jungle*, the play belongs to the period that preceded his exposure to Marxism in the mid 1920s. He did not stage it in the GDR, and it certainly did not have '*Modell*' status. Indeed, the play itself was written with the intention of problematizing questions of motivation and explanations of the action. The plot, broadly speaking, concerns a fight, set in Chicago, between Shlink, a Malay timber merchant, and Garga, who works in a lending library. The fight, which Shlink provokes without any suggestion of a reason, costs him his business and ultimately his life, while Garga loses his lover and his family. The various strategies undertaken by both combatants often suggest little about their provenance. This puzzling play had two different appeals. To Weigel, at a meeting in 1969, it was of political interest because she believed the West was under the impression that the BE was not allowed to stage the early, pre-Marxist Brecht. (She was also concerned that the BE was running out of plays by Brecht that had not already been performed at the BE.) Berghaus had already reported that SED's District Leadership in Berlin

[32] See Jörg Mihan, 'Bertolt Brecht – *Die Gewehre der Frau Carrar*, die Aufführung am Berliner Ensemble und ihre Wirkung beim jugendlichen Publikum. Probleme der ästhetischen Erziehung der Schüler', *Studien*, 1 (1973), supplement to *Theater der Zeit*, 2 (1973), pp. 1–16 (11).

[33] See Jörg Mihan, 'Foyergespräch', p. 3.

would support a production.[34] To Berghaus, writing in advance of the meeting, the play presented a challenge to locate social material buried under a veneer that apparently removed all social context. She noted that the play's struggles 'serve to obscure the circumstances: identifying the social situation in which the individual lives'.[35] Berghaus was thus interested in carrying out an analysis of the play in order to reveal a social connection between states of conflict amongst the characters and states of conflict within capitalist society.

The problem for the director was that there was precious little social material to be found in the text, and so Berghaus sought to develop a way of creating relationships on stage without direct reference to the play's text. Instead, she fashioned a physical language whose point of reference was itself, so that gestures and their variations became their own system of making meaning. Dramaturge Hans-Jochen Irmer called the foundation of Berghaus's approach the 'the comparative nature of the events [with each other]'.[36] The attempt to engineer a production based on its own gestural codes did not, however, mean that Berghaus was involved in a flight of artistic fancy. In the third scene, for example, Garga has a conversation with his mother which Berghaus described as 'two monologues without an ultimate aim'.[37] However, assistant Jürgen Kern noted at the same time that if these open-ended speeches should not be generalized into a portrayal of a timeless mother/son relationship, 'then our socially concrete *Arrangements* and proposals for *Gestus* and *Haltungen* make clear in which social order such behaviour has its roots'.[38] The assistant clearly signals the use of orthodox Brechtian terms, applied to material that does not vouchsafe their relationship to a concrete understanding of society. Berghaus was investigating the possibilities of a Brechtian theatre under conditions of profound uncertainty, generated by a text that did not provide interpretive keys to the material it represented.

Jungle premiered on 28 January 1971 and presented the audience with a production that diverged greatly from the BE's usual fare. The set for the production at the BE, designed by Andreas Reinhardt (with whom Berghaus collaborated extensively over the years), did not replicate the jungle of a city in any sort of realistic detail (see Fig. 8.1). Rather, it presented a jungle of metal frames, ladders, and scaffolds. This formless, physical metaphor corresponded to the performance style perfectly:

---

[34] See Weigel and Berghaus, in Anon., 'Inhaltsverzeichnis zum Tonband der Leitungssitzung vom 28.11.69', undated, 8 pages (5 and 4, respectively), HWA 164.
[35] Berghaus, '*Im Dickicht der Städte*', 22 October 1969, n.p., BEA File 53.
[36] Hans-Jochen Irmer, '*ImDickicht der Städte*', undated, 5 pages (4), ibid.
[37] Berghaus, in Jürgen Kern, 'Zum 3. Bild', undated, n.p., ibid.
[38] Jürgen Kern, ibid.

Fig. 8.1. The city as symbolic jungle: the urban sprawl of Brecht's fictional Chicago is presented as a mass of metal. *In the Jungle of the Cities*, January 1971.

it connoted a series of complex relationships without fixing them in the external world. The actors demonstrated their relationships to each other by creating (sometimes highly acrobatic) spatial images which were repeated or varied to allow the audience to compare *Gestus* and *Haltung*. Yet these physical indices were not guaranteed by the conventional markers of context, and thus the images created their own meanings by establishing their own visual language.

Berghaus, who came from a background in dance, wanted to introduce physicality as a way of expanding the performance's horizons beyond the text: 'the athletic emphasis on the actors' movements must feature strongly to counter the literary character of the play'.[39] The foregrounding of the actor's body as a performing entity, not merely asking it to create readable signs, again indicates how Berghaus wanted to short-circuit a purely intellectual reception of the production and engender more visceral responses as well. Such an approach corresponded to the director's belief that the material could not merely be assimilated by the mind, but had to be experienced, too.

---

[39] Anon., 'Notate über *Dickicht* – Gespräche vom 13.6. u. 16.6.70', undated, n.p., AdK RBA 12.

Berghaus wanted to create a socially engaged theatre that retained as much of Brecht's method and philosophy as the epistemological situation of the time could support. This was a production that maintained a link with a society that she still considered dialectical. However, the production was not able to articulate contradiction as something eminently readable and presentable in terms of binary oppositions, as Brecht had sometimes done. Instead, contradictions proliferated on stage, unresolved, yet present. This production thus provides an example of a reinterpretation of Brecht's method, yet the method is radically updated for a society in which Brecht's socialist certainties were no longer clearly evident. I have termed this reconfiguration 'post-Brechtian',[40] in that it seeks to preserve a commitment to dialectics while finding new means to supplant the binary oppositions that ran through Brecht's practice at the BE. The retention of ideas of *Gestus* and *Haltung*, for example, reflect the need to connect the body to society, but Berghaus then problematized them by relating the carefully articulated gestures and movements not to 'reality', but a system of signs generated in rehearsal. This 'opening up' of the dialectic and the shift away from implicit meaning pervades Berghaus's more experimental work with the BE.

A final point to bear in mind when examining Berghaus's stage practice is that it was not programmatic. While Brecht started with *Arrangements*, then courted offers from his actors to establish *Gestus* and *Haltung*, Berghaus realized that each production required its own organization of the Brechtian elements because the material and the epistemological conditions surrounding the realization process were so unstable. As she put it:

Since our work has an experimental character, the play brings with it particular complications, and as *Notate* at the BE can be freely consulted, we must not give the impression that this is a theory for dealing with Brecht's early plays.[41]

She was not working with anything approaching the concept of a *Modell*, that is, a process that could be replicated or recycled. As such, Berghaus's approach had an important effect on the documentation she produced, too. In more orthodox productions at the BE, documentation served as a blueprint for future work; it set out a model of how one could realize a play. Here Berghaus signalled that documentation could only describe and reflect on a particular process in order to understand its

---

40 See David Barnett, 'Toward a Definition of Post-Brechtian Performance: The Example of *In the Jungle of the Cities* at the Berliner Ensemble, 1971', *Modern Drama*, 54: 3 (2011), pp. 333–55.
41 Berghaus, in Anon., 'Regie-Gespräch über *Dickicht* am 3.11.1970', undated, 4 pages (4), BEA File 53.

specific outcomes. It no longer offered a vista onto future productions. And although Brechtian terminology and devices were in her blood, she insisted on being able to augment and extend them according to the needs of the text and the creative team. As Sigrid Neef writes, the *Intendantin* made it possible 'for plays to be radically interrogated without prejudice'.[42] For the most part, this was her artistic credo at the BE, yet it would create great problems for her and ultimately lead to her dismissal in 1977.

Dissatisfaction with the *Modell* production of *Galileo*

Well before 1977, Berghaus found herself faced with a problem unique to the BE. On various occasions since the mid 1960s, the company that owed its success and reputation to Brecht's theatre reforms and innovations had been called a 'Brecht Museum'. *Jungle* and *Carrar* certainly challenged this impression, yet the *Intendantin* was also hampered by plans developed by her predecessor. The one that appeared in Berghaus's first full season in charge of the BE was a production of Brecht's *Life of Galileo*. Fritz Bennewitz, who had successfully promoted Brecht's work outside Berlin, was the head director in Weimar, and he had been charged with directing the production at the BE with veteran actor Wolfgang Heinz playing the lead.

A meeting in March 1971, that is, while Weigel was still alive, was designed to persuade Bennewitz to stage a *Modell* production, something he opposed. He also reported that Heinz's views diverged even further from the *Modell* than his. However, as dramaturge Manfred Hocke noted, Bennewitz's ideas were actually quite close to Brecht's of 1956.[43] Bennewitz also objected to the presence of the copper scenery used for that production as it would have associated the new production far too closely with the old one. However, by the beginning of rehearsals in May 1971, the copper scenery had been installed, and Bennewitz had signed up to the *Modell*, however unwillingly. Notes on the concept behind the production present a rather vague interpretation: 'today Galileo means nothing different from what he did in 1956, but the same and more. We need to find the relevance to today of the dilemma Galileo faced'.[44]

---

[42] Sigrid Neef, *Das Theater der Ruth Berghaus* (Frankfurt/Main: Fischer, 1989), p. 75.

[43] See Manfred Hocke, 'Bericht über die Fahrt nach Weimar am 30.3.1971 zu Besprechungen über die geplante *Galilei*-Inszenierung zu Fritz Bennewitz', undated, 3 pages, BEA File 55.

[44] Klaus Schwalm, 'Zum Beginn der Probenarbeit *Galilei*', undated, 2 pages (1), ibid.

It seems that Bennewitz found himself at a loss working with the actors of the BE and Heinz as a guest. Heinz was more or less an orthodox Stanislavskian actor[45] and early on he was criticized for creating unreadable, naturalistic gestures 'by doing too much'.[46] Indeed, many of the early notes describe how messy the work was. Bennewitz may well have had success with his productions of Brecht's plays outside Berlin, but when he worked with the BE, he found that they spoke a different performative language, based on experiences steeped in a Brechtian orthodoxy developed primarily by Manfred Wekwerth. Work in June was marked by what the BE would have considered sloppiness. A run in early July revealed 'a certain unawareness of basic *Gestus* and comportment' amongst the actors.[47] The assistant suggested going through Käthe Rülicke's *Notate* of 1956 to make the characterizations and an understanding of the scenes more precise.

Bennewitz returned to the BE after the summer break, but by September he had been sent back to Weimar. Berghaus, and later Pintzka and Schall had taken over what were termed 'Korrekturproben' ('corrective rehearsals').[48] Berghaus did not intervene to radicalize the production; it was too late for that. She and the other directors did their best to fill the *Modell* with freshness and energy without sacrificing precision. The work seems to have been a partial success. Two West German reviewers denied that the production was a museum-piece despite its indebtedness to the past.[49] But while *Neues Deutschland* breathed an implicit sigh of relief that *Galileo* had not gone the way of *Carrar* or *Jungle*, Ernst Schumacher rued the fact that the BE had opted 'more for a copy than its dialectical progression, as Brecht's theory of the *Modell* suggests'.[50]

The production of *Galileo* confirmed to Berghaus how outdated the *Modell* idea had become. In the official BE brochure marking its twenty-fifth anniversary in 1974, Karl Mickel wrote, clearly with the approval of his *Intendantin*:

---

[45] Hans Jochen Irmer was against Heinz playing The Actor in a plan for a new version of *Der Messingkauf* for that very reason: Irmer, unpublished interview with the author, 3 November 2010.

[46] Entry for 2 June 1971, in Anon., 'Notate zur Inszenierung von *Leben des Galilei*', undated, 12 pages (1), BEA File 55.

[47] Jürgen Pörschmann, 'Zur Probe am 7.7.71 (Durchlauf)', 8 July 1971, 2 pages (2), ibid.

[48] Entry for 21 September 1971, in Anon., untitled *Notate*, undated, 10 pages (1), ibid.

[49] See Jürgen Beckelmann, 'Galilei – leicht und beschwingt', *Frankfurter Rundschau*, 15 October 1971; and Hans J. Beck, 'Sozialismus: vorwiegend heiter', *Deutsche Volkszeitung*, 21 October 1971.

[50] See Rainer Kerndl, 'Großartiger Galilei', *Neues Deutschland*, 7 October 1971; and Ernst Schumacher, 'Bedeutungsvoll wie je', *Berliner Zeitung*, 9 October 1971, respectively.

The imitation of the *Modell* production [of *Galileo*] became the gauge for the change in the conditions of reception; a different reception produces a different play from the same text of the reproduced production. The conclusion drawn from this experience is the new production of *The Mother*.[51]

While I will turn to *The Mother* in the next chapter, it is worth reflecting on the way Berghaus (and those who shared her vision of a post-Brechtian theatre) reacted to the process of producing *Galileo*. She had found herself locked into a production that she would not have chosen to direct. But she also appreciated that she could do nothing with what Bennewitz had wrought, but attempt to improve it on the *Modell*'s own terms. The result convinced her that work in that mode, with that philosophy did little more than pay homage to Brecht, rather than to serve him. The BE could not be a museum; it had to be opened up to new methods.

An interest in new writing

Berghaus was only interim *Intendantin* when a plan to stage Heiner Müller's *Der Bau* (*The Building Site*) and Volker Braun's *Hinze und Kunze* (roughly: *Tom, Dick and Harry*) was discussed in the summer of 1971.[52] Both plays were written by talented GDR playwrights and both were controversial. *The Building Site*, for example, had been banned from performance at the Deutsches Theater in 1965 in the wake of the SED's XI Plenum. It would only be premiered in 1980: the authorities ruled against the plan at the BE in 1972.[53] The early suggestion of staging both works indicates how the BE under Berghaus started to cast the repertoire's net wider, beyond Brecht and the classics, to plays that dealt with the GDR and its problems. The focus on the GDR was important, and in a speech on the occasion of Brecht's seventy-fifth birthday, Berghaus criticized the fact that contemporary West German playwrights had been performed at the BE in the past. Here she not only singled out Manfred Wekwerth's production of Heinar Kipphardt's *In der Sache J. Robert Oppenheimer* (*In the Matter of J. Robert Oppenheimer*) in 1965, but her own staging of Peter Weiss's *Vietnamdiskurs* (*Vietnam Discourse*) in 1968.[54] In

---

[51] Karl Mickel, 'Die Tradition und das neue Programm', in Hans-Jochen Irmer (ed.), *Berliner Ensemble. 1949–74* (Berlin: Berliner Ensemble, 1974), pp. 16 and 18, here p. 18.

[52] See Manfred Hocke, 'Stellungnahme zum Spielplanvorschlag', 28 June 1971, 2 pages, BEA File 'Projekte 1–70er'.

[53] Irene Ebel, 'für [*sic*] Regie- und Dramaturgie-Sitzung', 6 December 1972, 5 pages (1), BBA uncatalogued File 'Arbeitsberichte'.

[54] See Berghaus, '[Speech to the Verband der Theaterschaffenden on 11 February 1973]', undated, 3 pages (2), BEA File 'Berghaus Protokolle (Verwaltungs Mat.) 1971 72/73'.

this, she found herself in agreement with Wekwerth, who had advocated developing Brecht's work at the BE not by performing more Brecht, but by applying his methods to contemporary socialist drama. What divided the two, however, were their contrasting views of what Brecht's method implied and how it might be applied to other dramatists' plays, something I will consider in more detail below in the discussion of Heiner Müller's *Zement (Cement)* on pp. 253–9.

The first piece of new writing staged under and by Berghaus was a short piece, dramaturge Karl Mickel's *Wolokolamsker Chaussee (The Road to Volokolamsk)*. The play is not to be confused with the better known play cycle by Heiner Müller, although both are based on Alexander Bek's Soviet novel of the same name, written in 1944. In Mickel's version, the commander of the Soviet forces defending Moscow from the advancing Nazi *Wehrmacht* recalls six episodes from the battle to a journalist. The play thus resembled Brecht's *Lehrstück*, or learning play, in which distance is created on stage by consciously re-telling painful events of the past in the present in order to reach judgements in the auditorium.

There are precious few notes in the BE's dossier on the production, and so it is impossible to chart Berghaus's rehearsal process, but the staging featured the BE's principal male actor, Ekkehard Schall, as commander Momysch-Uli. The show premiered at a GDR air force base on 1 February 1972. While the venue may strike the reader as unusual, it betokens the BE's desire to connect military themes with military personnel. Hans-Jochen Irmer noted that Schall dominated the performance, to the detriment of Wolfgang Holz, sidelined as the journalist and relegated to someone who merely gave the lead his cues.[55] Back at the BE, the production was praised for the clarity of the commander's *Haltungen* which engaged the audience's imagination because the scene remained the commander's living room throughout.[56] The same reviewer was also impressed by the clear performance of dialectical contradiction, of argument and counterargument. Another enjoyed how Schall triumphed 'in a cleverly disciplined dynamic... rich in variety, precisely gauging the line between emotion and exaltation, sketching the portrait of a man of provocative passion, between quick anger and cool reflection'.[57] The confluence of precision and the containment of emotion was typical of Berghaus's direction in that it acknowledged human passions while framing them in the discourse of the play. She was able to provide Schall with

[55] See Hans-Jochen Irmer, 'Notiz zur Generalprobe und zur Aufführung *Die Gewehre der Frau Carrar, Wolokolamsker Chaussee* am 1. Februar 1972 in Marxwalde', 4 February 1972, 4 pages (2), BEA File 56.
[56] See Christoph Funke, 'Unruhe und große Fragen', *Der Morgen*, 22 March 1972.
[57] Helmut Ullrich, 'Das Gespräch mit dem Kommandeur', *Neue Zeit*, 22 March 1972.

the parameters within which he could produce work that was intellectually lucid without neglecting his subjectivity and physicality.

This, however, was a studio production, small-scale and often performed together with *Carrar*, as they shared the theme of armed struggle against fascist oppression. A more challenging new play was to follow, and again Berghaus chose to direct. Peter Hacks, who, together with Heiner Müller and Volker Braun, was one of the GDR's most talented and prominent playwrights, had been working on adapting classical myths for the contemporary stage, something he termed in the 1960s 'socialist classicism'. This he viewed as a type of drama that eschewed 'any restorative or apologetic traits' in order to treat classical *topoi* through the lens of socialism.[58]

Omphale took a lesser-known myth involving Heracles, who, having killed Iphitus, does penance by becoming Omphale's slave for a fixed period of three years. Hacks used the material to examine gender and the nature of love. A central moment in the play is when Heracles and Omphale 'swap' roles with Heracles dressing and behaving as a woman and Omphale wielding a sword. Through this, Heracles experiences what it feels like to be on the female side of a heterosexual relationship. Hacks deliberately called his version a comedy.

As Irmer noted in a preparatory discussion of the play, interest at the BE centred on redressing the traditional sexual imbalance that favoured the masculine: 'how does woman escape the role attributed to her in all societies? The feminine not as medium, but as active agent, woman with her own room to act as subject'. In addition, Irmer registered a desire that saw the gender exchange as metonymic of something far more expansive: 'experimenting with all possible role-changes in human society'.[59] The proposition was that socialist society allowed for such flexibility.

In rehearsal, Berghaus, as in *Jungle*, insisted on the primacy of the theatrical over the literary.[60] The theme of role-play, present in *Volokolamsk*, returned as Heracles and Omphale were directed to find the role-reversal difficult and fall out of character on several occasions. The gender-swap was '*intentional* play' in that each party provoked the other with gambits to understand better the nature of gender relations.[61] Irmer, however, reported that Schall as Heracles took exception to the more philosophical

---

[58] Peter Hacks, *Die Maßgaben der Kunst*, vol. 1 (Berlin: Eulenspiegel, 2003), pp. 20–36 (35). First published in 1960.
[59] Both quotations: Hans-Jochen Irmer, 'Notiz zu unseren *Omphale*-Besprechungen', 18 December 1971, 8 pages (2), AdK RBA 570.
[60] See Peter Konwitschny, 'Notate zu *Omphale* bis 4.6.72', undated, 4 pages (1), AdK RBA 580.
[61] Peter Konwitschny, 'Notate zu *Omphale* 20.9.72', undated, 2 pages (1), ibid.

passages and themes, dismissing them as "'the chatter of philologists'".[62] Irmer advised Schall to be wary of crowd-pleasing success and to engage with the loftier moments in the play as well.

The text and the performance style clearly took advantage of the apparent liberalism of Honecker's cultural policy, even though the BE had been in discussion with Hacks over a year before Honecker's speech eschewing taboos in art.[63] The play was politically unproblematic, but its aesthetics certainly caused consternation amongst reviewers. As already noted, Berghaus was not a director who valued a consistent artistic vision, but rather sought to play off different performance registers in a bid to keep contradictory material contradictory rather than harmonized. Most reviewers acknowledged the discontinuous nature of the production while rating it negatively. One GDR critic found that the production 'is too weighty for an evening's entertainment, too overdone and in love with itself for a play with engaging ideas for a contemporary audience'.[64] Only one reviewer from the West fully enjoyed the 'the play in a grotesque fairytale land' for its use of diverse theatrical forms and its blend of the low and the high.[65] Berghaus was experimenting with a postmodern montage of styles and approaches, each of which was designed to call the other into question and prevent the passive consumption of complex material.

Berghaus's *Intendanz* would see further contemporary drama grace the repertoire over the coming years, yet she did not neglect Brecht and also looked back to the drama of the previous century. Her capacity to craft a repertoire that realized her reformist ambitions was, however, curtailed by senior staff at the BE. While she endeavoured to place progressive forces in influential positions, she still had to deal with colleagues who shared neither her vision nor her ability.

The old and the new: staff politics under Berghaus

When Berghaus took charge of the BE, she did not suddenly introduce a new team who would support her plans, but had to accept the staff she found there. As it happened, she benefitted from changes made by Weigel in the wake of the crisis in the late 1960s. Weigel had employed Karl Mickel, who started off as 'wissenschaftlicher Mitarbeiter' ('academic collaborator'), but was soon reclassified as a dramaturge, and

[62] Schall, in Irmer, 'Probennotiz 13.–29.9.1972', 30 September 1972, 4 pages (3), ibid.
[63] See [Weigel] to Berghaus, Werner Hecht, Karl Mickel and Wolfgang Pintzka, 12 September 1970, BEA File '57/60: Schriftwechsel *Omphale/Zement*'.
[64] Christoph Funke, 'Der Held will Mensch sein', *Der Morgen*, 5 October 1972.
[65] Rolf Michaelis, 'Die Helden sind müde', *Frankfurter AllgemeineZeitung*, 5 October 1972.

Hans-Jochen Irmer, in 1970. Both were sympathetic to Berghaus's work and aspirations. Weigel also brought back Wolfgang Pintzka to the management of the BE and invited Peter Kupke to join. Both men had been *Intendanten* themselves, at Gera and Potsdam, respectively, and both were experienced directors. While Weigel knew Pintzka of old, she probably became aware of Kupke through his well-received 1966 production of *The Caucasian Chalk Circle* in Potsdam. Kupke, however, could not free himself of his commitments there until the beginning of the 1971/72 season,[66] by which time Weigel had died. As already noted, Pintzka, Weigel's choice as successor, supported Berghaus upon her installation as *Intendantin*. Kupke, too, played his part in defending the BE's new direction. In early 1972, for example, he attacked a review of *Jungle* in *Theater der Zeit* at a meeting of the Theaterverband (Theater Association).[67] However, Pintzka and Kupke were more traditionalist directors, especially of Brecht, and, over time, their aesthetic divergences from Berghaus's innovative colleagues become increasingly apparent.

Once in post, Berghaus introduced new members to the dramaturgy department who would help shore up support for her agenda. Karl von Appen, the BE's main designer, had recommended Friedrich Dieckmann to Weigel in 1969.[68] By 1972, Dieckmann had made Berghaus's acquaintance through Mickel and was duly appointed that year.[69] The *Intendantin* also hired playwright Heiner Müller as dramaturge a year later. He believed that she needed someone to 'advise her'.[70] This appointment was more difficult for her to push through: minutes of a meeting in January 1973 express the wish to employ Müller, but note that the proposal was still being discussed at the Ministry of Culture.[71] The playwright had had two productions cancelled, *The Building Site* in 1965, mentioned above, and, before that, *The Resettler* in 1961. He was yet to be rehabilitated and was still considered a risky figure in GDR theatre.

Ironically, Müller's questionable status with the authorities led to the appointment of an altogether more dubious dramaturge. While in Magdeburg, Hans-Diether Meves had wanted to produce Müller's

---

[66] See Peter Kupke to Berghaus, 22 April and 10 June 1971, BBA uncatalogued file 'HW RB Haus 1971 1972'.

[67] See Peter Kupke, '*Dickicht* im Theaterverband', 11 March 1972, n.p., BEA File 'Berghaus Protokolle (Verwaltungs. Mat.) 1971 72/73'.

[68] See [Weigel] to Tenschert, 27 November 1969, BBA uncatalogued file 'HW Haus 69'.

[69] Friedrich Dieckmann, unpublished interview with the author, 17 November 2010.

[70] See Heiner Müller, in Jan-Christoph Hauschild, *Heiner Müller oder Das Prinzip Zweifel. Eine Biographie* (Berlin: Aufbau, 2003), p. 292. On the same page Hauschild mistakenly asserts that Müller started work at the BE in 1970.

[71] See Margit Vestner, 'Protokoll der Regie- und Dramaturgiesitzung am Mittwoch, 13.1.73', undated, 4 pages (2), BEA File 'Protokolle 60er und 70er Jahre'.

Mauser (named after the handgun of the same name), the only play of his *oeuvre* that had been issued with an official written ban, according to Müller.[72] Meves's insistence on the production led to his being relieved of his post at the theatre. In a communication from the then head of the Central Committee's Cultural Department, Hans-Joachim Hoffmann,[73] to Kurt Hager, Hoffmann recommended in early 1973 that this maverick should work 'in a politically secure theatre'.[74] Meves, however, was not a maverick at all; he was actually a Stasi informer, 'Saint Just', a self-aggrandizing pseudonym that associates him with the political fanaticism of the same character in Büchner's *Danton's Death*. The question then arises as to whether the debacle over *Mauser* was in fact a Stasi ruse to confer the credibility and respect on Meves required if he were to work at the BE. There is no direct evidence to confirm this plan in the Stasi's archives, but, as Laura Bradley notes, the Stasi set up director Jürgen Gosch to direct a controversial production of *As You Like It* in order to have it banned and Gosch dismissed.[75] It was thus not beyond the wit of the Stasi to orchestrate such stunts in order to achieve its ends, which, in Meves's case, meant positioning a reliable informer in the upper echelons of the GDR's most internationally recognized cultural commodity. Whether the Stasi was or was not behind the abandoned production of *Mauser*, Meves certainly ended up at the BE in 1973. Quite what he did there, however, is unclear: his two-volume Stasi file has been filleted of almost all its content.[76]

One final change occurred in the higher levels of the BE in 1974. Werner Hecht, a dramaturge appointed by Weigel in 1959, had been made leader of the dramaturgy department in 1970 when Joachim Tenschert quit. Yet he clashed with Dieckmann in 1972 and 1973,[77] and left in 1974 when he found himself sidelined by Berghaus and in disagreement with the programme she wanted to pursue with the BE.[78] When Irmer took over as Head Dramaturge, Berghaus had a dramaturgy department that was broadly behind her. However, under the pressure of events following the production of *The Mother* in October 1974, this solidity would soon start to fragment.

---

[72] See Heiner Müller, *Krieg ohne Schlacht, Werke* 9:203.
[73] He became Minister of Culture later than year.
[74] Hans-Joachim Hoffmann to Kurt Hager, 9 January 1973, BArch DY 30/18985.
[75] See Laura Bradley, *Cooperation and Conflict*, p. 137.
[76] See BStU BV Bln. AIM 6049/91.
[77] See Werner Hecht to Berghaus, 17 November 1972, BBA uncatalogued file 'HW RB Haus 1971 1972'; and Dieckmann, 'Zu "Bemerkungen zum Werbeheft" von Werner Hecht', 14 June 1973, 5 pages, BBA uncatalogued file 'RB Haus 1973'.
[78] Werner Hecht, unpublished interview with the author, 8 June 2011.

Aesthetic fault-lines 1: the persistence of conventionality

Even before the turning point of *The Mother*, two very different directions in the company's productions can be detected. I will discuss this contrast by considering two examples: Brecht's *Turandot* (premiere 10 February 1973) and Müller's *Cement* (premiere 12 October 1973). Despite the closeness of their performance dates, their styles and approaches diverged greatly, something that can be traced back to the ideas and capabilities of their directors.

Turandot was the final full-length play Brecht completed before his death in 1956. It has never been particularly popular and had not been staged at the BE previously. Set in imperial China, its main plot line concerns the emperor and his monopoly on cotton. At the beginning of the play, he discovers that the price has slumped due to overproduction and he thus decides to stash it away to drive up the price. Subsequently, he convenes a congress at which his intellectuals (the 'Tuis') will cover up the real reason for the cotton shortage and offer alternative, credible explanations instead. The Tui with the best story will marry his daughter, Turandot. The play is thus mainly concerned with the relationship between power and the mind, and how politics can corrupt the sharpest of ideas. *Turandot* had its world premiere in Zurich on 5 February 1969, directed by Benno Besson and Horst Sagert, and while the directors' work was mostly praised, the play itself received a lukewarm reception from Western critics.[79] It is indeed a difficult text, laden with potential problems for directors regarding weakness in the plotting and characterization.

The production at the BE had a long and difficult gestation. Preparatory discussions started on 27 May 1971 and continued with analyses of individual scenes for a month.[80] Yet even by July, Wolfgang Pintzka was still heartened that he and co-director Peter Kupke had more time for 'a thorough analysis and preparation' before rehearsals were due to start.[81] At this stage, the minutes suggest that while the directors wanted to stage *Turandot*, they did not know how and, more importantly, why. The day after the meeting, Pintzka, Kupke and Werner Hecht prepared a *Konzeption* (conceptual plan) for the production although its main points were hardly radical: that the ruling class exploited intellectuals and that revolutionary relief from feudal poverty had to come from the people.[82] The lack of direction was confirmed in August when the minutes of

[79] See The Editors on the production's reception in BFA, 9: 407–8.
[80] Minutes of these meetings are to be found in BEA File 59.
[81] Wolfgang Pintzka, in Margit Vestner, 'Regie- und Dramaturgiesitzung am 9.7.1971', 9 July 1971, 7 pages (2), ibid.
[82] See Hecht, Kupke and Pintzka, 'Zur Konzeption von *Turandot oder der Kongress der Weißwäscher*', 10 July 1971, 3 pages (1), ibid.

another meeting noted: 'a directorial vision is missing. A new reading of the play is still not in sight'.[83] Rehearsals started on 5 November, but were suspended on 2 March 1972 after a not inconsiderable seventy-six sessions. They resumed on 23 October, and after another fifty-four rehearsals, the production premiered on Brecht's birthday, 10 February, in 1973. However, by late January Berghaus had already started to rehearse in place of the two directors. Her reported directorial instructions have a similar creative suggestiveness as Brecht's of the early 1950s. For example, when working with Turandot herself, Berghaus described her as an 'overripe pear that hasn't been picked' whose basic *Gestus* was: 'when on earth is something interesting going to happen in my life?'.[84] The attempt to rescue the production came, as with *Galileo* before it, too late. One critic found precision and rhythmic elegance,[85] something that came about through the emergency rehearsals. Almost every other reviewer registered deflation and a sense that intellectual intentions had not been realized.[86] Any positive comments were reserved for the actors rather than the directors, and a West German critic felt that the BE was turning back into the museum Berghaus had sought to demolish.[87]

The blame for the underwhelming production can be laid at the doors of the co-directors. From the start of the process they lacked vision and a sense of purpose, and one has then to ask whether they were actually capable of dealing with such a difficult play. Actor Heinrich Buttchereit called Kupke's introductory talk to open the rehearsals vague and limited, and noted that questions asked of the directors were either evaded or treated as unimportant. He described how rehearsals involved trying out 'new positions (instead of *Haltungen*)'; the directors apparently worked like alchemists 'who throw a bit of this and a bit of that into the pot, always in the hope that one day a bit of gold might finally come out'.[88] He concluded that the work contradicted all the experiences the ensemble had made with its previous directors and he wondered whether Kupke actually understood the relationship between director and actor 'as Brecht understood it'.[89]

---

[83]   Margit Vestner, 'Arbeitsgespräch *Turandot* am 18.8.71', 23 August 1971, 5 pages (1), ibid.

[84]   Berghaus, in Margit Vestner, 'Probe *Turandot* am 26.1.73', undated, 2 pages (1), ibid.

[85]   See Helmut Ullrich, 'Der Geist und die Geschäfte', *Neue Zeit*, 13 February 1973.

[86]   See, for example, Heinz Ritter, 'Ein Fest für BERTOLT?', *Der Abend*, 12 February 1973; or Jürgen Beckelmann, 'Die siebengescheiten Weißwäscher', *Süddeutsche Zeitung*, 15 February 1973.

[87]   See Rolf Michaelis, 'Kleine Brötchen zu Brechts Geburt', *Frankfurter Allgemeine Zeitung*, 14 February 1973.

[88]   Heinrich Buttchereit, 'Gedanken zur Arbeit am Projekt *Turandot*', undated, 4 pages (3), BEA File 59.

[89]   Ibid., p. 4.

The extended rehearsal period and the failure of the production caused ructions within the BE, too. A Stasi report indicated that the leadership at the company was in disarray after the premiere with the unnamed source suggesting that Berghaus had given the directors a task they could not satisfactorily complete. The source further noted that Heiner Müller had reportedly said that Berghaus wanted to prove their incompetence with the production and then remove them from the BE's management.[90] It is difficult to know whether to believe the source's claims concerning Müller here; Müller was certainly one to embellish a story and enjoyed intrigues in the theatre (see Chapter 13). However, a more reliable informer, Walter Braunroth, the BE's technical director, reported that Ekkehard Schall had gathered signatures against Pintzka and Kupke, an action prevented by the local Party at the BE. The real problem Braunroth identified was that the leadership remained stonily silent on the matter, something that indicated a tacit agreement with Schall.[91] So, it is possible that Berghaus wanted to use the production to teach the two directors a lesson, but that even she was unable to come out of the episode in a positive light because her own attempts at salvaging the production could not undo the damage done.

Pintzka directed one further production under Berghaus, George Bernard Shaw's *Mrs Warren's Profession* at the end of 1973. Kupke directed two major Brecht plays, *Puntila* in February 1975 and *The Caucasian Chalk Circle* in April 1976. None of these productions offered innovative approaches to the text. *Mrs Warren*, for example, was supported by Friedrich Dieckmann as dramaturge, and he had formulated some interesting ideas on how one might approach the play in the GDR, using Brechtian methods to expose the compact between bourgeois morality and prostitution.[92] Pintzka was not able to take up or realize Dieckmann's positions, and reviewers mainly found the production harmless.[93] As one critic noted: 'the programme promises a lot more than the production delivers'.[94] Pintzka, who had experienced Brecht's direction as an intern, went on to consider Erich Engel his 'most important teacher'.[95] As noted

---

[90] See [Major Müller], 'Bericht', 7 March 1973, file pp. 233–4 (233), BStU MfS AP 4578/71 (Beifügung).

[91] See Wilhelm Girod, 'Information', 20 March 1973, file p. 50, BStU MfS 20750/80, vol. 1.

[92] See Friedrich Dieckmann, 'Dies und das nach der Leseprobe', 24 October 1973, 4 pages; and Dieckmann, '*Frau Warrens Beruf*', 11 December 1973, 3 pages, BEA File 64.

[93] See, for example, Ernst Schumacher, '*Frau Warrens Beruf*', *Berliner Zeitung*, 27 December 1973.

[94] Jürgen Beckelmann, '*Frau Warrens Beruf*', *Frankfurter Rundschau*, 3 January 1974.

[95] Wolfgang Pintzka, *Von Sibirien in die Synagoge*, p. 117.

earlier, Engel could hardly be considered a very Brechtian director, and even Brecht believed that he did not understand his theatre. Kupke's Brecht productions added little to Brecht's own of the 1950s. This is surprising, given that his *Chalk Circle* in Potsdam had been so fêted. A charitable explanation would suggest that Kupke simply could not direct well under the glare of the BE's great reputation; directing at a world-famous company made demands he was unable to fulfil. B. K. Tragelehn, whose work as a director at the BE will be considered on pp. 259–62, offers a more critical opinion. He calls Kupke's productions in Berlin 'opportunism. He clearly thought he had a chance of taking over the shop'.[96] The reasons for this supposition will be discussed in the next chapter.

Aesthetic fault-lines 2: the experimental impulse

Although a play called *Cement* may not sound the most exciting, the production was one of the high points of Berghaus's *Intendanz*. Heiner Müller's adaptation of a classic Soviet novel of the same name by Fyo-dor Gladkov (published in 1925) is a radical and critical appropriation of another author's material. Set after the Russian Civil War, the play points more to open wounds and persistent social problems, rather than looking forward to a rosy socialist future. A pointed example of Müller's uncompromising stance concerned one of the central relationships:

Gleb: model – the return of Odysseus. Dasha: counter-model – Penelope, who confronts her husband with her own fully formed social power. Dasha, who in her own eyes is a model, is a figure from the future who rises up into the present, while Gleb paves the way from the past into the future.[97]

This brief sketch drafts contradictions that play off mutually exclusive conceptions of gender relations against each other. They are contextualized in vastly different understandings of historical time, yet all is predicated on the progressive premise that the new Soviet society has gender equality at its heart. Müller's reference to myth, which, already in the brief excerpt, signals a further dimension to the play, finds more direct expression in sections of the play in which no speaker is attributed to texts and classical figures such as Heracles, Achilles and Prometheus erupt into the action. Such an approach to the Soviet past was not going to make official approval of the script easy, and the very nature of the

---

[96] B. K. Tragelehn, in Irmer and Schmidt, *Die Bühnenrepublik*, p. 89.
[97] Heiner Müller, 'Exposé zu einem Drama nach Motiven des Romans *Zement* von Fjodor Gladkow', 10 January 1971, 4 pages (4), BEA File 60.

text, in which contradictions are exposed, left unresolved and re-echoed in narrative passages taken from classical mythology, also had serious formal implications for performance.

The play text's birth was long and arduous. Initial negotiations for *Cement* took place under Weigel, yet a letter with a full draft was only sent to senior party members at the Central Committee, Ministry of Culture and Berlin's District Leadership in March 1973.[98] In an interview, Müller recounted how the text was threatened with a ban, was actually banned, and then approved for performance.[99] While there is no evidence of a formal ban in the extant documents, there was a great deal of anxiety about the play. It should not be forgotten that Soviet history was a highly sensitive topic at the time: Volker Braun's *Lenins Tod* (*Lenin's Death*) had been banned in the early 1970s for depicting real figures from history.[100] Müller's choice of staging purely fictional characters at least offered the possibility of approval. A report in June 1973 criticized Müller's insistence on picking out points of conflict, rather than harmony and noted that academic Werner Mittenzwei found it to be Müller's best play, but still unplayable on a GDR stage.[101] The report acknowledged that changes had been discussed with Berghaus and that while she agreed to two major ones, she did not fully accept a call to tone down the sexual antagonisms between Gleb and Dasha.[102] A more thorough critique, written a couple of weeks afterwards, took particular issue with the unattributed mythological texts for the way in which they led 'inevitably to false ideas and metaphors', by 'confusing' two utterly different periods of human history.[103] In a paper written by the BE, the author acknowledged how *Cement* would eventually reach the stage through intense cooperation between the company, the District Leadership and the Ministry.[104] Quite how this manifested itself, is, however, unclear, and the positive term 'cooperation' may well have hidden a more difficult relationship.

---

[98] See [Berghaus] to Hans-Joachim Hoffmann, 12 March 1973, BEA File '57/60 Schriftwechsel *Omphale/Zement*'.

[99] See Heiner Müller, 'Stasi-Konstrukt oder das sollten Sie nicht persönlich nehmen', *Werke*, 12: 339.

[100] See, for example, Grublitz, 'Operative Information Nr. [blank] / 73', 19 September 1973, file pp. 62–3 (62), BStU MfS AOP 15582/83, vol. 2. This document registers internal GDR concerns, although the Soviets also frowned upon the text, see Kurt Hager, *Erinnerungen* (Leipzig: Faber & Faber, 1996), p. 343.

[101] See Hans Kießig, 'Information, Betr.: *Zement* von Heiner Müller nach dem Roman von Gladkow', 13 June 1973, 4 pages (2), LAB C Rep 902 3622.

[102] See ibid., p. 3.

[103] Marlis Helmschrott, 'Bemerkungen zu Heiner Müllers *Zement*', 28 June 1973, 8 pages (7), ibid.

[104] See Anon., 'Resultate', [October 1973?], 4 pages (1), ibid.

While the approval of the text caused *Intendantin* Berghaus many a problem, staging the text for director Berghaus was no less a challenge. In a meeting in August 1973, Müller noted: 'it isn't easy to understand the longer passages in terms of a single strand of the *Fabel*; the *Haltungen* change line by line'.[105] He also criticized the actors' reverence towards the text, something he implicitly felt restricted their performance, enlarging on the point in a meeting held a few weeks after the premiere: 'the actors don't take enough of the [play's] language from their own bodies . . . This gives rise to the impression that literature is being shown'.[106] At the earlier meeting, Berghaus also realized: 'the *Arrangements* are still too rigid'.[107] In short, both Müller's and Berghaus's comments point to limitations of orthodox Brechtian practices when working with a text that was so unwilling to reach judgement or frame its contradictions neatly. Berghaus had to find innovative ways of moving from the Brechtian to the post-Brechtian again, using the particularities of Müller's play, rather than relying on strategies she had employed previously.

Rehearsals began on 29 March 1973, well before the text had been roundly criticized by the authorities. Berghaus's initial position on her protagonist Gleb was that the qualities viewed in his first entrance had to be fully 'taken apart' in the course of events.[108] In a later rehearsal of the same scene, the tension between *Arrangement* and what it is trying to convey is evident. Under Brecht, the *Arrangement* was a concrete narrative element – the audience was supposed to watch one *Arrangement* after the other and understand the movement of the *Fabel* from tableau to tableau. Under Berghaus, the *Arrangement* worked as a broader frame that required further investigation itself from the audience: 'this is the situation in this scene: there is a huge amount of movement, but it's completely disordered. Everyone looks after their own interest, and so there is no harmony'.[109] Thus, while the concept of *Arrangement* had not been jettisoned, its function had changed: it provided a context, but did not vouchsafe its own content. All the same, the action itself did not neglect social detail: in the following scene, a machine operator is the first character to view Gleb as a worker; the women of the previous scene had only viewed him as a man.[110] His social classification was not immediately

[105] Müller, in Anon., 'Zwischenwertung *Zement* in der Leitung am 1. August 1973', undated, 9 pages (5), BEA File '57/60 Schriftwechsel *Omphale/Zement*'.
[106] Müller, in Irene Ebel, 'Protokoll einer Leitungssitzung am 14. November 1973', undated, 6 pages (2), BEA File 'Protokolle Leitungssitzungen 1973–76'.
[107] Berghaus, in Anon., 'Zwischenwertung', p. 9.
[108] Margit Vestner, 'Probe *Zement* am 29.3.73 – Probenbeginn', undated, 2 pages (1), BEA File 60.
[109] Vestner, 'Probe *Zement* am 6.4.73', undated, 2 pages (1), ibid.   [110] See ibid., p. 2.

obvious, as had previously been the case of the family in *Carrar*, but something that was allowed to emerge. The personal dimension, however, was also present. A note reported that Gleb often used revolutionary arguments to give himself confidence to act.[111] The decision to drive a wedge between the text and its meaning to open up other vistas meant that the characters as a whole offered more than one meaning to the audience at any one time, complicating simple understanding and easy consumption of Müller's difficult speeches.

The play placed its characters at the limits of their capabilities. They were trying to realize a communist utopia, while finding themselves confronted by a society in ruins, suffused with the vestiges of a previous age. This contradiction also bled into the actors' work: having been brought up on the BE's traditions of clearly articulating definitive meanings, they were being asked to perform more physically and *not* to have all the answers when constructing contradictions on stage. Berghaus also picked up the Brechtian predilection for contrast between actor and role in a bid to enrich the production's network of contradictions. Christine Gloger, for example, registered her dislike for her character, Dasha, but Berghaus chose to exploit the tension, rather than to cover it over.[112] Even veteran BE actor Martin Flörchinger acknowledged how situations could appear confusing and could only be understood in retrospect: 'here we have to put more trust in the spectator's imagination'.[113]

The documentation of Berghaus's rehearsal process shows that she was just as concerned with realism as Brecht, but that her understanding of human beings in concrete situations was less influenced by received class wisdom. She counselled against a clichéd understanding of a White Russian officer, for example, preferring to derive his qualities from his social provenance and the exigencies of the text;[114] he was not simply to be labelled 'negative' because he was fighting against the revolutionaries. Berghaus was, however, also prepared to admit moments when understanding simply was not possible. In one scene, she exhorted the actors to have the courage to carry long pauses: 'the people have nothing to say. They are worlds apart'.[115] The team traced the centrality of the characters, their social positions and their texts back to the form of

---

[111] See Vestner, 'Probe *Zement* am 12.4.73', undated, 2 pages(1), ibid.
[112] See Christine Gloger, 'Was sie für richtig hielt, hat sie auch gemacht', in Irene Bazinger (ed.), *Regie: Ruth Berghaus. Geschichtenaus der Produktion* (Berlin: Rotbuch, 2010), pp. 167–76 (171).
[113] Martin Flörchinger, in Vestner, 'Probe *Zement* am 10.5.73', undated 2 pages (2), BEA File 60.
[114] See Vestner, 'Probe *Zement* am 26.5.73', undated, 2 pages (2), ibid.
[115] Vestner, 'Probe *Zement* am 19.9.73', undated, n.p., ibid.

the play itself, which was described before rehearsals began as 'light on action'.[116]

A little under a month before the premiere on 12 October 1973, the BE sent a final draft of the play to three different authorities for approval.[117] A couple of weeks later a member of the Central Committee's Cultural Department wrote approvingly of a run-through and praised the fact that the BE had worked 'seriously on the partisan realization of the new play'.[118] 'Partisan' here means that the production broadly supported the characters' aspirations to build the Soviet Union, despite the multifarious contradictions. In a piece of pre-publicity, Berghaus praised the play for the way it allowed the team 'to think through experiences of existing performance modes anew and to find appropriate responses'.[119] Here she was preparing the audience for the ways in which she had re-processed the Brechtian approaches with which they were familiar at the BE. The reviews point to the complexity she hinted at, in that most critics found the production engaging and innovative (see Fig. 8.2) while, inevitably, signalling their own difficulties with certain directorial decisions or aspects of the play itself. The premiere was certainly a success with the audience: it received thirty-two curtain calls.[120]

Dramaturge Karl Mickel considered the achievements of such an ambitious project in a document written a month after the premiere: he concluded that the production represented the culmination of the work started in 1970 and returned the BE to the status of a first-class company that could no longer be ignored.[121] While this estimation may well have been true at the time, it would be called into question by none other than Manfred Wekwerth. He had directed his own adaptation of Gladkov's novel as a TV film that also carried the title *Cement*. This was a far more orthodox and positive version, and the BE's publicity department acknowledged that the film's broadcast had greatly diverted interest from the theatre production.[122] Wekwerth would go on the offensive against Berghaus's BE in 1975 and ultimately return as *Intendant* in 1977, and so the question arises as to whether this was a first salvo in a nascent

---

[116] Entry for 20 March 1973, in Anon., 'Arbeitsgespräch *Zement*', undated, n.p., AdK RBA 374.
[117] See, for example, Anon. to Peter Heldt, 14 September 1973, BEA File '57/60 Schriftwechsel *Omphale/Zement*'.
[118] Peter Heldt to Kurt Hager, 3 October 1973, BArch DY 30/18986.
[119] Berghaus, in Manfred Heidicke, 'Heute Abend: *Zement*', *Berliner Zeitung*, 12 October 1973.
[120] See Anon., '32 Vorhänge', *BZ am Abend*, 13 October 1973.
[121] See Karl Mickel, untitled, 15 November 1973, 2 pages (2), BEA File '57/60 Schriftwechsel *Omphale/Zement*'.
[122] See Klaus D. Winzer, 'Vorschläge zu *Zement*', 23 January 1974, 2 pages, ibid.

Fig. 8.2. Metatheatrical battle: Müller's stylized figures fight on the BE's lowered lighting gantry. *Cement*, October 1973.

campaign. In interviews, both Wekwerth and his male lead Hilmar Thate considered the overlap pure chance,[123] and the evidence appears to bear this out. Wekwerth noted that he was considering a *Cement* project in February 1971,[124] a month after Müller sketched his thoughts on the same play at the BE. While rehearsals only began at the end of March 1973 at the BE, Wekwerth wrote that his team had finished work on the two-part film earlier that month.[125] That the BE production was

---

[123] Manfred Wekwerth and Hilmar Thate, unpublished interviews with the author, 14 June 2011 and 19 July 2011, respectively.
[124] See Wekwerth, 'Arbeitsstenogramm', *Sonntag*, 14 February 1971.
[125] See Wekwerth, 'Tschumalow und die Barrikaden des Alltags', *Neues Deutschland*, 13 March 1973.

often in danger of being cancelled also gives credence to the claim that Wekwerth's project was not envisaged as competition for the BE, even though it managed to eclipse the radical production. On the other hand, this seems like a remarkable coincidence, and it is difficult to believe that each project was in some way hermetically sealed within a relatively small artistic community. It is perhaps more likely that there was an element of competition, but that the eventual triumph of the TV film took both sides by surprise.

Mickel's assessment of *Cement*'s place in Ruth Berghaus's BE points to the fragility of experimental work at the time. The newness of its forms did not guarantee long-term success – *Cement* remained in the repertoire until 1976, but it ran to a mere forty-one performances. The only other major provider of innovative theatre work in early 1970s' East Germany was Berlin's Volksbühne, a venue also closely associated with Heiner Müller. Yet even there, the experiments were not as radical or challenging as Berghaus's. Audiences in the FRG were growing used to the dominance of the director over the text, a phenomenon known as *Regietheater*, that had gathered pace in the late 1960s. Companies like the West Berlin Schaubühne, led by director Peter Stein, had revolution-ized the processes of rehearsing classic texts in the FRG by integrating the cast into certain fundamental decisions concerning a production, for example. Yet its successes appear to have had little impact on the BE, partly because of the physical barrier of the Berlin Wall, partly because the BE was rediscovering its own ways of approaching plays afresh. SED control in the GDR, however, had made divergences from the orthodoxy of socialist realism far more difficult to realize, and so even well-received productions like *Cement* were few and far between. The production prob-ably deserved to do far better in the GDR, but was a victim of its own uncompromising approach to staging the dramatic material. Such pro-ductions were important introductions to new ways of making theatre, but without a tradition or more extensive exposure, they had to make their own way, something that, by its very nature, was a difficult task.

Augmenting experimentation: B. K. Tragelehn and Einar Schleef

Before moving on to the season that sealed Berghaus's fate as *Intendantin*, it is worth considering two further additions to Berghaus's creative staff: B. K. Tragelehn and Einar Schleef. Tragelehn had been Brecht's last *Meisterschüler*, appointed in 1955. He is most famous, however, for direct-ing Müller's *The Resettler* with students in September 1961, a production that was banned after its premiere. Tragelehn found himself a *persona non grata* before he was allowed to return to creative work. Berghaus had met him through her husband, the composer Paul Dessau, and it was Karl Mickel who had introduced him to Dessau.[126] His first production at the BE was Erwin Strittmatter's *Katzgraben* (the name of a rural village), which he originally directed with Ilona Freyer as set designer. However, during rehearsals in early autumn 1972, Freyer absconded from the GDR. Karl von Appen brought in his own *Meisterschüler*, Schleef, as a replacement while Ruth Berghaus was away on tour with the BE in Munich. Berghaus was angry that she had not been consulted on the matter, but found Schleef's work to be good and so let it lie.[127] Schleef's contribution to *Katzgraben* extended beyond merely designing the sets. According to Tragelehn, Schleef mostly observed rehearsals with his sketchpad open, and drafted a comic-strip-like storyboard that then fed into the production. *Katzgraben* itself was not a great success: there was a great deal of tension between the directors and the ensemble, and the BE's leadership pushed for the production against the will of the actors.[128] Berghaus, however, was not displeased with the work and kept the guests on for two further productions; a third could not be realized, as discussed in the next chapter.

The pair reconvened to stage *Frühlings Erwachen* (*Spring Awakening*) by Frank Wedekind. Published in 1891, the play features a host of teenage characters who experience sexual awakening in a variety of ways, yet the play's subtitle, 'a children's tragedy', indicates that things do not turn out well for the three main characters. Tragelehn and Schleef both directed the production which, at Berghaus's suggestion, was to be acted by real schoolchildren with members of the BE playing the adult roles.[129] The play itself is not uncontroversial: it contains a scene including sado-masochism between two of the teenagers, one scene with male homo-sexuality, and two with masturbation. However, the BE found it could defend itself on two fronts. First, Wedekind was an acknowledged influence on Brecht, and Brecht had apparently wanted to stage the same play at the BE in the early 1950s.[130] In addition, when the Ministry of Culture confronted the BE with criticisms regarding the text, dramaturge Hans-Jochen Irmer, the GDR's foremost expert on Wedekind at that time,

---

[126] B. K. Tragelehn, unpublished interview with the author, 9 November 2010.
[127] This story was confirmed by both Tragelehn and Friedrich Dieckmann, unpublished interview with the author, 17 November 2010.
[128] See Margit Vestner, 'Protokoll der Regie- und Dramaturgiesitzung am 6.12.72', undated, 8 pages (2), BEA File 'Protokolle 60er und 70er Jahre'.
[129] See Tragelehn, in Irmer and Schmidt, *Die Bühnenrepublik*, p. 81.
[130] The claim is made in Hans-Jochen Irmer, B. K. Tragelehn and Einar Schleef, 'Frühlingserwachen. . . . Kulturpolitische Zielsetzung einer Inszenierung 1973/74 am Berliner Ensemble', 13 July 1973, 4 pages (1), AdK Einar-Schleef-Archiv 1640.

demonstrated that the suggested cuts were remarkably similar to those made in Wilhelmine Germany at the turn of the century.[131] Unwilling to be tarred with that brush, the Ministry relented.

Nonetheless, the BE provided a document for the authorities in order to sketch the production's aims and intentions. This type of document, known broadly as a *Konzeption*, became increasingly important to the Ministry of Culture as a way of monitoring theatres' plans. Brecht, as noted in earlier chapters, did not work like this, preferring to plumb a text's depths for contradictions, a practice that Berghaus continued, albeit in a more radical fashion. Tragelehn and Schleef were similarly inclined to this approach, which is why their *Konzeption* for the production carried an interesting note. Schleef had handwritten: 'text only for cultural politics – a tactic (Tragelehn); me: hogwash . . . '.[132] The pair were clearly letting the authorities read what they wanted to read while negotiating the text on their own terms.

Unfortunately, there are no rehearsal documents. Reviews of and commentaries on the production, that premiered on 1 March 1974, tended to welcome the teenage amateurs for their freshness and lack of actorly trappings, while also mostly noting that the execution was not perfect.[133] The reviewer at *Neues Deutschland*, however, felt that he was being offered an unhistoricized clash of the generations, suggesting that such nineteenth-century problems persisted in the GDR[134] (which, of course, they did). The scenes with the adults tended to attract fewer plaudits because of their satirical forms. All the same, Mickel welcomed the debate because it focused on the artistic means being used by the BE, rather than on the play's content.[135]

The experiment with the amateurs was a radicalization of Brecht's understanding of naïvety on stage. While Brecht sought to use his actors to allow the audience to view situations afresh, or naïvely, Tragelehn and Schleef relied on their amateur actors' real inexperience of difficult texts and complex action to leave the performed material more open for the audience. According to Irmer, Tragelehn wanted to connect the old and the new dialectically, Schleef preferred to cleave them apart.[136] Either way, this insistence on contrasting more spontaneous

[131] Hans-Jochen Irmer, unpublished interview with the author, 3 November 2010.
[132] Schleef, in Irmer *et al.*, '*Frühlingserwachen*', p. 4.
[133] See, for example, Ernst Schumacher, '*Frühlings Erwachen*', *Berliner Zeitung*, 5 March 1974.
[134] See Rainer Kerndl, 'Stilistisches Experiment mit Frank Wedekind', *Neues Deutschland*, 9 March 1974.
[135] See Karl Mickel, 'Die Tradition und das neue Programm', p. 18.
[136] See Irmer, 'Ein Frühlings Erwachen im Berliner Ensemble', *Theater der Zeit*, 1 (2002), pp. 57–9 (59).

performances which were not inhibited by the directors did not find favour with actor Ekkehard Schall who reportedly opposed the production, although not to the extent that he prevented his daughter Johanna from acting in it.[137]

The relatively warm reception of the production with critics and audiences (it ran for 116 performances) seemed to maintain the impetus of Berghaus's reforms in 1974. Her first three seasons had been moderately successful. As a director she had developed her own practice as a constructive modification of Brecht's approaches, appropriate to the uncertainties of her own society. As *Intendantin* she had enabled new directors and dramaturges to work on engaging projects while she still tolerated the more conventional approaches of staff favoured by Helene Weigel. The authorities were certainly not disappointed by her at this stage. She managed to navigate the BE through a potentially sensitive tour to Munich in 1972, for example. Munich was the first German city to host the Olympic Games after Hitler's infamous Berlin Olympics of 1936. The GDR thus wanted to disassociate itself from a sense of shared responsibility for the historical catastrophe because it saw itself as the inheritor of Germany's progressive, not reactionary traditions. On the other hand, the GDR and the FRG found themselves at the start of a process of détente. As Merrilyn Thomas notes: 'détente . . . allowed and encouraged the GDR to function as a relatively normal state' as well as having advantages for the FRG.[138] The SED thus had to be careful not to alienate the FRG at one of the first major occasions on which the two states would be on show together. Once the tour was over, the SED was certainly pleased with the BE and the way it presented itself in Munich. Minister Gysi wrote to *Intendantin* Berghaus that he had been told 'that you have run your tour with great prudence, commitment and discipline. With this you have made a valuable contribution to raising the GDR's prestige along with our excellent sportsmen and women'.[139] To the Minister, the line between asserting the GDR's cultural independence and not instigating inter-German tension had been expertly negotiated, and Berghaus had thus proved herself as a responsible leader in the early years of her tenure.

---

[137] Hans-Jochen Irmer, unpublished interview with the author, 3 November 2010.
[138] Merrilyn Thomas, '"Aggression in Felt Slippers." Normalisation and the Ideological Struggle in the Context of Détente and *Ostpolitik*', in Mary Fulbrook (ed.), *Power and Society in the GDR 1961–1979. The 'Normalisation of Rule'?* (New York: Berghahn, 2009), pp. 33–51 (51).
[139] Gysi to Ruth Berghaus, 22 September 1972, BEA File 'Tourneen [unnumbered]'.

In 1974, the head of Berlin's District Leadership of the SED praised Berghaus and the company, citing in particular the BE's increased productivity and its higher audience numbers.[140] Productivity at the BE increased from its dismal rates in the 1950s and 1960s with three premieres in the 1972/73 season and six in 1973/74. As already noted, the BE's low productivity had been offset by the high quality of productions that had been in development for long periods. Trouble arose when the balance between the two became skewed. Berghaus was painfully aware of the problems associated with a low number of annual premieres. In 1972, when rehearsals of *Turandot* were already in trouble, she expressed how she wished to combat this 'old habit' of only producing one major premiere per year.[141]

Berghaus's efforts were concerted, and her early *Intendanz* was marked by a desire to read Brecht and his theatre in a new light for a new time. It would be difficult to say that all was rosy at the BE, however. The company effectively had only one short-lived hit, *Cement* in 1973, its experiments were by their very nature uneven, and there had been serious tensions amongst the senior staff regarding the artistic direction of the company. Yet it is hard to ignore the huge pressure Berghaus was under. She had taken over the most significant theatre in the GDR, about which everyone had an opinion, and tried to introduce new working practices to enliven what was a moribund institution. Yet the goodwill from which Berghaus had benefitted was soon to dissipate, and the next chapter considers the productions that would lead to her dismissal and the forces that brought it about.

---

[140] See Konrad Naumann, 'Rede vor dem Berliner Ensemble am 20.2.1974 anläßlich der Auszeichnung mit dem Orden "Banner der Arbeit"', in Irmer (ed.), *Berliner Ensemble. 1949–74*, p. 21.

[141] Berghaus, in Irene Ebel, 'Gespräch am 2. Februar 1972...', undated, 7 pages (5), BEA File 59.

9   A new crisis: 1974–1977

The turning point: Berghaus's production of *The Mother*

The 1974/75 season would prove to be fateful, indeed fatal for Berghaus as *Intendantin* due to the staging and reception of two of the season's four premieres: Berghaus's production of Brecht's *The Mother* and Tragelehn and Schleef's production of Strindberg's *Miss Julie*. Both shows brought one issue in particular to a head: how the BE treated Brecht's legacy. Berghaus's reading of *The Mother* focused conservatives' criticism on her interpretation and the forms she employed, while *Miss Julie*, a play not written by Brecht, suggested to this faction that the BE's direction was increasingly diverging from Brecht's aims and methods in general.

The Mother had a special status in the BE's history. Although the original production as a *Modell* in 1951 had been subject to SED criticism, its revival in 1967 had hardly caused a stir. Nonetheless, the show attained almost mythical status in the repertoire on account of Helene Weigel's performance as the eponymous lead. Not only did the role allow her to embody a spirited proletarian revolutionary, it also proved to be her last, given in Paris on a tour to mark the centenary of the Commune, a month before her death. Divergences from the hallowed production provided more evidence in certain quarters for Berghaus's perceived heresy.

The creative team set out its intentions in preparatory material for the show's actors, and I have paraphrased and summarized them thus:

1. Socialist society is founded on the workers' material needs, which, by definition, are not a priority under capitalism.
2. The behaviour of the mother and her comrades provides a model of why and under which circumstances people devote themselves to the class struggle.
3. Human relationships are not timeless, but dependent on common or differentiated social aims.
4. A contemporary reading of the play has tragic elements.
5. Departure from the 1951 *Modell* is deliberate and consistent.

6. There is no need to represent the mother's milieu, rather the direct depiction of experiences.
7. The production will use the first version of Hanns Eisler's music, understood as ballads for a single voice or as a one-voice chorus.[1]

The list demonstrates its commitments to dialectical politics and the effects of material privation on the actions of working people. The corporeality identified in Berghaus's previous productions is also present here, in that privation manifests itself in the suffering of the body. However, the presence of tragedy already points to interpretive divergences from Brecht's production of 1951 (see pp. 89–92, Chapter 3), which presented an optimistic depiction of the class struggle and its ultimate triumph. Berghaus and her team, on the other hand, emphasize the difficulties and the costs involved in attaining class consciousness and bringing about a revolution. This was underlined by locating their reading in the here and now, rather than in an idealized past. That decision had implications for the production's aesthetics. The departure from the *Modell* suggests the valorization of the characters' subjectivity – the characters cannot be generalized as such, but are to be treated as models of individual behaviour. In addition, the unwillingness to engage with milieu is reminiscent of the approach to *Carrar*: using real social relations, but abstracting them from naturalistic settings to engender an experience of the struggle, rather than an accurate representation of, in the case of *The Mother*, pre-Revolutionary Russia. Berghaus later defended this shift with direct reference to Brecht in a document archived by the Ministry of Culture: 'the *Fabel* should reflect the "issues of the day". Experiences modify the issues; the [production's] aesthetics are derived from the demands of the class struggle'.[2]

The new interpretation of the play was certainly at odds with SED and indeed Leninist theory in general. There, the party had the special role of providing an ideological and practical vanguard for the proletariat, whereas the new production proposed material poverty and its physical consequences as the point of departure. This can be found in the scene in which peasants stone the mother when she tries to disseminate propaganda material. In a note made during rehearsal, one finds, with respect to the mother: 'she discovers the peasants' problems, she has to experience on her own body the way in which urban and rural workers tear each other apart. . . . Unity in theory is a long way from unity in practice'.[3] The

---

[1] See Berghaus, Karl Mickel, Thomas Günther and Andreas Reinhardt, '*Die Mutter*', undated, 27 pages (2–3), BEA File 67.
[2] Berghaus, 'Die Neuinszenierung *Die Mutter* von Bertolt Brecht', undated, 3 pages (1), BArch DR 1/17547.
[3] Thomas Günther, untitled, 5 September 1974, n.p., AdK RBA 915.

Mother gains knowledge through material suffering; ideas alone are not enough to change the world. In another scene, in which three women try to console the Mother after her son Pavel has been shot dead, the production explored how good intentions could not overcome real class division: 'the women were out of their depth; they couldn't give consolation any more because the [class] situation doesn't permit consolation any more. But they themselves didn't recognize that'.[4] Dialectical tensions between the classes prevent communication of the most fundamental kind.

In order to bring out the tragic dimension, Berghaus cut the final two scenes to emphasize the importance of revolutionary activity rather than to confirm its success in the final scene's report of mass strikes across Russia. In the new ending, the Mother was knocked to the ground during a demonstration and even sympathetic workers rejected the propaganda she tried to distribute. Beaten and laid low, she offered what was now her curtain line: 'remember what will happen if you fail!'. The revolutionary moment was no longer guaranteed, but left open as a challenge to the audience. Laura Bradley identifies this reading as suggesting 'disillusionment with the regime's rhetoric of success', making the new ending fresh and contemporary.[5] The line was followed by the song 'In Praise of Dialectics', which preaches that the world is never stable and always subject to change. Thus the tragedy of the Mother's apparent defeat was neither inevitable nor final.

Aesthetically, the decision to reject more realistic settings also disturbed the traditionalists. In scene seven, for example, a plan to use prison bars to divide the Mother and Pavel was replaced by simply dividing the two with a prison guard. The production thus suggested: 'the division between the two is the product of people and their ways of thinking'.[6] The production was interested in presenting visual metaphors of social contradictions. This strategy aimed at provoking interpretation from the audience, rather than presenting it with representations that could simply be 'read'. More generally, the set itself dispensed with milieu: Andreas Reinhardt had designed a junkyard to serve as a multipurpose backdrop to the production as a whole (see Fig. 9.1). The decision to abolish Brecht's metonymic sets moved the production into a more metaphorical space, alive with associations. This scenic mode had already been employed in Carrar, yet its implementation in a major play of many

---

[4] Günther, ibid.

[5] Laura Bradley, *Brecht and Political Theater*, p. 104. For a description and summary of the other textual changes, see pp. 109–10.

[6] [Thomas Günther?], 'Szene 7', 26 August 1974, ibid. Bradley offers an analysis of this scene, including Berghaus's innovative use of lighting, in *Brecht and Political Theatre*, pp. 121 and 125.

Fig. 9.1. Abstract materialism: a metaphorical set, designed to spark associations between the mother's poverty, her thoughts and her actions. *The Mother*, October 1974.

scenes and locations caused further consternation amongst the production's critics.

One reviewer at the premiere on 18 October 1974 registered both thunderous applause and boos.[7] That reception was mirrored in the papers over the following days. Those supporting the production praised the relevance of the new reading and the appropriateness of the formal means used to realize it. Wolfgang Gersch noted the shifting perspective: 'proximity and distance. Bloody detail and "ritualized" image'.[8] Erika Stephan enjoyed the way that the production acknowledged the audience's familiarity with the play in order to resist a simple restatement of its meaning.[9] Another East German critic observed how the more abstract set and interactions promoted associations; he saw mothers in Chile and South Africa, and the Mother's cradling of the worker Smilgin reminded him of the memorials at the former concentration camps of Buchenwald

---

[7] See Anon., 'Gegenentwurf?', *BZ am Abend*, 19 October 1974.
[8] Wolfgang Gersch, 'Aktueller Versuch mit Brecht im BE', *Tribüne*, 23 October 1974.
[9] See Erika Stephan, '*Die Mutter*', *Sonntag*, 8 December 1974.

and Ravensbrück.[10] Yet many found the performance choices puzzling and counterproductive. Ernst Schumacher saw the production's attractiveness solely in its formal presentation because he felt Berghaus had nothing more to say to a play with which the audience was so familiar; a West German colleague considered the new form 'an end in itself', rather than a means to probe the play further.[11] More conservative voices criticized the ways in which the production diverged from how they were used to seeing Brecht at the BE.[12]

Behind the scenes, criticism had already been made in the BE's management group. Director Peter Kupke had asked shortly before rehearsals began 'why we want to change already successful productions'.[13] This remarkable question seems to undermine the very point of making art at the BE, preferring to revive old favourites, rather than to challenge with new explorations. At the Ministry of Culture, however, the verdict on the production was surprisingly even-handed. While criticizing what he considered a certain pathos running through the show, Jochen Genzel concluded that *The Mother* had realized its political goals, invited the audience to consider its artistic means and brought 'Brecht's play back into the debate at a high level'.[14] For the most part, it did not seem as though the critics or officials had registered anything approaching a milestone production. Yet, as reviewer Christoph Funke put it: 'with this production of *The Mother* begins a new chapter in the history of the Berliner Ensemble'.[15] His prediction was certainly correct, but for all the wrong reasons.

The rise of the Brecht estate

It was neither the BE's management nor the SED that caused the greatest problems for Berghaus after *The Mother*; it was Brecht's heirs in the form of his daughter and son-in-law, Barbara Brecht-Schall and Ekkehard Schall. Up until her death in 1971, Helene Weigel as widow had been the main representative of the Brecht estate, and she had followed

[10] See Rolf-Dieter Eichler, 'Die andere *Mutter* – die anderen Mütter', *Nationalzeitung*, 22 October 1974.

[11] See Ernst Schumacher, '*Die Mutter*', *Berliner Zeitung*, 22 October 1974; and Peter Hans Göpfert, 'Mutter Corsage', *Der Abend*, 23 October 1974.

[12] See, for example, Günther Bellmann, 'Wo ist der Weg?', *BZ am Abend*, 25 October 1974.

[13] Peter Kupke, in Irene Ebel, 'Protokoll zur Leitungssitzung am 13. Juni 1974', undated, 5 pages (2), BEA File 'Protokolle Leitungssitzungen 1973–76'.

[14] Jochen Genzel, 'Information über die *Mutter*-Premiere im Berliner Ensemble', 21 October 1974, 2 pages (2), BArch DR1/17548.

[15] Christoph Funke, 'Bekannte Fabel in neuer Sicht', *Der Morgen*, 20 October 1974.

Brecht's lead in terms of dealing with performance rights to his plays. Brecht had signed a contract with the Henschel publishing house permitting it to administer performing rights in the GDR, but decided himself which theatres in Berlin would perform his plays. GDR legal opinion later termed this a 'Gewohnheitsrecht' ('customary right'),[16] that is, a right with no necessary legal basis as such, but brought about through habitual practice.

When Weigel died, the GDR moved very quickly to bring the rights under its own jurisdiction. A mere four days after her death, Minister of Culture Klaus Gysi signed a resolution 'on the safe-keeping, nurturing [Pflege] and protection of the dramatic and literary work and the estate of Bertolt Brecht as well as the estate of Helene Weigel'.[17] The language here suggests a paternalistic, conservative relationship to Brecht's work, and the term 'Pflege' ('nurturing') will recur later in the discussion of how the BE was to treat Brecht. The resolution transferred authority to the GDR's Academy of Arts while guaranteeing the heirs their financial due.[18] As Erdmut Wizisla notes, the resolution marked 'a striking breach of international law' concerning copyright,[19] even if the State tried to buy off those it attempted to disappropriate by respecting their internationally guaranteed earnings. The speed with which the resolution was readied, signed and approved by the Council of Ministers betrays the fact that the matter had presented a concern for the State for some time. The reasons for the move are to be found in another document. The SED was anxious that the rights to Brecht's work might move beyond the GDR's borders after Weigel's death, as only one of his three children, Barbara, was a GDR citizen; Stefan Brecht and Hanne Hiob lived in the USA and the FRG, respectively. And while the document states that the decision was taken 'to protect [Brecht's] political reputation', it also acknowledges that the State wanted to prevent 'unsuitable publications'.[20] Poems and journal entries critical of the GDR had not yet been published there, and the regime hoped to keep things that way.

The transfer of rights to the State was not one uniquely applied to Brecht; the SED had done the same to the intellectual property of the first president of the academy, Arnold Zweig, on his death in 1968.[21] Brecht, however, presented a special case to the authorities: he was by far the most important cultural figure to have been associated with the

[16] See Hager to Honecker, 21 June 1983, BArch DR 1/13525a.
[17] Klaus Gysi, untitled, 10 May 1971, n.p., BArch DR1/9851.
[18] See Anon., 'Beschluß über die Sicherung...', undated, 2 pages, ibid.
[19] Erdmut Wizisla, 'Private or Public? The Brecht Archive as an Object of Desire', in Bradley and Leeder (eds.), *Brecht and the GDR*, pp. 103–24 (116).
[20] Anon., 'Begründung', undated, n.p., BArch DR1/9851.   [21] See ibid.

GDR, and the State feared losing control of him, having done its best to portray him as an unequivocally loyal supporter of the GDR. The resolution made no reference, however, to the importance of performing rights. Presumably, these were not considered an issue worth mentioning: theatres in the GDR would continue to stage Brecht as they had done in the past. As it would turn out, this very aspect became central to the State's ability to run its most prestigious cultural commodity, the BE, as will become evident later in this chapter.[22]

Brecht-Schall had already threatened to deprive the BE of its connection to Brecht if the Ministry of Culture brought Wekwerth back to lead the company in 1971. With this sabre-rattling in mind, Berghaus was perhaps wary of causing bad relations with the estate and courted its favour early in her *Intendanz*. She offered Brecht-Schall, who had only played one lead role with the BE (Pegeen Mike in *Playboy of the Western World* in 1956), the eponymous lead in *Turandot* in 1971.[23] As it happened, Brecht-Schall withdrew due to illness in late 1972.[24] In addition, Berghaus proposed Ekkehard Schall (together with designer Andreas Reinhardt) for membership of the Academy of Arts in 1972.[25] Schall, of course, was a great artist, and so there can be no doubt about the merits of his candidature, yet Berghaus may well have sought to raise herself in his estimation by initiating the process. And in the 1973/74 season, she even allowed Schall and Brecht-Schall to co-direct Brecht's *Leben Eduards des Zweiten von England* (*The Life of Edward II of England*) on the BE's main stage. Yet all the goodwill gestures came to nothing when she offended the heirs' sensibilities on the matter of staging Brecht at the BE.

The premiere of *The Mother* did not immediately trigger a response from the estate. The first documented protest occurred in April 1975. The date of the meeting is significant in that Berghaus was in the USA on a visit to inspect two theatres that might host the first tour of any GDR theatre to that most symbolic of Western nations. Brecht-Schall told the SED's District Leadership in Berlin that she could no longer sit on the sidelines and had to protest 'against the political mutilation of Brecht by Ruth Berghaus's productions'.[26] It is worth lingering on this concern. Berghaus's production was hardly an example of *l'art pour l'art*;

---

[22] Further discussion of the ramifications of the resolution is to be found later in this chapter on pp. 289–92, and on pp. 333–5, Chapter 11.

[23] See Pilka Häntzsche, 'Notiz über ein Gespräch mit Barbara Schall am 22.9.71', 28 December 1971, n.p., BBA uncatalogued file 'Korr 54–66'.

[24] See [unclear signature] to 'dear colleagues', 30 November 1972, BEA File 59.

[25] See Berghaus to Manfred Wekwerth, 7 March 1972, AdK Adk-O 1172.

[26] Hans Kießig, 'Betr.: Vorgänge am Berliner Ensemble', 4 April 1975, 3 pages (2), LAB C Rep 902 3622.

the documentation clearly shows her materialist aesthetic *and* the need to employ new forms of performance to work against the accepted view of the play. Brecht-Schall's point is that Berghaus's politics, which she chose to reject, diverged from the conventional treatment of Brecht on stage, especially at the BE. The same sentiment can be found in a Stasi document whose information was provided by a dramaturge in the BE's publicity department. He reported that Brecht-Schall had reproached Berghaus 'for leading the theatre away from Brecht *Pflege*'.[27] The *Pflege* argument was closely allied to notions of Brecht's practices that ceased in 1956, yet the term implied perpetuating them and, indeed, reifying them in order to create an orthodoxy from which deviation was considered sacrilege. Berghaus and her supporters actively sought to resist such impositions. In a forthright report written in support of Berghaus's early *Intendanz*, the anonymous writer compares Brecht's plight in the early 1950s to the BE's in the early 1970s: 'as [Brecht] was countered with Stanislavsky back then, so we are reproached with "the real Brecht"'.[28] Brecht-Schall also feared that other directors would follow Berghaus's lead by making cuts and adding material to Brecht's work in performance if she permitted the production of *The Mother* as it stood.

Brecht-Schall's critique as a whole is interesting because it is predicated on two factors: the style of Berghaus's production and the treatment of the text. The first would seemingly go beyond the remit of a rights holder, whereas the second certainly concerned what had or had not been licensed. However, the first factor was Brecht-Schall's responsibility, as she saw it, due to Brecht's practice (which, by definition, was not a legal right) of choosing which theatres in Berlin staged his plays. That is, she believed that she had been entrusted with perpetuating the tradition of the *Modell* at the BE because Brecht had developed it there, to the exclusion of all other companies in Berlin. Brecht-Schall could wield great power over a repertoire that based itself on Brecht's drama and she threatened to ban *The Mother* at the BE unless Berghaus made changes. In addition, the success of the American tour also seemed to rest on the BE's ability to deliver a new production of *The Threepenny Opera*. This was because it was the play whose songs were best known and consequently offered the US promoters the best prospect of attracting large audiences to offset the expense of hosting the BE.[29] Brecht-Schall told the Party that she would not grant the BE rights to this show due to the exception she had

[27] Wilhelm Girod, 'Operative Information Nr. [blank]/75', 29 April 1975, file pp. 90–2 (90), BStU MfS Bln. Abt. XX A 480–11.

[28] Anon., 'Berliner Ensemble', [end of 1972?], 19 pages (18), BArch DR 1/18047.

[29] See Anon., 'Bericht über die Vorreise in die USA zur Vorbereitung eines Gastspiels des Berliner Ensembles', 7 April 1975, 6 pages (3 and 4), BEA File 'Tourneen [unnumbered]'.

taken to *The Mother*.[30] As it happened, the planned tour collapsed under the burgeoning costs the promoters could not cover.[31] And at the same meeting at which Brecht-Schall expressed her disapproval and threatened the BE's repertoire, Ekkehard Schall also criticized Berghaus's leadership style, which he found dictatorial and exclusionary. He was also troubled by the artistic direction the company was taking.[32]

A new power had emerged. Berghaus was no longer only struggling with elements of her own management team and the government's cultural agencies, but with the Brecht estate as well. The implications of this new player went beyond the BE, however: the SED had much interest in making sure that Brecht was successfully allied to the GDR, as confirmed by the resolution passed by the Council of Ministers in 1971. A major crisis was certainly in the offing for the State if Brecht's own theatre company was no longer allowed to stage him. As a result, the Ministry and the Central Committee involved themselves in attempts at mediation in the coming years in a bid to retain the BE as its Brecht theatre.

Miss Julie: an experiment too far

The meeting between Brecht's estate and the District Leadership, discussed above, took place scarcely a week before the premiere of Strindberg's *Miss Julie* on 10 April 1975, under the direction of B. K. Tragelehn and Einar Schleef. Berghaus had been away from the BE and the GDR, reconnoitring theatres in New York and Washington, DC, or Washington state. As a result, she may not have been aware that *The Mother* was the subject of debate and that *Julie* was already causing concern back in East Berlin. A Stasi report written after the premiere noted that she had paid the production little attention in the run-up to what would become the BE's most controversial show under her *Intendanz*.[33] The crisis that ensued primarily involved the convergence of three factors: Berghaus's promotion of experiment and experimenters, conservatism from the Brecht estate, and the lack of a unified response from the GDR's cultural agencies.

The production itself was certainly unconventional. Tragelehn had divided the text into three parts: the first ended when Jean and Julie exited before the peasants performed their midsummer night's dance.

---

[30] See Kießig, 'Betr.: Vorgänge', p. 3.
[31] See Alexander Cohen to Berghaus, 30 April 1975; and Harvey Lichtenstein to Berghaus, 30 October 1975, both in BEA File 'Tourneen [unnumbered]'.
[32] See Kießig, 'Betr.: Vorgänge', p. 1.
[33] See Wilhelm Girod, 'Operative Information Nr. [blank]/75', 20 June 1975, file pp. 109–10 (109), BStU MfS AIM 20750/80, vol. 1.

The second started with their return to the stage post coitus and concluded just before Julie returned, having dressed for flight with Jean. The final part ran from there until the final line. Not a word of this short play was cut. The first phase explored the relationships between Miss Julie, Jean the valet, and Christine the cook. Although these relationships were unstable and generated a number of possibilities, none defined the way the characters related to each other in the sections that followed. The second phase took place, as Tragelehn put it, "'in the mind'".[34] Here Julie and Jean playfully tried out the different avenues available to them after their love-making. This section included experiments with role-reversal, with the actors exchanging lines with each other, amongst other things. The lack of a resolution was derived from the text itself: the pair do not undertake any of the plans they discuss. The final section dealt with the aftermath of the crisis and was played against almost blinding light from backstage that prevented the audience from seeing the action clearly and cast the actors' bodies into shadow for the most part. Here Brecht's visual clarity was deliberately forsaken in favour of a suggestive play of light and dark, of silhouettes provoking greater concentration on the speeches themselves. The finale, whose usual interpretation is that Jean, at Julie's behest, orders her to exit and kill herself, was read quite differently by the team. The text does not instruct Julie to commit suicide, just to leave, which was what she did, by climbing down from the stage, over the rows of seats in the stalls with the help of the audience, and leaving the theatre through one of the auditorium's doors. This final action with the spectators reinforced the production's desire to connect with them and their experience by actively involving them in the action.[35]

This description may well give the impression that Tragelehn and Schleef were involved in something un- or apolitical, or at least self-absorbed, but the production's notes reveal that not to have been the case. In one comment, the creative team wrote:

Main thematic point: psychology of the master/servant relationship. Representation of Strindberg's psychology as having political content; the most private, particular and singular as the general, historical and political. Formally: projection of the inner life outwards, in physicalized *Haltungen*.[36]

[34] Tragelehn, in Christoph Müller, 'Geschichte und Gegenwart auf der Bühne', in B. K. Tragelehn, *Roter Stern in den Wolken. Aufsätze, Reden, Gedichte, Gespräche und ein Theaterstück. Ein Lesebuch*, ed. by. Gerhard Ahrens (Berlin: Theater der Zeit, 2006), pp. 137–65 (142).

[35] For more information on the production itself, see the 'documentation' in *Theater der Zeit*, 7 (1990), pp. 28–33.

[36] B. K. Tragelehn, Einar Schleef and Hans-Jochen Irmer, 'Zu Strindberg/*Fräulein Julie*', October 1974, n.p., BEA File 70.

As noted in the previous chapter, Tragelehn and Schleef had previously treated such conceptual musings cynically, yet here, the central points can be detected in the finished production, although they made use of suggestive post-Brechtian forms, rather than Brecht's more epistemologically stable stagecraft. Tragelehn did not work on concrete political or social contextualization as he believed that it need not be formulated for the audience:[37] the point of connection between gender tensions of the late nineteenth century and the contemporary GDR were implicit. In a fictional dialogue, dramaturge Friedrich Dieckmann gestured to inequalities with a candour that is surprising for a GDR publication of 1975:

A: You mean that power relations between the sexes haven't disappeared, however far we are from bourgeois or even feudal class structures?
B: Indeed. Women's economic and social emancipation has still not been adequately dealt with in the private sphere and can't be . . . Even our State is a male one when it comes to the important functionaries.[38]

The production thus engaged with a series of relationships between the sexes predicated upon specific social structures that the team believed had persisted despite the GDR's declarations to the contrary. The inability to reach a conclusion on the gender issue, due to its complexity, points to the post-Brechtian politics and approaches to performance taken by the team.[39]

In addition, the directors sought communication with the audience in the present. They thus asked the actor playing Christine to sing a contemporary popular song on her first entrance, for example, and introduced a stage full of teenagers dancing to beat music instead of the traditional melodies of peasants' dance. Assistant Thomas Günther mused in the wake of the premiere: 'the actors and the directors have brought their experiences into the work'.[40] Dramaturge Jörg Mihan confirmed the success of the approach when assessing the second performance in which he observed: 'not confrontation, but communion. . . . What appeared mannered and "clever" in rehearsal became rounded, humane, serious and

---

[37] B. K. Tragelehn, unpublished interview with the author, 9 November 2010.

[38] Friedrich Dieckmann, 'Diskurs über *Fräulein Julie*', in Dieckmann, *Streifzüge. Aufsätze und Kritiken* (Berlin: Aufbau, 1977), pp. 141–70 (143). Originally published in *Sinn und Form*, 27 (1975), pp. 1305–19.

[39] For a more detailed discussion of this aspect, see David Barnett, 'Encountering a Classic as Other in Post-Brechtian Performance: A Radical *Fräulein Julie* at the Berliner Ensemble in 1975', in Nina Birkner, Andrea Geier and Urte Helduser, *Spielräume des Anderen. Geschlecht und Alterität im postdramatischen Theater* (Bielefeld: transcript, 2014), pp. 111–28.

[40] Thomas Günther, 'Versuch einer Selbstverständigung anläßlich der Inszenierung *Fräulein Julie*', June 1975, n.p., BEA File 70.

direct in this performance'.[41] Mihan's conclusion was not shared by all, indeed, it was hardly shared by anyone beyond the supporters of experimentation at the BE.

Disapproval within the institution came from two quarters: Berghaus as *Intendantin* and the more conservative wing. Berghaus was concerned about the clarity of the production, not the experimental aesthetics that had been adopted. This she expressed at a meeting held two days before the premiere: 'I'm all for different modes of performance, but not for accentuating opacity'.[42] She also counselled against making too radical a leap in the style of the production because the audience simply would not be able to make connections any more.[43] The second section in particular drew criticism, but Berghaus asked Tragelehn to explain his decisions with a view to bringing about constructive changes.

The more conservative voices had both general and particular reservations. Finance director Rolf Stiska asked whether working people could possibly understand what was happening on stage.[44] Hans-Jochen Irmer felt that it was 'wrong to reduce the text to the status of a mere draft for performance'.[45] A day later, after the dress rehearsal, more staff gathered to consider whether the premiere would take place at all. A Stasi report noted that Berghaus had deliberately filled the meeting with her supporters (such as Heiner Müller and Friedrich Dieckmann, themselves not members of the BE's management) to rig the vote on the production in her favour.[46] Peter Kupke read out a letter from Ekkehard Schall to Berghaus that accused her of permitting a production that had come about 'without any consideration for Brecht'.[47] That Kupke was charged with reading out the letter shows his close connection to Schall and the estate. One can only speculate that Kupke's decision to vote in favour of the premiere taking place as planned on the following day was a move to expose the production's failings. Müller replied to Schall's charge with the observation that nobody asked about a connection to Brecht when the BE staged *Mrs Warren's Profession*.[48] Berghaus supported *Miss Julie*'s post-Brechtian approach without mentioning the term by name:

[41] Jörg Mihan, 'Zur *Julie*-Vorstellung am 12. April 1975, 13 April 1975, 8 pages (1), ibid.
[42] Berghaus, in Irene Ebel, 'Besprechung am 8. April 1975 bei Frau Berghaus über *Fräulein Julie* . . .', undated, 7 pages (1), ibid.
[43] Ibid., p. 4.   [44] See Rolf Stiska, in ibid. p. 1.
[45] Hans-Jochen Irmer, in ibid., p. 4.
[46] See Girod, 'Operative Information Nr. [blank]/75', 20 June 1975, file p. 109.
[47] See Peter Kupke, in Irene Ebel, 'Besprechung am 9. April 1975 bei Frau Berghaus nach der Generalprobe *Julie*', undated, 11 pages, here p. 3, BEA File 70. The letter itself can be found here: Ekkehard Schall to Berghaus, 9 April 1975, AdK Einar-Schleef-Archiv 5561. The minutes misquote the letter and so I have quoted from it in the original.
[48] See Heiner Müller, in Ebel, 'Besprechung am 9. April', p. 4.

'we want to realize the broad spectrum [of practices] Brecht left us and make them useful for us today, and that is very complicated'.[49] Looking back in 1996, Karl Mickel acknowledged that *Miss Julie* would never have made it onto the stage if it were not for Berghaus. While she was not a fan of Strindberg, she rated her colleagues' work and valued 'the educative properties of uneasiness'.[50] She also suggested an eight-day postponement of the premiere in order for further changes to be made.[51] Instead, the decision was taken to allow the premiere to take place as planned, with traditionalists relishing a public debacle while the experimentalists hoped that the production would prove its own worth with the audience.

Gisela Holan of the Ministry of Culture was also present at the meeting and voted against the premiere. It is perhaps surprising that the authorities did not reserve the right to a veto. The deferral, in this case, to a more democratic process was in line with the Ministry's stated view on the function of theatres' repertoires at that time. Minister Hoffmann had declared in January 1975 that he considered the repertoire 'an ideological instrument of management' in that its construction resulted from the leadership of the *Intendant* working in concert with a broad range of colleagues.[52] This openness tended to apply to productions of classic texts only, however, and the Ministry continued to suppress the work of Heiner Müller and Volker Braun, for example, without any reference to an open discussion process. That the Ministry did not have the final say on the premiere of *Miss Julie* can be traced to negotiations that had already taken place; Berghaus confirmed successful discussions with the Ministry in December 1974.[53] Its opinions, however, had changed by the date set for the premiere, when it recommended cancellation or at the very least 'a complete rethink'.[54] The same document noted that representatives of the cultural sections of the Central Committee, Berlin's Municipal Authority and District Leadership were all present at the run-through. Such a high-ranking audience was also more the exception than the rule for a production of a classic text, and its presence indicates just how seriously the party was taking the work. A report for the District Leadership stated that all the agencies opposed the premiere,

[49] Berghaus, in ibid., p. 4.
[50] Karl Mickel, 'Das Berliner Ensemble der Ruth Berghaus', *Theater der Zeit*, 2 (1996), pp. 50–1 (51).
[51] See Berghaus, in Ebel, 'Besprechung am 9. April', p. 4.
[52] Hans-Joachim Hoffmann, 'Theater in unserer Zeit', *Theater der Zeit*, 1 (1975), pp. 2–4 (4).
[53] See Berghaus to 'dear colleagues', 16 December 1974, BEA File 70.
[54] Jochen Genzel, 'Betr.: *Fräulein Julie* von August Strindberg im Berliner Ensemble', 10 April 1975, 3 pages (3), BArch DR 1/17548.

something that raises the question of why it was not banned. The same report acknowledged, however, that the minister had granted Berghaus the discretion to authorize the production because it did not contravene any important points of cultural policy or contain 'hostile positions' regarding the SED or the GDR.[55] By 'cultural policy', one may assume that *Miss Julie* could go ahead because the play had not been proscribed, yet the production itself paid little heed to the State's aesthetic norms of socialist realism, and it was this aspect that caused the major problem in the context of the BE and its traditions.

This was never more clearly stated than in the Stasi's summation of the production, composed by the officer with responsibility for the BE, Wilhelm Girod, but based on unnamed overt and covert sources. He traced a line from *The Mother* and *Spring Awakening* to *Julie*. This new direction was to be seen as a deliberate attempt to destroy the image of the BE as a Brecht museum, but only by making 'politically useless theatre'.[56] Of course, when a Stasi officer criticizes the political efficacy of art, it is art viewed through the narrowest of propagandist lenses. He noted that performances were sold out, something used as evidence of subversion, rather than success. The inclusion of the wider context led Girod to suggest 'a review of the *Intentantin*'s leadership as well as her real political conception of the BE'.[57]

Girod was not the only person to shift the blame from the directors to the theatre's leadership. The production was withdrawn from the repertoire after a mere ten performances. A Stasi informant noted that Berghaus had carried this out 'on her own authority', although Tragelehn was also said to have felt sorry for the *Intendantin* for having to make this decision.[58] Indeed, in early 1976, a Ministry document noted that Berghaus still regretted cancelling *Miss Julie*.[59] It would seem, then, that it was not solely her decision. There is no definitive documentary evidence to confirm who put Berghaus under pressure, but there is one pointer that indicates that the Brecht estate was the instigator. In a reply to a query from Kurt Hager about Barbara Brecht-Schall, the head of the Central Committee's Cultural Department, Ursula Ragwitz, acknowledged the heirs' power with respect to the BE and the fact that they

[55] Hans Kießig to Konrad Naumann, 10 April 1975, LAB C Rep 902 3622.
[56] Wilhelm Girod, 'Bericht über die Premiere im Berliner Ensemble *Fräulein Julie*...', 6 May 1975, file pp. 94–5 (94), BStU MfS Bln. Abt. XX A 480–11.
[57] Ibid., file p. 95.
[58] IM Klein, untitled, 18 July 1975, file pp. 145–8 (147), BStU MfS Bln. Abt. XX A 480–11.
[59] See Jochen Genzel, 'Zur Situation im Berliner Ensemble nach den Parteiwahlen', 15 January 1976, 5 pages (2), BArch DR 1/17548.

could destroy the company's 'profile and future' if they withdrew new rights to Brecht productions.[60] This had already been hinted at when Brecht-Schall refused to grant Berghaus the rights to *The Threepenny Opera* in the USA. Ragwitz noted that Berghaus had already made concessions on *The Mother* and that *Miss Julie* would not appear in the new season's repertoire. This is the clearest suggestion that the estate had brought about the enforced foreshortening of the run. Head dramaturge Hans-Jochen Irmer agreed; in addition, he told me that when Berghaus cancelled *Miss Julie*, she also cancelled her *Intendanz*.[61] By this he meant that by giving in to the estate, she had effectively surrendered her ability to run the BE.

A climate of panic

The fall-out from the criticism of *The Mother* and the cancellation of *Miss Julie* took a variety of forms, although not all the BE's woes were due to the intervention of the Brecht estate. As already noted, the tour of the USA, which may have appeared to have collapsed due to the rights issue surrounding *The Threepenny Opera*, actually foundered on the promoters' inability to fund such an expensive undertaking. Similarly, a tour to Recklinghausen in the FRG of June 1975 looked like it was in jeopardy due to reservations from Schall and Brecht-Schall. The former was unhappy that only Berghaus's productions were to go on tour.[62] At the time of the complaint, only *Cement* and *The Mother* were mentioned, that is, there would be no major roles for Schall. Earlier, in March, he had protested that the plan for the tour had only been casually mentioned at a management meeting as a *fait accompli*.[63] Brecht-Schall had criticized the text of *The Mother* ahead of the tour and insisted on the complete restitution of excised passages.[64] However, the tour actually came to nothing due to a larger political quarrel between the GDR and the FRG. The festival at Recklinghausen was funded by the FRG's confederation of trade unions, the DGB. That body had apparently caused affront to the GDR's confederation, the FDGB, at a congress in Hamburg not long

---

[60] Ursula Ragwitz to Kurt Hager, 1 July 1975, SAPMO BArch DY 30/IV B 2/9.06/69.

[61] Hans-Jochen Irmer, unpublished interview with the author, 3 November 2010.

[62] See Wilhelm Girod, 'Operative Information Nr. [blank]/75', 29 April 1975, file pp. 90–2 (90), BStU MfS Bln. Abt. XX A 480–11.

[63] See Hans Kießig, 'Betr.: Vorgänge am Berliner Ensemble', 4 April, 1975, 3 pages (2), LAB C Rep 902 3622.

[64] See Hans Kießig, 'Betr.: Situation am Berliner Ensemble', 21 July 1975, 4 pages (1), ibid.

before the tour.[65] At very short notice, the GDR authorities cancelled the tour in solidarity with the FDGB. While Berghaus was disappointed that her preparations had been in vain, she conceded that the decision had been 'necessary and justified'.[66] She nonetheless drew criticism from the chair of the local Party at the BE, Wolfgang Holz, for 'the unprofessional way' in which she informed the ensemble.[67] Her manner of leadership was not helping her to court allies at this crucial phase.

Even if Brecht's heirs had not been responsible for the two failed tours, their comments and criticisms applied a steady stream of pressure. For example, Ekkehard Schall, the BE's best-known actor, resigned from the ensemble in a letter of 27 March 1975. Yet his letter had not been sent to Berghaus, but to Minister Hoffmann.[68] It was clear that he no longer considered Berghaus the appropriate recipient for such communication. Indeed, this would become the primary mode of communication for the heirs, preferring to deal with the true wielders of power, rather than their representatives. Berghaus had still not seen the letter in June,[69] something that suggests that Schall was using the resignation as a lever, much as Wekwerth had with Weigel in 1968, rather than as a genuine attempt to leave the BE at the time. Indeed, by July, Schall had postponed the decision to leave, something Friedrich Dieckmann interpreted in a letter to Schall as '"an instrument of power" to extinguish artistic conceptions you see standing in contradiction with Brecht'.[70] Schall then worked behind the scenes to secure his aims, and resubmitted his resignation only in July 1976,[71] when he needed to move against Berghaus more openly. The resignation was accepted the following month.[72] All the same, Schall continued playing his roles in existing BE productions as a guest star, rather than as a formal member of the ensemble.

Problems at the company at this time extended to Berghaus's relationship with her once-trusted dramaturgy department. Dieckmann had been in touch with Jerzy Jarocki of the Stary Teatr Krakow with a view to staging Witkiewicz's play *The Shoemakers* for the GDR's festival of Polish

---

[65] See Anon., handwritten letter to Maud Klevenow, undated, BEA File 'Tourneen [unnumbered]'.

[66] Berghaus, in Anon. enclosure from Harald Bühl to Harry Tisch, 'Information des Zentralvorstandes der Gewerkschaft Kunst über die Probleme der Gewerkschaftsarbeit im Berliner Ensemble', 25 July 1975, 3 pages (1), SAPMO BArchDY 34/10670.

[67] Wolfgang Holz, in Otto Richter, 'Kurzinformation', 16 June 1975, 2 pages (1), ibid.

[68] See Kießig, 'Betr.: Vorgänge', p. 1.

[69] See Otto Richter to Rudolf Höppner, 25 June 1975, LAB C Rep 902 3622.

[70] Dieckmann to Schall, 16 July 1975, AdK FDA 'Dramaturgische Papiere'.

[71] See Irene Ebel, 'Protokoll zur Leitungssitzung am 1. Juli 1976, undated, 8 pages (1), BEA File 'Protokolle Leitungssitzungen 1973–76'.

[72] See Irene Ebel, 'Protokoll zur Leitungssitzung am 19.8.1976', undated, 7 pages (1), ibid.

theatre in October 1975.[73] In March, Dieckmann gained the Ministry's approval, but by April both this plan and one for an evening featuring the work of Tadeusz Różewicz were both in jeopardy due to Berghaus's doubts.[74] Dieckmann and Hans-Diether Meves encouraged Berghaus not to lose heart in the projects which seemed to have 'slipped into the tide of self-doubt that's gripped our ensemble'. Such aversion to risk was an immediate consequence of the *Miss Julie* affair. Approved projects were no longer safe, and Irmer joined the other two dramaturges to protest.[75] Dieckmann then courted Schall with the script of *The Shoemakers* and asked him which role he wanted to play.[76] This was a curious move in that it appeared that Dieckmann was siding with Schall against Berghaus in the greater scheme of things. However, Dieckmann was not a terribly partisan person – he continued to offer good advice to Berghaus on the situation at the BE – and so this letter may actually betoken his attempt to keep alive a project in which he believed. His gambit failed, however, and the play was never to be produced at the BE. Dieckmann left the company in 1976, and Irmer followed, both of their own free will.

Perhaps the most visible indicator of instability can be found in what would become Berghaus's final production with the BE. In July 1975, a report for the District Leadership noted that she had withdrawn her plan to stage Helmut Baierl's *Der Sommerbürger* (*The Summer Resident*). Apparently, encouraged by the *Intendantin*'s doubt, ensemble members openly attacked the play, and only Schall spoke in favour, offering to play a major role.[77] Berghaus then withdrew her withdrawal and cast Jürgen Holtz, who had played Jean in *Miss Julie*, to play the lead, Schotte. This, in turn, created more friction with the Brecht estate, as Holtz had also been cast as the Singer in Peter Kupke's production of *Chalk Circle*, although this was decided without actually consulting Holtz.[78] By November, Holtz said that he could not take both parts and not surprisingly opted for Berghaus over Kupke. Brecht-Schall reportedly read this as a boycott of the Brecht production, and verbal threats followed from Schall, who

[73] See Dieckmann to Jerzy Jarocki, 7 February 1975, AdK FDA 'Dramaturgische Papiere'.
[74] See Dieckmann to Jerzy Jarocki, 14 March 1975; and Dieckmann and Hans-Diether Meves to Berghaus, 16 April 1975, both ibid. The following quotation comes for the co-authored letter.
[75] See Hans-Jochen Irmer, Dieckmann and Hans-Diether Meves to Berghaus, 18 April 1975, ibid.
[76] See Dieckmann to Schall, 13 May 1975, ibid.
[77] See Hans Kießig, 'Betr.: Situation', p. 3.
[78] Information on this incident here and below is to be found in Jochen Genzel, 'Aktennotiz über ein Gespräch mit der Genossin Ruth Berghaus am 2.11.1975', 6 November 1975, pp. 5, BArch DR 1/17548; and Sepp Müller to Roland Bauer, 13 November 1975, LAB C Rep 902 3622.

said he would not play Azdak, and from Brecht-Schall, who asserted that the BE had lost the right to call itself the BE. Brecht-Schall believed Holtz's behaviour represented a breach of contract and demanded that Berghaus suspend rehearsals, something she undertook on 12 November until matters were clarified. There was, however, an additional problem: the ensemble itself was unhappy with Kupke's rehearsals, a situation that echoed the one noted in the discussion of *Turandot* on pp. 250–2, Chapter 8. An important internal committee had recommended that rehearsals be suspended until Kupke either prepared more effectively or took Schall as co-director. The BE's management, however, turned down the latter proposal. The result, unsurprisingly, was a further drop in morale.

As was already clear, *The Summer Resident* was not a popular choice. Although it was an example of an officially approved contemporary GDR play, it had already attracted criticism in Dresden where rehearsals began before those of the BE, although they were not to lead to a premiere. A document forwarded from Dresden to the Stasi in Berlin noted that the problems explored in the play were only 'pseudo-problems' and that Schotte had no real conflict with any other character or group.[79] Such a critique is worryingly reminiscent of Baierl's *Johanna von Döbeln*, staged at the BE in 1969 (see pp. 220–1, Chapter 7). It is thus hard to fathom why Berghaus returned to *The Summer Resident*. A clue is given in a document written before Berghaus tried to distance herself from the text in the first place. According to voices within the ensemble, Berghaus had initially been persuaded to direct the play 'auf "höhere Empfehlung"' ('by "higher decree"').[80] While the German word 'Empfehlung' actually translates as 'recommendation', there can be little doubt as to the force that lay behind such official recommendations. It can only be assumed that the authorities prevailed upon Berghaus to revive their plan, and while one might speculate about whether she was being set up for a fall, I will argue anon that the Ministry did not want her to fail. On the contrary, one could surmise that the Ministry was trying to offer her a project that would bring her back to the socialist realist fold and thus protect her from the attacks made on her aesthetics by the Brecht estate, the press and the Party.

Unfortunately, the production realized the Ministry's aims all too well. Its own report, written after a run-through four days before the premiere on 12 March 1976, acknowledged the weakness of the text and how 'Ruth

---

[79] Gerhard Piens, 'Protokoll', 19 September 1975, file pp. 35–8 (37), BStU MfS BV Bln. AIM 6210/91, vol. II/2.
[80] IM Klein, untitled, 18 July 1975, file p. 146.

Berghaus broadly foregoes extraneous effects in the production . . . This is a reassuring sign for the development of the BE'.[81] However, the reviewer was quick to note that the combination of understated direction and a poor piece of writing was 'unsatisfying', and predicted that the production would not be a great success. And this was the case: *The Summer Resident* ran for a mere twenty-four performances and had left the repertoire by the end of the year. It is interesting to observe that while the Ministry praised Berghaus's directorial restraint, it tacitly understood that such a play actually required her more imaginative approach to make it work. The newspapers were more charitable to Berghaus than to the play, and tended to praise 'Berghaus's performance artistry' and the interplay of human warmth and satire.[82] The real problems came in the wake of the production's lukewarm reception. A Stasi report noted that three factions had emerged within the ensemble: a small one supportive of Berghaus, a larger one gathered around the Brecht estate, and one for Kupke, whose solid, but hardly innovative *Chalk Circle* was seen as a success, not least due to Schall's performance as Azdak.[83] Berghaus was accused of being unable to direct 'Sprechtheater', the German term for 'dramatic theatre'. This was another critique of her directorial abilities and one that was deployed to contrast itself with her success as a director of opera. The report concluded that most of the ensemble believed 'that *Intendantin* Berghaus had now finally lost her reputation with the BE' and that the majority of party members at the company were in favour of a change of leader.[84] The campaign to oust Berghaus was gaining momentum, but it had been unofficially inaugurated the previous year.

A series of public attacks on Berghaus

The fall of Ruth Berghaus was orchestrated in public and in private. The public element helped to create an environment critical of Berghaus's work and her leadership of the BE; the private element sought to lobby and apply pressure to GDR cultural agencies in support of Berghaus's removal. It would, however, be a mistake to believe that the ultimate success of the campaign lay in a coordinated master plan. Indeed, one

[81] Jochen Genzel, 'Bericht über die Hauptprobe *Der Sommerbürger* im Berliner Ensemble am 8.3.1976', 12 March 1976, 2 pages (1, as is the following quotation), BArch DR 1/17548.
[82] A. W. Mytze, 'Sommerbürger Helmut Baierl', *Süddeutsche Zeitung*, 17 March 1976; and see Werner Pfelling, 'Rentnertick und Kämpferherz', *Junge Welt*, 16 March 1976.
[83] See Anon., 'Information 498/76', 11 May 1976, file pp. 108–9 (108), BStU MfS Bln. Abt. XX A 480–11.
[84] Ibid., file p. 109.

could conclude that it took two whole years to remove Berghaus precisely because her two main opponents only joined forces in the second half of 1976.

Manfred Wekwerth, having directed at the Deutsches Theater, in London and Zurich, was appointed the head of a new establishment dedicated to the professional training of directors in East Berlin in 1975, the Regieinstitut. This position anchored him back in the cultural life of the GDR, and he opened a front against Berghaus's BE in August 1975. On the twenty-ninth anniversary of Brecht's death, Wekwerth published an article in *Neues Deutschland* on the subject of directing. Without naming either the director or the production, it was clear that he was referring to Berghaus's *The Mother* in his article and criticized its politics for what he perceived to be its undialectical premises.[85] That said, an article discussing a forthcoming conference of the Association of Theatre-Makers (Verband der Theaterschaffenden) noted unrest at Wekwerth's comments, and the author assured those troubled that Wekwerth was referring to recent productions at the BE only.[86] There can be no doubt, though, that Wekwerth's was a veiled attack on *The Mother*; a letter to GDR film-maker Gerhard Scheumann called the changes at the BE under Berghaus 'dilettante regressions to the sins of the bourgeois theatre; they change Brecht because they're incapable of staging him correctly'.[87] The use of the word 'correctly' allies Wekwerth with a sense of orthodoxy and his own rightness, attitudes he shared with Brecht-Schall. In the same letter, Wekwerth directly attacked Berghaus's production of *The Mother* for turning a play about the victorious proletariat into a tragedy. (It is worth noting how Wekwerth, who, as will become clear, is a keen revisionist of his own biography, went on to defend Berghaus's production in 1999: 'I did not find... resignation there, rather a playful exhortation to save, not to demolish the GDR'.[88] He made no mention of the beliefs he previously held.)

Wekwerth also published an open letter to the BE's dramaturgy department in the August number of *Theater der Zeit*.[89] He had sent the strident and occasionally haughty letter privately to the BE in June, and Dieckmann passed it on to Berghaus with an accompanying note that

---

[85] See Manfred Wekwerth, 'Das Buch Hiob oder die Fragen der Schöpfer', *Neues Deutschland*, 13 August 1975.

[86] See Klaus Pfützner, 'Beobachtungen, Erfahrungen, Tendenzen', *Theater der Zeit*, 11 (1975), pp. 1–2 (1).

[87] Wekwerth to Gerhard Scheumann, 14 May 1975, AdK MWA 'Korr. Privat A-Z'.

[88] Wekwerth, '*Die Mutter* war Ermutigung', *Neues Deutschland*, 6 May 1999.

[89] See Wekwerth, 'Eine Richtigstellung', *Theater der Zeit*, 8 (1975), pp. 43–4.

read Wekwerth's missive as an attack on her ability to lead and to direct.[90] Dieckmann wrote a letter of complaint to the magazine and requested his right to reply.[91] His counter-piece was a reasoned argument that both accepted Wekwerth's critique of a quotation taken from Berghaus and defended the BE's departure from Brecht's *Modell*. It appeared in the November issue.[92] That, however, was not the end of the story. Wekwerth's original letter to the BE was reprinted in a collection of Wekwerth's writings in 1976; yet this volume was published by a house in the FRG, giving his critique an even wider readership.[93] Berghaus was so angered by this that she took legal advice; her lawyer sent a letter to Wekwerth in October 1976 protesting about both the in-house sources cited in his original letter and his unwillingness to reprint Dieckmann's reply.[94] The lawyer added that the BE was not going to press charges, but asked Wekwerth to consider the appropriateness of his words. Wekwerth was not cowed and replied that his critiques were at one with many other party members concerned about the reception of Brecht in the GDR.[95]

Another voice in the public debate was a completely unexpected one. Kenneth Tynan, the fêted British theatre critic and champion of Brecht and his work, came to East Berlin in October 1975. He interviewed key figures at the BE while Berghaus was on sick leave with a broken ankle and published his findings as a major article in the *New York Times* in January 1976, and later that year in the British theatre magazine *Plays and Players*.[96] It would be difficult to call the piece partisan, as it presents all its interviewees in a fair light; rather it is an attempt to diagnose the 'crisis' that 'concerns anyone who cares about theatre'. Tynan names some of his interlocutors, like Wekwerth, Karl von Appen, and Brecht-Schall, while hiding people like Heiner Müller and Werner Hecht behind the generic terms 'an East German playwright' and 'a dramaturge', respectively. The view that arises is that the BE is in decline and in need of urgent help. Müller predicted an alliance between the Brecht estate and Wekwerth 'against the Ruth Berghaus regime'. Tynan wondered

---

[90] See Dieckmann to Berghaus, 11 June 1975, AdK FDA 'Dramaturgische Papiere'.
[91] See Dieckmann to Hans-Rainer John, 16 August 1975, ibid.
[92] See Dieckmann, 'Eine Antwort', *Theater der Zeit*, 11 (1975), pp. 45–6. It was also sent personally to Wekwerth on 15 July 1975, AdK MWA 'Korr. mit Institutionen'.
[93] See Wekwerth, *Brecht? Berichte, Erfahrungen, Polemik* (Munich and Vienna: Hanser, 1976), pp. 157–60.
[94] See Friedrich Karl Kaul to Wekwerth, 21 October 1976, AdK MWA 'Korr. Privat A-Z'.
[95] See Wekwerth to Friedrich Karl Kaul, 26 October 1976, ibid.
[96] See Kenneth Tynan, 'Brecht would not applaud his Theater [*sic*] today', *The New York Times*, 11 January 1976; and 'Brecht's Theatre at the Crossroads' in *Plays and Players*, March 1976, pp. 12–16. Subsequent references are taken from these sources.

whether Wekwerth's new Regieinstitut might provide 'the perfect launching pad . . . for a guerrilla movement aimed at infiltrating the Ensemble'. Appen openly criticized Berghaus's taste for experiment. Wekwerth and Joachim Tenschert both pleaded for a return to orthodox Brechtianism. Barbara Brecht-Schall was reported to have wanted to see her husband and Wekwerth 'back together at the Ensemble', and Hecht, implicitly referring to that point, ironically praised Berghaus for uniting 'people who used to be sworn enemies'.

While there is no evidence and, indeed, no reason to suggest that Tynan was playing anyone's game in writing the piece, it nonetheless served various parties' agendas. It gave Wekwerth and Brecht-Schall an international platform, and for all his fairness, Tynan was clear that something had to change in order to restore Brechtianism, as he understood it, to the BE. Wekwerth sent the *Plays and Players* version of the article to Politburo member Werner Lambertz in May 1976, together with a letter protesting against the perceived de-politicization of the BE's work.[97] Yet while Wekwerth was lobbying senior Party members, his public utterances had alienated sections of the BE. Both his allusions to *The Mother* in *Neues Deutschland* and the interview with Tynan were cited as bones of contention at a meeting of the acting ensemble.[98] Berghaus, on the other hand, used Tynan's article to show Kurt Hager how the BE had come under attack from the GDR's own people in a publication written in the West.[99] The conditions surrounding the interviews also gave Berghaus the opportunity to put her house in order; she could identify the loose tongues at the BE and considered initiating a disciplinary process against Appen.[100] There is no evidence, however, that this actually took place. The Ministry nonetheless hoped that she would be able to assert authority 'with all her energy'.[101]

Ekkehard Schall also made his feelings known publicly, although he only began his open criticism once he had formally resigned from the BE. He launched the opening salvo on GDR television together with none other than Wekwerth. Schall roundly criticized the contemporary reception of Brecht 'primarily in Berlin',[102] which could only mean at the BE.

[97] See Wekwerth to Werner Lambertz, 13 May 1976, SAPMO BArch DY 30/IV 2/2.033/115.
[98] See Wolfgang Pintzka to Ursula Ragwitz, 14 May 1976, BArch DR 1/17548.
[99] See Berghaus to Hager, 30 January 1976, SAPMO BArch DY 30/IV B 2/2.024/102.
[100] See Marlis Helmschrott to Roland Bauer, 23 October 1975, LAB C Rep 902 3622.
[101] Jochen Genzel, 'Aktennotiz', p. 1.
[102] Schall, in Anon., 'Studiogespräch mit Manfred Wekwerth und Ekkehard Schall', *Kulturmagazin*, August 1976, undated transcription, 9 pages (9), AdK MWA 'Texte 1970–1975'.

Wekwerth, while echoing Schall's views, was not as specific in his criticism. The important aspect, far beyond the interviewees' comments, was that Wekwerth and Schall actually appeared together, a clear signal that old animosities concerning the crisis of the late 1960s had at least been put to one side in a show of unity against Berghaus. Schall later wrote an article in *Theater der Zeit* that repeated and varied his critique of contemporary Brechtianism in the GDR, but this time without mentioning Berlin.[103] Wekwerth, too, published an article in *Neues Deutschland* on Brecht to commemorate the twentieth anniversary of his death in August 1976, which criticized BE productions, again without naming names.[104] In the wake of the article, a reporter in West Berlin viewed Wekwerth very much as an *Intendant*-in-waiting.[105]

Perhaps the most interesting thing about the various articles discussed here was the time-lag between the date on which Tynan's was published and Berghaus's removal from office. Tynan's piece first appeared in January 1976, yet its picture of the BE as a company in crisis did not change until Berghaus was finally dismissed in April 1977. In hindsight, it reads like a chronicle of a death foretold, to quote the novella by García Márquez. One thus has to ask why it took sixteen months for the inevitable to happen, even despite the marriage of convenience between the Brecht estate and Wekwerth in the summer of 1976. The complex answer is to be found out of the public's sight in the GDR's corridors of power.

Wekwerth's gambit for a return to the BE

In order to understand the nature of the politics that played out behind closed doors, it is worth reacquainting the reader with the structures that confronted the various parties. If one excludes the smallest administrative unit, the Local Leadership (Kreisleitung) of Berlin Mitte, which only dealt with issues concerning the BE's local Party,[106] cultural matters were administered and/or monitored by four agencies. These were, in order of importance, the Central Committee's Cultural Department, the Ministry of Culture, Berlin's District Leadership and its Municipal Authority. The Central Committee, however, consisted of a further two strata: there was the Cultural Department itself, but that unit always had to defer to

---

[103] See Schall, 'Ausblick nach vorn', *Theater der Zeit*, 9 (1976), pp. 31 and 33.
[104] See Wekwerth, 'Er hat Vorschläge gemacht . . .', *Neues Deutschland*, 14/15 August 1976.
[105] See transcription of a broadcast on West Berlin's radio station RIAS by Horst Wenderoth, 24 August 1976, 2 pages, SAPMO BArch DY 30/IV B 2/9.06/69.
[106] See, for example, Anon., 'Information über den Stand der Parteiarbeit in den Berliner Theatern', undated, 15 pages, LAB C Rep 903–01–04 1237.

Kurt Hager, who was the defining voice in science, the academy and culture, and was a member of the Politburo, the Central Committee's governing executive body. The Minister of Culture also had a small raft of deputies with special responsibilities within the cultural brief. Werner Rackwitz was one such deputy who took the theatre portfolio from 1969 until 1981. Joachim Walther notes that the Central Committee always trumped the Ministry in terms of power, and so the head of the Cultural Department was more important than the more public face of cultural policy, the Minister.[107] That would mean that Hans-Joachim Hoffmann effectively took a demotion when he was appointed Minister of Culture in 1973, having been the head of the Cultural Department earlier that year. While Walther is not wrong about the pecking order in principle, the everyday running of the two units was not quite as hierarchical as his assertion might suggest. For the most part, the Ministry dealt with the cultural issues of the day as a trusted associate, and the Central Committee was happy to defer most decisions to this larger apparatus. In more difficult matters, as was the case with the leadership of the BE, the Central Committee became an important player itself, due to its role as ultimate arbiter, more in the figure of Kurt Hager than in the head of the Cultural Department, however.

As discussed on pp. 217–18, Chapter 7, responsibility for East Berlin's main theatres passed from the Ministry to the Municipal Authority in 1968. Erich Honecker, who came to power in May 1971, reversed that decision five months later,[108] preferring centralization to regionalism. Not all the theatres transferred to the Municipal Authority reverted to the Ministry, and this created a two-tier system, with those theatres left under the Authority feeling like second-class institutions.[109] The BE, as the GDR's premiere company, was not one of these, and thus the Municipal Authority no longer played that important a role since Berghaus was appointed *Intendantin*. The joker in the pack was the District Leadership. This resembled a local version of the Central Committee in that it oversaw more political and ideological issues in its designated territory. The term 'fiefdom', however, may be more appropriate, as the first secretaries of these bodies tended to build power bases in their administrative districts. Yet the District Leadership in Berlin was a slightly different type

---

[107] See Walther, *Sicherungsbereich Literatur*, pp. 45 and 47.
[108] See Anon., 'Beschluß über die Änderung der Unterstellung von Berliner Theatern', undated, n.p., BArch DR 1/9851. The document reports that the Central Committee approved the decision on 29 October 1971; the transfer took place on 1 January 1972.
[109] See Anon., 'Ergänzende Informationen zur BL-Vorlage: "Über den Stand der Parteiarbeit in den Berliner Theatern"', 22 September 1978, 4 pages, LAB C Rep 903–01–04 1237.

of administration because it found itself in the same city as the seat of all major government agencies. Its influence on the BE was thus not as great as that of other District Offices, further from Berlin, on their own theatres. That said, it still had a voice and still had power; indeed the length of Berghaus's tenure at the BE can in part be accounted for by her closeness to and the support from the District Leadership.

The final state apparatus that should not be forgotten is the Stasi. This organ did not have any formal responsibility for the BE, although it assigned an officer to monitor the company in this period, Wilhelm Girod. However, the Stasi was clearly a part of the GDR's power structures and, as a result, Berghaus sought its help in a bid to defend herself, too. It should be noted, however, that, as far as can be ascertained from the archive, Wekwerth made no use of his Stasi connections to act against Berghaus; he preferred to use official channels. For example, after his fall from grace in 1969, Wekwerth was initially given short shrift by the Ministry of Culture. The volume collecting various essays, his *Notate* and his doctoral thesis was initially refused publication by Minister Gysi in August 1971.[110] The issue was resolved in October, after Honecker himself enquired about the problem. Wekwerth had previously contacted Politburo member Werner Lambertz to address the matter. Wekwerth believed that the book had been banned because his views on Brecht were deemed to undermine the new leadership at the BE.[111] The point to note here is that Wekwerth went straight to the top, and it was with the upper echelon that he had most contact in the period prior to his ultimate appointment as *Intendant* in 1977.

Wekwerth has always maintained that he did not want to become the BE's *Intendant*, and in an interview with me, he said that he had no interest in theatre at the time and preferred to make films.[112] While the documents show that he did not overtly covet the *Intendanz* itself, they nonetheless contradict the position that he wanted nothing to do with the company that had taught him so much and at which he had staged world-famous productions. Wekwerth was already in contact with the Brecht heirs in the late summer of 1976, as evidenced in the TV appearance with Ekkehard Schall. While Barbara Brecht-Schall was against the Ministry appointing Wekwerth *Intendant* that September, the Ministry's man who reported this opinion at a meeting in her flat noticed that Wekwerth and

---

[110] See Johannes Hörnig to Hager, 26 October 1971, SAPMO BArch DY 30/IV A 2/2.024/32.

[111] See Wekwerth, in Hans-Dieter Schütt, *Manfred Wekwerth* (Frankfurt/Oder: Frankfurt Oder Editionen, 1995), p. 165.

[112] See Wekwerth, in ibid., p. 281; Wekwerth, unpublished interview with the author, 1 July 2011.

his wife were looking for the heiress as he left.[113] By October, Wekwerth was actively lobbying the Central Committee for a return to the BE. He referred to a discussion paper he wrote in 1968 with respect to the leadership of the BE in which he proposed as *Intendant* a cultural functionary while reserving the position of artistic director for himself.[114] In effect he wanted to play the role of Brecht to the new *Intendant*'s Weigel. He saw his Regieinstitut as a feeder for new directors at the BE and noted: 'but I can't function as a theatre director in the long run without my own ensemble', so there is no suggestion that he had turned his back on the stage. He also portrayed himself as a loyal party member in an enclosure to the letter, in which he said he was happy to keep his communications private so that they would not be used against the GDR by a hostile Western press. Wekwerth continued his campaign in a letter to Hager in January 1977, which echoed the sentiments reported above. Here, however, he explicitly stated that he did not want to return to the BE as a guest, but craved 'real work in the theatre'.[115] This clearly involved a change of leadership, as Wekwerth acknowledged in the same letter, but he was also taking advantage of the pressure the Brecht estate had been applying to Berghaus's position: at the time, he lacked that kind of power himself.

Dealing with Barbara Brecht-Schall

Barbara Brecht-Schall started to intervene in the workings of the BE in April 1975 in response to Berghaus's production of *The Mother*. The influence she wielded, of course, rested solely on the chance of her birth, but this historical accident, coupled with a very determined personality, allowed her to cause a great many problems. Not only could she deny the BE performing rights to Brecht, something that would effectively prevent it from retaining its international profile as Brecht's theatre, but she could also affect the way the GDR as a whole performed Brecht because she controlled his performance rights. Initially, it seems, she was content to become a part of the BE's structures through the formation of an 'Arbeitsgruppe' (Working Group). The group represents a way of integrating Brecht-Schall into decision-making at the company and placating her at the same time in the wake of the resolution of 1971.

---

[113] See Jochen Genzel, 'Aktennotiz', [written after the meeting of 7 September 1976], 4 pages (3–4), BArch DR 1/1746.

[114] See Wekwerth to Ursula Ragwitz, 3 October 1976, SAPMO BArch DY 30/IV 2/2.033/115. The following quotation and reference to the enclosure are also taken from this source.

[115] Wekwerth to Hager, 2 January 1977, SAPMO BArch DY 30/IV B 2/9.06/69.

Records indicate that the group sat for the first time on 1 September 1975, and Berghaus sent invitations to a representative of the Ministry (Jochen Genzel), Brecht-Schall, Hecht, Kupke, Pintzka and Schall. Berghaus saw it as 'a new level of management . . . a small management forum in which all questions can be discussed'.[116] Genzel proposed that the Group establish a theoretical platform for the development of the BE, something with which Brecht-Schall agreed, without, however, being able to formulate one herself.[117]

The Group's work was interrupted by Berghaus's ankle injury at the end of 1975. By March 1976, the Group was already in trouble, and now included a representative from the Central Committee's Cultural Department. Schall described the body as 'pointless', as it had not sat since Berghaus's absence, and Kupke wanted to leave it because he felt that Berghaus was reaching decisions without consultation with the Group in any case.[118] A further item at the meeting concerned granting other Berlin theatres performing rights to Brecht's plays. Brecht-Schall argued that a decision to break the BE's monopoly would indicate that the Ministry had also lost faith in the BE. Schall opposed this move.[119] Its very discussion, however, set alarm bells ringing at the Ministry because of the way a private individual was using her power to influence State theatre policy. This anxiety led to the implementation of a desperate measure later than year.

Minister Hoffmann sought refuge from the potential damage Brecht-Schall could wreak in the resolution passed by the Council of Ministers in 1971 and advised all *Intendanten* to apply for performing rights to Brecht through the Academy of Arts.[120] The heiress reacted almost immediately by instructing the agency that organized the GDR's touring schedule not to make any further contracts permitting GDR theatres to take productions of Brecht's plays abroad.[121] She repealed the ban only in April 1977,[122] once the new leadership of the BE had been confirmed. Erdmut Wizisla considers that Hoffmann's actions were 'beyond doubt . . . ideologically motivated', something he reads in the language of key documents concerning the rights issue.[123] While the ideological

---

[116] Berghaus, in Anon., 'Notizen zum Gespräch der Arbeitsgruppe am 1. September 1975', 2 September 1975, 4 pages (1), BArch DR 1/17547.
[117] See Genzel and Brecht-Schall, in ibid., p. 2.
[118] See Schall and Kupke, in Jochen Genzel, 'Arbeitsgruppe Berliner Ensemble', 5 March 1976, 5 pages (both 1), ibid.
[119] See Brecht-Schall and Schall, in ibid., p. 3.
[120] See Hoffmann to Hager, 4 November 1976, SAPMO BArch DY 30/ IV B 2/2.024/102.
[121] See Brecht-Schall to Hermann Falk, 8 November 1976, ibid.
[122] See Hager to Erich Honecker, 21 April 1977, ibid.
[123] Wizisla, 'Private or Public?', in Bradley and Leeder (eds.), *Brecht and the GDR*, p. 118.

argument was certainly a part of the Minister's rhetoric, it should not be forgotten that the move to secure the rights for the GDR also had a more pragmatic element: the defence of the SED's monopoly on power in matters of cultural policy.

Werner Hecht wrote an analysis of the Working Group in June 1976 which drew the conclusion that it had been a failure for two main reasons: it had not established any real basis or criteria for further discussion and it had succeeded in intensifying existing conflicts.[124] Although Berghaus disputed his conclusions,[125] they were difficult to deny. The Group was formally dissolved in January 1977 by Deputy Minister Rackwitz with a view to establishing a new Advisory Group in its stead (see pp. 320–1, Chapter 10).[126]

Since the demise of the GDR, Brecht-Schall has continually denied playing any part in Berghaus's downfall,[127] and has also portrayed herself as a victim of the SED, citing the resolution in evidence.[128] This is a remarkable piece of post-Wall revisionism. While the SED may not have liked her, it was certainly in fear of her, and the prospect of losing its claim to Brecht in print and on the stage made it willing to accommodate her in a variety of ways. The decline of the Working Group, which had been set up for her benefit, led to more sustained contact between the estate and senior Party members. She had enviable access to the highest of offices, and what she said there was anything but mild or conciliatory with respect to Berghaus.

In a meeting with Minister Hoffmann of September 1976, Brecht-Schall acknowledged that she had initially supported the appointment of Berghaus, but now considered it a mistake. She had three people in mind as potential successors, and although she kept those names to herself at the time, she believed that Wekwerth would make a bad *Intendant*.[129] If one needed any more evidence of Brecht-Schall's move to oust Berghaus, it came in October where the minutes of a meeting with Hager read:

---

[124] See Werner Hecht, 'Bemerkungen zur Arbeit der "Arbeitsgruppe Berliner Ensemble"', 21 June 1976, n.p., BArch DR 1/17547.

[125] See Berghaus to Hecht, 13 August 1976, ibid.

[126] See Berghaus to members of the Group, 11 January 1977, ibid.

[127] See, for example, Brecht-Schall, 'Letter from Barbara Brecht-Schall', *Brecht Yearbook*, 22 (1997), p. 46.

[128] See Brecht-Schall, in Ingeborg Pietzsch and Martin Linzer, 'Familien-Geschichten', *Theater der Zeit*, 6 (1994), pp. 12–15 (15).

[129] See Brecht-Schall, in Jochen Genzel, 'Gedächtnis-Protokoll eines Gespräches zwischen dem Minister für Kultur und Frau Barbara Brecht-Schall am 29.9.1976', 30 September 1976, 8 pages (4 and 7), SAPMO BArch DY 30/IV B 2/2.024/102.

Mrs Brecht-Schall declares her complete rejection of the BE's leadership. The *Intendantin* has forfeited the BE's right to be the exclusive place for Brecht's plays in Berlin through her productions and her policies regarding the repertoire.[130]

At the same meeting, she stated that she would not grant new rights to Berghaus, a decision that effectively rendered the *Intendantin* incapable of running a theatre dedicated to Brecht's work. By January 1977, Ursula Ragwitz had been informed of Brecht-Schall's demand 'that Mrs Berghaus should be relieved [of her post]'.[131] Brecht-Schall finally got her way in March 1977, yet before discussing the removal of Berghaus from the BE, I will consider why the authorities vacillated for so long, and the efforts Berghaus made to retain her position.

The failure of Berghaus's defence

In July 1975, in the wake of the cancellation of *Miss Julie*, the Ministry took stock of the situation at the BE. Functionary Jochen Genzel accounted for the BE's successes of the 1950s and 1960s in terms of its 'conceptual and artistic unity of purpose', something he no longer found at the company.[132] The Ministry wanted the BE to discover Brecht for the present day, but also to preserve the Brecht it recognized. The paper discussed how the company should return to its rightful position as a unit that made exemplary productions: in particular in the staging of Brecht, something the Ministry allied to the *Modell*, and in general in the staging of drama, something it found lacking in *Miss Julie*.[133] The need to stabilize the BE was, in part, implicit in a note in the same document that mentioned Brecht's eightieth birthday celebrations in 1978. The GDR was very keen to mark anniversaries because they were a means of demonstrating its prestige, and the authorities endeavoured to do whatever was necessary to ensure flawless jubilation. That the Brecht anniversary was being considered this far in advance indicates the importance attached to the project. The two obstacles to a successful event were clear: unorthodox productions that would not reflect the Brecht the GDR wanted to portray and the ability of the Brecht estate to frustrate the State's plans by withdrawing strategic performing rights. This is why the Ministry sought to clip the BE's experimental wings in a bid to bring back a semblance of

---

[130]   Erika Hinckel, 'Notiz über Gespräch, das Genosse Kurt Hager am 5.10.76 mit Frau Brecht-Schall führte', 12 October 1976, 3 pages (2), ibid.

[131]   [Siegfried Otto?], 'Information: Betr. Angelegenheit Barbara Schall', 27 January 1977, n.p., ibid.

[132]   Jochen Genzel, 'Gedanken zur Aussprache über die Arbeit des Berliner Ensembles', 18 July 1975, 4 pages (1), BArch DR 1/17548.

[133]   See ibid., p. 3.

order; such a move would make the company's output more consistent while bringing the estate back on board. Yet as Laura Bradley notes, this imperative actually had the opposite effect: 'discussions in the BE [in the run-up to 1978] show that anniversaries themselves were starting to contribute to stagnation in the repertoire'.[134] Rather than 'normalizing' the work, the pressure actually drove down its quality.

The threat from the estate went beyond the eightieth birthday plans; the control of the rights had a direct effect on the *Intendantin*'s ability to run her own theatre, something she was supposed to undertake together with the State, not with private citizens. The fear of bolstering Brecht-Schall's power can be felt in the documents of the Central Committee[135] and the Ministry in the first half of 1976. Minister Hoffmann was clear that changing the *Intendantin* would give Brecht-Schall a fillip, although he also noted that such a move *would* be possible after 1978.[136] Thus, he was not so much interested in saving Berghaus than defending the State against the estate. Both the Central Committee and the Ministry thought they could support Berghaus by strengthening the ideological 'reliability' of the BE's dramaturgy department: Karl Mickel appears in both documents referenced above, Friedrich Dieckmann in the first and Heiner Müller in the second, as candidates for dismissal. The need to furnish Berghaus with approved political advisors was a key concern, yet the authorities were not aware that Dieckmann had already lost faith in Berghaus[137] and would actually leave of his own accord later in 1976.

Berghaus also tried to defend herself against attack. In the late 1960s, when she was BE Party Secretary, she had had a great deal of contact with Berlin's District Leadership, especially in connection with the problems surrounding *Johann Faustus* and *Seven against Thebes* (see pp. 209–11 and 215–20, Chapter 7). So, while Wekwerth had friends in the Central Committee, Berghaus had her backers in the regional Party. She was also married to an influential figure, the composer Paul Dessau, who had worked with Brecht as musical collaborator at the BE. He complained to Harry Tisch, a member of the Politburo, in 1976 about Berghaus's treatment by both Party members and the press, something he found 'unseemly'.[138] In another document, the author noted that Dessau was going to speak

[134] Laura Bradley, 'Remembering Brecht: Anniversaries at the Berliner Ensemble', in Bradley and Leeder (eds.), *Brecht and the GDR*, pp. 125–44 (135).

[135] See, for example, Ursula Ragwitz, 'Einige Gedanken für das Gespräch mit Ruth Berghaus', 19 January 1976, 2 pages (2), SAPMO BArch DY 30/IV B 2/2.024/102.

[136] See Hoffmann to Hager, 5 June 1976, SAPMO BArch DY 30/IV B 2/9.06/69.

[137] See the intercepted letter from Dieckmann to BE Leadership, 25 March 1976, BStU MfS AOP 6418/87, vol. 2.

[138] Paul Dessau to Harry Tisch, 20 October 1976, SAPMO BArch DY 34/10670.

to Erich Honecker about the matter because he had support from both the GDR's trade union confederation and the District Leadership.[139] According to Hecht, Dessau was also on first name terms with Kurt Hager.[140]

However, Berghaus did not merely rely on the connections and reputation of her husband. Her own campaign to retain her position involved a number of meetings. She allegedly cultivated a friendly relationship with Deputy Minister Rackwitz in 1975.[141] Corinna Holtz reads the Stasi file that reports this as an early indication that she had been discussing her resignation at the meeting, but the document actually only mentions a rumour that she might be bound for one of East Berlin's two opera houses.[142] Relations with the Minister were cordial, and Rackwitz solicited Berghaus's opinions on the future of the BE as late as January 1977.[143] She also defended herself in the Working Group when she found the minutes of one meeting that she had not approved one-sided and incomplete, and thus did not represent her views.[144]

In a bid to shore up more support, she arranged a meeting with a senior Stasi officer connected with the BE in September 1975, yet her attempt to win him over had the opposite effect. She tried to argue that attacks on the BE frustrated GDR cultural policy. The officer, reflecting on the interview, surmised that she was trying to paint criticism of her aesthetics as 'a politically construed defamation' and dismissed her arguments.[145] Turning her attention to more significant figures, Berghaus wrote to Honecker in January 1976 to apprise him of her position. She confirmed her commitment to the GDR's core leadership value of democratic centralism while noting her inability to exercise this due to the interventions of Brecht-Schall.[146] Berghaus also sent Hager a self-penned report on the BE's recent tour to Italy in September 1976.[147] She had hoped to use international esteem as a means of persuading Hager that things were not all bad with the BE. However, she failed to understand that the BE's

---

[139] See Harald Bühl to Harry Tisch, 13 December 1976, ibid.

[140] Werner Hecht, unpublished interview with the author, 8 June 2011.

[141] See Arnold Klemer, 'Operative Information Nr. 1206/75', 1 August 1975, file pp. 5–7 (7), BStU MfS AIM 14525/85, vol. 2/2.

[142] See Holtz, *Ruth Berghaus*, p. 194.

[143] See Werner Rackwitz to Berghaus, 3 January 1977, BArch DR 1/17548.

[144] See Berghaus, 'Protokoll zur Beratung der Arbeitsgruppe am 18. März 1976', 19 March 1976, 3 pages (1), BArch DR 1/17547.

[145] Arnold Klemer, 'Bericht', 17 September 1975, file pp. 86–7 (87), BStU MfS Bln. Abt. XX A 480–11.

[146] See Berghaus to Honecker, 12 January 1976, SAPMO BArch DY 30/IV B 2/2.024/102.

[147] See Berghaus to Hager, 24 September 1976, SAPMO BArch DY 30/IV B 2/2.024/79.

performance on tour was never a reliable indicator of its domestic standing: foreign audiences saw the BE so rarely that its work almost always seemed fresh, even when it was flagging at home.

Berghaus spent a lot of time looking for help, but allowed her potential power base at the BE to dissipate. She also lacked either the strength or the resolution to stand up to Brecht-Schall or at least to call her bluff on the issue of the BE losing its monopoly of Brecht productions in Berlin. Dieckmann had counselled her to renounce the BE's exclusivity as a way of asserting her authority and demonstrating her ability to act. He maintained that an experimental approach to staging Brecht 'precludes the notion of a theatre with a house style'.[148] Berghaus still argued that the link with Brecht was the BE's distinguishing feature and could not be given up,[149] something that ultimately condemned her to dependence on the wishes of the Brecht estate.

However, conditions at the BE itself were so disorganized that even the possibility of action there was much diminished. Productivity and quality had slumped; the 1975/76 season saw three premieres, two of which ran for less than half a year. The company had only filled 84.5 per cent of its seats in 1975 as opposed to its target of 93 per cent.[150] The following season produced one single premiere. A sign of the chaos at the BE could be found in its plans for the repertoire, too. None of the plays mentioned in either of the production plan's two versions would go on to be produced:[151] Berghaus was thus unable to carry out the most basic tasks of a theatre's leader. However, she certainly behaved 'correctly' in the face of the GDR's last great crisis before the fall of the Berlin Wall in 1989. When the oppositional singer Wolf Biermann was expatriated from the GDR in November 1976, artists signed a petition in protest against the measure. The GDR authorities sought to limit the damage as much as possible by compelling the signatories to retract their names. Berghaus, who was not a signatory herself, demonstratively toed the party line in two meetings of the BE's senior management.[152] Yet while the District

---

[148] Dieckmann to Berghaus, 9 May 1975, AdK FDA 'Dramaturgische Papiere'.

[149] See Berghaus, in Irene Ebel, 'Protokoll zur Beratung der Arbeitsgruppe am 18. März 1976', 19 March 1976, 3 pages (2), BEA File 'Protokolle Leitungssitzungen 1973–76'.

[150] See Anon., 'Abrechnung – Plan der Aufgaben 1975', undated, n.p., BArch DR 1/17548.

[151] See Irene Ebel, 'Protokoll zur Leitungssitzung am 19.8.1976', undated, 7 pages; and Ebel, 'Protokoll zur Leitungssitzung am 21. Oktober 1976', 22 October 1976, 5 pages, both documents BEA File 'Protokolle Leitungssitzungen 1973–76'.

[152] See Irene Ebel, 'Protokoll zur Leitungssitzung am 25. November 1976', undated, 8 pages; and Ebel, 'Protokoll zur Leitungssitzung am 16. Dezember 1976', undated, 10 pages, ibid.

Leadership praised the BE's response,[153] informer Saint Just reported to the Stasi that Berghaus's argumentation to one protester had been 'flawed'.[154] It is thus difficult to know whether Berghaus's stock rose with the SED during this crucial phase.

In the end, however, Berghaus's efforts to defend herself against the power of the Brecht estate and Wekwerth failed. At a meeting of late March 1977, convened by Kurt Hager and attended by Wekwerth, Schall, Brecht-Schall, Minister Hoffmann and Ursula Ragwitz, the die was finally cast.[155] Wekwerth was to be named *Intendant* and supported by a Kollegium (Council) on which Brecht-Schall, amongst others, would sit. The latter, only a couple of weeks earlier, had still been arguing against giving Wekwerth too much power at the BE.[156] Here she suggested Peter Kupke as head director, something that explains Tragelehn's opinion of the previous chapter (see p. 253) that Kupke's uninspiring production work at the BE was opportunist. That is, he was currying favour with Brecht-Schall by promulgating her aesthetic conservatism in *Puntila* and *Chalk Circle*. Wekwerth in his autobiography recounts how Kupke believed he was to inherit the BE in 1977.[157] The SED's decision to back Wekwerth was a compromise that Brecht-Schall had to accept in order to drive out Berghaus. Hager orchestrated the public-relations side of the coup, saying that it should be emphasized 'that R. Berghaus has left the BE at her own behest on health grounds. There must be no criticism whatsoever of R. Berghaus. She is a good Communist and must not encounter any difficulties in her new position at the State Opera House'.[158]

The years of radical experiment at the BE had come to an end. The conclusion hinted at in Kenneth Tynan's article of January 1976 had finally come to pass. Berghaus's tenure as *Intendantin* had not been easy, and while her attempts to develop a post-Brechtian theatre appeared to be in tune with Honecker's cultural policies in 1971, the Party had turned on her by 1977. Ultimately, it is Berghaus's ambitious work at the BE, that both she and her protégées directed, that will be remembered. Her tactical skills, however, were not the finest: she was unable to build a

[153] See J. Kleeburg, 'Betr.: Information zur Diskussion, zu Stimmen und Meinungen zur Aberkennung der Staatsbürgerschaft von Wolf Biermann im Bereich der kulturell-künstlerischen Einrichtung... Berlin-Mitte', 22 November 1976, 10 pages (4), LAB C Rep 902 3614.

[154] Wilhelm Girod, 'Operative Information Nr. 1314/76', 2 December 1976, file p. 132, BStU MfS Bln. Abt. XX A 480–11.

[155] See Hager, 'Aktennotiz über die Fragen der Leitung des Berliner Ensembles', 29 March 1977, 2 pages, SAPMO BArch DY 30/IV B 2/2.024/102.

[156] See Hoffmann to Hager, undated, but received by Hager on 16 March 1976, ibid.

[157] See Wekwerth, *Erinnern ist Leben*, p. 288.   [158] Hager, 'Aktennotiz', p. 2.

bedrock of support at the company with which she might have combatted attacks from the Party and the estate, and her decision to commit to the BE's monopoly on staging Brecht in East Berlin made her hostage to a fortune predicated on the desires of Barbara Brecht-Schall.

The SED had backed a new *Intendant* who was politically reliable, and the SED believed that it had forged a partnership between their man and the Brecht estate in a bid to stabilize the BE and lead it back to its pre-eminent position in the GDR's cultural landscape. The compromise, however, did not solve the problem, and the stability that ensued would often be confused with stagnation.

10   A safe pair of hands: 1977–1981

Minor friction, not major tension: the initial relationship with the Brecht estate

The SED backed Manfred Wekwerth not only because he was politically reliable, but also because he was professionally capable of discharging his duties as *Intendant* of the GDR's showpiece theatre company. Wekwerth's wealth of experience as a director at the Berliner Ensemble and as the head of the Regieinstitut meant that it would be difficult for Barbara Brecht-Schall to suggest a credible alternative. While she was reported as saying that she wanted a cultural functionary to head the BE,[1] Wekwerth has written that her first choice was actually her husband, Ekkehard Schall.[2] The veracity of this claim is hinted at in comments made in the years following the upheaval of 1977. In 1979, Brecht-Schall was publicly cagey about how she viewed Wekwerth's leadership and believed that it could only be evaluated 'after several years'.[3] In a document written for the Stasi later that year, she was reported to have said that she considered Wekwerth's appointment as merely 'an "interim solution"' that would run its course in two or three years' time.[4] As it would turn out, the predicted date coincided with a moment of crisis around the BE's production of Brecht's *Trommeln in der Nacht* (*Drums in the Night*) in late 1982, an episode discussed on pp. 326–32, Chapter 11. Regardless of whether Brecht-Schall did or did not want to install Schall as *Intendant*, a move that would have given her unique access to the leadership of the BE, he was appointed Wekwerth's deputy in 1977. With him as second-in-command, any subsequent change of *Intendant* could have led to a promotion. Schall and his wife also sat on the BE's new Council, a body

---

[1] See Hoffmann to Hager, undated, but received by Hager on 16 March 1976, SAPMO BArch DY 30/IV B 2/2.024/102.

[2] See Manfred Wekwerth, *Erinnern ist Leben*, p. 288.

[3] Barbara Brecht-Schall, in Werner Hecht, '"... das muß mal gesagt werden"', *notate*, 2 (1979), pp. 1–2 (1).

[4] Arnold Klemer, 'Operative Information', 22 August 1979, file p. 129, BStU MfS AOP 15582/83, vol. 5.

not that far removed from Berghaus's ill-fated Working Group. The new leadership was without doubt a 'compromise', as Joachim Tenschert, Wekwerth's old dramaturgical collaborator, called it.[5] It reconciled the ambitions of the SED and the Brecht estate, yet a compromise, by its very nature, suggests that both sides were not entirely satisfied with the arrangement.

An early sign of the friction between the two can be found at Wekwerth's inauguration on 14 April 1977. Schall already had a commitment on this day and was unable to attend. Brecht-Schall reportedly took the SED's refusal to change the date in light of this as 'an affront' and threatened to prevent the upcoming BE tour to Venice as a sign of her disapproval.[6] The ceremony itself was low-key. As a Stasi report recorded, the change of *Intendant* 'passes off, contrary to expectations from the West, in an unsensational way i.e. without incident'.[7] Both Wekwerth and Berghaus were present, and the outgoing *Intendantin* received her due from Minister Hoffmann in his official speech. He noted how her bid to update Brecht had been undertaken 'courageously' and that this approach accounted for the 'successes and failures' of her time at the helm.[8] The relationship between the State and the Brecht estate was still uncertain, yet the Minister did add: 'the BE has to be the centre of Brecht *Pflege*'.[9] This was a nod to the heirs; the term *Pflege* ('nurture') was, as noted in the previous chapter, a conservative one, concerned more with preserving a certain tradition than with innovating. The Stasi report also notes that Hoffmann gave Wekwerth an impromptu word of warning. Apparently the Minister commented that Wekwerth left the BE 'under a cloud' and added 'we can't deny we've all got older, but you can't always equate age with wisdom'.[10] The informant acknowledged the long applause for the departing Berghaus and Wekwerth's own short and cautious speech. It is true that the speech was light on specifics, but this was only to be expected, given the time the new incumbent had to prepare. He promised a repertoire of 'diversity and fun' and observed: 'stability without change equals stagnation'.[11] Wekwerth was looking

[5] Joachim Tenschert, in Erdmut Wizisla, 'Gespräch mit Joachim Tenschert über Helene Weigel am 21.11.1983 [with Matthias Braun]', undated, 24 pages (8), HWA FH 65.
[6] Gisela Holan to Hans-Joachim Hoffmann, 11 April 1977, BArch DR 1/10124.
[7] IM Klein, 'Bericht', 9 May 1977, file pp. 4–7 (4), BStU MfS HA XX 10818.
[8] Hans-Joachim Hoffmann, 'Zur Einführung des neuen Intendanten, Gen. Prof. Dr. Manfred Wekwerth am 14.4.1977', undated, 10 pages (5), BArch DR 1/13059, vol. 1.
[9] Ibid., p. 9.
[10] Hoffmann, in IM Klein, 'Bericht', file p. 5. The following reference is taken from the same page.
[11] Wekwerth, 'Entdeckungen und Spaß', *Sonntag*, 25 April 1977.

forward to developing the BE in the context of greater coherence in its artistic direction.

Coherence was not only an artistic, but an institutional concern, and this was the reason for the establishment of the Council; the aim was to reconcile the aspirations of the State with those of the estate. By the end of 1977, Brecht-Schall said that the Council had met twice and only considered secondary issues, something confirmed by extant records. This she considered a marginalization of her influence.[12] However, when the Ministry asked Brecht-Schall to approve a document on the Council's work, which she did, she requested that two paragraphs be deleted 'because they could strain her precarious relationship with Prof. Dr Wekwerth at this time'.[13] This show of tact indicates that she understood her own position as uncertain and did not want to push her agenda too hard, something that would not be the case later in Wekwerth's *Intendanz*. In the following year, Wekwerth reminded her of the Council's duties as set out in his certificate of appointment: 'the Council will give advice to the *Intendant* in all conceptual, strategic and cultural-political matters concerning the development and further development of the BE as Brecht's theatre'.[14] Wekwerth was keen to stress that the Council's role was advisory, not managerial. Brecht-Schall, in reply to Wekwerth's letter, proposed a wider sphere of activity, including issues such as casting, new appointments and productions selected for touring, categories that clearly tried to extend the Council's role beyond its defined remit of discussing Brecht productions at the BE. She did, however, add that she agreed that the Council should function in an advisory capacity and 'nor do I think that *I* am the Council and that everything has to be discussed with *me*'.[15] This self-effacement may, again, owe something to the nascent nature of her relationship with Wekwerth as the State-backed *Intendant*. In the early 1980s, she would claim a position that collapsed the distinction between her private self and the Council.

The start of the relationship between Wekwerth and Brecht-Schall was marked by a certain tentativeness on both sides. Brecht-Schall clearly did not want to derail Wekwerth's plans from the start but, having flexed her muscles in the removal of Berghaus, she did not want to sideline herself either.

[12] See Brecht-Schall, reported in Jochen Genzel to Hoffmann, 20 December 1977, BArch DR 1/10124.
[13] [Jochen Genzel?], undated, 2 pages (1), ibid.
[14] Wekwerth to Brecht-Schall, [c. early 1978], AdK MWA 'Korr. Brecht-Erben 1977–83'.
[15] Brecht-Schall to Wekwerth, 29 January 1978, ibid.

Wekwerth's first full season: restoration and innovation

Wekwerth's first full season was an important one, not only because he sought to re-establish himself and the BE, but also because it included Brecht's eightieth birthday celebrations: the *Intendant* was charged with marking the anniversary without controversy. When the new management was announced in the spring of 1977, the West German theatre journal *Theater heute* considered Wekwerth, Schall and Brecht-Schall 'keepers of the tradition'.[16] This attribution was mostly accurate, as will be seen both in Wekwerth's production of *Galileo* and other aspects of his new repertoire, but also, true to his pledge in his inaugural speech, he introduced changes to allow young talent to direct more challenging plays.

The first new production under Wekwerth's leadership in the 1977/78 season had already been scheduled by Berghaus. Peter Kupke, one of Brecht-Schall's favourite directors, staged Brecht's adaptation of *The Tutor* in October 1977. The reading material he provided for the actors indicated that they should research the 1950 production of the play by consulting the official documentation in *Theaterarbeit* as well as the unpublished *Notate* appended, the *Modellbuch* and the reviews held in the BE's archive.[17] The backwards-looking focus roundly informed the production itself: critics argued that Kupke had been intimidated by the BE's own 'classicism', a reference to Brecht's exhortation to resist such a relationship to canonical dramas, made in 1954 with regard to his own production of *Urfaust*.[18] Other reviewers found a distinct lack of bite, a result of the reverence Kupke showed towards Brecht's *Modell*.[19] While the work was 'in no way lacking verve on the part of the actors',[20] the bulk of the reviewers felt that they were watching something limited and measured, rather than vibrant and fresh. The new leadership, however, was keen to play up the first production despite its shortcomings. Wekwerth's wife, Renate Richter, proclaimed that 'the first battle's been won' and the *Intendant* himself declared 'the BE is back!'[21]

---

[16] Anon., untitled, *Theater heute*, 5 (1977), p. 58.

[17] See Anon., '*Der Hofmeister*', undated, 56 pages (2), BEA File 75.

[18] See, for example, Peter Hans Göpfert, 'Misere im deutschen Land oder Einschüchterung durch Klassizität', *Die Welt*, 8 October 1977. Brecht's essay can be found in BFA, 23: 316–18; *BoT*, pp. 275–7.

[19] See, for example, Hans-Dieter Schütt, 'Ironisches Zeitgemälde', *Junge Welt*, 11 October 1977; and Christoph Funke, 'Ironie der Genauigkeit', *Der Morgen*, 11 October 1977.

[20] Ernst Schumacher, '*Der Hofmeister* wieder im BE', *Berliner Zeitung*, 10 October 1977.

[21] Renate Richter and Wekwerth, in Michael Stone, 'Jubel beim Berliner Ensemble', *Der Tagesspiegel*, 13 October 1977.

The next two premieres promised more because they were to be directed by fresh talent in the form of student directors, even though the productions ran the risk of being backwards-looking because the two short plays were written by GDR dramatists in the 1950s. The shows were grouped together as a double-bill under the title *Die Anfänge* ('Beginnings'). The project involved four third-year students from Wekwerth's Regieinstitut, directing in pairs on the BE's rehearsal stage. Matthias Renner and Axel Richter were allocated Heiner Müller's *Der Lohndrücker* (*The Wage Sinker*);[22] Christoph Brück and Wolf Bunge Helmut Baierl's *Die Feststellung* (*The Statement of Fact*). Bunge told me that there was no application process as such; the four directors were selected by the Regieinstitut's management.[23]

Before turning to the productions themselves, I will briefly consider Wekwerth's agenda for the project. First, he realized a plan that had been set out back in 1976 that saw the Regieinstitut as a feeder for the BE.[24] Second, he re-introduced Brecht's practice of 'learning by doing' for younger staff. Although the students were not 'assistants' as such, they were supervised by one of Wekwerth's trusted colleagues, Konrad Zschiedrich. Third, training took place in pairs with a view to developing teams, rather than individuals, as was the case in the BE of the 1960s. Berghaus wanted to encourage her young directors to find their own signature style (in German, 'Handschrift').[25] Wekwerth countered: 'a director's originality consists in his [sic] knowing his craft, himself and his times . . . In short, the blather about signature styles should be replaced by a discussion of ability'.[26] That is, he, like Brecht before him, considered that a director did not require a 'vision', but had to master the tools of the trade and combine them with a concrete relationship to the world.

This point can be seen in notes written by young director Axel Richter after the premiere of *The Wage Sinker* in January 1978. His reconstruction of the preparations he made reads like an orthodox completion of Brechtian tasks. The team first set about identifying turning points in the scenes, then moved on to work on the *Fabel*, an exercise that was

[22] The published English translation is *The Scab*, but I have chosen to offer my more literal version.
[23] Wolf Bunge, unpublished interview with the author, 18 August 2011.
[24] See Wekwerth to Ursula Ragwitz, 3 October 1976, SAPMO BArch DY 30/IV 2/2.033/115.
[25] Berghaus, in Anon., 'Sieben Fragen an Ruth Berghaus', in Irmer (ed.), *Berliner Ensemble. 1949–74*, p. 21.
[26] Wekwerth, *Theater in Diskussion: Notate Gespräche Polemiken* (Berlin: Henschel, 1982), p. 186. Essay originally published in 1978.

augmented by Richter's structural analysis of the text.[27] Rehearsals then dealt with *Arrangements* and *Gestus* as one would have expected. Yet while this process may sound mechanistic, the results were lively and engaging. A West German critic provided arguably the best sketch of the project's outcome: 'all of a sudden, you saw the Brecht School as it once was. [The directors] explored the plays with curiosity and naïvety, let loose their playfulness and included enough critical moments to make you reflect'.[28] The double-bill thus betokened orthodox Brechtianism at its fresh and inquisitive best, and confirmed Wekwerth's hopes for a generation of directors without a 'Handschrift'.

Wekwerth continued more or less with the format the following season, with one student directing *Lisa* by Paul Grazik and two directing *Prognose* (*Prognosis*) by Alfred Matusche on the rehearsal stage in April 1979. This time the project was called 'Entwicklungen' ('Developments') to convey a sense of movement with respect to the 'Beginnings' of the previous year. While the productions were far from being failures and reviewers recognized the young directors' talent, the critics also pointed to the limitations of the Brechtian process when applied to plays that did not necessarily suit it.[29] *Lisa* only ran for ten performances, *Prognose* for five, whereas the previous two shows managed twenty-two and nineteen performances, respectively. There was no third outing for the format, yet Wekwerth still supported the students once they had graduated by integrating them into the BE as directors.

The showpiece production of the anniversary season was Brecht's *Galileo Galilei*, a staging of the version written in Denmark in 1938–9 that had premiered in Zurich under this title, rather than the more familiar *Life of Galileo*. It was directed by Wekwerth and Joachim Tenschert, Wekwerth's former directing partner at the BE in the 1960s, who had been brought back as Head Dramaturge. The production team also took advice from Werner Mittenzwei, an academic and Brecht specialist, whose previously occasional relationship with the BE was formalized to run alongside his university commitments.[30] The production premiered, as one would expect, on Brecht's birthday, 10 February 1978. The version of the script completed in Denmark was far more focused on the physicist's struggle to establish the truth of his discoveries and

---

[27] See Axel Richter, 'Rekonstruktion einer Inszenierungsarbeit', February–March 1978, 15 pages (4–6), AdK Theaterdokumentation ID 900.

[28] Günther Rühle, 'Was wollt Ihr noch mit Brecht?', *Frankfurter Allgemeine Zeitung*, 18 February 1978.

[29] See, for example, Helmut Ullrich, 'Probleme zwingen zum Nachdenken', *Neue Zeit*, 11 April 1979.

[30] See Mittenzwei to Wekwerth, 18 May 1978, BEA File 83.

his attempts to disseminate them; it did not arraign him for betraying his principles as Brecht had done in 1956. The new mantra was that Galileo could only continue his work by recanting to the Inquisition.[31] Although the team was happy to work on the Danish version, Mittenzwei nonetheless acknowledged that the later version of the text would be used to supplement the original's technical weaknesses.[32]

The emphasis on Galileo's rationality bled into the production as a whole, in particular, into the carnival scene. As Wekwerth explained, the grotesque masks 'are the common people's view of their ghostly superiors. For us they are metaphors, reminiscent of Goya's painting "The Sleep of Reason Produces Monsters"'.[33] Thus, a scene that could unleash corporeality and sensuality was constrained by an insistence on metaphor (see Fig. 10.1). This detail marks an important moment in Wekwerth's direction as a whole: the body was always an index, a pointer to meaning, rather than meaning or a part of that meaning itself. His notion of *Gestus* centred on readability, not physicality. It is difficult to know quite whence his emphasis on rationality came, but it is perhaps worth noting that Wekwerth trained as a teacher of mathematics before he was invited to join the BE in 1951.

The reception of the production was mostly divided by the Berlin Wall. East German critics enjoyed a version of the text with which they were, on the whole, unfamiliar.[34] In this sense, Wekwerth was offering something new and fitting for Brecht's anniversary. In the West, however, the critics, who, of course, had greater licence, pointed to the production's political impotence with reference to the way it treated its eponymous hero. Sibylle Wirsing noted: 'the topicality of the dissident in the clutches of the authorities, at their mercy in such a way that he will always be the victim... is hardly even hinted at'.[35] This lack of a meta-level can be seen in connection with Brecht's essay 'Five Difficulties in Writing the Truth' in which the fifth difficulty is described as 'the cunning to spread the truth amongst many'.[36] There is, however, no sense that Wekwerth

[31] See Werner Mittenzwei, '*Galileo Galilei*'; and Wekwerth, 'Regie 77', in Gert Hof (ed.), '*Galileo Galilei*' von Bertolt Brecht: EineDokumentation der Aufführung des Berliner Ensembles 1978 (Berlin: Verband der Theaterschaffenden, 1982), p. 5 and pp. 18–22 (21), respectively.
[32] See Mittenzwei, '*Galileo Galilei*', in ibid., pp. 9–17 (12).
[33] Wekwerth, 'Regie 77', p. 22.
[34] See, for example, Rainer Kerndl, 'Zeittheater – parteilich und kunstvoll', *Neues Deutschland*, 13 February 1978; or Rolf-Dieter Eichler, 'Wahrheit ist gefunden – wer setzt sie durch?', *Nationalzeitung*, 13 February 1978.
[35] Sibylle Wirsing, 'Brechts Theater als gute Stube', *Frankfurter Allgemeine Zeitung*, 13 February 1978.
[36] Brecht, 'Fünf Schwierigkeiten beim Schreiben der Wahrheit', BFA, 22: 74–89 (81); *Brecht on Art and Politics*, pp. 141–56 (148).

Fig. 10.1. Wekwerth's rationalist impulse: carnival without the carniva-lesque. *Galileo Galilei*, February 1978.

was interested in a reading that reflected badly on the GDR, such as one that equated the Inquisition with the Politburo. In 1990, he noted that theatres in the GDR 'became – especially in the final years – meeting places that broke taboos every evening'.[37] Quite whether this can be applied to the BE of the late 1980s is questionable (see Chapter 11), but it was certainly not the case in 1978. The only meta-level visible to one West German reviewer was quite unintentional. He considered that Wekwerth's production was 'an expression of the embarrassment in which the GDR finds itself with respect to intellectuals and the classic

---

[37] Wekwerth, 'Revolution und Restauration', *Theater heute*, Jahrbuch (1990), pp. 144–5 (144).

author Brecht'.[38] With reference to the production's isolation from the social situation that surrounded it, one Western critic observed 'the Brecht museum is still open'.[39]

In many ways, this production is indicative of the BE's treatment of Brecht under Wekwerth's *Intendanz* as a whole. Wekwerth tried to realize a 'philosophisches Volkstheater' ('philosophical theatre for the people'), a term he traced back to his last conversations with Brecht.[40] This was not to be a cerebral theatre for intellectuals,[41] but a theatre that made philosophical issues accessible to a wider audience. In practice, however, such a theatre eschewed the corporeal and the indeterminate, and emphasized the rational, while avoiding connections with the issues of the day in the GDR. The reading of the text may have varied from Brecht's production of 1956, but the formal measures used to realize it differed little from the scheme outlined by directing student Axel Richter, above.

An aspect of the production that went unseen was Wekwerth's relationship to Brecht-Schall. In late 1977, she reportedly complained that she had not approved the Danish version the BE was using and considered this a mark of disrespect.[42] It appears, however, that Wekwerth was not deterred by the contractual position concerning the rights and went ahead with the premiere regardless. The rights were only granted in October 1978,[43] apparently because Ekkehard Schall had won praise as Galileo.[44] The point here was that Wekwerth was not afraid of Brecht-Schall and used the production itself as an argument. This strategy was frequently deployed in his dealings with the estate and distinguishes him from Ruth Berghaus, who never took on the heiress directly.

A final point to note about Wekwerth's first year in charge is that he re-introduced the format of the 'Brecht-Abend' ('Brecht Evening'), discussed on pp. 176–80, Chapter 6, and developed it to include other authors, too. That is, he promoted collections of songs, poems or short scenes that could be produced with little fuss in order to offer variety to the repertoire at relatively small cost. The 1977/78 season included two such events: one dedicated to Brecht's work for children ('Onkel Ede

[38] Heinz Ritter, 'Meister der List', *Der Abend*, 11 February 1978.
[39] Peter Hans Göpfert, 'Die Sinnlichkeit eines Schriftgelehrten', *Die Welt*, 13 February 1978.
[40] See Wekwerth, *Erinnern ist Leben*, p. 50.
[41] See Wekwerth to Schall, 11 October 1983, AdK ESA 'Dienstschreiben/Korr.', in which Wekwerth counsels against a production of Heiner Müller's *Quartett* (*Quartet*) at the BE because he thought it would only appeal to a narrow audience of intellectuals.
[42] See Jochen Genzel to Hoffmann, 20 December 1977, BArch DR 1/10124.
[43] See Wekwerth to Jürgen Gentz, 4 March 1983, BArch DR 1/1746.
[44] Wekwerth, unpublished interview with the author, 1 July 2011.

hat einen Schnurrbart...' – 'Uncle Eddy's got a Moustache...') and one to the poems and songs of GDR author Volker Braun. The latter premiered in February 1978 and was billed as 'Volker Braun Abend Nr. 1', suggesting the first in a series. Braun was a writer who had had his fair share of difficulties with the authorities. He was, however, becoming increasingly well known internationally, and so the SED was interested in bringing him back to the GDR's fold. A Stasi report reveals that the *Evening* was in fact part of a larger strategy to bind the writer more closely to the nation. Officer Wilhelm Girod noted that the show 'was able to be secured by GMS "Manfred" and official points of contact'.[45] 'Secured' meant that there was no possibility that the writings selected for the performance could provoke reactions hostile to the Party. A second *Evening* followed, but the author had to wait over two years before it premiered. Even though Braun found its content to be 'more challenging',[46] the Stasi had sent its operative, code name 'Lisa Müller', to help shape the programme in late 1978.[47] The following section considers Braun's early relationship with the BE in the light of a series of manipulations behind the scenes.

Volker Braun's first years at the BE, or the discrete charm of the Stasi

The Stasi archive contains eleven full volumes detailing operation 'Erbe' ('Legacy'). They trace the surveillance of and attempts to influence Volker Braun that started in 1975. The documents, like much in this archive, attempted to record meetings and opinions accurately, otherwise they would have had little value as intelligence. However, one should not forget that such documents were also written with intent and were pervaded by paranoid impulses and ideological inflections. The following argument thus seeks to navigate between the two aspects in order to understand the interaction between the BE and both overt and covert organs of the State.

Braun had already found himself on the wrong side of the SED in the 1960s when his play *Trucker Paul Bauch* was subject to censure at the

---

[45] Wilhelm Girod, 'Aktenvermerk für den OV "Erbe"', 27 February 1978, file pp. 185–6 (186), BStU MfS AOP 15582/83, vol. 4. All subsequent references to the many volumes on Volker Braun will appear as 'BStU Braun' followed by a volume number. The term 'GMS' is explained on p. 213, Chapter 7.

[46] Entry for 21 January 1980, in Volker Braun, *Werktage 1977–1989: Arbeitsbuch* (Frankfurt/Main: Suhrkamp, 2009), p. 262.

[47] See Girod, 'Operativplan zum OV "Erbe"', 20 November 1978, file pp. 151–8 (153), BStU Braun, vol. 1.

XI Plenum in 1965 (see p. 197, Chapter 6). It was later prevented from being performed at the BE in 1969.[48] By early 1977, two further plays, *Tinka* and *Guevara, oder der Sonnenstaat* (*Guevara, or The Sun State*) had been cancelled pre-premiere in Potsdam and at the Deutsches Theater, respectively. Braun was not an oppositional writer as such; he was a committed socialist and a member of the SED as well. However, his views of socialism were the views of an artist – curious and interrogative – qualities that would not find favour in a dogmatic totalitarian state. The authorities did not, however, view him as a lost cause and sought to reintegrate him into the GDR. This difficult end was approved as policy by the Ministry of Culture,[49] which attempted to realize its ambitions together with the Stasi. The aim was both to prevent Braun from becoming perceived as a dissident and to encourage him to identify with the GDR by experiencing the benefits of allegiance.

Joachim Walther, who has written the standard work on the Stasi's activities in the literary field, notes that after détente in the early 1970s, the Stasi started to treat the subjects of its surveillance in a deliberately differentiated fashion.[50] This meant banning some authors while publishing others, permitting some dramatists productions in the FRG while refusing others a stage in the GDR, and so forth. This approach followed a classic 'divide and conquer' strategy, and this was made explicit in a document of 1979. The document was not, however, the report of a cabal of covert agents (IMs) and Stasi handlers; it was a protocol of a meeting at the Ministry of Culture, attended by senior figures including Minister Hoffmann, and leaked to the Stasi by its own mole in the Ministry, IM Fritz. The convergence of the Ministry's and the Stasi's intentions is clear:

Continue to treat Volker Braun as an individual according to the tried and tested method, and have our efforts appear as if we concern ourselves with every individual, lest a platform for similarly minded authors take shape in this area.[51]

Walther lists a range of options open to the Stasi in its pursuit of this end, taken from a document used in training. He quotes 'singular preferment in certain negotiations' amongst other ways of gratifying writers in

[48] See [Weigel?] to Joachim Tenschert, 11 November 1969, BBA uncatalogued file 'HW Haus 69'.
[49] See Gisela Holan, 'Zum Stück *Der Große Frieden* von Volker Braun in der Inszenierung von Professor Manfred Wekwerth am Berliner Ensemble', [early 1979], 6 pages (6), SAPMO BArch DY 30/IV B 2/2/024/86.
[50] See Walther, *Sicherungsbereich Literatur*, pp. 97, 101 and 109.
[51] Captain Müller, 'Operative Information', 30 January 1979, file pp. 313–14 (314), BStU Braun, vol. 4.

order to promote 'exaggerated ambition, pronounced need for recognition . . . an overly high opinion of oneself, vanity, egotism and other such things'.[52] The Stasi was engaged in psychological warfare, and this was one weapon in its diverse armoury: flattering writers into sympathy with the GDR, its politics and its systems. And while Braun was not given carte blanche by the State and was later prevented from having certain plays performed in the GDR in the early and mid 1980s, this strategy broadly applied until 1982.

The Stasi's main instrument of influencing events and its target authors was the deployment of IMs. Manfred Wekwerth had been informing for the Stasi since 1956 as IM Manfred, and so he was in the perfect position to execute the State's plans. Later, other IMs, within and without the BE, also made their contribution. Wekwerth worked swiftly: Braun records in his diary that he was contacted in early April 1977 by the man who was still to be officially installed as *Intendant* with an offer of a permanent position at the BE.[53] Officer Girod praised Wekwerth's efforts in appointing Braun.[54] This was an important move, as another informer had reported in March that Braun considered himself relegated to the status of *persona non grata* after the cancellation of *Guevara*.[55] However, Wekwerth's role in the manipulation of Braun would assume far greater proportions in connection with the State's main project, which was – after the disappointments of early 1977 – to have Braun's work performed in the GDR and thus prevent him from playing or being cast as a dissident.

Braun's latest play, *Großer Frieden* (*The Great Peace*), had been read in draft form by IM Verlag (the German for 'publishing house') in late 1976.[56] IM Verlag was one Karl-Heinz Schmidt, a chief editor at Henschel, the GDR's only theatre publisher.[57] His work on this project extended beyond merely supplying opinions on the text, as will become clear below. The Stasi compiled an analytical report of the play in the summer of 1977 and found that Braun used his 'ideologically diffuse positions' to criticize socialism in the GDR.[58] The State found itself

52 Walther, *Sicherungsbereich Literatur*, p. 387.
53 See Braun, entry for 6 April 1977, *Werktage*, p. 48.
54 Wilhelm Girod, 'Sachstandsbericht OV "Erbe"', 12 October 1978, file pp. 145–50 (145), BStU Braun, vol. 1.
55 See Manfred Wild, 'Information', 30 March 1977, file pp. 74–5 (74), BStU Braun, vol. 4.
56 See Arnold Klemer, 'Operative Information Nr. 10/77', 5 January 1977, file pp. 6–7 (6), ibid.
57 His 'Erklärung' ('declaration') of 1967 to keep his covert discussions and reports secret is to be found on file p. 18, BStU Mfs AIM 2949/88. vol. I/1.
58 Wilhelm Girod, 'Sachstandsbericht zum OV "Erbe" – XV 760/75', 31 August 1977, file pp. 126–42 (132), BStU Braun, vol. 1.

confronted with a challenge: to produce a 'difficult' play in such a way that would not damage the GDR while convincing Braun that his work was valued and performable in the East. The report continued by both identifying and solving the problem in quick succession: 'it was necessary to find a director who can continue to work with V. Braun to dismantle these negative positions. Through covert methods, the new *Intendant* of the Berliner Ensemble was enlisted for this production'.[59] Wekwerth has directly denied any involvement in the Stasi's plans for the play,[60] although a range of documents contradict this position.

Wekwerth certainly had his work cut out. *Peace* is a play that is both thematically and formally challenging. It deals with revolution in general and explores its failure in ancient China in particular. The reasons for this failure are complex, and so the text offers little that is concrete in terms of cause and effect. The way the play treats its themes is episodic, and the language is dense, allusory and metaphorical; it is thus difficult to vouchsafe the lines' meaning. In several ways, then, *Peace* resembles Heiner Müller's *Cement*, whose production was discussed on pp. 253–9, Chapter 8. Yet Wekwerth's approach to directing associative, politically ambiguous material diverged greatly from Berghaus's. Braun had hoped for a visceral, corporeal production in which the texts were almost spoken 'in passing'.[61] That is, Braun was happy for definitive meaning to be suspended, to allow the speeches to be given without interpretation so that this process might take place in the auditorium, rather than on the stage. This, of course, was an utterly untenable position for the SED, which sought to replace ambiguity with clearly defined and readable performances.

Braun wrote in his diary that the authorities had contacted Wekwerth in January 1979: Deputy Minister Rackwitz wanted to know whether the BE still wanted to stage the play, Minister Hoffmann demanded a copy of the text, and Gisela Holan a *Konzeption* (conceptual outline).[62] Braun also noted that while Wekwerth said he would not allow officials into the theatre to monitor rehearsals, the director himself almost immediately changed one of the scenes so as to portray critical events in a more positive light. On the very same day, Wekwerth wrote to Hager to tell him that he was working hard 'to clarify the action residing in the subtext, or even to make it up'.[63] Such moves would be welcomed and encouraged

[59] Ibid.
[60] See Wekwerth, in Holger Kulick, 'Volker Braun und das Stasi-Theater', *Der Spiegel*, 26 October 2000.
[61] Entry for 27 October 1978, in Braun, *Werktage*, p. 167.
[62] Entry for 24 January 1979, ibid., p. 176.
[63] Wekwerth to Hager, 24 January 1979, SPMO BArch DY 30/IV B 2/2.024/86.

a month later. Ministry functionaries Gisela Holan and Jochen Genzel met with senior members of the BE's management, Wekwerth, Schall, Joachim Tenschert and Werner Mittenzwei, in February 1979. Braun, of course, was not in attendance. The meeting set out what was expected of the production. This can be summed up as follows:

1. Braun's 'sententiae' need to be organized into a *'story'*.
2. Volker Braun's 'mistakes' have to become the mistakes of the main character.
3. The conclusion, the failure of the revolution, is not to be portrayed as tragic, but to be historicized as unrealizable in its time.
4. The openness of Braun's language has to be closed down to prevent 'wrong interpretations'.
5. The necessity of treating the scenes 'contrary to Volker Braun's intentions' to achieve the Ministry's ideological ends.[64]

In short, every effort had to be made to turn ambiguity into certainty and the negative into the positive. The document combines practical measures with the Stasi's more general desire to allow Braun to be performed in the GDR. As a result, it would not be unfair to assert that the Ministry, the Stasi and Wekwerth co-directed *The Great Peace*.

Rehearsals started at the end of October 1978. Both Braun's diary and Stasi reports register his discomfort with the process. He noted in that same month that the directors 'want to weaken the text'.[65] Later, he was quoted as finding the production '"lacking in radicalism"' and regretted 'a serious "reduction of the relationships with the present day"'.[66] This last point could be seen in the following directorial shift of emphasis. Initially, the plan had been not to focus too much on the representation of China in order to emphasize more general issues about revolution.[67] By January 1979, the Ministry reportedly considered it important that 'Volker Braun's aspiration to update the play to address the GDR be pushed in the direction of China'.[68] That is, the Ministry wanted to criticize the Chinese party's policies of the time, rather than turn attention to its own shortcomings.

---

[64] Jochen Genzel, 'Information über ein Gespräch mit der Leitung des Berliner Ensembles zu *Großer Frieden* von Volker Braun', [received by the Ministry on 28 February 1979], 3 pages (1–2), BArch DR 1/18325.
[65] Entry for 27 January 1979, in Braun, *Werktage*, p. 178.
[66] Braun, in [Arnold Klemer?], 'Operative Information', 26 March 1979, file p. 47, BStU Braun, vol. 5.
[67] See Heinz Joswiakowski, 'Notiz zum Arbeitsgespräch *Grosser Frieden* am 16.6.1978', undated, 2 pages (1), BEA File 83.
[68] Captain Müller, 'Operative Information', 30 January 1979, file pp. 313–14 (314), BStU Braun, vol. 4.

The Ministry was certainly satisfied with the results of the rehearsal process. Gisela Holan saw the dress rehearsal and praised how the directors had found visual and poetic images 'for making the very sparse text intelligible' and approvingly acknowledged that the production avoided 'false political topicality'.[69] She also reported that she had met with a representative of the Central Committee's Cultural Department at the run-through and that they had agreed that the production could go ahead with its planned premiere on 22 April. Braun's reception of the dress rehearsal diverged somewhat from Holan's in its evaluation of the same points she had identified: 'no one could understand the play, now they're all smiles at what they've "made out of it"'.[70] While Braun also praised the scenic work that had been done and the commitment of the ensemble, it is hard to mistake his frustration at the way in which his lines had been collapsed into definitive meaning, rather than left as associative textual particles.

The production was certainly well received in the GDR. Even Friedrich Dieckmann, who, as noted in the previous chapter, had had his problems with Wekwerth while working as a dramaturge at the BE, praised Wekwerth for rescuing Brecht's theatre with his direction.[71] That the reviewers in the East reacted so favourably says much about the conditions under which they were working. The successful realization of a complex play like *Peace* led to plaudits even though, as shown above, the directors actively worked against the polysemy and ambitions of the wild text to produce a piece that had effectively been 'domesticated'.

The positive reception at home had positive effects for the BE and Braun. According to Barrie Baker, the Ministry instituted a regulation in 1978 that required the Minister's signature before any new play could be staged.[72] Wekwerth has often claimed that the Ministry never formally approved the play and thus let the BE take responsibility for the production.[73] To an extent, this is true insofar as approval was never given, yet the SED was never going to sever the link between State and theatre in the mere hope that the BE would come good. Instead, a document archived at the Ministry tells of how the company had been

---

[69] Gisela Holan, 'Betr.: Uraufführung *Großer Frieden* von Volker Braun am Berliner Ensemble', 19 April 1979, 2 pages (1), BArch DR 1/18325.
[70] Entry for 18 April 1979, in Braun, *Werktage*, p. 196.
[71] See Friedrich Dieckmann, '*Der große Frieden*', *Thüringische Landeszeitung*, 25 April 1979.
[72] See Barrie Baker, *Censorship in Honecker's Germany. From Volker Braun to Samuel Beckett* (Oxford: Peter Lang, 2007), p. 61.
[73] See, for example, Wekwerth, 'Eine Odyssee oder Der Ehrenplatz zwischen den Stühlen', in Frank Hörnigk (ed.), *Volker Braun. Arbeitsbuch* (Berlin: Theater der Zeit, 1999), pp. 140–2 (140).

granted a 'Regelung' ('dispensation') that charged it 'with making the as yet undeveloped play performable through the rehearsal process so that a production is possible'.[74] Minister Hoffmann said as much in a letter to Kurt Hager, noting that the undertaking was 'a test, to an extent' for the BE and that 'we' should do as much as possible to make it successful.[75] So, while there was indeed no official approval of the problematic text, there was no lack of official input. Such 'support' was also offered by the Stasi.

Three minor actors in the show's cast were instructed to report on anyone outside the BE who was interested in the play and to identify any moments in the text that could be turned against the GDR.[76] One of these informers was also told to investigate anyone who acted 'provocatively' at post-show discussions.[77] Wekwerth's disavowal of State participation in the production of *Peace* tacitly distanced him from interaction with official and unofficial channels. This veneer was maintained by two elements: the successful production itself, which suggested the BE's own independence as theatrical producer, and a documentation of the work, published three years after the premiere.[78] Its editor was none other than Karl-Heinz Schmidt, aka. IM Verlag, a fact noted approvingly in Braun's Stasi file.[79] There would thus be no evidence of State interference, which was, of course, to be expected, but also an assiduous cleansing of any doubt or scepticism registered by the playwright himself. Yet despite the success of the premiere and the supposedly positive effects it was to have on Braun, a secret report to the District Leadership noted in 1980 that Braun had 'reservations' with respect to his main points of contact at the BE: Wekwerth, Werner Mittenzwei and Wolfgang Pintzka.[80] It seems that the grand plan of winning Braun over to the GDR had not born the expected fruit.

It is tempting to see the Stasi as an important player behind the scenes at the BE in the light of the *Peace* affair, but this is, to my knowledge, the only time that that Ministry deliberately and extensively interfered in the

[74] Anon., 'Entwurf: Berliner Intendanten-Tagung am 6.3.1979', undated, 14 pages (9), BArch DR 1/10211.
[75] Hoffmann to Hager, 1 February 1979, SAPMO BArch DY 30/IV B 2/2.024/86.
[76] See Girod, 'Operativplan zum OV "Erbe"', file p. 155.
[77] Girod, 'Maßnahmenplan zum OV "Erbe"', 6 March 1980, file pp. 167–73 (170), BStU Braun, vol. 1.
[78] See Karl-Heinz Schmidt (ed.), *'Großer Frieden' von Volker Braun: Eine Dokumentation der Aufführung des Berliner Ensembles 1979* (Berlin: Verband der Theaterschaffenden, 1982).
[79] See Werner Muck, 'Bericht – Volker Braun', 23 December 1981, file p. 280, BStU Braun, vol. 5.
[80] [Girod], 'Parteiinformation', 27 August 1980, file pp. 188–91 (188), BStU Braun, vol. 1.

company's production work. The Stasi certainly criticized many aspects of the BE's output over the years, yet there is little evidence to suggest that it effected changes on stage directly. And while the BE provided a perfect environment for staging *Peace*, given both its traditions and the compliance of its *Intendant*, the larger operation was focused on Braun, rather than the theatre itself. Braun may have temporarily benefitted from the plan to support his work in the GDR. His even more difficult play[81] *Simplex Deutsch* was staged on the BE's rehearsal stage in April 1980 by Piet Drescher, reportedly because Braun did not want Wekwerth to water down the play as he had done with *Peace*.[82] There were still problems with the text two days before the premiere,[83] but the production hardly caused a stir and received a mixed reception with the critics. In 1982, however, Braun was offered a deal: *Tinka*, cancelled in 1977, could be performed at the BE only if he forbade a theatre in the FRG from performing his *Dmitri*, which had been proscribed in the GDR.[84] Braun refused, and the production was nonetheless staged at the BE, although Braun laconically described it as 'not good'.[85] The Stasi's attempts to influence Braun had failed. The production of *Peace* that was supposed to anchor the playwright to the SED's cultural agenda had not wholly satisfied him, and he was aware that the play's potential had not been fully realized. If such expenditure of resources on the SED's part could not secure a positive result, then future plans were also unlikely to succeed. The Stasi did not lose interest in Braun, but had to revise its objectives downwards to damage limitation: to prevent him from becoming a public dissident, rather than to convert him into an uncritical Party supporter. The idea that the manipulation of a theatrical production could bring about a fundamental change in its author proved to be completely flawed.

Notable productions in Wekwerth's early *Intendanz*

The work at the BE in Wekwerth's first four seasons was mostly solid, if not overly adventurous. It included plays from the Renaissance to the contemporary period, and there were also a couple of surprises in the repertory at this time. Wekwerth invited young directors Wolf Bunge and

---

[81] One IM called it 'counter-revolutionary' on reading the text: see IMS Peter Steinhaus, 'Information zum Berliner Ensemble', 26 February 1980, file pp. 143–4 (144), BStU Braun, vol. 5.

[82] See Manfred Wild, 'Information', 6 February 1980, file pp. 134–7 (137), ibid.

[83] See Jochen Ziller, 'Notat zur Diskussion am 24.4.1980. 14.00 Uhr', 24 April 1980, n.p., BEA File 92.

[84] See entry for 5 February 1982, in Braun, *Werktage*, p. 439.

[85] Entry for 4 December 1982, ibid., p. 497.

Christoph Brück to direct *The Taming of the Shrew*. In any other theatre, this would have been a thoroughly ordinary decision. But when one considers the extensive preparation and rehearsal of the BE's first (and as yet only) production of Shakespeare, *Coriolan* in 1964, it seems remarkable that the playwright Brecht rated above all others was entrusted to two novices. The pair had already directed the play in Cottbus as their final-year graduation project for the Regieinstitut, but found transferring their ideas to the BE difficult. Bunge told me that the ensemble had problems with improvising, and the team, in a written reflection on a difficult rehearsal process, noted that they found criticism from the actors made them 'more uncertain and inhibited'.[86] The production, which premiered in April 1980, received a lukewarm reception, no doubt partly as a result of the awkward relationship between the directors and the cast. The unsatisfactory result can also be attributed to the fact that production had become more industrial at the BE; the days of overly long rehearsals had finally gone, and a once-prized perfectionism had deferred to the need to produce more theatre.

And while the BE's output in this period mainly conformed to the SED's ideological line, the actors themselves occasionally took the opportunity to engage in more direct contact with the audience. Dario Fo's *Can't Pay? Won't Pay!* was staged in December 1978. Werner Mittenzwei wrote a report on the text that effectively saw it as a satire on consumerism in the capitalist West.[87] In performance, however, the Stasi noticed how certain of Fo's words, like 'Party' or 'government', were being used to refer to the GDR, rather than to Italy, and later that improvised, topical changes to the lines elicited spontaneous applause from the audience.[88] It seems that the BE was indeed able to enter into a dialogue with its audience through the actors' own exploitation of the live nature of performance.

The 1980/81 season opened with a contemporary Soviet play, *Blaue Pferde auf rotem Gras* (*Blue Horses on Red Grass*), written in 1979 by Mikhail Shatrov and premiered on 3 October 1980. The play is the retelling of a normal day in the life of Lenin, and seeks to present the revolutionary leader in a light that overturns official clichés. The play's

---

[86] Wolf Bunge, unpublished interview with the author, 18 August 2011; and Christoph Brück and Wolf Bunge, 'Einschätzung des Inszenierungsprozesses von *Die Zähmung der Widerspenstigen*', 17 June 1980, n.p., BEA File 93.

[87] See Mittenzwei, 'Anmerkungen zu einem Stück und zur Spielweise: *Bezahlt wird nicht von Dario Fo*', April 1978, 5 pages (2–3), BEA File 82.

[88] Anon., 'Anlage 1', [late 1979], file p. 38, BStU MfS HA XX 10818; and see Girod, 'Information', 10 December 1980, file pp. 170–1 (170), BStU MfS BV Bln. AIM 2827/89, vol. 2/1, respectively.

Fig. 10.2. Looking for the 'real' Lenin: acting students struggle with official aggrandizement and cultural dogma. *Blue Horses on Red Grass*, October 1980.

title refers to an obviously non-realistic depiction of a familiar scene. Literally, the picture is sent to Lenin, and although he says he would prefer to see brown horses on green grass, he adds that his tastes cannot become dogma. Metaphorically, the picture's unorthodox representational style reflects the aims of the play with respect to Lenin and Soviet Communism. The production was directed by Christoph Schroth as a guest from the theatre in Schwerin. From there, he had attracted Wekwerth's attention for his version of a 'philosophisches Volkstheater'.[89] Schroth was keen to engage with the provocation of the play's title and included a large troupe of students from East Berlin's drama school (that changed its name to 'Ernst Busch' in 1981). They injected a contemporary element into the production as they set about discovering the 'real' Lenin. The first scene, for example, involved the youths 'invading' a stage strewn with a plethora of Lenin busts and viewing this standardized representation with incredulity (see Fig. 10.2). They cleared the stage of the monuments and sought an escape from the institutionalized politician. Ekkehard Schall originally played Lenin, but left after a week's rehearsal.

[89] Wekwerth, 'Christoph Schroth am Berliner Ensemble', in Martin Linzer, Peter and Renate Ullrich, and Esther Undisz (eds.), *Wo ich bin, ist keine Provinz. Der Regisseur Christoph Schroth* (Berlin: Förderverein Theaterdokumentation, 2003), pp. 112–18 (112).

According to one student actor, this was because he did not agree with Schroth's approach to direction.[90] Barbara Brecht-Schall maintained that there was too little time to prepare for the premiere and that Schall withdrew due to illness.[91] Whatever the real reason was, the relationship between Brecht-Schall and Schroth would become one element in the crisis around *Drums in the Night*, discussed on pp. 326–32 of the next chapter. Schall's replacement was Arno Wyzniewski, an actor who did not resemble Lenin in the slightest. This decision further enhanced the production's central metaphor concerning the mimetic accuracy of representation.

Schroth's directorial ideas and additions were received more positively than Shatrov's more journalistic and dramaturgically weak text.[92] The production was not, however, concerned with a dialectical exploration, but proceeded 'with such easygoing directness, such freshness and passion'.[93] The agit-prop aesthetic drew plaudits from the East and amazement from the West that such directness might be used to highlight the discrepancy 'between the challenge the production presents and everyday reality [in the GDR]'.[94] The playwright himself praised Schroth's work, having seen many other productions beforehand.[95] This piece also proved remarkably popular with the audience, running for 248 performances up until March 1990 – the longest run by far of a play not written by Brecht at the BE. On the surface, then, Schroth's work represented an object lesson in iconoclasm. Yet there was more to it than met the eye.

The authorities were remarkably supportive of the play, and in January 1980 Deputy Minister Werner Rackwitz approved its place in the BE's repertoire in the year of Lenin's 110th birthday without reservation.[96] The Kreisleitung (Local Leadership) in Berlin also welcomed the play as well suited 'for educational work with our youth'.[97] The initial enthusiasm was followed up by yet more official support: Rackwitz reportedly 'considers that the play has been staged with an unmistakably

[90] See Manuel Soubeyrand, '*Blaue Pferde auf rotem Gras* oder wie ich einen Alptraum hatte', in ibid., pp. 119–24 (122–3).
[91] See Brecht-Schall to the Council and Management, 12 June 1980, AdK MWA 'Korr. Brecht-Erben 1977–83'.
[92] See, for example, Anne Braun, 'Im Namen des Glücks', *Wochenpost*, 26 September 1980.
[93] Christoph Funke, 'Ein Tag im Leben Lenins', *Der Morgen*, 6 October 1980.
[94] Michael Stone, 'Ein Tag im Leben Lenins', *Der Tagesspiegel*, 19 October 1980. The review's title is indeed the same as Funke's in the previous footnote.
[95] See Mikhail Shatrov, in Uwe-Eckart Böttger, 'Für einen praktischen Nutzen der Kunst', *Neue Zeit*, 14 February 1981.
[96] See Werner Rackwitz to Wekwerth, 3 January 1980, BArch DR 1/10215.
[97] Gotthard Schicker to Lothar Witt, 26 February 1980, LAB C Rep 903–01–04 1237.

positive political message'.[98] Two IMs with great theatrical experience provided the Stasi with the opinion that the play was being directed 'politically responsibly',[99] which meant that it did not criticize SED or Soviet policies, although the report also noted that 'politically negatively minded spectators' might applaud points when Lenin attacked dogma and bureaucracy. After the premiere, no less a figure than Kurt Hager was reported to have enjoyed the show.[100] That said, rumours circulated that the production was to be cancelled after a closed performance for the Central Committee in December 1980.[101] The production clearly caused an amount of anxiety, but was deemed performable all the same. Indeed, the head of the Central Committee's Cultural Section recommended Shatrov's next play on Lenin to the BE in 1982.[102] What one might conclude about this production is that it offered a simulacrum of political theatre, a feel-good show that gave the illusion of change while the GDR went about its normal business. This opinion is confirmed by the date of the production's removal from the repertoire. Schroth himself insisted on its immediate withdrawal three months after the fall of the Berlin Wall claiming that 'with the best will in the world [the production] no longer keeps up with the demands of the times'.[103] The environment that had been so conducive to the production's success had changed too radically for even the director himself to approve further performance.

A production of a rather different hue led to immediate censure in 1981, however. Perhaps the word 'production' is a little overblown here: the controversy concerned a BE project that was not intended for the general public. In mid 1980, Wekwerth made a proposal to the Ministry of People's Education. He wanted the BE to stage one of Brecht's learning plays with school pupils for National Teacher's Day in February 1981, with a possible plan to film their work to support teaching.[104] Later that year, the plan had slightly changed in that the pupils from different schools would stage scenes from Brecht's *Furcht und Elend des Dritten*

[98]   Anon., 'Vermerk', 1 August 1980, file p. 47, BStU HA XX 10818.
[99]   Girod, 'Information – Aufführung des Theaterstückes *Blaue Pferde auf rotem Gras* von Michail Schatrow im Berliner Ensemble', 12 September 1980, file pp. 42–3 (43), ibid.
[100] See First Lieutenant Feig, 'die [*sic*] Inszenierung des Berliner Ensemble [*sic*], *Blaue Pferde auf rotem Gras*', 5 November 1980, file pp. 50–1 (50), ibid.
[101] See Anon., 'Information über eine Inszenierung des Berliner Ensemble [*sic*]', 29 December 1980, file p. 53, ibid.
[102] See Wekwerth to Hoffmann, 8 February 1982, BEA File 'Wekwerth 1977–90 BE Gesch.'
[103] Christoph Schroth to the BE Management, 8 February 1990, BEA File 'Schriftverkehr Christoph Schroth'.
[104] See Liesel Rumland, 'Aktennotiz über ein Gespräch bei Genossen Prof. Wekwerth am 20.6.80 in Beantwortung seines Briefes an die Genn. Minister vom 18.3.80', 24 June 1980, 2 pages, BArch DR 2/51844.

Reiches (*Fear and Misery of the Third Reich*).[105] Wekwerth outlined the aims of the project in an interview:

> we believe that fascism gets dangerous when it isn't recognized as such any more . . . People think they know all about it and they no longer concern themselves with the bacillus that infiltrates people's everyday lives and families.[106]

Unfortunately for Wekwerth, these aims were to be realized all too well by one group of pupils.

Six groups from different schools in East Berlin, ranging from the second to the tenth class, were involved in the one-off performance on 28 March 1981 entitled 'Schüler spielen für Schüler' ('Pupils Perform for Pupils'). Everything went well until the final section, which included the episode 'Der Spitzel' ('The Spy'). Brecht's scene deals with the suspicion within a family that their child is a secret Nazi informer. An anonymous report written after a 'debate conducted with great passion' that followed the performances, noted that the scenes were 'directly linked to contemporary material from today's pupils about their dissatisfaction and problems with socialist schooling and the State; their programme could just as well have been called *Fear and Misery of the GDR*'.[107] The author reported that the scenes themselves were well received, and that director Günter Schmidt and the pupils blamed each other for providing the impetus behind the work. The post-mortem in the Ministry of People's Education concluded that the scenes were 'judged objectively as a political provocation'.[108] While blame still shuttled back and forth between director and pupils, the Ministry maintained that the latter at least had learned an important lesson: 'that even in the creative field, you can't do whatever you want'.[109]

This project was, of course, minor – a single performance on a single day, never intended to be repeated. A published report and a series of documents on the project made no reference the debacle, of course.[110] Yet the scenes acted out by one group drew too close a connection between the everyday fascism of the Nazis and the pupils' experience

---

[105] See Liesel Rumland, 'Aktennotiz zur Zusammenarbeit der Volksbildung mit dem Brecht-Zentrum und dem Berliner Ensemble', 11 September 1980, 3 pages (2), ibid.

[106] Wekwerth, in Werner Hecht, 'Wie es mit dem Berliner Ensemble weitergeht', *notate*, 5 (1980), pp. 1–3 (2).

[107] Anon., '"Nur danenben – oder bitterer Eigentor?"', 29 March 1981, file pp. 241–3 (241), BStU MfS BV Bln. AIM 2827/89, vol. 2/1.

[108] Dr Bauer, 'Aktennotiz zur Klärung der im Zusammenhang mit der Schüleraufführung am Berliner Ensemble in der Kl. 10b der Karl-Grünberg-Oberschule aufgetretenen politisch-ideologischen Probleme', 26 May 1981, 3 pages (1), BArch DR 2/51844.

[109] Ibid., p. 2.

[110] See Anon., 'Schüler spielen für Schüler', *notate*, 4 (1981), pp. 3–5.

of life in the GDR. *Blue Horses* and this project exemplify the limits of political theatre at this time: the former's *apparently* critical treatment would always trump the latter's direct engagement with the issues of the day.

Waiting in the wings: the muted activities of Barbara Brecht-Schall

The Brecht estate was content to give Wekwerth time to establish himself at the BE, and despite the initial problem with the rights to *Galileo Galilei*, Brecht-Schall did not initiate any major actions against the new leadership in its first four seasons. At the time, she was not only involved in the BE's Council, but also in an Advisory Group. This was set up in 1977 in connection with the Academy of Arts to deal with issues concerning rights to staging Brecht's plays after the ructions of late 1976 (see pp. 289–91, Chapter 9). The SED originally planned to integrate Brecht-Schall into the thinking behind the resolution passed by the Council of Ministers in 1971 so that the Academy could administer the rights in concert with the heiress. The underlying criterion for approval was that proposed productions were staged through 'the realization of Brecht's socialist realist position'.[111] That the draft document was passed to Erich Honecker for approval shows just how important the matter was to the Party as a whole.[112] Reportedly, Brecht-Schall found the Group superfluous, but would support it if she had the final say.[113] Minister Hoffmann was reluctant to give her such power in an earlier discussion of the Group's remit,[114] although she gained it all the same after a visit to Honecker in 1978.[115] It should be remembered that most of the discussions took place before Wekwerth was appointed *Intendant*, and once he took up that position, the Advisory Group mainly carried out its work as intended. The next chapter will consider how Brecht-Schall tried to use it to influence BE policy more directly.

However, even while the Group was running fairly smoothly, Brecht-Schall still sought to expand her role in decision-making at the BE. Having reproached Wekwerth for passing on her private correspondence

---

[111] Anon., 'Arbeitsordnung der Beratergruppe "Bertolt Brecht"', undated, 3 pages (2), SAPMO BArch DY 30/IV B 2/2.024/102.
[112] See Ursula Ragwitz to Erich Honecker, 28 February 1977, ibid.
[113] See Hoffmann to Hager, received by Hager on 16 March 1977, ibid.
[114] See Hoffmann to Hager, 2 December 1976, ibid.
[115] See Anon., 'Information zur Entwicklung der Kontroverse zwischen Frau Barbara Brecht-Schall und dem Berliner Ensemble über die Inszenierung von *Trommeln in der Nacht*', [March or April 1983], 5 pages (5), SAPMO BArch DY 30/27409.

on Council business to a third party in the SED in January 1980,[116] she revised her opinion in July, grasping the opportunity to go beyond the Council on matters concerning Brecht and the BE. She was now of the opinion 'that the Ministry can only act properly if it's informed at all times by all sides'.[117] She had previously been in contact with the Ministry on a variety of matters, however, and put forward her plans for plays by Brecht for the 1979/80 season when she found that his work did not appear in the BE's original document, for example.[118] One of her hobby horses was finding work for director Peter Kupke, whom Wekwerth would not permit to direct *The Threepenny Opera* in 1978.[119] Wekwerth had already tried to rescue Kupke's *Tutor* in 1977 by taking over the final rehearsals.[120] Kupke directed *Mother Courage* in 1978, again with Wekwerth's help as the premiere approached,[121] but his directorial career at the BE came to an end when Wekwerth cancelled his production of Ben Jonson's *Bartholomew Fair* in late 1979, due to its poor quality.[122] Kupke subsequently worked abroad in Scandinavia and the Baltic before leaving the GDR illegally in May 1982. At that time, the authorities would not grant him a long-term visa.[123] Unfortunately for Kupke, the Central Committee did not esteem his talents as commensurate with those of directors like Manfred Karge or B. K. Tragelehn, who had been issued with the relevant documents, and Hager insisted he either return to the GDR or renounce his citizenship.[124] The only support he received, according to a Stasi report, came from the Brecht estate.[125] Wolfgang Pintzka, another of Brecht-Schall's favoured directors, was also being given little to do at the BE, and he too started directing in Scandinavia in the early 1980s.

Instead of engaging Brecht-Schall's favourites, Wekwerth promoted directors he trusted and whose work he valued, such as Regieinstitut

---

[116] See Brecht-Schall to Wekwerth, 15 January 1980, AdK MWA 'Korr. Brecht-Erben 1977–83'.
[117] Brecht-Schall to Wekwerth, 9 July 1980, ibid.
[118] See Jochen Genzel, 'Gespräch mit Barbara Schall am 15.1.1979', undated, pp. 3 (1–2), BArch DR 1/1746.
[119] See Brecht-Schall to Wekwerth, 22 January 1978, AdK MWA 'Korr. Brecht-Erben 1977–83'.
[120] Wekwerth, unpublished interview with the author, 1 July 2011.
[121] See Wekwerth, 'Brief an Gisela May [of 11 September 1978]', in Gert Hof (ed.), *'Mutter Courage und ihre Kinder' von Bertolt Brecht: Eine Dokumentation der Aufführung des Berliner Ensembles 1978* (Berlin: Verband der Theaterschaffenden, 1981), pp. 64–5.
[122] See entry for 1 November 1979, in Braun, *Werktage*, p. 235.
[123] Peter Kupke to Ursula Ragwitz, 11 January 1982, SAPMO BArch DY 30/23261.
[124] See Hager to Ragwitz, 28 January 1982, ibid.
[125] See Girod, 'Operative Information', 24 March 1982, file p. 314, BStU MfS BV Bln. AIM 2827/89, vol. 2/1.

director Konrad Zschiedrich and recent graduate Carlos Medina, a Chilean refugee from Augusto Pinochet's regime. The depletion of allies amongst the directors at the BE meant that Brecht-Schall had less possibility of realizing her plans because she could not nominate directors she preferred. The combination of this marginalization and her own thoughts on Wekwerth's 'interim' status as *Intendant* proved explosive in 1982 when she tried to prevent the production of an early play by Brecht.

11 Crisis and stagnation: 1981–1989

A series of flops

Wekwerth's final production of the 1980/81 season, directed together with Joachim Tenschert, was the notoriously difficult *Turandot*. One analysis written in preparation for the show pointed out that 'Tui *Haltungen* as we encounter them even today in the GDR often conceal themselves by calling themselves "socialist"'.[1] This potentially critical stance was not realized in the final production, presumably because it broke the implicit compact between theatre and State, and the lengthy premiere on 22 March 1981 elicited boos and an inappropriate gesture (a raised middle finger) from Wekwerth in reply.[2] The production ran for a mere seventeen performances. Brecht, as the centrepiece of the BE's repertoire, was no longer the dynamo that powered the company forward. The lack of confidence in staging Brecht may be found in a proposal for future productions in 1982: Brecht was represented once, in his complicated fragment *Fatzer*, and then only as the last of six plays under consideration.[3] As it turned out, *Fatzer* was finally staged five years later, but it fared better than the five other suggestions: to my knowledge none even entered the rehearsal phase. Barbara Brecht-Schall was not at all pleased with the planning document and, in a letter to Wekwerth, wrote of her incredulity on hearing the following from Wekwerth and Tenschert: *'we can't do anything with Brecht any more, we thus have to make use of other authors and plays'*.[4] The Ministry was also disappointed with the BE. Minister Hoffmann wrote to his counterpart in the USSR to apologize for the fact that the BE would not be touring the Soviet Union as

---

[1] Anon., 'Zur Fassung 1980', undated, n.p., BEA File 97.
[2] See Jürgen Beckelmann, 'Die Kunst des Speichelleckens', *Süddeutsche Zeitung*, 1 April 1981; and Ernst Schumacher, 'Es tanzten die Puppen aber nicht der Kongreß', *Berliner Zeitung*, 26 March 1981.
[3] See Anon., 'Spielplan für die Produktionszeit 1982', undated, 6 pages, LAB C Rep 902 4573.
[4] Brecht-Schall to Wekwerth, 20 January 1982, SAPMO BArch DY 30/18986.

planned 'because, due to staff problems, we cannot currently guarantee the requisite quality in the work of the Ensemble'.[5]

The potential solution to the problem of staging Brecht in an original and engaging way came later in 1982. Initially, the BE had sought to realize a plan that dated back to 1980. The influential Italian director of Brecht, Giorgio Strehler, had been invited to direct *The Threepenny Opera*, but the plan had been put back to 1981.[6] Brecht had seen Strehler's production of the same play in 1956 and, as a mark of his approval, jokingly invited the director to stage his complete works.[7] By mid 1980, the plan had changed, but nonetheless bubbled with novelty and energy: Dario Fo was to replace Strehler, and Brecht-Schall was excited and keen to see what the commentators would make of such a production in the theatre they had labelled a museum.[8] Critics in the West often blame the Brecht estate for preventing Fo from modernizing the text and the songs,[9] but this, perhaps surprisingly, was not the case. Fo had been in discussion with the BE and had proposed to update the text for a contemporary capitalist setting. He foresaw an emphasis on the drugs market as an example of how gangsters administer the product and banks provide funding while remaining in the shadows.[10] The estate agreed to textual changes 'while keeping for the most part to Brecht's original'.[11] Fo met senior staff and Brecht-Schall in early March 1981, and the meetings appear to have gone well. The problem was not with Brecht's estate, but with Kurt Weill's. Brecht-Schall had apparently gained tacit approval to change orchestration and tempi from Lotte Lenya, Weill's widow, in a telephone conversation.[12] However, Lenya was adamant that this was not that case and forbade Fo's plan to modernize the music.[13] When Fo arrived on 13 April 1981, he brought an Italian version of the first half of his adaptation that only retained 30 per cent of Brecht's lines. He intended to complete the second half during rehearsal. The version

---

[5] Hoffmann to Piotr Demichev, 16 July 1982, SAPMO BArch DY 30/18778.
[6] See Werner Rackwitz to Wekwerth, 3 January 1980, BArch DR 1/10215.
[7] See Brecht to Giorgio Strehler, 10 February 1956, BFA, 30: 428.
[8] See Brecht-Schall to Wekwerth, 1 July 1980, AdK MWA 'Korr. Brecht-Erben 1977–1983'.
[9] See, for example, Anon., 'ADN-Information', 10 July 1981, 2 pages, DY 30/18986; or Jürgen Beckelmann, 'Politischer Wert gleich Null', *Süddeutsche Zeitung*, 10 October 1981.
[10] See Jochen Ziller, '*Dreigroschenoper* – Gespräch am 28.2.1981', 2 March 1981, 2 pages (1), BEA File 'Dario Fo + DGO'.
[11] This and subsequent information is found in S. Wirsching, 'Information zur Spielplanvorhaben *Dreigroschenoper*', 19 April 1981, 3 pages, LAB C Rep 902 4573.
[12] See Brecht-Schall to Alfred Schlee, 6 March 1981, BEA File 'Dario Fo + DGO'.
[13] See Lenya's view, reported in Oktavian von Spitzmüller to Wolfgang Schuch, 10 March 1981, ibid.

pleased nobody at the BE because it strayed too far from Brecht's text and was simply considered 'not acceptable'.[14] After another meeting with Fo, Brecht-Schall suggested that they pursue one of two avenues. The BE could continue with a production of *The Threepenny Opera* 'after Bertolt Brecht by Dario Fo', but that would require both Lotte Lenya's permission for Weill's music to be used in a new setting and the input of one of the GDR's best writers to translate the new text into a German worthy of Brecht.[15] The other option involved a new staging of the play as written, yet Brecht-Schall believed that the BE did not have a suitable director and told Wekwerth: 'and don't even think about [Konrad] Zschiedrich', who had directed Brecht's *Man Equals Man* at the BE that February. Presented with the choice, most of the management and the ensemble were reported to have preferred the second option although Fo was invited to return to his text with a view to returning to his plans in early 1982. Fo remained in Italy with a work called *L'Opera Dello Sghignazzo* (*The Opera of the Sneering Laugh*), 'the freest of adaptations of *The Threepenny Opera*', as Paolo Puppa puts it.[16]

The BE was left with an obligation to stage *The Threepenny Opera* because the company had agreed to take it with them on tour to Greece in the summer of 1981 in return for valuable hard foreign currency. Wekwerth and Zschiedrich assembled all the directors they could muster to stage the production as a seven-person collective, with Ekkehard Schall playing the lead, Mack the Knife. The Greek reviews were overwhelmingly positive.[17] Wolf Bunge, who was part of the directing team, told me that the plan had been merely to cobble together the production for Greece and to leave it at that.[18] Wekwerth, however, brought the production back to East Berlin where it premiered on 2 October 1982 and received a thorough panning. Critics understandably resented the fact that the 1928 production had served as a model,[19] called the booing of Schall 'understandable', and noted that none of the directors dared to appear at the curtain call.[20] By March 1982, Schall dropped out and

[14] Karl-Claus Hahn, 'Hitparade mit zuviel Zwischentext', *notate* 5 (1981), pp. 8–9 (8).
[15] Brecht-Schall to Wekwerth [April 1981], AdK MWA 'Korr. Brecht-Erben 1977–1983'. The following quotation is also taken from this letter.
[16] Paolo Puppa, 'Tradition, Traditions, and Dario Fo', in Joseph Farrell and Antonio Scuderi (eds.), *Dario Fo: Stage, Text, and Tradition* (Cardondale: Southern Illinois University Press, 2000), pp. 181–96 (184).
[17] For a selection, see Anon., 'Sorgfältig gearbeitet, aber . . . ', *notate*, 1 (1982), p. 8.
[18] Wolf Bunge, unpublished interview with the author, 18 August 2011.
[19] See, for example, Ernst Schumacher, '"Harmlos!" heißt das Stichwort', *Berliner Zeitung*, 6 October 1981.
[20] Christoph Funke, 'Ohne Schärfe, Spaß und Protest', *Der Morgen*, 5 October 1981.

was replaced by Stefan Lisewski.[21] A project with such high hopes had not merely failed, it had failed spectacularly. Unlike the unwieldy *Turandot*, *The Threepenny Opera* was an absolute favourite, and the impotent production very much suggested that the BE had run out of ideas with respect to its founder and inspiration.

The rest of the season was uneven. An adaptation of Antoine de Saint-Exupery's *The Little Prince*, directed by Carlos Medina, was a decent success with a thoroughly respectable 158 performances and a gently positive response from the critics, but the production of Friedrich Dürrenmatt's *Die Physiker* (*The Physicists*) was a critical disaster. In the original, a physicist makes a discovery so great that he voluntarily signs himself into a care home to prevent his ideas from falling into the hands of the superpowers. Agents from the USA and the USSR infiltrate the home and, to Dürrenmatt, they are both as bad as each other. Such a position was impossible to represent in the GDR, as a conceptual document made clear. The BE refused 'a lack of ambiguity since we consider it an inadmissible simplification'.[22] According to one review, the Western agent was clearly Western, while the Eastern one's provenance was left unclear.[23] Another bemoaned the lack of edge and precision, the trademarks of the BE.[24] The sloppy, aimless work did nothing to enhance the company's profile. The next major production was also a disappointment. Schall had proposed Hanns Eisler's *Johann Faustus*, the text that had been banned as a rehearsed reading at the BE in 1968 (see pp. 209–11, Chapter 7). Wekwerth defended it to the Minister in February 1982,[25] and it premiered on 2 October. This grand coup, however, was nothing of the sort, and critics contrasted its sumptuous set and stage machinery with its empty content; one reviewer called the production a 'Torso'.[26] The lack of a solid success, let alone a hit at the BE, led to consternation, particularly from the Brecht estate. Against a background of disappointment, Brecht-Schall decided to move against the next major Brecht project.

A molehill becomes a mountain: the BE's second attempt at the early Brecht

Brecht's *Trommeln in der Nacht* (*Drums in the Night*), a play written in 1919 against the background of the Spartacist Uprising when workers

[21] See Anon., 'Übernahme', *notate* 2 (1982), p. 12.
[22] Freya Klier, 'Konzeption', undated, 7 pages (5), BEA File 100.
[23] See Ernst Schumacher, '*Die Physiker* ohne Nutzen', *Berliner Zeitung*, 1 April 1982.
[24] See Helmut Ullrich, 'Halbherzig und ohne Aussagekraft', *Neue Zeit*, 6 April 1982.
[25] See Wekwerth to Hoffmann, 8 February 1982, BEA File 'Wekwerth 1977–90 BE Gesch.'.
[26] Ingrid Seyfahrt, 'Eislers *Johann Faustus*', *Sonntag*, 24 October 1982.

tried to seize power in Germany, had its premiere late in the GDR: on 30 January 1982. It was directed by Christoph Schroth at the theatre in which he had made his name, the Mecklenburgisches Staatstheater in Schwerin. Wekwerth had greeted Brecht-Schall's approval of the project in 1981 and signalled his intention to use the production as a test-run for a production at the BE.[27] Schroth's *Drums* was a success, and so, on the back of that and the popularity of his BE hit *Blue Horses* (discussed on pp. 315–18, Chapter 10) the director was invited to direct as a guest and to use his production in Schwerin as a basis for work at the BE.

Brecht-Schall first intervened privately with Wekwerth in early October 1982. She criticized the casting of Martin Seifert (see Fig. 11.1), whose Saxon accent displeased her, and invoked what she called her 'most wide-ranging right of veto'.[28] In the same letter, she acknowledged that a compromise would be possible with Schroth, a director she admired. Her view was made public shortly afterwards at a meeting of the BE's Council. Here she was the only one to raise an objection, and Wekwerth reminded her that the Council played a purely advisory role. She, in turn, reminded the Council that she had the right to withdraw the performing rights, which had not actually been granted at the time.[29] A day earlier, the Ministry held a meeting with the BE's management at which Wekwerth reportedly spoke, with respect to Brecht-Schall's objection, 'of an attempted power struggle'. Deputy Minister Martin Meyer assured Wekwerth of the Ministry's full support for him and confirmed that casting was 'the sole responsibility of the *Intendant*'.[30] Further official backing emerged when Gisela Holan wrote to Brecht-Schall in November, telling her that the Ministry considered Seifert 'sound' as the male lead, Kragler. Holan also emphasized how important it was to have a new Brecht production for his eighty-fifth birthday the following year.[31] Again, it is worth noting how the GDR's fixation with marking anniversaries played right into Brecht-Schall's hands: while the rhetorical tactic was designed to pressurize the rights holder by laying a potential failure squarely at her door, it actually revealed how desperate the State was to celebrate without incident.

By February 1983, an attempt at a compromise had been reached. Brecht-Schall was to see a run-through as evidence of the good work done

---

[27] See Wekwerth to Brecht-Schall, 25 September 1981, AdK MWA 'Korr. Brecht-Erben 1977–1983'.

[28] Brecht-Schall to Wekwerth, 4 October 1982, ibid.

[29] Heinz Joswiakowski, 'Ergänzung zum Protokoll der Kollegiumssitzung vom 6.10.1982', 18 October 1982, n.p., ibid.

[30] Both quotations: Bernd Spitzer, 'Aktennotiz', 8 October 1982, 2 pages (1), BArch DR 1/1746. The meeting itself took place on 5 October 1982.

[31] Gisela Holan to Brecht-Schall, 15 November 1982, ibid.

Fig. 11.1. Problematic protagonist: Martin Seifert plays Kragler, a decision that provoked Barbara Brecht-Schall into action. *Drums in the
Night*, March 1983.

so far. The afternoon, however, was not a success: she criticized Seifert, the set design and the inclusion of songs, but again she was the only dissenting voice.[32] In a letter to Wekwerth, Brecht-Schall acknowledged that they needed to find a way of cooperating that involved her accepting his rights as *Intendant* and he respecting hers as rights holder and head of the Academy's Advisory Group on Brecht.[33] This call for balance was actually nothing of the sort. Wekwerth had a theatre to run and was sanctioned to make a series of artistic decisions by his employer, the State. Brecht-Schall, on the other hand, had the single right to permit or to refuse the performing rights to Brecht's works in Berlin. This is because the main rights issue for the rest of the GDR was settled by Brecht himself in a general agreement with the GDR publisher Henschel.[34] Brecht-Schall, however, had given herself the right to approve the director and the lead actors in productions of Brecht's plays in Berlin and, as noted in the previous chapter, had been lobbying for a more active role for the Council in more general matters concerning the running of the BE. She had cleverly engineered herself into a position of great influence at the BE by exploiting her limited power regarding rights in Berlin.

The premiere, originally planned for Brecht's birthday on 10 February, had now been pushed back to 19 March. Ahead of that date, Brecht-Schall's lawyer contacted Wekwerth to remind him that no contract granting the rights to *Drums* had been signed by his client.[35] Wekwerth replied by return and set out his position. The BE had supplied the Advisory Group with the relevant papers at the end of October 1982 to approve or contest the production, but the Group only met on 10 January 1983, a mere month before the intended premiere. He wrote that the criterion used by the Group, that Brecht be performed in the context of the politics he had supported, had been satisfied. He also reminded the lawyer of the precedent established in 1978 regarding *Galileo*, in which many performances took place ahead of official approval.[36] This was a robust rebuttal, and shortly afterwards Wekwerth instructed his head of administration, Rolf Stiska, to go ahead with the premiere because there were neither copyright not artistic reasons to block it. He also noted that the stakes were high; while he acknowledged the estate's important contribution to the Council, he contemplated the consequences of a triumph for Brecht-Schall: 'in such an event, I no longer see myself able to lead the

[32] See Sigrid Kunze, 'Protokoll einer Beratung mit Mitgliedern der Leitung, der Parteileitung, des Kollegiums und des KÖR am 3.2.1983', undated, 2 pages (2), ibid.
[33] See Brecht-Schall to Wekwerth, 3 February 1982, ibid.
[34] See Hager to Honecker, 21 June 1983, BArch DR 1/13525a.
[35] See Jürgen Gentz to Wekwerth, 3 March 1983, BArch DR 1/1746.
[36] See Wekwerth to Jürgen Gentz, 4 March 1983, ibid.

Berliner Ensemble in accordance with my socialist duties and would have to call for my immediate removal'.[37] Wekwerth has described the *Drums* affair as 'Krach' ('a quarrel'), not 'Krise' ('a crisis'),[38] but this document shows just how precarious the situation was. One wonders whether it ever dawned on Wekwerth that the boot was now on the other foot: having allied himself with Brecht-Schall to depose Ruth Berghaus, he now found *himself* fighting a battle for survival as *Intendant* at the hands of the estate. He had, however, an ace or two up his sleeve that gave him the confidence to stand up to Brecht-Schall. The matter of the rights had already been assessed by the Academy for the prospect of an appearance in court, and it found that the BE had a water-tight case.[39] Similarly, the Ministry concluded that a civil action was unlikely to succeed given the way the BE had behaved with respect to applying for the rights and following proper procedure.[40]

Brecht-Schall was also applying pressure to the highest office of the State. She wrote to Erich Honecker twice in March. On the first occasion, she proposed that the Advisory Group be dissolved and that she be handed sole responsibility for approving the rights to Brecht productions in East Berlin.[41] She then informed Honecker about the plan to stage *Drums* without a contract, just for his information, as it were.[42] As a result, Honecker involved the SED's cultural supremo, Kurt Hager. He wrote to Brecht-Schall to tell her that the Central Committee was neither able nor obliged to intervene in a matter between the estate and the BE, and suggested a meeting with the Minister instead. He also asked her to wait until the premiere to see what the audience made of the production.[43] She, however, had already dismissed this argument the day before in a letter to Wekwerth in which she reminded him that the production of *Miss Julie* in 1975 had been a great success with the audience despite its major artistic and political failings in her eyes.[44] On the eve of the premiere, she threatened a lawsuit that strove for an injunction preventing the performance and used an argument similar to those used by Weigel in the struggle for the *Probenhaus* in 1954 (see pp. 125–6, Chapter 4): that

[37] Wekwerth to Rolf Stiska, 7 March 1983, AdK MWA 'Korr. Brecht-Erben 1977–1983'.
[38] Wekwerth, unpublished interview with the author, 1 July 2011.
[39] See Wekwerth to Gisela Holan, 8 March 1983, AdK MWA 'Korr. Brecht-Erben 1977–1983'.
[40] See Erika Zeißler, untitled, 15 March 1983, n.p., ibid.
[41] See Brecht-Schall to Honecker, 1 March 1983, SAPMO BArch DY 30/27409.
[42] See Brecht-Schall to Honecker, 14 March 1983, ibid.
[43] See Hager to Brecht-Schall, 17 March 1983, ibid.
[44] See Brecht-Schall to Wekwerth, 16 March 1983, AdK MWA 'Korr. Brecht-Erben 1977–1983'.

such ructions would draw the attention from the eyes of the world.[45] For the time being, the authorities remained undaunted, and the production went ahead as planned.

To the outside world, the premiere took place as usual, and there was no reference, even in the Western media, that had at times gained privileged information through contacts at the BE,[46] to the struggle that had unfolded behind the scenes. The production was mostly received as weaker than Schroth's celebrated *Drums* in Schwerin.[47] Seifert himself drew no criticism; reviewers only noted that his character had been presented more sympathetically than critically in Berlin.[48] Schroth had merely demonstrated that he had found it difficult to make the leap from the provinces to the capital and provided another middling production for a theatre used to better.

The battle for the premiere revealed a number of interesting aspects. Brecht-Schall was no longer prepared to use the argument deployed against Berghaus's Brecht productions – that they misrepresented Brecht's political aims. This principle was the central criterion for the Advisory Group, but could not be deployed against *Drums*. Her other argument against Berghaus, that she had adulterated Brecht's play (in that case, *The Mother*), had also been discarded, albeit tacitly. The following year, Brecht-Schall permitted *enfant terrible* Frank Castorf to direct *Drums* in Anklam. The production was cancelled because of tensions between the local SED and Castorf himself; it was thus not for his maverick treatment of the text, and Laura Bradley reports how Brecht-Schall actually viewed the party's ban as an attack on Brecht.[49] What emerges is that she was serving her own ends and not necessarily those she had previously imputed to Brecht, and that she would use whichever strategies were required to achieve them.

With respect to *Drums* at the BE, these 'ends' are not unambiguous. The Minister's own analysis is illuminating here. He observed that Brecht-Schall's attacks on Wekwerth had increased since he was elected president of the Academy of Arts in the summer of 1982. Hoffmann

---

[45] See Brecht-Schall to Hoffmann, 17 March 1983, BArch DR 1/13525a.
[46] See, for example, Wilhelm Girod, 'Abschlußbericht', 28 April 1982, file p. 288, BStU MfS AIM 6538/71, vol. 1. Here the Stasi handler acknowledged that an IM at the BE had become unreliable and had been passing on information to the West Berlin journalist Horst Wenderoth.
[47] See, for example, Christoph Funke, 'Psychologie des Spießbürgers', *Der Morgen*, 22 March 1983; or Michael Stone, 'Absage an die Revolution', *Der Tagesspiegel*, 8 April 1983.
[48] See, for example, Ernst Schumacher, 'Gedämpfter Trommeln Klang', *Berliner Zeitung*, 24 March 1983.
[49] See Bradley, *Cooperation and Conflict*, p. 225.

believed that such an official vote of confidence in Wekwerth suggested a diminution of Brecht-Schall's influence at the BE and the possibility of realizing 'her old plan to install Ekkehard Schall as *Intendant*'.[50] He also noted after a meeting with Brecht-Schall that she not only positioned herself 'as the immediate successor to Brecht and Weigel concerning the rights, but also that only she was competent to judge whether Brecht was being correctly staged and acted at the BE'. It may be, then, that Brecht-Schall used the relatively minor premiere to assert different, but related aspects of her role as heiress. She chose both to fight to have her voice heard by the management of the BE and to establish herself as an authority on the performance of Brecht's plays. Suffice it to say, neither of these were rights, nor were they borne out by any ostensible talent in these areas on Brecht-Schall's part.

The response from the authorities is also worth noting. The attempt to cool down the altercation was unusually sensible. For example, Hager chose to show Brecht-Schall that letters to high places did not elicit panic-stricken knee-jerk reactions. Instead, the Central Committee deferred responsibility and hoped that an amicable solution could be found between the opposing parties. The premiere should have marked an end to the dispute, but Brecht-Schall felt that there was considerable business left unfinished.

The aftershocks

Wekwerth had again stood up to the Brecht estate and again won through. This he did because he believed he was in the right as *Intendant* to stage productions of Brecht, or indeed anyone else, in the spirit of the SED's cultural agenda. Such resolve was not to go unpunished. In May 1983, Brecht-Schall refused to grant the BE rights to a new production of Brecht's *The Days of the Commune* until the *Drums* rights had been sorted out. She also threatened future performances of existing Brecht productions in the BE repertoire by not renewing contracts for the following season.[51] The issue was resolved later that year when she granted the BE the rights to *Commune* provisionally with the enigmatic comment 'on political grounds'.[52]

---

[50] Hoffmann to Hager, 15 June 1983, SAPMO BArch DY 30/27409. The following quotation is also taken from this letter.

[51] See Brecht-Schall to Hoffmann, 9 May 1983, BArch DR 1/1746. See also Brecht-Schall to Wekwerth, 6 June 1983, AdK MWA 'Korr. Brecht-Erben 1977–1983'.

[52] Brecht-Schall to Rolf Stiska, 14 December 1983, BArch DR 1/1746.

In July, the rights to *Drums* had finally been settled,[53] but Brecht-Schall sought to capitalize on the way in which the BE had initially circumvented her approval. In February 1984, she demanded an extra 5 per cent on top of the existing 10 per cent royalties for *Drums* in damages.[54] The BE continued to resist her claim, but as time went on, the authorities took a peculiar decision: from July 1984, the BE was no longer considered to be 'selbständige Person' ('an independent entity'),[55] and this meant that the Ministry officially ran the BE, not Wekwerth, something that, in practice, mostly affected the signing of contracts.[56] This move shows just how seriously the Ministry viewed Brecht-Schall's machinations and sought to bypass the personal animosity between her and Wekwerth that had been identified by Hoffmann.[57] With power now with the Ministry, Wekwerth wrote to Hager at the Central Committee, not to Minister Hoffmann, to tell him that Brecht-Schall had withdrawn the rights to *Galileo* which was due to be taken on the BE's first trip to the Edinburgh Festival at the end of summer 1984. Wekwerth did not believe that she would deliver on the promised threat because the tour would fall apart without it and because her husband was playing the lead. Instead he opined: 'she wants to blackmail us'.[58] The rights were granted, as Wekwerth had predicted. The condition was that the BE finally pay the extra 5 per cent and remove *Drums* from the repertoire that season.[59] The not terribly popular show was certainly cancelled, yet it is not clear from the documentary evidence whether or not the BE paid the damages.

While the argument concerning the rights to *Drums* rumbled on in 1984, Brecht-Schall had opened another front in her battle to exert more influence over Brecht and the BE the previous year. Her proposal to Honecker to dissolve the Advisory Group also had implications for the resolution made by the Council of Ministers in 1971 that effectively 'nationalized' the rights to Brecht. A meeting in June 1983 led only to a retrenchment of positions: Brecht-Schall insisted on her right to approve Brecht's plays in East Berlin and that this right modified the resolution's universal ambit. Minister Hoffmann countered that theatres' repertoires could not be determined by authorial rights holders.[60] One of the most

---

[53] See Wekwerth to Erika Hinckel, 6 July 1983, BArch DR 1/13525a.
[54] See Brecht-Schall to Hoffmann, 1 February 1984, BArch DR 1/1747.
[55] Wekwerth to Gregor Gysi, 6 July 1984, ibid.
[56] See Brecht-Schall to Martin Meyer, 9 July 1984, ibid.
[57] See Hoffmann to Hager, 15 June 1983, SAPMO BArch DY 30/27409.
[58] Wekwerth to Hager, 31 July 1984, SAMPO BArch DY 30/26313.
[59] See Wekwerth to Hager, 1 September 1984, ibid.
[60] See Anon., 'Notiz über eine Aussprache mit den Brecht-Erben über die Wahrnehmung von Aufführungsrechten am Berliner Ensemble', 14 June 1983, 3 pages. BArch DR 1/13525a.

absurd elements of the whole confrontation was noted in the attendance list: Wekwerth appeared for the Academy, which, according to the resolution, administered the rights, and Ekkehard Schall appeared for the Brecht estate. Yet both, as the protocol acknowledged 'represented, at the same time, the Berliner Ensemble'.[61] Officially, Schall was arguing for two opposing interests. The meeting ended in deadlock. Three days later, Brecht-Schall increased the pressure when she phoned the Ministry's legal advisor. She told him that she planned to take action in the courtrooms of the GDR (Leipzig) and the FRG (Frankfurt am Main). Yet the advisor counselled a measured response; her quarrel was with the GDR, and so the Frankfurt option was not relevant.[62] Brecht-Schall hung up midway through the conversation, and there was no further reference to lawsuits in further communication, although the threat itself initiated a revision of the State's position.

The Ministry started to weigh the legal implications of Brecht-Schall's demands. Their own expert identified a contradiction in the constitution: rights holders enjoyed the protection of the State *and* those rights could not run counter to the interests of society.[63] This tension led to the proposal to give Brecht-Schall 'full authority' to decide on Brecht plays in East Berlin, with the proviso that she had to give a 'rationale' for her decisions.[64] Against this background, Hager wrote to Honecker saying that the GDR had little to lose by granting Brecht-Schall rights to decide which of Brecht's plays were staged in the capital. By retaining the resolution and dissolving the Advisory Group, the SED would keep its legal principle in place while appearing to accede to Brecht-Schall's demands. Wekwerth agreed to the ruling and hoped that they could all get on with their work.[65]

This was not, however, the end of the story. Brecht-Schall was still looking for ways to overturn the resolution itself and thought she had found a precedent. She wrote directly to Honecker in September 1983, having come upon the case of the GDR's first Minister of Culture, Johannes R. Becher.[66] She had discovered that the rights to his work remained with his estate, despite a resolution passed by the GDR's Council of Ministers. On closer inspection, however, the Ministry's legal expert observed

---

[61]   Ibid., p. 1.

[62]   See Wolfgang England, 'Vermerk für Genosse Minister Hoffmann über einen Anruf von Frau Schall-Brecht [*sic*] am 14.6.83, 11.00 Uhr', 14 June 1983, n.p., SAPMO BArch DY 30/27409.

[63]   See Wolfgang England, 'Vorschlag für eine Regelung der Entscheidung über Aufführungsrechte', 22 June 1983, n.p., BArch DR 1/13525a.

[64]   Anon., '[Draft agreement on rights]', undated, n.p., ibid.

[65]   See Wekwerth to Erika Hinckel, 6 July 1983, ibid.

[66]   See Brecht-Schall to Honecker, 13 September 1983, SAPMO BArch DY 30/27409.

that while this was true, it had taken place before a new copyright law was introduced in 1965 that charged the State with responsibility for the 'protection and nurture' of significant estates.[67] The resolution regarding Brecht still stood. Hoffmann forwarded the information to Hager, but believed that little would deflect Brecht-Schall from realizing her goal 'of clawing back all the rights to herself'.[68]

Things remained quiet until the BE had returned from its trip to the Edinburgh Festival. Hoffmann wrote that having met with Brecht-Schall in August, he believed everything had been settled, but now, in September, she reportedly complained that there was not enough Brecht at the BE and that her husband was underused as its lead actor. She proposed removing Wekwerth and replacing him with Schall, with herself as his deputy. She reportedly concluded that if these matters were not dealt with, it would be better 'to turn the Berliner Ensemble back into a Theater am Schiffbauerdamm'.[69] Brecht-Schall maintained the pressure when she predicted that Wekwerth and the BE would be in a similar position to that of Berghaus in a year or two's time.[70] As noted above, Wekwerth certainly contemplated the consequences of a victory for Brecht-Schall over the State, yet resolve on his and the SED's part meant that he continued as *Intendant* until 1991; Brecht-Schall was unable to effect any great changes at the BE.

Yet all the time she had been struggling with the authorities and Wekwerth, she had also been using her position to extract benefits and privileges from the regime, something that runs counter to her own narrative in which she painted herself as someone 'out of favour' with the SED.[71] She had a certificate, personally approved by Honecker in 1977 and renewed in 1986, allowing her to avoid GDR customs and was, according to the Head of the Department for Security Affairs in the Central Committee, the only GDR citizen who had one.[72] Hager had also intervened to have Brecht-Schall and her husband treated at the Government's Hospital in 1982,[73] and he had one of her daughters approved for treatment there later that year. And in the run-up to her attempt to oust Wekwerth, she asked Honecker whether he was able to exempt her, Schall and her children from paying inheritance tax in June 1984.[74] The approval of this

---

67 Wolfgang England, 'Stellungnahme zum Schreiben der Brecht-Erben (Barbara Schall) an Genossen Honecker vom 13.9.83', 22 September 1983, 3 pages (1), ibid.
68 Hoffmann to Hager, 29 September 1983, BArch DR 1/13154.
69 Hoffman to Hager, 7 September 1984, BArch DR 1/13154a.
70 See Brecht-Schall to Hoffmann, 27 September 1984, BArch DR 1/1747.
71 Brecht-Schall, in Pietzsch and Linzer, 'Familien-Geschichten', p. 15.
72 See Wolfgang Herber to Hager, 14 July 1989, SAPMO BArch DY 30/989.
73 See Brecht-Schall to Hager, 30 September 1982, SAPMO BArch DY 30/27409.
74 See Brecht-Schall to Honecker, 5 June 1984, ibid.

measure, however, was tied securely to the GDR's retention of Brecht's archive.[75]

The regime was also keen to keep Brecht-Schall sweet. In 1986, for example, she vigorously opposed the award of the Helene-Weigel-Medal to actor Ursula Karusseit. Hoffmann did not want to antagonize her, especially with Brecht's ninetieth birthday two years away, when the BE planned to stage four of Brecht's plays. With this in mind, he enquired whether she would countenance the medal going to her own husband instead. Hoffmann reported: 'Mrs Barbara Brecht-Schall agreed to that'.[76] He received the award on 27 March 1986. Soft soap was required to bring about a successful anniversary.

It is difficult to view Brecht-Schall as a victim of the regime, despite its attempt to control the way she granted rights to the theatres of East Berlin. She was a skilled operator who knew how to exploit the power she wielded and the fear it evoked, in order to use it to establish connections with the most powerful players in the GDR. In the process, she accumulated some remarkable privileges of which fellow citizens could only dream.

As it happened, Wekwerth won a final tussle with Brecht-Schall in an episode that demonstrates how the heiress sought to extend her influence at the BE to areas beyond granting rights to Brecht's plays. A plan dating back to 1983 proposed Schall as the eponymous lead in *Timon of Athens* in a production mooted for 1985.[77] In 1985 Brecht-Schall wrote to Hoffmann saying that she wanted the British director David Leveaux to direct the play and said that Wekwerth appeared to support the plan although she suspected he might withdraw his backing later.[78] In early 1988, she was still lobbying Wekwerth for its inclusion in the repertoire,[79] and Wekwerth agreed to direct with Tenschert.[80] Yet by July, she asked the Central Committee to intervene in the matter.[81] In October 1989, Wekwerth wrote to Schall postponing the plan in the light of the GDR's plight: he noted that the BE could not condemn a wealthy man when the nation itself was crying out for resources itself.[82] The plan that had been

[75] See Strasberg and Siegert, 'Vermögensangelegenheit von Frau Barbara Brecht-Schall', undated, 2 pages (1), ibid.

[76] Hoffmann to Ursula Ragwitz, 20 February 1986, BArch Dr 1/8408.

[77] See Joachim Tenschert, 'Zur "Gesamtkonzeption der Berliner Bühnen" (Vorlage des MfK, 20.4.1983), Punkte 2.1. und 2.2.', 31 May 1983, 7 pages (4), AdK JTA 'BE-Dramaturgie u.a. interne Korr. ab 1978'.

[78] See Brecht-Schall to Hoffmann, 25 October 1985, BArch DR 1/1747.

[79] See Brecht-Schall to Wekwerth, 17 February 1988, AdK ESA 'BE Int. A-Z'.

[80] See Wekwerth to Brecht-Schall, 29 February 1988, ibid.

[81] See Brecht-Schall to Ursula Ragwitz, 15 July 1988, SAPMO BArch DY 30/23093.

[82] See Wekwerth to Ekkehard Schall, 16 October 1989, AdK ESA 'Wekwerth'.

so dear to Brecht-Schall had finally been shelved, and this represented a small victory in a long battle.

Heinz Uwe Haus contends that 'it is a fact that [Brecht-Schall] exercised absolute control over all decisions dealing with the program of a theater which was, however, a state and not a private theater'.[83] It is evident from the relationship sketched above that the repertoire was actually a highly contested area. The State used its power to appease and cajole Brecht-Schall into positions that at least allowed the *Intendant* to carry out his duties. For the most part, it succeeded in negotiating a workable ceasefire between the opposing personalities in the interests of preserving the integrity of what was still regarded internationally as the GDR's showpiece theatre.

The allegation of stagnation

The widely divergent receptions of *The Threepenny Opera* in 1981 in East Berlin and in Greece point to the radically different contexts in which the BE performed. The domestic audience found the production tired, devoid of political edge, and miscast, especially with respect to the play's male lead, Mack the Knife. In Greece, reviewers raved, something that may have convinced Wekwerth to abandon the plan to view the work as temporary and bring it back to East Berlin to open the 1981/82 season. The Greek example was not an exception; it is difficult to find evidence of any tour that was poorly received. This suggests that the BE clearly offered something that was not available to most foreign audiences (and to the many foreign spectators the BE continued to draw to East Berlin): high technical skill, tight ensemble playing, and interpretations based on performing a contradictory *Fabel*, rather than the psychological travails of individuals. In addition, the company was inextricably associated with Brecht and was thus able to ally its programmes with a sense of political critique that very much appealed to critics and audiences alike in the Cold War days of the 1980s. Today, one would perhaps call this constellation a 'unique selling point', yet at home precisely this uniqueness, seen day-in, day-out, had the opposite effect – familiarity was breeding contempt. Martin Linzer characterized one aspect of Wekwerth's *Intendanz* as being marked 'by museum-like ossification',[84] a view that tends to define the BE of the 1980s. This and the following section will account for why this

---

[83] Heinz Uwe Haus, 'Brecht in Post-Wall Germany', in Lyon and Breuer, *Brecht Unbound*, pp. 89–97 (94).

[84] Martin Linzer, 'Thoughts on a Walking Corpse: The Berliner Ensemble Five Years after the Wende', *Brecht Yearbook*, 21 (1996), pp. 289–300 (289).

may have been the case, although the section that follows them shows why the BE cannot exclusively be considered stagnant in this period.

The authorities were well aware of a problem at the BE. In a letter sent to Hager in 1984, Ursula Ragwitz, Head of the Central Committee's Cultural Department, wrote that the BE had had no real success in the past few seasons and that it was other GDR theatres that were developing Brecht in the GDR, not the BE.[85] Ragwitz identified Brecht-Schall's caprice as an inhibiting factor, but also that Wekwerth's array of directors were an obstacle. Wekwerth, back in 1975 when he unveiled the new Regieinstitut, commented: 'the young people we're training shouldn't just make theatre, but rather change the theatre, as they'll be making theatre in the 1980s'.[86] Wekwerth's hope was certainly realized, at the BE at least, but the change he foresaw was not terribly positive. In the 1980s, the Regieinstitut had indeed become a feeder for the BE, yet the establishment had been set up by Wekwerth and his notions of Brechtian direction pervaded it. As a result, the directors chosen for the BE came from a background of Brechtian orthodoxy in the Wekwerth mould. The lack of aesthetic dissent kept the BE on an even keel, but did not produce interesting deviations for the most part. The Chilean directors Carlos Medina and later Alejandro Quintana brought a certain lightness and flair from a non-European tradition, but were, at base, also products of the Regieinstitut. For example, Quintana's first solo production, Lorca's *Play without a Title*, that premiered on the BE's rehearsal stage in February 1986, was something of a coup in terms of the GDR's cultural politics (and it was only first produced in Spain in 1989). The experimental text, that mixes a theatrical performance with an apparently real revolution, was a brave choice and, as the reviews make clear, the director did not baulk at the challenge. Yet as one reviewer noted: 'the direction pulled out all the stops the play had to offer', yet even that was not enough.[87] The characteristic BE precision was certainly present – *Neues Deutschland* called the production 'as beautiful as it was consistent' – but even the Party newspaper concluded that the production lacked the bite that might have accompanied the play fifty years earlier.[88] The production was a technical triumph, yet it did not make a connection with its audience and the situation of the day.

---

[85]   See Ursula Ragwitz to Hager, 15 June 1984, SAPMP BArch DY 30/26313.
[86]   Wekwerth, in Jochen Gleiß, 'Theatermachen für die achtziger Jahre', *Theater der Zeit*, 8 (1975), pp. 53–4 (54).
[87]   Michael Stone, 'Einbruch der Wirklichkeit', *Der Tagesspiegel*, undated.
[88]   Gerhard Ebert, 'Begegnung mit dem letzten Stück von García Lorca', *Neues Deutschland*, 25 February 1986.

This innovative addition to the repertoire indicates a desire to take risks, yet that desire also had its limits. Wekwerth joined the Central Committee in 1986,[89] a move he would later rue.[90] A speech he wrote for the eleventh party conference in the same year was unashamedly positive.[91] It is unimportant whether the speech did or did not convey Wekwerth's real opinions; he was playing his role in the grand scheme of things, and this extended to his management of the repertoire as well. In the letter from Ragwitz to Hager, referenced above, Ragwitz made a couple of suggestions to improve the situation at the BE. One was to draft in new directors, a move that proved only partly successful, in that both Fritz Marquardt (seconded from the Volksbühne in 1985) and Christoph Schroth (seconded from Schwerin in 1988) failed to change the BE's direction that radically. The other was to develop Volker Braun as a playwright, although she noted that Wekwerth considered his play *Die Übergangsgesellschaft* (*Society in Transition*) unperformable in 1984.[92] This view was hardly surprising at that time; even the play's title was political dynamite in that it asserted that the GDR had not arrived at its historical destination, as asserted by Party dogma, but was still in transit. Yet even by 1987, when a thaw had set in that allowed a freer treatment of taboo subjects in most GDR theatres' repertoires,[93] Wekwerth reported that Braun and guest director Schroth preferred the playwright's *Lenin's Death* to *Society in Transition* as it showed 'not only our commitment to the Leninist direction of the Revolution, but in this play more than in his later ones, Braun proves himself to be a political propagandist'.[94] This line of conservatism and political loyalty meant that the more controversial play premiered at the Maxim-Gorki-Theater in March 1988 to much acclaim, while *Lenin's Death*, a controversial play itself back in the early 1970s, was dismissed as largely dull later that year.[95]

The personnel problem, identified in terms of the directors, also pervaded the ensemble. The actors' greatest strength – their inductive Brechtian training – was also their greatest weakness, in that they lacked the flexibility to go beyond it. Bunge and Brück encountered that when

[89] He was never, however, a member of the Politburo, as Carola Stern alleges, in *Männer lieben anders*, p. 204.
[90] See Wekwerth, in Hans-Dieter Schütt, *Manfred Wekwerth*, p. 291.
[91] See Wekwerth, 'Diskussionsbeitrag zum XI.', [spring 1986], 6 pages (1), SAPMO BArch DY 30/18550.
[92] See Ursula Ragwitz to Hager, 15 June 1984, SAPMO BArch DY 30/26313.
[93] See Bradley, *Cooperation and Conflict*, p. 231.
[94] Wekwerth to Hager, 27 August 1987, SAMPO BArch DY 30/27350.
[95] See, for example, André Plath, 'Wie aber geht man mit Geschichte um?', *Junge Welt*, 30 September 1988; or Rolf-Dieter Eichler, 'Bruchstücke aus einem großen Zusammenhang', *Nationalzeitung*, 4 October 1988.

they tried to encourage improvisation in the production of *The Taming of the Shrew*. Actor Corinna Harfouch joined the BE to perform in *Urfaust* in 1984. Her impression was that the actors 'executed their work, in my eyes, mechanically as if they were on the assembly line in a factory. Wekwerth had probably broken them all'.[96] Actor Angelika Ritter concurs: '[when directing] Manfred Wekwerth forced people into such a tight framework, so I was never really free'.[97] The comments reflect a move away from the integrated interactions that developed between Brecht, his assistants and the actors in the 1950s to a more top-down relationship in the 1980s. While the actors could be relied upon to deliver performance modes associated with Brecht's theatre, such as the implementation of *Gestus* and *Haltung*, they now mostly served the directors' wishes, rather than arriving at solutions together.

Ritter also notes that there may have been structural reasons for the lack of creativity in the ensemble: GDR actors could not be fired after a certain number of years at a theatre.[98] Tragelehn told me that, in his experience, GDR actors felt that they had reached their career's peak if they landed a full-time contract at a major Berlin theatre like the BE, and this led to complacency.[99] Wekwerth was certainly aware of this problem on his appointment in 1977. He had experienced a freer system when he worked in Switzerland and saw how new *Intendanten* regularly brought their own creative team and actors with them upon taking up a new position. He regretted not being able to do so at the BE.[100] A Stasi report, written a few months after Wekwerth's inauguration, noted how his talk of challenging the actors' 'job for life' status had ruffled feathers in the ensemble.[101] It seems, however, that Wekwerth was powerless to challenge GDR employment law, and so the ensemble became ever more passive over time.

In addition, Wekwerth, too, seemed to be stuck in a rut. As already acknowledged, he preferred to direct in a team, in order to generate productive tensions. This had very much been the case in 1959 when he and Peter Palitzsch staged *Ui* to global acclaim. By 1964 he had

[96] Corinna Harfouch, in Sabine Zolchow, 'Protokoll der Gespräche zwischen Corinna Harfouch und Sabine Zolchow am 30.6. und 11.7.06 in Böhmerheide', 4 September 2008, unpublished typescript, 30 pages (3).

[97] Angelika Ritter, in Margaret Setje-Eilers, 'The Berliner Ensemble Interviews: Angelika Ritter, Eva Boehm, Ursula Ziebarth, Angela Winkler', *Communications from the International Brecht Society*, 38 (2009), pp. 118–53 (123).

[98] See Ritter, in ibid., pp. 118–19.

[99] B. K. Tragelehn, unpublished interview with the author, 9 November 2010.

[100] Wekwerth, unpublished interview with the author, 1 July 2011.

[101] See IM Klein, 'Zur Situation am Berliner Ensemble', 20 September 1977, 4 pages (2), BStU MfS HA XX 10818.

joined with Head Dramaturge Joachim Tenschert to direct the BE's next great hit, *Coriolan*, although this production also included the input of Ruth Berghaus and a battery of assistants. Wekwerth had brought back Tenschert to lead the dramaturgy department in 1977 and re-formed the team for *Galileo* in 1978. He and Tenschert remained together for almost all the productions Wekwerth directed at the BE in the 1980s. However, as dramaturge Holger Teschke observes, the two were too similar to produce creative sparks of dissent.[102] The relationship was asymmetrical: Wekwerth implemented his theories and interpretations as practice, and Tenschert offered sharp critiques and analyses of that process, without exploring what might lie beyond it. Consequently, the creative heart of the BE was somewhat sclerotic.

It is perhaps Wekwerth's own response to Brecht that most clearly signalled the lack of verve at the BE in the 1980s. Wekwerth's extensive writings give the impression that he was as able a theorist as he was a practitioner. However, his reading of Brecht was hardly radical and, at times, quite mistaken. For instance, in a bid to persuade Brecht-Schall to authorize performance of the *Lehrstück* (learning play) *Die Maßnahme* (translated as both *The Measures Taken* and *The Decision*), Wekwerth used some rather peculiar examples to justify extreme political decisions as an analogy to the play's final action in which four comrades murder a fifth in the name of the revolution. These included the expatriation of Wolf Biermann in 1976 and Ayatollah Khomeni's defence of killing the Shah's former secret policemen.[103] The interesting part of the argument is that Wekwerth believed that the *Lehrstück*'s purpose was to justify the four comrades' deed. This, however, was the main reason why Brecht had prevented performance in 1956.[104] That is, he did not want to see the play as a mere justification of political murder for a paying audience. Instead, the form was designed to open up the questions and allow the performers, who were simultaneously spectators, to experience the action *and* to reflect on it.[105] In Wekwerth's opinion, this radical openness was to be shut down to push home a political point. He still held this view in 2010.[106] My argument here is that Wekwerth represents, in his own

---

[102] Holger Teschke, unpublished interview with the author, 11 March 2011.

[103] See Wekwerth to Brecht-Schall, 1 October 1979, AdK MWA 'Korr. Brecht-Erben 1977–1983'.

[104] See Brecht to Wilfried Ziemann, 4 February 1956; and Brecht to Paul Patera, 21 April 1956: BFA, 30: 422 and 447 respectively.

[105] See Brecht, 'Zur Theorie des Lehrstücks', BFA, 22: 351; and 'Anmerkung zu den Lehrstücken', BFA, 23: 418.

[106] See Wekwerth, in Joachim Lang, *Neues vom alten Brecht. Manfred Wekwerth im Gespräch*, ed. by Valentin F. Lang and Karoline Sprenger (Berlin: Aurora, 2010), p. 80.

thoughts on Brecht, positions that both neglect Brecht's theoretical openness and push an agenda that valorizes the stage as a site of authority that then transmits its lessons to the audience.

This lack of theoretical development can also be found in a volume of 1989 that was supposed to show how Brecht could be imagined for the coming decade. However, rather than drafting a blueprint for a post-Brechtian theatre, the book restated existing positions and was, in fact, mostly a compilation of previously published material, going back as far as 1985.[107] Wekwerth's own views were vague: 'we are keen to have Brecht's method appear in its diversity, as lively and multi-coloured'.[108] It is tempting to think that Wekwerth was a hostage of the GDR's own normative staging practices at the time, yet this was no longer the case. Just around the corner, at the Deutsches Theater, Heiner Müller had staged his play *The Wage Sinker* in January 1988 in which the once clear dialectical scenes were left radically open for the audience actively to ponder.[109] Indeed, Müller and other GDR directors had challenged the norm for about a decade.

A failure to develop: Brecht productions in the late 1980s

In order to understand the practical nature of Brecht productions at the BE, I will focus on the three that surrounded Brecht's ninetieth anniversary in the years 1987 and 1988. The celebrations in 1988, that culminated in a production of *The Mother* on Brecht's birthday, were prefaced by productions of plays that had never been staged at the BE: *Fatzer* and *Baal*. *Untergang des Egoisten Johann Fatzer* (*Downfall of the Egoist Johann Fatzer*), to give it the title under which Brecht planned to publish a short selection of texts in 1930, was far and away the most ambitious project. The text itself is a sprawling fragment, written in dramatic scenes and epic commentaries over several years. The full collection of extant material covers over 140 sides in the standard edition,[110] and there is, a little like Büchner's much shorter *Woyzeck*, but to a far greater degree, no sense of a correct order or montage of the competing elements. Broadly speaking, the play is concerned with four deserters from the battlefields of World

[107] See Wekwerth (compiler), *Theater nach Brecht: Baukasten für eine Theorie und Praxis des Berliner Ensembles in den neunziger Jahren* (Berlin: no publisher credited, 1989), unpaginated page detailing sources.

[108] Wekwerth, 'Brecht spielen – gestern – heute – morgen', in ibid., pp. 41–51 (47).

[109] See David Barnett, '"I have to change myself instead of interpreting myself." Heiner Müller as Post-Brechtian Director', *Contemporary Theatre Review*, 20:1 (2010), pp. 6–20 (14–18) for a fuller discussion of the production.

[110] See Brecht, *Fatzer*, BFA, 10: 387–529.

War One. They come to Mülheim in a tank and await a revolution that fails to materialize. Fatzer, the individualist, is finally shot dead by his former comrades for leaving the group and following his own interests. The others die in an explosion.

In an interview in 1978, Wekwerth stated that the BE was interested in *The Measures Taken* and *Fatzer*: 'we will be producing these plays primarily to bolster the BE's workshop character'.[111] Of course, much can change over nine years, but the aspiration to stage *Fatzer* in a rough, rather than a polished form seemed to have remained when directors Wekwerth and Tenschert decided to use Heiner Müller's version, which is conspicuous for its refusal to connect the texts.[112] As Moray McGowan comments: 'for Müller, Brecht's text and theatrical practice were not models to be faithfully followed but . . . a set of processes, methods, ideas, and forms to be worked through critically in order to free theater from false accretions and discover new possibilities'.[113] Wekwerth, however, was not interested in associative texts or fragmentariness. The first words of his first article in a documentation of the production reads: '*Fatzer* is not incomprehensible and not abstract, either'.[114] Later Werner Mittenzwei noted: 'in contrast to Müller, [Wekwerth] was interested in organizing the *Fabel*. . . Wekwerth is after a dramatic quality that's not realized in the fragment, that's only there in embryo'.[115] Thus, the disparate fragments were carefully re-connected in order to impose a *Fabel*, a narrative cohesion. The aim was to deprive the complex of its interpretive openness and establish clear lines of action and meaning.

Mittenzwei went on to comment: 'firstly, the texts had to lose their strikingly quotable, sententious quality to allow a gestic rendition, to make them ready for the actors'.[116] Here it is clear that the team believed that such texts simply could not be delivered by the ensemble as they stood and had to be made to bend to accommodate the actors' usual approaches to their craft. This paternalistic view goes unchallenged in the documentation. An alternative and more radical stance to the

---

[111] Wekwerth, in John Fuegi, 'Interview mit Manfred Wekwerth', *Brecht Yearbook*, 8 (1978), pp. 120–8 (125).

[112] See Brecht, *Der [sic] Untergang des Egoisten Johann Fatzer*, ed. by Heiner Müller (Leipzig: Suhrkamp, 1994), originally compiled in 1978.

[113] Moray McGowan, 'Fatzer's Footprints: Brecht's *Fatzer* and the GDR Theater [sic]', in Bradley and Leeder (eds.), *Brecht and the GDR*, pp. 201–21 (208).

[114] Wekwerth, 'Notizen aus Gesprächen', in Peter Kraft (ed.), '*Untergang des Egoisten Johann Fatzer von Bertolt Brecht: Eine Dokumentation der Aufführung des Berliner Ensembles 1987* (Berlin: Verband der Theaterschaffenden, 1987), pp. 12–13 (12).

[115] Werner Mittenzwei, '*Fatzer* oder die Möglichkeit des Theaters im Umgang mit einem Fragment', in ibid., pp. 114–26 (115).

[116] Ibid., p. 117.

material could have seen *Fatzer* as a provocation to the cast that might have revealed something about the actors' relationship to a difficult, unwieldy text. Müller himself took this option in his own production of the fragment (see pp. 387–9, Chapter 13). Once Wekwerth had filed down the fragment's awkward edges into something that resembled a more crafted and conventional piece of drama, the usual BE process took over: 'the directors and the actors saw their main task as exposing the characters' contradictory *Haltungen* and integrating them into the thread of the *Fabel*'.[117]

In the published documentation, Wekwerth had stated that the team had worked '"without a conceptual plan"'.[118] The BE's own dossier tells a different story. In the preparatory phase, the director suggested that they eliminate the *Lehrstück* qualities from Müller's version and instead deal with '"archetypes in a time of upheaval" or "unready times – unready people"'.[119] The interpretive framework was certainly in place. Judith Wilke wrote that the team sought 'to demonstrate in exemplary fashion the drama as a battle between the strongest man, the individualist Fatzer, and a ruthless thinker, Koch, and, in doing this, model false and correct behaviours'.[120] *Fatzer* had been tamed and treated like any other drama at the BE. Its radical potential for anarchy, for showing the join between actor and role, and for delegating meaning to the audience, had been collapsed. Müller, looking back at Wekwerth's approach to directing as a whole, criticized it for its insistence on explication, that every word had to be understood: 'we know what the text is saying. That's when the text has no power any more'.[121] The refusal to enter into a dialogue with the audience, or the retention of the stage's position of authority, was a central component in the BE's productions of Brecht in the 1980s. They looked tired because the directors had not engaged in a dialogue with Brecht in order to update him.

Baal is another anarchic play and tells, in a series of episodes, the story of an artist who refuses to conform to the norms of society. Originally, the BE planned to stage the play with a guest director, Alexander Lang. He had been at the BE in the late 1960s, but left in 1969, like so many others, when the theatre went into crisis. He had directed the GDR premiere

[117] Ibid., p. 123.
[118] Wekwerth, '*Fatzer* mit veränderter Chorfunktion (4. Vorstellung), 26.9.1987', in ibid., pp. 142–3 (142).
[119] Wekwerth to Mittenzwei, 14 October 1986, BEA File 128.
[120] Judith Wilke, *Brechts 'Fatzer'-Fragment. Lektüren zum Verhältnis Dokument und Kommentar* (Bielefeld: Aisthesis, 1998), p. 248.
[121] Müller, 'Über Brecht', *Werke* 12: 523.

of Brecht's *Die Rundköpfe und die Spitzköpfe* (*Round Heads and Pointed Heads*) at the Deutsches Theater in September 1983 to great acclaim and was a much sought-after director. The choice of Lang was certainly an unexpected one, especially as the BE's management had previously criticized the production of *Round Heads*.[122] However, when Lang was invited to stage *Baal* his reply came back immediately: he would not work with Ekkehard Schall as the eponymous hero.[123] Apparently, Wekwerth had sent the hardly diplomatic Brecht-Schall to Munich, where Lang was working at the time, to talk him round. However, when the theatre in Munich denied her entry to the building,[124] she then visited him at his digs, threatened him with legal consequences and reportedly 'made him aware of her influence with the Party's leadership'.[125] Alejandro Quintana stepped into the breach to direct the play, but his work, which premiered on 12 December 1987, was hardly lauded. One critic noted that while the GDR premiere in Erfurt had been full of 'revelations', the BE version was muddy and vague, that it was difficult to understand Schall's relationship to the character, and that one saw Schall rather than Baal on stage.[126] The actor drew criticism for not showing why people on stage were so attracted to Baal – his anti-social behaviour was clear, but his charm and sensuality were missing.[127] A Western reviewer used the production to diagnose 'the BE's old malady: whatever doesn't suit ideologically is denounced and pushed to absurd extremes'.[128] The one positive outcome of the production was a personal one: Quintana had now established himself in Brecht-Schall's artistic affections, like Peter Kupke and Wolfgang Pintzka before him.[129] As should be obvious by now, however, she was not so much concerned with artistic quality as with the 'loyalty' of directors prepared to work with Schall and to deliver productions that did not take risks.

The crowning glory of the anniversary was supposed to have been Wekwerth and Tenschert's production of *The Mother*, premiered on Brecht's birthday in 1988. It was not reviewed that badly, but the critics noted the usual qualities associated with the BE at the time (an emphasis

[122] See entry for 27 January 1984, in Braun, *Werktage*, p. 583.
[123] See Hilde Schmidt, 'Zum Brief von Genossin Ellen Brombacher', [March 1987], n.p., SAPMO BArch DY 30/27496.
[124] See Karl Heinz Hafranke, 'Notiz', 13 March 1987, n.p., ibid.
[125] Hilde Schmidt, 'Notiz', 7 April 1987, 2 pages (1) ibid.
[126] Rolf-Dieter Eichler, 'Versuch mit *Baal* am Baal gescheitert', *National Zeitung*, 15 December 1987.
[127] See Joachim Bohlmann, 'Ein Baal ohne Sinnlichkeit', *Tribüne*, 15 December 1987.
[128] Michael Stone, 'Die alte Krankheit', *Der Tagesspiegel*, 20 December 1987.
[129] See Brecht-Schall to Wekwerth, 10 September 1990, AdK ESA 'BE Int. A-Z'.

on rationality, clarity, and technical precision),[130] rather than any stunning new readings. That such a potentially important production ran for a mere twenty performances probably speaks more succinctly about the state of the BE's Brecht reception in the late 1980s.

Glimmers of light

In reply to an article written in 1998 by Brecht expert Jan Knopf, Wekwerth defended himself against the charge that he had been responsible for the BE's slow decline in the 1980s. He noted an emphasis in his repertoire on 'world premieres and experiments'.[131] As noted above, the example of Lorca showed that even though this was an experimental GDR premiere, that label was not enough to allow the production to break out of the BE's performance orthodoxies. However, one dismisses Wekwerth's claim at one's peril. The repertoire under his *Intendanz* could be vibrant and, although its ambitions may have been undermined by the in-house style that he defined and over which he presided, there were some notable exceptions to this rule.

One of the most unexpected successes for the BE came in 1984, and this was a result of Wekwerth's initiative,[132] although the production itself had little to do with the BE's approach to making theatre at the time. The decision to invite director and designer Horst Sagert to stage a production was not without risk. His set design for Lorca's *Doña Rosita* at the Deutscher Theater in 1971 had attracted criticism for its bold approach and led him reportedly to ask the taboo question: "'is the GDR really so weak that it can't even deal with surrealism?'".[133] Sagert's open flouting of GDR design norms should have consigned him to artistic limbo and, indeed, in the GDR he found little work, yet he was allowed to function internationally, something that Friedrich Dieckmann reportedly ascribed to the intervention of none other than Kurt Hager.[134] That he had such a high-ranking benefactor may account for why he was finally permitted to work again in the GDR.

---

[130] See Gerhard Ebert, 'Rationale Kraft und poetische Frische Brechtscher Gedanken', *Neues Deutschland*, 12 February 1988; Ingrid Seyfahrt, '*Die Mutter*', *Sonntag*, 28 February 1988; and Ernst Schumacher, 'Besuch der alten Mutter', *Berliner Zeitung*, 20–21 February 1988.

[131] Wekwerth, 'Zum Artikel "Ein Werk, das standhält" – Brecht zwischen Ost und West – von Prof. Jan Knopf im *3GH* 3/98', *Dreigroschenheft* 1 (1999), pp. 46–7 (46).

[132] See Horst Sagert to Hager, [received on 23 October 1986], SAPMO BArch DY 30/23352.

[133] Horst Sagert, in Wilhelm Girod, 'Aktenvermerk', 21 June 1971, file p. 19, BStU MfS BV Bln. AIM 6210/91, vol. 2/1.

[134] See Dieckmann, in [IM Sumatic], untitled report, [c. July 1977], file pp. 303–5 (305), ibid.

Fig. 11.2. Sights unseen (at the BE): Sagert's production presents new approaches to staging the classics. *Faust Scenes (Urfaust)*, March 1984.

His *Faust-Szenen (Urfaust)* (*Faust Scenes (Urfaust)*) had nothing to do with Monk and Brecht's controversial productions of 1952–3 although the show used the same text. Instead Sagert engaged with mythical and magical motifs, such as Prometheus and Lucifer,[135] and these were set against lavish, sensuous stage sets (see Fig. 11.2). Early discussions signalled Sagert's aspiration to work as freely as possible with the material, as a dramaturge commented: 'the way of working, the collectivity of the project, his unconditional boundaries'.[136] Actor Hermann Beyer, who played Faust, remarked that it became clear to the cast very quickly that Sagert possessed a rare quality: 'the ability to forge an ensemble'.[137] He also gave the actors expressive freedom in rehearsal to explore his own visionary ideas. A further planning discussion at the BE revealed the dimensions of the work: 'on the Faust character: the world is defined by him. He seeks to and does everything spectacularly wrongly . . . A theatrical figure that explains little'.[138] Sagert actively worked against the BE's principles, as he reported in 1987: 'many of [the actors] were tired of

[135] See Anon., 'Anregungen', n.p., AdK Theaterdokumentation ID 578.
[136] Jochen Ziller, '*Urfaust*-Gespräch am 14.5.1982', 16 May 1982, 2 pages (2), BEA File 112.
[137] Hermann Beyer, in Dieter Kranz, *Berliner Theater*, p. 390.
[138] Ziller, '*Urfaust*-Gespräch am 8.9.82', 13 September 1982, n.p., BEA File 112.

theatre as enlightening and scientific. And I, too, thought that [the BE] was in danger of becoming a barracks of *Modelle* that went through the philosophical motions'.[139] From these short indications and opinions, one can see that Sagert's approach completely contradicted the BE's usual modes of realizing plays. And this was reflected in the production itself.

Neues Deutschland certainly gave *Faust Scenes*, which premiered on 31 March 1984, a mixed reception: 'a lot of naturalistic bits and bobs, wonderful scenic ideas'.[140] Another reviewer from the East was also sceptical: 'total theatre can only be justified after all when the totality is focused on the flow of the drama',[141] levelling the old charge of 'formalism' in a new vocabulary. One may ask how a production like this fitted into the BE's political programme. Holger Teschke told me that Brecht-Schall and her husband walked out of the premiere,[142] something that confirmed the work's contravention of the company's aesthetic and thematic mantras. Yet it was this very point that made *Faust Scenes* political, beyond the simplistic interpretation of the term as meaning connected to political subject matter. Instead, the production was a silent, but sustained attack on the GDR's cultural politics and their insistence on making things understandable. The production was not an assemblage of wilful obscurity – too many commentators acknowledged its beauty and its inner logic[143] – but an attempt to draft an alternative theatre in one of the most hallowed centres of rationalism and interpretive clarity. The production pleaded for a more imaginative theatre, unfettered by the GDR's aesthetic dogma of socialist realism. However, despite the radicalism of the form and performances, Sagert was not to return to the BE. Wekwerth found him difficult to work with and maintained that Brecht-Schall overruled a future production on the grounds that Sagert's work was too costly.[144] The Ministry was unequivocal in its correspondence with the Central Committee two years after the premiere: 'we are of the

---

[139] Sagert, in Kranz, *Berliner Theater*, p. 389.

[140] Gerhard Ebert, 'Undurchsichtiges Mysterium um Margerete', *Neues Deutschland*, 4 April 1984.

[141] Horst Heitzenröther, '*Faust-Szenen* mit bildnerischer Fülle', *Nationalzeitung*, 10 April 1984.

[142] Holger Teschke, unpublished interview with the author, 11 March 2011.

[143] See, for example, Ernst Schumacher, 'Voll von Zeichen und unterhaltend', *Berliner Zeitung*, 4 April 1984; or Michael Stone, 'Weiße und schwarze Engel', *Der Tagesspiegel*, 5 April 1984.

[144] Wekwerth, unpublished interview with the author, 1 July 2011. Holger Teschke, in the interview referenced above, told me that Heiner Müller was also interested in bringing Sagert back to the BE in the early 1990s, but also had reservations about Sagert being difficult to work with.

opinion that work by Horst Sagert at a Berlin theatre will not be scheduled and that such work will always be associated with difficulties'.[145]

Commentator Martin Linzer, who viewed the BE in the 1980s as marked on the one hand 'by museum-like paralysis', noted, on the other hand, how Wekwerth used his power as President of the Academy of Arts and member of the Central Committee to engineer an 'opening of creative space' for the company.[146] This is more than evident in the BE's championing of GDR playwright Georg Seidel. Wekwerth pushed the playwright onto the stage against the will of both his deputy, Schall, and his Head Dramaturge, Tenschert.[147] In addition, there is the possibility that the dramaturge closest to Seidel, Jochen Ziller, was actually a Stasi *agent provocateur* (in the mould of Hans-Diether Meves – see pp. 248–9, Chapter 8), encouraging dissent to arraign the dissenters. This suggestion was made by the director of Seidel's *Villa Jugend* (*Youth Villa*), Fritz Marquardt, in an interview a couple years after Ziller's death in 2001.[148] This was, however, only a suggestion and was not backed up by evidence. Ziller had an interesting background as an informer. He signed his 'Verpflichtung' ('obligation' to keep secret meetings with the Stasi to himself) in 1975,[149] but his handler discovered he was working for army intelligence at the same time and was instructed to restrict operational activity with Ziller to his work at the Henschel publishing house.[150] His career as an informer for the Berlin Stasi formally ended in 1978.[151] He was, however, explicitly mentioned as an informer in 1979, together with Peter Kupke.[152] Extant files do not currently support the view that Ziller informed on Seidel, however.

While the BE produced three of Seidel's dramas between 1985 and 1990, the most controversial was its first, *Jochen Schanotta*. The play is about the disaffected youth of the title and his problems with the

---

[145] Hoffmann to Ursula Ragwitz, 2 December 1986, SAPMO BArch DY 30/23352.

[146] Martin Linzer, 'Orakel aus dem Brecht-Tempel', *Theater der Zeit*, 1 (1993), pp. 19–22 (20).

[147] See Schall to Wekwerth, 28 September 1990, AdK ESA 'BE Int. A–Z'; and Joachim Tenschert to Wekwerth, 12 August 1988, AdK MWA 'BE Korr. ab 1970'.

[148] See Fritz Marquardt, in Sabine Zolchow, 'Protokoll der Gespräche zwischen Fritz Marquardt und Sabine Zolchow am 28.08.2005 und am 15.01.2006 in Amalienhof und Prenzlau', 26 March 2007, 32 pages (2), AdK TiW 1308.

[149] See Jochen Ziller, 'Verpflichtung', 25 September 1975, file p. 16, BStU MfS AIM 8207/78.

[150] See Hans Holm, 'Vermerk über eine Absprache zu Ziller, Jochen', 2 November 1976, file p. 99, ibid.

[151] See Hans Holm, 'Vorschlag zur Einstellung des IM-Vorlaufes "Vermittler"...', 10 April 1978, file p. 100, ibid.

[152] See Steffens, 'Übersicht zu inoffiziellen Quellen zum OV "Lyrik"...', 31 July 1979, file p. 146, BStu ASt Halle AOP 2358/82, vol. 1.

350 A History of the Berliner Ensemble

GDR. As a result, it was not only the usual government agencies that were interested in the production, but also the Ministry of People's Education, which attended rehearsals to monitor the way the play was being treated.[153] Dramaturge Jörg Mihan believed that this Ministry was by far the most difficult to deal with during the rehearsal process.[154] Wekwerth, an undeniable supporter of the project,[155] was nonetheless cautious. He gave Minister Margot Honecker a copy of Brecht's *The Days of the Commune* as evidence of the work the BE did and told her that *Schanotta* would be directed 'with great responsibility'.[156] In other words, he assured her that the BE would not let negative qualities stand freely, but contextualize them. Again one notes how a play's potential for systemic critique was blunted by the *Intendant*'s intervention.

Seidel is not an experimental writer, and his dialogues are fairly naturalistic. In a letter to the directing team, however, he noted an interesting contradiction: 'for me, theatre isn't a representation of reality; I use the manifestations of reality to write plays'.[157] He was inviting the directors Wolf Bunge and Christoph Brück to see beyond the dialogue's form in order to produce something that would not be mistaken for superficial naturalism. In the same letter, he also signalled the impulses that drove his apparently negative depictions: 'to say it one more time: I don't want to generate pessimism, I want to use pessimism to unsettle people'. Both Wekwerth and dramaturge Mihan saw the way of circumventing a negative reading of the character by understanding Schanotta's anarchic behaviour as a '"productive force"'.[158]

Before rehearsals began, the BE had contacted the two-man musical theatre group Karls Enkel (Karl [Marx's] Grandchildren) to offer what the directors considered 'a so-called "commentary level" that engages critically with Schanotta's exploits'.[159] Hans-Eckhardt Wenzel, a member of the duo, remembers that they were given the task of developing 'a parallel story' of songs and scenes to offset Seidel's naturalism.[160] The move upset Seidel who found that the texts they had written 'destroy the

---

[153] See Hans Kießig to Konrad Naumann, 1 February 1985, SAPMO BArch DY 34/13255.
[154] Jörg Mihan, unpublished interview with the author, 12 July 2011.
[155] See Funke and Jansen, *Theater am Schiffbauerdamm*, pp. 198–9.
[156] Wekwerth, unpublished interview with the author, 1 July 2011.
[157] Georg Seidel to Wolf Bunge and Christoph Brück, undated, AdK Georg-Seidel-Archiv 96.
[158] Jörg Mihan, 'Zu *Schanotta* – Fassung vom Mai 1984', 8 May 1984, 3 pages (1); and see Wekwerth to Christoph Brück and Wolf Bunge, 12 March 1984, both BEA File 117.
[159] Wolf Bunge and Christoph Brück, untitled, undated, n.p., ibid.
[160] Unpublished email from Hans-Eckardt Wenzel to the author, 9 August 2012.

play's aesthetics, denounce the characters, denounce the play, and consequently denounce the playwright'.[161] After a meeting in mid December 1984, he backed down slightly and accepted the use of music and song, but nothing more from the group.[162]

Schanotta premiered on 23 February 1985. By this time, Wolf Bunge had left the directing team, and so it was Christoph Brück alone who had to endure a mauling from certain quarters of the GDR press. *Neues Deutschland*, the most important official arbiter by far, considered Schanotta himself 'not a rewarding subject for drama'.[163] The GDR's main paper for young people, *Junge Welt*, was similarly damning, and the sentiments were echoed in the *National Zeitung*,[164] although other GDR critics were more charitable. Ernst Schumacher found the play had 'today's sound' in its dialogue.[165] Comments on the musical accompaniment varied, but Martin Linzer, looking back at the production in 1992, believed that the contribution from Karls Enkel, a duo he rated highly, had pushed Seidel's play 'almost to the point of being unrecognizable'.[166] It is important not to overrate this production's place in the BE's repertoire, however, and reviewer Wolfgang Giersch helps to contextualize it: 'it's not a great, but a necessary production'.[167] It was not going to change the way the nation saw itself, but made a small contribution to shifting perspectives that moved away from the State-sanctioned view of young people to something that approached their everyday experience a little more closely.

A desire to engage with more established, quality GDR playwrights was also sometimes a feature of the BE's repertoire. The presence of Volker Braun was also attributable to Wekwerth's interventions at times, although, as seen above in 1987, the decision to stage *Lenin's Death* over *Society in Transition* was hardly an act of managerial daring. In the season that preceded the fall of the Berlin Wall, the BE did stage a play long prevented from being performed in the GDR, Heiner Müller's *Germania Tod in Berlin* (*Germania Death in Berlin*). The play is mostly a montage of scenes from German and, more specifically, East German

---

[161] Georg Seidel to Wekwerth, 11 December 1984, AdK Georg-Seidel-Archiv 96.

[162] See Seidel to Brück and Bunge, 13 December 1984, ibid.

[163] Gerhard Ebert, 'Auf Gammeltour durch unsere Wirklichkeit', *Neues Deutschland*, 9–10 April 1985.

[164] See Henryk Goldberg, 'Weshalb mich Schanotta nicht interessiert', *Junge Welt*, 5 March 1985; and Rolf-Dieter Eichler, 'Ins Ziellose', *Nationalzeitung*, 27 February 1985.

[165] Ernst Schumacher, 'Von Struktur kaleidoskopisch', *Berliner Zeitung*, 28 February 1985.

[166] Martin Linzer, 'Anmerkungen zu Georg Seidels Werk und Wirken', in Seidel, *Villa Jugend: Das dramatische Werk in einem Band*, ed. by Andreas Leusink (Berlin and Frankfurt/Main: Henschel and Verlag der Autoren, 1992), pp. 381–9 (387).

[167] Wolfgang Gersch, 'Von einer Suche ohne Ankunft', *Tribüne*, 28 February 1985.

history. Minister Hoffmann told Hager in 1978 that the play could not be published without changes to a pair of scenes entitled 'Hommage à Stalin' and to passages in the curtain scene relating to Rosa Luxemburg.[168] An application to stage the play at the Deutsches Theater was rejected in 1982 on the grounds of Müller's 'false' understanding of history and the play's philosophical positions.[169] Director Fritz Marquardt attests that the play was not officially approved by the Ministry, but that Wekwerth wrestled 'a toleration [of the play], bound to my name'.[170] Marquardt was a friend of Müller's and had successfully directed some of his more controversial plays in the GDR. Wekwerth himself was no great fan of the GDR's most talented and internationally renowned playwright, but noted in a letter to Brecht-Schall that Müller was a potential Nobel laureate and that the BE had neglected the author over the years.[171] Yet after the struggle to bring *Germania* to the BE, the production itself, which premiered in January 1989, was an understated affair. Müller himself sums it up thus:

Marquardt consciously forsook the cabaret element, against expectations. When a play that's been banned for eighteen years is premiered, people expect something like a bomb going off. Marquardt's production was a refusal. But he was deeply shocked when [Deputy Minister Klaus] Höpcke said that it wasn't clear to him any more why he'd banned the play in the first place.[172]

The threatened *coup de théâtre* failed to materialize.

One final aspect of Wekwerth's management that is worthy of mention is his promotion of innovative, smaller projects. I noted his reintroduction and extension of the '*Brecht Evening*' format in the previous chapter, but he also made sure that a series of shorter plays, scenes, and one-handers added depth and variety to the programme of main stage productions. By their very nature, these shorter productions were able to experiment with various forms because they required fewer resources and often had very small casts. Over the years these projects included a show that reconstructed composer Hanns Eisler's appearance before the House Un-American Activities Committee, based on documentary material; Manfred Karge's *Jacke wie Hose* (*Man to Man*); Patrick Süskind's *Der Kontrabaß* (*The Double Bass*); and a specially adapted version of Jorge Diaz's *Diese ganz lange Nacht* (*This Long, Long Night*), that

---

[168] See Hoffmann to Hager, 26 April 1978, SAPMO BArch DY 30/23306.

[169] See Ursula Ragwitz to Erika Hinckel, 7 May 1982, SAPMO BArch DY 30/18988.

[170] Fritz Marquardt, in Zolchow, 'Protokoll der Gespräche zwischen Fritz Marquardt und Sabine Zolchow', p. 5.

[171] See Wekwerth to Brecht-Schall, 18 January 1989, AdK ESA 'BE Int. A-Z'.

[172] Heiner Müller, *Krieg ohne Schlacht*, *Werke* 9: 201.

dramatized the authentic experience of four female Chilean actors in police detention.

The two most culturally significant shows, however, were Samuel Beckett's *Play* and Heiner Müller's *Verkommenes Ufer Medeamaterial Landschaft mit Argonauten* (*Waterfront Wasteland Medea Material Landscape with Argonauts*). While again it is important not to overstate the importance of these productions (*Play* only ran for five performances, for example), they represent a shift in repertoire policy, unthinkable earlier in the decade. Beckett had been the antithesis of all the GDR held holy in terms of aesthetics. His ahistorical plays and their lack of an overt politics made his work synonymous with Western 'decadence', and he only started to be performed in the GDR of the mid 1980s. *Krapp's Last Tape* premiered in July 1986 in Berlin, and it was followed by the much-awaited *Waiting for Godot* in March of the following year in Dresden. The BE's *Play* in November 1987 was a small addition to the author's presence in the East, but it was still a sign that the BE was prepared to countenance a figure who had previously been reviled. Indeed, in the 1960s, the State made sure that academic Werner Mittenzwei appeared for Brecht and the GDR in a debate about Brecht and Beckett at the Experimenta Festival in Frankfurt am Main.[173] By 1987, the GDR did not, however, institute a policy for shaping repertoires along the lines of 'anything goes'. A mark of the resistance to *Play* can be found in a Western review that quoted lines from the GDR youth paper, *Junge Welt*: 'why do they have to stage Beckett to prove that Brecht's closer to us? We knew that already'.[174]

The inclusion of Müller's *Waterfront Wasteland* in the BE's repertoire signals another weakening of the front that prevented his more experimental work from being staged in the GDR. The play consists of three sections, two of which are not attributed to either characters or speakers. The production, given in the same month as the Beckett, was not officially a BE production – it was directed by a former assistant to Ruth Berghaus, Peter Konwitschny, and featured as its only performer Hanneliese Shantin from Rostock. Both were guest artists at the BE. The director submitted a *Konzeption* to the Ministry that was replete with the language it wanted to hear regarding 'exemplary situations of historical significance' and how Müller's texts were to be interpreted 'in our sense' for 'our gain'. He, however, noted that dramaturge Jochen

---

[173] See [Weigel?] to Hans Giersch, 28 May 1966, BBA uncatalogued file 'HW Haus 1966'. Central Committee member Alexander Abusch was reported to have supported this move.

[174] WM, 'Beckett mit Musik', *Volksblatt*, undated.

Ziller could tweak the text 'in the light of its usefulness'.[175] Konwitschny was clearly communicating that whatever they wrote in the final document should serve the purpose of having the play staged. The *Konzeption*, demanded by the Ministry, had become a parody of itself. The production, regardless of what it took to bring it to the stage, was a lively affair, with Shantin slipping in and out of roles, playing with the text's own theatricality while acknowledging the not unserious themes of historical disasters and potential apocalypse.[176]

Yet despite the small gems in Wekwerth's repertoire over the years, the BE was mostly lumbering its way towards what would become known as the *Wende* ('turn' or 'change'), the collapse of the Berlin Wall and the GDR.

[175] Peter Konwitschny to Jochen Ziller, 19 October 1987, AdK Theaterdokumentation ID 626.
[176] For a fuller discussion of the production, see David Barnett, *Literature versus Theatre. Textual Problems and Theatrical Realization in the Later Plays of Heiner Müller* (Frankfurt/Main: Peter Lang, 1998), pp. 234–8.

12   Wekwerth's last stand: 1989–1991

The Berliner Ensemble before and after the fall of the Wall

The fall of the Berlin Wall on 9 November 1989 may have surprised many, but signs of its cracks were visible beforehand. The accession of Mikhail Gorbachev to the position of General Secretary of the Soviet Communist Party in 1985 paved the way to gradual liberalization in the Soviet Union and other socialist states. The GDR, however, displayed and effected resistance to the reforms taking place in Moscow. The sometimes violent repression of demonstrations in September and October 1989 were presaged by arrests made at an annual rally on 18 January 1988, the GDR's designated day to commemorate the murder of communist leaders Rosa Luxemburg and Karl Liebknecht in 1919. Dissidents who had used the occasion to call for freedom of thought and human rights were bundled into a police van. In the cultural sphere, a somewhat tepid thaw can be seen in the more challenging plays staged from 1986 onwards, as discussed in the previous chapter. There were other signs of change for the GDR, too, and two of these came in quick succession.

Readers of the FRG's premiere theatre magazine, *Theater heute*, may have been taken aback by the candour of Minister Hoffmann in an interview that appeared in its 1988 Yearbook. The extensive discussion headed a series of eleven articles grouped under the title 'Glasnost in the GDR's Theatres' and made some remarkable claims. Perhaps the most unexpected was that Hoffman believed 'that the theatre system can't be run centrally'.[1] The interview's title 'The Surest Thing Change' was a quotation from the Minister himself, and he perhaps jokingly asked his interlocutors *not* to use it as a title. His dialectical assertion acknowledged an almost inevitable upheaval that lay ahead after so many years of stagnation. In a preface to the interview, the two journalists who conducted

---

[1] Hoffmann, in Peter von Becker and Michael Merschmeier, '"Das Sicherste ist die Veränderung." *Theater heute*-Gespräch mit dem DDR-Kulturminister Hans-Joachim Hoffmann', *Theater heute*, Jahrbuch (1988), pp. 10–20 (12).

it nonetheless advised their readership not to read too much into the Minister's comments, noting that Kurt Hager was 'more powerful than all the Hoffmanns'.[2] They did not realize how true their words would prove to be.

The head of the Central Committee's Cultural Department, Ursula Ragwitz, wrote directly to Hager with an admittedly fair description of the interview in September 1988.[3] At the time of publication, Hoffmann was actually in Havana at a conference, but was summoned to see Hager virtually as he got off the plane in East Berlin.[4] The 'meeting' was actually a one-sided dressing down. It ended with a self-abasing confession of weakness from the Minister: 'Comrade Hoffmann replied that he was aware of his peculiar position and . . . now had to say that he was fully committed to the direction and politics of the Party'.[5] Reportedly, Hoffmann was so shaken by the encounter that he passed out and was rushed to hospital. News of the incident got out, and he retained his position due to the wave of sympathy his condition elicited.[6] The SED had not, however, finished with him yet. In a letter to Erich Honecker, he took full responsibility for all his alleged mistakes and offered to read the letter out loud in front of the Central Committee should Honecker so desire.[7]

Theater heute, in its January 1989 number, noted that the Yearbook had been prevented from appearing in the GDR.[8] A similar ban had been issued to the Soviet digest *Sputnik* in November 1988. The magazine collected articles from the Soviet press, and it became a pro-Glasnost publication in the GDR for the openness with which it dealt with taboo topics. According to Hager, Honecker banned *Sputnik* unilaterally.[9] Hager himself was no supporter of liberalization in the USSR, however, a position made infamous when he commented that one does not change one's wallpaper simply because one's neighbour has done so.[10]

---

[2] Ibid., p. 10.

[3] See Ragwitz to Hager, 23 September 1988, SAPMO BArch DY 30/18732.

[4] See Hermann-Ernst Schauer, 'Der verdächtige Demokrat', in Gertraude Hoffmann and Klaus Höpcke (eds.), *'Das Sicherste ist die Veränderung'. Hans-Joachim Hoffmann: Kulturminister der DDR und häufig verdächtigter Demokrat* (Berlin: Dietz, 2003), pp. 10–24 (20).

[5] Anon., 'Gespräch des Genossen Hager mit dem Genossen Hans-Joachim Hoffmann am 12.10.1988', undated, 3 pages (2), SAPMO BArch DY 30/26314.

[6] See Thomas Flierl, 'Vorwort', in Hoffmann and Höpcke (eds.), *'Das Sicherste'*, pp. 7–9 (8).

[7] See Hoffmann to Honecker, 2 December 1988, BArch DR 1/13157.

[8] See Peter von Becker, 'Glasnost', *Theater heute*, 1 (1989), p. 1.

[9] See Hager, *Erinnerungen*, p. 389.

[10] The interview appeared in the West German news magazine *Stern* on 9 April 1987 and was reprinted in *Neues Deutschland* the following day.

The question arises as to how these events were received at the BE. Actor Corinna Harfouch claims that Wekwerth had a message she displayed on a BE notice-board protesting against the *Sputnik* ban removed scarcely a day after she posted it.[11] This may have been Wekwerth's public response, yet behind the scenes he was anything but supportive of the government's recent repressive action. Less than a week after the ban was announced, Wekwerth called the measure painful to Ragwitz.[12] An anonymous report on a local Party meeting at the BE noted that Wekwerth openly criticized the decision on *Sputnik* as 'idiotic' and treated Hoffmann's interview 'really positively'.[13] Hager sent the report to Honecker and wrote that he would have words with Wekwerth before the next Central Committee plenum.[14]

By August 1989, pressure was building as GDR citizens exploited the summer holidays and the travel possibilities they brought with them by seeking flight to the FRG via Hungary. Wekwerth learned in the same month that an interview he had given would no longer appear in the *Neue Berliner Illustrierte*.[15] He protested to Hager's office in September, emphasizing that the interview had been given before the summer holidays and demanded reasons for the ban in plain language.[16] He also wrote to Hager shortly afterwards and directly criticized the GDR's distorting media apparatus.[17] The interview finally appeared under a programmatic title, taken from *Galileo*: 'Victory of Reason – Victory of Rational People', and included a remark about how trust needed to be regained.[18] What one finds in both Wekwerth's critique to Hager and the interview itself is a position common to many SED loyalists: the need for honesty and renewal *in* the context of the Party and GDR socialism, not a dismantling of the system or its replacement with democratic pluralism, a position not unlike Brecht's with respect to the uprising of 17 June 1953.

As fate would have it, the Theater am Schiffbauerdamm, the Berliner Ensemble's home since 1954, was closed for renovation for six months in 1989 and only re-opened to the public on 11 October. The ensemble was

[11] See Corinna Harfouch, in Zolchow, 'Protokoll der Gespräche zwischen Corinna Harfouch und Sabine Zolchow', p. 8.
[12] See Wekwerth to Ragwitz, 23 November 1988, SAPMO BArch DY 30/23430.
[13] Anon., 'Information über die Berichtswahlversammlung der Parteiorganisation im Berliner Ensemble', [October or November 1988], 4 pages (2 and 3, respectively), SAPMO BArch DY 30/27350.
[14] See Hager to Honecker, 15 November 1988, ibid.
[15] See Joachim Maaß to Wekwerth, 15 August 1989, ibid.
[16] See Wekwerth to Hilde Schmidt, 19 September 1989, ibid.
[17] See Wekwerth to Hager, 22 September 1989, ibid.
[18] Joachim Maaß, 'Sieg der Vernunft – Sieg der Vernünftigen', *Neue Berliner Illustrierte*, 40 (1989), pp. 2–3.

nonetheless able to find space to meet and discuss the historic changes. The BE issued a public statement regarding recent events in the GDR on 29 September 1989. The declaration called for openness in debate, the re-establishment of trust between the government and the people, and the need for change to ensure the survival of socialism.[19] Wekwerth wrote to Ragwitz shortly afterwards assuring her that he had promoted a text that made suggestions, rather than complaints.[20] That Wekwerth was publicly protesting had an amount of symbolic value, too, and, in some quarters, sanctioned protest by other artists.[21] A mass demonstration, held on Berlin's Alexanderplatz on 4 November 1989, had been primarily organized by the Deutsches Theater,[22] although other Berlin theatres, including the BE, contributed to its planning and successful execution. Wekwerth was not at the demonstration himself, however, something that may raise the question as to just how committed he was to public protest in the light of his allegiance to the SED. He accounts for his absence by saying that Stasi officers Girod and Werner pressurized him to stay away. In response, he had a heart attack and was rushed to hospital, and that prevented him from attending.[23] While Wekwerth can sometimes portray his biography in a rosier hue in hindsight, there is little reason to doubt his version of events here: a letter from Tenschert to Wekwerth was sent to a GDR hospital two days after the momentous demonstration.[24]

That the theatres had been a focus for the protests is undeniable. However, as Laura Bradley wisely notes, while they stepped into the breach when official institutions failed, they were later still lobbying for reform while protesters were calling for reunification with the FRG.[25] A sign of how theatre was already out of step with its audience can be found in the BE's first new production of the 1989/90 season: a performance of all five parts of Heiner Müller's *Wolokolamsker Chaussee* (*The Road of Tanks*) on 16 December 1989. The cycle included both a scene set on the day of the workers' uprising, 17 June 1953, and a grotesque in which a Stasi official becomes one with his or her writing desk. Reviewers were generally disappointed: Ernst Schumacher believed that the theatricality diluted the impact of the text, and Sibylle Wirsing that the material

---

[19] See Anon., 'Berliner Ensemble', in Angela Kuberski (ed.), *Wir treten aus unseren Rollen heraus: Dokumente des Aufbruchs Herbst '89* (Berlin: Verband der Theaterschaffenden, 1990), pp. 22–3.

[20] See Wekwerth to Ragwitz, 2 October 1989, SAPMO BArch DY 30/26313.

[21] See Bradley, *Cooperation and Conflict*, p. 285.

[22] See Hans Rübesame (ed.), *Antrag auf Demonstration: Die Protestsammlung im Deutschen Theater am 15. Oktober 1989* (Berlin: Christoph Links, 2010).

[23] See Wekwerth, *Erinnern ist Leben*, p. 362.

[24] See Tenschert to Wekwerth, 6 November 1989, AdK MWA 'BE Korr. ab 1970'.

[25] See Bradley, *Cooperation and Conflict*, pp. 285 and 287.

remained solidly in the past, rather than resonating in the present.[26] Theatre, of course, can be a slow and cumbersome beast, and the view that it could respond quickly and eloquently to an historical moment that had taken the world by surprise was more wishful thinking than a reflection of what one might realistically expect from the institution. Indeed, a response to the *Wende* would prove difficult for the BE to articulate, both in terms of repertoire and its understanding of its own identity once the political structure that had nurtured and supported it started to crumble.

Reacting to a revolution

The most immediate response from the BE to the fall of the Wall was a special programme dedicated to the victims of Stalinism. The evening was planned in mid October as a joint project between the theatres of East Berlin to be staged at the BE.[27] It was performed with deliberate irony on the 110th anniversary of Stalin's self-proclaimed birthday,[28] on 21 December, and broadcast on GDR television the following day as 'Erinnerung – Das Recht auf Gedächtnis' ('Remembrance – The Right to Memory'). The six-hour marathon included spoken tributes, actors' complaints at their treatment by the police and the Stasi that autumn, and passages from books banned from publication in the East.[29] One reviewer noted how the theatre's role had shifted in the past months: 'GDR theatre, once the harbinger of the "*Wende*", is currently its voice of suffering'.[30] This special evening, of course, was a one-off event; the BE's more formal plans proved more difficult to manage.

The post-*Wende* period was not an easy one for theatres in East Berlin in general and for the BE in particular. The shock to the body politic and the fast-paced events that led to the dissolution of the GDR less than a year after the border was opened meant that the theatres simply did not have the time to respond to the ever-changing landscape. Indeed, even today, the speed of the transformation is breathtaking. While the faithful

---

[26] See Ernst Schumacher, 'Abmarsch von der Wolokolamsker', *Berliner Zeitung*, 19 December 1989; and Sibylle Wirsing, 'An der langen Straße nach Nirgendwo', *Frankfurter Allgemeine Zeitung*, 28 December 1989.

[27] See Wekwerth to Heinz Adamek, 25 October 1989, BEA File 'Schriftverkehr Christoph Schroth'.

[28] According to Church records, Stalin was born on 18 December 1878, yet he later maintained that the date was 21 December 1879, see Roman Brackman, *The Secret File of Joseph Stalin: A Hidden Life* (London: Frank Cass, 2001), p. 2. It is unclear why he chose to do this.

[29] See BEA File 'Stalin 21.12.89'.

[30] Heinz Kersten, 'Trauerarbeit', *Frankfurter Rundschau*, undated.

were talking about reforming socialism, GDR citizens had already voted for the Deutschmark and reunification. Each month drove on the inexorable transformation, and the theatres, like much of the populace, were at a loss to keep up. However, *Intendanten* at least had to acknowledge that a major change had taken place if production work was to attempt to comment on the upheavals. In 1995, Wekwerth was still of the opinion that the *Wende* was not a revolution.[31] His three productions following the fall of the Wall, Kleist's classic *Prinz Friedrich von Homburg* (*Prince Friedrich of Homburg*) in June 1990, Brecht's *Schweyk im Zweiten Weltkrieg* (*Schweyk in the Second World War*) in September 1991 and Labiche's farce *Florentiner Strohhut* (*An Italian Straw Hat*) in December 1991 were not terribly popular. They ran, on average, for fewer than twenty performances per production, and were mainly received poorly, although the farce did garner the odd plaudit.

The BE needed to re-establish itself once the GDR was officially dissolved and incorporated into the FRG on 3 October 1990. In a crisis meeting on 25 September, the management struggled with the fact that its latest premiere, Thomas Brasch's *Rotter*, due to go up four days later, had sold all of forty tickets.[32] Christoph Schroth directed the play, a reflection on its eponymous lead, an accommodating careerist in Nazi Germany and the GDR, with care so that it avoided both anchoring itself to its own historical periods and trying to comment directly on the events of the present. This was certainly a solid production, but was simply in the wrong place at the wrong time. Wekwerth, who had been away directing in Vienna in September, returned to the BE in October and wondered whether plays about the GDR could find an audience at this time.[33] The other drama under discussion at the meeting was Georg Seidel's *Youth Villa*. This is perhaps Seidel's Chekhovian masterpiece, an elegiac reflection on an East German family's disintegration. The metaphorical dimension was not missed by the critics, and the play that Seidel feared would be invalidated by the fall of the Wall,[34] actually became all the more painful and relevant. Seidel never lived to see the production itself; he died on 3 June 1990, half a year before the premiere of 19 January 1991, and the play was still unfinished. Dramaturge Jochen Ziller retrieved extra material from Seidel's computer and, together with director Fritz Marquardt, set about integrating the scenes into the text. The reviews were

---

[31] See Wekwerth, in Hans-Dieter Schütt, *Manfred Wekwerth*, p. 222.
[32] See Corrinna Wojtek, 'Krisensitzung 25.9.1990', 25 September 1990, AdK ESA 'BE Int. A-Z'.
[33] See Wekwerth, in Sigrid Kunze, 'Leitungssitzung am 4.10.1990', 3 pages (1), ibid.
[34] See Fritz Marquardt, in Zolchow, 'Protokoll der Gespräche' zwischen Fritz Marquardt und Sabine Zolchow, p. 1.

universally supportive of the production's sensitive treatment of its subject matter, which did not denounce the characters' personal weaknesses,
but allowed them to be fully explored as they approached dissolution.[35]
Perhaps the best description of the constellation on stage is offered by dramaturge Jörg Mihan: 'I see a late-socialist play in a post-socialist period
made by pro-socialist people. It is a stimulating encounter between text,
time and performance'.[36] The play was invited to Mülheim that summer,
a festival for the six best new dramas in the German-speaking theatre,
and there it won first prize. Yet even that could not prevent it from leaving
the repertoire; topical, high-quality, award-winning drama was finding it
hard to attract audiences in the early 1990s.

Yet it was not so much the BE's repertoire that was causing anxiety in
the immediate period after the *Wende*, but what the BE actually meant in
its new post-Wall context. Towards the end of 1989 and the beginning
of 1990, various groups began thinking about what the BE would look
like and how it should function. A document drafted by Fritz Marquardt
and Jochen Ziller was bold and radical: 'the BE's shift from a site of
experimentation to a State-owned repertory theatre must be brought to
an end'.[37] They acknowledged that even though they could not turn back
the clock, Brecht's organizational structures were highly productive, and
they proposed the formation of 'working groups' as 'an attempt at real
collaboration between those responsible for a production'.[38] Wekwerth,
together with dramaturge Holger Teschke, also drafted a proposal whose
gestation lasted from January 1990 until the end of that year. The finished document was finally published in the May/June 1991 issue of the
left-wing magazine *Das Argument*. Wekwerth opened the essay by making
the distinction between a theatre based on Brecht's principles and one
that merely based its repertoire on the playwright.[39] He proposed that
the BE become a focus for left-leaning theatre-makers from the whole
of Europe, yet his terms were strictly those that had accompanied his
Intendanz for the past decade: he wanted to further his 'philosophical
theatre for the people' and its rationalist basis.[40] Brecht-Schall criticized

---

[35] See, for example, Christoph Funke, 'Vom unaufhaltsamen Sterben', *Der Morgen*,
21 January 1991; or Sibylle Wirsing, 'Neue Bekanntschaften mit altem Schrecken',
Frankfurter Allgemeine Zeitung, 24 January 1991.

[36] Jörg Mihan, 'Zu *Villa Jugend* – 1. Hauptprobe am 16.1.1991', 17 January 1991, pp. 4
(2), AdK Theaterdokumentation ID 669.

[37] Fritz Marquardt and Jochen Ziller, 'Thesen zum BE', [1989?], 3 pages (1), AdK ESA
'BE Int. A-Z'.

[38] Ibid., p. 2.

[39] See Wekwerth, 'Über eine Weiterarbeit des Berliner Ensembles', *Das Argument*, 187
(1991), pp. 421–30 (421).

[40] Ibid., pp. 423 and 425.

one of Wekwerth's strategies back in the drafting stage: she said that he could not call on the BE's good name, countering that their reputation was actually being used against them in the new Germany.[41] Joachim Tenschert also formulated a series of ideas, which would feed into Wekwerth's document, yet these were roundly repudiated by Jörg Mihan. He noted that Tenschert's use of the word 'experiment' was vague, that his understanding of Brecht did not correspond to the BE's recent productions, which were anything but critical, and that his list of directors for a new centre for left-wing theatre was so diverse that it made the political category meaningless.[42] Mihan had exposed Tenschert's clichés and demanded more precision. It is clear from this brief survey that Wekwerth and Tenschert were merely trying to repackage the existing BE and imagine its future as a pulsing heart of left-wing theatre-making while Marquardt and Ziller at least considered how structural reform might promote new ways of working and new types of productions.

Although the FRG had guaranteed the BE's subsidies in the run-up to reunification,[43] the levels were significantly lower than those given to former West German theatres due to wage differentials and lower running costs in the East. By October 1990, the BE had received advice from the Deutscher Bühnenverein, the body that represents the interests of theatres and other performing arts in the FRG. It unequivocally instructed the BE to drive down production costs, something the company interpreted as job cuts in administration, to prevent losses to its creative staff.[44] The BE, like other former GDR theatres, was entering a different kind of financial climate and sought expertise from the 'other' Germany in the form of René Serge Mund, a native Maltese who had spent all his adult life in the FRG and had previously run the somewhat minor touring theatre of Remscheid. Mund set out his ideas to Wekwerth, a day after discussions with the *Intendant*, in October 1990. These included a flexible financial model that promoted innovation and a plan to attract sponsors.[45] As will become evident in the next chapter, his concept was not that far from the one that was supposed to lead to the rebirth of the BE in 1993.

[41] See Brecht-Schall to Wekwerth, 7 March 1990, AdK ESA 'BE Int. A-Z'.
[42] See Jörg Mihan, 'Bemerkungen zu den "Gesichtspunkten zu Grundverständnis des Berliner Ensembles in unserer Zeit"', 5 April 1990, 9 pages (4 and 6), AdK JTA 'BE-Dramaturgie u.a. interne Korr. ab 1978'.
[43] See Corrinna Wojtek, 'Besprechung Theaterleitung und Betriebsrat 17.9.1990', 17 September 1990, 2 pages (1), AdK ESA 'BE Int. A-Z'.
[44] See Sigrid Kunze, 'Leitungssitzung am 11.10.90', 12 October 1990, 3 pages (1), ibid.
[45] See René Mund to Wekwerth, 17 October 1990, ibid.

According to Wekwerth, who first employed Mund as 'advisor to the *Intendant* in matters of finance and administration' in November,[46] it was the Ministry of Culture that brought him to the BE's attention.[47] Mund took over as Head of Administration on 1 April 1991 after the previous incumbent, Bernd Gerwien, left.[48] Gerwien, whom Wekwerth had appointed in the late 1980s, had fallen out of favour after botching the BE's tour to Mexico in the summer of 1990. He had not realized that the Germans needed US visas even though they were only stopping over in the country; the surcharge was hefty and had to be paid in hard currency.[49] While Mund, at the time, appeared to be a sensible replacement for Gerwien, another new face at the BE drew criticism. The company was looking for a new Head of PR, and in July 1990 Wekwerth had simply appointed one: Thomas Wedel, who had been a press and cultural attaché for the GDR in Greece. Tenschert protested: 'I'm in favour of an application process. I'm in favour of an expert with integrity and proven experience in the West'.[50] The new appointment did not last long; Tenschert wrote that Wedel had shown himself to be 'a complete mistake' by September.[51] Wekwerth's abilities to function as a competent *Intendant* were starting to be questioned by one of his closest associates.

Others, however, were also critical of Wekwerth's judgement, as he tried to find a way of ensuring the BE's financial viability after the collapse of the GDR. The *Intendant* had taken seriously the advice given by the GDR's last Minister of Culture, Herbert Schirmer, that he should seek new partners. In the summer of 1990, he entered into talks with firms in the US and Japan. He wrote to Brecht-Schall to elicit agreement from her on his new plan, known as the 'New Venture',[52] because his potential backers specifically wanted to support the BE for its productions of Brecht's plays. They were offering high-quality video recordings and long-playing records of BE productions, and the publication of documentations in various forms. They would also organize tours to the highest international standards and make loans at 0 per cent interest to

---

[46] See Sigrid Kunze, 'Kurzprotokoll über die Leitungssitzung am 15.11.1990', 19 November 1990, 2 pages (1), ibid.

[47] Wekwerth, unpublished interview with the author, 1 July 2011.

[48] See Wekwerth to the BE Staff Council, 14 November 1990, AdK ESA 'Leitung (Korr., Protokolle) 1990/91'.

[49] Wekwerth, unpublished interview with the author, 1 July 2011.

[50] Tenschert to Wekwerth, 13 July 1990, AdK JTA 'BE-Dramaturgie u.a. interne Korr. ab 1978'.

[51] Tenschert to Wekwerth, 1 September 1990, ibid.

[52] The statement of agreement, dated 31 June 1990, 18 pages, is in AdK ESA 'BE Int. A-Z'.

run over ten years.[53] The offer, from today's perspective, seems too good to be true, but to Wekwerth, a man with little experience of the capitalist West, the terms were favourable, and he was clearly enthusiastic. He believed that the potential shareholders would bring the BE up to 2 million marks (or roughly €1 million in 2014), a subsidy he considered would not only ensure survival, but improve the ensemble's salaries. Just over a year later, the Berlin Senate agreed to subsidize the BE to the tune of 14.9 million marks.[54] The discrepancy between the two sums says much about how little Wekwerth understood of the practical aspects of running a major theatre in the new FRG. He also valued the financial and political independence he believed the loans would bring from what he called, without a hint of irony, the 'new authoritarian state'.[55] Brecht-Schall, a far shrewder player when it came to money, protested in the strongest possible terms to the BE's leadership and insisted that a lawyer read the terms of the New Venture contract Wekwerth was so keen to sign.[56] Wekwerth's own naïvety in these matters was revealed in his reply in which he tacitly acknowledged that the agreement had yet not been seen by a German legal expert.[57] The lack of further reference to the plan suggests that good financial sense prevailed, and Wekwerth desisted. His days, however, were numbered. Not only did dissatisfaction from within the BE manifest itself, someone more powerful than Brecht-Schall from the 'new authoritarian state' was eyeing his scalp.

The West German senator and the East German *Intendant*

The German theatre system is the most highly subsidized in Europe. After the fall of the Wall and subsequent reunification, the FRG found that the number of theatres in Berlin had rapidly increased, and this situation exerted pressure on the City of Berlin's cultural budget. In late 1990, the Theater im Palast, the venue that staged the first Beckett in the GDR, was selling off its equipment and the BE showed interest in purchasing its rostra.[58] Nervousness with respect to the future was also felt in the BE where the question of jobs and even the existence of the company made

---

[53] See Wekwerth to Brecht-Schall, 22 July 1990, ibid.
[54] See dpa, 'Brecht umbrochen', *die tageszeitung*, 30 August 1991.
[55] Wekwerth to Tenschert, 27 July 1990, AdK JTA 'BE-Dramaturgie u.a. interne Korr. ab 1978'.
[56] See Brecht-Schall to BE Leadership, 11 September 1990, AdK ESA 'BE Int. A-Z'.
[57] See Wekwerth to Brecht-Schall, 12 September 1990, ibid.
[58] See Sigrid Kunze, 'Kurzprotokoll über die Leitungssitzung am 22.11.1990' undated, 2 pages (2), ibid.

production work difficult and caused a general air of anxiety. Tenschert's description of the BE to Wekwerth on his return from directing in Vienna in September 1990 was bleak: staff felt isolated and at risk, especially in the light of the New Venture project,[59] a gambit that was designed to ease financial pressure on the theatre, but that would then leave staffing levels at the mercy of private investors. The ensemble had good reason to be fearful as politicians holding the purse strings addressed the number of Berlin theatres and their financial feasibility.

The Berlin City parliament elected Ulrich Roloff-Momin Senator for Culture in early 1991. A month after he was appointed, he commissioned a report on Berlin theatres that was written by the respected critic, director and *Intendant* Ivan Nagel, together with three other experts on theatre in the East and West. They were given a mere three weeks to complete their task. Nagel told him that the report would be a description of the institutional landscape and would not, on principle, recommend any closures.[60] Before considering Nagel's report, I will turn briefly to one compiled by the GDR's Ministry of Culture months before the State was dissolved. In it, the authors divided the city's theatres into two categories: ones able to survive the *Wende* on their own strengths and ones that needed to define their own niche.[61] The BE, unsurprisingly, belonged to the former category. The financial statistics found in the report also make interesting reading. Theatres in the East received 105 million marks in subsidy for a seating capacity of 11,500 seats while those in the West received 200 million for 8,000. That is, the East annually subsidized each seat to the tune of 9,130 marks while the West almost trebled that sum with 25,000 marks per seat. This statistic already signals why Roloff-Momin's plans eventually led to the closure of West Berlin's Schiller-Theater in 1993 instead of any of the major East Berlin theatres.

Nagel's report focused, as set out in its own terms of reference, on '*profiling every single institution; the diversity of a metropolis*'.[62] While acknowledging that Berlin would have to close three venues if it funded the theatres without support from the Federal government, the report unambiguously called the possibility of this measure a three-fold "'cultural

[59] See Tenschert to Wekwerth, 1 September 1990, AdK JTA 'BE-Dramaturgie u.a. interne Korr. ab 1978'.
[60] See Ulrich Roloff-Momin, *Zuletzt: Kultur* (Berlin: Aufbau, 1997), p. 40.
[61] See Bernhard Karthens and Rainer Roßner, 'Eine Weltstadt und ihr Theater – Studie zu Gegenwart und Zukunft der Berliner Theater', [June 1990], n.p., AdK TiW 1856. All subsequent references are taken from this source.
[62] Friedrich Dieckmann, Michael Merschmeier, Ivan Nagel, Henning Rischbieter, 'Überlegungen zur Situation der Beliner Theater', ed. by Nagel, 6 April 1991, 20 pages (4), AdK TiW 1755.

disgrace"'.[63] However, as Sabine Zolchow notes 'everything the experts feared occurred'; two theatres and an orchestra closed and Federal funding remained uncertain.[64] Later in the document, the authors' discussion of the BE did not make happy reading for Wekwerth. They considered appraising the theatre company one of their most difficult tasks and called for a renewal of the BE's Brechtian mission and, by extension, its *Intendant*.[65] They also suggested three further options: first, that the BE officially become a 'Brecht Museum... with nothing but counterfeit originals' because none of its current productions had actually been directed by Brecht; second, that a theatre school devoted to the methods of the epic theatre be annexed to the company; third, that the BE become a private theatre, run 'as a family business' as 'a monument for theatre historians, home-grown keepers of the Old Faith, overseas tourists'. The final option, replete with ironic language, was an attempt to address the possibility of passing the company to Brecht-Schall. Friedrich Dieckmann was the only co-author from the GDR and he submitted an appendix that stated he was not always in agreement with his three Western colleagues.[66] There was nothing there, however, to suggest that the quartet diverged on the question of the BE.

In a press release sent to the Deutsche Presseagentur, the FRG's news service, Wekwerth dismissed Nagel's report as inconsequential.[67] Other leaders of Berlin theatres also considered that the document had been written far too quickly and was 'often superficial'.[68] Their views had been expressed at a hearing into the report conducted by the SPD, Germany's major left-of-centre party. Wekwerth did not attend, something that led actor Carmen-Maja Antoni, the chair of the Personalrat (Staff Council), who represented the BE there, to call the company leaderless.[69] The reason for Wekwerth's absence may be found in the Senator's plans for the *Intendant*. One of the peculiar attributes of this position was that the Senator had the power to appoint or dismiss *Intendanten* without consultation or due process, not unlike the GDR's Minister of Culture. And while he was prepared to use this power, he actually sought a different route to rid himself of Wekwerth.

---

[63] Ibid., p. 6.
[64] Sabine Zolchow, 'The Island of Berlin', in Denise Varney (ed.), *Theatre in the Berlin Republic. German Drama since Reunification* (Bern: Peter Lang, 2008), pp. 55–80 (66).
[65] Dieckmann *et al.*, 'Überlegungen', p. 13, as are the following quotations.
[66] See Dieckmann, 'Besondere Aspekte', 5 pages (1), in ibid.
[67] See Wekwerth, 'Stellungnahme zu dem "Theatergutachten"', 11 April 1991, n.p., Adk TiW 689.
[68] dpa/lbn, 'Widerstand der Betroffenen gegen Theatergutachten', *Volksblatt*, 30 April 1991.
[69] See ibid.

To this day, Wekwerth has ascribed his removal from the BE to his 'foolishness' in making public his plans to turn the BE into a centre for left-wing theatre.[70] Yet while Wekwerth and his collaborators *drafted* the essay for *Das Argument* in 1990, it was only published in the May/June issue of the magazine in 1991. Roloff-Momin already had Wekwerth in his sights before that time and demanded his resignation at a meeting of 18 March 1991. According to the Senator, he was surprised at how little had changed at the BE after the *Wende*. Wekwerth allegedly told him that he saw no great difference between GDR and FRG cultural policy, at which point Roloff-Momin asked him to quit.[71] Wekwerth's private comments on the FRG, quoted above, would seem to confirm Roloff-Momin's account. However, Wekwerth was not prepared to go quietly, and in a report to the Staff Council about the meeting, he only noted that the Senator had supported the BE's continued existence and the move to pay-equalization with theatres in West Berlin.[72] What he omitted was Roloff-Momin's main complaint with Wekwerth: his connections to the SED's apparatus. As President of the Academy of Arts and a member of the Central Committee, he had simply been too close to the heart of power in a repressive regime. However, Roloff-Momin's view was not inflexible, and he retained the services of Albert Hetterle, a member of the SED's District Leadership in Berlin since 1967. He, as *Intendant* of the Maxim-Gorki-Theater, had approved the production of Volker Braun's *Society in Transition*, for example. High-ranking SED membership was thus not an automatic ground for dismissal.

The future of the BE and its leader was discussed at a staff meeting in April 1991. Christoph Schroth, who had come to the BE in 1988 with a handful of his colleagues from Schwerin, insisted on Brecht as the company's focal point, but attacked the Brecht estate for its restrictive treatment of the performing rights. He also said he would find it appropriate if both Wekwerth and Tenschert resigned.[73] Actor Hermann Beyer thought that the West German director and *Intendant* Peter Zadek might make a good replacement, and director Fritz Marquardt argued for a 2- to 3-year moratorium on staging Brecht as a way of taking the estate out of the BE's equation.[74] Around this time, Roloff-Momin went on the offensive. He publicly demanded that Wekwerth resign due to his

---

[70] See, for example, Wekwerth, 'Zum Artikel', p. 47; Wekwerth, unpublished interview with the author, 1 July 2011.
[71] See Roloff-Momin, *Zuletzt: Kultur*, p. 54.
[72] See Wekwerth to the Staff Council, 21 March 1991, AdK TiW 690.
[73] See Christoph Schroth, in Anon., [in pencil: 'Spartenversammlung/Protokoll'], [in pencil: April 1991], 9 pages (1 and 2), AdK TiW 693.
[74] See Hermann Beyer and Fritz Marquardt, in ibid. (4 and 8, respectively).

support for a regime that curtailed, rather than promoted freedom of expression.[75] Wekwerth insisted on his legal rights under FRG employment law and said he wanted a formal dismissal. Thus, the two were engaged in a moral battle. There was no doubt about Wekwerth's departure, it was more a question of who would effect it. Unwilling to pander to Wekwerth's vanity, the Staff Council demanded Wekwerth's resignation on 8 May 1991.[76] It had previously discussed Wekwerth's position with Brecht-Schall as the rights holder to Brecht's plays in Berlin and found that she was no longer in favour of Wekwerth retaining the *Intendanz*. Instead, she put herself forward for the job, although she acknowledged that the Senate had rejected the proposal.[77] By mid May, the Staff Council reported that Wekwerth had agreed to resign at the end of July and that he had handed the BE over to René Serge Mund, something the Council found unlawful as Wekwerth was still legally responsible for the company.[78] Mund chaired a meeting of directors and dramaturges in June at which it was confirmed that he would serve as interim *Intendant* for the 1991/92 season and that he would be in discussion with Antoni and Marquardt about future cooperation. He also announced that he had signed a contract with Wekwerth to keep him on as a director,[79] a unilateral move made without consultation.

Wekwerth's *Intendanz* had been a mostly steadying and steady affair, yet this was also its main weakness. The lack of development that dogged the BE's Brecht reception can be put down to the in-house style re-established over these years and the directors that Wekwerth lined up from the Regieinstitut. In addition, there was no real desire to make theatre that could meaningfully discuss the GDR itself. The complicity between theatre and State that pervaded the production of *The Great Peace* in 1979 (see pp. 309–14, Chapter 10) tacitly became the norm in the 1980s. Only in 1990, with *Youth Villa*, did the BE begin a proper exploration of the GDR. While there were certainly high points in Wekwerth's *Intendanz*, they were few and far between. That Wekwerth championed exciting new writing from playwrights like Georg Seidel and Volker Braun was a mark of his commitment, but, conversely, he did

[75] This and the subsequent position from Wekwerth are quoted in 'Wie können Sie das mit Ihrem Gewissen vereinbaren, Herr Wekwerth? Treten Sie zurück', *BZ*, 26 April 1991. NB The *BZ* is the West Berlin *Berliner Zeitung* and this abbreviation will be used to differentiate between the East and West newspapers of the same name.

[76] See Staff Council to Wekwerth, 8 May 1991, AdK TiW 690.

[77] See Anon., 'Gesprächsprotokoll des Personalrates mit Frau Barbara Brecht-Schall am 26.4.1991, 10 Uhr', 27 April 1991, 6 pages (1, 4 and 5), AdK TiW 692.

[78] See Anon., 'Personalratssitzung 15.5.[1991]', undated, n.p., ibid.

[79] See Sigrid Kunze, 'Protokoll über die Regie- und Dramaturgensitzung am 19.6.1991', 20 June 1991, 4 pages (1), AdK ESA 'BE Int. A-Z'.

not seek to use these writers to open up the fault lines running through the GDR. The lack of ideas and direction after the *Wende* left him a sitting target for Roloff-Momin, and once the Senator's mind had been made up, Wekwerth's time was up.

Wekwerth's ejection from the *Intendanz* in the summer of 1991 led to administrative chaos over the coming months. Antoni, Marquardt and Mund announced that they would run the BE together in a temporary capacity once Wekwerth formally left at the end of July.[80] By the end of August, Mund remained the interim *Intendant*, but Marquardt was now the artistic director and Bärbel Jaksch the head of the dramaturgy department.[81] Yet shortly after this management structure had been made public, Marquardt and Jaksch privately resigned their positions because of disagreements with Mund, and a new leadership of Heiner Müller, Marquardt and Jaksch was announced on 24 October.[82] The day before, Mund had been sacked for 'overstepping his authority and budgetary responsibilities'.[83] Mund had raised salaries without consultation with the Senate, according to two BE members,[84] and his own style had been secretive, as evidenced by the contract he signed to retain Wekwerth at the BE as guest director.[85] By the end of the year, the newspapers reported that Peter Palitzsch, one-time assistant to Brecht, would be relieving Müller and Marquardt, and leading the BE himself.[86] The situation was a mess and required a solution quickly. Roloff-Momin's response was as surprising and ambitious as it would be unsuccessful.

---

[80] See Anon., 'Wir übernehmen das Brecht-Theater', *BZ*, 31 June 1991.

[81] See Volker Oesterreich, 'Mit Wekwerth und Brechts *Schwejk* in die neue Saison', *Berliner Morgenpost*, 29 August 1991.

[82] See dpa/JW, 'Das "schwierige Theater"', *Junge Welt*, 24 October 1991.

[83] Tsp., 'Interimsleitung für Berliner Ensemble', *Der Tagesspiegel* 23 October 1991.

[84] See Axel Werner, in Sabine Zolchow, 'Protokoll des Gesprächs zwischen Axel Werner und Sabine Zolchow am 12.12.2005 in Berlin', 29 August 2007, 23 pages (9), AdK TiW 1350; and Christoph Schroth, in Zolchow, 'Protokoll eines Gespräches zwischen Christoph Schroth und Sabine Zolchow am 25.2.2010 in Berlin', 4 November 2010, 25 pages (23), AdK TiW 1801. Schroth went on to employ Mund as the business manager at the theatre in Cottbus, whither Schroth went as *Intendant* after leaving the BE.

[85] See Fritz Marquardt, in Zolchow, 'Protokoll der Gespräche', p. 22.

[86] See dpa, 'Palitzsch wird Leiter des Berliner Ensembles', *Der Tagesspiegel*, 31 December 1991.

13   From gang of five to power of one: 1992–1995

A five-headed beast

In the second half of 1991, Fritz Marquardt, Heiner Müller and Peter Palitzsch had all been named in the various configurations of the BE's leadership, however fleetingly. In the summer of 1991, a newspaper also reported that Matthias Langhoff, who had directed at the BE together with Manfred Karge in the 1960s, was also being tipped as a possible *Intendant*.[1] Peter Zadek, one of the FRG's most important directors and *Intendanten*, had not been mentioned as a potential head, although he did have a connection with the company. In 1990, he had offered to direct Goethe's *Faust* in either 1992 or 1993,[2] and that plan was made public in the same month as the speculation about Langhoff's possible *Intendanz*.[3] In September 1991, Senator Ulrich Roloff-Momin announced that the five men would *all* come together to form a collective *Intendanz* for the BE,[4] although the arrangements were far from agreed.

The new line-up, a complete novelty in terms of managing a major German theatre, combined experience from every decade of the BE's history. Palitzsch had learned his craft under Brecht in the 1950s, Langhoff had directed his first productions at the BE in the 1960s, Müller had been a key dramaturgical advisor to Ruth Berghaus in the 1970s, and Marquardt had joined Wekwerth's team in the 1980s. Zadek was the only 'outsider', yet he had a more personal relationship to the BE: he had seen the famous tour of London in 1956 and, thereafter and into the 1960s, had found the company to be 'the only German theatre that interested me'.[5]

The accounts of how this structure came about are contradictory. According to actor Hermann Beyer, Langhoff was originally offered the

---

[1] See Sibylle Wirsing, 'Die Restauration im Reformkleid', *Der Tagesspiegel*, 25 May 1991.
[2] See Sigrid Kunze, 'Kurzprotokoll über die Leitungssitzung am 15.11.1990', 19 November 1990, 2 pages (2), AdK ESA 'BE Int. A–Z'.
[3] See Rüdiger Schaper, 'Wekwerth geht', *Süddeutsche Zeitung*, 15 May 1991.
[4] See dpa, 'Neue Leitung für Berliner Ensemble', *Neues Deutschland*, 7 September 1991.
[5] Peter Zadek, *Das wilde Ufer: Ein Theaterbuch*, compiled by Laszlo Kornitzer, expanded edition (Cologne: Kiepenheuer & Witsch, 1994), p. 333.

Intendanz alone, but he then discussed the possibility of expanding the membership of the leadership with Ivan Nagel, the lead author of the report on Berlin's theatres, hurriedly commissioned by Roloff-Momin.[6] Fritz Marquardt, on the other hand, asserts that Langhoff denied instigating the five-man model, and so Marquardt believes that Nagel was behind the plan.[7] Roloff-Momin's account also supports this view, although he also includes his own input into the design of the new model.[8] The Senator's version of events starts with him consulting exclusively with Müller, who then demurred to take over the BE alone. Nagel then suggested Langhoff.[9] Stephan Suschke, Müller's assistant at the time, maintains, however, that the Senator did not want to appoint Müller alone.[10] Müller's biographer slightly alters this narrative by claiming that Müller suggested Langhoff to the Senate and that the Senate was not keen for the two to work together.[11] One of these last two variants seems more likely than the one suggesting that Müller did not want the *Intendanz*. As will become clear later in this chapter, Müller vigorously defended himself as potential leader against Peter Zadek. Müller had always been central to Langhoff's plan. In a letter written to Roloff-Momin of June 1991, Langhoff imagined a future BE and looked back to its heyday. He said that in contemporary Germany there was only one person capable of filling Brecht's shoes, and that was Müller.[12] In this he understood his old friend as the most innovative and dynamic political playwright writing in German, who also had several high-quality directing credits to his name. Zadek records that Nagel invited him to join the experiment.[13] The team was to be known as the *Direktorium* (Directorate), although the popular press preferred to call it the 'Fünferbande' ('the gang of five').[14]

The full line-up had an international flavour: Marquardt represented the GDR, together with Müller, although the latter had been permitted to travel freely since the mid 1970s and was the most well-known

---

[6] See Hermann Beyer, in Sabine Zolchow, 'Protokoll eines Gespräches zwischen Hermann Beyer und Sabine Zolchow am 11.8.2004 in Berlin', 25 November 2005, 28 pages (18–19), AdK TiW 1348.

[7] See Fritz Marquardt, in Sabine Zolchow, 'Protokoll der Gespräche zwischen Fritz Marquardt und Sabine Zolchow', pp. 21–2, AdK TiW 1308.

[8] See Roloff-Momin, *Zuletzt: Kultur*, p. 57.   [9] See ibid., p. 55.

[10] See Stephan Suschke, in Sabine Zolchow, 'Protokoll eines Gespräches zwischen Stephan Suschke und Sabine Zolchow am 29.06.2004 in Berlin', 29 June 2006, 29 pages (4), AdK TiW 1307.

[11] See Hauschild, *Heiner Müller oder das Prinzip Zweifel*, p. 473.

[12] See Matthias Langhoff, 'Brief an einen Senator', *Drucksache*, 1 (1993), pp. 11–24 (16).

[13] See Peter Zadek, *Die Wanderjahre: 1980–2009*, ed. by Elisabeth Plessen (Cologne: Kiepenheuer & Witsch, 2010), p. 217.

[14] For example, Urs Jenny, 'Brecht, ein auslaufendes Modell', *Der Spiegel*, 2 March 1992.

contemporary German playwright on the world's stage. Palitzsch had directed in the FRG, and Zadek had made his name there in the late 1960s, continuing to stage important productions ever since. Zadek had also directed in England, the country to which his parents had fled the Nazis as persecuted Jews, and thus had started his career in a very different tradition. Langhoff had left the German-speaking countries to direct in France in the 1980s and so brought his experiences of a theatre system that greatly diverged from the German model, and these in particular profoundly influenced the BE's immediate future. Only Langhoff was under sixty at the time of the Directorate's appointment, something that reflected an investment in experience, rather than fresh, young talent. It is hard to overlook the fact that Roloff-Momin had opted for an all-male line-up. Women had run the BE for almost thirty years, but the Senator had clearly neglected this particular tradition in his deliberations. Ruth Berghaus, a potential candidate suggested by name in Nagel's report, certainly had the requisite experience, but there is no record of her even being approached. Instead, the Senator put his faith in a patriarchal model.

Roloff-Momin saw the team as deliberately angular: 'for me, these five people, highly esteemed artists to a man, embodied Germany with all its highs and lows, its contradictions and hopes, its abysses and ambitions'.[15] This statement also encodes the Senator's utopian aspiration for the BE: that it would function as a microcosm of the new Germany – not as a model of harmony, but as one in which constructive tensions bring about new and wonderful things. Tension was certainly at the heart of the line-up, and the most obvious one was between Müller and Zadek as artists at very different ends of the creative spectrum. Müller was austere, presenting dialectical material to his audience without offering solutions; Zadek was more populist, combining seriousness with humour and irony. The fall of the Wall had also created two new 'types' of Germans: so-called 'Ossis' from the East and 'Wessis' from the West, and Müller and Zadek were to become their respective representatives in an inter-German rivalry over the coming years. Yet at the start of the new leadership model, both sides viewed each other with a mutual respect of sorts[16] and committed to the common cause of making the arrangement work.

A meeting at Zadek's villa in Lucca, Italy, in the summer of 1992 allowed the team to discuss fundamental issues before taking the reins. The initial plan was for each director to bring one assistant and to do away with a dramaturgy department as such. As it would turn out, both

[15] Roloff-Momin, *Zuletzt: Kultur*, p. 58.
[16] See Zadek, *Das wilde Ufer*, p. 334; and Müller, 'Überleben ist alles', *Werke* 12: 254.

types of creative unit lived side-by-side. Langhoff told the press that they all acknowledged that the new structure would be difficult to implement, especially as their preferred business manager, Rolf Stiska, the BE's Head of Administration from 1973 to 1988, declined to involve himself in the project.[17] Stiska told me that he simply did not believe that the structure could work.[18] In addition, however, division was already evident. According to Stephan Suschke, 'Zadek gave Marquardt the once-over, and Marquardt immediately felt the wealthy farmer looking down on the lowly peasant'.[19] Both Palitzsch and Marquardt confirm the story.[20] This marked the start of a tension between the two that came to a head in 1994.

Stiska's prediction for the overall success of the project was largely shared by the media and others.[21] The title of an article by Ernst Schumacher looked back to the French Revolution, as he wondered 'will a Napoleon follow the Directorate [?]'.[22] He clearly felt that struggles within the group could ultimately lead to the triumph of a single director, something history was to prove correct. Barbara Brecht-Schall was also critical of the five-man structure. She had so little faith in the new order that she withdrew the company's monopoly on staging Brecht in Berlin, although she still reserved the right to approve who directed and starred in lead roles of plays by Brecht at the BE.[23] This was a somewhat incongruous position, as Brecht-Schall later stated that she considered the continued use of the name 'Berliner Ensemble' under the new management 'ridiculous',[24] presumably because she believed that the new regime had betrayed the BE's Brechtian traditions as she interpreted them. She thus simultaneously viewed the BE as a 'special' theatre by insisting on laying down conditions when it wanted to stage Brecht while nonetheless treating it like any other theatre in Berlin by declaring open season on the rights. The BE was now in competition for Brecht with the other Berlin stages. It should not be forgotten, however, that the new

---

[17] Ernst Schumacher, 'Gewinnen oder Scheitern – mit neuen Aufführungen', *Berliner Zeitung*, 2 July 1992.

[18] Rolf Stiska, unpublished interview with the author, 13 July 2011.

[19] Stephan Suschke, in Zolchow, 'Protokoll eines Gespräches zwischen Stefan Suschke und Sabine Zolchow', p. 7.

[20] See Palitzsch, in Iden, *Peter Palitzsch*, p. 94; and Marquardt, in Zolchow, 'Protokoll der Gespräche zwischen Fritz Marquardt und Sabine Zolchow', p. 26.

[21] See, for example, Peter von Becker, 'Das Phantom im Theater', *Theater heute*, 10 (1992), p. 4.

[22] Ernst Schumacher, 'Folgt dem Direktorium ein Napoleon – oder: Was wird aus Brechts Bühne', *Berliner Zeitung*, 18 September 1991.

[23] See Brecht-Schall, in NZ/ADN, 'Brecht nun überall in Berlin', *Neue Zeit*, 11 February 1992.

[24] Brecht-Schall, 'Letter from Barbara Brecht-Schall', p. 461.

leadership chose not to escape its historical association with Brecht and still sought to make the playwright and his political theatre the centrepiece of the repertoire.

Yet while Brecht-Schall and the majority of public opinion was dismissive of the BE's future, not everyone was keen to condemn the new management model. Critic Martin Linzer saw the time as right for a 'new start',[25] and BE actor Axel Werner looked back to the Volksbühne of the 1970s when a diverse leadership brought about a lively and varied programme.[26] At that time, however, the Volksbühne had a single *Intendant*, not a five-man Directorate, and the aim to establish the new model was made all the more difficult by the BE's new organizational plans. It is perhaps worth restating that it is still difficult, even today, to fathom the logic that led to the formation of the Directorate. No accounts, either contemporaneous or retrospective, shed much light on the rationale for or the confidence in what was a unique experiment in German theatre management.

Left-leaning directors embrace neo-liberal practices

Matthias Langhoff, fresh from his experiences of the French theatre system, proposed introducing a radical shake-up to the way the BE made and performed plays. Not unlike René Serge Mund in 1990, he sought a structure that would be flexible and would rethink the existing repertory system that dominated German public theatres. He proposed that the BE start producing work in blocks or *en suite* as the French put it, with a smaller permanent ensemble of actors and a greater use of guest artists. Each year the theatre would stage two or three shows: 'blocks have the benefit of emphasizing the fleeting and ephemeral quality of productions; in that way theatre takes more risks, is more playful and experimental'.[27] In a discussion paper, a ratio of 1:2 was proposed between permanent and temporary staff, with seventy people employed in the former category, including only twenty actors.[28] The means with which Langhoff set about realizing this departure from the conventional theatre system's norms, however, involved a separation of theatre and State; a kind of financial independence was necessary, but one that would not cut the umbilical cord of public subsidy, without which an institution like the BE could not exist.

---

[25] Linzer, 'Orakel aus dem Brecht-Tempel', pp. 21–2.
[26] See Axel Werner, in Sabine Zolchow, 'Protokoll des Gesprächs zwischen Axel Werner und Sabine Zolchow', p. 14.
[27] Langhoff, 'Brief an einen Senator', p. 20.
[28] See Anon., 'Matthias Papier', undated, 3 pages (1), AdK HMA 7803.

According to Roloff-Momin, the decision to privatize the BE came at around the same time as the Directorate was conceptualized in the summer of 1991.[29] The plan was for the BE to become a *Gesellschaft mit beschränkter Haftung* (limited liability company, or GmbH) with each of the five directors paying the, for them, modest sum of 20,000 marks (or roughly €10, 000 in 2014) for a 20 per cent stake in the new concern. The financial advantages of a GmbH were that subsidies could be allocated in a flexible manner: money that went unspent on a particular production could then be used on another, something not permitted under the State system.[30] In short, the BE would function in almost the same way as any other public German theatre in that it received a generous subsidy, but had more control over its budgets and remained outside the Senator's public remit to the extent that he was no longer able to hire and fire its Directors. However, as Suschke notes, the new flexibility, which pleased the Senate, led to internal squabbles amongst the Directors about differences between the budgets for their own productions at an early stage.[31]

An initial proposal recommended that the BE fire all its staff because the old structure would no longer exist, and a completely new one would take its place. Staff would thus have to re-apply for their own jobs. Another 'advantage' of privatization was that the new company would be free of national pay agreements, and this was actually seen as the main reason for the move by one of the GmbH's architects, Rolf Paulin.[32] Paulin was the business manager of the Thalia Theater in Hamburg, and he gave his advice unpaid in order to replicate and improve upon the structure at his own theatre, which had also turned itself into a GmbH.[33] The BE duly left the Deutscher Bühnenverein, the body that looked after the interests of public theatres.[34] This did not, however, free the new company from all its financial obligations. Ensemble members represented by the union IG Medien wanted to use the BE's national importance as a bargaining chip in the fight for fair wages,[35] and a long series of negotiations with the union finally broke down in January 1995.[36] In addition, the BE also severed its links with the Staatliche Werkstätten

---

[29] See Roloff-Momin, *Zuletzt: Kultur*, p. 57.
[30] See FAZ, 'Berliner Ensemble mgH', *Frankfurter Allgemeine Zeitung*, 6 October 1992.
[31] See Stephan Suschke, in Zolchow, 'Protokoll eines Gespräches zwischen Stephan Suschke und Sabine Zolchow', p. 5.
[32] See Peter Raue to Müller, 11 November 1991, AdK HMA 7803, in which Raue summarizes a meeting involving Paulin, amongst others.
[33] Peter Raue, unpublished interview with the author, 13 September 2012.
[34] See Suschke, in Zolchow, 'Protokoll eines Gespräches', p. 6.
[35] See Peter Sauerbaum to the BE Shareholders, 15 December 1992, AdK HMA 7806.
[36] See Peter Sauerbaum to Roloff-Momin, 10 January 1995, AdK HMA 7814.

(the State Workshops).[37] The Workshops had served the BE for many decades, and although, at times, they could be overworked and thus unreliable, the quality of their work was high, based on their years of specialist experience. The free-market mantra that was driving the BE's new agenda dictated that costs could be cut by picking and choosing suppliers, rather than by relying on a single provider. That proved to be a mistake, as noted by seasoned BE carpenter Wolfgang Bömelburg.[38] Stephan Suschke concurred and observed that the new sets either did not fit the stage, fell apart, and/or arrived late.[39]

Unsurprisingly, the GmbH went down very badly with rank-and-file members. A letter to the chairs of Berlin's main political parties of March 1992 affirmed the ensemble's support for the new Directorate, but not for the GmbH.[40] The mood had not changed four months later, when the management sought to fire the majority of the sixty-strong acting ensemble.[41] By October, Ernst Schumacher reported that forty actors were due to be made redundant,[42] although a Berlin court later ruled that actors with over fifteen years' experience could not be summarily dismissed.[43] The initial plan to make a clean break with past structures had already run into legislative trouble. Things were not going well in the management, either. Peter Sauerbaum had been appointed as the new company's business manager after Rolf Stiska declined the position, but by the autumn of 1992, he had already tendered his resignation after clashing with Langhoff.[44] Sauerbaum came from the Senate's own cultural administration as an expert in theatre matters, and so it is possible that his background and its effects on the way he ran the BE were too 'conventional' for Langhoff. As it would turn out, Sauerbaum stayed on at the BE far longer than Langhoff.

The radical upheavals at the BE that took it from a public theatre to a private company are little short of remarkable, given the political credentials of the Directorate. The plan they pursued would have gained approval from many a free-marketeer and neo-liberal supporter of deregulation. The abandonment of free collective bargaining, the introduction of a flexible labour policy, and the outsourcing of service provision would all seem to run counter to Directors who might at least be described as

[37] See Anon., 'Matthias Papier', p. 3.   [38] See Bömelburg, *Hobellied*, p. 108.
[39] See Suschke, in Zolchow, 'Protokoll eines Gespräches', p. 6.
[40] See eb, 'BE gegen Privatisierung', *Berliner Zeitung*, 10 March 1992.
[41] See BM/dpa, '"Konflikt liegt auf dem Tisch" am Berliner Ensemble', *Berliner Morgenpost*, 4 July 1992.
[42] See Ernst Schumacher, 'Weite und Vielfalt oder Etikettenschwindel?', *Berliner Zeitung*, 22 October 1992.
[43] See Tsp., 'Kündigungen am BE sind unwirksam', *Der Tagesspiegel*, 15 December 1992.
[44] See Peter Sauerbaum to the BE Shareholders, 12 October 1992, AdK HMA 7806.

'left-leaning' and at most as 'socialists'. It is possible, however, that some quarters of the Directorate did not actually understand the implications of the decisions. Heiner Müller, for example, made this peculiar statement in 1992: 'it's our common interest to remove the theatre from the market... We have utopian conceptions of another kind of theatre. That's where the idea for a GmbH came from'.[45] His logic is hard to fathom; one of the advantages of the German theatre system with its large subsidies is precisely that it allows productions to fail, as was more than clear in the recent history of the BE itself. Distance from the market was an integral element of the public system, yet it was that aspect that had also led to artistic stagnation. If anything, Langhoff wanted to introduce deregulated mechanisms in order for the BE to break out of the complacency the state system could engender. He certainly advocated this position in a meeting with the ensemble in September 1992. Müller called a halt to the gathering, however, when the possibility of meaningful dialogue broke down.[46] All the same, Langhoff's brave new theatre would not crystallize in the ways he predicted.

A difficult first season

The 'old' Berliner Ensemble formally closed on 12 July 1992 with a final performance of *The Threepenny Opera* and planned to re-open on 1 January 1993. The interim period was used to update the sound and lighting systems at a cost to the Senate of 3.5 million marks.[47] This was a part of the contract that constituted the GmbH,[48] and so one can see that the authorities were keen to demonstrate their continued financial support for the BE with up-to-date facilities. The new Directorate also understood the closure as a symbolic hiatus and an opportunity to prepare for the first season.[49] As it happened, the BE re-opened on 10 January, precisely one day after author Dieter Schulze had alleged that Heiner Müller was a Stasi informer. Although any suggestion that Müller was an informer at all and had betrayed anyone were thoroughly

---

[45] Müller, 'Überleben ist alles', *Werke* 12: 253.
[46] See BM, 'Vollversammlung mit Krach, Wut und Kündigung', *Berliner Morgenpost*, 6 September 1992.
[47] See Anon., 'Berliner Ensemble: Pause bis Januar', *Berliner Kurier*, 2 July 1992.
[48] See Anon., 'Entwurf: Vertrag zwischen dem Land Berlin... und dem Berliner Ensemble GmbH', [fax dated 20 October 1992], 6 pages (5), AdK HMA 7803. Although this is only a draft, it is the final draft of many in this file, and it can be assumed that the clause remained as the work was indeed carried out.
[49] See Renate Ziemer, 'Protokoll der Leitungssitzung im Berliner Ensemble am 23.2.1992', 27 February 1992, 10 pages (1), AdK HMA 7805.

dismissed later that year,[50] the (primarily West) German press was keen to gloat uncritically over the 'revelation' at the time. The episode very much exposed the East/West rift in that it showed just how keen Western journalists were to use any means at their disposal to disparage the GDR's cultural achievements. Suffice it to say, once the relevant documents had come to light, there was no collective *mea culpa* or apology forthcoming. Nonetheless, this was a bad start for the BE, but then so was the first production that Müller watched from the Directors' box.

One may have thought that the audience would have been treated to a bold, fresh reading of Brecht to raise the curtain on the Berliner Ensemble GmbH, but that was not that case. The Directorate had announced in early 1992 that it would not be taking over any of the 'old' BE's Brecht productions, something that shocked Barbara Brecht-Schall.[51] The rationale was clearly that the new company wanted to start afresh without the old BE's baggage. Müller pointed out his own reservations, calling the long-running production of *The Caucasian Chalk Circle* 'a shitty production, but full and "successful"'.[52] The inverted commas around 'successful' indicate his scorn for work that merely pleased the audience, rather than challenged it.

The season actually opened with Shakespeare's hardly crowd-pulling *Pericles*, directed neither by Zadek nor Müller, but Palitzsch. Dramaturge Holger Teschke, who also translated the play into German, told me that actor Volker Spengler considered Palitzsch to have played the role of a 'Frontschwein' here.[53] This slang term is taken from the military and denotes a person who continues to return to the front after several battles. Zadek and Müller had sent the veteran out to face the expectant crowd although the production was not of the highest standard. According to Teschke, Müller refused to save the production through his own intervention with the words 'I'm not Wekwerth'. He was prepared to see the production fail, rather than deploy directorial tricks to satisfy the audience.

In a way, there was a biographical reason for the choice of play: Palitzsch, like Pericles, had made a long and difficult journey back to his (spiritual) home, the BE. Yet this did little to justify the show to the critics. The BE had tried to frame the play as early epic theatre through

---

[50] See Andreas Schreier and Malte Daniljuk, 'Das Müller-Phantom', in Müller, *Krieg ohne Schlacht: Leben in zwei Diktaturen. Eine Autobiographie*, expanded edition (Cologne: Kiepenheuer & Witsch, 1994), pp. 470–6.

[51] See Brecht-Schall to Peter Palitzsch, 19 February 1992, AdK HMA 7827.

[52] Müller, in Ziemer, 'Protokoll der Leitungssitzung', p. 6.

[53] Holger Teschke, unpublished interview with the author, 11 March 2011.

Shakespeare's narrator figure, Gower.[54] It was Zadek's idea to use a traverse stage and to sit some of the spectators on the main stage. Palitzsch later noted that he had foolishly accepted this new way of positioning the audience.[55] While there was some praise, the reviewers were mostly disappointed by the lack of innovation or verve. Gerhard Stadelmaier, never a terribly charitable critic in general or towards leftist theatre in particular, believed that little had changed at the company: 'the actors perform like veteran administrators of the *Verfremdungseffekt*'.[56] Peter Iden found little Brechtian virtue in the production and regretted the lack of social interest, poor discipline from the cast, and the little that was offered to engage the audience's minds.[57] Volker Oesterreich perhaps best summed up the work: 'on the whole, an unusual, but not an exceptional theatre event'.[58]

Matters were hardly progressing well with the ensemble, either. A meeting of late January 1993 ended with many walking out when questions about pay and contracts were met with either vague or indeed no answers at all.[59] After a similarly disastrous meeting the previous September, mentioned above, the Directors decided to field Sauerbaum alone, perhaps with the intention of conducting business in a more business-like fashion, perhaps because their own appearance at the last meeting did little to persuade the anxious staff of their plan. However, the lack of senior representation at the meeting simply perpetuated the discontent.

The BE followed up the damp squib of *Pericles* with an altogether more radical production. One might have thought that, amongst a collective leadership of five experienced and successful directors, one of them might have staged the next work in the debut season, but this did not happen. It seems that Müller unilaterally invited Einar Schleef back to the BE, and he mentioned 'Schleef's project' without further detail at a meeting back in February 1992 as if it were common knowledge.[60] Schleef had not directed at the theatre since the fateful production of *Miss Julie* in 1975, and, indeed, had left the GDR in 1976. In the meantime he had

[54] See Holger Teschke, untitled, November 1992, n.p., BEA File 154.
[55] Palitzsch, in Peter Iden, *Peter Palitzsch*, p, 93.
[56] Gerhard Stadelmaier, 'Das harte Brot der toten Könige', *Frankfurter Allgemeine Zeitung*, 12 January 1993.
[57] See Peter Iden, 'Neubeginn im heulenden Elend', *Frankfurter Rundschau*, 12 January 1993.
[58] Volker Oesterreich, 'Brücke vom Gestern zum Heute', *Berliner Morgenpost*, 12 January 1993.
[59] See Corrinna Wojtek, 'Belegschaftsversammlung im Berliner Ensemble anläßlich der Übergangs in eine GmbH am 28.01.1993 auf der Probebühne', undated, n.p., AdK ESA 'BE-Korresp. etc.'.
[60] Müller, in Ziemer, 'Protokoll der Leitungssitzung', p. 5.

developed a theatre based on the dynamics of the chorus and wanted to experiment further with a most unlikely play, Rolf Hochhuth's *Wessis in Weimar*. Subtitled 'Scenes from an Occupied Country', *Wessis* is a thesis play in the worst sense of the term. Rather than exploring the situation of the former GDR, it uses documentary material, largely taken from newspapers, and dramatizes highly partisan approaches to themes such as unemployment and the restitution of confiscated property. It makes its points in the most inelegant of ways and sacrifices its own aesthetic of realism in order to make them. The play hit the headlines before it was finished when its first scene was published in *Manager Magazine* in the middle of 1992. The prologue to the play argues that the assassination of the head of the Treuhand, the institution entrusted with overseeing the privatization of GDR business and industry, was in some way justified. This provocation, which was clearly designed to solicit attention for the play, had its desired effects, but the result was that the play would become a victim of its own notoriety in Hochhuth's eyes.

Schleef was named director in a letter to the play's publishers in July 1992.[61] Yet by October, Hochhuth was already getting nervous about Schleef because he had heard that the director was rehearsing songs when there were none in the text itself. He requested that Zadek take over the production.[62] Zadek replied that he could not intervene in a production already in rehearsal and would not because he stood 'in great loyalty' with his fellow Directors.[63] At the same time, October 1992, however, Zadek privately wrote to the Directorate that he did not approve of playing around with a text and noted that while he was looking forward to the production, he could not help worrying that actors had started leaving the project.[64] The record shows that at least two performers objected to the manner and style of Schleef's direction, but also that another wondered whether she could join the cast, although it was late in the day.[65] Hochhuth signed the contract agreeing to Schleef's cuts to five of his (lengthy) scenes in November while nonetheless registering his uneasiness that, according to an actor he knew, no word of his play had been rehearsed even though they had been working on the project since 2 October.[66]

[61] See Bärbel Jaksch to Corinna Brocher and Michael Neumann, 10 July 1992, BEA File 'Spielplan: Produktionen ab 92/93/sonstige Veranstaltungen'.
[62] See Peter Sauerbaum to the Directorate, 26 October 1992, ibid.
[63] Peter Zadek to Rolf Hochhuth, 30 October 1992, ibid.
[64] See Zadek to BE Leadership, 30 October 1992, AdK Einar-Schleef-Archiv 5362.
[65] The three letters are in ibid. 5369.
[66] See Hochhuth to Sauerbaum, 4 November 1992, BEA File 'Spielplan: Produktionen ab 92/93/sonstige Veranstaltungen'.

Six days before the premiere of 10 February 1993, Hochhuth attended a rehearsal unannounced and was horrified.[67] The morning after, he appeared on a television breakfast show in high dudgeon. His main objections were that characters' dialogues were being delivered by choruses; his extensive stage directions and notes to actors were being performed on stage; roughly ten per cent of his text actually appeared in the production; and other material, from Goethe, Schiller and Brecht amongst others, was present without any apparent reason.[68] Despite threatening to ban the production, Hochhuth found that his hands were tied. This was because he had signed a contract agreeing to Schleef as director, and Schleef had a reputation that already suggested the kind of aesthetics he would employ. Schleef said as much in a sworn statement,[69] although it appears that the document was written pre-emptively, before Hochhuth realized that he would not be able to secure an injunction.

The irate playwright insisted on *Werktreue*, a term loosely translated into English as 'faithfulness to the text'. That is, Hochhuth wanted the scenes to be realized as he had intended them and insisted that Schleef's directorial input skewed what he had written. This position, however, is a contentious one because a play text, by its very nature, does not, and indeed cannot, delimit how it is performed, since performance is a wholly different category. *Werktreue* is thus an impossible ambition, but this has not stopped a variety of authors citing it when criticizing directors' work.[70] The cleavage between text and performance in this production appears to be enormous, yet Schleef defended his decisions in an interview published a week or so after the opening night. In it, he expressed nothing but admiration for Hochhuth's original play, of which little was to be seen in the final printed version, for saying what no one else had dared to say. Schleef maintained: 'what Hochhuth gave us to read was nothing short of a call to civil war, perhaps a terror-ridden scenario of an approaching civil war in Germany following unification'.[71] He believed that Hochhuth was 'intoxicated' by political violence and asserted that 'to him, murder becomes an heroic act', a position that is not contradicted by some of the scenes in the final script. With these ideas in mind, one can start to understand that Schleef's production was not an example of

---

[67] See Anon., 'Notiz zu *Wessis*', 4 February 1993, ibid.

[68] See Anon., 'Hochhuth contra *Wessis* am BE', *Der Tagesspiegel*, 6 February 1993.

[69] See Anon., '[unsigned and corrected] Eidesstattliche Versicherung', February 1993, n.p., AdK Einar-Schleef-Archiv 5371.

[70] See David Barnett, 'Offending the Playwright. Directors' Theatre and the *Werktreue* Debate', *German Monitor*, 77 (2013), pp. 75–97, for a fuller discussion.

[71] Schleef, in Rolf Michaelis, 'Hochhuth ist ein Feigling', *Die Zeit*, 19 February 1993. The following quotations are also taken from this source.

directorial arbitrariness that merely happened to make use of selections from Hochhuth's play. Instead, the production represented a carefully considered reflection on a subject matter that was present in the text, although its means were not at all sanctioned by the playwright. This was Schleef's understanding of *Werktreue*.

The BE placated Hochhuth by agreeing to his demand to provide each member of the premiere's audience with a free copy of his play and to have his protest registered in the *Wessis* programme. Langhoff, Marquardt and Müller, however, issued a press release on the day of the premiere saying that, while the company printed Hochhuth's 'Entgegnung' ('riposte'), they distanced themselves from both its form and content.[72] The production ran for forty-three performances *en suite* until mid May 1993 and was invited to German theatre's most prestigious festival, the Berlin Theatertreffen. The critics were in no doubt about the relationship between text and performance. Petra Kohse, who reflected many other reviewers' responses noted: 'the deceived author should be grateful that his lines play a part here'.[73] Schleef deployed massed choruses in a deliberately confrontational fashion to highlight both the implicit violence of reunification and the kinds of social structures it was starting to spawn. The four-hour-long production was certainly hard work, for both the performers and the audience, but there was very much the sense that it had transformed its weak source material into an utterly compelling theatrical experience.

The battle with Hochhuth had been won, and the production offered Müller, as the show's 'sponsor', precisely the kind of theatre he wanted to see at the BE: topical and difficult themes transformed into visceral theatrical performance. In 1975, Müller, like Brecht before him,[74] had made a distinction between 'Erfolg und Wirkung' ('success and impact'),[75] a view still evident in his comments on *The Caucasian Chalk Circle*, quoted above. Müller believed that it was more important to have the latter, which was necessarily the result of a challenging production, rather than the former. The bonus with *Wessis* was that impact and success went hand in hand. Peter Zadek, however, begged to differ. He had not signed the BE's press release criticizing Hochhuth, and this was because he objected

[72] See Langhoff, Marquardt and Müller, [untitled press release], 10 February 1993, n.p., BEA File 155.
[73] Petra Kohse, 'Archaische Rituale im besetzten Land', *General-Anzeiger*, 12 February 1993.
[74] See Brecht, 'Kleines Privatissimum für meinen Freund Max Gorelik', BFA, 23: 37; *BoT*, pp. 146–7.
[75] Müller, 'Literatur muß das Theater Widerstand leisten', *Werke* 10: 62.

in the strongest terms to what he considered a theatre that was reminiscent of a Nuremberg rally.[76] While he could not stop the production, he did threaten to leave the BE if Schleef was allowed to direct there again.[77] Palitzsch, too, did not sign the press release, but it was the tension between the BE's most important directors, Zadek and Müller, that boded ill. *Wessis* marked a point of moral and aesthetic fracture between the two that went on to reach a breaking point within a couple of years.

The new BE's first season had three more productions to come. The first, Peter Turrini's *Grillparzer im Pornoladen* (*Grillparzer in the Sex Shop*), was premiered shortly after *Wessis* and staged at a new venue for the BE, the Ballhaus Rixdorf, in the Kreuzberg district of Berlin. The theatre both extended the BE's performance possibilities with a new studio space and signalled that the BE was not just a theatre for the old East, because Kreuzberg was a part of former West Berlin. Again, Palitzsch was the director, and again this minor work, which was played in the round, received mixed reviews. While a couple of critics enjoyed the piece,[78] most were disappointed.[79] Yet disappointment was not limited to the audience.

In mid March 1993, Matthias Langhoff resigned from the Directorate, reducing the gang of five to a quartet. The official reasons he gave concerned his health and a desire to spend more time with his family.[80] It was only a couple of weeks later, however, that the news was made public, and although this lag might appear to indicate that the other Directors sought to persuade him to stay, he actually did not want to distract attention from the next premiere.[81] The irony that Langhoff, the motor behind the reforms at the company, was the first to go before a single season had passed, was not lost on the press.[82] His vague grounds for quitting sounded like a politician going through the motions, and thus one might look for other factors that led to such a sudden exit. Later, Langhoff himself revised his reasons citing both his objections to 'greater ambitions' amongst the Directors and a focus on intra-German tensions, rather than global ones after the fall of the Wall.[83] There has,

---

[76] See Zadek, *Die Wanderjahre*, p. 225.   [77] See ibid., p. 226.

[78] See, for example, Rüdiger Schaper, 'Souffleur mit Peitsche', *Süddeutsche Zeitung*, 22 February 1993.

[79] See Hartmut Lange, 'Zweimal Turrini: Des einen Leid, des andern Kampf', *Die Welt*, 27 February 1993; or Gerhard Ebert, 'Wer eine Provokation erwartet hatte, sah sich enttäuscht', *Neues Deutschland*, 23 February 1993.

[80] See Langhoff to the BE, 17 March 1993, BEA File 'C-D'.

[81] See Langhoff to Directorate, 15 March 1993, AdK HMA 7808.

[82] See, for example, g.r. [sic], 'Die Vorgänge im Berliner Ensemble', *Der Tagesspiegel*, 31 March 1993.

[83] Langhoff, in Roland Koberg, 'Der letzte Dissident', *Berliner Zeitung*, 30 March 1999.

however, been no shortage of additional theories. Stephan Suschke believed that a rift with Langhoff's old friend Müller lay at the heart of the decision. They were initially going to co-direct a production, but found they did not share the same aesthetic agenda, and Müller began working with set designer Mark Lammert behind Langhoff's back.[84] This possible cause is all the more credible given Langhoff's original plan to build the new BE around Müller. Roloff-Momin connected the departure to the tensions surrounding the production of *Wessis*, but also wondered whether the persistence of the German theatre system's structures had got the better of Langhoff.[85] Zadek raised the possibility that the friction with the representative of the old system, Peter Sauerbaum, had had an effect, and noted that Langhoff might have seen less possibility of directing his own productions if Müller was already approaching directors like Schleef from outside the Directorate.[86]

All these reasons given after the resignation could have been contributory factors. What was certain was that the BE had returned to crisis mode while the GmbH was still in its infancy. The first meeting of the management to follow Langhoff's departure established several important responses to his decision. First, the option of appointing a fifth Director was deferred with Sauerbaum suggesting, and Zadek supporting, the proposition that each existing Director invest a further 5,000 marks to buy out Langhoff. Müller proposed that the fifth person should not be a theatre director, but someone who was able to organize the remaining four shareholders.[87] Müller had already realized that the five-way pull was potentially destructive. Zadek was keen to maintain a veneer of harmony and proposed regular press releases 'that contain the agreed views of the management, so to speak'.[88] The spirit of unity was also to be found in a proposed collaboration, between Zadek as director and Müller as adapter, on Marlowe's *Tamburlaine*. Palitzsch, rather than Marquardt, was charged by Zadek with directing the BE's first Brecht in the hope that he would make sure that it worked, and Palitzsch was also invited to have a 'polite conversation' with director Peter Stein, who, via the Senate, had suggested that he direct both parts of Goethe's *Faust* at the BE. The meeting also dismissed a proposal from Rolf Hochhuth that he become the fifth Director. This approach may have come as a surprise

---

[84] See Suschke, in Zolchow, 'Protokoll eines Gespräches zwischen Stephan Suschke und Sabine Zolchow', p. 12.
[85] See Roloff-Momin, *Zuletzt: Kultur*, p. 62.
[86] See Zadek, *Die Wanderjahre*, pp. 237 and 222, respectively.
[87] See Sigrid Kunze, 'Protokoll über die Leitungssitzung am 24.4.1993', 27 April 1993, 5 pages (1), AdK HMA 7807.
[88] Zadek, in ibid., p. 4.

to the Directors after the problems with *Wessis*, but this would not be the last the BE heard from the playwright.

The first season, designed to launch a new organizational structure, was failing before it had a chance to process its own contradictions. Two poor productions, one hit that split the Directorate, and one major resignation did not augur well for a radical experiment which, to the outside world, looked suspiciously like the old BE in its inability to connect with its new pan-German audience. Even critic Martin Linzer, one of the few voices to encourage the five-man structure, counselled that the time might have come to admit that it had been a mistake to appoint five leaders, in order for a truly new BE to emerge from the ongoing implosion.[89]

Contrary to Langhoff's planned radio silence, his departure had been made public before the next premiere on 9 April 1993, although one could not say that it made much difference to its reception. Fritz Marquardt directed Horváth's *Sladek oder die schwarze Armee* (*Sladek, or the Black Army*), and it fared even worse than *Grillparzer*, with one critic going so far as to demand its immediate removal from the repertoire.[90] Another, who was similarly damning, at least looked forward to what had been kept from the audience up until now: productions from Zadek and Müller.[91] Towards the end of the first season, the two directors had become the focus of interest. The tension between them had been evident after *Wessis*, but both sought to use it productively, as a way of offering contrasting yet mutually illuminating work.[92]

Untimely meditations: Zadek and Müller's first productions

The first season ended with Peter Zadek's long-awaited debut production. The second season opened with Heiner Müller's production. Zadek did not stage an existing drama, but adapted Cesare Zavattini's *Totò il Buono* (*Totò the Good*), the novel of 1940 that inspired Vittorio de Sica's neo-realist classic film *Miracolo a Milano* (*Miracle in Milan*) of 1951, as *Das Wunder von Mailand*. Zadek had originally planned to stage Goethe's *Faust* at the BE, but changed his plans in the light of right-wing violence

---

[89]   See Linzer, 'Orakel', p. 22.
[90]   See Dirk Nümann, 'Die Schonfrist ist jetzt um', *Junge Welt*, 14 April 1993.
[91]   See Roland H. Wiegenstein, 'Noch einmal die alten Ziehbilder', *Frankfurter Rundschau*, 14 April 1993.
[92]   See Müller and Zadek, writing separately, in Anon., 'Zwei Einsprüche aus dem Berliner Ensemble', *Der Tagesspiegel*, 1 April 1993.

and xenophobia in the new Germany,[93] so as to treat a more immediately relevant subject matter. He also noted how Brecht had written to the SED to have de Sica's film made available in the GDR.[94] Brecht himself drew attention to the 'miracle' of the film's title: 'I'm sure the mystical ending won't infect anyone with superstition, since here in the GDR everyone knows it doesn't take miracles to do away with intolerable conditions'.[95] The miracle itself involved Totò and his friends escaping poverty by flying away from Milan on broomsticks. Zadek's shift from Goethe to Zavattini represents his version of a commitment to Brecht and his aims, in that he was pursuing a clear social agenda instead of directing a classic. His magical realist aesthetic, however, was not Brecht's, and so Zadek was concerned with connecting his work with Brecht's content, rather than his form. Thus, rather than a tough Brechtian materialist analysis, Zadek employed gags, slapstick and lightness. The songs he introduced delivered social criticism, but this quality was not evident in the scenes themselves. He adopted the aesthetics of the revue as a way of treating themes of poverty and deprivation.

One of the appeals of coming to the BE for Zadek was the opportunity of working with actors from the East, versed in more stylized performance, and incorporating that into his more psychological theatre.[96] This proved to be a more difficult proposition than he first thought, and, in a show of unity, Müller, Palitzsch, Zadek and Marquardt wrote to East German actor Hermann Beyer imploring him to stay with a production that would fall apart without him.[97] Beyer was disappointed that he was acting not in *Faust*, but in *Wunder*, a film that he detested,[98] as Alfredo, the street-sweeper. The production, which premiered on 13 June 1993, was not that well received because it appeared that Zadek had merely been dabbling with fantastical froth. One review called the production 'a poetic, frivolous fairytale comedy', another dubbed his star actor Eva Mattes a 'holy mother of social romanticism'.[99] Something that should not be ignored is one critic's observation that 'Zadek puts all his

[93] See dpa, 'Zadeks neue Inszenierung', *Berliner Zeitung*, 2 December 1992.
[94] See Zadek, in Anon., 'Notizen aus dem Berliner Ensemble', undated, n.p., BEA File 158.
[95] Brecht to Anton Ackermann, 21 May 1954, BFA, 30: 251; *Letters*, p. 529.
[96] See Zadek, *Das wilde Ufer*, p. 334.
[97] See Müller, Palitzsch, Zadek and Marquardt to Hermann Beyer, 2 March 1993, BEA File 'Spielplan: Produktionen ab 92/93/sonstige Veranstaltungen'.
[98] See Hermann Beyer, in Zolchow, 'Protokoll eines Gespräches zwischen Hermann Beyer und Sabine Zolchow', p. 10.
[99] Dirk Nümann, 'Das Leben ist schön – tralala', *Junge Welt*, 15 June 1993; and Robin Detje, 'K(l)eine Wunder', *Die Zeit*, 18 June 1993.

faith in the production on the power of poetry, imagination and fairy-tale magic'.[100] This was not gritty social criticism, but an imaginative engagement that asked the audience to think beyond social realism and imagine a different world. The production was not perhaps escapism, but an attempt to use popular forms as a way of transforming the audience's relationship to reality.

It would be difficult to find a more different production at the BE than Müller's *Duell Traktor Fatzer*, a show made up of three of Müller's shorter plays (it also included *Der Findling – The Foundling*) together with a distillation of Brecht's *Fatzer. Duell* was due to premiere in March 1993, but a chest infection prevented Müller from rehearsing for a short period in February,[101] an early indication of approaching ill health. The premiere, however, was put back to 30 September as the relationship between Langhoff and Müller deteriorated, and rehearsals resumed with Müller directing alone in mid August.

Müller had lined up a remarkable cast, including the eighty-six-year-old Erwin Geschonneck, the actor who had played Matti in the BE's first production in 1949, and Ekkehard Schall. Stephan Suschke calls this a first example of Müller's 'theatre of biography',[102] an important term that requires explication and contextualization. Müller's hope was that the actors' long and complex biographies would also be visible on stage to create a metatheatrical effect. The actors did not merely play the characters, but also displayed their own relationships to texts that resonated in their own lives. Geschonneck, for example, was a committed communist who was incarcerated in a Nazi concentration camp in 1939 for his beliefs. In the playlet *Das Duell*, set against the workers uprising of 17 June 1953, Geschonneck was required to sing the song 'Madrid du Wunderbare' ('Madrid, You Wonderful Place'). Although Geschonneck was not a veteran of the Spanish Civil War, the text nonetheless connected with the revolutionary fervour of his past while he spoke it in the post-socialist present. The split between what a text says and how it is delivered is something that Brecht also valued, and I discussed his predilection for the difference between an actor's background and their role on pp. 11–12, Chapter 1. Müller radicalized Brecht's position by casting actors with whom the audience would have been familiar and exploiting their biographies to achieve contrastive ends in performance. He sought to

---

[100] Bernd Lubowski, 'Ein Wunder am Schiffbauerdamm', *Berliner Morgenpost*, 15 June 1993.

[101] See Peter Sauerbaum to the cast, 19 February 1993, BEA File 'C-D'.

[102] Stephan Suschke, *Müller macht Theater: Zehn Inszenierungen und ein Epilog* (Berlin: Theater der Zeit, 2003), p. 163.

establish political and historical disjunctions that were deliberately left open for the audience.

One of the prerequisites for such work was to let the actor's own relationship with the lines emerge and not to bury it beneath a skilled and masterful interpretation. Zadek criticized Müller for patronizing Eva Mattes when telling her she need not understand the difficult texts of *Fatzer* in order to deliver them.[103] Müller was actually asking her to defer interpretation and to pass that task on to the audience, as was the case with the other members of the cast, too. Her own 'ignorance' was to provide a productive challenge; she should not pretend she fully understood either the text or the problems it treated, but rather show how difficult the situation was through her own difficulties as an actor. An assistant reported that the plan worked on the very first day of rehearsal: 'yet the resistant text challenges the actors in a productive way. Rehearsals at high intensity'.[104] However, this did not mean that uninflected delivery should be boring, but that it should expose the tension between actor and text.[105] The aim, when such delivery was executed correctly, was noted by Hans-Friedrich Bormann: 'there is no need to explain. Direct perception: watching is thinking'.[106] Yet there were also parts of the actors' biographies that Müller chose to ignore. When directing Jaecki Schwarz, who had performed in the BE's *Fatzer* of 1987, Müller told him to forget Wekwerth.[107] This was no time to resurrect old practices, but to engage with Müller's attempts to frustrate immediate comprehension.

Müller was also concerned with generating associations by deferring interpretation and suggesting connections. He saw the *Fatzer* fragment as an allegory of the dynamics of terrorist cells and sought to associate the four deserters with the Baader-Meinhof faction as well as the FRG's more playful Kommune 1 group of the late 1960s, for example.[108] Similarly, when asked whence the hatred came between the individualist Fatzer and the intellectual Koch, Müller replied 'it's the hatred between Trotsky and Stalin, Robespierre and Danton, that's always there. The free man against the thinker'.[109] The clash was thus not a personal one as such, but one that existed in the realm of the political, concerning whose ideas would

[103] See Zadek, *Die Wanderjahre*, p. 239.
[104] Entry for 8 February 1993, in Markus Thebe, 'Brecht Müller *Fatzer 1 Germania 2* Probenprotokolle 8/2/93–17/3/93', 22 March 1993, 46 pages (1), BEA File 159.
[105] See entry for 25 September 1993, in Markus Thebe, 'Brecht Müller *Duell Traktor Fatzer*: Probenprotokoll 16/8/93–30/9/93', 11 February 1994, 120 pages (109), ibid.
[106] Hans-Friedrich Bormann, '*Fatzer*/11.02.1993', undated, n.p., ibid.
[107] See entry for 7 September 1993, in Thebe, 'Brecht Müller *Duell Traktor Fatzer*', p. 66.
[108] See entry for 12 February 1993, in ibid., pp. 5–6.
[109] Entry for 16 February 1993, in ibid., p. 13.

triumph in the greater scheme of things. Müller's was also a gestic theatre, and in one scene, for example, Geschonneck was directed to hold a piece of paper aloft for a while, to emphasize the repressive State's insistence on bureaucracy.[110] The body was also the vessel of historical *Haltungen*, and Müller enjoyed Hermann Beyer's pose in a scene from *Traktor* when he stood hunched at the side of the stage: 'typical basic GDR *Haltung* – either attack or submit'.[111]

What should be evident from the rehearsal process is that Müller was working through a post-Brechtian approach to difficult material. Unlike Wekwerth and Tenschert before him, he did not seek to 'cheat' the difficult sections by integrating them into a *Fabel*, but to leave them open. One observer noted that the process lacked a 'basic idea'.[112] Müller was not trying to realize an interpretation, but asked the actors to find interesting material in the lines themselves. That is, he was directing inductively, like Brecht once had, but in a fundamentally different epistemological context. For Brecht, socialism provided the interpretive frame, while for Müller, in post-Wall Germany, that was no longer a given. In the light of this philosophical position, the performances themselves represent a counterpoint to Zadek's: speeches were delivered with an almost brutal dryness; gestures existed as unnatural movements in themselves; and communication did not really take place on the stage, but was delegated to the spectators in the auditorium.

The production's deliberate coldness was not well received. Critics from the right and left dismissed it as deadly dull.[113] Yet Ernst Schumacher identified what he called 'pure "epic theatre"': dominance of the word, dissolution of roles, "*Haltungen*" in the place of action, embedded quotations'.[114] He added that he found the re-introduction of such approaches at the BE overdue, but wondered whether an audience would appreciate them. It is safe to say that it did not. Müller later characterized the production thus: 'it was an experiment with a cadaver. The corpse was the audience. On the stage the phantoms, the dead in the auditorium'.[115]

Zadek and Müller's first productions at the BE were thus, for the most part, rejected by critics and audiences alike. They were both, however, carefully crafted, if aesthetically opposing pieces, that strove to address

---

[110] See entry for 17 February 1993, in ibid., p. 15.
[111] Entry for 5 March 1993, in ibid., p. 18.
[112] [Unclear signature], 'Vom Glauben an Jerichow', undated, n.p., BEA File 159.
[113] See, for example, Gerhard Stadelmaier, 'Abgestanden in Ruinen', *Frankfurter Allgemeine Zeitung*, 3 October 1993; or Peter Iden, 'Vorhang zu und keine Fragen', *Frankfurter Rundschau*, 4 October 1993.
[114] Ernst Schumacher, 'Die Leichen steigen aus dem Keller', *Berliner Zeitung*, 2–3 October 1993.
[115] Müller, 'Die Wahrheit, leise und unerträglich', *Werke*, 12: 764.

social and historical questions. It is possible that, had they been staged
at some other time, at some other theatre, they would have been more
warmly received and appreciated. It is difficult to understand quite why
they were so vehemently rejected. One can perhaps conclude that the
audience had certain ideas of what the BE should have been doing after
the fall of the Wall, and that both directors' productions did not satisfy
that particular desire. Today, both may be seen as valiant attempts to
interrogate the possibilities of political action against a backdrop of indif-
ference and helplessness generated by the uncertainties that followed
reunification.

What the BE did next, or the problems of an invisible profile

The Berliner Ensemble, despite all its difficulties, was still one of the
most well-known theatre companies in the world, and its reputation was,
of course, based on its Brechtian traditions. It is thus perhaps a little
surprising to find that it had become so directionless. However, imagining just what a home for dialectical theatre might look like against the
backdrop of a world in which socialism appeared to have been thoroughly
discredited was a complex task in itself. Add to that the diverse interests
and means of the BE's directorial staff, and one finds a political and
aesthetic hotchpotch in which the BE's profile had become increasingly
indistinct.

The two seasons that followed the uncertain debut were certainly productive. In addition to Müller's *Fatzer*, there were twenty productions
that appeared on either the BE's main or its rehearsal stage, and the
plays were certainly diverse: Zadek directed Shakespeare; all bar Marquardt directed Brecht; Beckett, O'Casey, Edward Bond and Ibsen all
featured, together with a handful of better- and lesser-known playwrights.
In addition, a host of talks, discussions and small performances augmented the programme. Such scheduling was a far cry from the BE's
earlier practices of long rehearsals and three-figure performance runs.
On the surface, it looked liked diversity, breadth and energy were reflecting the positive qualities of the leadership, but this was far from the
case.

With regard to Brecht, things were precarious. Barbara Brecht-Schall
had decided to end the BE's monopoly on staging Brecht in the newly
reunified Berlin. This was not necessarily a bad thing; it could have
spurred the BE on to establish its own understanding or understandings
of what it meant to stage Brecht in a period of profound political uncertainty. In doing so, it could then distinguish itself from the other theatres

in Berlin. The BE was, however, unable to set out its aesthetic stall in this new competitive marketplace due to a lack of coherence and, indeed, a lack of vision.

As it turned out, Palitzsch did not direct the first Brecht of the BE's new era as planned; that honour went to Thomas Heise, a director I will discuss in the following section. Palitzsch's production of *Lebenslauf des Mannes Baal* (*Life Story of the Man Baal*), the 1926 revision of Brecht's first full-length play, attempted to contextualize the unusual and unexpected aspects of the poet's life in the concrete contexts of his society in a bid to rob him of the aura of genius.[116] The dry production, which opened in November 1993, won few fans, with most reviewers noting that the actor playing Baal, Volker Spengler, seemed to be playing a version of himself, rather than the character, although some enjoyed the way this resisted the clichés associated with Baal.[117] The antiseptic feel of the production did little to inject energy into the BE.

Two months later, Zadek approached his first Brecht in a long career of directing classic dramatists. His production of the pair of short *Lehrstücke*, *Der Jasager/Der Neinsager* (*He who Says Yes/He who Says No*), was, in his own words, rehearsed in a mere ten days.[118] The overwhelming response was to view the two complementary pieces as weak, empty gestures. Only the reviewer at *Neues Deutschland* considered he had rediscovered the works 'with a poetic, magically naïve production'.[119] Stephan Suschke notes Müller's response to the production: he called it the 'operetta version'.[120] He adds that Müller did not necessarily mean this in a nasty way, but that Zadek certainly took it like that, and this further fuelled the tension between them.

Zadek's reputation as a director was in part based on fresh new interpretations (of Shakespeare, in particular) and his musical productions that often dramatized novels and added songs. He was thus a perfect candidate to direct *The Threepenny Opera*, but had been refused the rights by Brecht-Schall, whose behaviour he later considered 'opaque and unpleasant'.[121] Thus, while she was happy to open up the Brecht market to all, she reserved the right to control it, as far as possible. It is

---

[116] See Palitzsch's director's note, in *Programme for Brecht's 'Lebenslauf des Mannes Baal'*, premiere 21 November 1993, p. 35.
[117] See, for example, Peter Laudenbach, 'Professionelle Abendunterhaltung', *Berliner Zeitung*, 23 November 1993.
[118] See Zadek, *Die Wanderjahre*, p. 212.
[119] Gerhard Ebert, 'Neu nachdenken in neuer Lage', *Neues Deutschland*, 20 December 1993.
[120] Suschke, in Zolchow, 'Protokoll eines Gespräches zwischen Stephan Suschke und Sabine Zolchow', p. 13.
[121] Zadek, *Die Wanderjahre*, p. 239.

nonetheless difficult to understand how someone as celebrated as Zadek, who proposed the distinguished actor Gerd Voss to play Mack the Knife, could be turned down. Reportedly, Brecht-Schall had already given the rights to another theatre,[122] although Berlin's Deutsches Theater only staged the play in September 1995,[123] long after Zadek had applied. Marquardt had also received a total ban on staging Brecht from Brecht-Schall. He diplomatically noted: 'I certainly place myself in the Brecht tradition, but she doesn't see it that way'.[124] The reason was not to be found in Marquardt's work as a director; his productions of Müller's plays were inflected by a focus on contradiction and the social. It is far more likely that his call for a moratorium on Brecht plays at the BE in 1991 (see p. 367, Chapter 12) created in Brecht-Schall an enemy who was known for her long memory.

Zadek revived an old production of *The Merchant of Venice* in January 1994 and brought a production of *Antony and Cleopatra* to the BE in October of that year, having unveiled it in Vienna in May. While neither was 'vintage' Zadek, they were solid, well received and, most important, did better business than the BE's other productions. One of the purported advantages of the GmbH model was that its financial flexibility could help the BE become a more efficient unit, capable of making savings, of putting money into risky productions, and then moving on if they failed. In the Directorate's second season, such promises were not delivering. By September 1993, Palitzsch criticized 'the ways in which money is apportioned and dealt with here'.[125] Two months later, low takings at the box office were reported,[126] something that caused a political as well as a financial problem. Zadek had originally insisted that ticket prices be set at a single standard price, so that at least their theatre would offer an alternative to a stratified society.[127] Price differentiation thus represented a subversion of the BE's egalitarian aims, and a sizeable increase could price potential spectators out of their seats. In January 1994, Sauerbaum publicly admitted that while the BE received 23.3 million marks in public subsidy, he still had to raise 2.7 million through

[122] See ibid., p. 240.
[123] See Deutscher Bühnenverein (ed.), *Wer spielte Was? Werkstatistik* (Darmstadt: Mykenae, 1998–2000) for the seasons 1995/6–1997/8.
[124] Marquardt, in Volker Oesterreich, 'Brecht ist Regisseur Fritz Marquardt verboten', *Berliner Morgenpost*, 13 September 1993.
[125] Palitzsch, in Sigrid Kunze, 'Protokoll über die Leitungssitzung am 3.9.1993', 6 September 1993, 3 pages (3), AdK HMA 7807.
[126] See Sigrid Kunze, 'Protokoll über die Leitungssitzung am 22.11.93', undated, n.p., ibid.
[127] See Zadek, *Die Wanderjahre*, p. 220.

ticket sales and other income-generating measures.[128] The BE, which used to boast filling around 90 per cent of its seating capacity, had fallen on hard times in recent years. The end of the GDR heralded a plunge in audience numbers. In 1991, the BE covered a mere 54 per cent of its seating, and this fell further to 49 per cent in 1992. A small bounce occurred in the mini season of 1993 (61 per cent), and this quotient rose with increased productivity in the 1993/94 season to 64 per cent. Yet the following season saw a low of 51 per cent,[129] a financially untenable position, and one far removed from the BE's glory days. This plummet can be accounted for by the poor quality of the productions, accompanying press hostility and the economic plight of many East Berliners, but the company was also missing something important.

Palitzsch complained that the BE did not understand its own function and asked which factors or perspectives were influencing production work. Müller's response was not exactly constructive: 'there isn't a political situation, there's only a vacuum, an emptiness, there's no human substance'. His only suggestion was that the turgid state of affairs required disruption, something he considered his own plays provided.[130] Müller admitted to Roloff-Momin in December 1994 that the BE had lost its public profile. The now four-headed model had led, in his words, to 'a mishmash and stagnation'. He also acknowledged that the BE's main competitors were in far better positions, mentioning the Deutsches Theater, 'that was working through its traditions' and the Volksbühne, 'that lives from a break with tradition'.[131] In other words, two major theatres with different foci nonetheless converged in their relationships to their pasts. Indeed, the Volksbühne had completely reinvented itself as an iconoclastic venue, but even here, there was no aesthetic uniformity: Frank Castorf's contemporary demolitions of classic texts sat side-by-side with Christoph Marthaler's gently repetitive productions and Johann Kresnik's biographical dance theatre. Diversity *and* a unity of purpose made the Volksbühne one of the most exciting theatres of the 1990s in Germany. For the BE, diversity meant the divergent interests of its directors, and there was clearly no unity of purpose, except for the desire to get the company out of the hole dug by the management structure Langhoff

---

[128] See Sauerbaum, in Peter Jacobs, '"Ich muß die Einnahmen steigern"', *Die Welt*, 19 January 1994.

[129] All statistics, rounded up or down to full percentages, are in Anon., [Untitled statistical data], undated, n.p., AdK TiW 698.

[130] See Palitzsch and Müller, respectively, in Sigrid Kunze, 'Protokoll über eine Leitungssitzung am 25.10.1993', 30 October 1993, n.p., AdK HMA 7807.

[131] Müller to Roloff-Momin, 6 December 1994, AdK HMA 7811.

had designed and promptly abandoned. Müller's need to refashion a profile for the company betokens his commitment to the BE's traditions in general and his own post-Brechtian theatre in particular. The BE found itself in a mire and had to reconcile itself with a new mode of production, one that did not see itself liberated from the market, as Müller had once hoped, but ever more dependent upon it.

Making theatre under straitened circumstances

Both of Zadek's Shakespeare productions at the BE were listed as co-productions, which meant that funding had come from other sources, too. In November 1993, Palitzsch suggested that in a time of economic recession, the Directors, who were already paid the handsome sum of 120,000 marks a year, should either forego their salary when directing or reduce their director's fee.[132] In December, the GmbH designated Müller a private individual in order for him to invest the princely sum of 200,000 marks into the 500,000 mark budget of his own production of his play, *Quartett*.[133] The production premiered in March 1994 and ran for 57 performances until 1997, which made it one of the BE's better received offerings, even with the critics,[134] although it was not universally applauded.

Yet while the BE's two main directors showed how they could contribute to offset the BE's ever worsening financial position, another used limited means as the basis for his work. As noted earlier, the original plan for the BE's new structures foresaw no dramaturges, but two-person teams – a director and his trusted assistant – who would set about realizing projects together. Fritz Marquardt brought film-maker Thomas Heise with him. By October 1993, he had already directed his first solo production, Brecht's *Der Brotladen* (*The Bread Shop*), the first Brecht production of the GmbH era. The play, a hit for the BE in 1967 when directed by Manfred Karge and Matthias Langhoff, was one of Brecht's fragments, and so Heise constructed a playable script from the Brecht archive. Heise emphasized its rough edges and unfinished nature by using BE actors, final-year acting students, two school pupils and technicians as performers on stage. Such 'economical' use of resources consciously displayed its own lack of virtuosity. One critic was caught between finding the production too amateurish for such a theatre like the BE while

[132] See Palitzsch to Sauerbaum, 16 November 1993, AdK HMA 7808.
[133] See Sauerbaum to the Directorate, 17 December 1993, ibid.
[134] See, for example, Peter Laudenbach, 'Sadomasochistische Endzeitsspiele', *Berliner Zeitung*, 14 March 1994; or Volker Oesterreich, 'Eine Verbeugung vor Marianne Hoppe', *Berliner Morgenpost*, 13 March 1994.

then wondering whether this was not an aggressive slap in the face for its comfortable audience.[135] Zadek suggested that Heise be given a full directing contract in the light of his obvious talent, regardless of the quality of *Der Brotladen*.[136] As if promotion from assistant to director were not indication enough, Zadek's remark clearly signals that Langhoff's initial model of a vanguard of experienced directors was dead and buried. While the BE was still run as a GmbH by its four surviving shareholders, its structure had now formally become one of pluralism with all artistically able hands on deck. Schleef's appearance as a guest director had already heralded the wider use of directors who were not the GmbH's Directors.

Heise's next production, premiered in September 1994, was Müller's *Cement*, the play that had rehabilitated the playwright, to an extent, in the GDR when Ruth Berghaus staged the world premiere at the BE in 1973. The site for the work was not, however, the BE's main stage, but a disused factory hall in the southeast of the city that was due to be demolished that October. While Müller's *Quartett* had a budget of 500,000 marks and a cast of five, *Cement* cost 212,000 marks with a cast of twenty-one. The BE contributed a mere 80,000 marks.[137] In a letter to a potential sponsor, Heise also noted that thirty-five people were sacrificing their time-off free of charge to realize the project. He was looking to cover a 50,000 mark shortfall in the budget.[138] In the same letter, Heise appealed to his potential sponsor, the chair of the PDS, the party that succeeded the SED, in the most strident of terms: this was a militantly Brechtian production that was not concerned with portraying milieu, but revolution. It is hard to overlook the irony, or perhaps the foregone conclusion, that the neo-liberal values enshrined in the founding of the GmbH were undermining such political ambitions: the revolution was to be paid for by actors and technicians working for no pay on a production starved of a decent budget and forced to go cap in hand to a series of external sponsors (the programme lists nineteen, the PDS was not one of them). While this certainly reflected the pressures on finance at the BE and did not prejudice the seriousness or commitment of the work, it was a far cry from Brecht's own harmonious working conditions in which supportive structures promoted active contributions from as many creative quarters as possible. Critics were divided by Heise's ascetic rigour, which echoed Müller's approach to *Fatzer*.

---

[135] See Reinhard Wengierek, 'Frag nicht, der Weg führt', *Neue Zeit*, 18 October 1993.
[136] See Sigrid Kunze, 'Protokoll über die Leitungssitzung am 6.10.1993', 7 October 1993, 4 pages (2), AdK HMA 7807.
[137] See Anon., 'Die Kalkulation', undated, n.p., BEA File 170.
[138] See Thomas Heise to Gregor Gysi, 24 August 1994, draft letter, ibid.

Heise's final low-budget production was staged in May 1995 and was a montage of texts by little-known playwright, Michael Wildenhain, collected as *Im Schlagschatten des Mondes Hänsel und Gretel* (*In the Shadow Cast by the Moon Hansel and Gretel*). Savings were made on the cast: the eleven actors were all school pupils aged between ten and eleven. It should be noted, however, that the savings were a financial fringe benefit, rather than the driver in the process of hiring cheaper actors. The decision allowed the director to engage with a different kind of post-Brechtian theatre than *Cement*, in which the actors delegated interpretation to the audience by not colouring speeches with everyday inflections. The children certainly engaged with meaning-making, but the distance between their own relationship to what they acted and how the audience understood it was large enough to create a productive disjunction. The children performed scenes about right-wing violence and xenophobia, written in poetic language. Heise wanted *their* take on the texts as a radically naïve approach to delivering text. He did not want to push them into interpretations that made sense to him as an adult and tried to enforce a single rule when they learned their lines at home: 'no parents'.[139] He sought to give his young actors expressive freedom so that they could work through their own relationship to the topical material, and this was to give the work integrity; he did not want the audience to patronize the children by feeling superior to them. Rather, the children had to commit to their own ensemble work if a credible performance were to emerge that would necessarily challenge the audience.

The nature of the material also meant that there was always a metatheatrical wedge that divided the stage and the auditorium. The themes of violence, the use of sexual images and 'adult' language could make an audience profoundly aware of the artifice involved in the production. Reviewer Günther Grack was unsettled by this aspect and wrote that '[the evening's] questionable moment starts when it oversteps the bounds of the child actors' experiences'.[140] Grack was raising the ethical question as to whether the children had in some way been exploited and corrupted by the material they were delivering and performing. As Nicholas Ridout observes about this seemingly perennial problem: 'the concern over exploitation focuses on whether or not the . . . children know what they are doing, whether they are capable of giving properly informed consent

---

[139] Thomas Heise, in Anon., 'Thomas Heise zu seiner Arbeit mit 10- und 11-Jährigen in *Im Schlagschatten des Mondes Hänsel und Gretel*: Interview am 4 September 1995 in der Kantine des Berliner Ensemble [sic]', undated, 8 pages (4), BEA File 181.

[140] Günther Grack, 'Der Charme der "Nagten wahrheit [sic]"', *Der Tagesspiegel*, 9 May 1995.

to their own participation and whether their lives will be in any way damaged by their appearance on stage'.[141] It is debatable whether ten- and eleven-year-olds have no conception of either the violence that was widely reported, 'bad language', or the adult world of sex. What Grack's point does indicate is that there was a productive frisson between the stage and the auditorium when potentially taboo issues were brought up. Such a frisson is self-reflective and frame-breaking because the spectator starts to ask about the ethics of the production, not what is happening on stage at the time. This confrontation was present throughout, in that children were almost exclusively playing the roles of adults without ever pretending to be grown-up. This is one of the ways in which Heise permanently engineered *Verfremdung* to resist the simple reception of the material on stage.

The deliberate cultivation of naïvety had implications for the longevity of the project. Heise noted that once the production had become a part of the repertoire at the BE, its radical naïvety would be compromised.[142] The sixteen performances over a four-month period gave the children a greater familiarity with one another, their texts and the theatre space. As they got more experienced and were more able to connect the difficult lines to their reality, the distance between speaker and spoken started to contract. When that happened, the production lost its edge and was retired.

Heise's experiences during the BE's 'gang of four' period show the effects of the GmbH structure on the business of production. An imagined fiscal flexibility translated into concrete financial austerity, and this started to run through the very ways in which theatre was made. Theatre is, of course, an expensive activity, yet the more one has to seek external funding and ask people to work either without payment or on fees that do not reflect the hours invested, the more the productions themselves become compromised. While this was not really the case with *In the Shadow*, where a performative virtue had been made out of a budgetary necessity, *The Bread Shop* and *Cement* both suffered under the pecuniary strains applied by the BE.

The quest for new forms, however, could make the BE inventive. While driving through Brandenburg, Zadek discovered a country pub with a space big enough to be used for performance.[143] He redirected *He who Says Yes* and sent it to the venue, the Gasthof Naase, where it was warmly

[141] Nicholas Ridout, *Stage Fright, Animals and Other Theatrical Problems* (Cambridge: Cambridge University Press, 2006), pp. 99–100.
[142] See Heise, in Anon., 'Thomas Heise zu seiner Arbeit', p. 7.
[143] See Zadek, *Die Wanderjahre*, p. 261.

received, and the run was virtually sold out.[144] His light, mobile company also took the production to schools and received several requests from local officials to continue and extend the practice. Post-show discussions were a regular feature, and so the audience could engage more fully with the piece afterwards. A production of Ionesco's *La Cantatrice Chauve* (*The Bald Primadonna*) followed in September 1994, and a project supervised by Zadek on the BE's main stage, *Ich bin das Volk* (*I Am the People*) by Franz Xaver Kroetz, was also redirected for touring in April 1995. Again, this represented a relatively cheap way of taking theatre beyond the city's borders. The BE's ability to take advantage of its reputation meant that the shows were usually very well attended.

The year 1994 was, however, a year in which attention was very much focused on the BE's failure to master its finances. At the end of April, Sauerbaum proposed setting up a second GmbH as a way of hiving off certain aspects of the privatized BE that had the potential to generate extra income. The terms of the original agreement envisaged the BE as a not-for-profit organization, and so an additional company could bypass that condition and seek to make money that could then be fed back into productions. Sauerbaum also saw the potential of using the new company to attract wealthy investors seeking to park their money and offset tax liabilities.[145] He noted that the great Max Reinhardt had run such a scheme with his brother, and it worked so well that his Deutsches Theater barely required state subsidy. He added, however, that the sister company also owned a lot of property. It is not clear whether this company was actually set up. Even if it was, it did not save the BE from financial peril.

By February 1995, Sauerbaum asked the shareholders whether they believed that they could maintain the BE as a going concern and confronted them with the possibility of declaring the GmbH bankrupt if they answered in the negative.[146] He subsequently proposed a registered association in April 1995 to encourage benefactions and sought to target seven high-profile patrons from large firms like the Commerzbank or Daimler Benz. The left-wing theatre was now courting big business. Sauerbaum added, however, that the association was nonetheless open to all.[147] The idea itself was Peter Raue's, a high-profile lawyer, and he

[144] See Elisabeth Gabriel and Thorsten Weckherlin to BE leadership, 22 April 1994, BEA File 'Spielplan: Produktionen ab 92/93/sonstige Veranstaltungen'.
[145] See Sauerbaum to the Shareholders, 29 April 1994, AdK HMA 7810.
[146] See Sauerbaum to the Shareholders, 8 February 1995, AdK HMA 7815.
[147] See Anon., 'Satzung des Vereins der "Freunde und Förderer des Berliner Ensembles"', 23 April 1995, 6 pages; and Sauberbaum to Müller, 7 May 1995, both documents: AdK HMA 7816.

told me that while most theatres had this kind of structured support, the BE did not set up the association in the end.[148]

The BE was always looking for ways to cut its costs. One such initiative was a bid to sever links with the Ballhaus Rixdorf. The BE had not made great use of the space for performance – indeed, it had only staged *Grillparzer* there in its first 'new' season and transferred one other production there temporarily. Sauerbaum had written to the Directors in November to inform them that they could save 369,000 marks by withdrawing from their contact with the venue.[149] The Ballhaus found the BE's reasons for breaking the contract unfounded and merely an excuse to remove themselves from a legally binding agreement.[150] A formal writ was sent to the Directors in December.[151] The lack of further documentation suggests that some kind of agreement or compromise was reached, but it is unlikely that the BE made the saving it originally envisaged.

The GmbH had proved to be a financial millstone, rather than an economic panacea. Self-governance had led to opacity regarding the allocation of budgets and this lack of transparency, brought about in part by cutting the regulated link to the State, made planning and budgeting difficult. The effect on the productions themselves cannot be ignored, and so the new system actually had the effect of both instigating and exacerbating the crisis at the company. Yet the crisis was not only of a financial or an artistic nature.

The Directorate's death knell

The five-Director structure was an experiment, and experiments, by their very nature, can lead to a variety of outcomes. However, experiments can at least allow for the possibility of a positive result. The question thus emerges as to what prerequisites might have led to the successful realization of the leadership model developed for the BE. Shows of unity, in the run-up to *Wessis* and in the wake of Langhoff's departure, were not really sufficient because they were merely shows, brought about by a sense of obligation. A successful experiment might, then, have been predicated on a more fundamental kind of understanding amongst the Directors, and this could have taken one of two forms. The first might have enshrined the five Directors, who were also stage directors, as equals: each with their own history and achievements, permitted to realize their

---

[148] Peter Raue, unpublished interview with the author, 13 September 2012.
[149] See Sauerbaum to the Directors and Eva Mattes, 9 November 1994, AdK HMA 7811.
[150] See Jörn Richter to Boden, Oppenhoff, Raso, Raue [the BE's lawyers], 11 November 1994, ibid.
[151] See Wolfgang Redel to the Directors, 19 December 1994, ibid.

theatrical visions on their own terms within the usual constraints defined by budget, space and time. This option was already tainted before the five men founded the GmbH: we know how Zadek looked down on Marquardt and how Langhoff wanted to build the BE around Müller. The other possibility was one based on accepting a hierarchy, or, putting it more bluntly, knowing one's place. In this scenario, the five-man leadership would not have fostered the illusion of equality, but seen itself as a graduated structure with, presumably, Zadek and Müller at its apex. Even in this configuration of the experiment, success would have been possible due to an acknowledgement that resources would not have been equally distributed, but allocated according to one's place in the pecking order. While not an egalitarian model, it could have established order by offering all the Directors a concrete sense of where they belonged and what they could expect. Instead, the experiment was doomed to failure because it combined elements of both versions in that it gave the illusion of equality while actually functioning as a hierarchy based around Zadek and Müller. It was this contradiction that led to the breakdown of the four-man leadership in early 1995.

The reasons for the collapse are, as discussed above, partly to be accounted for in terms of economics and a failure to re-establish the BE's artistic profile through its productions. Against a backdrop of fiscal constraint and uneven artistic performance, divisions became more manifest in the Directorate itself. While a key factor was the power struggle between Zadek and Müller, it is worth noting that all was not well elsewhere, either. Palitzsch had written to his fellow directors in May 1994 about his frustration at his lack of influence and announced that he wanted to resign as a Director before the year was out.[152] By this time, Marquardt was something of a silent partner himself. Yet while these two retreated to the sidelines, Peter Sauerbaum, the BE's business manager, became more active, and one of his joint initiatives was to bring an already difficult situation to a head.

The tension between Zadek and Müller had an ideological component, and this was evident in the differing responses to Schleef's *Wessis*: Zadek found it a brutal, neo-fascist event while Müller supported the confrontational aesthetic as an appropriate treatment of the violence surrounding reunification. However, Zadek prevailed in the ensuing debate about whether Schleef should return to direct at the BE after he threatened to leave the Directorate over the matter.[153] That said, Zadek did countenance Schleef's possible return in late 1993 when the Senate closed

---

[152] See Palitzsch to the Directors, 10 May 1994, AdK HMA 7810.
[153] See Zadek, *Die Wanderjahre*, p. 226.

West Berlin's Schiller-Theater, and the director found he had nowhere to perform his *Faust*. Yet Zadek insisted that he had to be present at any negotiation involving Schleef.[154] Schleef continued to remain a bone of contention in late 1994, something Müller ironically acknowledged in a letter to the other directors: 'Peter Zadek's fear of Schleef is as incomprehensible to me as, unfortunately, my plays are to him'.[155] However, the tension between the two was becoming more of a struggle for the way the BE was to be run at this time.

In September 1994, Müller was diagnosed with cancer of the gullet and underwent an operation in October to remove the tumour. In the following months he convalesced in California and returned to Berlin much weakened in March 1995. While he was away, he kept in contact by fax and letter, and found himself forced to respond to Zadek's bid for dominance. Zadek's gambit opened with a tactic observed earlier in the BE's history when Manfred Wekwerth and Ekkehard Schall tendered their resignations in 1968 and 1975, respectively. That is, he was applying pressure, rather than actually resigning in the first instance. Zadek submitted his resignation to Sauerbaum in November 1994.[156] Here he protested about Müller's absentee support for Schleef's proposal to stage Hauptmann's *Die Weber* (*The Weavers*) with a chorus of unemployed people declaiming their lines in Silesian dialect.[157] Zadek was supported in his objection to Schleef by the BE's lawyer, Peter Raue.[158] Raue was an important figure on Berlin's cultural scene in that he often took a leading role in helping to define it. He was instrumental in drafting the original GmbH contract and played an even more important part in late 1994. Before that, however, Müller wrote directly to Roloff-Momin, not only to complain about Zadek's resistance to Schleef, but to signal his critique of the four-man model and to warn against the potential mistake of allowing Zadek to take over as sole leader. He noted: 'Peter Zadek is a bank as a director, but a catastrophe as *Intendant*'.[159] He suggested that an administrator be appointed to the overall leadership in order to organize the existing Directors and to recruit high-profile guests such as Peter Brook, Giorgio Strehler, Peter Sellars and Robert Wilson. On the same day, Sauerbaum backed Zadek, believing that Zadek's departure would

---

[154] See Sigrid Kunze, 'Protokoll über eine Leitungssitzung am 6.10.1993', 7 October 1993, 4 pages (1), AdK HMA 7807.
[155] Müller to the Directorate, 10 November 1994, AdK HMA 7811.
[156] See Zadek to Sauerbaum, 23 November 1994, ibid.
[157] See Zadek to the Leadership, 22 November 1994, ibid.
[158] See Peter Raue to Müller, 2 December 1994, ibid.
[159] Müller to Roloff-Momin, 6 December 1994, ibid.

be too high a price to pay for employing Schleef.[160] The letter was sent to the Directors and the actor Eva Mattes. She had been brought to the ensemble by Zadek, as someone with whom he had worked extensively over the years, and had sat on the BE's management group as a Director (but not as a shareholder) since September 1994[161] in a bid to bolster Zadek's position in the decision-making process.

The pressure Raue and Sauerbaum applied to Müller was made concrete in a document they co-authored at the end of December 1994. Their proposal involved reconciling the visions of Müller and Zadek by dividing the pair. It proposed the creation of an entity, the 'BE-Werkstatt für Theater und Literatur' ('BE Workshop for Theatre and Literature'), independent of the GmbH, within which Müller and Marquardt could direct their own projects separately. The two would have to give back their shares in the GmbH, and the subsidy was to be set at up to 900,000 marks per year, although the question of where they would work remained open.[162] This was a radical proposition, but one remarkably disadvantageous to Müller and Marquardt. They would lose all control over the BE, receive a relative pittance in subsidy, and effectively remain isolated. Understandably, both rejected the proposal out of hand.[163] Zadek openly displayed his support for the coup, stating that it merely confirmed the status quo as he saw it: 'namely that of a theatre run by Peter Palitzsch and me, and financed by my productions'.[164] This interjection, of course, did not persuade Müller and Marquardt to accept the plan that now seemed dead in the water.

Sauerbaum, however, was keen to pursue it and submitted a modification to Müller at the end of January 1995. Here he proposed that the BE be expanded into two venues, the Theater am Schiffbauerdamm and the newly redeveloped boiler house of the Kulturbrauerei in Berlin's Prenzlauer Berg district, that could seat 300 people. The structure of the BE's leadership would remain unchanged and the directors would decide who directed where.[165] This was certainly a more palatable version for Müller, although the old plan re-emerged in a further variation of early February. The proposal now designated Zadek and Müller as the

[160] See Sauerbaum to Directors and Eva Mattes, ibid.
[161] See Detlef Friedrich, 'Das Theaterbüro tagte und brach abends das Schweigen', Berliner Zeitung, 9 March 1995.
[162] See untitled document, enclosed with Peter Raue to Directors, 29 December 1994, AdK HMA 7811.
[163] See Marquardt to the Directors, 10 January 1995; and Müller to the Leadership, 11 January 1995, AdK HMA 7814.
[164] Zadek to Directors and Sauerbaum, 16 January 1994 [sic], ibid.
[165] See Sauerbaum, 'Variation der Konzeption Raue/Sauerbaum zur Leitungsstruktur des Berliner Ensemble [sic]', 27 January 1995, n.p., ibid.

BE's artistic directors with Palitzsch, Marquardt and Mattes as 'artistic advisors'. Zadek was to run the Schiffbauerdamm venue, Müller the Kulturbrauerei. The old budget attached to the 'Workshop' was retained at 900,000 marks.[166] However, Sauerbaum reported that both Müller and Zadek supported the plan and that he, Raue and Roloff-Momin had met to discuss it. The senator approved the plan, as long as existing funding could cover it.[167] Smelling victory, Zadek wanted the deal sealed by Müller's written agreement.[168] However, by mid February, Müller had changed his mind. In a letter to his fellow directors, he noted that the BE would not founder if Zadek left, proposed that the Kulturbrauerei plans be postponed, and he submitted ideas for the repertoire that included Schleef and the equally uncompromising Frank Castorf.[169] Müller was on the offensive, and a flurry of communication ensued.

Sauerbaum wrote to Müller on 23 February telling him that Zadek still insisted on Müller's signature.[170] Around the same time, Müller received letters of encouragement to stand his ground from director Thomas Heise, his personal assistant, Sigrid Kunze, and dramaturge Bärbel Jaksch.[171] On 24 February, the Directors received an ultimatum from Zadek that set out in no uncertain terms the conditions under which he would remain at the BE. The nine-point plan had at its centre the marginalization of Müller. While Zadek agreed that Müller could remain a Director, he wanted to limit his directing activity to one production a year and re-label him Head Dramaturge. Zadek and Palitzsch would share the role of *Intendant* with support from Sauerbaum and Mattes. Marquardt would not be allowed to direct any more and would be bought out as a Director. Zadek also sought to detach the BE from its traditions by insisting on a maximum of one Brecht and one Müller production per season.[172] Müller, unsurprisingly, considered the demands unacceptable, and while he lamented Zadek's departure because of his great directing talents, he believed it was now inevitable.[173] On 6 March Zadek demanded a reply to his ultimatum and said that he would have to assume that the Directorate stood behind Müller if he did not receive one

---

[166] See Sauerbaum, 'Variation der Konzeption Raue/Sauerbaum zur Leitungsstruktur des Berliner Ensemble [*sic*]', 3 February 1995, 2 pages, AdK HMA 7815.
[167] See Sauerbaum to the Directors and Mattes, 4 February 1995, ibid.
[168] See Sauerbaum to Müller, 6 February 1995, ibid.
[169] See Müller to the Leadership, 16 February 1995, ibid.
[170] See Sauerbaum to Müller, 23 February 1995, ibid.
[171] See Thomas Heise to Müller 23 February 1995; Sigrid Kunze to Müller, 24 February 1995; and Bärbel Jaksch to Müller, 25 February 1995, ibid.
[172] See Zadek to Directors, Mattes and Sauerbaum, 24 February 1995, AdK HMA 7816.
[173] See Müller to the Leadership [but not to Zadek], 26 February 1995, AdK HMA 7815.

within two days.[174] A day later, Palitzsch pleaded with Zadek to retract the document, whose terms he considered 'in part inhumane, in part unrealizable'. His subsequent question, 'aren't you aware of that?',[175] acknowledged the possibility that Zadek preferred to quit, rather than continue to work at the BE by setting out conditions that could never be accepted.

Zadek's deadline arrived, and an exceptional meeting of the BE's shareholders was convened. There Zadek agreed to leave the company on 31 July 1995, and it was decided that Sauerbaum could buy him out of his shares. Eva Mattes did thus not replace Zadek, but kept her seat on the management board all the same.[176] The news was made public the following day.[177] Slightly over a week later, the right-of-centre CDU party called for a single *Intendant* at the BE.[178] Palitzsch left the Directorate, but remained a director and shareholder. Stephan Suschke became the company's 'coordinator',[179] a position that helped to turn the different artistic ideas into a coherent programme while ensuring that organizational and communications issues were dealt with sensibly.[180] Müller officially took over as sole artistic director on 15 June,[181] a position he had implicitly held since Zadek's departure in March. Mattes then left the Directorate, which only continued to exist in name, but stayed at the BE as an actor. All the same, Müller was not happy at the outcome. In an interview in April, he said he did not consider himself the victor, adding 'we lose something with Zadek – Zadek loses something with this theatre'.[182]

After his departure, Zadek himself gave a variety of reasons for leaving the BE. He initially said that he had always been outvoted in meetings because Müller was at the BE's centre; he objected to the pessimism and cynicism he detected in Müller's work and the right-wing tendencies of Schleef; and later he said he found it impossible to talk to Müller once he was diagnosed with cancer as he was a different person afterwards.[183]

[174] See Zadek to Directors, Mattes and Sauerbaum, 6 March 1995, AdK HMA 7816.
[175] Palitzsch to Zadek, 7 March 1995, ibid.
[176] See Sigrid Kunze, 'Beschlußprotokoll', 8 March 1995, n.p., AdK TiW 696.
[177] See, for example, Friedrich, 'Das Theaterbüro tagte'.
[178] See BM/dpa, 'Soll nur noch ein Intendant das Berliner Ensemble leiten?', *Berliner Morgenpost*, 18 March 1995.
[179] See Lutz Hoyer, 'Fünf-Köpfe-Modell beendet', *Berliner Zeitung*, 16 March 1995.
[180] Email from Stephan Suschke to the author, 16 August 2012.
[181] See JW, 'BEerdigung?', *Junge Welt*, 16 June 1995.
[182] Müller, in Harald Biskup, '"Landeplätze für Geier sind geräumig"', *Kölner Stadt-Anzeiger*, 20 April 1995.
[183] See Zadek, in Karin Kathrein, '"Diese generelle Unkultur wird unerträglich"', *Die Welt* 10 March 1995; Marianne Heuwagen, '"Ich bin immer ein Optimist"', *Süddeutsche Zeitung* 14 March 1995; Georgia Tornow and Michael Maier, '"Bei Menschen und bei

Yet he had clearly been able to discuss transplanting Müller to the Kulturbrauerei.

The experiment with the five-, and then four-man leadership had run its course. Müller, echoing the terms of Roloff-Momin's initial plan to combine East and West in one theatre, believed that it was Germany that divided himself and Zadek.[184] This claim has a ring of truth about it: despite its grand scale, it acknowledges that the two came from two different traditions and addressed two different sets of problems. Their contrasting biographies, formed by two distinct experiences of theatre and its possibilities, did not spark off each other, but led to antagonism. Another factor, of course, was one based on power and the desire to control a famous theatre. Stephan Suschke offers one further contributory factor: space. He contends that the BE was physically too small for five Directors.[185] All five were rarely present together, and thus the most basic aspects of communication were prevented. It is not by chance that so much of the story of Zadek's departure was carried out by letter and fax. The opportunity for regular exchange was severely limited and so, when things started to go wrong, positions were developed on paper, rather than in person. This combination of factors sealed the original model's fate. Once it had broken down, central figures agreed that, in hindsight, they would not have approved the plan.[186]

Müller had won the battle for primacy at the BE, but it is difficult to see why he was not made sole *Intendant* back in 1992. This was effectively Langhoff's aim, and the voices of criticism surrounding the establishment of the 'gang of five' mean that this was not merely an opinion voiced after the fact. Müller's reputation as an innovative post-Brechtian director meant that the BE could have preserved its traditions while dragging them into the new political landscape of a reunified Germany. His vision of a theatre after Brecht was not dogmatic, either; he supported Schleef and Castorf as exemplars of radical contemporary political theatre, rather than insisting on his own stripped-down version, for example. Müller was also well connected in the theatre world and had productive relationships with the internationally fêted directors mentioned above. They were thus more likely to accept invitations to work as guests at the new BE. The confrontation with Zadek showed that he knew how to fight his corner. He was also able to nurture new talent, as can be seen in the development

---

Schauspielern gibt es nur eines, das mich wirklich interessiert: Das Echte'", *Berliner Zeitung*, 11–12 May 1996.

[184] See Müller, 'Die Wahrheit, leise und unerträglich', *Werke*, 12: 760.

[185] Stephan Suschke, unpublished interview with the author, 28 April 2011.

[186] See, for example, Müller, 'Die Wahrheit', *Werke* 12: 761; Roloff-Momin, *Zuletzt: Kultur*, p. 69.

of Thomas Heise. Potentially productive years had been wasted by a series of battles that could have been prevented by the appointment of Müller as a single, suitable *Intendant* in the first place. Yet by March 1995, it seemed that the BE had finally reached a point at which it could both stabilize itself and develop a concerted strategy for regaining lost ground and time. These efforts, however, were to be frustrated when a new front was opened against the BE by a most unexpected enemy.

As one battle ends, another begins: Hochhuth's attack on the BE

The end of the power struggle with Peter Zadek seemed to have left the BE ready to face the future with new resolve. Even before Zadek had resigned, a Müller-driven plan for the coming season had been drafted, and it prominently featured plays by Brecht and Müller, as well as a wish-list of guest directors, including Schleef, Wilson, Heiner Goebbels, Dimiter Gotscheff, and, most unexpectedly, Woody Allen.[187] However, before the dust could settle, the BE found itself embroiled in a new crisis, instigated by Rolf Hochhuth, the dramatist who tried to stop the company's production of *Wessis in Weimar*. Hochhuth had approached the BE on three separate occasions to join the Directorate: once after Langhoff left, then later in 1993, and again after Zadek left.[188] His applications were not approved. Then, without warning, the *Berliner Morgenpost* newspaper broke the story that would further distract the BE from its primary task of steadying the ship and developing further.

Rolf Hochhuth, whose stature as a dramatist was questioned by the reviewers of *Wessis*, is nonetheless an excellent researcher. He had discovered that the Berlin authorities did not own the BE's main building, and he tracked down the person who did. The *Morgenpost* revealed on 28 April 1995 that Hochhuth's foundation, the Ilse-Holzapfel-Stiftung, had acquired the rights to buy the Theater am Schiffbauerdamm with a down-payment of one million marks of the total 4.5 million mark selling price. Hochhuth's plan was to take over the BE as an 'Autorentheater', a 'theatre for playwrights', although the only playwright he named was himself. Sauerbaum was said to be completely astounded by the news because he was not aware that there were outstanding problems

---

[187] See Anon., untitled, 1 March 1995, pp. 2–5, BEA File 'Spielplan: Produktionen ab 92/92/sonstige Veranstaltungen'.

[188] See Sigrid Kunze, 'Protokoll über die Leitungssitzung am 24.4.1993', 27 April 1993, 5 pages (1), AdK HMA 7807; Rolf Hochhuth to Marquardt, Müller, Palitzsch and Zadek, 28 October 1993, AdK HMA 7829; and Hochhuth to Müller, 14 April 1995, AdK HMA 7834, respectively.

concerning the property.[189] The City owned all the site around the main house, yet that most important of buildings was still in private hands. Officials in the GDR were well aware of this fact. They agreed a rental price shortly before the BE moved into its new home in 1954,[190] and the Ministry of Culture contacted its owner, Klaus Wertheim, by that time a US citizen, to agree the BE's full usage of the building in 1964. The Ministry valued it at just under half a million marks and agreed to maintain it so that it retained its value.[191]

According to Roloff-Momin, he was aware of the anomaly early in his tenure, but when he brought it to the attention of the Senator for Finance, he received no reply.[192] This assertion is dubious because it is contradicted by the final draft of the contract constituting the GmbH, written in autumn 1992.[193] The document includes a clause explicitly stating that the land belongs to the City of Berlin, and thus Roloff-Momin either deliberately signed something he knew to be untrue or was in fact unaware of the problem with the deeds. He also noted that Hochhuth had been on the hunt for a theatre to stage his plays in Berlin for some time. Roloff-Momin had offered him the Konrad-Wolf-Saal shortly before Hochhuth announced his intention to buy the BE,[194] but Hochhuth then demanded a further two million marks to refurbish it.[195] Indeed, newspapers reported that the playwright had looked elsewhere, too. He had made a bid for the Deutsches Theater in the winter of 1991/92, but had been turned down by Gottfried Reinhardt, the son of Max Reinhardt.[196] He then tried to acquire Berlin's Schloßparktheater.[197] However, after Roloff-Momin made enquiries in Stuttgart, where the Holzapfel-Stiftung had been registered, he came to the conclusion that the foundation had been set up exclusively with the aim of staging Hochhuth's plays at the BE.[198]

Müller's defence was two-fold. First, he accused Hochhuth of hypocrisy: 'Saint George has become the dragon; Rolf Hochhuth takes the stage in the garb of the Treuhand'.[199] That is, Hochhuth's *Wessis* was

---

[189] See Peter Schubert, 'Rolf Hochhuth will das Brecht-Theater kaufen', *Berliner Morgenpost*, 28 April 1995.
[190] See Dr Münzer, 'Vermerk', 9 February 1954, 2 pages, BArch DR 1/18162.
[191] See Gärtner to Rubner, 18 December 1964, BArch DR 1/18164.
[192] See Roloff-Momin, *Zuletzt: Kultur*, p. 66.
[193] See Anon., 'Entwurf: Vertrag zwischen dem Land Berlin', p. 5.
[194] See how, '20 Ansprüche, keine Unterlagen', *Die Welt*, 16 May 1995.
[195] See Roloff-Momin, *Zuletzt: Kultur*, p. 67.
[196] See FAZ, 'Großer Hunger', *Frankfurter Allgemeine Zeitung*, 9 June 1995.
[197] See tll., 'BE wehrt sich gegen Hochhuths Kaufpläne', *Berliner Morgenpost*, 29 April 1995.
[198] See Roloff-Momin, *Zuletzt: Kultur*, p. 67.
[199] Müller, in Anon., 'Der heilige Georg', *Berliner Morgenpost*, 29 April 1995.

all about Western speculators and other interest groups buying up assets and property in the former GDR through the institution that managed the sell-off, the Treuhand, and now Wessi Hochhuth was behaving in the same way as those he had previously condemned. Second, Müller claimed that the BE did not fear Hochhuth because he did not have the money to run a theatre. Subsidy was the only way to make one like the BE work.[200] This was obviously the more powerful argument: the City could simply turn off the money supply and leave Hochhuth high and dry as the owner of a theatre that could not afford to stage productions.

Yet even with that argument in mind, Roloff-Momin still tried to cut a deal with Wertheim and asked him to name his price in May 1995.[201] Wertheim did not switch buyers, but Hochhuth could not tie up the deal quickly, revealing in December that he was still looking for backers to raise the capital.[202] However, even before the deal was completed, Hochhuth offered pronouncements on the BE as if he already owned it. For example, he noted that the current four-person leadership should remain in place, with Müller at its head, but with Hochhuth as its fifth member.[203]

The story rumbled on for the next couple of years. The playwright officially assumed ownership of the building in March 1996,[204] but it took longer to reach agreement on terms with the City. It seemed as if everything had been settled in January 1998: the Stiftung would receive rent of 360,000 marks, considerably less than Hochhuth's original stipulation of 1.3 million,[205] and the Stiftung, at its own cost, was allowed to stage what it wanted for five weeks during the theatre's summer break.[206] However, by October, the Senate was so outraged by the way Hochhuth continued to impinge on the BE's artistic autonomy, it considered moving the company from the Theater am Schiffbauerdamm to the now vacant Freie Volksbühne in former West Berlin.[207] Perhaps conceding to this threat from the Senate, Hochhuth finally signed a thirty-year contract at the end of the month on the terms described above.[208]

---

[200] See Müller, 'Verwaltungsakte produzieren keine Erfahrungen', *Werke*, 12: 713.
[201] See BM/dpa, 'Kultursenator wandte sich an John Wertheim', *Berliner Morgenpost*, 12 May 1995.
[202] See jal, 'Hochhuth: BE großenteils erworben', *Der Tagesspiegel*, 2 December 1995.
[203] See Volker Oesterreich, 'Rolf Hochhuth: "Die jetzige Crew soll lange bleiben"', *Berliner Morgenpost*, 21 May 1995.
[204] See dpa/ND, 'BE geht an Hochhuths Stiftung', *Neues Deutschland*, 8 March 1996.
[205] See Tsp, 'Berliner Ensemble: Hochhuth und Senat vor Einigung', *Der Tagesspiegel*, 6 January 1998.
[206] See Tsp, 'Mietvertrag fürs BE unter Dach und Fach', *Der Tagesspiegel*, 8 January 1998.
[207] See ADN, 'Krise am BE: Kultursenat fühlt sich erpreßt', *Der Tagesspiegel* 8 October 1998.
[208] See dpa, 'Peymann kommt', *Frankfurter Allgemeine Zeitung* 30 October 1998.

Despite Hochhuth's public protestations to the contrary, he very much wanted to influence the way the BE ran and the plays it staged. On the one hand, there was a noble aim behind this: Klaus Wertheim and his parents had emigrated to the United States because they were Jews in Nazi Germany, and Hochhuth proposed a statutory performance of his own anti-Nazi play *Der Stellvertreter* (translated in English as *The Representative* and *The Deputy*) on 16 October every year to mark the first deportation of Jews from Berlin. On the other hand, he wanted to stage as many of his own plays as possible, something that may not have generated terribly large audiences, given their overall quality. Hochhuth's victory, which did not grant him the possibility of making artistic decisions at the BE, was thus pyrrhic. Yet the whole process had cost the company a great deal of time and effort in order to defend its artistic integrity against Hochhuth's ambush.

Müller's final months

Once Müller effectively took over as *Intendant*, he set about implementing a programme that would give the BE the coherence it lacked. Eighteen productions of plays exclusively by Brecht, Müller and Shakespeare appeared in a draft plan for a repertoire that covered the coming three seasons. Six further 'new plays' supplemented these three playwrights. Schleef was to direct four productions and Ruth Berghaus was also mooted to stage *As You Like It* in 1998.[209] A brochure previewing the 1995/96 season mostly stuck to the 'Brecht Müller Shakespeare' programme and included Schleef directing *Puntila* and a project entitled '*Faust III* (after Müller and Ulbricht)'.[210] Frank Castorf was also to direct Müller's *Der Auftrag (The Mission)*.

By early June 1995, Zadek's touring theatre venture, based around the Gasthof Naase, seemed to have come to an end. Despite its popularity amongst local audiences, the BE said that it could no longer finance the project.[211] However, it was saved by lottery funding in August.[212] In October a secondary school complained about a change of programme that substituted two short plays for a production Zadek originally supervised.[213] It would seem that all traces of Zadek's work were slowly being expunged from the BE, although the brochure, mentioned

---

[209] Anon., 'Spielplan-Entwurf für die Spielzeiten 95/96, 96/97, 97/98', 20 April 1995, n.p., BEA File 'Spielplan: Produktionen ab 92/93/sonstige Verantstaltungen'.
[210] See Bärbel Jaksch (ed.), [untitled brochure for the season 95/6], 40 pages (3).
[211] See Anon., 'BE zum letzten Mal in Gaststätte', *Berliner Kurier*, 8 June 1995.
[212] See Anon., 'Gerettet: Das BE-Tourneetheater', *Berliner Zeitung*, 27 August 1995.
[213] See Axel Hoeppner to Müller, 10 October 1995, AdK HMA 7836.

above, included his *Merchant of Venice* and *Moonlight* by Harold Pinter. The *Merchant*, however, only lasted until the end of October 1995, while *Moonlight* finished earlier, in April of that year. The touring theatre initiative did survive Zadek, and new productions were added in the 1995/96 season.

The new leadership now had a chance to fashion the repertoire in its own image, yet it was still constrained by the financial imperative to generate ticket sales and other revenue. In April 1995, Sauerbaum noted that Zadek's popular Shakespeare productions were running at a loss of 37,590 marks (*Antony and Cleopatra* – roughly €18,000 in 2014) and 45,000 marks (*The Merchant of Venice* – roughly €23,000 in 2014).[214] Zadek replied that this was relatively cheap, given that many of the other productions had deficits that ran to six figures.[215] The pressure was on to find productions that could attract large audiences, and so, in 1994, Müller agreed to direct Brecht's *Arturo Ui*, not because he particularly liked the play, but because it was more commercial than the one he really wanted to stage, Brecht's *The Measures Taken*.[216] However, Müller, was very ill late in that year, and so the BE sought to transfer the production to Palitzsch in October because contracts had been signed and rehearsals were due to start.[217] Brecht-Schall would not permit this change and, having phoned Müller and his wife, discovered that the operation had gone well and that he would return in January. She thus refused to allow Palitzsch to take over.[218] Müller did not return to Berlin in January, yet he did start rehearsals once back in Berlin, on 17 March 1995, and *Ui* premiered on 3 June.

Müller had worked with actor Martin Wuttke on *Quartett* and invited him to play the lead in *Ui*, a role he first found 'not very interesting'.[219] That Wuttke made his name with this role says much about the production and his performance. *Ui* was the BE's greatest success since *Coriolan* of 1964 in its critical, popular, and international reception. Indeed, by the summer of 2014, the production has been performed 399 times.

Initially, Müller located the action in a series of Brechtian contradictions. For example, when Ui first encounters the Actor who teaches him deportment and oratory, Müller wanted Ui to doff his hat, 'a bourgeois reflex that clearly shows Ui the gangster with his great ambitions for

[214] See Sauerbaum to the Directorate and Mattes, 3 April 1995, AdK HMA 7816.
[215] See Zadek to Sauerbaum, 5 April 1995, ibid.
[216] See Müller, 'Die Wahrheit, leise und unerträglich', *Werke*, 12: 763.
[217] See Peter Raue to Wilhelm Nordemann, 10 October 1994, BEA File 'Spielplan: Produktionen ab 92/93/sonstige Veranstaltungen'.
[218] See Nordemann to Raue, 14 October 1995, ibid.
[219] Martin Wuttke, in Suschke, *Müller macht Theater*, pp. 242–8 (243).

power as a philistine'.[220] Ui was also to retain 'his harsh Ui tone' when declaiming the Marc Antony speech to produce 'in all the character's ridiculousness, his menace, too'. This was the same tension found in the BE's classic production of 1959. Elsewhere, other dialectical ideas ran through the central character's construction: 'Ui doesn't have a personality of his own, he's actually a nobody who always has to be constructed by others according to the principle: other people make the king'.[221] The irony of quoting this principle is that it was one of Wekwerth's favourite sayings, too.[222]

Yet Müller was not content merely to offer a calm dialectical dissection of Ui and his environment for the audience. An early note registered Müller's desire 'to demolish order; to destroy Brecht's harmony'.[223] This plan was realized through direction that injected a more visceral element into the piece: 'the pervading mood is one of panic, fear and nervousness. Everyone is scared of everyone else... They all indeed appear to be cool, but they aren't relaxed, on the contrary, beneath this apparent casualness they are very alert'.[224] The reason for this fear is the uncontrolled violence of Ui's rise. This became an element in the production as a whole that resisted explication. Violence was a part of the plan to install Ui as a puppet, but 'now violence has caught up with [those people] and destroyed them'.[225] Later it was noted: 'we see clearly: once violence has been established it has its own attraction – a pull that most people can't resist'.[226] Thus Müller sought to offset a solid Brechtian basis with factors that could not be accounted for in purely rational terms.

Günther Heeg has discussed the tension between Brecht and Müller in the production by drawing attention to the relationship between the 1959 and the 1995 productions. Heeg notes that Müller, in contrast to Wekwerth and Palitzsch, sought to destroy the clear communication of information, and one of the ways he executed this intention was by constructing Brechtian tableaux in order to frustrate their ability to mediate

[220] Margit Vestner, 'Notat Der Aufstieg des Arturo Ui – Schauspielerszene', 25 March 1995, n.p., BEA File 182. The following quotation is also taken from this source.
[221] Vestner, 'Der Aufstieg des Arturo Ui: 5. Bild – Stadthaus', 8 April 1995, n.p., BEA File 182.
[222] See, for example, Wekwerth speaking in relation to Coriolanus, in Hans-Dieter Schütt, Manfred Wekwerth, p. 38.
[223] Müller, in Krischan Schroth, 'Arturo Ui', 8 March 1995, n.p., BEA File 182.
[224] Margit Vestner, 'Probennotat Der Aufstieg des Arturo Ui 1. Bild – 18.4.95', undated, 2 pages (2), ibid.
[225] Vestner, 'Probennotat Ui 21.4.95 Blumenladen – Mausoleum', undated, 2 pages (2), ibid.
[226] Vestner, 'Probennotat Der Aufstieg des Arturo Ui: 13. Bild – Mausoleum – 27.4.95', undated, 2 pages (2), ibid.

Fig. 13.1. A post-Brechtian *Ui*: director Heiner Müller makes use of frames on stage to open them up and break them down. *The Resistible Rise of Arturo Ui*, June 1995.

meaning (see Fig. 13.1).[227] The main disruptive element was Martin Wuttke as Ui. His physical versatility, range of performative registers, and inability to be contained by the stage's various scenographic frames made him the great question mark of the production: how does this nobody attain such power and charisma? In addition, there was an extra, more metatheatrical dimension to the production. The cast was largely made up of the BE's permanent ensemble. Wuttke was a recent recruit and had not been subject to the BE's acting orthodoxies. He felt that the rest of the cast were not really responding to him in rehearsal and asked Müller whether this was deliberate because he came from the West. Müller reportedly replied: 'Nah, they're always like that'.[228] Actor Axel Werner maintains that Müller concentrated on Wuttke to the detriment to the rest of the cast, although he also concedes that this contributed to the production's success.[229] Actor Hermann Beyer, who had worked

---

[227] See Günther Heeg, *Klopfzeichen aus dem Mausoleum. Brechtschulung am Berliner Ensemble*, ed. by Stefan Schnabel (Berlin: Vorwerk, 2000), pp. 32–6.

[228] Wuttke, in Suschke, *Müller macht Theater*, p. 244.

[229] See Axel Werner, in Sabine Zolchow, 'Protokoll des Gesprächs zwischen Axel Werner und Sabine Zolchow', p. 13.

productively with Müller in the 1980s, is less forgiving: he found the extensive cuts to the text a contributory factor to 'the ensemble's castration',[230] quit the production and left the BE at the end of the 1995/96 season.[231] It would seem, then, that part of Müller's strategy was to contrast the 'old' BE with the 'new' to produce his post-Brechtian reading – Wuttke was the foreign body exposing the limitations and shortcomings of yesterday's Brechtianism. Müller even initially tried to short-circuit the play's enlightenment title by excising the 'resistible' from it, but Brecht-Schall insisted on its restitution.[232]

The production itself mainly took place on the BE's illuminated bare stage, its sides plunged into darkness, with steel girders forming two avenues of industrial pillars stage right and left. Müller appears to have warmed to the 'resistible' theme of the play because he included, at relevant moments, the sound of a train departing. This was an aural motif that suggested a certain course of action had been set in motion, that a decision or an action had caused the further events. By definition, the play would have turned out differently if something had prevented the particular decision or action.

The show opened with a bold image: Ui stripped to his waist with bloody tongue, perched upon an engine. The show as a whole used the visual and the visceral to transcend a purely semiotic mode of communication: Ui was not only to be 'decoded', but also experienced. Wuttke's physicality was both alluring and repelling – he had the ability to charm and to unsettle, and it was this tension that made him so fascinating. The trimmed text focused attention on the central character, yet the elaborate *Haltungen* of the supporting cast integrated them into the narrative as cogs in the larger social machine.

The critics were almost universally impressed. One celebrated 'a burial of Brecht of the very highest order', while another noted that Wuttke's Ui was no longer merely a copy of Hitler, but the character 'boisterously asserts a life of its own'.[233] Müller, who had made the distinction between 'impact' and 'success', soberly believed that his *Ui* had had the latter while foregoing the former.[234] While one can understand his position – that the aura conferred by popular success precludes an intense

---

[230] Hermann Beyer, in Suschke, *Müller macht Theater*, p. 245.
[231] See Hermann Beyer to Sauerbaum, 28 October 1995, AdK HMA 7817.
[232] See Sauerbaum to Müller, 5 September 1994, BEA File 'Spielplan: Produktionen ab 92/93/sonstige Veranstaltungen'.
[233] Rüdiger Schaper, 'Schüsse am Schiffbauerdamm', *Süddeutsche Zeitung*. 6 June 1995; and Peter Hans Göpfert, 'Die Figur behauptet frech ihr Eigenleben', *Berliner Morgenpost*, 6 June 1995, respectively.
[234] See Müller, in Ute Scharfenberg, 'Protokoll eines Gespräches zwischen Heiner Müller und Ute Scharfenberg am 16.09.1995', undated, pp. 10–29 (15), AdK HMA 7813.

414   A History of the Berliner Ensemble

engagement with the work itself – it may not necessarily reflect the audience's experience. My point here is that the incommensurable nature of Wuttke's performance does not allow for simple consumption or categorization, and so Müller's opposition might break down in this case. However the audience may have experienced the production, it had two major effects on the BE: it brought in the revenue the BE craved, and it proved that the company, and in particular its *Intendant*, could stage sophisticated, high quality and attractive work.

It seemed that the BE now had a foundation on which to build. Schleef and Castorf, as a guest director from his Volksbühne, were set to direct Brecht and Müller in the coming season, and Müller's new play, *Germania 3* was to have its world premiere. The BE also resurrected the 'Brecht-Abend' series in October 1995 when Manfred Karge presented an evening of lesser-known poems and songs as *Über die Herrenmode und andere Katastrophen* (*On Fashion for Men and Other Disasters*). In addition, Josef Szeiler, an experimental director, who had staged innovative and challenging productions of Brecht and Müller, was to take on Müller's *Philoktet* (*Philoctetes*). Szeiler had filled a gap in the schedule left when Müller was unable to direct the play himself through illness. In an interview he said he relished the thought of a short, intensive rehearsal period and working with Fritz Marquardt, who had not acted for years, and Nino Sander, who was not an actor himself. He did not consider the first night of 17 November 1995 as a premiere, but 'the first experiment in public'.[235] Part of the stage was built over the seats in the stalls, and the three actors played virtually naked, with only Marquardt wearing jeans and, indeed, reading his lines from a script in his hand. One reviewer noted that he had asked the BE for a photograph of the production and was only supplied with an image that did not show the actors: 'the said photo is actually the perfect expression of this non-production'.[236] Every other critic agreed: the dull deliveries and empty gestures were very badly received. The production, whose flyer listed a further five performances, was cancelled after its second; the BE declared the experiment 'a failure'.[237] Dramaturge Holger Teschke told me that the production had only been allowed to go ahead because Müller feared it would be his last chance to see the play performed.[238] Sadly, he was right. A bout of flu had weakened the ailing playwright, and he died on 30 December, a

---

[235] Josef Szeiler, in Hans-Dieter Schütt, 'Wach sein. Müde sein. Durcheinanderkommen', *Neues Deutschland*, 14 November 1995.

[236] Reinhard Wengierek, 'Kein Theater im Theater', *Die Welt*, 20 November 1995.

[237] See Karin Graf, [press release], 21 November 1995, n.p., BEA File 184.

[238] Holger Teschke, unpublished interview with the author, 11 March 2011.

fact announced to the audience before the production of *Ui* that night at the BE. At a time when the company appeared to be getting itself back on track, despite the blip of *Philoctetes*, it had lost its figurehead. After less than a year of renewed confidence and energy, it found itself plunged back into uncertainty.

14   The last hurrahs: 1996–1999

The search for a new *Intendant*

The BE's immediate response to the death of Heiner Müller was to organize an eight-day reading marathon in the theatre's first-floor foyer area. The event ran from 2 to 9 January 1996 and was organized by Stephan Wetzel, Holger Teschke and Paul Plamper.[1] Actors, staff, friends and others read extracts of Müller's plays, scenes, poems and writings in a show of collective grief and mourning. The funeral took place on 16 January. Meanwhile, behind the scenes, the management looked for a new *Intendant*, now that the model of collective artistic leadership had proven itself divisive and unworkable.

Rolf Hochhuth, who, at the time, was yet to secure ownership of the BE's main building, offered to serve as a Director at the BE in a radio interview of 5 January. This was his fourth attempt to date. Business manager and director Peter Sauerbaum called him 'irreverent' for trying to acquire Müller's shares shortly after the death had been announced. Hochhuth denied the accusation vehemently,[2] but his name had been sullied, and he was forced to withdraw his unwelcome offer. Müller's widow, Brigitte Mayer, was now in possession of her late husband's shares.

The problem of the succession at the BE was that there was no obvious candidate for the vacant post. *Die Zeit* had asked Einar Schleef about the position shortly before Müller died,[3] and once it had become a possibility, Schleef was certainly interested, according to Stephan Suschke. However, a move merely to get him onto the Board of Directors failed due to resistance from the company's shareholders, Peter Palitzsch, Fritz Marquardt, Sauerbaum and Mayer.[4] Hochhuth still wanted to play puppet-master and suggested the wholly unqualified Wolf Biermann as

---

[1] See Anon., 'Lesung Heiner Müller im Foyer des Berliner Ensembles', flyer, n.p.
[2] See BM/dpa, 'Hochhuth: Kann mir keine Mitarbeit mehr denken', *Berliner Morgenpost*, 6 January 1996.
[3] See Rolf Michaelis, 'Theater muß man von hinter der Bühne sehen', *Die Zeit*, 29 December 1995.
[4] See Stephan Suschke, in Zolchow, 'Protokoll eines Gespräches zwischen Stephan Suschke und Sabine Zolchow', p. 19.

Intendant on TV in mid January, something the singer himself called 'an absurd idea'.[5] Others also threw in their two penn'orth,[6] and these included Peter Kupke, the director who staged solid yet uninspiring productions of Brecht under Ruth Berghaus and Manfred Wekwerth in the 1970s. He offered himself as a guest director, not an *Intendant*, but it is hard to believe that the BE would be interested in someone so conventional at this time.[7]

Only one contender openly announced his candidacy for the *Intendanz*: actor Ulrich Mühe, known to many today as Stasi officer Gerd Wiesler in the Oscar-winning film *Das Leben der Anderen* (*The Lives of Others* – 2006) and as an actor at the Schaubühne in the early twenty-first century, had worked closely with Müller in the 1980s.[8] This was a surprising move, given that Mühe had no experience of managing a theatre and had not yet even directed a play. It was more his close connection to Müller than proven ability that led to the application. How ironic, then, for the BE to announce on 26 January that Martin Wuttke, Müller's Arturo Ui, was to take over and lead the BE. Wuttke had the same shortfall in relevant qualifications as Mühe; his only advantage over Mühe was that he had worked more recently with Müller at the company. Suschke later opined that if Wuttke could play Hitler and Ui, then Wuttke could also play the BE's *Intendant*.[9] This rather curious rationale says something about the BE's mood at the time; a prominent figurehead was more valuable than managerial ability.

Wuttke was, however, to have solid support: Suschke, who had formerly coordinated the BE's affairs, became his deputy; Sauerbaum offered continuity as the business manager; and a new face also joined the team. Karl Hegemann, formerly of Berlin's wildly successful Volksbühne, was named head dramaturge. Hegemann had actually been on Suschke's radar earlier in 1995 as a person who could help strengthen the BE after Zadek's departure,[10] and so his eventual appointment realized an existing aim.

However, despite the cohesion of the new management, all was not well. Wuttke's appointment had antagonized the only director, apart

---

5 Wolf Biermann, in dpa, 'Biermann will nicht ans Berliner Ensemble', *Süddeutsche Zeitung*, 19 January 1996.
6 See, for example, Anon., 'Vorschlag: Heise als BE-Intendant', *Berliner Morgenpost*, 23 January 1996.
7 See Peter Kupke, 'Zur Erprobung von Standards', *Frankfurter Rundschau*, 20 January 1996.
8 See dpa/FR, 'Mühe bewirbt sich – Wuttke im Gespräch', *Frankfurter Rundschau*, 26 January 1996.
9 See Suschke, in Zolchow, 'Protokoll eines Gespräches zwischen Stephan Suschke und Sabine Zolchow', p. 22.
10 See Suschke to Palitzsch, Marquardt and Müller, 21 August 1995, AdK HMA 7817.

from Müller, who had had any real success at the BE since 1992: Einar Schleef. Wuttke's acting career owed much to the director's influence, and the two had become acquainted with each other in Frankfurt in the late 1980s.[11] Schleef was obviously the master to Wuttke's apprentice at that time, but that pecking order, however eroded it may have become by Wuttke's own successes, was still in Schleef's mind when he entered into discussion with the BE following Müller's death. To find that not he but Wuttke had been appointed did not sit well with someone who clearly felt he had more right to the top job than the actor. His anger at the affront had not abated by the end of Wuttke's brief stewardship, as will be seen below.

Personnel changes were not, however, limited to the BE. Senator for Culture Ulrich Roloff-Momin found himself friendless after the CDU became the largest party in elections to Berlin's city parliament in October 1995, and Peter Radunski took over the position the following January.[12] Although the new senator was an unknown quantity, an initial meeting between Wuttke and Radunski was reported to have been 'very positive', and a plan to secure funding until 2002 was passed on to the Senate for approval.[13] The need to move quickly was imperative. A CDU politician had already opined that the BE would have to solve its problems soon because a 20 million mark saving was always attractive.[14] Wuttke appeared to allay immediate fears of indecision in a major interview early in 1996. He said that he would be continuing with the 'Brecht Müller Shakespeare' programme although he did not want to canonize the more extreme methods Müller had employed in some of his productions.[15] Yet as well as being responsible for preparing new productions, Wuttke also inherited plans fashioned by Müller, and so his first few months were made a little easier in this respect.

Wuttke's short *Intendanz*

In early 1996, the BE was affected by another prominent death: Ruth Berghaus passed away on 25 January. A special matinee of readings and

[11] See Martin Wuttke and Karl Hegemann, '"Das ist doch kein Drama", in Gabriele Gerecke, Harald Müller and Hans-Ulrich Müller-Schwefe (eds.), *Einar Schleef: Arbeitsbuch* (Berlin: Theater der Zeit, 2004), pp. 193–6 for a discussion of Wuttke's early work with Schleef.
[12] See Roloff-Momin, *Zuletzt: Kultur*, p. 239.
[13] Michael Horst, 'Mit Sicherheitslinie auf dünnem Eis', *Berliner Morgenpost*, 27 January 1996.
[14] See Franz Wille, 'Erbe der Zukunft', *Theater heute*, 2 (1996), pp. 46–8 (48).
[15] See Martin Wuttke, in Franz Wille, 'Einfach kompliziert', *Theater heute*, 3 (1996), pp. 8–9 (8 and 9).

recordings was hurriedly organized for 11 February. The short period between Müller's and Berghaus's funerals was, of course, nothing but an unhappy coincidence, but the loss of the two figures in quick succession also threw the credentials of the new *Intendant* into relief. Müller and Berghaus may not have been great administrators, but they did have a strong sense of what theatre could and should do, and without that quality, the BE could slide back into artistic vagueness and indistinctiveness.

The first major production after Müller's death could have both represented a fitting monument to the playwright and signalled a statement of intent. Thomas Heise, whose track record at the BE had certainly shown great promise, directed Müller's *Der Bau* (*The Building Site*), and it premiered on 3 February 1996. The production was already in preparation in June 1995, and even then, it had assumed very 'Müllerian' dimensions. Heise included Müller's *Die Hamletmaschine* (*The Hamletmachine*) as a way of paralleling the tension in the play between the male Hasselbein and the female Schlee.[16] By the time of the performance itself, the play had become a 20-minute monologue, stripped of dramatic interaction. Heise also included Kafka's short story 'Der Bau' ('The Burrow') to play on the associativity of Müller's title, and continued Müller's 'theatre of biography'. The cast included veteran actor Erwin Geschonneck, who had already performed in Müller's *Fatzer*, yet here he appeared on video, as the Old Comrade. Heise was insistent that the BE assert its own identity in order to survive,[17] and thus *The Building Site* was intended to develop the aesthetic of constructive disjunction. The disjunction, however, together with a lengthy running time, was mostly dismissed as uninspired. One critic summarized the evening, which was divided by two intervals, thus: (1) 'prime Manfred Wekwerth in his final phase'; (2) 'now we're done for – the director suddenly wants to make great art'; and (3) 'a touch of kitsch regarding an extramarital pregnancy'.[18] The press was certainly not in reverential mood with respect to the dead playwright, not, of course, that it should have been. Heise's uncompromising position that insisted on offering spectators material they did not necessarily want to see[19] was swiftly compromised in response to the negative reception; he rearranged the order of proceedings by chopping and changing the disparate elements, and adding an extra interval a few

[16] See Enrico Stolzenburg, 'Bühnenbildsitzungen *Der Bau* Berliner Ensemble 1995 Heise, Winter', undated, 33 pages (21), BEA File 188.
[17] See Thomas Heise, in corrected draft of Anon., 'Das Profil heißt Müller', 1 January 1996, n.p., ibid.
[18] Peter Laudenbach, 'Spur der Gebeine', *Berliner Zeitung*, 5 February 1996.
[19] See Heise, 'Die Eiszeit', *Der Tagesspiegel*, 2 February 1996.

days after the premiere.[20] In addition, Heise once again found himself directing a production partly funded by sponsorship. The play, set in the GDR of the 1960s, was in the 1990s supported by former GDR spirit and cigarette manufacturers. It is possible that the conspicuous use of their products on stage (and, indeed, in the auditorium, when a bottle of vodka was passed amongst the spectators after an onstage topping-out ceremony) acted as a creative disjunction between the two economic systems. Alternatively, the product placement may have undermined the production's attempt at engaging with socialism.

The next premiere was directed by Schleef and proved to be just as controversial as his *Wessis in Weimar*, earlier. Müller had invited Schleef to direct *Mr Puntila and His Man Matti*, something that initially left him nonplussed.[21] His aggressive choral theatre appeared to have little in common with the dialectical humour of *Puntila* until he went to the archive. There he read one of Brecht's first versions, written in 1940, that is, shortly after the outbreak of World War Two.[22] *Puntila* was inspired by the stories of Hella Wuolijoki, but in this crucial historical phase, Brecht also looked back to the end of World War One in Finland. At this time, the class struggle manifested itself in a bloody civil war between left-wing forces inspired by revolutionary Russia and right-wing militarists from Finland, who prevailed. Brecht's early drafts thus emphasized Finland's traumatic and class-riven past and were thus no longer that light. Franz Wille notes: 'instead of the knowing comic look back to the victory over the disasters of war and Hitler in 1948–9, [one finds] the look forward from 1940 into the inescapable catastrophe'.[23] Wille's reading points to Schleef's materialist aesthetics: for all the formal precision and abstraction of Schleef's production, the starting point was concrete and historical. As Ute Scharfenberg notes: 'Schleef's discovery of the play's "language of the exile" offers him an important point of departure for his production's rationale'.[24] That is, the earlier version allowed Schleef the opportunity to disorientate the audience by uncovering impulses later expunged and make them the basis for a new approach to the material. The threat of fascism, more pronounced in the 1940 version, cast a wholly different mood over the production, for example.

---

[20] See Heise to the cast and crew, undated, BEA File 188.

[21] See aro [*sic*], 'Nach einer riesigen nationalen Tragödie', *Frankfurter Allgemeine Zeitung*, 16 February 1996.

[22] Schleef consulted File 178 in the Brecht-Archiv. The script he submitted to Barbara Brecht-Schall for permission is available in the Berliner Ensemble Archive in File 190.

[23] Franz Wille, 'Der Untergangsdirigent', *Theater heute*, 4 (1996), pp. 6–12 (12).

[24] [Ute Scharfenberg], [Documentation of Scheef's *Puntila*], undated, 42 pages (3), in AdK, Inszenierungsdokumentation ID 569.

In addition, Schleef was interested in the treatment of the female characters in the earlier version. He was keen to counter Eva's relegation as a mere appendage to the male leads in the later version and he contended that Eva had not always been an Aunt Sally figure in the play.[25] Schleef sought to reintegrate the female characters; he noted the importance of Puntila's housekeeper, Hanna, in the earlier version and viewed her as a concrete antagonist to her master. He also insisted that the two other female members of Puntila's staff, Fina and Laina, were on stage more frequently, often observing the action and maintaining their presence. The other important change of emphasis, from a textual point of view, was the role of Matti, the usual antagonist. Günther Heeg writes that this conflict was in fact a convenient way of demonstrating proletarian superiority in the later version: 'the dialectic of master and servant is replaced by the cooperation between the author and a character who represents him in the play: Mr Brecht and his dramaturgical lackey Matti'.[26] Matti's superiority is ideological and loads the dialectic in favour of the oppressed underdog. A part of the post-Brechtian impulse is a desire to retain the dialectic while opening it up in all its complexity without ideological pressures. Schleef thus underplayed and re-functioned Matti's status as a privileged character. Eva and Hanna became more central figures, while Matti played a wholly different role as a choral extension of Puntila's will.

The play itself was radically rearranged. Schleef divided it up into four sections, in which, for example, the first section included material from the standard version's first, third, fourth and eighth scenes. The diffuse texts ran into each other without a nod to the spectators. The logical unfolding of the *Fabel* gave way to the experience of the words, shouted or declaimed by Puntila for the most part or by the choruses of women and Mattis. Such a presentation of the text opened it up for the audience, although a power relation – between Puntila and everyone else on stage – defined a constant dialectical tension. Thus the text did not float entirely freely as text, but was linked to the class-based antagonisms at the heart of Schleef's reading.

With this amount of textual adulteration, it is difficult to believe that Brecht-Schall allowed Schleef to stage the play at all. However, it was the lead actor that concerned her most: 'with the greatest of reservations and the unpleasant feeling of having been coerced, I hereby grant you

---

[25] See Einar Schleef, in Rolf Michaelis, 'Theater muß man von hinter der Bühne sehen', *Die Zeit*, 29 December 1995.
[26] Günther Heeg, 'Herr und Knecht, Furcht und Arbeit, Mann und Frau: Einar Schleefs archäologische Lektüre von Brechts *Puntila*', in *Brecht Yearbook*, 23 (1997), pp. 147–52 (147).

permission for Einar Schleef to play Puntila'.[27] Wuttke himself was due to star, but an injury had ruled him out.[28] As it happened, Schleef produced a breathtaking performance as a brutally despotic Puntila who barked orders at a chorus of Mattis while also playing himself as an onstage director, marshalling the actors round the stage at times.

Controversy lay in his brash dictatorial approach with its fascist over-tones. Puntila marched the Mattis round the stage as if at a right-wing training camp.[29] More negative reviewers believed that Schleef was pay-ing lip service to the far right: 'Brecht's *Volksstück* has become an antique and fascistoid motorway pile-up in a freestyle of Greco-Roman forms'.[30] Schleef did not limit the power of the fascist imagery he employed, but this was hardly a tacit expression of support. Instead, he allowed the full implications of such barbarity to be presented on stage. While one reviewer noted that 'somehow, somewhere, everything's connected to class consciousness and the class struggle', others were more specific.[31] Brecht expert Ernst Schumacher wrote that he considered the production 'the most radical realization of an epic theatre ... In all ... this produc-tion demands in the strongest of terms that one think rethink Brechtian performance, a task to which no other theatre is more especially called than the Berliner Ensemble'.[32] A 'radical' epic theatre loses its ideologi-cal strictures without forsaking its dialectical basis. It thus appeared that Müller's post-Brechtian theatre was being advanced with Schleef's own iconoclastic, materialist aesthetic.

The final two major productions of the 1995/96 season, both of which premiered in June, held much promise: guest director Frank Cas-torf directed Müller's *Der Auftrag* (*The Mission*), and surprise director Wuttke staged Müller's final play, *Germania 3*. Both, however, disap-pointed expectations, but for different reasons. Most of the critics could not understand why Castorf had bothered to direct *Der Auftrag*,[33] a play he had previously produced with great flair in Anklam, the small provin-cial theatre at which he had made his name, in the 1980s. Wuttke, on

[27] Brecht-Schall to Sauerbaum, 2 February 1996, AdK Einar-Schleef-Archiv 6139.
[28] See Schleef, in Petra Kohse, '"Gegen die allmähliche Erstarrung"', *die tageszeitung*, 20 November 1996.
[29] See, for example, Klaus Dermutz, 'Paramilitärische Grundausbildung', *Frankfurter Rundschau*, 20 February 1996.
[30] Michael Berger, 'Die Inszenierung', *Die Woche*, 23 February 1996.
[31] Peter Hans Göpfert, 'Irgendwie geht es um Klassenkampf', *Berliner Morgenpost*, 19 February 1996.
[32] Ernst Schumacher, 'Wer kennt den wahren Puntila?', *Berliner Zeitung*, 28 February 1996.
[33] See, for example, Manuel Brug, 'Revolte im Kinderzimmer', *Der Tagesspiegel*, 7 June 1996.

the other hand, had never directed a play before and found himself confronted with one of Müller's difficult historical montages. *Germania 3* is a series of tenuously related scenes and monologues that, compared with other examples from Müller's *oeuvre*, such as *Germania Tod in Berlin* (*German Death in Berlin*), did not really acquit themselves. Wuttke himself said that the task was the fulfilment of one of Müller's final wishes, but also an opportunity to acquaint himself in the most concrete of ways with the work and workings of the BE.[34] Unfortunately, good intentions were simply not enough.

Müller had actually started planning the production in the autumn of 1995, and he experimented with the set on the main stage on 28 September. The photos taken only hint at the possible scenarios he had in mind,[35] but the flat-colour divisions of space, designed by Mark Lammert, indicate a varied interplay between the scenes. Müller also wanted to invite the real Wekwerth and Palitzsch to join his 'theatre of biography' by playing themselves in a scene set in the BE after Brecht's death in 1956.[36] It is, however, almost impossible to imagine them agreeing to the request. In any case, Müller was unable to make it, yet when Wuttke took over, he did not take over any of Müller's ideas and worked with a different set designer, too. The record of his rehearsals[37] reveal little depth to the work. Rather, Wuttke appeared to be directing very much in an immanent style, trying to solve immediate problems, rather than fashioning a rhythm within the scenes or their arrangement as a whole.

Leander Haussmann had directed the world premiere less than a month earlier in Bochum, and so comparisons echoed through the reviews. Critics were surprised that Haussmann's four-hour epic was more than double the length of Wuttke's production in Berlin, but they also regretted the latter's lack of lavishness.[38] Wuttke had stripped down the production on a predominantly black stage, and preferred a more statuesque declamatory style, addressed to the audience. One reviewer believed he put too much faith in Müller's language, neglecting his own input as a director.[39] The production was not a disaster, and the audience appeared to appreciate the effort the novice director had expended: he

---

[34] See Wuttke, in Wille, 'Einfach kompliziert', p. 9.
[35] Nine colour photos, taken by Brigitte Mayer, are to be found in Grischa Meyer (ed.), *Drucksache*, 20 (1996), pp. 813–29.
[36] See Müller, in Paul Plamper, 'Nomadenlager in Gefangenschaft', in Suschke, *Müller macht Theater*, pp. 256–8 (256).
[37] See the descriptive notes made by Margit Vestner in BEA File 193.
[38] See, for example, Günther Grack, 'Gespensterreigen', *Der Tagesspiegel*, 20 June 1996.
[39] See Gerhard Ebert, 'Stalingrad aus der Loge betrachtet', *Neues Deutschland*, 21 June 1996.

received special applause, together with three of the actors, on the opening night.[40] The production had a decent run, twenty-eight performances over the course of the next twelve months, but it was not exceptional.

There were no major premieres in the autumn of Wuttke's first full season in charge, and I will return below to discuss the one-woman show, *Eva Hitlers Geliebte* (*Eva, Hitler's Lover*), that premiered in November. That month was to make headlines for reasons that were not, however, related to the lack of work on the main stage. The BE's financial problems had been a cause for concern for some time. Suschke said that when Wuttke took over, the company was running 1 million marks' worth of debt.[41] Wuttke had stated in early 1996 that a condition for his accepting the *Intendanz* was Peter Radunski's schedule of annual public subsidies until 2002.[42] However, by November, Sauerbaum reported in a newspaper article that the subsidy agreement that Radunski had previously passed to the Senator for Finance for approval, had not been signed. This was because the City had discovered a large hole in its finances.[43] Sauerbaum also noted that Einar Schleef was due to start rehearsing a new production in November. The two, seemingly unrelated stories were to converge very shortly.

Wuttke brought the financial issue to a head in early November and threatened to resign if a contract guaranteeing subsidies until 2002 were not forthcoming. Radunski had assured him that he would have a contract until 1998, a particularly important year for the BE in that it marked Brecht's centenary, but this did not satisfy the *Intendant*.[44] Wuttke gave a deadline of 1 December for his ultimatum. He later decided to extend the deadline,[45] yet on 4 December, he announced to a meeting of BE staff that he would be stepping down.[46] At the same time, the BE also fired Einar Schleef as a director after he cancelled a run of his *Puntila* the day before it was due to start. A BE spokesperson described the swift action as 'regrettable, but unavoidable'.[47] Wuttke mentioned both the financial issue and Schleef in a press release, calling Schleef's work

---

[40] See Grack, 'Gespensterreigen'.
[41] See Suschke, in Zolchow, 'Protokoll eines Gespräches zwischen Stephan Suschke und Sabine Zolchow', p. 19.
[42] See Wuttke, in Wille, 'Einfact kompliziert', p. 8.
[43] See Volker Oesterreich, '"Wir repräsentieren die ganze Stadt"', *Berliner Morgenpost*, 17 October 1996.
[44] See Petra Kohse, 'Chef des Berliner Ensembles droht mit Rücktritt', *die tageszeitung*, 8 November 1996.
[45] See kob, 'Wuttke vertagt sein Ultimatum', *Berliner Zeitung*, 3 December 1996.
[46] See Roland Koberg, 'Ende eines Befreiungskampfes nach innen', *Berliner Zeitung*, 5 December 1996.
[47] Anon., 'Einar Schleef wurde fristlos gekündigt', *Frankfurter Rundschau*, 5 December 1996.

at the BE 'a further condition for my continuing as *Intendant*'.[48] Thus, virtually simultaneously, two power struggles unfolded and both ended in the (self-)removal of the *acteur* in question.

To take Schleef first: it is unclear quite what Schleef wanted to achieve with the cancellation of *Puntila*. He may have merely been flexing his muscles to see what kind of power he wielded at the BE. After all, his two productions there had generated headlines and audiences, and he was clearly an asset to the creative team. He may also have been signalling his own independence of action to the *Intendant*, a position he believed he and not Wuttke should have held. On the other hand, he may have been provoking his own dismissal by going too far: cancelling a run without notice would have cost the BE dearly. *Puntila* had been successful *en suite* and, after some months off the stage, it was likely to have filled the auditorium for its intensive five-day run. The management had no choice but to sack Schleef; such a breach of discipline and flagrant disrespect for the theatre could not become the norm because it would make a nonsense of any future plans involving Schleef.

On the surface, Wuttke's resignation crystallized two issues. The *Intendant* required financial guarantees to run his theatre and demanded a dependable partner in Schleef. Radunski, for his part, had assured Wuttke that he would have 42 million marks in total to cover the next two seasons and, more generally, that he could not imagine the City cutting all subsidy to a company like the BE.[49] To an extent, this is true, although the conservative politician had said in the same interview that he very much believed in the devolved revenue model of funding – that is, in a system in which theatres were free to spend public money as they saw fit, within the realms of good practice. However, such apparently liberal inclinations often transfer fiscal responsibility from the provider to the consumer, and fail to take account of the provider's responsibilities for the actual level of funding. Wuttke may then have been correct to insist on a concrete long-term agreement, rather than a two-year assurance followed by vague promises. On the other hand, the narrow window Wuttke opened for a satisfactory resolution of the subsidy issue suggests that he may have had other motives. One might speculate that Wuttke was having second thoughts about the office of *Intendant*. After all, he was primarily an actor. His brief stint as *Intendant* had not revealed a great administrative gift: the new season had not even opened with a

---

[48] Wuttke, [press release], 4 December 1996, n.p., BEA File 'Müller Aufführungen/ Wuttke – Intendant'.
[49] See Radunski, in Michael Merschmeier, Franz Wille and Bernd Feuchtner, 'Landschaftsgärtner oder Totengräber?', *Theater heute*, 1 (1997), pp. 30–3 (33).

major production and he was required rapidly to develop a range of skills necessary to promote and develop one of the world's most famous theatre companies. Whatever the reason or reasons for the resignation, the BE again found itself leaderless, less than a year after Müller had died.

Picking up the pieces

There was no shortage of potential candidates to fill the vacant post of *Intendant*. The press mentioned directors Peter Stein, Leander Haussmann, Katharina Thalbach (who had started as an actor at the BE in the late 1960s) and Claus Peymann.[50] Rolf Hochhuth, as proprietor-in-waiting, was also keen to make another of his suggestions, and, as earlier with Biermann, it was similarly laughable. He proposed a team of Palitzsch, Marquardt and Wekwerth to take over the leadership.[51] Hochhuth was seemingly unaware that the experiment with a multi-headed management, run by ageing directors, had already failed. Instead of appointing a named *Intendant*, the management decided to close ranks. Suschke became artistic director and Sauerbaum continued to run the business. Suschke stuck to the now familiar mantra of developing a programme at the BE that would make the company 'unmistakable and necessary'.[52] The consciously interim leadership also included head dramaturge Karl Hegemann. In characteristic rhetorical bluster, he announced in January 1997 that the new management 'is preparing for its own failure'.[53] By this he meant that they had been given something of a fool's licence; they were merely 'minding the shop' and so could take risks for the short period of their existence.

The risk-taking had actually started in 1996, although it was not quite the kamikaze experimentation suggested by Hegemann. A first performance of a one-off show written by Jörg-Michael Koerbl called *Adolf Hitler* was postponed in October 1996, reportedly due to illness.[54] The plan, however, had not been shelved, and an unsigned contract foresaw a premiere in April 1997.[55] By that time, Suschke had removed the play,

---

[50] See, for example, Volker Oesterreich, 'Wer will nochmal, wer hat noch nicht?', *Berliner Morgenpost*, 6 December 1996.

[51] See Rolf Hochhuth, 'Holt Manfred Wekwerth zurück!', *Berliner Morgenpost*, 7 December 1996.

[52] Suschke, in Hans-Dieter Schütt, 'Was ausrichten. Was hinrichten', *Neues Deutschland*, 9 December 1996.

[53] Karl Hegemann, 'Scheitern am Berliner Ensemble', *Der Tagesspiegel*, 12 January 1997.

[54] See ADN, 'BE: *Adolf Hitler* von Michael Koerbl entfällt', *Die Welt*, 9 October 1996.

[55] See Anon., [unsigned contract for *Adolf Hitler*], undated, n.p., BEA File 'Spielplan neue Projekte ab 1995 . . . '.

whose details remain unclear today, from the repertoire. He considered that the BE had been 'too naïve' about the project and reported that there had been a worryingly intense interest from Israeli journalists.[56] Suschke told me that he cancelled purely out of fear because of the negative press that surrounded Schleef's *Puntila* and its imputed connections to fascism.[57] However, another Nazi-themed show had also raised eyebrows.

Suschke had proposed directing a one-woman piece, *Eva Hitlers Geliebte (Eva, Hitler's Lover)* while Müller was still *Intendant*.[58] Eva Braun was played by Corinna Harfouch, who delivered a roughly 90-minute monologue on the BE's main stage. Suschke commissioned Stefan Kolditz, better known as a television screenplay writer, to compose the text. Suschke hoped: 'she simply tells us the stories of yesterday – her version and not the ones produced by ideology and time'.[59] Kolditz added: '*Eva* is the greatest German love story of the twentieth century'.[60] The two statements hardly suggested a critical representation of a most problematic affair. Suschke's insistence on telling things 'as they were' sounds at best naïve and at worst remiss, while Kolditz's emphasis on a great love story would seem to have forgotten some rather important contextual details. Suschke told me that his intention had actually been to stage an inverted *Verfremdung* in that understanding Eva necessarily produced horror.[61] Reviewers of the show, which premiered on 29 November 1996, did not find the complexities Suschke suggested. Some called it a 'trivialization of the Nazis', others found the direction uncritical in that did not interrogate the single voice on stage.[62] Harfouch reported that a meeting with representatives of Berlin's Jewish Community revealed how applause for Eva Braun on a German stage left them with a bitter taste in their mouths. She also insisted that the shows were followed by discussions.[63] This would indicate that the performance itself could not stand alone, but required further qualification. However, it certainly did good business, with its first twenty performances mainly attracting over

---

[56] See df/kob, 'Suschke übernimmt *Umsiedlerin*', *Berliner Zeitung*, 11 April 1997.

[57] Suschke, unpublished interview with the author, 28 April 2011.

[58] See Suschke to Palitzsch, Marquardt and Müller, 21 August 1995, AdK HMA 7817.

[59] Suschke, in Stephan Wetzel, 'Totenfest mit Eva Braun', *Der Tagesspiegel*, 24 November 1996.

[60] Stefan Kolditz, in ibid.

[61] Suschke, unpublished interview with the author, 28 April 2011.

[62] See Irene Bazinger, 'Hack-Stücke-Narzisse', *Junge Welt*, 3 December 1996; and Lothar Schmidt-Mühlisch, 'Blondchen will nach Hollywood', *Die Welt*, 2 December 1996.

[63] See Corinna Harfouch, in Sabine Zolchow, 'Protokoll der Gespräche', pp. 28–9.

450 spectators per show,[64] a very solid statistic for the BE at the time. Commercial success overcame moral reservation.

The kinds of risks Hegemann envisaged were evident in the summer of 1997. A year before Brecht's centenary, the BE staged its own Brecht festival, the 'Brecht Sommer' ('Summer of Brecht'), mostly in the last week of June and the first week of July. There were regular concerts and two guest performances of *The Caucasian Chalk Circle* from France (Terrain Vague) and the UK (Theatre de Complicité), yet the centre-piece was a collection of fragments, excavated from the Brecht Archive and performed for the first time in ten different venues over the course of an evening. It was impossible to see all fourteen pieces together, and so spectators had to pick and choose their route through the timetable, guided mostly, one presumes, by the sound of the little-known works' titles themselves or the reputations of the fragments' directors. Not sur-prisingly, the critics found the project a very mixed bag. Only one pro-duction, *Aus Nichts wird Nichts* (*Nothing Ever Comes of Nothing*), was deemed tightly directed,[65] but it was the anarchy and playfulness of work by directors like Leander Haussmann and Christoph Schlingensief that caught the imagination.[66] This was experimentalism in all its highs and lows, and it was to act as a curtain-raiser for the centenary itself.

The liberty of the lame ducks

In November 1962, an unknown student director wrote to the BE's dramaturgy department to invite its members to his production of *Der Tag des großen Gelehrten Wu* (*The Day of Wu, the Great Scholar*) in West Berlin. The original production had been developed at the BE by Peter Palitzsch and Carl Weber, and the young director wanted to show the esteemed company his version, which had won first prize at a compe-tition in Erlangen and had been praised at a student drama festival in Zagreb. The director, who hoped the BE would allow him and his cast to see the original *Modellbuch*, was Claus Peymann.[67] Little could he have dreamt that, nearly four decades later, he would be taking over the once illustrious theatre. In March 1997, journalists started to connect the fact that Peymann, a much-celebrated director and *Intendant*, was set to leave the prestigious Burgtheater of Vienna in the summer of 1999

---

[64] See BEA File 'E-F'.

[65] See Klaus Dermutz, 'Spaß mit dem armen B.B.', *Frankfurter Rundschau*, 2 July 1997.

[66] See Peter Hans Göpfert, 'Fragment! Fragment! Brecht! Brecht!', *Berliner Morgenpost*, 29 June 1997.

[67] See Claus Peymann to the BE's dramaturgy department, 10 November 1962, BBA uncatalogued file 'Korr 54–66'.

and that the BE was also looking for a new head to start around the same time.[68] In April 1997, the newspapers reported that Peymann had met Senator Radunski and that he openly acknowledged his interest 'to take over the *Intendanz* at the Theater am Schiffbauerdamm from autumn 1999'.[69] It is important to note here that Peymann avoided referring to the theatre as the 'Berliner Ensemble'. From the outset, he did not want to associate his work that closely with that of Brecht and preferred to relativize the new company by calling it 'Das Berliner Ensemble im Theater am Schiffbauerdamm'. Negotiations lasted roughly a year and the new *Intendant*-designate was presented to the media on 1 May 1998. Peymann bought out Palitzsch and Marquardt and used City funds to extend and renovate the theatre before its first production in January 2000.[70]

Suschke notes that everything changed at the BE once Peymann became a serious proposition in August 1997.[71] Head dramaturge Karl Hegemann left the leadership in September, citing both Peymann's potential arrival and what he perceived to be Sauerbaum's interference in artistic matters as his grounds.[72] Suschke and Sauerbaum thus had to look after the BE themselves in the fixed period until Peymann's arrival. In theory, this was a lame-duck leadership, unable to build itself a better future, but condemned to spin out its remaining time. However, such a finite period also meant that the BE could enjoy what it had left, especially with the centenary celebrations just around the corner. As it would turn out, the remaining two seasons were inflected differently: the first was conspicuous for its energy and the verve surrounding Brecht, the second was more understated, and it seemed like the members of the ensemble were either waiting for Peymann to start up the BE afresh or afeared that he might dismiss them.

The BE had attracted good money to support Brecht's centenary season, and the programme was rich and varied. The season certainly opened with a coup: *The Measures Taken*, a play Brecht had banned in 1956, was finally to receive its first public performance. This is technically true although there had been opportunities to see the play earlier. A production by students of Berlin's prestigious Ernst-Busch-Schule in February 1995 circumvented restrictions by not charging a fee, but

---

[68] See GG, 'Der Weg ist frei', *Der Tagesspiegel*, 5 March 1997.
[69] Rüdiger Schaper, 'Grüß Gott, Herr Exorzist', *Süddeutsche Zeitung*, 23 April 1997.
[70] See Günther Grack, '"Aufklärerische Anstalt"', *Der Tagesspiegel*, 2 May 1998.
[71] See Suschke, in Zolchow, 'Protokoll eines Gespräches zwischen Stephan Suschke und Sabine Zolchow', p. 2.
[72] See Karl Hegemann, in Petra Kohse, '"Wir wollten den Knechtgeist austreiben": Zwischen Macht und Müller-Erbe', *Die Tageszeitung*, 20 September 1997.

Fig. 14.1. A politically playful curtain-raiser to Brecht's centenary: young idealists sing against a jaded chorus. *The Measures Taken*, September 1997.

soliciting voluntary contributions. A sung production was also staged in English by Stephen Unwin at London's Almeida Theatre in 1987. Back in Berlin, director Klaus Emmerich was praised for the way he negotiated the difficult text. Rather than offering an investigation of how a Young Comrade consents to his own murder in the name of a successful revolution, he chose to focus on the relationship between the four Agitators and the Control Chorus to which they have to answer.

All four Agitators played the Young Comrade in different scenes, as Brecht instructed. While the Agitators sang and marked out their relationships in abstracted form downstage, the Chorus reflected the problems of communism in 1998 behind them (see Fig. 14.1). The four Agitators embodied the idealistic hope of a younger generation while the Chorus, made up of older singers and actors, was jaded and critical. Take, for example, the way in which certain lines were exploited to comic effect. One reviewer reported an example of how Freudian slips pointed to the Chorus' problems with the Party line: 'Klug ist, der seine Fehler schnell zu vergesse . . . verbessern versteht' ('wise is the person who knows how to forget . . . correct their mistakes').[73] Critics found the production

---

[73] In Nikolaus Merck, 'Vorwärts und nicht verbessern!', *die tageszeitung*, 17 September 1997.

refreshing in its approach,[74] in that it did not turn Brecht's text on its head, but probed it by playfully contrasting the political attitudes of the two antagonists on stage.

The Measures Taken was followed by Life of Galileo, directed by B. K. Tragelehn, and it premiered on 12 December 1997. This was Tragelehn's first production at the BE since Miss Julie of 1975. Tragelehn's return was not as glorious as that of his erstwhile directing partner, Einar Schleef. Tragelehn viewed the play as Brecht's most personal and found in Galileo a version of Brecht himself. Yet despite this reading and the impressive Josef Bierbichler in the title role as a guest at the BE, the production was considered flat and uninspiring. Indeed, one reviewer criticized Bierbichler for his lack of Brechtian pedigree, finding him too close to the role and undialectical.[75] Others did not consider that the proximity shed any light on Tragelehn's equation of Galileo and Brecht.[76] Shortly afterwards, on 20 December, the BE presented the world premiere of Brecht's fragment Die Judith von Shimoda (Judith of Shimoda). However, this production, too, was not well received with reviewers stating that they now understood why the play had never been staged before,[77] and criticizing the directing team of Judith Kuckart and Jörg Aufenanger for filling the short text with business that obscured the play itself.[78] Despite the poor press, it is perhaps worth noting that the BE was at least trying to offer new material to its audience in the run-up to the centenary itself.

The next part of the schedule was the realization of a plan hatched back in 1995: to get the pioneering American director Robert Wilson to the BE. Müller thought it would be interesting for Wilson to direct a Lehrstück, and Wilson liked Der Ozeanflug (The Flight across the Ocean) because the protagonist did not speak to other characters, but 'rather with cities, ships, machines, and with the elements'.[79] However, the play did not stand alone. Dramaturge Holger Teschke proposed the addition of Müller's text 'Landschaft mit Argonauten' ('Landscape with Argonauts') to offset Brecht's optimistic view of technology, and Wolfgang Wiens suggested passages from Dostoevsky's Notes from Underground not

[74] See, for example, Anja Nioduschewski, 'Zeichen aber kein Fanal', Junge Welt, 16 September 1997.
[75] See Gerhard Ebert, 'Wenig Hoffnung für die Wissenschaft', Neues Deutschland, 15 December 1997.
[76] See, for example, Peter Hans Göpfert, 'Ein mürrischer Allerweltstyp', Berliner Morgenpost, 14 December 1997.
[77] See Gerhart Ebert, 'Okichis Heldentat', Neues Deutschland, 23 December 1997.
[78] See Peter Hans Göpfert, 'Ein Hoch auf die Milch', Berliner Morgenpost, 22 December 1997.
[79] Robert Wilson, in Holger Teschke, 'Brecht's Learning Plays – A Dance Floor for an Epic Dramaturgy', Theatre Forum, 14 (1999), pp. 10–16 (11).

only to give the production the quality of a triptych,[80] but also to move from Brecht's light to proper darkness.[81] Wilson's full diary meant that although Brecht-Schall approved the rights to the production in July 1996,[82] it only reached the stage on 28 January 1998. In an interview, Wilson conjectured that his theatre was both close to and distant from Brecht's. This he based on his own belief that each element in a theatrical production had equal value.[83] That is, he expressed both an affinity with Brecht's desire for a separation of the elements in the epic theatre and a radical distance because his use of theatrical means was usually evacuated of Brecht's interpretive strategies. Wilson thus invited more input from the spectators than for them merely to reassemble related pieces. Nonetheless, reviewers found that the stripped-down and disconnected material did open dialectical readings of the three parts,[84] precisely because the elements were presented, rather than interpreted. The press generally warmed to Wilson's cooled down theatre and enjoyed its humour as well as its precision.

More Brecht and Brecht-themed events followed, including the *Berliner Example*, a satirical 'Kongreß der brechtmäßigen Erben' ('conference of Brecht-related heirs'), another world premiere of a fragment (*Jae Fleischhacker*, directed by Thomas Heise), and an evening of Brecht songs and poems with new musical accompaniment, directed by Peter Palitzsch. This was Palitzsch's only opportunity to work with Brecht, as the director had been banned from actually staging Brecht's plays by Brecht-Schall after the production of *Baal* in 1993.[85] The response to the offerings was predictably mixed: *Fleischhacker* was mostly well received as a deliberately angular production that embraced its status as fragment,[86] while Palitzsch's evening of song was generally deemed to have been let down by the new music.[87] All in all, the centenary was an engaging mélange of hits and misses, and reflected a programming ethic, already present in the

---

[80] See ibid., pp. 12–13.
[81] See Teschke, in Christine Gerberding, 'Aufstieg und Absturz', *Berliner Morgenpost*, 28 January 1998.
[82] See Holger Teschke to Robert Wilson, 10 July 1996, BEA File 207.
[83] See Wilson, in Holger Teschke, 'Mit dem Körper hören, mit dem Körper sprechen', *Spiel-Zeit*, supplement of *Der Tagesspiegel*, February 1998.
[84] See, for example, Anja Nioduschewski, 'Drei Stücke im Überflug', *Junge Welt*, 30 January 1998; or Esther Slevogt, 'Die Frechheit des Menschen', *Freitag*, 30 January 1998.
[85] See Volker Oesterreich, 'pp huldigt bb', *Berliner Morgenpost*, 5 May 1998.
[86] See, for example, Klaus Dermutz, 'Stadtansicht', *Frankfurter Rundschau*, 25 March 1998; or Petra Kohse, 'Dem fröhlichen Irgendwie fröhnen', *die tageszeitung*, 26 March 1998.
[87] See, for example, Detlef Friedrich, 'Brecht unter den Klangteppich gekehrt', *Berliner Zeitung*, 5 May 1998; or Carsten Gerhard, 'Oh, du schöne Hoffnungslosigkeit', *Die Welt*, 5 May 1998.

'Brecht Sommer', of taking a broad range of ideas, supporting them, and seeing what worked and what did not. The difference between this celebration and those staged in the GDR could not be more pronounced: in 1998, the sense of reverence and duty was missing. While the plan could not be considered frivolous, the different elements were opened up to a broad spectrum of input, and the idea of a unifying 'house style' was absent. An attempt to impose orthodoxy or even to present a delimited breadth of Brechtian possibilities did not inform the events consciously. Such an approach is, of course, perfectly reasonable, yet it indicates that the BE's traditional role in defining a certain type of philosophical or aesthetic response to staging Brecht was no longer desired or indeed required.

The final production of the 1997/98 season, Shakespeare's *The Tempest*, directed by Suschke in June 1998, marks the start of the shift from energetic anarchy to the resigned waiting for Peymann. One reviewer stated that despite the initial storm on stage, the production itself 'is stuck in the doldrums'.[88] Klaus Emmerich then returned to direct Brecht's *Die Rundköpfe und die Spitzköpfe* (*Round Head and Pointed Heads*), the first major production of the new season in September 1998, as a kind of metatheatrical work-in-progress. The actors performed as if in rehearsal in front of scaffolding, on which hung a sign pointing to the BE's promised rebirth: 'the Berlin Senate, with federal support, is building the new BE'. The production thus communicated its own provisional status. The playful approach met with a mixed reception, primarily because the play deals with racial issues and alludes to the Nazis' persecution of the Jews. Some reviewers thus felt that the lightness was inappropriate.[89] Others enjoyed the lack of historicization and prosthetics to denote the different head shapes of the play's title because Emmerich's approach shifted the emphasis away from the theme of racism to the other plotline, the political manipulation of public opinion.[90]

Emmerich was supposed to follow up the relaxed production, that made a virtue out of its 'unfinished' aesthetic, with an altogether more serious project, Heiner Müller's reworking of Shakespeare, *Anatomie Titus Fall of Rome*. However, by February 1999, the actors accused the

[88] Peter Hans Göpfert, 'Der Typ mit der Tolle', *Berliner Morgenpost*, 9 June 1998.
[89] See, for example, Lothar Müller, 'Flachschädel', *Frankfurter Allgemeine Zeitung*, 22 September 1998; or Detlef Friedrich, 'Nicht faul, sondern bedürftig', *Berliner Zeitung*, 21 September 1998.
[90] See, for example, Christa Hasselhorst, 'Machtwechsel hin, Machtwechsel her', *Die Welt*, 18 September 1998; or Gerhard Ebert, 'Reich und reich gesellt sich gern', *Neues Deutschland*, 23 September 1998.

director of being poorly prepared for rehearsal.[91] The production was cancelled, and Wuttke reportedly left it after four weeks of rehearsal.[92] Emmerich persuaded the cast to work on the BE's final project on the main stage in March 1999, that compiled Müller's three different approaches to the Heracles myth. *Anatomie* was not, however, the only project to be abandoned that season. Suschke wanted to stage a version of Jean-Luc Godard's film *Les Carabiniers* involving a rehearsal process based on improvisation, yet, according to Suschke, the actors wanted to work within the Brechtian categories of *Arrangement* and *Gestus*.[93] For their part, the actors claimed they found the text 'too flat', and the premiere, scheduled for December, was cancelled in November 1998.[94]

The final homage to Müller, *Philoctetes*, was directed by Suschke on the rehearsal stage in April. It was mostly judged a fitting final production in all its sobriety,[95] as a resigned farewell to the BE before Peymann's arrival. The show ran to ten performances, and most were sold out. Both Müller projects ended their short runs on 28 April, and the BE finally closed the doors on its current incarnation with an evening entitled 'Geschichten aus der Klebekolonne' ('Tales from the Team of Gluers'). The title referred to the labour expended by the assistants at the BE who glued photos and text into the many *Modellbücher* in the 1950s. Holger Teschke chaired the conversation with former assistants Peter Palitzsch and Peter Voigt on 30 April 1999.

By the end of this fiftieth season, the BE had a very different relationship to its Brechtian heritage from that of the past decades. The sense of duty or reverence was certainly gone, and this may well have been a good thing. Its replacement by a more playful approach to producing Brecht's works may, however, have merely reflected uncertain times and the lack of a concrete political culture within which to make theatre politically. Even Brecht-Schall seemed to acknowledge this by permitting the long-banned *Measures Taken* and approving Robert Wilson's experimental production. There was little discussion of grander plans for the treatment of Brecht or Müller on stage at the company, and the BE's status as a theatre with a politico-aesthetic mission had all but eroded by 1999. The BE was becoming simply one of a number of Berlin theatres that staged plays

---

[91] See voe, 'Berliner Ensemble will ins Schiller-Theater', *Berliner Morgenpost*, 3 February 1999.

[92] See Henrike Thomsen, 'Augiasstall ist müde', *Berliner Zeitung*, 10 March 1999.

[93] Suschke, unpublished interview with the author, 28 April 2011.

[94] Anon., 'Berliner Ensemble sagt Premiere ab', *Berliner Morgenpost*, 19 November 1998.

[95] See, for example, Christoph Funke, 'Müller in Schwarz-Weiß', *Der Tagesspiegel*, 3 April 1999.

by Bertolt Brecht. The BE's final seasons, then, reflect the company's gradual shift from a distinctive unit, based on a shared set of theoretical and practical political principles, to a more general purveyor of theatre productions. It is difficult singularly to account for this shift: the contributory factors are many and varied. It is possible that the BE had run out of ways to approach Brecht's legacy without a major figure like Müller or Schleef to direct and inspire new post-Brechtian productions. The organization was also uncertain of itself as a unit; Suschke did not apply for the *Intendanz* Peymann was to assume and he knew that he was in charge of a company he was destined to forsake. Commercial factors also exerted a not inconsiderable pressure that made the development of new directors in the Brechtian tradition both difficult and financially perilous. The BE closed before Peymann's renovations, not with a bang, but T. S. Eliot's whimper. From 2000, the BE would no longer even implicitly suggest an obligation to Brecht's theatrical methods, even though it staged his plays on regular occasions.

Conclusion

The parabola of the Berliner Ensemble's achievements

Like that of many innovative theatre companies, the Berliner Ensemble's upward trajectory was steep: Bertolt Brecht and Erich Engel's *Mother Courage* of January 1949 prepared the way for work that went on to impress audiences and critics alike, once the BE was founded in September of that year. The achievements of a dialectical theatre attracted interest from various quarters, and there is a palpable sense of excitement in the reports, letters and memoires of members of the young company. Even in the face of SED censure, Brecht and his assistants remained loyal to developing their 'realistic' approach that finally received its international due in the mid 1950s; the BE had been 'discovered', and it would never really lose its special status overseas. Even Brecht's death in 1956 could not halt the BE's ascendancy; the modes of working were so firmly established, yet open to further development, that the former assistants were able to apply them to as yet untried and unperformed plays from Brecht's canon. That the successes continued to come until the mid 1960s pays tribute to the flexibility of the dialectical method. However, the BE's rapid decline into a tired troupe going through the Brechtian motions at the end of Helene Weigel's *Intendanz* nonetheless had its roots in practices that preceded it.

The seeds of the decline were sown as early as 1956. The triumvirate of erstwhile assistants who 'inherited' the BE could not replace Brecht's prodigious talent singularly. Benno Besson may have had lightness, Manfred Wekwerth precision, and Peter Palitzsch revolutionary drive, but the company needed them to combine forces to offer the political sharpness, the corporeal sensuousness, and the visual inventiveness of Brecht's classic productions. The staggered departures of Besson and Palitzsch meant that the BE then had to rely on one creative source who had been initiated into the Brechtian method first-hand, and this simply was not enough to generate the diversity and freshness that had marked the work of the early BE. Productivity was also low. This was because directors strove to attain

436

performative perfection in the name of staging the *Fabel* with the utmost clarity. Such orthodoxy imbued productions with a 'can't fail' status that, for the BE, was fine as long as it lasted, but proved catastrophic when *Saint Joan* flopped. It says much for this strategy that it could succeed for so long: the landmark productions of *Ui* and *Coriolan* were premiered five years apart, yet they still helped to cement the BE's reputation as a purveyor of innovative theatre. The absence of a more eclectic dialectical approach to staging major productions, a strategy that entailed more risk, but promised more variety, almost inevitably led to the accusations that the BE was turning into a Brecht museum.

The late 1960s saw the rise of what became known as *Regietheater* in the FRG. This phenomenon, a 'theatre of direction', suggests the imposition of directorial vision upon a usually classic text with a view radically to reinterpret it. *Regietheater* came in a variety of flavours, from the inventive to the indulgent, but was, by definition, something that could never take root in the BE of the 1960s, where inductive rehearsal, with its exploration of a text's contradictions, precludes the imposition of directorial 'vision'. It is tempting, then, to view Ruth Berghaus's productions, and those of Tragelehn and Schleef, as the late implementation of an approach to directing that enlivened theatres on the other side of the Berlin Wall. However, as discussed earlier, their work was also rooted in the dialectical and materialist tradition, and so it is difficult to understand their innovations as imports from the West. They were reviving the Brechtian tradition through their own fresh methods.

The BE after Brecht nonetheless represents a move away from what Fredric Jameson has called 'one continuous master class, to which a paying public is invited only on selected occasions'.[1] His point is that the company was originally more a giant workshop, experimenting with theatrical forms and ways of working, rather than a theatre that only staged plays. Over time, then, the BE *became* a theatre company; it did not start off as one in the conventional sense of the term. The sacrifice of its workshop character and the search for new forms to address new social formations in the 1960s was countered, briefly, by Berghaus and her favoured directors, although she, too, pushed forward a BE that raised the annual number of productions. This concession to the more conventional practices of running a theatre continues to this day. Wekwerth's tenure introduced few innovations and showed no signs of developing the Brechtianism evident in the 1960s. His production of *Fatzer* in 1987 amply demonstrates the conservative desire to 'tame' an unruly text and impose order on disorder. The chaos of the 1990s reflects a company at

---

[1] Jameson, *Brecht and Method*, p. 63.

a loss to address the issues Brecht raised back in the 1950s. At times, Heiner Müller's productions offered perspectives on updating Brecht's methods and retained the 'workshop' character of unfinished, open productions, yet he was unable to infuse the company itself with such a spirit. The work that followed his death took a somewhat scattergun approach to staging Brecht and Müller.

The history of the BE charts the possibilities of working with the dialectical method of interrogating dramatic material, or 'Brechtianism', as I termed it on pp. 37–8, Chapter 1. The 1950s presented Brecht with the material conditions required to revolutionize theatre-making. He embraced them and reformed not only approaches to staging plays, but also institutional structures. The interchange between director, creative team, ensemble, and other staff was the prerequisite for establishing his 'workshop' theatre and developing his method. Once the director started to assume a more dominant role, directing an ensemble trained in Brecht's gestic, anti-psychological theatre, the structures of the conventional theatre started to return. With these came the BE's gradual transformation from a radical institution into a more hierarchical and traditional one.

The Berliner Ensemble as a 'Brecht Theatre'

At its inception, the Berliner Ensemble was unlike any theatre in either East or West Germany. The defining position of Brecht as artistic director, stage director, theorist and playwright had a pervasive impact on the way the company worked and made theatre. However, as seen in the example of Berthold Viertel's *Vassa Zheleznova* and Brecht's unsuccessful attempts to attract other directors, the BE was not originally conceived as a 'Brecht theatre'. Over a relatively short period of time, the BE became such an institution, primarily through its ever-evolving method of staging both Brecht's and other dramatists' plays. The dominance of multipurpose, dialectical inquiry was the product of Brecht's hands-on relationship with the work at the theatre. He was unable to resist 'correcting' Therese Giehse's *Broken Jug*, Ernst Busch's *Kremlin Chimes* or Emil Burian's *Battle in Winter*. The failure to cultivate other directing styles also led to a focus on Brecht's ideas. In addition, Brecht had instituted a 'learning by doing' training regime in which talented young men and women observed his own practice as exemplary and were invited to contribute to, critique, and further it. At the time of Brecht's death in 1956, the BE had developed a workable and learnable method, and it had grown famous and admired as a result.

Usually, when an *Intendant* (or in this case, artistic director) leaves a German theatre, the theatre changes because of the dominant status of the *Intendant*. In the FRG, important *Intendanten* tend to attract actors, directors and/or dramaturges, and take members of that team with them when they move to new theatre, firing existing staff on arrival. In the GDR, the situation was not quite the same, due to more worker-friendly employment laws; *Intendanten* moved around, often at the behest of the SED, but then had to work with an existing ensemble. While this reduced the speed of change, it nonetheless took place. Unusually, then, Brecht's death did not bring about a new artistic direction. Helene Weigel remained *Intendantin* and served as the keeper of the Brechtian flame, although the BE's main directors also wanted to continue exploring the method they had found so enlivening. Consequently, the company became the 'Brecht theatre'. However, in such a capacity, the BE often found itself duty-bound to continue the tradition, something that became a millstone around the necks of even the most fervent Brechtians in the late 1960s. Indeed, in 1968, Wekwerth signalled an interest in directing in Brecht's hometown of Augsburg, but added that he did not want to work on a play by Brecht.[2] Brecht, the BE's boon, had become its bane. The Brechtian assumed the quality of an imagined yardstick by which all work was measured, yet precisely what 'Brechtian' meant and how one was to realize its tenets over time caused great strife, both within and without the company.

One of the problems the BE encountered as a 'Brecht theatre' was that Brecht's own practice provided a blueprint for the work that followed his death, yet this practice itself had developed a certain conservatism while Brecht still was alive. His more ambitious writings on theatre of the late 1920s and 1930s, in which, for example, he proposed the abolition of the barrier between the stage and the audience in the *Lehrstück* or showed little more than contempt for Stanislavsky, seemed to meet sober reality when he finally found himself artistic director of his own company in the GDR. The rigours of running a real theatre at least contributed to the diminution of Brecht's more radical ideas.

Brecht found he had a fairly well-functioning apparatus. He was, however, working with a group of actors untrained in and unfamiliar with his approaches to making theatre, and he was aware that not only the actors, but also the audience needed time to understand the changes he wanted to introduce. Regine Lutz reports that Brecht, after the BE's second production,

---

[2] See Wekwerth to Peter Ebert, 15 August 1968, BEA File 'Dramaturgie Wekwerth Allgemeines – Schriftwechsel 1964–68/69'.

summarized: theatre is nothing other than a business. The spectator is the customer, and the customer is always right. You may well be able to influence the
customers, but to do so you need time, prudence and patience. He himself gave
the ensemble ten years until the spectators had reached the point at which they
could accept his theatre fully.[3]

Brecht was under no illusions about the task that stood before him and
realized that theatre, even in a socialist state, conformed to the laws of the
market. Spectators did not simply go to the BE out of loyalty, and they
needed to be convinced by the merits of Brecht's challenge to character-
based, empathetic theatre. The audience had to learn a new way of watching performance, something that Brecht called 'Zuschaukunst' ('the art
of spectatorship'),[4] and acclimatize itself to the shifts of emphasis in his
understanding of a realistic theatre. However, Brecht's 'ten-year' forecast
suggests an ongoing process of development, one that would not merely
stop after a couple of successes. He realized that the unanimously positive reception of the BE's first production, *Puntila*, was not an indefinite
seal of approval. By 1954, Brecht reflected on the achievements of his
lead actors rehearsing *Chalk Circle* and believed that their performance
should not be ascribed to the input of the director, but to the five years of
hard work at the BE.[5] Brecht's long-term plan was, of course, cut short
in 1956, but by then, an approach to staging plays dialectically had been
established, and this provided the model for practice post-mortem.

In the context of the compromises Brecht made, it is tempting to
quote the dictum Heiner Müller puts in the mouth of the Hamlet-like
Hasselbein in his play *The Building Site*: 'practice, devourer of utopias'.[6]
Yet practicality was not the only factor that hamstrung Brecht's work. It
would be difficult to say that Brecht had fully delivered on his desire to
inflect performance with the full possibilities of the dialectic, and this can
be seen in two different yet related strategies that limited the dialectic's
scope and efficacy. First, the productions of *The Mother* and *Katzgraben*,
for example, 'loaded' the dialectic in such a way that the audience was
no longer the honoured co-producer of meaning, weighing up the contradictions presented on stage. Instead it became the receiver of implied
syntheses. Second, Brecht introduced a hierarchy into the formulation of
the dialectic after his reading of Mao in 1954. Both modifications affected
the dialectic's productive potential in ways that could unduly influence
its reception in the auditorium. These restrictions were not the result of

[3] Lutz, *Schauspieler – der schönste Beruf*, p. 239.
[4] Brecht, '[Es gilt zwei Künste zu entwickeln]', BFA, 23: 191.
[5] See Brecht, journal entry for 7 February 1954, BFA, 27: 349; *Journals*, p. 457.
[6] Müller, *Der Bau, Werke* 3: 343.

the material pressures of working in a real theatre; they were considered decisions Brecht had taken. And while they may have had their roots in making a new kind of dialectical theatre for a socialist society, they compromised Brecht's desire to activate his spectators and imbue them with critical attitudes that they could deploy outside the theatre.

It would not be fair to suggest that subsequent directors at the BE simply aped Brecht's dialectical predilections. The productions of *Ui* and *Coriolan*, to name the two most prominent in the ten years following Brecht's death, introduced practices that enriched the terms of the dialectic, but the dominance of the economic aspect certainly informed the changes of emphasis in *Ui*. More generally, however, the BE's dialectics in this period and in the 1980s remained tied to a binarism, an either/or, and such a structure led to a restriction of possibilities for audience response. The dialectic's complexities offered radical theatre-makers a wealth of options, but Brecht chose to limit these. His *Schüler*, most prominently Wekwerth, due to the longevity of his stay at the BE, perpetuated this 'narrow' dialectic, and a failure to embrace its richness can be seen in the criticism of the BE in crisis as a 'Brecht museum'.

The Berliner Ensemble, the GDR and the SED

It should be evident that the BE's relationship with the GDR differed from its relationship with the SED. Brecht very much endorsed the GDR and famously retorted to some rather silly accusatory questions from a West German author in November 1952: 'I don't have my opinions because I'm here, on the contrary, I'm here because I have my opinions'.[7] This bold pledge of allegiance does not quite tell the whole story of Brecht's journey to the GDR. He did not act immediately on Soviet inducements to resettle in the East and bided his time in Switzerland until 1948.[8] Plans to settle in Salzburg and Munich earlier that year came to nothing,[9] and so, what was to become the GDR was hardly Brecht's first choice of destination.

However, it is difficult to dismiss his reply, either. The GDR, as evidenced by Brecht's thoughts on 17 June 1953, was the only alternative to the capitalist FRG, but this position also meant having to endure what he might have considered its 'teething' period. Consequently, there is perhaps a surprising degree of understanding on Brecht's part for the

---

[7] Brecht, '[Antworten auf Fragen des Schriftstellers Wolfgang Weyrauch]', BFA, 23: 220.
[8] See David Bronsen, 'Brechts Rückkehr 1948', *Die Zeit*, 8 November 1968.
[9] See Stern, *Männer lieben anders*, p. 147.

cancellation of his *Lukullus* at the Staatsoper in 1951.[10] Around the same time, Brecht also mused on his divided position as an artist in the GDR. In Marxist terms he acknowledged that the 'dictatorship of the proletariat is not a good time for art' because of the primacy of politics over art.[11] Three days earlier, however, he had unfavourably compared the SED with the Communist Party of the Soviet Union (which he surprisingly believed actively sought artists' help for its political mission), and Käthe Rülicke noted: 'Brecht doesn't want to learn how to write from Ulbricht'.[12] The conflict between a broad acceptance of the GDR despite its (as Brecht considered them, temporary) injustices, and a concrete problem with the way the state was being run specifically, echoes down through the BE's history in its first decades.

Helene Weigel allowed herself to appear as a candidate for the SED in elections in West Berlin in 1954–5.[13] She was prepared to lend her famous face to the official campaign, which was more a gesture of solidarity with the GDR because she was not, and never became, a member of the SED. Both Brecht and Weigel had the opportunity of leaving the GDR whenever they wanted – in Weigel's case after the erection of the Berlin Wall as well. Neither chose to do so. While both were privileged within GDR society, due to their incomes from home and abroad, and their international profiles, they still had to submit to the SED's authority. Brecht certainly had his problems with the Party and in early 1953 bemoaned its failure to promote the BE in the press, for example.[14] The formalism campaign left him incredulous, but the triumph in Paris gave the BE such a firm footing that subsequent sniping and censure rarely led to major problems.

By the time Wekwerth became the *de facto* artistic director in the early 1960s, the Party had in him a far more loyal figure and one whose profile at this stage was less influential than Brecht's. At times, he was not uncritical of SED cultural policy: in 1962 he wrote to a member of the Central Committee that there was no single interpretation of Marxism-Leninism and that this should be respected in the theatre.[15] On the other hand, he could also actively get behind hard-line positions, backing

---

[10] See Brecht, journal entry for 23 March 1951, BFA, 27: 318; *Journals*, p. 433.
[11] Brecht, in Rülicke, 'Brecht zu Scherchen März 51 (nach *Lukullus*)', [7 April 1951], BBA 1340/47.
[12] Rülicke, 'Brecht: März/April 1951', [4 April 1951], BBA 1340/49.
[13] See Weigel to DEWAG [GDR print company], 9 November 1954, BBA uncatalogued file 'Korr 54–66'. She was not elected.
[14] See Brecht, journal entry for 4 March 1953, BFA, 27: 346; *Journals*, p. 454.
[15] See Wekwerth to Siegfried Wagner, 24 September 1962, AdK MWA 'Korrespondenz mit Institutionen'.

the thrust of the XI Plenum for theatres in 1965, for example.[16] Ruth Berghaus, for her part, was also a good servant of the State, although her aesthetics and approach to theatrical production ran counter to the official doctrine of socialist realism, and her taste for experiment led to her removal as *Intendantin*.

If one looks beyond the central personalities themselves, the BE as institution was, for the most part, a proud representative of the GDR. It enjoyed a unique position at home as the GDR's leading theatre, until that started to wane in the mid 1960s, and never really lost its appeal abroad. The BE, however tired or wounded, almost always offered foreign audiences high artistic quality together with an approach to performance that they could not find domestically.

Making theatre after Brecht

The BE's work between 1971 and 1999 offered what might appear to be contradictory manifestations under the different leaderships that succeeded Weigel's, yet from the progressive to the conservative, and the experimental to the traditional, the productions express both their debt to Brecht's methods and their dependency on historical conditions that differed greatly from those under which Brecht worked in the GDR. Ruth Berghaus attempted to introduce radical new ways of approaching the dialectical method and encountered both support and resistance from the company in her six years at the helm. Manfred Wekwerth ran a tighter ship, yet some important productions diverged greatly from his own more conventional methods that pervaded the BE's output from 1977 until 1991. And while aesthetic pluralism ran wild under the various heads of the BE between 1992 and 1995, Martin Wuttke and Stephan Suschke, following Müller's lead, returned to the Brechtian legacy in a variety of forms from 1996 to 1999 with varying degrees of success. However, the one unifying factor was that they were all involved in creating theatre after, but not without Brecht.

Making theatre after Brecht was a different kind of endeavour than making it with Brecht. He had introduced the practice of rigorous production documentation in a bid to analyse, reflect on and further the practical means available to dialectical directors, dramaturges and actors. The importance of writing such *Notate* continued well into the 1960s, a time at which Ruth Berghaus publicly called for their manufacture by other GDR theatres at the conference that founded the Verband der

---

[16] See Wekwerth to Franz Henschel, 29 December 1965, BEA File 'Dramaturgie Wekwerth Allgemeines – Schriftwechsel 1964–68/69'.

Theaterschaffenden (Association of Theatre-Makers) and cited Brecht as her inspiration.[17] However, by 1971, Berghaus had already realized that her experiments were not repeatable and that her documentation could only capture the particulars of a singular process, rather than more generic approaches that could be reused by others. The decline in documentation also accompanied the work of more conservative directors in the 1970s and 1980s, and by the 1990s, the vast majority of the BE's production dossiers held little more than newspaper reviews for the most part. The drop in the amount and quality of documentation over time can be accounted for in three ways. The first has already been mentioned: the experimental nature of post-Brechtian theatre meant that it was not repeatable and thus had little pedagogical value to subsequent theatre-makers. The second is that Brecht's method had already been tried and tested for over two decades, and, so, recording it further held no inherent value in itself, indeed, it could expose just how conventional rehearsals had become at times. The third is that the BE's productivity increased under Berghaus and Wekwerth, and this meant that fewer resources could be devoted to the often arduous process of documentation. Taken together, however, the reasons indicate that the BE increasingly resembled an 'ordinary' theatre, rather than a 'special' one: its existing practices had lost their sheen, and even innovative work was not connected to the development of a transferable 'method' any more. The BE was no longer concerned about its legacy as such – rivalling Brecht's discoveries may have proven to be a vain pursuit – but was more focused on making theatre in the here and now. It had hits and flops like any other theatre, but the hits did not necessarily betoken a wondrous new approach that was worth telegraphing further. The BE's change of status indicates the different context in which the various heads that succeeded Weigel were working. As other GDR theatres began to develop their profiles with fresh, new productions, the BE became aware of the fact that while it still had a distinctive place as the GDR's 'Brecht theatre', this status was not necessarily enough to guarantee the quality of its work alone.

Along with its triumphs, its crises, its in-fighting, and its sometimes fraught relationships with various authorities, what makes the BE worthy of study in the period 1971–99 are the ways in which it deals with the burden of tradition. Despite flashes of brilliance, the company never recaptured its reputation of the 1950s and 1960s domestically. The BE

---

[17] See Ruth Berghaus, in Anon., 'Stenografische Niederschrift: Kongreß zur Gründung des Verbandes der Theaterschaffenden der DDR am 11. und 12. Dezember 1966', uncorrected text, undated, 95 pages (84), AdK Verband der Theaterschaffenden 7.

thus found itself in a peculiar place. Unlike other companies that reach a peak and then fall into obscurity, the BE never lost its allure because it was always wedded to notions of Brecht, his methods and his plays. The BE was not allowed to die either by those who held the purse strings or those who sought to loosen them, and the peculiar relationship between the institution and its history provided the life-support for the sometimes ailing company. Audiences, too, both at home and abroad, continued to foster a hope that the BE could fashion new, engaging and relevant connections to Brecht and return to the glory days of a politicized theatre that rarely ceased to dazzle.

When is the Berliner Ensemble not the Berliner Ensemble?

Over the course of the Berliner Ensemble's history, the question has been asked as to whether its name at some point merely denoted a theatrical brand, having lost a vital connection to the company's founding principles. My decision to conclude this study in 1999, when Claus Peymann relieved Stephan Suschke and Peter Sauerbaum of the company's leadership, is a deliberate one: this was the point at which the BE as such ceased to be the BE.

Friedrich Dieckmann, in an article of 1999, tries to ascertain when the BE 'ended'. He asks whether Helene Weigel's death in 1971 marked the end of the BE, calling the BE under Weigel 'a subsidized family theatre' that then became one implicitly, co-run by Berghaus and Brecht-Schall.[18] He then wonders whether the 'gang of five' ultimately laid the BE to rest because the name had become instrumentalized at that time. That is, he proposes that the 'gang' was merely using the name to further certain commercial ends while neglecting the BE's artistic mission. Theatre commentator Martin Linzer called the BE 'a walking corpse' in the mid 1990s,[19] already suggesting that the company was condemned to stalk the stage as a husk of Brechtianism, bereft of verve and vitality. Others have also rung the death knell for the BE, including Barbara Brecht-Schall and Manfred Wekwerth, who believed the BE should be renamed the 'Berliner Gästehaus' ('Berlin Guesthouse') in 1995.[20]

Dieckmann and Linzer both focus on the BE's artistic mission as a way of understanding the validity of the name 'Berliner Ensemble'. Lurking

[18] See Friedrich Dieckmann, *Wer war Brecht? Erkundungen und Erörterungen* (Berlin: Aufbau, 2003), p. 201.
[19] See Linzer, 'Thoughts on a Walking Corpse', pp. 289–300.
[20] Wekwerth, in Schütt, *Manfred Wekwerth*, p. 250.

behind both Brecht-Schall's and Wekwerth's pronouncements is also a sense that 'the BE is not making theatre in the Brechtian mould as I understand it'. Clearly definitions of this kind are too narrow and rest on the personal tastes of those making the accusations, yet likewise, Dieckmann and Linzer do not explicate their understanding of a Brechtian tradition sufficiently enough to qualify the terms of the BE's demise. In order to locate a broader, less subjective basis, it is worth considering Marvin Carlson's concept of the theatre as 'haunted house'.[21] Carlson considers the ways in which particular theatre institutions or companies either consciously or inadvertently generate effects predicated upon their past that then influence reception in the present. He cites Wagner's Bayreuth as 'a somewhat extreme example of what one might call a pilgrimage theatre, in which for the faithful . . . each new season is ghosted by memories'. Elsewhere he considers a different kind of ghosting associated with theatres whose reputations go so far before them that spectators 'encountering them for the first time . . . inevitably find that experience haunted by the cultural construction of . . . persons or places'. In both examples, Carlson focuses on how spectators' responses to theatres can be interpenetrated by history and its associations. Both facets clearly apply to the BE, whose (international) profile and history have drawn audiences in much the same way as Bayreuth and have affected expectations of new visitors to the BE by teasing them with the promise of viewing theatre as Brecht might have made it, regardless of what that might actually mean.

It may be helpful, however, when establishing the circumstances of the 'end' of the BE, to treat the 'haunting' as an *internal* process and focus on those making, rather than attending the theatre. In order to ascertain the time at which the BE ceased to be the BE, one might ask how long the spirit of Brecht 'haunted' the house itself. By this I mean, for how long was he able to dominate the ways in which the BE thought about, approached and made theatre. Such a question is not predicated on *how well* directors realize their ideas, but whether theatre-makers still consider the ideas important and worth working on in a more or less systematic manner. Thus, despite Brecht-Schall's concerns, I have demonstrated that Berghaus was very much committed to Brecht's ideas, but sought to take them beyond Brecht's own interpretive limitations. Wekwerth, too, instituted a return to practices developed in the 1960s when he took over the BE in 1977. While his work markedly differed from that of Berghaus, both were drawing from the same source and, more importantly, wanted to inform the work of the BE as a whole with a relationship to Brecht's method.

Even while Wekwerth was pilloried in 1991 for turning the BE into a museum, one of his main detractors, Ivan Nagel, still held on to Wekwerth's fundamental position, namely, that the BE could still be run along Brechtian lines. Nagel, the man commissioned to author the report on Berlin's theatres for Senator Roloff-Momin, was asked why he had wanted to back the BE as a Brecht theatre, when the report itself was so concerned with innovation. He replied: 'the most established name is Brecht's... His legacy can only be protected if it's separated from the familial control of his estate'.[22] At this time, the emphasis was still on realizing Brecht's theatre after what Nagel considered the stagnant years of Wekwerth's *Intendanz* and the constant interference of Brecht-Schall. The appointment of five heads led to aimlessness, and one could rightly argue that for the first time in its history, the BE was not singularly inflected by a commitment to Brecht's method. However, Müller, Marquardt and Palitzsch all, to a varying degree, worked through Brechtian principles. Only Müller actually managed to execute this in a sustained manner, and when he finally emerged as the victor over Zadek, he swiftly sought to align the BE under the 'Brecht Müller Shakespeare' programme. Wuttke, and later Suschke, continued Müller's direction not only by scheduling Brecht and Müller regularly, but by promoting different ways of directing them that were not in some way arbitrary, but that tried to connect with various Brechtian and post-Brechtian impulses. However, after the dismissal of the poorly behaved Einar Schleef, it was only impulses that could be detected, and the failure to develop an approach on the part of the BE's leadership represented the practical inability of a company to pursue anything approaching a cohesive method by the 1990s. The Brechtian had fractured into a plurality of ideas and could no longer support a single method in the unstable and uncertain world of post-Wall Germany. The varying interpretations of post-Brechtian theatre criticized certain positions associated with Brecht's work at the BE and could thus not be considered a 'method' in their own right. However, post-Brechtianism clearly derives its approaches from Brechtian tenets, and so making theatre in this mould still acknowledged a commitment to Brecht's aims of refashioning the world through theatre.

Brecht, of course, can be performed in ways that are neither Brechtian nor post-Brechtian. This is why it is important to note Claus Peymann's

[22] Ivan Nagel, in Esther Slevogt, 'Es wurde viel zuwenig geschrien', *die tageszeitung*, 17 April 1991.

early indication that he was interested in taking over 'the *Intendanz* at the Theater am Schiffbauerdamm'.[23] Indeed, the title of the newspaper article from which the quotation is taken translates as 'Good day, Mr Exorcist'. It was clear even back in 1997 that Peymann was not coming to the BE to continue the tradition, but to break with it in favour of his own ideas and conceptions about how to run such a theatre. Rumour has it that Peymann wanted to go ahead with returning the theatre to its pre-BE name, 'das Theater am Schiffbauerdamm', but was prevented by the Berlin Senate because the association with the company's famous name still brought in sizeable audiences.[24] Whether this is true or not is less important than Peymann's desire to drive out the ghosts of the past from the BE's staff itself, if not from the minds of its audience.

Peymann certainly did not neglect Brecht in the repertoire and opened both Brecht's and Weigel's offices to visiting spectators, but, crucially, he and his fellow directors did not actively seek to perform Brecht in accordance with methods developed at the BE over the years. As Carlson notes: 'Peymann's plan was apparently to acknowledge Brecht but resist the "Brecht-house" mentality long associated with the theatre'.[25] Indeed, he has engendered a pluralist repertoire whose criterion for success is rarely critical, but public acclaim. He has been so successful in this light that the Berlin Senate extended his contract in 2010 and, again, in 2013. Such a body was always going to welcome a strong and steady income from this theatre after the deficits of the 1990s. Laura Bradley notes that Peymann 'remains committed to the Schillerian concept of theatre as a moral institution, explaining that he wants to enlighten spectators in the tradition of Lessing, Schiller and Brecht'.[26] He is thus not so much concerned with Brecht's theatrical forms than with a more general social purpose, associated with progressive artists from the German canon. In addition, Peymann's established directorial penchants for Peter Handke, Thomas Bernhard and George Tabori have provided at least regular rivals for Brecht in the repertoire. In short, the BE is now another major theatre in Berlin that stages Brecht, amongst other playwrights. Peymann has made the theatre remarkably popular with theatre-goers, but has no wish to continue the BE's production traditions. It was only in 2000, then, that Peymann finally exorcized Brecht's ghost from the mindset of

[23] Rüdiger Schaper, 'Grüß Gott, Herr Exorzist', *Süddeutsche Zeitung*, 23 April 1997.
[24] See Werner Hecht, 'Berliner Ensemble: Einzug der Gladiatoren in das Theater am Schiffbauerdamm', *Dreigroschenheft*, 2 (2000), pp. 5–15 (8). I have found no evidence to support these contentions, especially regarding the Senate's alleged intervention.
[25] Marvin Carlson, 'Claus Peymann and the Performance of Scandal', *Contemporary Theatre Review*, 18:2 (2008), pp. 193–207 (205).
[26] Laura Bradley, 'Contemporary Theatre? Brecht, Peymann & Co. at the Berliner Ensemble', *Contemporary Theatre Review*, 18:1 (2008), pp. 69–79 (74).

the creative staff. However, in December 2014, it was announced that Peymann would be stepping down in 2017 and would be replaced by Oliver Reese, the *Intendant* of Frankfurt's major theatre. From his early pronouncements, it seems that the new head will also not be seeking to take up the Brechtian mantle.[27]

The BE had run its course. Its irresistible rise in the early GDR could not be sustained, and it declined in the late 1960s. Berghaus attempted to revive its fortunes, but her experiments were too distant from what both the Brecht estate and the SED considered to be 'Brecht's theatre', although they were, of course, not necessarily the best judges. The reaction to Berghaus's risks was a return to the security of an organized interpretive method in a theatre run by someone who would become the President of the GDR's Academy of Arts and a member of the Central Committee. The challenge to Wekwerth's definition of Brechtianism was the uncoordinated directorship of the gang of five. While the focus was narrowed under Müller's half-year reign, all that was left to Wuttke and Suschke was a managed decline as the BE gradually lost its Brechtian bearings. Peymann marks the logical conclusion to the company's life cycle; he was not interested in carrying on its traditions, and the Senate endorsed this artistic position by appointing him. With Peymann, the chain was broken and, perhaps over the years, spectators will gradually stop expecting to find Brecht staged 'authentically', whatever that might mean today, at the Theater am Schiffbauerdamm.

The BE's legacy, however, remains. This was a company that broke the mould by adopting, developing, modifying, reinstating and rethinking Brecht's method. The method, rather than the devices associated with it, involved establishing the centrality of the dialectic in the process of making performance and consequently integrating the audience into the activity of meaning-making. This complex clearly went through a number of incarnations until it no longer presented a tenable theatrical programme. Yet it should not be forgotten that even as late as 1995, Müller's *Arturo Ui* continued to satisfy the method's axioms, although the production differed greatly, in its form, ambition and context, from Palitzsch and Wekwerth's equally formidable version of 1959. It is unlikely that audiences will see a company of the Berliner Ensemble's like again: the combination of innovation in rehearsal and performance, reform of institutional structure, and ample funding seems impossible to replicate on such a grand scale under current economic conditions. However, the Berliner Ensemble's triumphs, and its defeats, may yet serve as productive examples for future theatre-makers seeking to further art's engagement with politics and society.

[27] 'See Anon., 'Reese folgt auf Peymann', *Süddeutsche Zeitung*, 1 December 2014.

Appendix: Productions of the Berliner Ensemble, 1949–1999

All information kindly provided by the Berliner Ensemble Archive. All attempts have been made to fill gaps in the table, although some, inevitably, persist. The list does not include revivals.

Season 1949/50

1   Bertolt Brecht   Premiere: 12 November 1949
     MR PUNTILA AND HIS MAN   100 performances to 20 November 1953
     MATTI
     Directors: Bertolt Brecht/Erich Engel

2   Maxim Gorky   Premiere: 23 December 1949
     VASSA ZHELEZNOVA   50 performances to 15 April 1951
     Director: Berthold Viertel

3   After Jakob Michael Reinhold Lenz   Premiere: 15 April 1950
     THE TUTOR   72 performances to 17 April 1951
     Directors: Bertolt Brecht/Caspar Neher

Season 1950/51

4   Bertolt Brecht   Premiere: 13 January 1951
     THE MOTHER   113 performances to 31 May1955
     Director: Bertolt Brecht

5   After Gerhart Hauptmann   Premiere: 24 March 1951
     THE BEAVER COAT AND   14 performances to 22 April 1951
     CONFLAGRATION
     Director: Egon Monk

Season 1951/52

6   Heinrich von Kleist   Premiere: 23 January 1952
     THE BROKEN JUG   107 peformances to 13 June1953
     Directors: Therese Giehse (/Bertolt
     Brecht)

7   N. F. Pogodin   Premiere: 28 March 1952
     THE KREMLIN CHIMES   51 performances to 13 June 1953
     Directors: Ernst Busch (/Bertolt Brecht)

8   Johann Wolfgang von Goethe   Premiere: 23 April 1952
     URFAUST   19 performances to 5 May 1953
     Director: Egon Monk

Season 1952/53

9   Bertolt Brecht   Premiere: 16 November 1952
    SEÑORA CARRER'S RIFLES   49 performances to March 1955
    Director: Egon Monk

10   After Anna Seghers   Premiere: 23 November 1952
    THE TRIAL OF JOAN OF ARC AT   33 performances to 13 June 1954
    ROUEN, 1431
    Director: Benno Besson

11   Erwin Strittmatter   Premiere: 23 May 1953
    KATZGRABEN   37 performances to 26 April 1955
    Director: Bertolt Brecht

12   Ashakh Tokayev   Premiere: 27 June 1953
    A STRANGE CHILD   8 performances to 23 October 1953
    Director: Wolfgang Böttcher

Season 1953/54

13   After Martinus Hayeccius   Premiere: 4 March 1954
    HANS PFRIEM, OR BOLDNESS   5 performances to 2 October 1955
    PAYS OFF
    Director: Käthe Rülicke

14   Scenes adapted by Angelika Hurwicz   Premiere: 1954
    COBBLER PINNE IN A PICKLE
    Director: Angelika Hurwicz

15   After Moliére   Premiere: 19 March 1954
    DON JUAN   80 performances to 31 August 1955
    Director: Benno Besson

16   After Lo Ding, Chang Fan, Chu   Premiere: 1 April 1954
    Jin-Nan   77 performances to 7 March 1957
    MILLET FOR THE EIGHTH ARMY
    Director: Manfred Wekwerth

Season 1954/55

17   Bertolt Brecht   Premiere:7 October 1954
    THE CAUCASIAN CHALK CIRCLE   175 performances to 22 December 1958
    Director: Bertolt Brecht

18   After Johannes R. Becher   Premiere: 12 January 1955
    BATTLE IN WINTER   115 performances to 10 July 1957
    Directors: Bertolt Brecht/Manfred
    Wekwerth

Season 1955/56

19   After George Farquhar   Premiere: 19 September 1955
    TRUMPETS AND DRUMS   165 performances to 10 July 1958
    Director: Benno Besson

20   Adapted by Peter Palitzsch and Carl   Premiere: 8 November 1955
    Weber   43 performances to 7 March 1957
    THE DAY OF WU, THE GREAT
    SCHOLAR
    Directors: Peter Palitzsch/Carl Weber

21   Alexander Ostrovsky   Premiere: 12 December 1955
     THE FOSTER DAUGHTER, OR   52 performances to 24 January 1957
     GOOD DEEDS HURT
     Director: Angelika Hurwicz
22   After John Millington Synge   Premiere: 11 May 1956
     THE PLAYBOY OF THE WESTERN   135 performances to 9 May 1961
     WORLD
     Directors: Manfred Wekwerth/Peter
     Palitzsch

Season 1956/57
23   Bertolt Brecht   Premiere:15 January 1957
     LIFE OF GALILEO   242 performances to 2 December 1961
     Directors: Erich Engel/Bertolt Brecht
24   Bertolt Brecht   Premiere: 15 February 1957
     FEAR AND MISERY OF THE   84 performances to 10 July 1959
     THIRD REICH
     Directors: Lothar Bellag/Peter
     Palitzsch/Käthe Rülicke/Konrad
     Swinarski/Carl Weber

Season 1957/58
25   Bertolt Brecht   Premiere: 5 October 1957
     THE GOOD PERSON OF   109 performances to 4 July 1959
     SZECHWAN
     Director: Benno Besson
26   After Vsevolod Vishnevsky   Premiere: 1 April 1958
     OPTIMISTIC TRAGEDY   63 performances to 26 May 1960
     Directors: Peter Palitzsch/Manfred
     Wekwerth

Season 1958/59
27   Bertolt Brecht   Premiere 23 March 1959
     THE RESISTIBLE RISE OF   532 performances to 13 January 1974
     ARTURO UI
     Directors: Peter Palitzsch/Manfred
     Wekwerth

Season 1959/60
28   Bertolt Brecht/Kurt Weill   Premiere: 23 April 1960
     THE THREEPENNY OPERA   497 performances to 10 July 1971
     Director: Erich Engel

Season 1960/61
29   Helmut Baierl   Premiere: 8 May 1961
     FRAU FLINZ   94 performances to 23 March 1963
     Directors: Manfred Wekwerth/Peter
     Palitzsch

Season 1961/62

30   BRECHT EVENING NR. 1: SONGS   Premiere: 26 April 1962
      AND POEMS 1914–1956   53 performances to 6 May 1966
      Led by: Manfred Karge/Isot
      Kilian/Matthias Langhoff /Manfred
      Wekwerth

Season 1962/63

31   After Bertolt Brecht   Premiere: 7 October 1962
      THE DAYS OF THE COMMUNE   188 performances to 13 June 1971
      Directors: Manfred Wekwerth/Joachim
      Tenschert
32   Bertolt Brecht   Premiere: 31 December 1962
      SCHWEYK IN THE SECOND   674 performances to 23 June 1981
      WORLD WAR
      Directors: Erich Engel/Wolfgang
      Pintzka
33   BRECHT EVENING NR. 2: ON THE   Premiere: 10 February 1963
      GREAT CITIES/THE LITTLE   51 performances to 6 April 1968
      MAHAGONNY
      Directors: Manfred Karge/Matthias
      Langhoff

Season 1963/64

34   BRECHT EVENING NR. 3: THE   Premiere: 12 October 1963
      MESSINGKAUF   100 performances to 17 June 1970
      Directors: Uta Birnbaum/Guy de
      Chambure/Werner Hecht/Manfred
      Karge /Matthias Langhoff /Hans-Georg
      Simmgen/Kurt Veth/Manfred Wekwerth

Season 1964/65

35   After William Shakespeare   Premiere: 25 September 1964
      CORIOLAN   276 performances to 8 February 1979
      Directors: Manfred Wekwerth/Joachim
      Tenschert
      Battle scenes director: Ruth Berghaus
36   DON'TCHA KNOW (REVUE)   Premiere: 10 February 1965
      Director: Manfred Wekwerth
37   Heinar Kipphardt   Premiere: 12 April 1965
      IN THE MATTER OF J. ROBERT   75 performances to 30 June 1969
      OPPENHEIMER
      Directors: Manfred Wekwerth/Joachim
      Tenschert

Season 1965/66

38   Sean O'Casey   Premiere: 14 February 1966
      PURPLE DUST   296 performances to 29 March 1978
      Directors: Hans-Georg Simmgen/
      Manfred Wekwerth

Season 1966/67

39 Bertolt Brecht
REFUGEE CONVERSATIONS
Led by: Manfred Wekwerth/Joachim
Tenschert

Premiere: 11 October 1966
6 performances to 7 December 1966

40 Bertolt Brecht
MAN EQUALS MAN
Director: Uta Birnbaum

Premiere: 10 February 1967
113 performances to 6 June 1970

41 BRECHT EVENING NR. 4: THE
BREAD SHOP
Directors: Manfred Karge/Matthias
Langhoff

Premiere: 13 April 1967
107 performances to 14 October 1972

42 Paul Dessau
THE DISTANT WAR (REVUE)
Musical director: Paul Dessau

Premiere: 26 April 1967

Season 1967/68

43 Peter Weiss
VIETNAM DISCOURSE
Director: Ruth Berghaus

Premiere: 30 April 1968
20 performances to 9 May 1969

44 Alexander Lang
THE DWARVES
Directors: Uta Birnbaum/Helmut Rabe

Premiere: 4 May 1968
3 performances to 1 June 1968

45 Bertolt Brecht
SAINT JOAN OF THE
STOCKYARDS
Directors: Manfred Wekwerth/Joachim
Tenschert

Premiere: 12 June 1968
50 performances to 12 January 1972

Season 1968/69

46 Helmut Baierl
JOHANNA VON DÖBELN
Director: Manfred Wekwerth

Premiere: 1 April 1969
40 performances to 19 June 1970

47 Aeschylus
SEVEN AGAINST THEBES
Directors: Manfred Karge/Matthias
Langhoff

Premiere: 28 May 1969
10 performances to 25 October 1969

Season 1969/70

48 BRECHT EVENING NR. 5: THE
MANIFESTO
Directors: Klaus Erforth/Alexander
Stillmark

Premiere: 1 October 1969
8 performances to 5 December 1969

49 Georg Büchner
WOYZECK
Director: Helmut Nitzschke

Premiere: 11 April 1970
65 performances to 16 October 1974

Season 1970/71

50   Sean O'Casey   Premiere: 5 January 1971
     COCK-A-DOODLE DANDY   19 performances to 18 December 1971
     Directors: Werner Hecht/Hans-Georg
     Voigt

51   Bertolt Brecht   Premiere: 28 January 1971
     IN THE JUNGLE OF THE CITIES   73 performances to 11 January 1977
     Director: Ruth Berghaus

52   Bertolt Brecht   Premiere: 15 June 1971
     SEÑORA CARRAR'S RIFLES   101 performances to 30 June 1978
     Director: Ruth Berghaus

Season 1971/72

53   Bertolt Brecht   Premiere: 5 October 1971
     LIFE OF GALILEO   93 performances to 30 October 1974
     Director: Fritz Bennewitz

54   Karl Mickel after Alexander Bek   Premiere: 1 February 1972
     THE ROAD TO VOLOKOLAMSK   20 performances to 8 October 1973
     Director: Ruth Berghaus

Season 1972/73

55   Peter Hacks   Premiere: 3 October 1972
     OMPHALE   66 performances to 3 April 1977
     Director: Ruth Berghaus

56   Erwin Strittmatter   Premiere: 10 November 1972
     KATZGRABEN   33 performances to 24 June 1975
     Director: B. K. Tragelehn

57   Bertolt Brecht   Premiere: 10 February 1973
     TURANDOT   67 performances to 30 December 1976
     Directors: Peter Kupke/Wolfgang
     Pintzka

Season 1973/74

58   Bertolt Brecht   Premiere: 4 August 1973
     THE BADEN-BADEN LESSON ON   11 performances to 26 November 1974
     CONSENT
     Directors: Jürgen Pörschmann/Günther
     Schmidt

59   Heiner Müller after Fyodor Gladkov   Premiere: 12 October 1973
     CEMENT   41 performances to 14 October 1976
     Director: Ruth Berghaus

60   Helmut Baierl   Premiere: 21 October 1973
     ...PROUD OF 18 HOURS   14 performances to 20 February 1975
     Director: unknown

61   George Bernhard Shaw   Premiere: 21 December 1973
     MRS WARREN'S PROFESSION   141 performances to 4 December 1979
     Director: Wolfgang Pintzka

62   Frank Wedekind   Premiere: 1 March 1974
     SPRING AWAKENING   116 performances to 4 December 1976
     Directors: B. K. Tragelehn/Einar
     Schleef
63   Bertolt Brecht after Marlowe   Premiere: 18 June 1974
     THE LIFE OF EDWARD II OF   50 performances to 10 March 1978
     ENGLAND
     Directors: Ekkehard Schall/Barbara
     Brecht-Schall

Season 1974/75
64   Bertolt Brecht   Premiere: 18 October 1974
     THE MOTHER   53 performances to 1 April 1978
     Director: Ruth Berghaus
65   Karl Mickel after Fernando de Rojas   Premiere: 31 December 1974
     CELESTINA   68 performances to 18 June 1977
     Directors: Jürgen Pörschmann/Günther
     Schmidt
66   Bertolt Brecht   Premiere: 25 February 1975
     MR PUNTILA AND HIS MAN   190 performances to 5 February 1984
     MATTI
     Director: Peter Kupke
67   August Strindberg   Premiere: 10 April 1975
     MISS JULIE   10 performances to 23 June 1975
     Directors: B. K. Tragelehn/Einar
     Schleef

Season 1975/76
68   Leon Kruckowski   Premiere: 9 October 1975
     THE FIRST DAY OF FREEDOM   8 performances to 16 January 1976
     Directors: Jürgen Pörschmann/Günther
     Schmidt
69   BRECHT EVENING: I, BERTOLT   Premiere: 10 December 1975
     BRECHT   13 performances to 26 November 1976
     Directors: Jürgen Pörschmann/Günter
     Schmidt
70   Helmut Baierl   Premiere: 12 March 1976
     THE SOMMER RESIDENT   24 performances to 11 December 1976
     Director: Ruth Berghaus
71   Bertolt Brecht   Premiere: 20 April 1976
     THE CAUCASIAN CHALK CIRCLE   246 performances to 3 December 1992
     Director: Peter Kupke

Season 1976/77
72   Johann Nestroy   Premiere: 29 September 1976
     THE INSIGNIFICANT MAN   47 performances to 17 March 1978
     Directors: Karl von Appen/Hein Trilling

Season 1977/78

73 After Jakob Michael Reinhold Lenz
    THE TUTOR
    Director: Peter Kupke

Premiere: 6 October 1977
91 performances to 20 December 1980

74 Heiner Müller
    THE WAGE SINKER
    Directors: Matthias Renner/Axel
    Richter

Premiere: 17 January 1978
22 performances to 3 June 1979

75 Helmut Baierl
    THE STATEMENT OF FACT
    Directors: Christoph Brück/Wolf
    Bunge

Premiere: 17 January 1978
19 performances to 3 June 1979

76 Bertolt Brecht
    GALILEO GALILEI
    Directors: Manfred Wekwerth/Joachim
    Tenschert

Premiere: 10 February 1978
274 performances to 3 December 1992

77 VOLKER BRAUN EVENING NR.1
    Led by: Wolfgang Pintzka

Premiere: 11 February 1978
20 performances to 28 March 1979

78 Bertolt Brecht
    UNCLE EDDY'S GOT A
    MOUSTACHE...
    Directors: Jürgen Kern/Jörg
    Mihan/Matthias Stein

Premiere: 14 April 1978
36 performances to 3 June 1980

Season 1978/79

79 Bertolt Brecht
    MOTHER COURAGE AND HER
    CHILDREN
    Directors: Peter Kupke/Manfred
    Wekwerth

Premiere: 3 October 1978
217 performances to 30 April 1992

80 Dario Fo
    CAN'T PAY! WON'T PAY!
    Director: Konrad Zschiedrich

Premiere: 15 December 1978
243 performances to 21 December 1987

81 Paul Gratzik
    LISA
    Director: Helle Müller

Premiere: 6 April 1979
10 performances to 19 March 1980

82 Alfred Matusche
    PROGNOSIS
    Directors: Katrin Wolf/Hermann Schein

Premiere: 6 April 1979
5 performances to 24 November 1979

83 Volker Braun
    THE GREAT PEACE
    Directors: Manfred Wekwerth/Joachim
    Tenschert

Premiere: 22 April 1979
76 performances to 7 February 1987

Season 1979/80

84 BRECHT EVENING:
    WHEN I RETURNED
    Director: Wolfgang Pintzka

Premiere: 31 August 1979
5 performances to 12 January 1980

85	BRECHT PROGRAMME FOR WHAT AND AGAINST WHAT Director: Ekkehard Schall	Premiere: 5 October 1979 9 performances to 30 October 1979
86	BRECHT PROGRAMME: ON THE KINDNESS OF THE WORLD Director: Peter Konwitschny	Premiere: 21 November 1979 18 performances to 27 February 1983
87	Johannes Conrad KNUPPEPÜTZE Directors: Jürgen Kern/Hein Trilling	Premiere: 30 November 1979 53 performances to 19 June 1982
88	Maxim Gorky YEGOR BULYCHOV AND OTHERS Director: Manfred Wekwerth	Premiere: 14 December 1979 25 performances to 15 April 1981
89	VOLKER BRAUN EVENING NR. 2 Led by: Jochen Ziller	Premiere: 21 January 1980 5 performances to 25 March 1980
90	Bertolt Brecht THE EXCEPTION AND THE RULE Director: Carlos Medina	Premiere: 10 February 1980 52 performances to 19 March 1985
91	Volker Braun SIMPLEX DEUTSCH Director: Piet Drescher	Premiere: 26 April 1980 22 performances to 8 May 1981
92	William Shakespeare THE TAMING OF THE SHREW Directors: Christoph Brück/Wolf Bunge	Premiere: 29 April 1980 38 performances to 12 December 1981

Season 1980/81

93	Mikhail Shatrov BLUE HORSES ON RED GRASS Director: Christoph Schroth	Premiere: 3 October 1980 248 performances to 27 March 1990
94	STEPHAN HERMLIN EVENING NR. 1: Led by: Jochen Ziller	Premiere: 3 October 1980 2 performances to 1 December 1980
95	Bertolt Brecht MAN EQUALS MAN Director: Konrad Zschiedrich	Premiere: 27 February 1981 157 performances to 2 February 1988
96	Bertolt Brecht TURANDOT Directors: Manfred Wekwerth/Joachim Tenschert	Premiere: 22 March 1981 17 performances to 11 June 1982

Season 1981/82

97	Bertolt Brecht/Kurt Weill THE THREEPENNY OPERA Led by: Manfred Wekwerth/Konrad Zschiedrich	Premiere: 2 October 1981 118 performances to14 July 1985
98	Antoine de Saint-Exupéry THE LITTLE PRINCE Director: Carlos Medina	Premiere: 15 November 1981 158 performances to 24 March 1989

99	Friedrich Dürrenmatt THE PHYSICISTS Director: Jochen Ziller	Premiere: 25 March 1982 33 performances to 17 December 1983
100	WAR LIES IN MAN'S NATURE Montage by Wolfgang Pintzka Director: Wolfgang Pintzka	Premiere: 29 March 1982 2 performances to 27 April 1982
101	WHERE TRUE LOVE REIGNS, OR WWI NEVER TOOK PLACE Text by: Jürgen Hart Director: Christoph Brück	Premiere: 1 April 1982 35 performances to 24 January 1984
102	HUAC – THE CASE OF EISLER Montage by Gudrun und Hans Bunge Directors: Christoph Brück/Wolf Bunge	Premiere: 15 June 1982 27 performances to 14 December 1983

Season 1982/83

103	Hanns Eisler JOHANN FAUSTUS Directors: Manfred Wekwerth/Joachim Tenschert	Premiere: 2 October 1982 34 performances to 22 February 1986
104	Volker Braun TINKA Director: Konrad Zschiedrich	Premiere: 3 December 1982 27 performances to 6 March 1984
105	Bertolt Brecht DRUMS IN THE NIGHT Director: Christoph Schroth	Premiere: 19 March 1983 27 performances to 21 October 1984
106	Aeschylus THE PERSIANS Directors: Hans-Joachim Frank/Klaus Noack	Premiere: 22 March 1983 21 performances to 1 October 1984

Season 1983/84

107	Patrick Süskind THE DOUBLE BASS Directors: Jürgen Kern/Hein Trilling	Premiere: 8 October 1983 147 performances to 27 September 1992
108	Bertolt Brecht THE DAYS OF THE COMMUNE Director: Carlos Medina	Premiere: 18 December 1983 15 performances to 8 December 1984
109	Manfred Karge MAN TO MAN Director: Peter Konwitschny	Premiere: 11 February 1984 59 performances to 13 May 1988
110	Johann Wolfgang von Goethe FAUST SCENES (URFAUST) Director: Horst Sagert	Premiere: 31 March 1984 59 performances to 13 May 1988

Season 1984/95

111	DIDN'T YOU KNOW? DON'T YOU KNOW? (REVUE) Led by: Jürgen Kern/Hein Trilling	Premiere: 20 October 1984 82 performances to 31December 1987

112	Peter Weiss	Premiere: 18 November 1984
	THE NEW TRIAL	20 performances to 2 May 1986
	Director: Axel Richter	
113	KURT WEILL EVENING: FROM	Premiere: 19 January 1985
	THE SCHIFFBAUERDAMM TO	52 performances to 31 January 1992
	BROADWAY	
	Led by: Rainer Böhm/Jochen	
	Ziller/Jürgen Scherbera	
114	Georg Seidel	Premiere: 23 February 1985
	JOCHEN SCHANOTTA	18 performances to 27 March 1986
	Director: Christoph Brück	
115	STEPHAN HERMLIN EVENING	Premiere: 13 April 1985
	NR. 2	5 performances to 20 July 1986
	Led by: Jochen Ziller	
116	William Shakespeare	Premiere: 15 June 1985
	TROILUS AND CRESSIDA	52 performances to 1 February 1989
	Directors: Manfred Wekwerth/Joachim	
	Tenschert	

Season 1985/86

117	PETER WEISS EVENING	Premiere: 8 October 1985
	Led by: Jochen Ziller	5 performances to 20 July 1986
118	Carl Sternheim	Premiere: 14 November 1985
	CITIZEN SCHIPPEL	62 performances to 19 March 1989
	Director: Fritz Marquardt	
119	After Maurice Maeterlinck	Premiere: 1 February 1986
	CHAMBER MUSIC VII: THE BLIND	8 performances
	Led by: Paul-Heinz Dittrich/Hans-	
	Joachim Frank/Klaus Noack/Jörg Mihan	
120	Federico Garcia Lorca	Premiere: 18 February 1986
	PLAY WITHOUT A TITLE	12 performances to 7 March 1987
	Director: Alejandro Quintana	
121	PRAISING THE REVOLUTIONARY,	Premiere: 5 April 1986
	OR THE UTILITY OF DIALECTICS	20 performances to 20 April 1986
	Directors: Christoph Brück/Günther	
	Schmidt	
122	Uwe Saeger	Premiere: 7 April 1986
	BEYOND GUILT	42 performances to 3 January 1990
	Directors: Jürgen Kern/Hein Trilling	

Season 1986/87

123	Carl Zuckmayer	Premiere: 9 October 1986
	THE CAPTAIN OF KÖPENICK	137 performances to 8 July 1992
	Director: Christoph Brück	
124	Dario Fo	Premiere: 7 December 1986
	ELISABETH, ALMOST BY	60 performances to 18 July 1989
	CHANCE A WOMAN	
	Directors: Manfred Wekwerth/	
	Alejandro Quintana	

125	Jorge Diaz	Premiere: 12 February 1987
	THIS LONG, LONG NIGHT	11 performances to 4 November 1988
	Director: Alejandro Quintana	
126	Bertolt Brecht	Premiere: 16 June 1987
	DOWNFALL OF THE EGOIST	44 performances to 20 February 1991
	JOHANN FATZER	
	Directors: Manfred Wekwerth/Joachim	
	Tenschert	

Season 1987/88

127	Marieluise Fleißer	Premiere: 30 October 1987
	PURGATORY IN INGOLSTADT	15 performances to 12 November 1988
	Director: Axel Richter	
128	Samuel Beckett	Premiere: 17 November 1987
	PLAY	5 performances to 21 February 1988
	Led by: Paul-Heinz Dittrich/	
	Hans-Joachim Frank/Klaus Noack/	
	Jörg Mihan	
129	Heiner Müller	Premiere: 29 November 1987
	WATERFRONT WASTELAND	
	MEDEAMATERIAL LANDSCAPE	
	WITH ARGONAUTS	
	Director: Peter Konwitschny	
130	Bertolt Brecht	Premiere: 12 December 1987
	BAAL	62 performances to 19 July 1992
	Director: Alejandro Quintana	
131	Bertolt Brecht	Premiere: 10 February 1988
	THE MOTHER	20 performances to 30 March 1989
	Directors: Manfred Wekwerth/Joachim	
	Tenschert	

Season 1988/89

132	Volker Braun	Premiere: 28 September 1988
	LENIN'S DEATH	40 performances to 19 July 1990
	Director: Christoph Schroth	
133	Heiner Müller	Premiere: 20 January 1989
	GERMANIA DEATH IN BERLIN	48 performances to 7 April 1991
	Director: Fritz Marquardt	
134	Nikolai Erdman	Premiere: 26 March 1989
	THE SUICIDE	38 performances to 12 April 1992
	Director: Manfred Wekwerth	
135	Georg Seidel	Premiere: 6 May 1989
	CARMEN KITTEL	25 performances to 7 July 1990
	Director: Jochen Ziller	
136	Sergei Tretyakov	Premiere: 22 July 1989
	I WANT A BABY!	10 performances to 6 August 1989
	Director: Günter Schmidt	

Season 1989/90

137 Heiner Müller   Premiere: 16 December 1989
     THE ROAD OF TANKS I–V   22 performances to 22 May 1990
     Director: Christoph Schroth
138 DON'T YOU BELIEVE IT! (REVUE)   Premiere: 10 March 1990
     Led by: Anna-Christine Naumann   8 performances to 14 July 1990
139 Walter Jens   Premiere: 25 March 1990
     THE CASE OF JUDAS   16 performances to 17 June 1992
     Director: Holger Teschke
140 Slawomir Mrozek   Premiere: 28 April 1990
     TANGO   33 performances to 11 May 1992
     Director: Herbert Olschok
141 Heinrich von Kleist   Premiere: 16 June 1990
     PRINCE FRIEDRICH OF   19 performances to 21 April 1991
     HOMBURG
     Director: Manfred Wekwerth

Season 1990/91

142 Thomas Brasch   Premiere: 29 September 1990
     ROTTER   21 performances to 25 October 1991
     Director: Christoph Schroth
143 Georg Seidel   Premiere: 19 January 1991
     YOUTH VILLA   55 performances to 29 April 1996
     Director: Fritz Marquardt
144 Raymond Cousse   Premiere: 23 February 1991
     THE PIG'S STRATEGY   16 performances to 30 May 1992
     Director: Aljoscha Westermann
145 Bertolt Brecht   Premiere: 29 March 1991
     THE GOOD PERSON OF   50 performances to 11 December 1992
     SZECHWAN
     Director: Alejandro Quintana
146 Bertolt Brecht   Premiere: 10 April 1991
     LOVE AND REVOLUTION   42 performances to 15 March 1997
     Led by: Carmen-Maja
     Antoni/Hans-Peter
     Reinecke/Karl-Heinz Nehring

Season 1991/92

147 Bertolt Brecht   Premiere: 3 September 1991
     SCHWEYK   27 performances to 10 July 1992
     Director: Manfred Wekwerth
148 Heinrich von Kleist   Premiere: 8 September 1991
     THE SCHROFFENSTEIN FAMILY   31 performances to 5 December 1992
     Director: Christoph Schroth
149 José Sanchis Sinisterra   Premiere: 1 October 1991
     AY, CARMELA!   23 performances to 17 June 1992
     Director: Alejandro Quintana
150 Eugène Labiche   Premiere: 31 December 1991
     AN ITALIAN STRAW HAT   12 performances to 7 July 1992
     Director: Manfred Wekwerth

151	Ernst Barlach	Premiere: 2 February 1992
	THE POOR COUSIN	12 performances to 26 June 1992
	Director: Fritz Marquardt	
152	Werner Schwab	Premiere: 4 April 1992
	PEOPLE ANNIHILATION, OR MY	63 performances to 19 January 1996
	LIVER IS USELESS	
	Director: Herbert Olschok	
153	Gerhart Hauptmann	Premiere: 4 June 1992
	BEFORE SUNRISE	18 performances to 9 December 1992
	Director: Christoph Schroth	

Season 1992/93

154	William Shakespeare	Premiere: 10 January 1993
	PERICLES	35 performances to 2 June 1993
	Director: Peter Palitzsch	
155	Rolf Hochhuth	Premiere: 10 February 1993
	WESSIS IN WEIMAR	43 performances to 15 May 1993
	Director: Einar Schleef	
156	Peter Turrini	Premiere: 20 February 1993
	GRILLPARZER IN THE SEX SHOP	29 performances to 25 May 1994
	Director: Peter Palitzsch	
157	Ödön von Horváth	Premiere: 9 April 1993
	SLADEK, OR THE BLACK ARMY	22 performances to 18 April 1994
	Director: Fritz Marquardt	
158	After Cesare Zavattini	Premiere: 13 June 1993
	MIRACLE IN MILAN	59 performances to 11 June 1995
	Director: Peter Zadek	

Season 1993/94

159	Bertolt Brecht/Heiner Müller	Premiere: 30 September 1993
	DUEL TRACTOR FATZER	34 performances to 11 December 1996
	Director: Heiner Müller	
160	Bertolt Brecht	Premiere: 15 October 1993
	THE BREAD SHOP	18 performances to 28 May 1994
	Director: Thomas Heise	
161	Bertolt Brecht	Premiere: 21 November 1993
	LIFE STORY OF THE MAN BAAL	
	Director: Peter Palitzsch	
162	Sean O'Casey	Premiere: 13 December 1993
	JUNO AND THE PAYCOCK	19 performances to 21 May 1994
	Director: Fritz Marquardt	
163	Bertolt Brecht	Premiere: 18 December 1993
	HE WHO SAYS YES AND HE WHO	20 performances to 14 November 1994
	SAYS NO	
	Director: Peter Zadek	
164	William Shakespeare	Premiere: 8 January 1994
	THE MERCHANT OF VENICE	63 performances to 29 October 1995
	Director: Peter Zadek	

165	Heiner Müller	Premiere: 11 March 1994
	QUARTETT	57 performances to 21 September 1997
	Director: Heiner Müller	
166	Tankred Dorst	Premiere: 23 April 1994
	FERNANDO KRAPP HAS	7 performances
	WRITTEN ME THIS LETTER	
	Director: Peter Palitzsch	
167	Friedrich Hölderlin	Premiere 2 June 1994
	PHARSALIA	21 performances to 10 June 1995
	Director: Stephan Suschke	

Season 1994/95

168	Eugène Ionesco	Premiere: 9 September 1994
	THE BALD PRIMADONNA	
	Director: Elisabeth Gabriel	
169	Edward Bond	Premiere: 23 September 1994
	OLLY'S PRISON	20 performances to 20 January 1995
	Director: Peter Palitzsch	
170	Heiner Müller	Premiere: 24 September 1994
	CEMENT	9 performances to 7 October 1994
	Director: Thomas Heise	
171	William Shakespeare	Premiere: 14 October 1994
	ANTONY AND CLEOPATRA	43 performances to 14 February 1995
	Director: Peter Zadek	
172	After Else Lasker-Schüler	Premiere: 9 November 1994
	THE TRIP TO JERUSALEM	43 performances to 28 August 1998
	Director: Brigitte Landes	
173	LOVE LETTERS TO HITLER	Premiere: 12 November 1994
	Director: Stephan Suschke	12 performances to 21 January 1996
174	Franz Xaver Kroetz	Premiere: 21 December 1994
	I AM THE PEOPLE	25 performances to 12 June 1995
	Led by: Peter Zadek	
175	Henrik Ibsen	Premiere: 25 January 1995
	EYOLF	49 performances to 25 April 1999
	Director: Fritz Marquardt	
176	Brendan Behan	Premiere: 10 March 1995
	THE HOSTAGE	8 performances to 30 April 1995
	Directors: Elisabeth Gabriel/Ulrike	
	Maack	
177	Samuel Beckett	Premiere: 19 March 1995
	ENDGAME	34 performances to 15 June 1996
	Directors: Peter Palitzsch/Karl Kneidl	
178	Franz Xaver Kroetz	Premiere: 7 April 1995
	DAS NEST	12 performances to 25 June 1995
	Director: Nino Sandow	
179	Harold Pinter	Premiere: 26 April 1995
	MOONLIGHT	
	Director: Peter Zadek	

180	Michael Wildenhain IN THE SHADOW CAST BY THE MOON HANSEL UND GRETEL Director: Thomas Heise	Premiere: 7 May 1995 16 performances to 14 November 1995
181	Bertolt Brecht THE RESISTIBLE RISE OF ARTURO UI Director: Heiner Müller	Premiere 3 June 1995 399 performances to Summer 2014

Season 1995/96

182	Bertolt Brecht ON FASHION FOR MEN AND OTHER DISASTERS Director: Manfred Karge	Premiere: 11 October 1995 10 performances to 14 April 1996
183	Heiner Müller PHILOCTETES Director: Josef Szeiler	Premiere: 17 November 1995 2 performances to 20 November 1995
184	Manfred Karge KILLER FISH Director: Claudia Bosse	Premiere: 2 December 1995
185	STERNTALER IN SLOB WOOD Director: Corinna Harfouch	Premiere: 6 December 1995 13 performances to 30 December 1995
186	Heiner Müller THE BUILDING SITE Director: Thomas Heise	Premiere: 3 February 1996 23 performances to 30 October 1996
187	Anna Langhoff SCHMIDT DEUTSCHLAND THE PINK GIANT Director: Anna Langhoff	Premiere: 9 February 1996
188	Thomas Brasch MERCEDES Director: Veit Schubert	Premiere: 15 February 1996
189	Bertolt Brecht MR PUNTILA AND HIS MAN MATTI Director: Einar Schleef	Premiere: 17 February 1996 38 performances to 2 October 1996
190	Lothar Trolle THE TRENCH Director: Armin Petras	Premiere: 3 April 1996 11 performances to 2 June 1996
191	Heiner Müller THE MISSION Director: Frank Castorf	Premiere: 5 June 1996 20 performances to 18 June 1997
192	Heiner Müller GERMANIA 3 GHOSTS AT DEAD MAN Director: Martin Wuttke	Premiere: 19 June 1996 28 performances to 15 June 1997

466   Appendix

Season 1996/97

193	Eugène Ionesco THE KING DIES Director: Karin Henkel	Premiere: 12 November 1996 21 performances to 19 June 1997
194	BRECHT MAYAKOVSKY HANS ALBERS Singer: Nino Sandow	Premiere: 15 November 1996 42 performances to 8 April 1999
195	Stefan Kolditz EVA, HITLER'S LOVER Director: Stephan Suschke	Premiere: 29 November 1996 37 performances to 15 May 1998
196	THE REST IS DISASTER HORROR OR LUST (REVUE) Director: Werner Schroeter	Premiere: 30 December 1996 7 performances to 16 February 1997
197	Charles Spencer Chaplin MONSIEUR VERDOUX Director: Werner Schroeter	Premiere: 19 January 1997 40 performances to 1 May 1998
198	Heiner Müller THE PEASANTS Director: Stephan Suschke	Premiere: 28 May 1997 24 performances to 30 April
199	Lothar Trolle THE HOMEWORKER Director: Vera Herzberg	Premiere: 13 June 1997 12 performances to 19 April 1998
200	Dorothy Lane/Kurt Weill HAPPY END Led by: Bärbel Jaksch	Premiere: 20 June 1997 11 performances to 6 May 1998
201	Bertolt Brecht BRECHT FRAGMENTS	Premiere: 27 June 1997 5 performances to 4 July 1997

Season 1997/98

202	Bertolt Brecht/Hans Eisler THE MEASURES TAKEN Director: Klaus Emmerich	Premiere: 13 September 1997 46 performances to 13 February 1999
203	PROJECT RAF Director: Paul Plamper	Premiere: 20 September 1997
204	Bertolt Brecht LIFE OF GALILEO Director: B. K. Tragelehn	Premiere: 12 December 1997 42 performances to 27 April 1999
205	Bertolt Brecht JUDITH OF SHIMODA Directors: Judith Kuckart/Jörg Aufenanger	Premiere: 20 December 1997 15 performances to 10 February 1998
206	Bertolt Brecht/Heiner Müller/Fyodor Dostoevsky THE FLIGHT ACROSS THE OCEAN. LANDSCAPE WITH ARGONAUTS. NOTES FROM UNDERGROUND. Director: Robert Wilson	Premiere: 28 January 1998 46 performances to 24 April 1999

207	Wolfgang Krause Zwieback BERLINER EXAMPLE Director: Wolfgang Krause Zwieback	Premiere: 3 March 1998 9 performances to 16 June 1998
208	Bertolt Brecht JAE FLEISCHHACKER Director: Thomas Heise	Premiere: 21 March 1998 10 performances to 14 June 1998
209	Bertolt Brecht I WANT TO LIVE! SUP YOUR SUN! Led by: Peter Palitzsch	Premiere: 3 May 1998 13 performances to 2 April 1999
210	William Shakespeare THE TEMPEST Director: Stephan Suschke	Premiere: 7 June 1998 30 performances to 21 April 1999
211	FAUSTUS 53 Director: Hans-Werner Kroesinger	Premiere: 16 June 1998 6 performances to 26 December 1998

Season 1998/99

212	Bertolt Brecht/Hanns Eisler ROUND HEADS AND POINTED HEADS Director: Klaus Emmerich	Premiere: 19 September 1998 24 performances to 29 April 1999
213	Georg Büchner DANTON'S DEATH Director: Robert Wilson	Premiere: 3 October 1998 25 performances to 5 November 1998
214	Bertolt Brecht I COMMAND MY HEART Director: Nino Sandow	Premiere: 28 November 1998 11 performances to 11 April 1999
215	Heiner Müller HERACLES Director: Klaus Emmerich	Premiere: 13 March 1999 10 performances to 28 April
216	Heiner Müller PHILOCTETES Director: Stephen Suschke	Premiere: 1 April 1999 10 performances to 28 April

Select bibliography

PRIMARY WORKS BY BRECHT AND WEIGEL

Berliner Ensemble/Helene Weigel (eds.), *Theaterarbeit: 6 Aufführungen des Berliner Ensembles* (Dresden: Dresdner Verlag, 1952).

Brecht, Bertolt, *Große kommentierte Berliner und Frankfurter Ausgabe*, ed. by Werner Hecht, Jan Knopf, Werner Mittenzwei and Klaus-Detlef Müller (Berlin and Frankfurt/Main: Aufbau and Suhrkamp, 1988–2000) (= Complete Works in German). References give volume and page numbers.

Brecht, Bertolt, *Letters 1913–1956*, ed. by John Willett (London: Methuen, 1990).

Brecht, Bertolt, *Journals 1934–1955*, ed. by John Willett (London: Methuen, 1993).

Brecht, Bertolt, *Collected Plays*, ed. by John Willett and Ralph Mannheim, vol. 6. (London: Methuen, 1994).

Brecht, Bertolt, *Der Untergang des Egoisten Johann Fatzer*, ed. by Heiner Müller (Leipzig: Suhrkamp, 1994).

Brecht, Bertolt, *Brecht on Art and Politics*, ed. by Tom Kuhn and Steve Giles (London: Methuen, 2003).

Brecht, Bertolt, *Brecht on Performance*, ed. by Tom Kuhn, Steve Giles and Marc Silberman (London: Bloomsbury, 2014).

Brecht, Bertolt, *Brecht on Theatre*, ed. by Marc Silberman, Steve Giles and Tom Kuhn, 3rd edn (London: Bloomsbury, 2014).

Brecht, Bertolt and Ruth Berlau, *Die Gewehre der Frau Carrar* (Dresden: Verlag der Kunst, 1952).

Weigel, Helene, 'Gemeinsam studieren', *Theater der Zeit*, 5 (1953), pp. 7–8.

Weigel, Helene, *'Wir sind zu berühmt, um überall zu hinzugehen': Briefwechsel 1935–1971*, ed. by Stefan Mahlke (Berlin: Theater der Zeit, 2000).

SECONDARY AND OTHER PRIMARY WORKS

Abusch, Alexander, 'Brecht im Geiste Brechts', *Neues Deutschland*, 17 February 1962.

ADN, 'BE: *Adolf Hitler* von Michael Koerbl entfällt', *Die Welt*, 9 October 1996.

ADN, 'Krise am BE: Kultursenat fühlt sich erpreßt', *Der Tagesspiegel*, 8 October 1998.

Anon., 'Das kommunistische ABC', *Telegraf*, 14 January 1951.

Anon., '*Mutter Courage* nicht in Venedig', *Informationen Deutsches Friedenskomitee*, 29 (1951), pp. 43–4.

Anon., 'Un Festival D'Erreurs', *L'Express*, 24 July 1954.

Anon., 'Irisches Lob für Berliner Ensemble', *Der Morgen*, 2 October 1960.

Anon., 'Begeisterung mit Brecht', *BZ am Abend*, 27 April 1962.

Anon., 'Berlin ehrt Bertolt Brecht', *Berliner Zeitung*, 11 February 1963.

Anon., 'Intendant Langhoff jetzt einfacher Schauspieler', *Hamburger Abendblatt*, 9 September 1963.

Anon., untitled, *Stuttgarter Zeitung*, 17 September 1963.

Anon., 'Krag will Brecht-Ensemble sehen', *Frankfurter Allgemeine Zeitung*, 23 September 1963.

Anon., 'Berliner Ensemble nach Kopenhagen', *Volksstimme Österreich*, 3 October 1963.

Anon., '32 Vorhänge', *BZ am Abend*, 13 October 1973.

Anon., 'Gegenentwurf?', *BZ am Abend*, 19 October 1974.

Anon., 'Sieben Fragen an Ruth Berghaus', in Hans-Jochen Irmer (ed.), *Berliner Ensemble:1949–74* (Berlin: Berliner Ensemble, 1974), p. 21.

Anon., untitled, *Theater heute*, 5 (1977), p. 58.

Anon., 'Über die Komik in *Don Juan*', in Werner Hecht (ed.), *Brecht im Gespräch: Diskussionen und Dialoge* (Berlin: Henschel, 1979), pp. 126–33.

Anon., 'Über die Arbeit am Berliner Ensemble', in Werner Hecht (ed.), *Brecht im Gespräch: Diskussionen und Dialoge* (Berlin: Henschel, 1979), pp. 154–74.

Anon., 'Schüler spielen für Schüler', *notate*, 4 (1981), pp. 3–5.

Anon., 'Sorgfältig gearbeitet, aber . . . ', *notate*, 1 (1982), p. 8.

Anon., 'Übernahme', *notate* 2 (1982), p. 12.

Anon., 'Gespräch mit Benno Besson am 17.11.1987 im Kleinen Saal der Akademie der Künste der DDR', *Material zum Theater*, 16 (1988), pp. 66–80.

Anon., 'Berliner Ensemble', in Angela Kuberski (ed.), *Wir treten aus unseren Rollen heraus: Dokumente des Aufbruchs Herbst '89* (Berlin: Verband der Theaterschaffenden, 1990), pp. 22–3.

Anon., 'Wir übernehmen das Brecht-Theater', *BZ*, 31 June 1991.

Anon., 'Berliner Ensemble: Pause bis Januar', *Berliner Kurier*, 2 July 1992.

Anon., 'Zwei Einsprüche aus dem Berliner Ensemble', *Der Tagesspiegel*, 1 April 1993.

Anon., 'Hochhuth contra Wessis am BE', *Der Tagesspiegel*, 6 February 1993.

Anon., 'Der heilige Georg', *Berliner Morgenpost*, 29 April 1995.

Anon., 'BE zum letzten Mal in Gaststätte', *Berliner Kurier*, 8 June 1995.

Anon., 'Gerettet: Das BE-Tourneetheater', *Berliner Zeitung*, 27 August 1995.

Anon., 'Vorschlag: Heise als BE-Intendant', *Berliner Morgenpost*, 23 January 1996.

Anon., 'Einar Schleef wurde fristlos gekündigt', *Frankfurter Rundschau*, 5 December 1996.

Anon., 'Berliner Ensemble sagt Premiere ab', *Berliner Morgenpost*, 19 November 1998.

Anon., '"Einige Stücke inszeniert man eben mehrmals"', in Christa Neubert-Herwig, *Benno Besson: Theater spielen in acht Ländern. Texte – Dokumente – Gespräche* (Berlin: Alexander, 1998), pp. 107–25.

Anon., 'Reese folgt auf Peymann', *Süddeutsche Zeitung*, 1 December 2014.

aro [*sic*], 'Nach einer riesigen nationalen Tragödie', *Frankfurter Allgemeine Zeitung*, 16 February 1996.

Auld, Tim, 'Public Enemy, at the Young Vic', *The Telegraph*, 18 May 2013.

Baker, Barrie, *Censorship in Honecker's Germany: From Volker Braun to Samuel Beckett* (Oxford: Peter Lang, 2007).

Barber, John, 'The Extraordinary Leading Lady who Startled London Last Night', *Daily Express*, 28 August 1956.

Barnett, David, *Literature versus Theatre: Textual Problems and Theatrical Realization in the Later Plays of Heiner Müller* (Frankfurt/Main: Peter Lang, 1998).

Barnett, David, *Rainer Werner Fassbinder and the German Theatre* (Cambridge: Cambridge University Press, 2005).

Barnett, David, '"I have to change myself instead of interpreting myself": Heiner Müller as Post-Brechtian Director', *Contemporary Theatre Review*, 20:1 (2010), pp. 6–20.

Barnett, David, 'Brechtian Theory as Practice: The Berliner Ensemble stages *Der Messingkauf* in 1963', *Theatre, Dance and Performance Training*, 2:1 (2011), pp. 4–17.

Barnett, David, 'Toward a Definition of Post-Brechtian Performance: The Example of *In the Jungle of the Cities* at the Berliner Ensemble, 1971', *Modern Drama*, 54:3 (2011), pp. 333–55.

Barnett, David, 'Undogmatic Marxism: Brecht as Director at the Berliner Ensemble', in Laura Bradley and Karen Leeder (eds.), *Brecht and the GDR: Politics, Culture, Posterity* (Rochester, NY: Camden House, 2011), pp. 25–43.

Barnett, David 'Offending the Playwright: Directors' Theatre and the *Werktreue* Debate', *German Monitor*, 77 (2013), pp. 75–97.

Barnett, David, *Brecht in Practice: Theatre, Theory and Performance* (London: Bloomsbury, 2014).

Barnett, David, 'Encountering a Classic as Other in Post-Brechtian Performance: A Radical Fräulein Julie at the Berliner Ensemble in 1975', in Nina Birkner, Andrea Geier and Urte Helduser, *Spielräume des Anderen: Geschlecht und Alterität im postdramatischen Theater* (Bielefeld: transcript, 2014), pp. 111–28.

Barnett, David, 'The Politics of an International Reputation: The Berliner Ensemble as a GDR Theatre on Tour', in Christopher Balme and Berenika Szymanski-Düll, *Theatre, Globalization and the Cold War* (Basingstoke: Palgrave, forthcoming).

Barthes, Roland, 'Théâtre Capital', *Observateur*, 8 July 1954.

Bazinger, Irene, 'Hack-Stücke-Narzisse', *Junge Welt*, 3 December 1996.

Beck, Hans J., 'Sozialismus: vorwiegend heiter', *Deutsche Volkszeitung*, 21 October 1971.

Beckelmann, Jürgen, 'Galilei – leicht und beschwingt', *Frankfurter Rundschau*, 15 October 1971.

Beckelmann, Jürgen, 'Die siebengescheiten Weißwäscher', *Süddeutsche Zeitung*, 15 February 1973.

Beckelmann, Jürgen, 'Frau Warrens Beruf', *Frankfurter Rundschau*, 3 January 1974.

Beckelmann, Jürgen, 'Die Kunst des Speichelleckens', *Süddeutsche Zeitung*, 1 April 1981.

Beckelmann, Jürgen, 'Politischer Wert gleich Null', *Süddeutsche Zeitung*, 10 October 1981.

Bellmann, Günther, 'Gewichte besser verteilt', *BZ am Abend*, 11 December 1969.

Bellmann, Günther, 'Wo ist der Weg?', *BZ am Abend*, 25 October 1974.

Bentley, Eric, *The Brecht Memoir* (Evanston, IL: Northwestern University Press, 1989).

Berger, Manfred, Manfred Nössig, Fritz Rödel, *et al.*, *Theater in der Zeitenwende: Zur Geschichte des Dramas und Schauspieltheaters in der Deutschen Demokratischen Republik 1945–1968*, vol. 1 (Berlin: Henschel, 1972).

Berger, Manfred *et al.*, *Kulturpolitisches Wörterbuch*, 2nd expanded edn (Berlin: Dietz, 1978).

Berger, Michael, 'Die Inszenierung', *Die Woche*, 23 February 1996.

Bernhardt, Heike, 'German Democratic Republic: Absorbing the Sins of the Fathers', in Jacob D. Lindy and Robert Jay Lifton (eds.), *Beyond Invisible Walls: The Psychological Legacy of Soviet Trauma* (New York: Taylor & Francis, 2001), pp. 59–89.

Billington, Michael, 'When Did "Brechtian" Become Such a Dirty Word?', *The Guardian*, 20 October 2009.

Bilstein, Michael, 'An die Gewehre', *Rheinische Merkur*, 9 July 1971.

Biskup, Harald, '"Landeplätze für Geier sind geräumig"', *Kölner Stadt-Anzeiger*, 20 April 1995.

BM, 'Vollversammlung mit Krach, Wut und Kündigung', *Berliner Morgenpost*, 6 September 1992.

BM/dpa, '"Konflikt liegt auf dem Tisch" am Berliner Ensemble', *Berliner Morgenpost*, 4 July 1992.

BM/dpa, 'Soll nur noch ein Intendant das Berliner Ensemble leiten?', *Berliner Morgenpost*, 18 March 1995.

BM/dpa, 'Kultursenator wandte sich an John Wertheim', *Berliner Morgenpost*, 12 May 1995.

BM/dpa, 'Hochhuth: Kann mir keine Mitarbeit mehr denken', *Berliner Morgenpost*, 6 January 1996.

Bohlmann, Joachim, 'Ein Baal ohne Sinnlichkeit', *Tribüne*, 15 December 1987.

Bömelburg, Wolfgang, *Hobellied für Bertolt Brecht: Ein Theatertischler erzählt* (Berlin: Eulenspiegel, 1997).

Böttger, Uwe-Eckart, 'Für einen praktischen Nutzen der Kunst', *Neue Zeit*, 14 February 1981.

Brackman, Roman, *The Secret File of Joseph Stalin: A Hidden Life* (London: Frank Cass, 2001).

Bradley, Laura, '"Prager Luft" at the Berliner Ensemble? The Censorship of *Sieben gegen Theben*, 1968–9', *German Life and Letters*, 58:1 (2005), pp. 41–54.

Bradley, Laura, 'A Different Political Forum: East German Theatre and the Construction of the Berlin Wall', *Journal of European Studies*, 36:2 (2006), pp. 139–56.

Bradley, Laura, *Brecht and Political Theatre: 'The Mother' on Stage* (Oxford: Oxford University Press, 2006).

Bradley, Laura, 'Contemporary Theatre? Brecht, Peymann & Co. at the Berliner Ensemble', *Contemporary Theatre Review*, 18:1 (2008), pp. 69–79.

Bradley, Laura, *Cooperation and Conflict: GDR Theatre Censorship 1961–1989* (Oxford: Oxford University Press, 2010).

Bradley, Laura, 'Remembering Brecht: Anniversaries at the Berliner Ensemble', in Laura Bradley and Karen Leeder (eds.), *Brecht and the GDR: Politics, Culture, Posterity* (Rochester, NY: Camden House, 2011), pp. 125–44.

Bradley, Laura, and Karen Leeder (eds.), *Brecht and the GDR: Politics, Culture, Posterity* (Rochester, NY: Camden House, 2011).

Braun, Anne, 'Im Namen des Glücks', *Wochenpost*, 26 September 1980.

Braun, Matthias, 'Berthold Viertels erste Berliner Nachkriegsinszenierung: *Wassa Schelesnowa* am Berliner Ensemble: Ein dokumentarischer Bericht', *Kleine Schriften der Gesellschaft für Theatergeschichte*, 36 (1991), pp. 31–51.

Braun, Volker, *Werktage 1977–1989: Arbeitsbuch* (Frankfurt/Main: Suhrkamp, 2009).

Brecht-Schall, Barbara, 'Letter from Barbara Brecht-Schall', *Brecht Yearbook*, 22 (1997), p. 46.

Bronsen, David, 'Brechts Rückkehr 1948', *Die Zeit*, 8 November 1968.

Brug, Manuel, 'Revolte im Kinderzimmer', *Der Tagesspiegel*, 7 June 1996.

Bryant-Bertail, Sarah, *Space and Time in Epic Theater: The Brechtian Legacy* (Rochester, NY: Camden House, 2000).

Bryden, Ronald, 'Off the Peg Coriolanus', *The Guardian*, 9 May 1971.

Buchmann, Ditte, Wera Küchenmeister and Claus Küchenmeister, *'Eine Begabung muß man entmutigen . . . '* (Berlin: Henschel, 1986).

Bunge, Hans, *Brechts Lai-Tu: Erinnerungen und Notate von Ruth Berlau* (Darmstadt: Luchterhand, 1985).

Bürger, Peter, *Theory of the Avant-Garde*, trans. by Michael Shaw (Minneapolis: University of Minnesota Press, 1984).

Buschey, Monika, *Wege zu Brecht: Wie Katharina Thalbach, Benno Besson, Sabine Thalbach, Regine Lutz, Manfred Wekwerth, Käthe Rülicke, Egon Monk und Barbara Brecht – Schall zum Berliner Ensemble fanden* (Berlin: Dittrich, 2007).

Carlson, Marvin, *The Haunted Stage: The Theatre as Memory Machine* (Ann Arbor: University of Michigan Press, 2001).

Carlson, Marvin, 'Claus Peymann and the Performance of Scandal', *Contemporary Theatre Review*, 18:2 (2008), pp. 193–207.

Cleve, Ingeborg, 'Subverted Heritage and Subversive Memory: Weimarer Klassik in the GDR and the Bauerbach Case', in Christian Emden and David Midgely (eds.), *German History, Literature and the Nation* (Berne: Peter Lang, 2004), pp. 355–80.

Daiber, Hans, *Deutsches Theater seit 1945: Bundesrepublik Deutschland, Deutsche Demokratische Republik, Österreich, Schweiz* (Stuttgart: Reclam, 1976).

de Ponte, Susanne, *Caspar Neher – Bertolt Brecht: Eine Bühne für das epische Theater*, ed. by the Deutsches Theatermuseum, Munich (Berlin: Henschel, 2006).

Dermutz, Klaus, 'Paramilitärische Grundausbildung', *Frankfurter Rundschau*, 20 February 1996.

Dermutz, Klaus, 'Spaß mit dem armen B.B.', *Frankfurter Rundschau*, 2 July 1997.

Dermutz, Klaus, 'Stadtansicht', *Frankfurter Rundschau*, 25 March 1998.

Deutscher Bühnenverein (ed.), *Wer spielte Was? Werkstatistik* (Darmstadt: Mykenae, 1998–2000).

df/kob, 'Suschke übernimmt *Umsiedlerin*', *Berliner Zeitung*, 11 April 1997.

Dieckmann, Friedrich, 'Die Tragödie des Coriolan: Shakespeare im Brecht-Theater', *Sinn und Form*, 17: 3 and 4 (1965), pp. 463–89.

Dieckmann, Friedrich, *Karl von Appens Bühnenbilder am Berliner Ensemble: Szenenbilder, Figurinen, Entwürfe und Szenenphotos zu achtzehn Aufführungen* (Berlin: Henschel, 1973).

Dieckmann, Friedrich, 'Eine Antwort', *Theater der Zeit*, 11 (1975), pp. 45–6.

Dieckmann, Friedrich, 'Diskurs über Fräulein Julie', in Dieckmann, *Streifzüge: Aufsätze und Kritiken* (Berlin: Aufbau, 1977), pp. 141–70.

Dieckmann, Friedrich, '*Der große Frieden*', *Thüringische Landeszeitung*, 25 April 1979.

Dieckmann, Friedrich, *Theaterbilder: Studien und Berichte* (Berlin: Henschel, 1979).

Dieckmann, Friedrich, 'Komponenten am Berliner Ensemble', in Dieckmann, *Die Freiheit – ein Augenblick: Texte aus vier Jahrzehnten*, ed. by Therese Hörnigk and Sebastian Kleinschmidt (Berlin: Theater der Zeit, 2002), pp. 85–95.

Dieckmann, Friedrich, *Wer war Brecht? Erkundungen und Erörterungen* (Berlin: Aufbau, 2003).

Dieckmann, Friedrich and Karl-Heinz Drescher (eds.), *Die Plakate des Berliner Ensembles 1949–1989* (Hamburg: Europäische Verlagsanstalt, 1992).

Ding, Loo, Fan Chang, Shin-nan Chu, Elisabeth Hauptmann, and Manfred Wekwerth, *Hirse für die Achte*, with additional material by Manfred Wekwerth (Leipzig: Friedrich Hoffmann, 1956).

Döderin, Karl Reinhold, 'Die Moritat vom bösen Kulaken', *Neue Zeit*, 3 June 1953.

Döderlin, Karl Reinhold, 'Am Anfang der wissenschaftlichen Epoche', *Neue Zeit*, 22 January 1956.

Doll, Alfred, 'Helene Weigel und das "Berliner Ensemble"', *Vorwärts*, 28 November 1949.

Doll, Alfred, 'Ihre Kunst gilt dem Volke', *Nachtexpreß*, 29 January 1951.

dpa, 'Brecht umbrochen', *die tageszeitung*, 30 August 1991.

dpa, 'Neue Leitung für Berliner Ensemble', *Neues Deutschland*, 7 September 1991.

dpa, 'Palitzsch wird Leiter des Berliner Ensembles', *Der Tagesspiegel*, 31 December 1991.

dpa, 'Zadeks neue Inszenierung', *Berliner Zeitung*, 2 December 1992.

dpa, 'Biermann will nicht ans Berliner Ensemble', *Süddeutsche Zeitung*, 19 January 1996.

dpa, 'Peymann kommt', *Frankfurter Allgemeine Zeitung* 30 October 1998.

dpa/FR, 'Mühe bewirbt sich – Wuttke im Gespräch', *Frankfurter Rundschau*, 26 January 1996.

dpa/lbn, 'Widerstand der Betroffenen gegen Theatergutachten', *Volksblatt*, 30 April 1991.

dpa/JW, 'Das "schwierige Theater"', *Junge Welt*, 24 October 1991.

dpa/ND, 'BE geht an Hochhuths Stiftung', *Neues Deutschland*, 8 March 1996.

Dymschitz, Alexander, 'Ein gewöhnliches Genie', *Theater der Zeit*, 14(1966), p. 14.

eb, 'BE gegen Privatisierung', *Berliner Zeitung*, 10 March 1992.

Ebert, Gerhard, 'Undurchsichtiges Mysterium um Margerete', *Neues Deutschland*, 4 April 1984.

Ebert, Gerhard, 'Auf Gammeltour durch unsere Wirklichkeit', *Neues Deutschland*, 9–10 April 1985.

Ebert, Gerhard, 'Begegnung mit dem letzten Stück von García Lorca', *Neues Deutschland*, 25 February 1986.

Ebert, Gerhard, 'Rationale Kraft und poetische Frische Brechtscher Gedanken', *Neues Deutschland*, 12 February 1988.

Ebert, Gerhard, 'Wer eine Provokation erwartet hatte, sah sich enttäuscht', *Neues Deutschland*, 23 February 1993.

Ebert, Gerhard, 'Neu nachdenken in neuer Lage', *Neues Deutschland*, 20 December 1993.

Ebert, Gerhard, 'Stalingrad aus der Loge betrachtet', *Neues Deutschland*, 21 June 1996.

Ebert, Gerhard, 'Wenig Hoffnung für die Wissenschaft', *Neues Deutschland*, 15 December 1997.

Ebert, Gerhart, 'Okichis Heldentat', *Neues Deutschland*, 23 December 1997.

Ebert, Gerhard, 'Reich und reich gesellt sich gern', *Neues Deutschland*, 23 September 1998.

Eichler, Rolf-Dieter, 'Die andere *Mutter* – die anderen Mütter', *National Zeitung*, 22 October 1974.

Eichler, Rolf-Dieter, 'Wahrheit ist gefunden – wer setzt sie durch?', *Nationalzeitung*, 13 February 1978.

Eichler, Rolf-Dieter, 'Ins Ziellose', *Nationalzeitung*, 27 February 1985.

Eichler, Rolf-Dieter, 'Versuch mit *Baal* am Baal gescheitert', *Nationalzeitung*, 15 December 1987.

Eichler, Rolf-Dieter, 'Bruchstücke aus einem großen Zusammenhang', *Nationalzeitung*, 4 October 1988.

Engel, Erich, 'Über die Neuinszenierung', in Werner Hecht (ed.), *Brechts 'Dreigroschenoper'* (Frankfurt/Main: Suhrkamp, 1985), pp. 168–71.

Engelmann, Roger, Bernd Florath, Helge Heidemeyer, Daniela Münkel, Arno Polzin and Walter Süß, *Das MfS-Lexikon: Begriffe, Personen und Strukturen der Staatssicherheit der DDR* (Berlin: Christoph Links, 2011).

Erpenbeck, Fritz, 'Einige Bemerkungen zu Brechts *Mutter Courage*', *Die Weltbühne*, 4:3 (1949), pp. 101–3.

Erpenbeck, Fritz, 'Mit unerbittlicher Konsequenz', *Neues Deutschland*, 24 December 1949.

Erpenbeck, Fritz, 'Anknüpfen – aber wie? Unser klassisches Erbe in Theorie und Praxis', *Theater der Zeit*, 9 (1951), pp. 4–8.

Erpenbeck, Fritz, 'Episches Theater oder Dramatik?', *Theater der Zeit*, 12 (1954), pp. 16–21.

FAZ, 'Berliner Ensemble mgH', *Frankfurter Allgemeine Zeitung*, 6 October 1992.

FAZ, 'Großer Hunger', *Frankfurter Allgemeine Zeitung*, 9 June 1995.

Ferran, Peter W., 'Molière's *Don Juan* adapted for Brecht's Berliner Ensemble', *Contemporary Theatre Review*, 6: 2 (1997), pp. 13–40.

Flierl, Thomas, 'Vorwort', in Gertraude Hoffmann and Klaus Höpcke (eds.), *'Das Sicherste ist die Veränderung': Hans-Joachim Hoffmann: Kulturminister der DDR und häufig verdächtigter Demokrat* (Berlin: Dietz, 2003), pp. 7–9.

Friedrich, Detlef, 'Das Theaterbüro tagte und brach abends das Schweigen', *Berliner Zeitung*, 9 March 1995.

Friedrich, Detlef, 'Brecht unter den Klangteppich gekehrt', *Berliner Zeitung*, 5 May 1998.

Friedrich, Detlef, 'Nicht faul, sondern bedürftig', *Berliner Zeitung*, 21 September 1998.

Fuegi, John, 'Interview mit Manfred Wekwerth', *Brecht Yearbook*, 8 (1978), pp. 120–8.

Fuegi, John, *Bertolt Brecht: Chaos according to Plan* (Cambridge: Cambridge University Press, 1987).

Funke, Christoph, 'Das Gangsterstück im großen Stil', *Der Morgen*, 25 March 1959.

Funke, Christoph, 'Also wissense, ja!', *Der Morgen*, 12 February 1965.

Funke, Christoph, 'Die Wissenschaft – ein Krüppel?', *Der Morgen*, 18 April 1965.

Funke, Christoph, 'Kühle Legende ohne Sinnlichkeit', *Der Morgen*, 21 June 1968.

Funke, Christoph, 'Der Dichter und seine Zeit', *Der Morgen*, 3 October 1969.

Funke, Christoph, 'Mißbrauch der Naivität', *Der Morgen*, 16 January 1970.

Funke, Christoph, 'Unruhe und große Fragen', *Der Morgen*, 22 March 1972.

Funke, Christoph, 'Der Held will Mensch sein', *Der Morgen*, 5 October 1972.

Funke, Christoph, 'Bekannte Fabel in neuer Sicht', *Der Morgen*, 20 October 1974.

Funke, Christoph, 'Ironie der Genauigkeit', *Der Morgen*, 11 October 1977.

Funke, Christoph, 'Ein Tag im Leben Lenins', *Der Morgen*, 6 October 1980.

Funke, Christoph, 'Ohne Schärfe, Spaß und Protest', *Der Morgen*, 5 October 1981.

Funke, Christoph, 'Psychologie des Spießbürgers', *Der Morgen*, 22 March 1983.

Funke, Christoph, 'Vom unaufhaltsamen Sterben', *Der Morgen*, 21 January 1991.

Funke, Christoph, 'Das Berliner Ensemble am Schiffbauerdamm 1954–1992', in Christoph Funke and Wolfgang Jansen, *Theater am Schiffbauerdamm: Die Geschichte einer Berliner Bühne* (Berlin: Christoph Links, 1992), pp. 165–207.

Funke, Christoph, 'Müller in Schwarz-Weiß', *Der Tagesspiegel*, 3 April 1999.

Funke, Christoph and Wolfgang Jansen, *Theater am Schiffbauerdamm: Die Geschichte einer Berliner Bühne* (Berlin: Christoph Links, 1992).

Galfert, Ilse, '*Theaterarbeit – Sechs Aufführungen des Berliner Ensembles*', *Theater der Zeit*, 11 (1952), pp. 14–17 (16).

Gautier, Jean-Jacques, 'Au Festival de Paris *Mère Courage* de Bertolt Brecht', *Le Figaro*, 1 July 1954.

Gautier, Jean-Jacques, 'L'Allemagne de l'est présente: *Le Cercle de Craie Caucasien*', *Le Figaro*, 22 June 1955.

Generlich, Helga, 'Stimmbildung und Sprecherziehung', in BE/Weigel (eds.), *Theaterarbeit*, pp. 390–3.

Gerberding, Christine, 'Aufstieg und Absturz', *Berliner Morgenpost*, 28 January 1998.

Gerhard, Carsten, 'Oh, du schöne Hoffnungslosigkeit', *Die Welt*, 5 May 1998.

Gersch, Wolfgang, 'Aktueller Versuch mit Brecht im BE', *Tribüne*, 23 October 1974.

Gersch, Wolfgang, 'Von einer Suche ohne Ankunft', *Tribüne*, 28 February 1985.

Geschonneck, Erwin, *Meine unruhigen Jahre*, ed. by Günter Agde (Berlin: Dietz, 1984).

GG, 'Der Weg ist frei', *Der Tagesspiegel*, 5 March 1997.

Gläss, Siegfried, 'Eine hilfreiche Hand für unsere Dramatischen Zirkel', *Neues Deutschland*, 27 April 1954.

Gleiß, Jochen, 'Theatermachen für die achtziger Jahre', *Theater der Zeit*, 8 (1975), pp. 53–4.

Gloger, Christine, 'Was sie für richtig hielt, hat sie auch gemacht', in Irene Bazinger (ed.), *Regie: Ruth Berghaus. Geschichten aus der Produktion* (Berlin: Rotbuch, 2010), pp. 167–76.

Goertz, Heinrich, 'Wie Brecht sich das "Schiff" unter den Nagel riß', *Die Welt*, 9 December 1972.

Goldberg, Henryk, 'Weshalb mich Schanotta nicht interessiert', *Junge Welt*, 5 March 1985.

Goldhahn, Johannes, 'Nachdenken über Naivität', Brecht-Zentrum der DDR (ed.), *Brecht 85: Zur Ästhetik Brechts. Fortsetzung eines Gesprächs über Brecht und Marxismus. Dokumentation* (Berlin: Henschel, 1986), pp. 212–23.

Göpfert, Peter Hans, 'Mutter Corsage', *Der Abend*, 23 October 1974.

Göpfert, Peter Hans, 'Misere im deutschen Land oder Einschüchterung durch Klassizität', *Die Welt*, 8 October 1977.

Göpfert, Peter Hans, 'Die Sinnlichkeit eines Schriftgelehrten', *Die Welt*, 13 February 1978.

Göpfert, Peter Hans, 'Die Figur behauptet frech ihr Eigenleben', *Berliner Morgenpost*, 6 June 1995.

Göpfert, Peter Hans, 'Irgendwie geht es um Klassenkampf', *Berliner Morgenpost*, 19 February 1996.

Göpfert, Peter Hans, 'Fragment! Fragment! Brecht! Brecht!', *Berliner Morgenpost*, 29 June 1997.

Göpfert, Peter Hans, 'Ein mürrischer Allerweltstyp', *Berliner Morgenpost*, 14 December 1997.

Göpfert, Peter Hans, 'Ein Hoch auf die Milch', *Berliner Morgenpost*, 22 December 1997.

Göpfert, Peter Hans, 'Der Typ mit der Tolle', *Berliner Morgenpost*, 9 June 1998.

g.r. [sic], 'Die Vorgänge im Berliner Ensemble', *Der Tagesspiegel*, 31 March 1993.

Grack, Günther, 'Der Charme der "Nagten wahrheit [sic]"', *Der Tagesspiegel*, 9 May 1995.

Grack, Günther, 'Gespensterreigen', *Der Tagesspiegel*, 20 June 1996.

Grack, Günther, '"Aufklärerische Anstalt"', *Der Tagesspiegel*, 2 May 1998.

G. W., 'Berliner Ensemble spielt *Urfaust*', *Neue Zeit* 26 April 1952.

Haas, Birgit, *Theater der Wende – Wendetheater* (Würzburg: Königshaus & Neumann, 2004).

Hacks, Peter, *Die Erzählungen* (Hamburg: Lutz Schulenburg, 1995).

Hacks, Peter, *Die Maßgaben der Kunst*, vol. 1 (Berlin: Eulenspiegel, 2003).

Hade, 'Gastspiel des "Berliner Ensembles"', *Märkische Union*, 26 April 1952.

Hager, Kurt, *Erinnerungen* (Leipzig: Faber & Faber, 1996).

Hahn, Karl-Claus, 'Hitparade mit zuviel Zwischentext', *notate* 5 (1981), pp. 8–9.

Hanssen, Paula, *Elizabeth Hauptmann: Brecht's Silent Collaborator* (Bern: Peter Lang, 1995).

Harich, Wolfgang, 'Trotz fortschrittlichen Wollens...', *Die Weltbühne*: 4: 6 (1949).

Harich, Wolfgang, 'Brief an Anton Ackermann', *Sinn und Form*, 50: 6 (1998), pp. 894–903.

Harich, Wolfgang, *Ahnenpass: Versuch einer Autobiographie*, ed. by Thomas Grimm (Berlin: Schwarzkopf & Schwarzkopf, 1999).

Harnisch, Rudolf, 'Gerupfter *Biberpelz* und *Roter Hahn*', *Tägliche Rundschau*, 29 March 1951.

Hasselhorst, Christa, 'Machtwechsel hin, Machtwechsel her', *Die Welt*, 18 September 1998.

Haus, Heinz Uwe, 'Brecht in Post-Wall Germany', in James K. Lyon and Hans-Peter Breuer, *Brecht Unbound: Presented at the International Bertolt Brecht Symposium held at the University of Delaware February 1992* (Newark: University of Delaware Press, 1995), pp. 89–97.

Hauschild, Jan-Christoph, *Heiner Müller oder Das Prinzip Zweifel: Eine Biographie* (Berlin: Aufbau, 2003).

Hayneccio, Martino, *Hans Pfriem der Kühnheit zahlt sich aus*, with *Notate* by Käthe Rülicke (Leipzig: Friedrich Hoffmann, 1955).

Hecht, Werner, *Aufsätze über Brecht* (Berlin: Henschel, 1970).

Hecht, Werner (ed.), *Brecht im Gespräch: Diskussionen und Dialoge* (Berlin: Henschel, 1979).

Hecht, Werner, '"... das muß mal gesagt werden"', *notate*, 2 (1979), pp. 1–2.

Hecht, Werner, 'Wie es mit dem Berliner Ensemble weitergeht', *notate*, 5 (1980), pp. 1–3.

Hecht, Werner, 'Das Vergnügen an einer ernsten Sache: Ein Leben im Dienste Brechts – Erinnerungen von und an Käthe Rülicke', *Der Tagesspiegel*, 3 November 1992.

Hecht, Werner, *Brecht Chronik 1898–1956* (Frankfurt/Main: Suhrkamp, 1997).

Hecht, Werner, '"Der Pudding bewährt sich beim Essen": Brechts "Prüfung" Stanislawskis 1953', in Ingrid Hentschel, Klaus Hoffmann and Florian Vaßen (eds.), *Brecht & Stanislawski und die Folgen: Anregungen für die Theaterarbeit* (Berlin: Henschel, 1997), pp. 57–71.

Hecht, Werner, 'Berliner Ensemble: Einzug der Gladiatoren in das Theater am Schiffbauerdamm', *Dreigroschenheft*, 2 (2000), pp. 5–15.

Hecht, Werner, *Helene Weigel: Eine grosse Frau des 20. Jahrhunderts* (Frankfurt/Main: Suhrkamp, 2000).

Hecht, Werner, *Brecht und die DDR: Die Mühen der Ebenen* (Berlin: Aufbau, 2013).

Heeg, Günther, 'Herr und Knecht, Furcht und Arbeit, Mann und Frau: Einar Schleefs archäologische Lektüre von Brechts Puntila', in *Brecht Yearbook*, 23 (1997), pp. 147–52.

Heeg, Günther, *Klopfzeichen aus dem Mausoleum: Brechtschulung am Berliner Ensemble*, ed. by Stefan Schnabel (Berlin: Vorwerk, 2000).

Hegemann, Karl, 'Scheitern am Berliner Ensemble', *Der Tagesspiegel*, 12 January 1997.

Heidicke, Manfred, 'Heute Abend: *Zement*', *Berliner Zeitung*, 12 October 1973.

Heinke, Lothar, 'Ohne Puder und Perücke', *Der Morgen*, 28 April 1962.

Heise, Thomas, 'Die Eiszeit', *Der Tagesspiegel*, 2 February 1996.

Heiser-Duron, Meredith A., 'Brecht's Political and Cultural Dilemma in the Summer of 1953', *Communications for the International Brecht Society*, 30: 1 and 2 (2001), pp. 47–57.

Heitzenröther, Horst, '*Faust-Szenen* mit bildnerischer Fülle', *National Zeitung*, 10 April 1984.

Hellberg, Martin, 'Armer Kean! Die anorganischen Thesen Bertolt Brechts', *Theater der Zeit*, 10 (1949), pp. 10 and 14 (14).

Herold, Christine, *Mutter des Ensembles: Helene Weigel – ein Leben mit Bertolt Brecht* (Cadolzburg: Ars Vivendi, 2001).

Hess-Wyneken, Susanne, 'Bert Brechts *Herr Puntila und sein Knecht*', *Berlin's* [sic] *Modenblatt*, 1 (1950), p. 22.

Heuwagen, Marianne, '"Ich bin immer ein Optimist"', *Süddeutsche Zeitung* 14 March 1995.

Hildebrandt, Dieter, 'Ist die Mauer eine Barrikade?', *Frankfurter Allgemeine Zeitung*, 24 October 1962.

Hildebrandt, Dieter, 'Oppenheimer, ein Nachfahrer des Galilei', *Frankfurter Allgemeine Zeitung*, 21 April 1965.

Hinz, Melanie, 'Vorspiel und Nachahmung auf Probe', in Hinz and Jens Roselt (eds.), *Chaos und Konzept: Proben und Probieren im Theater* (Berlin: Alexander, 2011), pp. 72–96.

Hochhuth, Rolf, 'Holt Manfred Wekwerth zurück!', *Berliner Morgenpost*, 7 December 1996.

Hof, Gert (ed.), '*Galileo Galilei*' *von Bertolt Brecht: Eine Dokumentation der Aufführung des Berliner Ensembles 1978* (Berlin: Verband der Theaterschaffenden, 1982).

Hof, Gert (ed.), '*Mutter Courage und ihre Kinder*' *von Bertolt Brecht: Eine Dokumentation der Aufführung des Berliner Ensembles 1978* (Berlin: Verband der Theaterschaffenden, 1981).

Hoffmann, Hans-Joachim, 'Theater in unserer Zeit', *Theater der Zeit*, 1 (1975), pp. 2–4.

Holtz, Corinne, *Ruth Berghaus: Ein Porträt* (Hamburg: Europäische Verlagsanstalt, 2005).

Honecker, Erich, 'Schlußwort auf der 4. Tagung des ZK der SED', *Neues Deutschland*, 18 December 1971.

Horst, Michael, 'Mit Sicherheitslinie auf dünnem Eis', *Berliner Morgenpost*, 27 January 1996.

how, '20 Ansprüche, keine Unterlagen', *Die Welt*, 16 May 1995.

Hoyer, Lutz, 'Fünf-Köpfe-Modell beendet', *Berliner Zeitung*, 16 March 1995.

Hurwicz, Angelika, 'Brechts Arbeit mit dem Schauspieler', in Hubert Witt (ed.), *Erinnerungen an Brecht* (Leipzig: Reclam, 1964), pp. 172–5.

Hurwicz, Angelika and Gerda Goedhart, *Brecht inszeniert: 'Der kaukasische Kreidekreis'* (Velber: Friedrich, 1964).

ic [*sic*], 'Aufgefrischter Sturm und Drang', *Neue Zeit*, 16 April 1950.

Iden, Peter, 'Neubeginn im heulenden Elend', *Frankfurter Rundschau*, 12 January 1993.

Iden, Peter, 'Vorhang zu und keine Fragen', *Frankfurter Rundschau*, 4 October 1993.

Iden, Peter, *Peter Palitzsch: Theater muß die Welt verändern* (Berlin: Henschel, 2005).

Irmer, Hans-Jochen, 'Ein Frühlings Erwachen im Berliner Ensemble', *Theater der Zeit* 1 (2002), pp. 57–9.

Irmer, Thomas and Matthias Schmidt, *Die Bühnenrepublik: Theater in der DDR*, ed. by Wolfgang Bergmann (Berlin: Alexander, 2003).

Jacobs, Peter, '"Ich muß die Einnahmen steigern"', *Die Welt*, 19 January 1994.

jal, 'Hochhuth: BE großenteils erworben', *Der Tagesspiegel*, 2 December 1995.

Jameson, Fredric, *Brecht and Method* (London: Verso, 1998).

Jenny, Urs, 'Der ersetzbare Held', *Süddeutsche Zeitung*, 28 September 1964.

Jenny, Urs, 'Pyrrussieg eines Theaterelefanten', *Süddeutsche Zeitung*, 13 February 1967.

Jenny, Urs, 'Brecht, ein auslaufendes Modell', *Der Spiegel*, 2 March 1992.

JW, 'BEerdigung?', *Junge Welt*, 16 June 1995.

Kaltofen, Günter, '*Die Winterschlacht*', *Theater der Zeit*, 2 (1955), pp. 53–5.

Kaiser, Gerhard, 'Eine verlöschende Welt', *BZ am Abend*, 22 December 1949.

Kathrein, Karin, '"Diese generelle Unkultur wird unerträglich"', *Die Welt* 10 March 1995.

Kebir, Sabine, *Helene Weigel: Abstieg in den Ruhm. Eine Biographie* (Berlin: Aufbau, 2000).

Keisch, Henryk, 'Bertolt Brechts *Leben des Galilei*', *Neues Deutschland*, 29 January 1956.

Keisch, Henryk, '"Lebensgefühl" gestern und heute', *Neues Deutschland*, 5 May 1960.

Kerndl, Rainer, 'Brecht-Abend des Berliner Ensembles', *Neues Deutschland*, 12 February 1962.

Kerndl, Rainer, 'Theater in Berlin', *Neues Deutschland*, 9 July 1971.

Kerndl, Rainer, 'Großartiger Galilei', *Neues Deutschland*, 7 October 1971.

Kerndl, Rainer, 'Stilistisches Experiment mit Frank Wedekind', *Neues Deutschland*, 9 March 1974.

Kerndl, Rainer, 'Zeittheater – parteilich und kunstvoll', *Neues Deutschland*, 13 February 1978.

Kersten, Heinz, 'Trauerarbeit', *Frankfurter Rundschau*, undated.

Kitching, Laurence, '*Der Hofmeister*': *A Critical Analysis of Bertolt Brecht's Adaptation of Jacob Michael Reinhold Lenz's Drama* (Munich: Wilhelm Fink, 1976).

Knietzsch, Horst, 'Eine deutsche Tragödie', *Neues Deutschland*, 18 January 1955.

Knopf, Jan, *Bertolt Brecht: Lebenskunst in finsteren Zeiten* (Munich: Hanser, 2012).

Knowles, Ric, *Reading the Material Theatre* (Cambridge: Cambridge University Press, 2004).

kob, 'Wuttke vertagt sein Ultimatum', *Berliner Zeitung*, 3 December 1996.

Koberg, Roland, 'Ende eines Befreiungskampfes nach innen', *Berliner Zeitung*, 5 December 1996.

Koberg, Roland, 'Der letzte Dissident', *Berliner Zeitung*. 30 March 1999.

Kohse, Petra, 'Archaische Rituale im besetzten Land', *General-Anzeiger*, 12 February 1993.

Kohse, Petra, 'Chef des Berliner Ensembles droht mit Rücktritt', *die tageszeitung*, 8 November 1996.

Kohse, Petra, '"Gegen die allmähliche Erstarrung"', *die tageszeitung*, 20 November 1996.

Kohse, Petra, '"Wir wollten den Knechtgeist austreiben": Zwischen Macht und Müller-Erbe', *Die Tageszeitung*, 20 September 1997.

Kohse, Petra, 'Dem fröhlichen Irgendwie fröhnen', *die tageszeitung*, 26 March 1998.

Kraft, Peter (ed.), '*Untergang des Egoisten Johann Fatzer von Bertolt Brecht: Eine Dokumentation der Aufführung des Berliner Ensembles 1987* (Berlin: Verband der Theaterschaffenden, 1987).

Kranz, Dieter, *Berliner Theater: 100 Aufführungen aus drei Jahrzehnten* (Berlin: Henschel, 1990).

Kuberski, Angela, 'Brechts Modellbücher und die Folgen', *notate*, 6 (1984), pp. 4–5.

Kuckhoff, Armin G., 'Unsere Stanislawski-Diskussion', *Theater der Zeit*, 8 (1953), pp. 19–23.

Kulick, Holger, 'Volker Braun und das Stasi-Theater', *Der Spiegel*, 26 October 2000.

Künstlerischer Beirat, 'Offener Brief an Peter Palitzsch', *Neues Deutschland*, 4 October 1961.

Kupke, Peter, 'Zur Erprobung von Standards', *Frankfurter Rundschau*, 20 January 1996.

Kusche, Lothar, '*Don Juan* am Schiffbauerdamm', *Die Weltbühne*, no date supplied, pp. 502–4.

Lang, Joachim, *Neues vom alten Brecht: Manfred Wekwerth im Gespräch*, ed. by Valentin F. Lang and Karoline Sprenger (Berlin: Aurora, 2010).

Lang, Joachim and Jürgen Hillesheim, '*Denken heißt verändern . . .* ': *Erinnerungen an Brecht* (Augsburg: Maro, 1997).

Lange, Hartmut, 'Zweimal Turrini: Des einen Leid, des andern Kampf', *Die Welt*, 27 February 1993.

Langhoff, Anna and Matthias Langhoff, '"Der Gummimensch kommt in Sicht"', *Theater der Zeit*, 3 (1998), pp. 36–9.

Langhoff, Matthias, 'Brief an einen Senator', *Drucksache*, 1 (1993), pp. 11–24.

Laudenbach, Peter, 'Professionelle Abendunterhaltung', *Berliner Zeitung*, 23 November 1993.

Laudenbach, Peter, 'Sadomasochistische Endzeitsspiele', *Berliner Zeitung*, 14 March 1994.

Laudenbach, Peter, 'Spur der Gebeine', *Berliner Zeitung*, 5 February 1996.

Lauter, Hans, *Der Kampf gegen den Formalismus in Kunst und Literatur, für eine fortschrittliche deutsche Kultur* (Berlin: Dietz, 1951).

Leclerc, Guy, 'Paris a Fait un Accueil Triumphal aux Acteurs Berlinois de *Mère Courage*', *L'Humanité*, 1 July 1954.

Leiser, Erwin, 'Der freundliche Frager', in Witt (ed.), *Gespräch auf der Probe* (Zurich: Sanssouci, 1961), pp. 42–8.

-ler [*sic*], 'Die Welt feiert unsern Brecht', *National Zeitung*, 12 February 1962.

Lietzmann, Sabine, 'Wenn die Wahrheit zum Angriff geht...', *Frankfurter Allgemeine Zeitung*, 18 January 1956.

Lietzmann, Sabine, 'Der Mann, was seinen Papa killte', *Frankfurter Allgemeine Zeitung*, 17 May 1956.

Lietzmann, Sabine, 'Der kunstvoll ausgestopfter Haifisch', *Frankfurter Allgemeine Zeitung*, 30 April 1960.

Linzer, Martin, 'Anmerkungen zu Georg Seidels Werk und Wirken', in G. Seidel, *Villa Jugend: Das dramatische Werk in einem Band*, ed. by Andreas Leusink (Berlin and Frankfurt/Main: Henschel and Verlag der Autoren, 1992), pp. 381–9.

Linzer, Martin, 'Orakel aus dem Brecht-Tempel', *Theater der Zeit*, 1 (1993), pp. 19–22.

Linzer, Martin, 'Thoughts on a Walking Corpse: the Berliner Ensemble Five Years after the Wende', *Brecht Yearbook*, 21 (1996), pp. 289–300.

Lommer, Horst, 'Zwei Welten', *Tägliche Rundschau*, 23 December 1949.

Lubowski, Bernd, 'Ein Wunder am Schiffbauerdamm', *Berliner Morgenpost*, 15 June 1993.

Lucchesi, Joachim (ed.), *Das Verhör in der Oper: Die Debatte um die Aufführung 'Das Verhör des Lukullus' von Bertolt Brecht und Paul Dessau* (Berlin: Basisdruck, 1993).

Lucchesi, Joachim and Ronald K. Schull, *Musik bei Brecht* (Frankfurt/Main: Suhrkamp, 1988).

Luckhurst, Mary, *Dramaturgy: A Revolution in Theatre* (Cambridge: Cambridge University Press, 2006).

Luckhurst, Mary, 'Revolutionising Theatre: Brecht's Reinvention of the Dramaturg', in Peter Thomson and Glendyr Sacks (eds.), *The Cambridge Companion to Brecht*, 2nd edn (Cambridge: Cambridge University Press, 1994), pp. 193–208.

Luft, Friedrich, 'Gorki: Stadien eines Verfalls', *Die neue Zeitung*, 23 December 1949.

Luft, Friedrich, 'Ein ABC der deutschen Misere', *Neue Zeitung*, 16 April 1950.

Luft, Friedrich, 'Brechts *Galileo Galilei* von beklemmender Aktualität', *Die Welt*, 17 January 1956.

Luft, Friedrich, '*Der aufhaltsame Aufstieg des Arturo Ui*', *Die Welt*, 26 March 1959.

Luft, Friedrich, 'Alte Theaterliebe rostet leider doch', *Die Welt*, 28 April 1960.

Lunn, Eugene, *Marxism and Modernism: An Historical Study of Lukács, Brecht, Benjamin and Adorno* (Berkeley and Los Angeles: University of California Press, 1982).

Lutz, Regine, *Schauspieler – der schönste Beruf: Einblicke in die Theaterarbeit* (Munich: Langen Müller, 1993).

Lyon, James K., 'Brecht in Postwar Germany: Dissident Conformist, Cultural Icon, Literary Dictator', in James K. Lyon and Hans-Peter Breuer (eds.), *Brecht Unbound: Presented at the International Bertolt Brecht Symposium held at the University of Delaware February 1992* (Newark: University of Delaware Press, 1995), pp. 76–88.

Maaß, Joachim, 'Sieg der Vernunft – Sieg der Vernünftigen', *Neue Berliner Illustrierte*, 40 (1989), pp. 2–3.

MacDonald, Ian, *Revolution in the Head: The Beatles' Records and the Sixties*, third, revised edition (London: Vintage, 2008).

Mahl, Bernd, *Brecht und Monks 'Urfaust'-Inszenierung mit dem Berliner Ensemble 1952/53* (Stuttgart and Zurich: Belser, 1986).

Mahlke, Stefan, 'Klassisch = Episch: Brecht als Agent seiner Produktion', in Birgit Dahlke, Martina Langermann and Thomas Taterka (eds.), *LiteraturGesellschaft [sic] DDR: Kanonkämpfe und ihre Geschichte(n)* (Stuttgart and Weimar: Metzler, 2000), pp. 146–72.

Martin, Hermann, 'In die Hölle mit Don Juan', *BZ am Abend*, 29 March, 1954.

Mayer, Hans, *Erinnerung an Brecht* (Frankfurt/Main: Suhrkamp, 1996).

McGowan, Moray, 'Fatzer's Footprints: Brecht's Fatzer and the GDR Theater [sic]', in Bradley and Leeder (eds.), *Brecht and the GDR: Politics, Culture, Posterity* (Rochester, NY: Camden House, 2011), pp. 201–21.

Mennerich, Karl, *'Die Tage der Kommune'*, *Freiheit*, 9 October 1962.

Merck, Nikolaus, 'Vorwärts und nicht verbessern!', *die tageszeitung*, 17 September 1997.

Merritt, Stephanie, 'Stewart Lee: Much A-Stew about Nothing – review', *The Observer*, 10 November 2013.

Merschmeier, Michael, Franz Wille and Bernd Feuchtner, 'Landschaftsgärtner oder Totengräber?', *Theater heute*, 1 (1997), pp. 30–3.

Meyer, Grischa (ed.), *Drucksache*, 20 (1996).

Michael, Nancy C., 'The Affinities of Adaptation: The Artistic Relationship between Brecht's *Coriolan* and Shakespeare's *Coriolanus*', *Brecht Yearbook*, 13 (1984), pp. 145–54.

Michaelis, Rolf, 'Ein Stück zum Parteitag', *Frankfurter Allgemeine Zeitung*, 19 June 1971.

Michaelis, Rolf, 'Die Helden sind müde', *Frankfurter Allgemeine Zeitung*, 5 October 1972.

Michaelis, Rolf, 'Kleine Brötchen zu Brechts Geburt', *Frankfurter Allgemeine Zeitung*, 14 February 1973.

Michaelis, Rolf, 'Hochhuth ist ein Feigling', *Die Zeit*, 19 February 1993.

Michaelis, Rolf, 'Theater muß man von hinter der Bühne sehen', *Die Zeit*, 29 December 1995.

Mickel, Karl, 'Die Tradition und das neue Programm', in Hans-Jochen Irmer (ed.), *Berliner Ensemble. 1949–74* (Berlin: Berliner Ensemble, 1974), pp. 16 and 18.

Mickel, Karl, 'Das Berliner Ensemble der Ruth Berghaus', *Theater der Zeit*, 2 (1996), pp. 50–1.

Mihan, Jörg, 'Bertolt Brecht – *Die Gewehre der Frau Carrar*, die Aufführung am Berliner Ensemble und ihre Wirkung beim jugendlichen Publikum: Probleme der ästhetischen Erziehung der Schüler', *Studien*, 1 (1973), supplement to *Theater der Zeit*, 2 (1973), pp. 1–16.

Misterek, Susanne, *Polnische Dramatik in Bühnen- und Buchverlagen der Bundesrepublik Deutschland und der DDR* (Wiesbaden: Harrassowitz, 2002).

Mittenzwei, Werner, *Der Realismus-Streit um Brecht: Grundriß der Brecht-Rezeption in der DDR 1945–1975* (Berlin and Weimar: Aufbau, 1978).

Mittenzwei, Werner, '*Galileo Galilei*', in Gert Hof (ed.), '*Galileo Galilei*' *von Bertolt Brecht: Eine Dokumentation der Aufführung des Berliner Ensembles 1978* (Berlin: Verband der Theaterschaffenden, 1982), p. 5.

Mittenzwei, Werner, 'Fatzer oder die Möglichkeit des Theaters im Umgang mit einem Fragment', in Peter Kraft (ed.), '*Untergang des Egoisten Johann Fatzer von Bertolt Brecht: Eine Dokumentation der Aufführung des Berliner Ensembles 1987* (Berlin: Verband der Theaterschaffenden, 1987), pp. 114–26.

Mittenzwei, Werner, *Das Leben des Bertolt Brecht oder der Umgang mit den Welträtseln*, 2 vols. (Berlin: Aufbau, 1997).

Mittenzwei, Werner, *Die Intellektuellen. Literatur und Politik in Ostdeutschland 1945–2000* (Berlin: Aufbau, 2003).

Mollenschott, Elvira, 'Große Kunst der kleinen Form', *Neues Deutschland*, 27 May 1962.

Mollenschott, Elvira, 'Vergnügliches Theatergespräch', *Neues Deutschland*, 28 September 1963.

Mollenschott, Elvira, 'Zweier großer Dramatiker würdig', *Neues Deutschland*, 27 September 1964.

Monk, Egon, 'Caspar Neher und Bertolt Brecht auf der Probe', *Frankfurter Rundschau*, 27 August 1966.

Monk, Egon, *Regie Egon Monk: Von 'Puntila' zu den Bertinis. Erinnerungen* (Berlin: Transit, 2007).

Müller, André, 'Gelächter – auf Kosten der Komödie', *Deutsche Volkszeitung*, 1 April 1966.

Müller, André, *Der Regisseur Benno Besson* (Berlin: Henschel, 1967).

Müller, Christoph, 'Geschichte und Gegenwart auf der Bühne', in B. K. Tragelehn, *Roter Stern in den Wolken: Aufsätze, Reden, Gedichte, Gespräche und ein Theaterstück. Ein Lesebuch*, ed. by. Gerhard Ahrens (Berlin: Theater der Zeit, 2006), pp. 137–65.

Müller, Heiner, *Werke*, ed. by Frank Hörnigk (Frankfurt/Main: Suhrkamp, 1998–2008). Notes give volume and page numbers.

Müller, Klaus-Detlef, 'Brechts Theatermodelle: Historische Begründung und Konzept', in Jean-Marie Valentin and Theo Buck (eds.), *Bertolt Brecht. Actes du Colloque Franco-Allemand tenu en Sorbonne...* (Bern: Peter Lang, 1990), pp. 315–32.

Müller, Lothar, 'Flachschädel', *Frankfurter Allgemeine Zeitung*, 22 September 1998.

Mumford, Meg, 'Brecht Studies Stanislavsky: Just a Tactical Move?', *New Theatre Quarterly*, 11: 43 (1995), pp. 241–58.

Mumford, Meg, *Showing the Gestus: A Study of Acting in Brecht's Theatre* (Unpublished PhD Thesis, University of Bristol, 1997).

Mumford, Meg, '"Dragging" Brecht's Gestus Onwards: A Feminist Challenge', in Steve Giles and Rodney Livingstone (eds.), *Bertolt Brecht Centenary Essays* (Amsterdam: Rodopi, 1998), pp. 240–57.

Mumford, Meg, 'Brecht on Acting for the 21st Century: Interrogating and Re-Inscribing the Fixed', *Communications from the International Brecht Society*, 29: 1 and 2 (2000), pp. 44–9.

Mumford, Meg, 'Gestic Masks and Brecht's Theater: A Testimony to the Contradictions and Parameters of a Realist Aesthetic', *Brecht Yearbook*, 26 (2001), pp. 143–71.

Mumford, Meg, *Bertolt Brecht* (Abingdon and New York: Routledge, 2009).

Mytze, A. W., 'Sommerbürger Helmut Baierl', *Süddeutsche Zeitung*, 17 March 1976.

Naumann, Konrad, 'Rede vor dem Berliner Ensemble am 20.2.1974 anläßlich der Auszeichnung mit dem Orden "Banner der Arbeit"', in Hans-Jochen Irmer (ed.), *Berliner Ensemble, 1949–74* (Berlin: Berliner Ensemble, 1974), p. 21.

Neef, Sigrid, *Das Theater der Ruth Berghaus* (Frankfurt/Main: Fischer, 1989).

Neubert-Herwig, Christa (ed.), *Benno Besson: Jahre mit Brecht* (Willisau: Theaterkultur, 1990).

Neubert-Herwig, Christa, *Benno Besson: Theater spielen in acht Ländern. Texte – Dokumente – Gespräche* (Berlin: Alexander, 1998).

Neubert-Herwig, Christa, '"Er wollte schon 1942 Theater machen"', in Christa Neubert-Herwig, *Benno Besso: Theater spielen in acht Ländern. Texte – Dokumente – Gespräche* (Berlin: Alexander, 1998), pp. 30–2.

Nioduschewski, Anja, 'Zeichen aber kein Fanal', *Junge Welt*, 16 September 1997.

Nioduschewski, Anja, 'Drei Stücke im Überflug', *Junge Welt*, 30 January 1998.

Nümann, Dirk, 'Die Schonfrist ist jetzt um', *Junge Welt*, 14 April 1993.

Nümann, Dirk, 'Das Leben ist schön – tralala', *Junge Welt*, 15 June 1993.

NZ/ADN, 'Brecht nun überall in Berlin', *Neue Zeit*, 11 February 1992.

Oesterreich, Volker, 'Mit Wekwerth und Brechts *Schwejk* in die neue Saison', *Berliner Morgenpost*, 29 August 1991.

Oesterreich, Volker, 'Brücke vom Gestern zum Heute', *Berliner Morgenpost*, 12 January 1993.

Oesterreich, Volker, 'Brecht ist Regisseur Fritz Marquardt verboten', *Berliner Morgenpost*, 13 September 1993.

Oesterreich, Volker, 'Eine Verbeugung vor Marianne Hoppe', *Berliner Morgenpost*, 13 March 1994.

Oesterreich, Volker, 'pp huldigt bb', *Berliner Morgenpost*, 5 May 1998.

Oesterreich, Volker, 'Rolf Hochhuth: "Die jetzige Crew soll lange bleiben"', *Berliner Morgenpost*, 21 May 1995.

Oesterreich, Volker, '"Wir repräsentieren die ganze Stadt"', *Berliner Morgenpost*, 17 October 1996.

Oesterreich, Volker, 'Wer will nochmal, wer hat noch nicht?', *Berliner Morgenpost*, 6 December 1996.

Palitzsch, Peter and Manfred Wekwerth, 'Leipziger Allerlei', *Theater der Zeit*, 3 (1955), pp. 19–23.

Parker, Stephen, 'What Was the Cause of Brecht's Death? Towards a Medical History', *Brecht Yearbook*, 35 (2010), pp. 291–307.

Parker, Stephen, 'A Life's Work Curtailed? The Ailing Brecht's Struggle with the SED Leadership over GDR Cultural Policy', in Laura Bradley and Karen Leeder (eds.), *Brecht and the GDR: Politics, Culture, Posterity* (Rochester, NY: Camden House, 2011), pp. 65–82.

Parker, Stephen and Matthew Philpotts, *Sinn und Form: The Anatomy of a Literary Journal* (Berlin and New York: de Gruyter, 2009).

Patterson, Michael, 'Brecht's Legacy', in Peter Thomson and Glendyr Sacks (eds.), *The Cambridge Companion to Brecht*, first edition (Cambridge: Cambridge University Press, 1994), pp. 273–87.

Pauli, Manfred, *Unterwegs zu Brecht: Rekonstruktion einer Annäherung* (Schkeuditz: Schkeuditzer Buchverlag, 2012).

Pfelling, Werner, 'Rentnertick und Kämpferherz', *Junge Welt*, 16 March 1976.

Pfützner, Klaus, 'Beobachtungen, Erfahrungen, Tendenzen', *Theater der Zeit*, 11 (1975), pp. 1–2.

Philpotts, Matthew, '"Aus so prosaischen Dingen wie Kartoffeln, Straßen, Traktoren werden poetische Dinge!": Brecht, *Sinn und Form*, and Strittmatter's *Katzgraben*', *German Life and Letters*, 56:1 (2003), pp. 56–71.

Pietzsch, Ingeborg and Martin Linzer, 'Familien-Geschichten', *Theater der Zeit*, 6 (1994), pp. 12–15.

Pintzka, Wolfgang, *Von Sibirien in die Synagoge: Erinnerungen aus zwei Welten* (Teetz: Hentrich & Hentrich, 2002).

Plath, André, 'Wie aber geht man mit Geschichte um?', *Junge Welt*, 30 September 1988.

Pollatschek, Walther, 'Die Bühne als Anleitung zum Handeln', *Tägliche Rundschau*, 14 January 1951.

Pollatschek, Walther, '*Tage der Kommune*', *Berliner Zeitung*, 10 October 1962.

Preuß, Joachim Werner, *Theater im ost-/westpolitischen Umfeld: Nahtstelle Berlin 1945–61* (Munich: iudicum, 2004).

Puppa, Paolo, 'Tradition, Traditions, and Dario Fo', in Joseph Farrell and Antonio Scuderi (eds.), *Dario Fo: Stage, Text, and Tradition* (Cardondale: Southern Illinois University Press, 2000), pp. 181–96.

Ridout, Nicholas, *Stage Fright, Animals and Other Theatrical Problems* (Cambridge: Cambridge University Press, 2006).

Rilla, Paul, *Essays: Kritische Beiträge zur Literatur* (Berlin: Henschel, 1955).

Ritter, Hans Martin, 'Bertolt Brecht – Unterm Strasberg begraben: Abwichlung oder Entwicklung der Brechtschen Theatertheorie in der Schauspielerausbildung?', *Brecht Yearbook*, 17 (1992), pp. 63–74.

Ritter, Heinz, 'Ein Fest für BERTOLT?', *Der Abend*, 12 February 1973.

Ritter, Heinz, 'Meister der List', *Der Abend*, 11 February 1978.

R.K., '*Biberpelz* und *Roter Hahn* von Gerhart Hauptmann', *Nacht-Expreß*, 24 March 1951.

Roloff-Momin, Ulrich, *Zuletzt: Kultur* (Berlin: Aufbau, 1997).

Rouse, John, 'Brecht and the Contradictory Actor', *Theatre Journal*, 36:1 (1984), pp. 25–42.

Rouse, John, *Brecht and the West German Theatre: The Practice and Politics of Interpretation* (Ann Arbor: UMI, 1989).

Rübesame, Hans (ed.), *Antrag auf Demonstration: Die Protestsammlung im Deutschen Theater am 15. Oktober 1989* (Berlin: Christoph Links, 2010).

Rudolph, Johanna, 'Wertvolle Bereicherung des Berliner Theaterlebens', *Neues Deutschland*, 14 January 1951.

Rudolph, Johanna, 'Weitere Bemerkungen zum *Faust*-Problem', *Neues Deutschland*, 27 May 1953.

Rühle, Günther, 'Was wollt Ihr noch mit Brecht?', *Frankfurter Allgemeine Zeitung*, 18 February 1978.

Rühle, Jürgen, '*Don Juan* – ausgegraben und aufgeputzt', *Sonntag*, 11 April 1954.

Rülicke, Käthe, 'Die Laienspielbrigade im Berliner Ensemble', *Volkskunst*, 2: 12 (1953), pp. 24–5.

Rülicke, Käthe, '*Leben des Galilei*: Bemerkungen zum Schlußszene', *Sinn und Form*, Zweites Sonderheft Bertolt Brecht (1957), pp. 269–321.

Rülicke-Weiler, Käthe, *Die Dramaturgie Brechts. Theater als Mittel der Veränderung* (Berlin: Henschel, 1966).

Rülicke-Weiler, Käthe, 'Historisierende Lesarten von J.R. Bechers *Winterschlacht*', *notate*, 1 (1988), pp. 18–19.

Rülicke-Weiler, Käthe, 'Anfänge des Berliner Ensembles', in Rainer Mennicken, *Peter Palitzsch* (Frankfurt/Main: Fischer, 1993), pp. 57–61.

Sander, H.-D., '*Don Juan*', *Theater der Zeit*, 5 (1954), pp. 44–6.

Schall, Ekkehard, 'Ausblick nach vorn', *Theater der Zeit*, 9 (1976), pp. 31 and 33.

Schaper, Rüdiger, 'Wekwerth geht', *Süddeutsche Zeitung*, 15 May 1991.

Schaper, Rüdiger, 'Souffleur mit Peitsche', *Süddeutsche Zeitung*, 22 February 1993.

Schaper, Rüdiger, 'Schüsse am Schiffbauerdamm', *Süddeutsche Zeitung*, 6 June 1995.

Schaper, Rüdiger, 'Grüß Gott, Herr Exorzist', *Süddeutsche Zeitung*, 23 April 1997.

Schauer, Hermann-Ernst, 'Der verdächtige Demokrat', in Gertraude Hoffmann and Klaus Höpcke (eds.), '*Das Sicherste ist die Veränderung*'. *Hans-Joachim Hoffmann: Kulturminister der DDR und häufig verdächtigter Demokrat* (Berlin: Dietz, 2003), pp. 10–24.

Schmidt, Karl-Heinz (ed.), '*Großer Frieden*' *von Volker Braun: Eine Dokumentation der Aufführung des Berliner Ensembles 1979* (Berlin: Verband der Theaterschaffenden, 1982).

Schmidt, Renate, *Therese Giehse: Na, dann wollen wir die Herrschaften mal was bieten! Biographie* (Munich: Langen Müller [*sic*], 2008).

Schmidt-Mühlisch, Lothar, 'Blondchen will nach Hollywood', *Die Welt*, 2 December 1996.

Schoenberner, Gerhard, 'Frühe Theaterarbeit', *Marburger Hefte zur Medienwissenschaft*, 21 (1995), pp. 6–18.

Schöttker, Detlev, 'Brechts *Theaterarbeit*: Ein Grundlagenwerk und seine Ausgrenzungen', *Weimarer Beiträge*, 53:3 (2007), pp. 438–51.

Schreier, Andreas and Malte Daniljuk, 'Das Müller-Phantom', in Müller, *Krieg ohne Schlacht: Leben in zwei Diktaturen. Eine Autobiographie*, expanded edition (Cologne: Kiepenheuer & Witsch, 1994), pp. 470–6.

Schubert, Peter, 'Rolf Hochhuth will das Brecht-Theater kaufen', *Berliner Morgenpost*, 28 April 1995.

Schumacher, Ernst, '*Die Gewehre der Frau Carrar*', *Berliner Zeitung*, 24 June 1971.

Schumacher, Ernst, 'Bedeutungsvoll wie je', *Berliner Zeitung*, 9 October 1971.

Schumacher, Ernst, '*Frau Warrens Beruf*', *Berliner Zeitung*, 27 December 1973.

Schumacher, Ernst, '*Frühlings Erwachen*', *Berliner Zeitung*, 5 March 1974.

Schumacher, Ernst, '*Die Mutter*', *Berliner Zeitung*, 22 October 1974.

Schumacher, Ernst, '*Der Hofmeister* wieder im BE', *Berliner Zeitung*, 10 October 1977.

Schumacher, Ernst, 'Es tanzten die Puppen aber nicht der Kongreß', *Berliner Zeitung*, 26 March 1981.

Schumacher, Ernst, '"Harmlos!" heißt das Stichwort', *Berliner Zeitung*, 6 October 1981.

Schumacher, Ernst, '*Die Physiker* ohne Nutzen', *Berliner Zeitung*, 1 April 1982.

Schumacher, Ernst, 'Gedämpfter Trommeln Klang', *Berliner Zeitung*, 24 March 1983.

Schumacher, Ernst, 'Voll von Zeichen und unterhaltend', *Berliner Zeitung*, 4 April 1984.

Schumacher, Ernst, 'Von Struktur kaleidoskopisch', *Berliner Zeitung*, 28 February 1985.

Schumacher, Ernst, 'Besuch der alten Mutter', *Berliner Zeitung*, 20–21 February 1988.

Schumacher, Ernst, 'Abmarsch von der Wolokolamsker', *Berliner Zeitung*, 19 December 1989.

Schumacher, Ernst, 'DDR-Dramatik und 11. Plenum', in Günter Agde (ed.), *Kahlschlag: Das 11. Plenum des ZK der SED 1965. Studien und Dokumente* (Berlin: Aufbau, 1991), pp. 93–104.

Schumacher, Ernst, 'Folgt dem Direktorium ein Napoleon – oder: Was wird aus Brechts Bühne', *Berliner Zeitung*, 18 September 1991.

Schumacher, Ernst, 'Gewinnen oder Scheitern – mit neuen Aufführungen', *Berliner Zeitung*, 2 July 1992.

Schumacher, Ernst, 'Weite und Vielfalt oder Etikettenschwindel?', *Berliner Zeitung*, 22 October 1992.

Schumacher, Ernst, 'Die Leichen steigen aus dem Keller', *Berliner Zeitung*, 2–3 October 1993.

Schumacher, Ernst, 'Wer kennt den wahren Puntila?', *Berliner Zeitung*, 28 February 1996.

Schütt, Hans-Dieter, 'Ironisches Zeitgemälde', *Junge Welt*, 11 October 1977.

Schütt, Hans-Dieter, *Manfred Wekwerth* (Frankfurt/Oder: Frankfurt Oder Editionen, 1995).

Schütt, Hans-Dieter, 'Wach sein. Müde sein. Durcheinanderkommen', *Neues Deutschland*, 14 November 1995.

Schütt, Hans-Dieter, 'Was ausrichten. Was hinrichten', *Neues Deutschland*, 9 December 1996.

SED-Parteiorganisation, 'An die Kulturredaktion der *Märkischen Volkstimme*', *Märkische Volksstimme*, 29 April 1952, in Mahl, *Brecht und Monks 'Urfaust'-Inszenierung*, p. 189.

Setje-Eilers, Margaret, 'The Berliner Ensemble Interviews: Angelika Ritter, Eva Boehm, Ursula Ziebarth, Angela Winkler', *Communications from the International Brecht Society*, 38 (2009), pp. 118–53.

Setje-Eilers, Margaret, '"Wochenend und Sonnenschein": In the Blind Spots of Censorship at the GDR's Cultural Authorities and the Berliner Ensemble', *Theater Journal*, 61: 3 (2009), pp. 363–86.

Seydel, Renate, . . . *gelebt für alle Zeiten: Schauspieler über sich und andere* (Berlin: Henschel, 1975).

Seyfahrt, Ingrid, 'Eislers *Johann Faustus*', *Sonntag*, 24 October 1982.

Seyfahrt, Ingrid, '*Die Mutter*', *Sonntag*, 28 February 1988.

sigy, 'Der *Urfaust* in Landesbühne Potsdam', *Märkische Volksstimme*, 29 April 1952.

Sippel, Karl, 'Kritik der Werktätigen am *Hofmeister*', *Das Volk*, 12 July 1950.

Slevogt, Esther, 'Es wurde viel zuwenig geschrien', *die tageszeitung*, 17 April 1991.

Slevogt, Esther, 'Die Frechheit des Menschen', *Freitag*, 30 January 1998.

Slevogt, Esther, 'Ritterschlag mit dem Damokelsschwert: Egon Monk und Bertolt Brecht, 1949–1953', *Brecht Yearbook*, 37 (2012), pp. 163–77.

Smith, James, 'Brecht, the Berliner Ensemble, and the British Government', *New Theatre Quarterly*, 22: 4 (2006), pp. 307–23.

Sodann, Peter, *Keine halben Sachen: Erinnerungen* (Berlin: Ullstein, 2009).

Soubeyrand, Manuel, '*Blaue Pferde auf rotem Gras* oder wie ich einen Alptraum hatte', in Martin Linzer, Peter and Renate Ullrich, and Esther Undisz (eds.), *Wo ich bin, ist keine Provinz: Der Regisseur Christoph Schroth* (Berlin: Förderverein Theaterdokumentation, 2003), pp. 119–24.

st, 'Wie können Sie das mit Ihrem Gewissen vereinbaren, Herr Wekwerth? Treten Sie zurück', *BZ*, 26 April 1991.

Staadt, Jochen, '"Arbeit mit Brecht" – "daß wir uns auf den Standpunkt der Gesellschaft stellen." Brecht, Weigel und die Staatliche Kommission für Kunstangelegenheiten', in Staadt (ed.), '*Die Eroberung der Kultur beginnt!' Die Staatliche Kunstkommission für Kunstangelegenheiten der DDR (1951–1953) und die Kulturpolitik der SED* (Frankfurt/Main: Peter Lang, 2011), pp. 351–78.

Stadelmaier, Gerhard, 'Das harte Brot der toten Könige', *Frankfurter Allgemeine Zeitung*, 12 January 1993.

Stadelmaier, Gerhard, 'Abgestanden in Ruinen', *Frankfurter Allgemeine Zeitung*, 3 October 1993.

Stephan, Erika, '*Die Mutter*', *Sonntag*, 8 December 1974.

Stern, Carola, *Männer lieben anders: Helene Weigel und Bertolt Brecht* (Reinbek: Rowohlt, 2000).

Stone, Michael, 'Perfektion als Selbstzweck', *Christ und Welt*, 12 July 1968.

Stone, Michael, 'Jubel beim Berliner Ensemble', *Der Tagesspiegel*, 13 October 1977.

Stone, Michael, 'Ein Tag im Leben Lenins', *Der Tagesspiegel*, 19 October 1980.

Stone, Michael, 'Absage an die Revolution', *Der Tagesspiegel*, 8 April 1983.

Stone, Michael, 'Weiße und schwarze Engel', *Der Tagesspiegel*, 5 April 1984.

Stone, Michael, 'Die alte Krankheit', *Der Tagesspiegel*, 20 December 1987.

Stone, Michael, 'Einbruch der Wirklichkeit', *Der Tagesspiegel*, undated.

Strasberg, Lee, *At the Actors Studio: Tape-Recorded Sessions*, ed. by Robert H. Hethman (New York: Viking, 1965).

Stuber, Petra, *Spielräume und Grenzen: Studien zum DDR-Theater* (Berlin: Christoph Links, 1998).

Stuber, Petra, 'Helene Weigel und ihre Rolle als Intendantin zwischen 1949 und 1954', *Brecht Yearbook*, 25 (2000), pp. 253–75.

Styan, J. L., *Max Reinhardt* (Cambridge: Cambridge University Press, 1982).

Subiotto, Arrigo, *Brecht's Adaptations for the Berliner Ensemble* (London: MHRA, 1975).

Suschke, Stephan, 'Ich hielt mich nie für ein Genie', *Theater der Zeit*, 2 (2002), pp. 30–2.

Suschke, Stephan, *Müller macht Theater: Zehn Inszenierungen und ein Epilog* (Berlin: Theater der Zeit, 2003).

Suvin, Darko, 'Brechtian or Pseudo-Brechtian: Mythical Estrangement in the Berlin Ensemble Adaptation of *Coriolanus*', *Asaph*, 3 (1986), pp. 135–58.

Tatlow, Antony, 'Bertolt Brecht Today: Problems in Aesthetics and Politics', in Tatlow and Tak-Wei Wong (eds.), *Brecht and East Asian Theatre* (Hong Kong: Hong Kong University Press, 1982), pp. 3–17.

Teschke, Holger, 'Mit dem Körper hören, mit dem Körper sprechen', *Spiel-Zeit*, supplement of *Der Tagesspiegel*, February 1998.

Teschke, Holger, 'Brecht's Learning Plays – A Dance Floor for an Epic Dramaturgy', *Theatre Forum*, 14 (1999), pp. 10–16.

Teschke, Holger, '"Bei Brecht gab's immer was zu lernen": Regine Lutz im Gespräch mit Holger Teschke', *Dreigroschenheft*, 1 (2009), pp. 5–7.

Thate, Hilmar, 'Versuch neuer Arbeitsweisen', *Theater der Zeit*, 3 (1960), pp. 47–50.

Thate, Hilmar, with Kerstin Retemeyer, *Neulich, als ich noch Kind war: Autobiografie – Versuch eines Zeitgenossen* (Bergisch Gladbach: Gustav Lübbe, 2006).

Thomas, Merrilyn, '"Aggression in Felt Slippers": Normalisation and the Ideological Struggle in the Context of Détente and Ostpolitik', in Mary Fulbrook (ed.), *Power and Society in the GDR 1961–1979. The 'Normalisation of Rule'?* (New York: Berghahn, 2009), pp. 33–51.

Thomas, Walter, 'Enthüllung der "teutschen Misere"', *BZ am Abend*, 15 April 1950.

Thomsen, Henrike, 'Augiasstall ist müde', *Berliner Zeitung*, 10 March 1999.

Thomson, Peter, *Brecht: 'Mother Courage and her Children'* (Cambridge: Cambridge University Press, 1997).

tll., 'BE wehrt sich gegen Hochhuths Kaufpläne', *Berliner Morgenpost*, 29 April 1995.

Tornow, Georgia and Michael Maier, '"Bei Menschen und bei Schauspielern gibt es nur eines, das mich wirklich interessiert: Das Echte"', *Berliner Zeitung*, 11–12 May 1996.

Tsp., 'Interimsleitung für Berliner Ensemble', *Der Tagesspiegel* 23 October 1991.

Tsp., 'Kündigungen am BE sind unwirksam', *Der Tagesspiegel*, 15 December 1992.

Tsp, 'Berliner Ensemble: Hochhuth und Senat vor Einigung', *Der Tagesspiegel*, 6 January 1998.

Tsp, 'Mietvertrag fürs BE unter Dach und Fach', *Der Tagesspiegel*, 8 January 1998.

Tynan, Kenneth, 'Braw and Brecht', *Observer*, 2 September 1956.

Tynan, Kenneth, 'Brecht would not applaud his Theater [*sic*] today', *The New York Times*, 11 January 1976.

Tynan, Kenneth, 'Brecht's Theatre at the Crossroads' in *Plays and Players*, March 1976, pp. 12–16.

Ullrich, Helmut, 'Auf den Barrikaden von Paris', *Neue Zeit*, 9 October 1962.

Ullrich, Helmut, 'Schlüsselfigur der Epoche', *Neue Zeit*, 15 April 1965.

Ullrich, Helmut, 'Nachts, wenn die Sintflut kommt', *Neue Zeit*, 17 February 1966.

Ullrich, Helmut, 'Das Gespräch mit dem Kommandeur', *Neue Zeit*, 22 March 1972.

Ullrich, Helmut, 'Der Geist und die Geschäfte', *Neue Zeit*, 13 February 1973.

Ullrich, Helmut, 'Probleme zwingen zum Nachdenken', *Neue Zeit*, 11 April 1979.

Ullrich, Helmut, 'Halbherzig und ohne Aussagekraft', *Neue Zeit*, 6 April 1982.

Ullrich, Renate, '"Und zudem bringt Ihr noch den genialen Stanislawski in Verruf": Zur Kanonisierung einer Schauspielmethode', in Birgit Dahlke, Martina Langermann and Thomas Taterka (eds.), *LiteraturGesellschaft [sic] DDR: Kanonkämpfe und ihre Geschichte(n)* (Stuttgart and Weimar: Metzler, 2000), pp. 104–45.

van Dijk, Maarten, 'Blocking Brecht', in Pia Kleber and Colin Visser (eds.), *Re-interpreting Brecht: His Influence on Contemporary Drama and Film* (Cambridge: Cambridge University Press, 1990), pp. 117–34.

voe, 'Berliner Ensemble will ins Schiller-Theater', *Berliner Morgenpost*, 3 February 1999.

Voigt, Peter, '*Der Zögling*. Ein Filmtext', *Sinn und Form*, 2 (2004), pp. 221–39.

Völker, Klaus, 'Wohin geht das Berliner Ensemble?', *Theater heute*, 11 (1964), pp. 34–5.

von Arnim, Ditte, *Brechts letzte Liebe: Das Leben der Isot Kilian* (Berlin: Transit, 2006).

von Becker, Peter, 'Das Phantom im Theater', *Theater heute*, 10 (1992), p. 4.

von Becker, Peter, 'Glasnost', *Theater heute*, 1 (1989), p. 1.

von Becker, Peter and Michael Merschmeier, '"Das Sicherste ist die Veränderung": *Theater heute*-Gespräch mit dem DDR-Kulturminister Hans-Joachim Hoffmann', *Theater heute*, Jahrbuch (1988), pp. 10–20.

Waller, Michael, *Democratic Centralism: An Historical Commentary* (Manchester: Manchester University Press, 1981).

Walther, Joachim, *Sicherungsbereich Literatur: Schriftsteller und Staatssicherheit in der Deutschen Demokratischen Republik*, revised edition (Berlin: Ullstein, 1999).

Weber, Carl, 'Brecht as Director', *The Drama Review*, 12:1 (1967), pp. 101–7.

Weber, Carl, 'The Actor and Brecht, or: The Truth Is Concrete', *Brecht Yearbook*, 13 (1984), pp. 63–74.

Weber, Carl, 'Brecht and the Berliner Ensemble – the Making of a Model', in Peter Thomson and Glendyr Sacks (eds.), *The Cambridge Companion to Brecht*, second edition (Cambridge: Cambridge University Press, 1994), pp. 175–92.

Wege, Carl, 'Spielplan(politik) und Inszenierungskalkül des Berliner Ensembles zwischen 1952 und 1956', in Thomas Jung (ed.), *Zweifel – Fragen – Vorschläge: Bertolt Brecht anläßlich des Hundersten* (Frankfurt/Main: Peter Lang, 1999), pp. 93–8.

Weidauer, Friedemann, 'Brecht's (Brush with) Maoism', *Brecht Yearbook*, 36 (2011), pp. 189–99.

Weinert, J., 'Wiederentdeckung eines deutschen Klassikers', *National Zeitung*, 29 January 1952.

Wekwerth, Manfred, *Wir arbeiten an Gerhart Hauptmanns Komödie 'Der Biberpelz'*, ed. by the Zentralhaus für Laienkunst (Halle: Mitteldeutscher Verlag, 1953).

Wekwerth, Manfred, *Theater in Veränderung* (Berlin: Aufbau, 1960).

Wekwerth, Manfred, 'Berliner Ensemble 1968. Oder: was blieb von Brecht?', *Theater heute*, 1 (1968), pp. 16–19.

Wekwerth, Manfred, 'Arbeitsstenogramm', *Sonntag*, 14 February 1971.

Wekwerth, Manfred, 'Tschumalow und die Barrikaden des Alltags', *Neues Deutschland*, 13 March 1973.

Wekwerth, Manfred, 'Anstatt einer Antwort', *Neues Deutschland*, 9 June 1993.

Wekwerth, Manfred, 'Eine Richtigstellung', *Theater der Zeit*, 8 (1975), pp. 43–4.

Wekwerth, Manfred, *Schriften: Arbeit mit Brecht*, second, revised and expanded edition (Berlin: Henschel, 1975).

Wekwerth, Manfred, 'Das Buch Hiob oder die Fragen der Schöpfer', *Neues Deutschland*, 13 August 1975.

Wekwerth, Manfred, *Brecht? Berichte, Erfahrungen, Polemik* (Munich and Vienna: Hanser, 1976).

Wekwerth, Manfred, 'Er hat Vorschläge gemacht . . .', *Neues Deutschland*, 14/15 August 1976.

Wekwerth, Manfred, 'Entdeckungen und Spaß', *Sonntag*, 25 April, 1977.

Wekwerth, Manfred, 'Brief an Gisela May [of 11 September 1978]', in Gert Hof (ed.), *'Mutter Courage und ihre Kinder' von Bertolt Brecht: Eine Dokumentation der Aufführung des Berliner Ensembles 1978* (Berlin: Verband der Theaterschaffenden, 1981), pp. 64–5.

Wekwerth, Manfred, 'Regie 77', in Gert Hof (ed.), *'Galileo Galilei' von Bertolt Brecht: Eine Dokumentation der Aufführung des Berliner Ensembles 1978* (Berlin: Verband der Theaterschaffenden, 1982), pp. 18–22.

Wekwerth, Manfred, *Theater in Diskussion: Notate Gespräche Polemiken* (Berlin: Henschel, 1982).

Wekwerth, Manfred, 'Notizen aus Gesprächen', in Peter Kraft (ed.), *'Untergang des Egoisten Johann Fatzer von Bertolt Brecht: Eine Dokumentation der Aufführung des Berliner Ensembles 1987* (Berlin: Verband der Theaterschaffenden, 1987), pp. 12–13.

Wekwerth, Manfred (compiler), *Theater nach Brecht: Baukasten für eine Theorie und Praxis des Berliner Ensembles in den neunziger Jahren* (Berlin no publisher credited, 1989).

Wekwerth, Manfred, 'Brecht spielen – gestern – heute – morgen', in Wekwerth (compiler), *Theater nach Brecht: Baukasten für eine Theorie und Praxis des Berliner Ensembles in den neunziger Jahren* (Berlin no publisher credited, 1989), pp. 41–51.

Wekwerth, Manfred, 'Revolution und Restauration', *Theater heute*, Jahrbuch (1990), pp. 144–5.

Wekwerth, Manfred, 'Über eine Weiterarbeit des Berliner Ensembles', *Das Argument*, 187 (1991), pp. 421–30.

Wekwerth, Manfred, 'Eine Odyssee oder Der Ehrenplatz zwischen den Stühlen', in Frank Hörnigk (ed.), *Volker Braun: Arbeitsbuch* (Berlin: Theater der Zeit, 1999), pp. 140–2.

Wekwerth, Manfred, 'Zum Artikel "Ein Werk, das standhält" – Brecht zwischen Ost und West – von Prof. Jan Knopf im *3GH* 3/98', *Dreigroschenheft*, 1 (1999), pp. 46–7.

Wekwerth, Manfred, *'Die Mutter* war Ermutigung', *Neues Deutschland*, 6 May 1999.

Wekwerth, Manfred, *Erinnern ist Leben: Eine dramatische Autobiographie* (Leipzig : Faber & Faber, 2000).

Wekwerth, Manfred, 'Christoph Schroth am Berliner Ensemble', in Martin Linzer, Peter and Renate Ullrich, and Esther Undisz (eds.), *Wo ich bin, ist keine Provinz: Der Regisseur Christoph Schroth* (Berlin: Förderverein Theaterdokumentation, 2003), pp. 112–18.

Wendt, Ernst, 'Konkurrenz der Tiere', *Stuttgarter Zeitung*, 4 March 1966.

Wengierek, Reinhard, 'Frag nicht, der Weg führt', *Neue Zeit*, 18 October 1993.

Wengierek, Reinhard, 'Kein Theater im Theater', *Die Welt*, 20 November 1995.

Wetzel, Stephan, 'Totenfest mit Eva Braun', *Der Tagesspiegel*, 24 November 1996.

White, John J., *Bertolt Brecht's Dramatic Theory* (Rochester, NY: Camden House, 2004).

Wiegenstein, Roland H., 'Noch einmal die alten Ziehbilder', *Frankfurter Rundschau*, 14 April 1993.

Wilke, Judith, *Brechts 'Fatzer'-Fragment: Lektüren zum Verhältnis Dokument und Kommentar* (Bielefeld: Aisthesis, 1998).

Wille, Franz, 'Erbe der Zukunft', *Theater heute*, 2 (1996), pp. 46–8.

Wille, Franz, 'Einfach kompliziert', *Theater heute*, 3 (1996), pp. 8–9.

Wille, Franz, 'Der Untergangsdirigent', *Theater heute*, 4 (1996), pp. 6–12.

Wirsing, Sibylle, 'Brechts Theater als gute Stube', *Frankfurter Allgemeine Zeitung*, 13 February 1978.

Wirsing, Sibylle, 'An der langen Straße nach Nirgendwo', *Frankfurter Allgemeine Zeitung*, 28 December 1989.

Wirsing, Sibylle, 'Neue Bekanntschaften mit altem Schrecken', *Frankfurter Allgemeine Zeitung*, 24 January 1991.

Wirsing, Sibylle, 'Die Restauration im Reformkleid', *Der Tagesspiegel*, 25 May 1991.

Witt, Clemens (ed.), *Gespräch auf der Probe* (Zurich: Sanssouci, 1961).

Wizisla, Erdmut, 'Private or Public? The Brecht Archive as an Object of Desire', in Bradley and Leeder (eds.), *Brecht and the GDR: Politics, Culture, Posterity* (Rochester, NY: Camden House, 2011), pp. 103–24.

WM, 'Beckett mit Musik', *Volksblatt*, undated.

Wüthrich, Werner, *Bertolt Brecht und die Schweiz* (Zurich: Chronos, 2003).

Wuttke, Martin and Karl Hegemann, '"Das ist doch kein Drama"', in Gabriele Gerecke, Harald Müller and Hans-Ulrich Müller-Schwefe (eds.), *Einar Schleef: Arbeitsbuch* (Berlin: Theater der Zeit, 2004), pp. 193–6.

Zadek, Peter, *Das wilde Ufer: Ein Theaterbuch*, compiled by Laszlo Kornitzer, expanded edition (Cologne: Kiepenheuer & Witsch, 1994).

Zadek, Peter, *Die Wanderjahre: 1980–2009*, ed. by Elisabeth Plessen (Cologne: Kiepenheuer & Witsch, 2010).

Zimmer, Dietmar E., 'Ohne antiamerikanische Spitze', *Die Zeit*, 16 April 1965.

Zolchow, Sabine, 'The Island of Berlin', in Denise Varney (ed.), *Theatre in the Berlin Republic: German Drama since Reunification* (Bern: Peter Lang, 2008), pp. 55–80.

Interviews

Uta Birnbaum, 28 August 2010
Wolf Bunge, 18 August 2011
Friedrich Dieckmann, 17 November 2010
Werner Hecht, 13 May 2010 and 8 June 2011
Werner Heinitz, 13 July 2010
Hans-Jochen Irmer, 3 November 2010
Claus Küchenmeister, 4 November 2010
Jörg Mihan, 12 July 2011
Peter Raue, 13 September 2012
Hans-Georg Simmgen, 21 July 2010
Rolf Stiska, 13 July 2011
Stephan Suschke, 28 April 2011
Vera Tenschert, 29 October 2010
Holger Teschke, 11 March 2011
Hilmar Thate, 19 July 2011
B. K. Tragelehn, 9 November 2010
Carl Weber, 28 May 2010
Manfred Wekwerth, 14 June and 1 July 2011

Index

CPSIA information can be obtained
at www.ICGtesting.com
Printed in the USA
LVOW10s2159080218
565818LV00011B/213/P